Dale and Appelbe's

Pharmacy Law and Ethics

EIGHTH EDITION

Gordon E Appelbe
LL B, PhD, MSc, BSc(Pharm), FRPharmS, Hon MPS(Aus), FCPP

Joy Wingfield
LL M, MPhil, BPharm, FRPharmS, Dip Ag Vet Pharm, FCPP

London • Chicago **Pharmaceutical Press**

Published by the Pharmaceutical Press
Publications division of the Royal Pharmaceutical Society of Great Britain

1 Lambeth High Street, London SE1 7JN, UK
100 South Atkinson Road, Suite 206, Grayslake, IL 60030-7820, USA

(P.P) is a trade mark of Pharmaceutical Press

First published 1976
Second edition 1979
Third edition 1983
Fourth edition 1989
Fifth edition 1993
Sixth edition 1997
Reprinted 1998, 1999
Seventh edition 2001
Reprinted 2003, 2004, 2005
Eighth edition 2005

Typeset by Photoprint, Torquay, Devon
Printed in Great Britain by TJ International, Padstow, Cornwall

ISBN 0 85369 604 7

A catalogue record for this book is available from the British
Library

Contents

Preface to the Eighth Edition

This book again seeks to provide in one volume an outline of the law that affects the practice of pharmacy in Great Britain, together with an account of the way in which British pharmacy has developed and maintained its standards of professional conduct. The authors hope that the book will prove useful not only to pharmacy undergraduates, pre-registration students and pharmacists in all branches of the profession, but also to others in Britain and overseas who may need some knowledge of contemporary British law relating to medicines and poisons, and of the development of professional ethics in British pharmacy.

The whole text has again been extensively revised for this edition, new material being added to most chapters. The chapters in this edition have been rearranged. All the statute law is now at the beginning of the book from Chapters 2 to 21. The major legislation affecting pharmacy – the Medicines Act (Chapters 1–15) and Misuse of Drugs Act (Chapter 16) – together with the regulations made thereunder, are dealt with in detail. With the loss of Crown immunity, it is important to stress that hospital pharmacists are aware that all this legislation now applies to NHS hospitals as well as to community pharmacies and hospitals in the private sector.

The Poisons Act and Regulations (Chapter 18), the Spirits Regulations (Chapter 19) and the Dangerous Substances Regulations (Chapter 20) now follow these chapters. In the chapter covering 'miscellaneous legislation' (Chapter 21), because of complexity and constantly changing detail, the sections on employment law, retail law and health and safety law have been simplified to give an overview of the scope and intention of the law with reference to relevant websites for more information. Other sections have been updated.

A new Chapter 1 deals for the first time with principles, sources of law and the administration of justice and incorporates Chapter 28 in previous editions dealing with European legislation. The law is that of Great Britain except where otherwise stated in the text. The aim has been to state the law as concisely as accuracy permits, but it should be borne in mind that only the courts can give a legally binding decision on any question of interpretation. The responsibility for the text and any views expressed therein lies with the authors.

Commenced before the publication of the previous edition, the changes underpinning the 'modernisation' of the Royal Pharmaceutical Society have still only been partially completed. A new charter was secured at the end of 2004 to clarify the professional role of the Society. The Section 60 Order under the Health Act 1999 to develop and strengthen the Society's regulatory powers was not available at the end of 2004 but an outline appears in Appendix 13. Much more legislation and amendment of the former bye-laws will be necessary before the process is complete.

The Section 60 Order will also provide the framework for modernisation of the Society's disciplinary role and the Statutory Committee. The chapters on professional conduct, and on the procedures and decisions of the Statutory Committee, have been rewritten with these issues in mind (Chapters 22–24), with recent cases being incorporated wherever possible into Chapter 24. In addition, the Council for the Regulation of Health Professionals has commenced its work to oversee the disciplinary processes of all health professionals.

The 'modernisation' of the NHS continues apace and each year between editions has seen a new Act to give powers to secure the detail of this modernisation. Measures to secure quality and collaboration have increased significantly and apply to both primary and secondary NHS care, and to private healthcare, so these changes are now brought together in one new chapter, Chapter 26.

The other healthcare professions are also undergoing change which will affect them variably, including a new Nursing and Midwifery Council to replace the UKCC and the new Health Professions Council, which has replaced the Council for the Professions Supplementary to Medicine (Chapter 25).

We gratefully acknowledge the help and advice we have received from numerous sources. Valuable help was received from Dr John Farwell, hospital pharmaceutical consultant, and Shelagh French, from the City Hospital, Nottingham, on matters concerning the NHS hospital service; from Edward Mallinson concerning the NHS in Scotland; from Sarah Cockbill concerning the NHS in Wales; and from Steve Lutener of the PSNC for his help on changes to the NHS contract and Terms of Service for community pharmacy.

In addition, thanks are due to Harold Gay, Pamela Kissman and Jeff Coombes of Boots The Chemists Ltd, Nottingham, with regard to employment, consumer and environmental legislation. Thanks also go, once again, to our publishers, in particular to Paul Weller and Charles Fry for their guidance and cheerfulness.

Gordon E Appelbe
Joy Wingfield

April 2005

Foreword

Preparing a new edition of any book concerning healthcare law and ethics gets no easier, even for authors with Gordon Appelbe's and Joy Wingfield's experience. Developments in science and technology, the continual modernisation of the NHS and the encroaching influence of Europe mean that no sooner is a draft chapter complete than it is out of date. Gordon Appelbe and Joy Wingfield continue to offer a beacon of light to pharmacists and all those interested in pharmacy law and ethics. Pharmacy has been a discipline somewhat neglected by scholars outside its boundaries. Change may be in the wind. I am honoured to be asked, once again, to write this Foreword.

There continues to be a flowering of interest in, and controversy surrounding, ethical and legal aspects of healthcare generally. Health professionals, with the doctors in the front line, have been confronted with critical analysis of their practice from diverse commentators outside their own professions. Lawyers, moral philosophers and social scientists queue up to offer their perspective on what does, and does not, constitute ethical and responsible professional practice. The rising tide of litigation has provoked fears of a malpractice crisis. The Shipman Inquiry, the several inquiries into organ retention and the many attacks on the quality of 'expert' evidence undermined medical morale and shook public confidence. Doctors felt besieged. Some resented the dissection of medical practice by scholars from other disciplines – scholars who do not ever have to face the reality of everyday practice. Even in 2005, pharmacists, while not immune from such developments, have so far appeared to attract less external *academic* criticism of their ethics and practice. With one or two notable exceptions, pharmacists, consciously or unconsciously, retain a relatively low profile. The Shipman Inquiry raised some questions about the conduct of a pharmacist given a great deal of publicity in the media. Ultimately any charges against the pharmacist were dismissed by the Royal Pharmaceutical Society who found there was no case to answer. That crucial fact received little publicity. The media thrives on tales of alleged malpractice. Nonetheless for the most part, the odium often attached to the 'bad' doctor passed the pharmacist by.

A number of reasons continue to explain the so-far happy lot of the pharmacist. A bad reason is that philosophers, social scientists and academic lawyers continue to demonstrate a worrying tendency to concentrate almost exclusively on ethical dilemmas of high drama and low incidence or even likelihood. The fate of the unfortunate patient in PVS, such as Terry Schiavo, the ethics of transplanting organs from genetically altered pigs to human recipients, reproductive cloning – these are the everyday menu of discourse in academic journals and university common rooms. Heartrending questions, for example, the sad case of Charlotte Wyatt are often transformed into media events. The daily round of the pharmacist in hospital or the community simply lacks that drama. Yet important though the ethics of caring for patients in PVS, or of transplantation, or disputes about the care of a terribly sick baby are, they are not the everyday stuff of life. They affect only a very few members of our society. The pharmacist's work reaches out to the entire community. The impact of his or her practice affects us all, but when pharmacists do their job properly, we barely even notice its importance.

Nevertheless, pharmacy is a risky business. No drug is one hundred per cent safe. All medication must be handled with care and respect. For most ills, great or small, some medication will be indicated. The pharmacist is the gatekeeper of that process. Whether dispensing a prescription medicine, or selling a medicinal product, pharmacists are the experts. We, the lay public, rely on the pharmacists, to ensure our welfare. We expect them to exercise not just technical skills, but to take steps to educate us in the safe use of our medicines. Do we accord them the professional status their training and discipline truly merits? The man or woman in the white coat is taken for granted by the customer rushing in and out of the pharmacy. And a form of intellectual snobbery, too, downgrades the provision of medicine, accepting the claims of medical practitioners that they are *the* crucial health profession. Heirs to the apothecaries of old, the pharmacists cannot entirely escape that ancient rivalry with the 'grander' physicians.

The pharmacy profession has long sought to enhance the image and status of the profession. The public are encouraged to seek advice from their pharmacists. The community pharmacist is so much more than a 'pedlar of pills'. Indeed, some of that part of the professional pharmacist's job is gradually being delegated to trained technicians. For many years now, the pharmacist has been an accessible, and usually local, source of care for minor ills and a professional able to help the layperson distinguish minor from major ills. In recent years, more and more licensed medicines have moved from Prescription Only to Pharmacy status. On their own authority, pharmacists grant access to more and more powerful medicines. The hospital pharmacist is encouraged to play a larger role as the hospital expert on medicines, a source of advice to his or her other professional colleagues. The modern pharmacist is a butterfly emerging from its constraining chrysalis. Other changes are making that metamorphosis less comfortable. The genuinely independent local pharmacist who lives in, and knows, his or her community is increasingly finding it hard to stay in business. The retail chains are increasing the number of in-house pharmacies. As medicines move from POM to P so they also move from P to GSL. Some patients perceiving themselves as informed consumers resent any gatekeeper, be they doctor or pharmacist.

Pharmacists are well aware that enlarged powers and enhanced status bring their disadvantages as well as advantages. Adopting a more fully advisory function and taking exclusive responsibility for providing a greater range of drugs necessarily increases the possibility of error, and consequent litigation. When medicines are sold, rather than dispensed on the NHS, the pharmacist guarantees the quality and safety of the medicines. In an increasingly litigious society, pharmacists must brace themselves for more lawsuits. Pharmacists in the community operate in the marketplace. They must run successful businesses as well as deliver professional services. They have to reconcile the demands of professional ethics with the desire to maximise profit. New regulations and developments in NHS policy grant pharmacists yet more independent powers including the management of repeat prescriptions and supplementary prescribing. In the community as well as in hospitals, pharmacists are looked to as the experts in medication with policy and advisory functions within Primary Care Trusts. Treated for decades as an NHS 'extra', pharmacists are coming into the fold in part but only in part. Some may feel that they now bear much greater burdens of regulation without either the status or the funds to match those burdens.

Pharmacists remain fortunate in two respects. First, one reason for the relative lack of controversy about pharmacy practice and the comparative rarity of litigation against pharmacists suggests a job done well. Second, pharmacists have for nearly 30 years benefited from a text which clearly and in great detail spells out their professional and legal obligations. *Dale and Appelbe's Pharmacy Law and Ethics* offers to every pharmacist a guide to ensure that he or she has no excuse for falling short of what their profession and the law requires. Written by authors who are themselves pharmacists, but with great legal and ethical expertise, this edition should be read and absorbed by every pharmacist. My first exposure to teaching health professionals was to deliver a term's lectures on law for pharmacists in the mid-1970s, when virtually no medical school in England taught medical law or ethics. Pharmacy recognised the need for pharmacists to understand the legal framework of their practice. Joe Dale and Gordon Appelbe sought to meet that need and, after Joe Dale's death, Joy Wingfield joined Gordon Appelbe in continuing that work. That far-sighted policy of anticipating the importance of professional appreciation of law and ethics has helped pharmacy avoid some of the pitfalls of their fellow professions. The need for this book today is even greater. New responsibilities mean that all pharmacists need greater understanding of both law and ethics. They need to be more aware of the law relating to consent confidentiality and access to records. Additionally, they need to appreciate that law simply sets the lowest common denominator of good practice. The professional must do more than just avoid unlawful conduct. He or she must aim for the highest standard of ethical behaviour. Pharmacists need education in ethics just as much as doctors do. They need to understand that a real appreciation of ethical practice requires more than simply being able to recite professional codes of practice. Education is more than training.

Dale and Appelbe offers education. The work gives its readers information and also prompts reflection. It is a book that has long affirmed the centrality of law in professional practice. It is an essential reference for the pharmacist and a key source for those of us outside pharmacy who do believe that pharmacy law and ethics is just as important as medical law and ethics.

Margaret Brazier
Professor of Law
School of Law
University of Manchester

May 2005

Introduction

Development of the law in relation to pharmacy, medicines and poisons

Between 1968 and 1978, the statutes relating to medicines, poisons and drugs were almost entirely repealed and replaced by new legislation. The Medicines Act 1968 controls the manufacture and distribution of medicines; the Poisons Act 1972 regulates the sale of non-medicinal poisons, while the Misuse of Drugs Act 1971 deals with the abuse of drugs. In 1973, the National Health Service Reorganisation Act brought about a major revision in the pharmaceutical services of the NHS. A new National Health Service Act in 1977 together with many amending Health Service Acts now regulate the pharmaceutical services. All these Acts are described in detail in later chapters together with the orders and regulations which have been made under them. This introduction gives a brief account of how the law developed to this point, including references to most of the early statutes, all of which have now been repealed either wholly or in part.

Before the middle of the nineteenth century, there were no legal restrictions in England on the sale of poisons or drugs, and anyone could describe themselves as a pharmaceutical chemist. Statutory control over sales was first applied to arsenic because, as the preamble to the Arsenic Act 1851 stated, *the unrestricted sale of arsenic facilitates the commission of crime*. The first statute relating to pharmacy followed the next year. The Pharmacy Act 1852 confirmed the charter of incorporation of the Pharmaceutical Society of Great Britain, hereinafter called *the Society*, which had been granted in 1843 (see p. 271). The 1852 Act established the framework of the Society and gave it power to hold examinations and to issue certificates. It also restricted the use of the title *pharmaceutical chemist* to members of the Society, although it did not restrict the use of the titles *chemist* or *druggist*. The Society received its *Royal* prefix in 1988.

The Pharmacy Act 1868 brought new developments. It introduced a Poisons List (with 15 entries) and empowered the Society to add other substances to it, subject to the approval of the Privy Council. A *poison* was defined as any substance included in the Poisons List. Articles and preparations containing poisons could be sold by retail only by *pharmaceutical chemists* or by a new legal class of *chemists and druggists*. Both titles were protected by the Act. The class of *chemists and druggists* comprised (a) all those who before the passing of the Act had been engaged *in the keeping of open shop for the compounding of the prescriptions of duly qualified medical practitioners*, and (b) all those persons who had been registered as *assistants* under the provisions of the Pharmacy Act 1852.

The registrar of the Society was thereafter required to keep registers of pharmaceutical chemists, of chemists and druggists, and of apprentices or students. The qualification of *chemist and druggist* (the *Minor* examination) became the statutory minimum for persons carrying on a business comprising the sale of poisons. Chemists and druggists were eligible to be elected members or associates of the Pharmaceutical Society, but did not have all the privileges of a member who had qualified as a pharmaceutical chemist (by passing the *Major* examination). That state of affairs continued – slightly modified by a statute of 1898 – until the Pharmacy Act 1953 combined the two qualifications in one Register of Pharmaceutical Chemists. The profession of pharmacy is now regulated by the Pharmacy Act 1954, which absorbed the 1953 Act. The 1954 Act is described in detail in Chapter 22.

The 1868 Act not only introduced the first list of poisons but also regulated the manner in which they could be sold, specifying more stringent restrictions on sale for the more dangerous poisons. Fixed penalties, recoverable in the civil courts, were prescribed for breaches of the Act. The list of poisons was extended by the Poisons and Pharmacy Act 1908, which also provided that poisons for agricultural and horticultural purposes could be sold by licensed dealers as well as by pharmacists. This Act also prescribed conditions under which corporate bodies could carry on the business of a chemist and druggist. This had become necessary because it had been held in the High Court in 1880 that an incorporated company was not covered by the word *person* as used in the 1868 Act, and was, therefore, not liable for penalties under the Act (*Pharmaceutical Society* v. *London and Provincial Supply Association Ltd*, see p. 390).

Under the Pharmacy and Poisons Act 1933, a Poisons Board was established to advise the Secretary of State on what should be included in the Poisons List. Poisons in Part I of the list could be sold by retail only at pharmacies; poisons in Part II could be sold also by traders on a local authority list. Poisons were further classified by means of the Schedules to the Poisons Rules made under the Act. Schedule 4, for example, comprised a class of poisons which could be supplied to the public only on the authority of a prescription written by a practitioner. A Register of Premises was set up under the Act, and all registered pharmacists were required to be members of the Pharmaceutical Society.

One of the main features of the 1933 Act was the establishment of a disciplinary body (the Statutory Committee) which had authority not only over pharmacists who committed misconduct but also over pharmacists and corporate bodies convicted of offences under the Pharmacy Act. The Society was placed under a duty to enforce the Act, and was authorised to appoint inspectors for the purpose. Proceedings under the Act were to be taken in courts of summary jurisdiction and not, as previously, in the civil courts. The Pharmacy and Poisons Act 1933 was repealed by the Medicines Act 1968. The Poisons Act 1972 deals only with non-medicinal poisons (Chapter 18). Chapter 24 deals with the powers of the Statutory Committee and includes reports of important Statutory Committee decisions.

Pharmacy and poisons were firmly linked together by statute, but the sale and manufacture of medicines was not regulated in any way except for medicines containing poisons. Some control over quality was provided by a series of Food and Drugs Acts, culminating in the Food and Drugs Act 1955. Under those Acts, it was an offence to sell adulterated drugs, or to sell, to the prejudice of the purchaser, any drug not of the nature, substance or quality demanded. The effectiveness of those provisions was limited by the fact that most drugs were of vegetable origin and, for many of them, there were no precise standards. Furthermore, a manufacturer of a proprietary medicine did not have to disclose its composition, provided that s/he paid the appropriate duty by way of fixing the appropriate excise stamps to each bottle or packet as required by the Medicine Stamp Acts. That state of affairs was changed by the Pharmacy and Medicines Act 1941, which abolished medicines stamp duty and required, instead, a disclosure of composition of each container. It also restricted the sale of medicines to shops (as distinct from market stalls etc.) and made it unlawful to advertise any article for the treatment of eight named diseases, including diabetes mellitus, epilepsy and tuberculosis. This was the first statute in which pharmacy and medicines were directly linked. The 1941 Act, however, did not apply to animal medicines.

The Therapeutic Substances Act 1925 controlled by licence the manufacture (but not the sale or supply) of a limited number of products the purity or potency of which could not be tested by chemical means (e.g. vaccines, sera, toxins, antitoxins and certain other substances). The list was greatly extended when antibiotics came into use. It had not been held necessary to restrict the retail sale or supply of vaccines, sera and antitoxins, but penicillin and most other antibiotics were found to be substances which were *capable of causing danger to the health of the community if used without proper safeguards.* Consequently, the Penicillin Act 1947 and the Therapeutic Substances (Prevention of Misuse) Act 1953 permitted the supply of antibiotics to the public only by practitioners, or from pharmacies on the authority of practitioners' prescriptions. The Therapeutic Substances Act 1956 replaced the earlier Acts, so bringing under the control of one statute both the manufacture and the supply of therapeutic substances. It could be regarded as the precursor to the Medicines Act 1968, which has now replaced it.

Legislation relating to medicines developed in a piecemeal manner, each problem being dealt with as it arose, and the law was scattered throughout a number of statutes. However, rapid developments in pharmaceutical research after the 1939–45 war made available an increasing number of potent substances for use in medicine, and a working party was set up by the Government in 1959 to examine the need for new controls. The thalidomide tragedy in 1961 almost certainly precipitated proposals for new legislation, which was published in 1967 in a White Paper entitled *Forthcoming Legislation on the Safety, Quality and Description of Drugs and Medicines* (Cmnd.3395). The Medicines Act 1968, which was designed to replace all earlier legislation relating to medicines, was based on the proposals in the White Paper. It is considered in detail in Chapters 2 to 15.

European Community legislation has had, and still has, a large impact on UK law. The Treaty of Rome and the issue of Regulations, Directives, Decisions and Recommendations by the Council of Ministers in Brussels has led to amendments of pharmacy law in Great Britain, particularly with regard to the mutual recognition of pharmaceutical qualifications and the manufacture and distribution of medicines. This is discussed in a new Chapter 1, which also includes the principles and sources of law and the administration of justice.

International agreement about the control of narcotics began with the International Opium Convention signed at the Hague in 1912, although the Convention was not implemented until after the 1914–18 war. A series of Dangerous Drugs Acts, beginning with the Dangerous Drugs Act 1920, brought the various international agreements into force in Great Britain. The Single Convention on Narcotic Drugs 1961 replaced all the earlier international agreements and was reflected in the Dangerous Drugs Act 1965.

The misuse of amphetamines and other psychotropic drugs widened the problems of abuse, and an International Convention on Psychotropic Substances was signed in 1971. In Great Britain, however, the Drugs (Prevention of Misuse) Act 1964 had provided a measure of control by making the unlawful possession of amphetamines, and certain other drugs, an offence. As problems of drug abuse continued to increase, the law was extended and recast in the Misuse of Drugs Act 1971, which repealed the various Dangerous Drugs Acts and the 1964 Act. The provision of the 1971 Act and the regulations made under it are described in detail in Chapter 17.

The National Health Service Act 1946 and the National Health Service (Scotland) Act 1947 provided for a comprehensive health service, including the provision of pharmaceutical services. There have since been numerous amending Acts particularly since the seventh edition of this book was published in 2001 In the present edition, because the primary and secondary healthcare systems are moving closer together, the opportunity has been taken to amalgamate the service requirements with those of the hospital service and create a new Chapter 26. Miscellaneous legislation impinging on pharmacy is dealt with in Chapter 21, professional matters in Chapters 22 and 23 and disciplinary matters in Chapter 24. A discussion on allied health professions is provided in Chapter 25.

List of Statutes

and Statutory Instruments

Statutes marked with an asterisk have been repealed.

ACCESS TO HEALTH RECORDS ACT 1990

AGRICULTURE ACT 1947

AGRICULTURE ACT 1970

ALCOHOLIC LIQUOR DUTIES ACT 1979

ANIMAL (CRUEL POISONS) ACT 1962
  SI 1963 No.1278   Animal (Cruel Poisons) Regulations 1963

ANIMAL HEALTH AND WELFARE ACT 1984

ANIMALS (SCIENTIFIC PROCEDURES) ACT 1986

APOTHECARIES ACT 1815

ARSENIC ACT 1851

BUSINESS NAMES ACT 1985

COMPETITION ACT 1998

COMPANIES ACT 1985

CONSUMER PROTECTION ACT 1987
  SI 1988 No.2078   Consumer Protection (Code of Practice for Traders on Price Indications) (Approved) Order 1988

Medicines

SI 1994 No.3119	—(Consequential Amendments – Medicines) Regulations 1994
SI 1994 No.3142	—(Marketing Authorisations for Veterinary Medicinal Products) Regulations 1994 amended 2002/269; 2004/3193; 2004/3224
SI 1994 No.3144	—(For Human Use) (Marketing Authorisations, etc.) Regulations 1994 amended 1998/3105; 2000/292; 2003/1618; 2004/3224
SI 1995 No.309	—(Advisory Board on the Registration of Homoeopathic Products) Order 1995
SI 1995 No.2321	—(Amendment) Regulations 1995
SI 1997 No.321	—(Registration of Homoeopathic Veterinary Medicinal Products) (Fees) Regulations 1997
SI 1997 No.322	—(Registration of Homoeopathic Veterinary Medicinal Products) Regulations 1997
SI 1997 No.1349	—(Registration of Homoeopathic Veterinary Medicinal Products) (General Sale List) Regulations 1997
SI 1997 No.1830	—(Prescription Only Medicines) (Human Use) Order 1997 amended 1997/2044; 1998/108; 1998/1178; 1998/2081; 1999/1044; 1999/3463; 2000/1917; 2000/2899; 2000/3231; 2001/2777; 2001/2889; 2001/3942; 2002/549; 2003/696; 2003/1590; 2003/2915; 2004/2; 2004/1189
SI 1998 No.1044	—(Exemptions for Merchants in Veterinary Drugs) Order 1998
SI 2000 No.7	—(Retailer Records for Veterinary Medicinal Products) Regulations 2000
SI 2000 No.1368	—(Aristolochia and Mu Tong, etc.) (Temporary Prohibition) Order 2000
SI 2000 No.2386	—(Data Sheets – Veterinary Drugs) Regulations 2000
SI 2001 No 2889	—The Prescription Only Medicines (Human Use)(Electronic Communications) Order 2001
SI 2002 No.236	—(Codification Amendments etc) Regulations 2002 amended 2002/542
SI 2002 No.3170	—The Medicines for Human Use (Kava-kava) (Prohibition) Order 2002
SI 2003 No.3141	—The Medicines (Pharmacies) (Application for Registration and Fees) Amendment Regulations 2003
SI 2004 No.1031	—The Medicines for Human Use (Clinical Trials) Regulations 2004
SI 2004 No.2779	—The Medicines (Vaccination Against Foot and Mouth Disease) Order 2004
SI 2004 No.3193	—The Marketing Authorisations for Veterinary Medicinal Products (Revocation of Confidentiality Provision) Regulations 2004

Abbreviations

AC—Appeal Court
All ER—All England Law Reports
Ch—Law Reports Chancery Division
CHIP—Chemical (Hazard Information and Packaging for Supply) (Regulations)
CHRE—Council for Health Care Regulatory Excellence
cm—centimetre
COSHH—Control of Substances Hazardous to Health (Regulations)
CPD—continuing professional development
DEFRA—Department of Environment, Food and Rural Affairs
EC—European Community
EEA—European Economic Area
EEC—European Economic Community
EMEA—European Agency for the Evaluation of Medicinal Products
EU—European Union
g—gram
GMC—General Medical Council
GP—General Practitioner
GSL—General Sale List
INN—international non-proprietary name
IU—international unit
KB—Law Reports King's Bench Division
kg—kilogram

LPC—local pharmaceutical committee
LT—Law Times reports
mdd—maximum daily dose
md—maximum dose
mg—milligram
MHRA–Medicines and Health Care Regulatory Authority
ml—millilitre
ms—maximum strength
NHS—National Health Service
PALS—Patient Advocacy and Liaison Service
PCT—Primary Care Trust
PGD—Patient Group Direction
Pharm J—Pharmaceutical Journal
PML—permitted licensed medicinal products
POM—Prescription Only Medicine
P—Pharmacy Medicine
QB—Law Reports Queen's Bench Division
r. (rr.)—rule (rules)
reg.—Regulation
s.—section
Sch.—Schedule
SI—Statutory Instrument
v/v—volume in volume
v/w—volume in weight
w/v—weight in volume
w/w—weight in weight

CHAPTER ONE

Sources of law

Since the accession of the UK (that is, England, Scotland, Wales and Northern Ireland) to the European Treaty of Rome in 1973, almost all legislation relevant to pharmacy and medicines derives from the European Union (EU) [formerly the European Economic Community (EEC)]. Therefore, Europe is the highest legal authority for such law in the UK. Law emanating from the EU has then to be enacted into 'domestic' legislation to take effect in the UK. Domestic legislation in the UK operates at two levels: 'primary' law, that is, Acts of Parliament, and 'secondary' law, that is, detailed provisions implementing the broad provisions of an Act. Public bodies are also subject to further 'Directions' made under the authority of primary and secondary law. This hierarchy is reflected in the processes by which law is made, how it is enforced and interpreted and how it may be challenged. This chapter provides an overview of aspects of UK law as they relate to pharmacy.

European law

Following the Second World War, there was felt to be a need for trading agreements between the countries of Europe. In 1957, six member states signed the Treaty of Rome, which established the EEC (now the EU). The UK acceded to the Treaty in 1973, along with Denmark and Ireland; Greece acceded in 1981 and Portugal and Spain followed in 1986. Sweden, Finland

and Austria signed up to the Treaty in 1996, and Latvia, Lithuania, Estonia, Cyprus, the Czech Republic, Slovakia, Poland, Hungary, Malta and Slovenia joined in May 2004, bringing the total number of member states to 25.

The Single European Act 1987 was designed to expedite a single internal market and to remove all the remaining barriers which exist to the free movement of people, goods, services and capital. It is the object of the EU to ensure that there is no impediment to these 'four freedoms' and, if there is, to remove it. Harmonisation is one method by which such obstacles can be overcome and this is shown in many of the Directives which have affected the production and distribution of pharmaceuticals.

The legislation implementing the Treaty is formulated by the Council of Ministers in four basic forms.

> *Regulations.* These have a direct effect and are binding on all member states and on individuals in every respect.
>
> *Directives.* These are binding as to their objectives but leave to member states the method of implementation. Such implementation may be legislative or administrative. Most directives include 'derogations' – a form of exception which member states may claim if they feel that their particular circumstances require it.
>
> *Decisions.* These are binding on those to whom they are addressed and are often of an administrative nature.
>
> *Recommendations.* These are self-evident and are persuasive.

The European institutions

There are five main institutions of the EU.

The Council of Ministers

The Council of Ministers is composed of politicians of each member state and in practice the minister attending changes according to the item under discussion. The Council makes the ultimate decisions on European law. The Council is supported by working parties which include civil servants from each state and which study proposals put forward by the Council or the Commission. The working party reports are sent to the Committee of Permanent Representatives, which makes the decision whether or not to put the proposal forward to a Council meeting.

The Commission

The Commission comprises Commissioners (civil servants), each with responsibilities for a particular area of interest (e.g. agriculture, internal affairs, environment, etc.). It has been called the Civil Service of the EU and proposes, executes and polices the policies of the EU as promulgated by the Council. Discussions between a Commissioner's department and interested parties can lead to the formation of draft proposals. These are discussed by the Commission as a whole, which then decides on the form of any final proposal to be laid before the Council.

The Parliament

The Parliament (Assembly) is a directly elected chamber of members from the 25 states; member state representation is related directly to population size. The Parliament has three main functions: control over the EU's budget, power of censure over the Commission and scrutiny of the legislative process. The last function has been of importance in the promulgation of Directives affecting pharmacy upon which the Parliament must be consulted. The detailed work is done by Standing Committees, who have a *rapporteur* responsible for preparing the draft response of the Committee and presenting it to the plenary session of the Parliament.

The Economic and Social Committee

The Economic and Social Committee comprises representatives of economic and social groups in the member states. It is divided into three groups: employers, workers (trade unions) and a variety of interest groups, which includes the professions. The Committee has to be consulted before any final decision can be taken on proposed legislation. The work is mainly done in various specialist expertise sections (e.g. agriculture, transport). Within each section, there are study groups which deal with specific proposals. The section produces an 'Opinion', which is presented to a plenary session of the Committee before being forwarded to the Council.

The European Court of Justice

The European Court of Justice is covered below (p. 7). European law usually results from a request for action from an EU member state. The Commission then drafts proposed legislation that passes through a lengthy debate, amendment and consultation process until the Council agrees the final form of the legislation.

British law

The scope of this book does not extend to Northern Ireland. Therefore, the law covered relates to England, Scotland and Wales only, although the law in Northern Ireland often replicates the British law. Law covering medicines and pharmacy practice generally applies across all of Britain but there is scope for differences. Law covering the administration of the National Health Service (NHS) differs significantly in the three component countries of Britain and is likely to diverge further over time. There are two primary divisions in British law: statute law and civil law (Table 1.1). These may commonly be referred to

Table 1.1 Summary of UK law with relevance to pharmacy

	Statutory law			Civil law: common law rights and duties, augmented by human rights
	Criminal legislation	Administrative legislation	Professional legislation	
Enforcement agencies	Police officers, RPSGB inspectors	Representatives of administrative body	Professional body, RPSGB inspectors	Direct action by plaintiff
Action for breach	Prosecution in the criminal courts	Appearance before relevant tribunal	Appearance before professional tribunal	Being sued in the civil courts
Sanctions available	Fines, imprisonment	Loss of remuneration, loss of contract, loss of position	Removal from professional register	Having to pay compensation
Redress available	Appeal	Judicial review	Appeal	Appeal

RPSGB, Royal Pharmaceutical Society of Great Britain.

as criminal and civil law, but there is a substantial body of statutory law that is not accompanied by criminal sanctions but rather by administrative or professional sanctions.

The arrangements for the NHS and for professional discipline fall into these two categories. Legislation in Britain is made in the name of the Crown – the Queen. Properties owned by, and activities carried out by the state on her behalf, have in the past been subject to *Crown immunity*.

Crown immunity means complete immunity from prosecution under statutory legislation. This concept prevailed in NHS hospitals for many years and many hospital pharmacists still have the false idea that it still applies and that they cannot be prosecuted for offences committed within NHS hospitals. This is not true as Crown immunity was formally removed from NHS hospital services in April 1991 and all the major pharmaceutical legislation now applies, including the Medicines Act and the Misuse of Drugs Acts together with the subordinate legislation made under these Acts. The prison health services and military health services are also expected to comply with UK legislation, other than in exceptional cases (Chapter 8).

Statute law

Statute law is referred to principally in Chapters 2–21. A statute, strictly speaking, is an Act of Parliament. There are two kinds: public and private, but this book is only concerned with public acts such as the Medicines Act, the Misuse of Drugs Act, the Poisons Act, etc. Acts are usually referred to as *primary* legislation since they are the primary authority for legislation in the UK. Statute law is also used to describe legislation which is subsidiary to an Act, normally in the form of Regulations or Orders. These are collectively known as Statutory Instruments (SIs) or *secondary* legislation. Proposals to introduce new legislation come forward in the form of a bill. Most are Government bills but sometimes they are put forward by individual Members of Parliament (private members' bills). Before a bill is proposed, the Government will normally signal its intentions in a 'white paper'. Sometimes this is preceded by a discussion document, called a 'green paper'. The programme of primary legislation is usually outlined in the Queen's speech when Parliament enters a new session in the autumn.

Each bill is normally introduced into the House of Commons at a formal first reading and then passes through a series of 'readings'. After the second reading, the content and objective of the bill is open to debate, following which the bill goes to a committee stage; this examines the detail clause by clause and any amendments suggested in debate. The House of Commons then considers the bill again at the report stage, followed by the third reading. These stages are then repeated in the House of Lords. Once a bill passes both Houses it is ready for Royal assent. Acts are most often 'enabling'; that is, they give powers to the Government, usually individual Secretaries of State, to do things. Major changes to an Act can normally only be made by another Act. An SI implements the detail of broad powers given by an Act. An SI does not go through parliamentary debate but is 'tabled' in Parliament in the name of the Minister and will be passed if no objections are raised.

Administrative law

Administrative law is discussed principally in Chapters 22 and 25. It is the body of law that regulates the activity of public bodies; such bodies include NHS Authorities such as Primary Care Trusts (PCTs) in England and local authorities and education authorities. Every NHS Trust and PCT is set up by individual Regulation, thus conferring statutory powers such as power to manage budgets, hire and fire staff and enter into contracts. Strategic Health Authorities, Ambulance and Mental Health Care Trusts are also individually created by statute. NHS Direct is a legally constituted Special Health Authority given power to enter into formal contracts with PCTs (England). Administrative law comprises statutes (Acts, Regulations, Orders) supplemented by a substantial body of 'Directions' made by senior civil servants acting under the authority of the relevant minister. Policy statements and guidelines, all of which describe the standards to which the public sector is expected to work, supplement the legal framework further. Initially, the public authority itself usually enforces administrative law; a good example would be the enforcement of the NHS dispensing contract by the PCTs in England. Enforcement is often also pursued through tribunals, appeal authorities and the courts.

Sanctions are administrative such as a fine (withholding of reimbursement for dispensing NHS scripts), which reverts to the public body, or loss of contract.

Action by public bodies is susceptible to *judicial review,* a process whereby a court determines whether the public body acted fairly and within its statutory powers, rather than reviewing the actual decision reached. Three types of criterion are considered regarding a decision made by a public body:

- was it lawful or not?
- was it reasonable and rational: had the body considered all the relevant facts and ignored those that were irrational?
- was it based on the correct procedures laid down in a particular case.

Decisions in Statutory Committee cases can be made subject to *judicial review,* particularly if there has been a breach of proper procedures or where the penalty imposed has been irrational or unreasonable (p. 331).

Professional law

Professional law is mainly discussed in Chapters 22–25. It comprises the law underpinning the powers to discipline health professionals such as pharmacists. The authority to discipline pharmacists lies in the Pharmacy Act 1954 with subordinate regulations made in 1978. The notion of an expected standard of care, which is also used in civil law cases (see below), is used by professional tribunals to judge whether a professional is guilty of professional misconduct. For pharmacists, these standards may principally be found in the profession's Code of ethics and in the standards, guidelines and protocols laid down for NHS care.

Civil law

Civil law is referred to in Chapters 22 and 25 and derives from the notion of duties and responsibilities owed between citizens (Latin *civitas,* citizen). In its turn, civil law has developed through court judgments based on 'common law'. The common law developed during the Middle Ages as the King's courts gradually took the rule of law out into the shires to make judgments over the affairs of 'common' people. Action under civil law allows an aggrieved party to sue for compensation from another citizen who is alleged to have 'wronged' him. This concept of 'a civil wrong' is known in law as *tort* (another archaic term from Old French). Some types of tort are now rarely seen in courts: breach of promise, for example. Libel, slander and trespass actions are all civil wrongs. In healthcare practice, the most likely actions are for clinical negligence and possibly breach of confidentiality and defamation. In a case of clinical negligence, the complainant (plaintiff) makes an allegation that the actions of another person (the respondent) has caused them damage or injury. To succeed, the plaintiff would have to prove that the health professional firstly owed him a duty of care, then that the duty had been breached (i.e. was lower than the standard expected) and finally that the breach had caused the injury alleged. A civil action for battery is also a possible tort if a patient is treated without consent.

The courts

The court of jurisdiction over EU law is the European Court of Justice. This settles legal disputes involving EU legislation and its judgments are binding on each member state. Much of its work now involves giving preliminary rulings on questions referred by the courts of the member states.

In addition, under the auspices of the Council of Europe, there is the European Court of Human Rights, which developed separately, before the EU Court, to enforce the European Convention on Human Rights. This was agreed in 1949 as a direct result of the human rights atrocities of the Second World War. The UK was a founder member but was the last of the original signatories to enact the convention into domestic law. This was principally because English common law conventions were held to embody adequate safeguards for human rights. Until 1998, any individual who wished to claim that their human rights had been violated had to complain for redress to the European Court of Human Rights. When the UK enacted the Convention in the Human Rights Act 1998, UK citizens then acquired the right to seek redress in the UK courts first, although the European Court of Human Rights remains an option if the complainant does not receive satisfaction in the UK

The structure of the Courts in England and Wales is shown in Table 1.2.

A strict hierarchical system of courts means that the lowest possible tier of the court system will first make a judgment on the particular facts of that case. This judgment becomes a precedent – or case law – for dealing with any similar cases, unless there are some significant facts that distinguish them from the first case. However, a higher court can disagree with the findings of a lower court and overturn them. More detail on the British legal system may be found under Further reading below.

Examples of European legislation affecting pharmacy, pharmacists and medicines are given below; further details may also be found in Further reading. Full details of British legislation appear in subsequent chapters of this book.

Examples of European law

Most of the current UK law applying to pharmacy practice derives from European legislation in the form of Directives although regulations have been made concerning the marketing authorisation of medicinal products (p. 9). The first set of digits in Directives refers to the year of enactment, the second

Table 1.2 The courts in England and Wales

Criminal division	Civil division
House of Lords: hears appeals from the Court of Appeal and sometimes direct from the Divisional Court	House of Lords: hears appeals from the Court of Appeal and sometimes direct from the High Court
Court of Appeal, Criminal Division: hears appeals from the Crown Court	Court of Appeal, Civil Division: hears appeals from the High Court and the County Court
Queen's Bench Division (Divisional Court)	High Court: Queen's Bench Division hears negligence cases (other divisions for family law and chancery – commercial matters)
Crown Court: hears cases committed to this court, and appeals, from the magistrate's court; has greater powers of sentencing than lower court	
Magistrates Court (Bench of lay Magistrates): may sometimes sit with a stipendiary or circuit judge	County Court: can deal with actions involving small sums of money (£5000–£10 000)

set refers to the number of this legal instrument within that year. All retain either the EC or the EEC suffix.

Free movement of pharmacists

In 1985, the Council of Ministers introduced two Directives, 85/432/EEC and 85/433/EEC, concerned with the free movement of pharmacists. Directive 85/432/EEC dealt with the education and training of the pharmacist and Directive 85/433/EEC dealt with a pharmacist's right to establishment within the member states. Each member state is obliged to recognise, without impediment, the list of degrees (or equivalent) laid down in the Directives. Registration as a pharmaceutical chemist in the UK is recognised. The competent authorities within the member states deal with the procedure; in the UK, those authorities are the Royal Pharmaceutical Society of Great Britain and its equivalent in Northern Ireland.

In order for a pharmacist to move freely throughout the EU, s/he must produce evidence from his/her own competent authority to the corresponding one in the host member state that s/he:

1   is a national of a member state of the Community or treated as such;
2   is qualified

    (a)   possesses a university degree (or equivalent) which was obtained following a course of study of not less than five years, at least four years of which comprised theoretical and practical training in a university, together with at least six months in-service training in a community or hospital pharmacy; or

(b)   has for at least three consecutive years during the previous five years been effectively and lawfully engaged in regulated pharmaceutical activity (e.g. a community pharmacy, hospital pharmacy, etc.); this is known as the *acquired rights* provision for those who cannot comply with (a) above;

3   is in good physical and mental health, if this is required in the host member state; and

4   is of good character, if this is required in the host member state.

The pharmacy degrees in the UK, together with the pre-registration year and the 'A' level at university entrance, are considered to be equivalent to the total five year requirement.

The Directives have been implemented in Great Britain by means of the Pharmaceutical Qualifications (European Community) Order 1987 (SI 1987 No.2202, as amended) and by section XIX(5) of the bye-laws of the Royal Pharmaceutical Society of Great Britain (see pp. 277–278 and Appendix 14). Pharmacists seeking free movement should contact the Royal Pharmaceutical Society.

Production and distribution of medicinal products for human use

Council Regulation 2309/93/EEC lays down EU procedures for the authorisation and supervision of medicinal products for human and veterinary use and established the European Agency for the Evaluation of Medicinal Products (EMEA). Directive 2001/83/EC, which in 2001 consolidated all the earlier Council Directives, states that the primary purpose of controls on the production and distribution of medicinal products is to safeguard public health. This consolidation has also required consequential amendments to the Medicines Act and the SIs in the UK, achieved by the Medicines (Codification Amendments etc.) Regulations 2002 No. 236. The Directive defines a medicinal product and establishes that a medicine must possess a licence or marketing authorisation, which had been granted on the basis of safety, quality, and efficacy, before that medicine can be put on the market. In addition, the Directive covers the labelling of medicines. Commission Directive 2003/94/EC lays down the principles and guidelines of *Good Manufacturing Practice*, which is applicable to all activities which require a licence under Council Directive 2001/83/EC. Good Manufacturing Practice means the part of quality assurance which ensures that products are consistently produced and controlled in accordance with the quality of standards appropriate to their intended use, the principles and guidelines of which are specified in Commission Directive 2003/94/EC. The Council Directive 65.65/EEC and its amending Directives were revoked by and consolidated in Council Directive 2001/83/EC. Council Regulation 2309/93/EEC, Council Directive 2001/

83/EC and Commission Directive 2003/94 have been implemented in the UK under the provisions of the Medicines Act (Chapter 2 and Appendices 1–7).

In 2004, the EU had completed its review of legislation regulating medicinal products and in April 2004 had published Council Directive 2004/27/EC, which amended Council Directive 2001/83/EC and Council Directive 2003/63/EC. Member states are obliged to amend their legislation to comply with the amending directive by October 2005. The amendments include changes to data exclusivity and generic products.

Council Regulation 2309/93/EC provides for marketing authorisations via the centralised procedures, the establishment of the European Agency for the Evaluation of Medicinal Products (EMEA) together with the setting up of a Committee for Veterinary Medicinal Products. The name of EMEA was changed to the European Medicines Agency by Council Regulation 726/2004/EC.

Analytical, toxicological and clinical standards for medicines for human use

Council Directive 2001/83/EC set up standards and protocols for the analysis and toxicological and pharmacological tests which had to be applied to medicinal products. Clinical trials are now controlled under Council Directive 2000/21EC.

High-technology medicinal products for human and animal use

Directive 93/41/EEC set up procedures to deal with applications for marketing authorisations involving high-technology medicinal products, in particular those derived from biotechnology.

Homoeopathic medicinal products

Council Directive 2001/83/EC is concerned with the authorisation for marketing and the labelling of homoeopathic medicinal products for human use. It also provides for a special simplified registration procedure for those traditional homoeopathic medicinal products which are placed on the market without therapeutic indications in a pharmaceutical form and dosage and which do not present a risk to the public. Directive 92/74/EEC relates to homoeopathic medicinal products for veterinary use. UK legislation implements both these Directives (Chapter 3).

In March 2004, the EU issued Council Directive 2004/24/EC, the Directive on Traditional Herbal Medicinal Products, to regulate herbal products. Member states must have a simplified registration scheme in force by October

2005. The Directive is based on long-standing use of the product and no clinical trial evidence will be required. All herbal products now on the market can remain so for seven years.

Advertising, labelling and leaflets

Council Directive 2001/83/EC deals with the labelling of medicinal products and the availability of package leaflets aimed at the public. It requires that 'information supplied to users should provide a high degree of consumer protection in order that medicinal products may be used correctly on the basis of full and comprehensible information'. This was implemented in the UK on 1 January 1994 (Chapter 15).

Council Directive 2001/83/EC deals with the advertising of medicinal products for human use both to the general public and to health professionals. It also deals with the question of hospitality related to sales promotion, samples, medical representatives, etc. (see Chapter 4).

Wholesale distribution

Council Directive 2001/83/EC covers the control of wholesale distribution of medicinal products for human use in the EU. It requires that such distribution should be subject to the possession of an authorisation to engage in the activity as a wholesaler in medicinal products and lays down the conditions for such an authorisation. Such activity is subject to licensing in the UK (Chapter 9).

Colouring of medicinal products

Directive 78/25/EEC controls the colouring agents which can and cannot be added to medicinal products.

Production of medicinal products for animal use

Directive 2001/82/EC, as amended by 2004/28/EC, provides that no veterinary medicinal product may be placed on the market of a member state unless a marketing authorisation has been granted by the competent authorities of that member state in accordance with these Directives or in accordance with Regulation EC/726/2004.

Directive 91/412/EEC introduced a legal requirement for a manufacturer of medicinal products for animal use to comply with the principles and guidelines of Good Manufacturing Practice.

Regulation 90/2377/EEC lays down procedures to establish maximum residue limits for animal medicines in foodstuffs of animal origin.

Controlled drugs

Council Directive 92/109/EEC applies to the manufacture and trade in scheduled substances within the EU and is implemented in the UK by the Controlled Drugs (Substances Useful for Manufacture) (Intra-Community Trade) Regulations 1993 as amended. It requires the person who manufactures or trades in these substances to be licensed and restricts the persons to whom supplies may be made. The 1993 UK regulations treat the provisions of Council Directive 92/109/EEC as if they were requirements of regulations made under section 13 of the 1990 Act.

Council Regulation 90/3677/EEC controls the import, export, recording and labelling of scheduled substances and the power to enter business premises to obtain evidence of irregularities. Records must be kept for two years. It also requires member states to adopt measures to enable them to obtain information on any orders for, or activities in, scheduled substances. There is a list of scheduled substances.

Data protection

Council Directive 95/46/EEC extends data protection to all data maintained manually and affects the way in which patient medication records are stored. This Directive was implemented in the UK by way of the Data Protection Act 1998, which came into force on 1 March 2000. All data, both electronic and manual, are now controlled under the 1998 Act (see p. 265).

Human rights

The Human Rights Act 1998 applies to public authorities such as the NHS or local authorities, but it also extends to 'private bodies exercising public functions'. So private contractors dispensing NHS prescriptions would be included. A full account of how the NHS is affected by the Act can be found on the Department of Health website. Since the Act came into force, all UK laws must be interpreted to respect and protect the human rights of all UK scitizens. Human rights go beyond common law: for example, they recognise a right to privacy that does not exist in the common law.

Human rights law departs from legal convention in the UK in three main ways.

1   Precedent will not necessarily bind judgments in human rights cases. The courts are expected to reflect concepts of human rights at the time of consideration rather than at the time of the complaint and thus will reflect present day attitudes and conditions.

2   Statutes will be interpreted as to intention rather than 'as written'. This is a major departure from UK conventions on interpretation of statutes.

3   The UK courts can challenge and overrule statute if not compatible with human rights; in other words, the judges may challenge Parliament in this area.

Key human rights in relation to healthcare practice

ARTICLE 2 'RIGHT TO LIFE'

Article 2 is really a right not to be deprived of life save in very special circumstances. The judicial sanction of capital punishment is not a special circumstances. It should be noted that this is not a right to unlimited healthcare in an effort to preserve life nor a right to death. Such rights may be cited in cases of assisted suicide or euthanasia and there are debates issues such as assisted conception, contraception and abortion. Debates can also arise over resource allocation and equity in availability of treatment to all patients.

ARTICLE 3 'RIGHT TO PROHIBITION OF TORTURE OR INHUMAN OR DEGRADING TREATMENT OR PUNISHMENT'

Article 3 is not obvious in relation to healthcare but arguments in some cases have asserted that aggressive treatment in terminal care or some treatments of the mentally handicapped are close to being inhuman.

ARTICLE 5 'RIGHT TO LIBERTY'

Article 5 is particularly relevant to the treatment of those with mental disorder and the use of 'sectioning'and compulsory treatment, and it is very relevant to consent to treatment.

ARTICLE 6 'RIGHT TO A FAIR TRIAL'

Article 6 is mostly relevant to disciplinary processes and to such principles as the right to know what one is charged with, time to prepare a defence, right to a defence, etc. In addition, any hearing has to be within a reasonable time without delay and with the right not to incriminate oneself. Pharmacy's processes (e.g. Statutory Committee procedures) do not appear yet to be fully compliant.

ARTICLE 8 'RIGHT FOR RESPECT FOR PRIVATE AND FAMILY LIFE'

Human rights issues may arise in the treatment of transsexuals and in the right to practise particular forms of sexuality. This right has also been cited in relation to the use of medical records in court. It is very relevant to issues of privacy in medical care, restrictions on disclosure of confidential information, and similar issues.

ARTICLE 9 'RIGHT TO FREEDOM OF THOUGHT, CONSCIENCE AND RELIGION'

Issues may arise where treatment is contrary to religious or cultural beliefs and practices. This also may be an issue for a 24-hour health service and religious restrictions on working at certain times or days.

Further reading

Louis, J.-V. (1990) *The Community Legal Order*. Office for Official Publications of the European Communities, Luxembourg.

Rules Governing Medicinal Products in the European Union, vol. 1: *Pharmaceutical Legislation, Human Medicinal Products*. The Stationery Office, London.

Rules Governing Medicinal Products in the European Union, vol. 5: *Pharmaceutical Legislation, Veterinary Medicinal Products*. The Stationery Office, London.

Textbooks on law

Beale H. *et al.* (eds) (2004) *Chitty on Contracts*, 29th edn. Sweet & Maxwell, London.

Dugdale A. M. *et al.* (eds) (2002) *Clerk & Lindsell on Torts*, 18th edn. Sweet & Maxwell, London.

Smith J. C. (2002) *Smith & Hogan Criminal Law*, 10th edn. Butterworths, London.

Wade E. C. S. and Bradley E. W. (1996) *Constitutional and Administrative Law*, 11th edn. Longman, London.

Websites

Legislation: http://www.hmso.gov.uk/legis.htm

CHAPTER TWO

Medicines Act 1968

Scope and administration

European Community Council Directives and Regulations together with the Medicines Act 1968 (from now on referred to as 'the Act') regulate the manufacture, distribution and importation of (a) medicines for human use, (b) medicines for administration to animals and (c) medicated animal feeding stuffs. At present their application to products for export is limited (Chapter 3). The Health and Agriculture Ministers of the UK are responsible for the administration of the Act and they have the benefit of advice from a Medicines Commission.

> It has been proposed that in October 2005 all the provisions in the Medicines Act 1968 relating to veterinary medicinal products, including medicated feeding stuffs and additives, will be replaced by a new veterinary medicinal products regulation (see p. 139).

Medicinal products placed on the market in the UK require a marketing authorisation, formerly called a product licence. Similarly the manufacture, wholesaling, importation and distribution of medicines are controlled through a licensing system operated by the Ministers and enforced by the *Medicines and Health Care Regulatory Authority* (MHRA) (see Chapter 3). Since the removal of Crown immunity in April 1991, manufacturing units in NHS hospitals are also within the licensing system and are subject to the oversight of the MHRA and its inspectorate. The animal medicines legislation is monitored by the Veterinary Medicines Directorate of the *Department of Environment, Food and Rural Affairs* (DEFRA).

The Act also deals with the registration of retail pharmacies and provides that medicines may be supplied to the public only from pharmacies, except those medicines which can with reasonable safety be sold without the supervision of a pharmacist. The Minister can make regulations relating to the labelling of medicines, the containers in which they are supplied and the manner in which their sale is promoted, whether by advertisement or oral representation.

In Great Britain, the Royal Pharmaceutical Society of Great Britain (referred to from now on as 'the Society') has duties of enforcement in connection with pharmacies and the retail distribution of medicines. Other enforcement duties may be given to the Society and to local authorities, as the appropriate Minister may decide (see p. 20).

Preparation of the *British Pharmacopoeia* and other books of standards also falls within the scope of the Act.

The Animal Health and Welfare Act 1984 (ss.13, 14 and 15) increased the powers under the Medicines Act to:

1   regulate the manufacture and sampling of animal feeding stuffs; and
2   provide for registration of suppliers of veterinary drugs and medicated feeding stuffs and for the maintenance of those registers in Great Britain by the Society.

Medicinal product

The term used is not *medicine* but *relevant medicinal product,* which means a medicinal product for human use to which provisions of the 2001 Directive applies (SI 2002 No.236). It is defined in Council Directive 2001/83 as:

1   Any substance or combination of substances presented for treating or preventing disease in human beings or animals.
2   Any substance or combination of substances which may be administered to human beings or animals with a view to making a medical diagnosis or to restoring, correcting, or modifying physiological functions in human beings or animals is likewise considered a medicinal product.

This is a broader definition than that in the Medicines Act and can be defined as being a medicinal product (a) by presentation and (b) by function.

The term *a medicinal product to which Chapters of the 2001 Directive apply* includes all medicinal products for human use *except* those prepared on the basis of a *magistral* or *official formula,* medicinal products intended for research or intermediate products intended for further processing by an authorised manufacturer (Council Directive 2001/83/EC, as amended).

Magistral means any medicinal product prepared in a pharmacy in accordance with a prescription for an individual patient.

Official formula means any medicinal product which is prepared in accordance with the prescriptions of a pharmacopoeia and is intended to be supplied directly to the patients served by the pharmacy in question.

Ingredient may be the sole active ingredient present in a medicinal product.

Hospital includes a clinic, nursing home or similar institution.

Animal includes any bird, fish or reptile.

Medicinal purpose means one or more of the following: (a) treating or preventing disease; (b) diagnosing disease or ascertaining the existence, degree or extent of a physiological condition; (c) contraception; (d) inducing anaesthesia; (e) otherwise preventing or interfering with the normal operation of a physiological function [s.130(2)].

Administer means administer to a human being or an animal, whether orally, by injection or by introduction into the body in any other way or by external application, a substance or article either in its existing state or after it has been dissolved or dispersed in, or diluted or mixed with, some other substance used as a vehicle [s.130(9)].

By ministerial order (s.104), the Act, or specified parts of the Act, can be applied to any article or substance which is not a medicinal product but is made wholly or partly for a medicinal purpose. In the past, Orders have been made in respect of surgical ligatures and sutures, dental filling substances, contact lenses and associated substances, and intrauterine contraceptive devices. However since 1994, these substances have been considered to be medical devices rather than medicines and are now controlled under the Medical Devices Regulations 1994 (SI 1994 No.3017, as amended) made under the Consumer Protection Act 1987 (p. 47).

An order may also be made (s.105) in respect of any substance which (a) is used as an ingredient in the manufacture of a medicinal product, or (b) is capable of causing danger to the health of the community or to the health of animals if used without proper safeguards. The order may specify which parts of the Act are to apply. Some substances used as ingredients in the manufacture of medicinal products, and certain other substances, have been controlled by orders of this kind (SIs 1971 No.1200, 1973 No.367 and 1985 No.1403) (Appendix 1).

Orders can also be made under the European Communities Act 1972, for example the Medicines for Human Use (Marketing Authorisations, etc.) Regulations 1994 (SI 1994 No.3144, as amended).

Certain things are specifically declared *not* to be medicinal products (s.130). These include:

1   Substances or articles manufactured for administration to human beings or animals in the course of the manufacturer's business, or in a laboratory on behalf of the manufacturer, solely by way of a test for ascertaining what effects they have, and in circumstances where the

manufacturer has no knowledge that the effects are likely to be beneficial.

2   Substances and articles as may be specified in a ministerial order. Chemical substances used to sterilise animals which are neither domestic nor held in captivity are not medicinal products (SI 1986 No.2177).

Breathing gases for human use in conditions in which respiration is adversely affected by abnormal atmospheric pressure or otherwise are not medicinal products when they are not administered for the treatment or diagnosis of disease. This exemption applies to oxygen, air, any mixture of both, or either or both with any inert gas or gases or with nitrogen (SI 1977 No.1488).

An animal feeding stuff into which a medicinal product has been incorporated is also classed as a medicinal product. Special provisions relate to such feeding stuffs (s.130).

Administration

The Medicines Act extends to Scotland and Northern Ireland, and the terms the *Health Ministers* and the *Agricultural Ministers* include the relevant Ministers of those countries (s.1), as well as those for England and Wales. All these Ministers, taken together, comprise the *Ministers* who act jointly in certain matters, for example the appointment of the Medicines Commission (s.2). The Ministers also make up the *licensing authority* (s.6), but these licensing functions are carried out by either the Medicines and Health Care Products Regulatory Agency (formed from the merger of the Medicines and Health Care products Regulatory Agency and the Medical Devices Agency; see Chapter 3) or the European Agency for the Evaluation of Medicinal Products.

The licensing authority is MHRA for the decentralised system (i.e. mutual recognition and national procedures) for market authorisations under the terms of the Council Directives (Chapter 3). It is also the licensing authority for all other licences required under the Act (e.g. manufacturers, wholesale dealers, etc.) and is also the enforcement authority for these matters in the UK.

The *European Agency for the Evaluation of Medicinal Products* (EMEA), established under EC Council Regulation 2309/93/EEC, was the licensing authority for the centralised procedures for market authorisations under the terms of the EC Council Directives (Chapter 3). Its name was changed to the *European Medicines Agency* by Council Regulation 726/2004/EC.

The *Veterinary Medicines Directorate* is the organisation for animal medicines equivalent to MHRA.

Before exercising any power to make Orders or Regulations, the Ministers must, except in certain cases of emergency, consult in advance organisations which appear to them (the Ministers) to represent interests likely to be affected (s.129). In relation to matters not connected with veterinary drugs or animal medicines, *appropriate Ministers* means the *Health Ministers*.

The *Medicines Commission* (s.2) is a body appointed by the Ministers to advise them on the administration of the Act and on any matters relating to medicinal products. It is a body corporate which must have at least eight members (there are in fact 19). It must include at least one member who, in relation to each of the following activities, has had wide and recent experience and has shown capacity in (a) the practice of medicine; (b) the practice of veterinary medicine; (c) the practice of pharmacy; (d) chemistry other than pharmaceutical chemistry; and (e) the pharmaceutical industry [s.2(3)]. The chairman is appointed by the Ministers from amongst the members of the Commission [s.2(4)].

The Commission is required to make recommendations to the Ministers about the numbers of committees required under section 4 (*appropriate committees*) and about their functions and membership [s.3(2)]. These committees may be set up by the Ministers for any purpose in connection with the execution of the Act, but specific reference is made to the establishment of committees (a) to give advice with respect to safety, quality or efficacy; (b) to promote the collection and investigation of information relating to adverse reactions; and (c) to prepare further editions of the *British Pharmacopoeia* and other compendia. The Commission itself is required to undertake any of these functions which have not been assigned to any committee.

Three section 4 committees are still functioning: the Committee on the Safety of Medicines (SI 1970 No.1257), the Veterinary Products Committee (SI 1970 No.1304), and the British Pharmacopoeia Commission (SIs 1970 No.1256 and 1982 No.1335).

The most recently established committee is the Advisory Board on the Registration of Homoeopathic Products, which gives advice with respect to the safety and quality of any homoeopathic product in respect of which a certificate of registration could be granted (SI 1995 No.309) (Chapter 3).

Administrative provisions relating to the Medicines Commission and the section 4 committees are in Schedule 1 to the Act and in regulations made thereunder (SI 1970 No.746). The Medicines Commission can appoint its own ad hoc committees, and section 4 committees can set up their own subcommittees.

The Ministers can extend the functions of the Medicines Commission and can vary or terminate any of the Commission's functions, subject to the approval of a resolution of both Houses of Parliament. Annual reports about the work of the Medicines Commission and its committees and of the committees set up under section 4 of the Act must be submitted to the Ministers (s.5).

In February 2004, a public consultation was started on a MHRA proposal to replace the Medicines Commission and the Committee on the Safety of Medicines with a new Commission on Human Medicines which will advise on policy matters relating to medicines regulation; the safety, quality and efficacy of medicines; the collection and investigation of adverse drug reaction data; and the establishment of section 4 committees under the Act. It is proposed to retain only two of the existing section 4 committees, namely the Veterinary Products Committee and the British Pharmacopoeia Commission. Therapeutic advisory groups will support the new Commission. There will be lay and patient representatives at all levels and no member will be allowed to hold personal company interests or represent the pharmaceutical industry (*Pharm J*. 21 February 2004 and 20 November 2004). These provisions now come into force in October 2005 (SI 2005 No. 1094).

Enforcement

The primary duty of enforcing the Act rests with the *appropriate Minister* in England and Wales [s.108(1)], the Secretary of State in Scotland [s.109(1)] and the Minister of Health and Social Services in Northern Ireland [s.110(1)]. There are provisions for these Ministers to delegate many of their functions to other authorities, but licensing requirements and those provisions which affect hospitals or the premises of practitioners are solely the responsibility of the Ministers. In England, Wales and Scotland, arrangements can be made or directions given whereby local food and drug authorities and/or the Royal Pharmaceutical Society can have certain duties or exercise certain powers, concurrently with the Ministers [s.108(2)]. In Scotland, these enforcement authorities cannot themselves institute proceedings (s.109).

Role of the Royal Pharmaceutical Society

The Society is responsible under this Act for the maintenance of the Register of Pharmacy Premises (Chapter 5) and for disciplinary control over bodies corporate and representatives of pharmacists carrying on retail pharmacy businesses (Chapter 22).

The Royal Pharmaceutical Society, concurrently with the Minister, is also required to enforce in Great Britain [ss.108(6) and 109(2)] the provisions relating to the following.

1   Sale and supply of medicinal products not on a General Sale List (s.52).
2   Sale, supply or administration of medicinal products on Prescription Only (s.58).
3   Regulations restricting sale, supply or administration of certain medicinal products except with the authority of specially certified practitioners (s.60).

4   Regulations restricting sale or supply of medicinal products to persons in a specified class (s.61).
5   Annual return of premises to the registrar (s.77).
6   Restrictions on use of titles, descriptions and emblems (s.78).
7   Regulations imposing further restrictions on titles [s.79(2)].

The appropriate Minister *must* arrange for the Society, and/or the Food and Drug Authorities (as designated in s.198 of the Local Government Act 1972) to have a power, or a duty, to enforce in connection with retail sale, supply, etc. of medicinal products provisions relating to the following.

8   Prohibition of sale, supply or importation of medicinal products specified by order (s.62) (Chapter 14).
9   Sale and supply and offer of sale or supply of adulterated medicinal products (s.63).
10   Sale of medicinal products not of the nature or quality demanded (s.64).
11   Compliance with standards specified in monographs in certain publications (s.65).
12   Regulations relating to labelling and marking of containers and packages [s.85(3),(4) and (5)].
13   Regulations relating to requirements for containers [s.87(2)].
14   Regulations relating to distinctive colours, shapes and marking of medicinal products [s.88(3)].
15   Regulations relating to display of information on automatic machines [s.89(2)].
16   Regulations relating to leaflets to be supplied with medicinal products [s.86(2) and (3)].
17   False or misleading representations or advertisements (s.93).
18   Advertisements requiring consent of product licence holder (s.94).
19   Regulations relating to issue of advertisements (s.95).

Such arrangements for enforcement have been made with the Society relating to items 9 to 13. Enforcement by the Society in respect of items 17, 18 and 19 is limited to premises, ships, aircraft, vehicles or places where retail sales take place, and to the display of advertisements in close proximity to automatic machines.

The Society and the Food and Drug Authorities *may* be given a power or duty to enforce provisions relating to:

20   Sale of medicinal products on the General Sale List (s.53).
21   Sale of medicinal products from automatic machines (s.54).
22   Regulations relating to premises where medicinal products are prepared or dispensed and to dealings in medicinal products including the supervision, storage, safekeeping, record keeping, disposal, supply as samples or precautions to be taken before sale, and to the construction etc. of automatic machines (s.66).

The Society has been given the power and is under a duty to enforce sections 53, 54 and 66 in respect of registered pharmacies and of premises where certain exempted veterinary drugs are sold (Chapter 13). Food and Drug Authorities have a power and are under a duty to enforce these sections in respect of all other premises (SI 1980 No.1923).

An enforcement authority must give 28 days' notice to the Minister before instituting proceedings under any of the sections in 8 to 22 above.

County Councils have a duty to enforce the provisions of the Act relating to the proper labelling and description of medicated animal feeding stuffs (ss.90 and 108). These authorities also have a duty to enforce any order made under section 62(1) prohibiting the sale, supply or importation of any specified animal feeding stuffs. The council of any county district which is not a Food and Drug Authority and the overseers of the Inner Temple and the Middle Temple may be required to enforce the regulations made under section 66 (see item 22 above).

Inspection and sampling

A right of entry and a right to inspect, take samples and seize goods and documents is given (ss.111 and 112) to *any person duly authorised in writing by an enforcement authority* in order to ascertain whether there has been a contravention of the Act. The right to inspect extends to any substance or article appearing to be a medicinal product; to any plant or equipment used to manufacture or assemble medicinal products; and to any labels, leaflets, containers or packages. An authorised person, having produced his/her credentials if required to do so, is empowered:

1   to enter any premises, stall or place other than any vehicle or home-going ship, to ascertain whether there has been a contravention of the Act, or generally for the purposes of performing the functions of the enforcement authority; and to enter any ship, aircraft or hover-vehicle to ascertain whether there is in it any article or substance imported in contravention of the Act;

2   to take a sample (by purchase or otherwise) of any medicinal product sold or supplied or any substance to be used in the manufacture of a medicinal product;

3   to require the production of any books or documents relating to the business;

4   to take copies of any entry in any such book or document; and

5   to seize and detain any substance or articles or any document which he has reasonable cause to believe may be required for proceedings under the Act (the person from whom the seizure is made must be informed).

A person duly authorised in writing by the licensing authority (i.e. an inspector of MHRA of the Department of Health) may exercise these rights in respect of the business of any applicant for a licence or certificate under Part II of the Act in order to verify any statement made in the application.

Twenty-four hours' notice must be given to the occupier if it is intended to enter any premises used only as a private dwelling house. In cases of urgency, where refusal is apprehended, where the giving of notice will defeat the object of entry or where the premises are unoccupied, a Justice of the Peace may issue a warrant authorising entry, by force if necessary. Any person entering any property in the exercise of a right of entry may take with him/her such other persons and such equipment as may be necessary. On vacating any unoccupied property entered in pursuance of a warrant, s/he must leave it as effectively secured as s/he found it.

It is an offence wilfully to obstruct a duly authorised person, or wilfully to fail to comply with any proper request made by him/her or, without reasonable cause, to fail to give him/her any assistance or information s/he may reasonably require within his/her functions under the Act. It is also an offence to give such a person false information (s.112).

A person who has exercised a right of entry and discloses to any other person, except in the performance of his/her duty, information about any manufacturing process or trade secret obtained by him/her in the premises commits an offence. It is similarly an offence for any person to disclose any information obtained by him/her in pursuance of the Acts (s.118).

A detailed procedure is set out in Schedule 3 for dealing with samples taken by a *sampling officer* (i.e. a person authorised by the relevant enforcement authority) either for any purpose in connection with that authority's functions under the Act or to ascertain whether there has been a contravention of the Act.

A sample must be divided forthwith into three parts, two being retained by the sampling officer and the third given to the vendor or dealer in the manner prescribed in the schedule, according to the circumstances. One of the parts retained by the sampling officer may be submitted for analysis to a public analyst, or to a laboratory with which an arrangement has been made by the enforcement authority with the approval of the Minister.

A certificate, in the prescribed form, specifying the result of the analysis must be issued by the person having control of the laboratory, or by the public analyst carrying out the analysis. The certificate must be signed by the person issuing it and, in any proceedings, a document purporting to be such a certificate shall be sufficient evidence of the facts stated in the document, unless the other party requires that the person who issued the certificates shall be called as a witness. The second part of the sample retained by the sampling officer must be produced as evidence and, if required by either party or at the direction of the court, must be submitted to the Government Chemist for analysis. The prescribed forms of certificates of analysis are in SI 1977 No.1399.

A sampling officer must pay the value of a sample if it is demanded by the person from whom it is taken; there is provision for arbitration about the value in case of a dispute. The taking of a sample by a sampling officer has effect as though it were a sale of a medicinal product and the provisions of section 64 of the Act relating to the protection of purchasers apply (Chapter 14).

Where a substance or article has been seized by a person exercising a right of seizure (referred to as an *authorised officer*) (s.113), s/he must either treat it as a sample or set aside part of it as a sample if requested to do so within 21 days by the person entitled to be informed of the seizure. This does not apply if the nature of the substance is such that it is not reasonably practicable to do either of these things. A substance or article treated as a sample under these provisions is subject to the procedure of division, analysis, etc. set out in Schedule 3 as described above.

Any person, other than a person authorised by an enforcement authority, who has purchased a medicinal product may submit a sample of it for analysis to the public analyst for the area where it was purchased, subject to the analyst's right to demand payment of the prescribed fee in advance. The public analyst must analyse the sample as soon as is practicable and issue a certificate in the form prescribed (s.115) (Appendix 7).

There are special enforcement and sampling provisions relating to animal feeding stuffs (s.117). The Agriculture Minister may by regulation modify the ordinary sampling procedure for use with animal feeding stuffs. These regulations may prescribe a method of analysis to be used in analysing samples of feeding stuffs and provide that the results of analysis by other methods shall not be admissible in evidence. The Agriculture Minister may by order specify the discrepancy which will be tolerated between the amount of medicinal product present in an animal feeding stuff and the amount declared on the label. Deficiencies or excesses within the prescribed limits are not regarded as contraventions of the Act.

Legal proceedings

Where a contravention is due to the default of another person, that person may be charged and convicted, whether or not proceedings are taken against the person committing the contravention. A person charged with an offence who proves to the satisfaction of the court (a) that s/he exercised all due diligence to prevent the contravention, and (b) that it was due to the act or default of another person, shall, subject to certain procedural requirements, be acquitted of the offence (s.121).

When an offence is committed by a body corporate, any director, manager, company secretary or other similar officer may be proceeded against, as well as the body corporate, if it is proved that the offence was committed with his/her consent and connivance or was attributable to his/her neglect. It is specifically provided that the superintendent pharmacist of a pharmacy company (whether or not a member of the board), and any pharmacist in personal control of a pharmacy and acting under his/her direction, shall be regarded as officers for this purpose (s.124).

Medicinal products and animal feeding stuffs that are proved to have been found on a vehicle from which those goods are sold are presumed to have been offered for sale, unless the contrary is proved (s.126). This presumption applies when the offences concern the offering for sale of (a) a medicated animal feeding stuff without the authority of a product licence, animal test certificate, or a veterinary direction (s.40); (b) a medicinal product contrary to the restriction on retail sales (ss.52 and 53); or (c) an adulterated medicinal product [s.63(b)]. There is also a presumption in respect of the possession of medicinal products or medicated animal feeding stuffs (or leaflets referring to them) on premises at which the person charged carries on a business including the supply of those goods.

When the offence concerns adulteration [s.63(b)], false or misleading labels or leaflets (ss.85 and 86), requirements as to containers (s.87) or requirements as to marking of medicinal products (s.88), a person is presumed, unless the contrary is proved, to have had medicinal products in his/her possession for the purpose of sale or supply. Warranty can be pleaded as a defence to a charge of contravening any of these sections, or of sections 64 and 65. These relate to sales made to the prejudice of the purchaser (s.64) or failure to comply with standards specified in official monographs (s.65).

Subject to certain formalities, a defendant can rely on warranty if s/he proves:

1   that s/he purchased the substance or article as one which could lawfully be sold, supplied or offered for sale and with a written warranty to that effect;
2   that at the time of the alleged offence s/he had no reason to believe that it was otherwise; and
3   that the substance or article was then in the same state as when s/he purchased it (s.122).

A defendant who is the servant of the person who purchased under warranty can rely on the same defence as his/her employer, and a name or description entered in an invoice is deemed to be written warranty that the article described can be sold under that description.

It is an offence for a person to give a false warranty unless s/he can prove that at the time s/he gave it s/he had reason to believe that the statement of description was accurate. It is also an offence wilfully to apply to any article or substance (a) a warranty or (b) a certificate of analysis issued under the Act (p. 23), if that warranty or certificate relates to a different substance or article.

Any document purporting to be an authorised copy of the *British Pharmacopoeia*, or a compendium or a list of names as described in Part VII of the Act or of an amendment thereto, shall be received in evidence as being a true copy of the subject matter contained therein and shall be evidence of the date on which it came into operation (s.102).

The validity of licences and licensing decisions is considered under licensing (Chapter 3), and certificates issued by the registrar relating to the premises are dealt with under pharmacies (Chapter 5).

Summary

- The legal sources for the marketing authorisations of medicinal products and the licensing of manufacturers, wholesalers and other distributors of medicines are the European Directives and the UK Medicines Act 1968.
- The advisory structure for the Ministers is a Medicines Commission and several statutory committees including the Committee on the Safety of Medicines. This will change in October 2005 (see p. 20)
- The two licensing authorities, MHRA and the European Medicines Agency deal, respectively, with the decentralised and centralised licensing procedures for medicinal products.
- The definition of a medicinal product is set out in Council Directive 2001/83/EC.
  Certain substances (e.g. surgical ligatures and sutures, dental fillings, contact lenses and intrauterine devices) are no longer controlled under the Medicines Act but under the Medical Devices Regulations made under the Consumer Protection Act.
- The enforcement of the Act and regulations fall upon MHRA and the Royal Pharmaceutical Society of Great Britain.
- The powers of the inspectors are laid down and stringent conditions relate to the taking of sampling within a sampling procedure.
- Those liable to commit offences under the Act are listed together with any defences that can be raised.

Further reading

AMELIA *Guidance Notes*. Veterinary Medicines Directorate, Addlestone, UK.
MAVIS (published regularly) *Advisory Leaflets*. Veterinary Medicines Directorate, Addlestone, UK.
MHRA (published bimonthly) *MAIL*. Medicines and Health Care Regulatory Authority Updating Service, London.
Rules Governing Medicinal Products in the European Union, vol. 1: *Pharmaceutical Legislation, Human Medicinal Products*. The Stationery Office, London.
Rules Governing Medicinal Products in the European Union, vol. 5: *Pharmaceutical Legislation, Veterinary Medicinal Products* The Stationery Office, London.

CHAPTER THREE

Medicines Act 1968

The licensing system

Licensing requirements are set out in EC Council Directives and Regulations and in the Medicines Act 1968, which provide for marketing authorisations, manufacturers' licences, wholesale dealers' licences, clinical trial certificates and animal test certificates. The licensing system applies to medicinal products and to substances incorporated in animal feeding stuffs for a medicinal purpose. (Retailers of licensed products, unless responsible for the composition of the products they sell, do not require any licences, but medicinal products which are not on a General Sale List may be sold or supplied by retail, subject to certain exemptions, only from registered pharmacies; Chapter 6.)

Without the appropriate marketing authorisation, licence or certificate, it is not lawful for any person, in the course of a business carried on by him/her, to manufacture, sell, supply, export or import into the UK any of these products unless some exemption is provided in the Act or regulations.

In this chapter, the provisions of the Directives and the Act and its Statutory Instruments (SIs) are collated and summarised under appropriate headings. The SIs mentioned are those in force on 7 February 2005. Explanatory leaflets are available from the MHRA in the case of human medicines and the Veterinary Medicines Directorate of DEFRA for medicines for animal use.

Issue of licences

Market authorisations and licences are issued by the licensing authorities; MHRA or the European Medicines Agency [see also Council Regulation 726/2004/EC. (p. 10)], who may grant, refuse, review, suspend, revoke or vary them (ss.20 and 28 and SI 1994 No.3144 as amended). They expire at the end of five years or such shorter period as is specified in the marketing authorisation/licence. If a marketing authorisation/licence, subsequent to its issue, contravenes any EU obligation, a notice terminating it may be served on the holder (s.24 and SI 1994 No.3144 as amended). The authority must send copies of licences to the appropriate section 4 committees (see p. 19). When an application for a marketing authorisation/licence is refused, the licensing authority must state the reasons for refusal in a notice served on the applicant. Refusal may not be based on any ground relating to the price of a product, and the licensing authority must consult the appropriate committee, that is the Committee on the Safety of Medicines or the Veterinary Products Committee, before refusing an application on grounds of safety, quality or efficacy (s.20).

Marketing authorisations for human medicines

The European Community issued proposals for a two-tiered system for obtaining marketing authorisations and this system was implemented in 1994, thus replacing earlier product licences with marketing authorisations. The system comprises a centralised system and a national (member state) system. The centralised licensing system is administered by the European Medicines Agency [was the European Agency for the Evaluation of Medicinal Products (EMEA)] and is used for new active substances and certain high-technology and biotechnology products. The centralised procedure is set out in Regulation 2309/93/EEC, which has direct effect on member states without any separate implementation by a member state.

The decentralised system, also known as the mutual recognition procedure, is for the other products and involves MHRA and its marketing authorisations may be recognised by the other member states. Council Directive 2001/83/EEC together with the other European pharmaceutical Directives, implemented by UK regulations (SI 1994 No.3144 as amended by SI 2002 No.236) establish the procedures for the decentralised system. The regulations implement the Directives concerned by cross-reference to the Directives themselves, rather than setting out the details in full.

No medicinal product may be placed on the market of a member state and no such product can be distributed by way of wholesale dealing unless a marketing authorisation has been issued by the MHRA or the EMEA. Medicinal products include immunological products, medicinal products based on human blood or blood constituents and medicinal products based on radioisotopes (radiopharmaceuticals). However, these provisions do not apply to whole human blood, plasma or blood cells of human origin, nor to a radiopharmaceutical in which the radionuclide is in a sealed source. Homoeopathic medicinal products are dealt with separately (see p. 31).

Proprietary medicinal product means any ready-prepared medicinal product placed on the market in the UK under a special name and in a special pack (Council Directive 2001/83/EC, Art.1 and 2).

Radiopharmaceutical means a medicinal product which, when ready for use, contains one or more radionuclides included for a medicinal purpose (SI 1992 No.604).

Blood product means any industrially prepared medicinal product for human use derived from human blood or blood plasma and includes albumin, coagulating factors and immunoglobulins of human origin but does not include whole blood, human plasma or blood cells of human origin (SI 1992 No.755).

The holder of a marketing authorisation for a medicinal product may (a) sell, supply or export the product; (b) procure its sale, supply or exportation; or (c) procure its manufacture or assembly, in accordance with the marketing authorisation.

In dealing with an application for a marketing authorisation, the licensing authority must give particular consideration to the safety, quality and efficacy of the products (s.19). Considerations of safety (s.132) are taken to include the extent to which the product:

1   if used without proper safeguards, is capable of causing danger to the health of the community, or of causing danger to the health of animals generally or of one or more species of animals; or
2   if administered to an animal, may be harmful to the animal or may induce disease in other animals or may leave a residue in the carcass or product of the animal which may be harmful to human beings; or
3   may interfere with the treatment, prevention or diagnosis of disease; or
4   may be harmful to the person administering it or (in the case of an instrument, apparatus or appliance) the person operating it.

When considering the *efficacy* of a product, the licensing authority must not take into account any question of the superior efficacy of another product (s.19), or refuse to grant a licence on any grounds relating to price (s.20).

For imported products, the licensing authority must have particular regard to the methods, standards and conditions of manufacture. The applicant may be required to produce one or more of the following:

1   an undertaking by the manufacturer that s/he will permit inspection by the licensing authority;

2   an undertaking by, or on behalf of, the manufacturer that s/he will comply with prescribed conditions (SI 1977 No.1038, as amended by SI 1992 No.2845) (see also Appendix 4);

3   a declaration by or on behalf of the manufacturer that the product has been manufactured in accordance with the law of the country where it was manufactured (s.19).

An application for a marketing authorisation for a medicinal product for human use in either of the procedures must be accompanied by the particulars set out in Council Directive 2001/83/EEC. Article 11 sets out the details of the Summary of Product Characteristics (SPC) (Appendix 3).

Summary of Product Characteristics means the information required to accompany any application for a marketing authorisation under Council Directive 2001/83/EEC (Art.11). (for details see p. 411).

Apart from the SPC, the particulars required to be given in a full application include the kind of activity to be undertaken (e.g. selling, procuring manufacture, etc.); the pharmaceutical form of the product; its composition, physical characteristics and medicinal use; method of manufacture and assembly; quality control procedures; containers and labelling; reports of experimental and biological studies and of clinical trials and studies; any adverse reactions; and, where the product is made abroad, documentary evidence of authorisation relating to manufacture, assembly, etc. Special additional conditions apply for applications concerning immunological products, radiopharmaceuticals and medicinal products derived from human blood or human plasma (Appendix 3).

Abridged applications are permitted where the relevant data have been submitted in an earlier application, or data about the kind of product in question are well documented. (Renewal applications for licenses and certificates are dealt with in SI 1994 No.3144, as amended.)

Standard conditions and obligations for marketing authorisations are prescribed in the relevant EC Directives (Appendix 5). These provisions are incorporated in the marketing authorisation unless the applicant desires that any of them shall be excluded or modified in respect of his/her product and his/her request is granted.

Revocation, suspension or variation

There is provision in the regulations for the marketing authorisation to be revoked, suspended or varied. The licensing authority may impose an urgency safety restriction on the holder of a marketing authorisation. Where this occurs, the holder shall implement the restriction within a specified period and apply to vary the authorisation so as to make the safety restriction immediately and in any event within 15 days (SI 2003 No.2321).

Variations are also covered by Regulation 1084/2003/EC and Council Directive 2003/63/EC.

Generic products

A product is defined as a generic medicinal product when it has: 'the same qualitative and quantitative composition in active substances and the same pharmaceutical form as the reference medicinal product, and whose bio-equivalence with the reference product has been demonstrated by appropriate bioavailability studies'.

There has to be a balance struck between allowing a person applying for a marketing authorisation for a follow-on product (e.g. a generic product) to be able to use the safety and efficacy data which have been used by the original innovator against the need for such an applicant being forced to repeat that data for the product when the information is already with the licensing authority. This balance is achieved by allowing a follow-on competitor to rely on the data for the original product only after the passage of a 'data exclusivity period'. The procedure under which a generic product can rely on the innovator's data after the end of data exclusivity period is known as an 'abridged procedure'.

The existing 'data exclusivity periods' under Council Directive 2001/83/EC vary from six to ten years across the EU and continue to apply until November 2005, after which the amending Directive 2004/27/EC takes effect. This harmonises the exclusivity period across the EU and is known as the 8+2+1 rule. The data can be used after eight years but the product cannot be marketed for a further two years. An extra year's protection can be added if the original product had therapeutic indications that were of 'significant benefit' over other remedies.

Borderline products

Where the licensing authority are of the opinion that a product is a relevant medicinal product, they may by notice in writing serve on any person who has placed the product on the market informing him/her that the product is a relevant medicinal product and needs to be licensed together with the reasons why they are so minded. Statutory provisions provide for initial representations to be made to the licensing authority and, if necessary, for further representations to be made to an independent review body. Once a final determination has been made, the licensing authority may serve notice requiring the person not to put the product on the market or to stop marketing it from a date specified. Detail procedures are set out in the legislation (SI 2000 No.292).

Registration certificates for homoeopathic medicines for human use

Homoeopathic medicinal products to which the 2001 Directive applies means a medicinal product (which may contain a number of principles) prepared from products, substances or compositions called homoeopathic stocks in accordance with a homoeopathic manufacturing procedure described by the *European Pharmacopoeia* or, in the absence thereof, by any pharmacopoeia used officially in a member state other than one prepared with a magistral or officinal formula (Council Directive 2001/83/EC).

Certificate of Registration means a certificate granted under the Medicines (Homoeopathic Medicinal Products for Human Use) Regulations 1994 (SI 1994 No.105, as amended by SI 2002 No.236).

In the case of a homoeopathic medicinal product, a marketing authorisation is not required provided that a certificate of registration has been granted (SI 1994 No.276). Only homoeopathic medicines which satisfy all of the following conditions may be subject to this simplified registration procedure:

1   they are administered orally or externally;
2   no specific therapeutic indication appears on the label of the product or in any information relating thereto; and
3   there is a sufficient degree of dilution to guarantee the safety of the product; in particular the product may not contain either more than one part per 10 000 of the mother tincture or more than 1/100th of the smallest dose used in allopathy with regard to active principles whose presence in an allopathic product would result in it requiring a doctor's prescription.

Applications for a certificate of registration for a homoeopathic medicinal product must be made in the manner prescribed in the regulations (SI 1994 No.105, as amended). The application must be in writing, in English, and include the particulars required by Council Directive 2001/83/EC (Appendix 3). Fees and standard variations are covered by SI 1998 No.574.

Product licences (parallel importing)

The importation from a member state of the EU of a medicinal product which is a version of one already the subject of a UK marketing authorisation is known as 'parallel importing'.

A modified form of licence application may be considered for such a product, subject to the following conditions:

1   the product to be imported must be a *proprietary medicinal product* (as defined in Article 1 of Council Directive 2001/83/EC) which is not a vaccine, toxin, serum; based on human blood or a blood constituent; a radioactive isotope; or a homoeopathic product, as specified in the Directive;
2   it must be covered by a currently valid market authorisation granted by the regulatory body of a European Community member state;
3   it must have no different therapeutic effect from the product covered by the UK licence; and

4   it must be made by, or under licence to, the UK manufacturer or by a member of the same group of companies.

A licence granted in these circumstances is known as a Product Licence (Parallel Import) [PL(PI)].

These requirements apply to the parallel importing of medicines for human use and are taken from an administrative document issued by the Department of Health and Social Security (MAL2/PI). Comparable requirements for veterinary medicines appear in the Medicines (Veterinary Drugs) (Exemption from Licences) (Importation) Order 1986 (SI 1986 No.228).

Marketing authorisations for animal medicines

At the time of going to press, there are proposals to consolidate and amend the UK regulations in regard to animal medicines. At present the provisions detailed below apply.

A *veterinary medicinal product* means

1   any substance or combination of substances presented as having properties for treating or preventing disease in animals, or,
2   any substances or combination of substances which may be used in, or administered to, animals with a view either to restoring, correcting or modifying physiological functions by exerting pharmacological, immunological or metabolic action, or by making a medical diagnosis. (Directive 2001/82/EC amended by Directive 2004/28/EC together known as the 'amending directive').

Although modified, the definition continues to apply to products that are said to be medicinal 'by presentation' or medicinal 'by function'.

The regulations do not apply to

1   inactivated immunological veterinary medicinal products that are manufactured from pathogens or antigens obtained from an animal and used for the treatment of that animal or other animals on the same site; or
2   veterinary medicines based on radioactive isotopes.

As with human medicines, there are three types of system, centralised, decentralised and national, with full data being required. The centralised procedure is obligatory for high-technology products and growth promoters (as defined in EU Regulation 726/2004) and is optional for other innovatory veterinary medicines. The decentralised scheme is available where the applicant wishes to license a product for more than one state and the national scheme where registration is only required in one state. New Veterinary Medicines Regulations 2005 (expected October 2005) will eventually revoke the Marketing Authorisations for Veterinary Medicinal Products Regulations

1994 (SI 1994 No.3142 as amended) and implement the amending Council Directive for the registration procedures. An application for a marketing authorisation for a medicinal product for animal use in any of the procedures must be accompanied by the particulars set out in Council Directive 2001/82/EEC and are similar to those for human medicines. The Committee for Veterinary Medicinal Products, established under Council Directive, gives advice to the Commission and to the national authorities.

Confidentiality was covered by Regulation 14 of SI 1994 No 3142, prohibiting any person from disclosing information learnt in pursuance of the regulations except in the performance of his/her duty. As from 1 January 2005, this prohibition has been revoked (SI 2004 No.3193).

Council Regulation 2377/90/EEC lays down the procedures for the evaluation of the safety of residues and the establishment of maximum residue limits in foodstuffs. Provisions for the renewal of applications are set out in SI 1994 No.3142.

Standard conditions for marketing authorisations are prescribed in the relevant Directives. These provisions are incorporated in the marketing authorisation unless the applicant desires that any of them shall be excluded or modified in respect of his/her product and his/her request is granted.

Registration certificates for homoeopathic medicines for animal use

No person may market a veterinary homoeopathic medicine for animals unless the product is registered in accordance with the provisions of EC Council Directives 2001/83/EC. Directive 92/74/EC sets out a simplified procedure for veterinary homoeopathic products similar to that for human medicines.

Manufacturer's licence

A manufacturer's licence is required by a person who, in the course of a business carried on by him/her, manufactures or assembles a medicinal product (s.8). The medicinal product to be manufactured or assembled must be the subject of a marketing authorisation unless some exemption is provided in the Act or regulations. The manufacturer must hold a marketing authorisation or be acting to the order of the marketing authorisation holder (s.23).

Manufacture includes any process carried out in the course of making the product but does not include dissolving or dispensing the product in, or diluting or mixing it with, some other substances used as a vehicle for administration.

Assemble means the enclosing of the products (with or without other medicinal products of the same description) in a container which is labelled before the product is sold or supplied or, where the product (with or without medicinal products of the same description) is already enclosed in a container in which it is to be sold or supplied, labelling the container before the product is sold or supplied in it (s.132). *Assembly* has a corresponding meaning.

A licence is not required for the manufacture of chemicals and other substances used in the manufacture of ingredients of medicinal products. Nor is a licence required for the manufacture of ingredients supplied in bulk to other manufacturers (see definition of medicinal products; p. 16). A manufacturer's licence covering assembly must be held for breaking bulk supplies of a medicinal product if it involves the enclosure of the product in different containers or labelling the containers.

In dealing with applications for manufacturer's licences, the licensing authority must, in particular, take into consideration [s.19(5)]:

1 the operations proposed to be carried out in pursuance of the licence;
2 the premises in which those operations are to be carried out;
3 the equipment which is or will be available on those premises for carrying out those operations;
4 the qualifications of the persons under whose supervision those operations will be carried out; and
5 the arrangements made or to be made for ensuring the safe-keeping of, and the maintenance of adequate records in respect of, medicinal products manufactured or assembled in pursuance of the licence.

Good manufacturing practice means the part of quality assurance which ensures that products are consistently produced and controlled in accordance with the quality of standards appropriate to their intended use; it is applicable to all activities which require a licence under Council Directive 2001/83/EC and the principles and guidelines are specified in Commission Directive 2003/94/EC (SI 2004 No.1678).

Applications must be made in the manner prescribed in the regulations (SI 1971 No.974 and SI 1977 No.1052, as amended) indicating whether the licence is to relate to manufacturing or assembly or to both, and giving the particulars mentioned in items 1 to 5 above. The applicant must describe the products to be manufactured or assembled and give details of any manufacturing operations to be carried out. The qualifications of the production manager and of the person in charge of quality control must be given, and the name and function of the person to whom they are responsible. Where relevant, the qualifications of the person in charge of animals, and of the person responsible for the culture of any living tissue, must also be given.

At least one *qualified person* is required to be nominated whose responsibilities are set out in the regulations (see Appendix 5). A qualified person means a person who in respect of qualification and experience satisfies the provisions of the 2001 Directive.

The standard provisions for a manufacturer's licence (Appendix 5) are incorporated in every licence unless the applicant has successfully applied for any to be excluded or modified (s.47). Renewal applications are dealt with in SI 1974 No.832, as amended.

Wholesale dealer's licence

Council Directive 2001/83/EC requires a wholesale dealer's licence to be held by any person who, in the course of a business carried on by him/her:

1   sells, or offers for sale, any medicinal products by way of wholesale dealing; or
2   distributes, otherwise than by way of sale, any medicinal product, ready made veterinary drug or industrially produced medicinal product other than a veterinary drug which has been imported, but was not consigned from a member state of the European Union (s.8 and SIs 1977 No.1050, 1983 No.1724 and 1992 No.604).

No person may distribute by way of wholesale any medicinal product which is subject to Directive 2001/83/EC (proprietary and generic medicinal products) except in accordance with a wholesale dealer's licence and from premises specified in that licence. The latter provision does not apply to whole human blood, plasma or blood cells of human origin, a radiopharmaceutical in which the radionuclide is in a sealed source, or a homoeopathic product. Neither does it apply to veterinary drugs which are immunological products, radio-pharmaceuticals, homoeopathic products, additives for animal feeding stuffs or a product specially prepared for a veterinary surgeon for an animal or herd under his/her care.

A wholesale dealer's licence is also required for exportation of any medicinal product which is subject to the 2001 Directive (Proprietary and Generic Medicinal Products) if it is to be exported to a member state of the EU (SI 1993 No.834).

No licence under item 2 is required by a person who provides facilities solely for the transport of the medicinal product or who, in the course of his/her business as an import agent, imports a medicinal product solely to the order of another person who intends to distribute it (SI 1990 No.566). Neither is a licence required by the holder of a marketing authorisation or by a person who has assembled the product to the order of the marketing authorisation holder and where the product has not left the premises of the manufacturer or assembler until the sale of the product (SI 1990 No.566).

Distribution of a medicinal product by way of wholesale dealing means:

1   selling or supplying it; or
2   procuring, holding or exporting it for the purposes of sale or supply to a person who receives it for the purposes of:

(a)   selling or supplying it; or
(b)   administering it, or causing it to be administered, to one or more human beings in the course of a business carried on by that person.

The term *business* includes a professional practice and any activity carried on by a body of persons, whether corporate or unincorporated (s.132). Consequently, all sales that are made to practitioners (whether medical or dental) for use in their practices constitute sales by way of wholesale dealing. The provision of services under the NHS is treated as the carrying on of a business by the appropriate Minister, Secretary of State or Ministry [s.131(5)].

Sales made by the manufacturer of a product are excluded from the definition of wholesale dealing so that s/he does not require a licence in order to sell his/her own products (s.131). A further concession is provided (SI 1972 No.640) in respect of wholesale sales made by a marketing authorisation holder who is not also the manufacturer, or by a person assembling to his/her order. Provided that such products do not leave the premises of the licensed manufacturer or licensed assembler until the actual sale, no wholesale dealer's licence is required.

The activities of a group of retailers or practitioners who buy medicinal products in bulk and divide the stock amongst themselves for resale does not normally require a licence. If the group has a separate legal identity of its own, or if purchases are made by it collectively for resale to members of the group, a wholesale dealer's licence may be necessary (see also Exemptions for pharmacists below).

In dealing with an application for a wholesale dealer's licence, the licensing authority must, in particular, take into consideration [s.19(6)]:

1   the premises on which medicinal products of the description to which the application relates will be stored;
2   the equipment which is or will be available for storing medicinal products on those premises;
3   the equipment and facilities which are or will be available for distributing medicinal products from those premises; and
4   the arrangements made or to be made for securing the safe-keeping of, and the manufacture of adequate records in respect of, medicinal products stored on or distributed from those premises.

Applications must be made in the manner prescribed in the regulations (SIs 1971 No.974 and 1977 No.1052) and state the classes of medicinal product which are the subject of the application and the uses for which they are intended, together with the particulars mentioned above. The applicant must also give the name and address and qualifications of the responsible person, details of an emergency plan for the recall of products and details for keeping records by way of invoices, on computer or in any other form relating to all products received or despatched (SI 1993 No.832).

The standard provisions for wholesale dealer's licences (Appendix 5) are incorporated in every licence unless the applicant has successfully applied for any to be excluded or modified (s.47 and SI 1971 No.972, as amended).

Fees

Holders of marketing authorisations, manufacturers' licences and wholesale dealers' licences have to pay a fee in connection with the holding of authorisations/licences in respect of each licence period. Such fees are prescribed in regulations made under the Medicines Act 1971, for human medicines (SI 1995 No.1116, as amended), for animal medicines (SI 1997 No.1469, as amended) and for homoeopathic medicines (SI 1996 No.482, as amended).

Clinical trial and animal test certificates

Clinical trial means an investigation or series of investigations consisting of the administration of one or more medicinal products, where there is evidence that they may be beneficial to a patient or patients, by one or more doctors or dentists for the purpose of ascertaining what effects, beneficial or harmful, the products have (s.31). (Chapter 2 discusses circumstances in which the administration of a substance does not constitute a clinical trial or bring the substance within the definition of a medicinal product.) For the manufacture or assembly of a medicinal product to be used only for the purpose of a clinical trial, a manufacturer's licence or a marketing authorisation is not required (s.35).

There is a comparable definition for *medicinal test on animals* (s.32). The provisions relating to clinical trials and medicinal tests on animals are in sections 31 to 39 of the Act. No person may, in the course of a business carried on by him/her, (a) sell or supply, (b) procure the sale or supply of, or (c) procure the manufacture of or assemble for the purpose of sale or supply a medicinal product for the purpose of a clinical trial or a medicinal test on animals unless s/he is, or acts to the order of, the holder of a marketing authorisation which authorises the clinical trial, or unless a clinical trial certificate or animal test certificate, as appropriate, has been issued and is in force, and the trial or test is to be carried out in accordance with it.

Exemptions for clinical trials

Clinical trials are controlled by procedures under Council Directive 2001/20/EC. A marketing authorisation or clinical trial certificate is not required for the sale, supply, manufacture or assembly of a medicinal product for the purpose of a clinical trial provided the conditions imposed by the exempting orders are met (SI 2004 No.1031). Notification of the supplier's intention must be sent to the licensing authority. The notice must be accompanied by particulars of the trial and summaries of pharmaceutical data and of reports made and tests performed as specified in Schedule 1 to the Order

(SI 2004 No.1031). There is provision for termination of the exemption in certain circumstances, usually on the grounds of safety.

A certificate is not required if the product to be the subject of the clinical trial is covered by a marketing authorisation and the conditions set out in SI 2004 No.1031 are met.

Similar conditions applicable to licensed products to be used in medicinal tests on animals are in SI 1977 No.161. The principal requirements are that the product is to be used strictly in accordance with the marketing authorisation and that the licensing authority is notified of any adverse reactions or effects.

A doctor or dentist wanting to have a product manufactured or imported for use in a clinical trial does not need a certificate if certain conditions are met. The products must have been manufactured or imported especially for the trial and only for administration to the practitioner's own patients. The trial must not have been arranged by, or at the request of, a third party [s.31(5) and (6) and SI 1972 No.1200]. A similar exemption applies where a product is specially manufactured for a veterinarian to use in a medicinal test on animals [s.33(2) and (3)].

When practitioners' prescriptions are dispensed in a registered pharmacy, hospital or health centre under the supervision of a pharmacist, there is no need for any certificate [ss.31(7) and 33(4)].

Exemptions for Tests on Animal Licences or Animal Test Certificates are not required for the sale, supply or administration of veterinary drugs (not including immunological drugs) for the purposes of medicinal tests on animals subject to the conditions set out in SI 1986 No.1180.

Exemptions for imports

No marketing authorisation is required for the importation of a medicinal product:

1   by any person for administration to him/herself or to any person or persons who are members of his/her household;
2   where it is specially imported by or to the order of a doctor or dentist (ss.9 and 13) for the purposes described in the section Exemptions for Practitioners (see below); or
3   is intended for re-export (see below).

No exemption exists for the veterinary surgeon, who may not import unlicensed veterinary medicines.

Marketing authorisations are not required for imported medicinal products which are to be exported in the form in which they were imported (see Exemptions for Exports below).

Exemptions for exports

The application of the licensing system to exports is postponed until a *special appointed day* at some time in the future (s.48). The result is that although a manufacturer's licence must be held in order to manufacture medicinal products for export, no marketing authorisations are required, except for certain products, the purity and potency of which cannot be adequately tested by chemical means. Those which are for human use are listed in SI 1971 No.1198, namely antigens, antitoxins, antisera, sera, toxins or vaccines. Those which are veterinary products are listed in SI 1971 No.1309, namely antigens, antisera, antitoxins, corticotrophin, heparin, hyaluronidase, insulin, plasma, preparations of pituitary (posterior lobe), sera, toxins, vaccines and other medicinal products or substances derived from animals.

Marketing authorisations are not required for imported medicinal products which are to be exported in the form in which they were imported and are either:

1   not assembled in a way different from the way in which they were assembled on being imported; or
2   assembled in a way different from the way they were assembled on being imported but, the assembler, being the holder of a manufacturer's licence and having supplied the licensing authority with required information, has been notified that s/he may import the product (s.13 and SIs 1971 No.1326 and 1977 No.640).

This exemption for re-exported products does not apply to the veterinary products listed in SI 1971 No.1309, which are set out in the paragraph above.

Exemptions for practitioners

A doctor, dentist or veterinarian does not require a licence of any kind in respect of medicinal products specially prepared by him/her for administration to a particular patient (sch.1 to SI 1994 No.3144). The exemption extends to the preparation of a medicinal product at the request of another practitioner for administration to one of his/her patients or to an animal or herd under his/her care.

There is no exemption from licensing for veterinary surgeons or veterinary practitioners in respect of any vaccine for administration to poultry, but there is exemption in respect of a vaccine for administration to an animal (other than poultry) provided it is an autogenous vaccine. Any plasma or serum specially prepared for administration to one or more animals in the herd from which it is derived is also exempt from licensing [s.9(3)].

A practitioner may hold a stock of medicinal products for the purposes described above without the need to hold marketing authorisations. The total stock of such products which may be held by him/her must not exceed 5 litres of fluids and 2.5 kg of solids (SI 1994 No.3144), and they must have been procured from a person holding an appropriate manufacturer's licence (SIs 1971 No.1450 and 1972 No.1200). (See also 'Special' Dispensing, Manufacturing and Assembly Exemptions, below.)

A doctor or dentist does not require any licence for any medicinal product specially imported by him/her or to his/her order for administration to a particular patient of his/hers or at the request of another doctor or dentist for administration to one of his/her patients (ss.9 and 13). There is a similar exemption from licensing for medicinal products imported by a hospital, wholesaler or retail pharmacy business provided the sale or supply is to a doctor or dentist for administration to a particular patient of his/hers. This exemption from licensing is subject to the requirements of SI 1994 No.3144, namely notification to the licensing authority, maintenance of written records including adverse drug reactions (for five years) and certain other conditions.

Exemptions for nurses and midwives

A registered nurse or a registered midwife is not required to have a manufacturer's licence in order to assemble medicinal products in the course of his/her profession (s.11).

Exemptions for pharmacists

The exemptions from licensing for pharmacists are contained in section 10 of the Act, to which a number of subsections were added by SI 1971 No.1445.

Subject to the work being done by or under the supervision of a pharmacist, no licence of any kind is required for any of the following activities being carried out in a registered pharmacy.

1   Preparing or dispensing a medicinal product in accordance with a prescription given by a practitioner, or preparing a stock of medicinal products for this purpose. The stock of medicinal products may be procured from a manufacturer holding the appropriate special licence (see 'Special' Dispensing, Manufacturing and Assembly Exemptions, below). This exemption also applies to hospitals and health centres [s.10(1) and (4) and SI 1972 No.1200]. In respect of vaccines, sera and plasma for administration to animals, the exemption from licensing for pharmacists is subject to the same limitation which applies to veterinarians (see Exemptions for Practitioners, above).
2   Preparing or dispensing a medicinal product in accordance with a specification furnished by the person to whom the product is to be sold for administration to that person, or to a person under his/her care, or an animal or herd under his/her control, or preparing a stock of medicinal products for these purposes [s.10(3)]. This exemption does not cover any vaccine, plasma or serum for animal use.

3 Preparing or dispensing a medicinal product for administration to a person when the pharmacist is requested by or on behalf of that person to do so in accordance with the pharmacist's own judgment as to the treatment required, and that person is present in the pharmacy at the time of the request (*counter prescribing*); a stock of medicinal products prepared in a registered pharmacy in accordance with 1 and 2 above and under this paragraph may be sold or supplied from any other registered pharmacy forming part of the same retail pharmacy business.

4 Preparing a medicinal product or a stock of medicinal products, not to the order of another person but with a view to retail sale or supply, provided that the sale or supply is made from the registered pharmacy where it was prepared and the product is not the subject of an advertisement [s.10(5)]. In this connection, *advertisement* does not include words appearing on the product or its container or package or the display of the product itself, but does include a show-card [s.10(8)].

5 Assembling a medicinal product [s.10(1)]. This exemption also applies to hospitals and health centres. When medicinal products are assembled in a registered pharmacy for retail sale or supply, they may not be the subject of any advertisement and may only be sold or supplied at the registered pharmacy where they are assembled or at some other registered pharmacy forming part of the same retail pharmacy business (SI 1971 No.1445).

6 Wholesale dealing, where such dealing constitutes no more than an inconsiderable part of the business carried on at that pharmacy. This covers occasional sales to practitioners or to other pharmacists (SI 1971 No.1445) (see p. 121).

A retail pharmacist who is responsible for the composition of a medicinal product which s/he intends to sell or supply in the course of his/her business must hold a marketing authorisation if his/her activities fall outside the exemptions set out above. S/he must also have a manufacturer's licence or arrange for the product to be made by a manufacturer who has an appropriate licence.

Exemptions for chiropodists and similar fields

A person who is either a member of a registering body or customarily administers medicinal products to human beings in the course of a business in the field of osteopathy, chiropody, naturopathy or other similar field does not require a manufacturer's licence to assemble medicinal products for human use which are on general sale. The product must be for administration to a particular person who has requested the naturopath or practitioner to use his/her own judgment as to the treatment required. Exemption is obtained by notification to the licensing authority (SI 1979 No.1114).

Exemptions for herbal remedies

> At the time of going to press, there are proposals via European directives to amend the legislation relating to herbal remedies.

A *herbal remedy* is defined (s.132) as a medicinal product consisting of a substance produced by subjecting a plant or plants to drying, crushing or any other process, or of a mixture whose sole ingredients are two or more substances so produced, or of a mixture whose sole ingredients are one or more substances so produced and water or some other inert substances.

No marketing authorisation/licence is required for the sale, supply, manufacture or assembly of any such herbal remedy in the course of a business in which the person carrying on the business sells or supplies the remedy for administration to a particular person after being requested by or on behalf of that person, and in that person's presence, to use his/her own judgment as to the treatment required. The person carrying on the business must be the occupier of the premises where the manufacture or assembly takes place and must be able to close them so as to exclude the public [s.12(1)].

No marketing authorisation/licence is required for the sale, supply, manufacture or assembly of those herbal remedies where the process to which the plant or plants are subjected consists only of drying, crushing or comminuting and the remedy is sold or supplied under a designation which only specifies the plant or plants and the process and does not apply any other name to the remedy; and without any written recommendation (whether by means of a labelled container or package or a leaflet or in any other way) as to the use of the remedy [s.12(2)]. This exemption does not extend to imported products.

Presumably, unless a herbal product is sold or supplied for a medicinal purpose, it is not even a medicinal product; no doubt there will be circumstances in which herbs of this kind will be sold for other than medicinal purposes.

Exemptions for wholesale dealing in confectionery

No wholesale dealer's licence is required for the sale, or offer for sale by way of wholesale dealing, of a medicinal product, other than a veterinary drug, which is for sale as confectionery if the marketing authorisation in respect of the medicinal product provides that the exemption shall apply, and if the medicinal product is not sold or offered for sale accompanied by or having in relation to it any particulars in writing specifying that product's curative or remedial function in relation to a disease specified, other than in relation to the relief of symptoms of coughs, colds or nasal congestion (SI 1975 No.762).

Exemptions for foods and cosmetics

It is provided by Orders (SIs 1971 No.1410 and 1973 No.2079) that licensing provisions do not apply to anything done in relation to a medicinal product which is wholly or mainly for use by being administered to one or more human beings and which is for sale, or is to be for sale, either for oral administration as a food or for external use as a cosmetic.

The definition of *food* includes beverages, confectionery, ingredients in the preparation of foods and advertised dietary supplements which contain added vitamins.

Vitamins are any of the following: vitamins A, B_1, B_2, B_6, C, D and E, biotin, nicotinamide, nicotinic acid, pantothenic acid and its salts, bioflavonoids, inositol, choline, p-aminobenzoic acid, cyanocobalamin or folic acid.

Vitamin preparation means any medicinal product, the active ingredients of which consist only of vitamins, or vitamins and mineral salts, that is, salts of any one or more of the following: iron, iodine, calcium, phosphorus, fluorine, copper, potassium, manganese, magnesium or zinc.

A *cosmetic* is defined as 'any substance or preparation intended to be applied to the various surfaces of the human body including epidermis, pilary system and hair, nails, lips and external genital organs, or the teeth and buccal mucosa, wholly or mainly for the purpose of perfuming them, cleansing them, protecting them, caring for them or keeping them in condition, modifying their appearance (whether for aesthetic purposes or otherwise) or combating body odours or normal body perspiration'.

This general exemption from licensing requirements does not apply if the food or cosmetic is sold with some particulars, in writing, specifying the product's curative or remedial function in relation to a specified disease, or the use of the product for such curative or remedial purposes. A marketing authorisation is required for any product promoted to practitioners. In addition, *no exemption* applies to the following.

1   Cosmetics for external use containing any antibiotic; or hexachlorophane (but not if less than 0.1 per cent and labelled with a statutory caution); any hormone in excess of 0.004 per cent (w/w); or resorcinol in excess of 1 per cent (w/w).

2   Any *vitamin preparation* for oral administration as a food in relation to which there are no written particulars or directions as to dosage.

3   Any *vitamin preparation* for oral administration as a food in relation to which there are written particulars or directions specifying a recommended daily dosage for adults involving a daily intake in excess of: vitamin A, 2500 iu; antirachitic activity, 250 iu; folic acid, 25 micrograms; or cyanocobalamin, 5 micrograms.

4   Any medicinal product for oral administration as a food, not being a *vitamin preparation*, to which one or more of the ingredients, vitamin A or D, folic acid or cyanocobalamin has been added; and in relation to

which product there are written particulars or directions as to recommended use of that substance which involves a daily intake in excess of the quantities and ingredients specified in 3.

5   Any medicinal product not covered by 2, 3 or 4 above, which is to be sold with, accompanied by, or having in relation to it any particulars in writing specifying the dosage relevant to that product's medicinal properties.

Exemption from marketing authorisations or licensing does not exempt a medicinal product from any labelling requirements which may be made under the Act (see Chapter 15).

Whether or not a substance or article is a medicinal product depends upon the purpose for which it is sold or supplied (Chapter 2). Some substances have both medicinal and non-medicinal uses. Although the exemptions for foods and cosmetics cover a wide field, borderline cases will inevitably occur where there is doubt as to the status of a product. A legally binding decision can only be given in the courts, but inquiries can be made of the MHRA about the status of any product which is being promoted in a particular way. It is quite possible that a slight alteration in wording of a label may alter the standing of a product under the Act.

Certain examples have been mentioned in the Department's leaflet MAL8. On the one hand, anti-smoking preparations which create an unpleasant taste in the mouth when the person taking them smokes tobacco and tablets and cachets sucked in order to freshen the breath are not considered to be medicinal products. On the other hand, hair restorers, whether to be taken orally or applied externally, and insect repellents for external application to cats and dogs are regarded as medicinal products.

Exemptions for ingredients

Ingredients used in pharmacies, in hospitals or in businesses where herbal remedies are sold and those used by practitioners are medicinal products (s.130), but they are exempted from licensing requirements (SI 1974 No.1150) provided particulars of the activity have been notified to the licensing authority by the manufacturer or supplier. The exemption may, in the interest of safety, be withdrawn by the licensing authority. Certain substances which are not themselves medicinal products but may be used as ingredients are subject to licensing. They are listed in SIs 1971 No.1200 and 1985 No.1403 (Appendix 1).

'Special' dispensing, manufacturing and assembly exemptions

In order *to fulfil special needs*, Council Directive 2001/83EC and SI 1994 No.3144 (sch.1) enable a *special* dispensing or manufacturing service to be provided in response to a bona fide unsolicited order, formulated in accordance with the specification of a doctor or dentist and for use by his/her individual patients on his/her direct personal responsibility without the need for the manufacturer to hold a marketing authorisation for the medicinal product concerned. The following conditions apply.

1   The medicinal product must be supplied to a doctor or dentist, or for use in a pharmacy, hospital or health centre under the supervision of a pharmacist.
2   The medicinal product must not be the subject of any advertisement or representation. However, the service provided may be advertised.
3   Manufacture or assembly must be carried out under the supervision of such staff and such precautions must be taken as are adequate to ensure that the product is of the character required by, and meets the specifications of, the doctor or dentist who requires it.
4   Written records as to the manufacture/assembly must be maintained and available to the licensing authority.
5   The medicinal product is manufactured/assembled by the holder of a manufacturer's licence.
6   The medicinal product is distributed by way of wholesale dealing by the holder of a wholesale dealer's licence.

Medicinal products to which these special licensing provisions apply and the circumstances in which they may be supplied are as follows.

1   Products supplied to a doctor or dentist for administration to a particular patient (but there is a limit on the amount of stock which may be held by a doctor or dentist; see p. 40).
2   Products, or stocks of products, supplied to retail pharmacists, hospitals or health centres for dispensing, or with a view to dispensing, practitioners' prescriptions.
3   Products, or stocks of products, supplied to retail pharmacists for administration to particular persons in accordance with the pharmacist's own judgment, or in accordance with the specification of a customer for administration to him/herself or a person under his/her care.
4   Herbal remedies supplied to a retailer for administration to a particular person in accordance with the retailer's own judgment.
5   Products (not being Prescription Only or Pharmacy Only products) supplied to a person for administration to him/herself or a member of his/her household.
6   Products (not being Prescription Only products) for sale or supply to a person exclusively for use by him/her in the course of his/her business for administration to human beings, but not by way of sale (e.g. a special formula for use in a first-aid room). These products must be prepared under the supervision of a pharmacist.
7   Products supplied to licensed wholesale dealers for supply in the circumstances specified in 1 to 6 above.

Hospitals

On 1 April 1991, by virtue of the National Health Service and Community Care Act 1990, all NHS hospitals lost their Crown immunity and became liable to the licensing provisions of the Medicines Act. The type of activities relating to manufacture, assembly, and wholesaling varies considerably from one hospital to another and whether any particular licence is required depends on the individual activity. Certain exemptions exist where an activity takes place under the supervision of a pharmacist either in a registered pharmacy (see p. 41) or in a hospital (s.10). MHRA (1992) issued a document entitled *Guidance to the NHS on the Licensing Requirements of the Medicines Act 1968*. Hospital pharmacists requiring further details should contact MHRA.

Export certificates

The licensing authority may, on the application of an exporter of medicinal products, issue to him/her a certificate containing such statements relating to the products as the authority considers appropriate, having regard to any requirements (whether having the force of law or not) which have effect in the country to which the products are to be exported and to the provisions of the Medicines Act, and to any licence granted or other things done by virtue of the Act (s.50).

Medical devices

Medical devices include intrauterine devices and diaphragms, dental fillings, contact lens care products, non-medicated dressings, sutures and ligatures, etc. These are no longer controlled under the Medicines Act but under consumer protection legislation (Medical Devices Regulations 1994, SI 1994 No.3017).

A *device* means a medical device, that is to say an instrument, apparatus, appliance, material or other article, whether used alone or in combination, together with any software necessary for its proper application which:

1   is intended by the manufacturer to be used for human beings for the purpose of:

    (a)   diagnosis, prevention, monitoring, treatment or alleviation of disease;

    (b)   diagnosis, monitoring, treatment or alleviation of or compensation for an injury or handicap;

    (c)   investigation, replacement or modification of the anatomy or of any physiological process; or

    (d)   control of contraception; and

2   does not achieve its principal intended action in or on the human body
by pharmacological, immunological or metabolic means, even if it is
assisted in its function by such means.

This holds even if the device is intended to administer a medicinal product as
defined in Council Directive 2001/83/EC or incorporates as an integral part of
a substance which, if used separately, would be a medicinal product and
which is liable to act upon the body with action ancillary to that of the
device.

Such devices must comply with the regulations with regard to the essential
requirements set out in Council Directive 93/42/EEC and with specific labelling. The former Medical Devices Agency, now merged with the former
Medicines Control Agency to form MHRA (Chapter 2), administers and
enforces the legislation. Manufacturers have to be registered and fees are
payable (SI 1995 No.449, as amended).

Summary

- All dealings in medicinal products are subject to a licensing system
  unless specifically exempted. Marketing authorisations or licences are
  needed to *place a medicine on the market*, to manufacture, wholesale or
  distribute medicinal products. Certification is needed for human and
  animal clinical trials.
- The national (decentralised) marketing authorisations are administered
  by MHRA and the centralised system by the European Medicines
  Agency .
- A simplified system of licensing (*certification*) applies to homoeopathic
  products.
- Stringent requirements, set out in a Guide to Good Manufacturing
  Practice, apply to manufacturing licences and introduce the concept of a
  qualified person. Similar conditions apply to wholesale dealers' licences,
  which have a *responsible person*.
- Clinical trials are subject to certification by the licensing authority unless
  specifically exempted.
- Certain exemptions from licensing exist for doctors, nurses, pharmacists, other health professionals and hospitals.
- No licences are required for certain activities carried out in a pharmacy
  under the supervision of a pharmacist.
- Certain products are exempt from licensing, e.g. herbal remedies, confectionery, food, cosmetics and vitamins.
- Provisions are made for *special* dispensing or manufacturing services.
- Medical devices (e.g. dental fillings, contact lenses, intrauterine devices)
  are now controlled under consumer protection legislation.

Further reading

AMELIA publications. Veterinary Medicines Directorate, Addlestone, UK.

European Industrial Pharmacists Group *Code of Practice for Qualified Persons*. The Royal Pharmaceutical Society of Great Britain, London.

MAVIS (published regularly) *Advisory Leaflets*. Veterinary Medicines Directorate, Addlestone, UK.

MHRA (published bimonthly) *MAIL*. Medicines and Health Care Regulatory Authority Updating Service, London.

MHRA *MAL Advisory Leaflets*. Medicines and Health Care Regulatory Authority, London.

Rules and Guidance for Pharmaceutical Manufacturers (GMP) (1997). The Stationery Office, London.

Rules Governing Medicinal Products in the European Union, vol. 1: *Pharmaceutical Legislation, Human Medicinal Products*. The Stationery Office, London.

Rules Governing Medicinal Products in the European Union, vol. 5: *Pharmaceutical Legislation, Veterinary Medicinal Products*. The Stationery Office, London.

CHAPTER FOUR

Medicines Act 1968

Sales promotion of medicinal products

Control of medicines advertising in the UK is based on a system of self-regulation underpinned by statutory powers under EU and UK law.

Advertisements and representations

The Medicines (Advertising) Regulations 1994 (SI 1994 No.1932, as amended by SIs 1999 No 267 and 2002 No.236) and the Medicines (Monitoring of Advertising) Regulations 1994 (SI 1994 No.1933, as amended by SI 2002 No.236) implement Council Directive 2001/83/EC and both sets of regulation supplement the existing controls under the Medicines Act (Part VI) and ensure that a relevant medicinal product is only promoted in accordance with its marketing authorisation.

A distinction is drawn between *advertisements* and *representations* in the Act (see below). In the regulations governing the advertising of relevant medicinal products (SI 1994 No.1932) the definition of advertisement includes a representation (see p. 52) but does not include reference material, factual, informative statements or announcements, a trade catalogue or a price list provided there is no product claim (cf. s.92 of the Act).

In the regulations, the word *representation* has the same meaning as in the Act, except it does not include the making of a factual, informative statement or announcement which includes no product claim.

Advertisement includes every form of advertising, whether in a publication; by the display of any notice; by means of any catalogue, price list, letter (whether circular or addressed to a particular person) or other document; by words inscribed on any article; by the exhibition of a photograph or a cinematograph film; by way of sound recording, sound broadcasting or television; or in any other way (s.92).

Representation means any statement or undertaking (whether constituting a condition or a warranty or not) which consists of spoken words other than words broadcast by way of sound recording, sound broadcasting or television, or forming part of a sound recording or embodied in a cinematograph film soundtrack [s.92(5)].

Words spoken, other than by way of sound or television broadcasting, or as part of a sound recording or film soundtrack, do not fall within the definition of advertisement. Similarly, unless provided for in regulations made under section 95, neither the sale or supply of a medicinal product in a labelled container nor the inclusion of a leaflet relating to a specific medicinal product constitute the issue of an advertisement (s.92).

Sound recording has the meaning assigned to it by section 12 of the Copyright Act 1956, that is 'the aggregate of the sounds embodied in, and capable of being reproduced by means of, a record of any description, other than a soundtrack associated with a cinematograph film'.

To ensure that adequate information is given about medicinal products, to promote safety in relation to them and to prevent the giving of misleading information about them, the appropriate Minister may impose by regulation any requirements which may be necessary or expedient. They may concern the form of any advertisement and the particulars contained therein and, in the case of television or cinematograph film advertisements, their duration and manner of exhibition may be controlled. Advertisements of particular kinds, as specified in the regulations, may be prohibited, either totally or subject to some exceptions [s.95(3)].

Control of advertisements and representations

No commercially interested party, and no person acting on his/her behalf, may issue an advertisement relating to a medicinal product without the consent of the holder of the marketing authorisation (s.94). The licensing authority may obtain up to 12 copies of any advertisement (including any data sheet) relating to medicinal products by serving a notice on the person who issued it or caused it to be issued (s.97).

The appropriate Ministers may, by regulation, prohibit the issue of advertisements (s.95):

1   relating to medicinal products of a specific description or class;
2   likely to lead to the use of any medicinal product, or any other substance or article, for the purpose of treating or preventing a specified disease, or

diagnosing a specified disease, or ascertaining the existence, degree or extent of a specified physiological condition, or permanently or temporarily preventing or otherwise interfering with the normal operation of a specified physiological function, or artificially inducing a specified condition of mind or body;

3   likely to lead to the use of a particular class of medicinal products, or other substances or articles, for the purposes set out in (b) below; or

4   relating to medicinal products and containing a specified word or phrase which, in the opinion of the Minister, is likely to mislead the public as to the nature or effects of the products, or as to any condition of mind or body in connection with which the products might be used.

The regulations may also extend the prohibitions mentioned in 2, 3 and 4 above to cover any representations made:

(a)   in connection with the sale or supply or offer for sale or supply of a medicinal product or other substance or article to which the regulations apply;

(b)   for the purpose of inducing any person to buy the medicinal product, substance or article from a retailer; or

(c)   to a practitioner, or a patient or client, for the purpose of inducing the practitioner to prescribe medicinal products of a specified description.

Regulations relating to advertisements for medicinal products for human use addressed to doctors or dentists and the public are in SI 1994 No.1932. Other regulations (SI 1979 No.1760) specify particulars which must be included in advertisements in the form of information sheets and sent to pharmacists and opticians about substances and fluids for use with contact lenses or blanks.

Advertising in general

Definitions

Certain terms used in advertising are further defined in SI 1994 No.1932 in relation to *relevant* medicinal products as follows.

Advertisement has the meaning as in section 92 of the Act (see p. 51), except that in relation to a relevant medicinal product (see p. 156): (a) provided that it makes no product claim, reference material, a factual informative statement or announcement, a trade catalogue or price list shall not be taken to be an advertisement; and (b) an advertisement includes a representation, and for the purposes of this representation has the meaning as in section 92 of the Act (see p. 51) except that it does not include the making of a factual informative statement or announcement which includes no product claim.

Essential information compatible with the summary of product characteristics (SPC) means essential information compatible with the SPC as set out in Title VIII of the 2001 Directive.

Promotional aid means a non-monetary gift made for a promotional purpose by a commercially interested party.

Reference material includes entries which are in the form of, and limited to, a brief description of a medicinal product, its uses and any relevant contra-indications and warnings appearing without charge in a publication consisting wholly or mainly of such entries where the publication is sent or delivered to persons qualified to prescribe or supply relevant medicinal products by a person who is not a commercially interested party.

General principles

The following general principles apply.

1   No person may issue an advertisement for a relevant medicinal product unless that product has a marketing authorisation. This general regulation does not apply to registered homoeopathic medicinal products (SI 1994 No.1932).
2   No person shall issue an advertisement relating to a relevant medicinal product unless that advertisement:

   (a)   complies with the particulars listed in the SPC, and
   (b)   encourages the rational use of that product by presenting it objectively and without exaggerating its properties (SI 1999 No.267).

3   No person shall issue a misleading advertisement relating to a relevant medicinal product (SI 1999 No.267).
4   No person shall issue an advertisement which is likely to lead to the use of a relevant medicinal product or substance or article for the purpose of inducing an abortion in women (SI 1994 No.1932).

Duties of holders of marketing authorisations

Any person who holds a marketing authorisation must (reg.4):

1   establish a scientific service to compile and collate all information, whether received from medical sales representatives employed by him/her or from any other source relating to that product;
2   ensure that, in relation to any such product which sales representatives promote, those medical sales representatives are given adequate training and have sufficient scientific knowledge to enable them to provide information which is as precise and as complete as possible about that product;
3   keep available for Health Ministers, or communicate to them within such period as may be specified in a notice served by them on him/her, a sample of any advertisement for which s/he is responsible relating to that product, together with a statement indicating the persons to whom the

advertisement is addressed, the method of dissemination and the date of its first dissemination (SI 1999 No.267); and

4   supply, within the period specified in a notice served by the Health Ministers on him/her, any information and assistance requested by them in order to carry out their functions under the regulations or the Monitoring of Advertising Regulations (SI 1999 No.267).

Advertising to persons qualified to prescribe or supply

Persons qualified to prescribe or supply includes persons, and employees of such persons, who in the course of their profession or in the course of a business may lawfully prescribe, sell by retail or supply in circumstances corresponding to retail sale relevant medicinal products.

The regulations (SI 1994 No.1932, as amended by SIs 1999 No.267 and 2002 No.236) implement Council Directive 2001/83/EC in connection with the control of advertising to persons who are qualified to prescribe or supply. The regulations do not relate to advertisements aimed at veterinary surgeons or veterinary practitioners.

No person may issue an advertisement relating to a relevant medicinal product and aimed at persons qualified to prescribe or supply unless the advertisement (reg.14 and Sch.2):

1   contains essential information compatible with the SPC; and
2   contains the following particulars:

(a)   the licence number of the product;
(b)   the name and address of the marketing authorisation holder which relates to the product or the business name and address of his/her business that is responsible for its sale or supply;
(c)   the classification of the product, i.e. Prescription Only, Pharmacy Only or General Sale List;
(d)   the name of the product and a list of active ingredients using the common name placed immediately adjacent to the most prominent display of the name;
(e)   the indications as within the terms of the licence;
(f)   a succinct statement of the entries in the SPC or where there is no SPC the data sheet, relating to side effects, precautions and relevant contra-indications;
(g)   a succinct statement of the entries in the SPC, or where there is no SPC the data sheet, relating to the dosage and method of use relevant to the indications shown. The method of administration should also be shown where this is not obvious;
(h)   a warning issued by the licensing authority under Part II of the Act which is required to be included;

(i)   the cost, excluding VAT, of either a specified package of the product, or a specified quantity or recommended daily dose, calculated by reference to any specified package of the product, except that the cost may be omitted in the case of an advertisement inserted in a publication which is printed in the UK but with a circulation outside the UK of more than 15 per cent of its total circulation; and

(j)   the particulars in paragraphs (f), (g) and (h) above shall be printed in a clear and legible manner and be placed in such a position in the advertisement that their relationship to the claims and indications for the product can readily be appreciated by the reader.

Abbreviated advertisements

Abbreviated advertisement means an advertisement, other than a loose insert, which does not exceed in size an area of 420 cm^2, in a publication sent or delivered wholly or mainly to persons qualified to prescribe or supply relevant medicinal products.

No person may issue such an advertisement unless it:

1   contains essential information compatible with the SPC; and,

2   the following particulars:

(a)   the name of the medicinal product and a list of the active ingredients using the common name placed immediately adjacent to the most prominent display of the name;

(b)   the name and address of the marketing authorisation holder or the business name and address of the part of the business responsible for the sale or supply;

(c)   the classification of the products, i.e. Prescription Only, Pharmacy Only or General Sale List;

(d)   a form of words which clearly indicates that further information is available on request to the licence holder or in the SPC or, if there is no SPC, the data sheet, relating to the product; and

(e)   any warning issued in relation to the product by the licensing authority.

Audiovisual advertisements

No person may issue in a programme service or video recording any advertisement unless the advertisement:

1   contains essential information compatible with the SPC;

2   contains the following particulars:

(a)   the licence number of the product,

(b)   the name and address of the marketing authorisation holder which relates to the product or the business name and address of his/her business that is responsible for its sale or supply;

(c)   the classification of the product, i.e. Prescription Only, Pharmacy Only, or General Sale List;

(d)   the name of the product and a list of active ingredients using the common name placed immediately adjacent to the most prominent mention or display of the name;

(e)   the indications as within the terms of the licence;

(f)   a succinct statement of the entries in the SPC or, where there is no SPC, the data sheet relating to side effects, precautions and relevant contra-indications;

(g)   a succinct statement of the entries in the SPC or, where there is no SPC, the data sheet relating to the dosage and method of use relevant to the indications shown; the method of administration should also be shown where this is not obvious; and

(h)   a warning issued by the licensing authority under Part II of the Act which is required to be included.

Promotional aids

The requirements set out above in relation to advertisements, abbreviated advertisements and audiovisual advertisements do not apply to promotional aids if:

1   the advertisement consists solely of the name of the product; and
2   the advertisement is intended solely as a reminder.

Written material accompanying promotions

No person may send or deliver to prescribers or suppliers of medicinal products as part of a promotion any written material unless it:

1   contains essential information compatible with the SPC;
2   contains the classification of the product, i.e. Prescription Only, Pharmacy Only, or General Sale List; and
3   states the date on which it was drawn up or last revised.

Any such written material shall be accurate, up-to-date, verifiable and complete and not state any quotation, table or other illustrative matter taken from a medical journal or other scientific work unless it is accurately reproduced and the precise source is indicated.

Free samples

A person may supply a sample only:

1   to a person qualified to prescribe medicinal products;
2   if the sample is not a narcotic or a psychotropic substance; and subject to the following:

(a)   the sample is supplied on an exceptional basis only;

(b)   a limited number only of samples of each product may be supplied in one year to one recipient;

(c)   samples supplied may only be in response to a written request, signed and dated from the recipient;

(d)   suppliers of samples must maintain an adequate system of control and accountability;

(e)   every sample shall be no bigger than the smallest presentation available for sale in the UK;

(f)   every sample must be marked 'free medical sample – not for resale' or bear a similar description; and

(g)   every sample must be accompanied by a copy of the SPC or, where there is no SPC, a copy of the data sheet.

Medical sales representatives

All sales representatives promoting medicinal products to prescribers or suppliers of medicines must give to all persons they visit a copy of the SPC or, in the absence of a SPC, a copy of the data sheet. Such representatives must report all information which they receive from prescribers, including any adverse drug reactions, to the scientific service established under the regulations.

Inducements and hospitality

When products are being promoted to health professionals, no person may supply, offer or promise any gift, pecuniary advantage or benefit in kind unless it is inexpensive and relevant to the practice of medicine or pharmacy.

Hospitality may be offered at events for purely professional or scientific purposes and/or for medicine promotion only to health professionals and provided that such hospitality is reasonable in level and is subordinate to the main scientific objective or main purpose of the meeting.

It is an offence for a health professional to solicit or accept any gift, pecuniary advantage, benefit in kind, hospitality or sponsorship prohibited by the regulations.

Advertisements directed to the public

The regulations dealing with advertisements which are directed to the public relating to medicinal products for human use (SI 1994 No.1932, as amended) impose a range of prohibitions, restrictions and requirements which are set out below.

No advertisement may be issued which is likely to lead to the use of a relevant medicinal product:

1   which is a Controlled Drug which is listed in Schedules I, II or IV of the Narcotic Drugs Convention or Schedules I–IV of the Psychotropic Substances Convention (reg.8);

2   which is for human use and is a Prescription Only Medicine (reg.7);

3   which is any other medicinal product, substance or article for the purpose of inducing an abortion in women (reg.6); and

4   which is for the purpose of treatment, prevention or diagnosis of any of the following diseases (SI 2004 No.1480, reg.6, as amended)

- chronic insomnia
- diabetes and other metabolic diseases
- malignant diseases
- serious infectious diseases including HIV-related diseases and tuberculosis
- sexually transmitted diseases.

NB The prohibition under 4 above does not apply to advertisements which lead to the use of a medicinal product for the purpose of:

(a)   the prevention of neural tube defects (reg.6), or

(b)   the treatment of sprains or strains, or

(c)   the treatment of the symptoms of rheumatic or non-serious arthritic conditions (SI 1996 No.1552).

Prohibition of certain material in advertisements

No person shall issue an advertisement relating to a relevant medicinal product which contains any material which (reg.9):

1   gives the impression that a medical consultation or surgical operation is unnecessary, in particular by offering a telephone number;

2   suggests that the effects of taking the medicinal product are guaranteed, are unaccompanied by side effects or are better than, or equivalent to, those of another identifiable treatment or medicinal product;

3   suggests that health can be enhanced by taking the medicinal product;

4   suggests that health could be affected by not taking the product;

5   is directed exclusively or principally at children;

6   refers to a recommendation by scientists, health professionals or persons who are neither of the foregoing but who, because of their celebrity, could encourage the consumption of medicinal products;

7   suggests that the medicinal product is a foodstuff, cosmetic, or other consumer product;

8   suggests that the safety and efficacy of the medicinal product is due to the fact that it is natural;

9   might, by a description or detailed representation of a case history, lead to erroneous self-diagnosis;

10   refers, in improper, alarming or misleading terms, or pictorial representations of changes in the human body caused by disease or injury, or

of the action of a medicinal product on the human body or parts thereof; or

11   mentions that the medicinal product has been granted a marketing authorisation.

Form and contents of advertisements

No person shall issue an advertisement relating to a relevant medicinal product unless that advertisement (reg.10):

1   is set out in such a way that it is clear that the message is an advertisement and so that the product is clearly identified as a medicinal product, and
2   excluding advertisements for homoeopathic medicinal products, includes the following:

   (a)   the name of the medicinal product;
   (b)   if it contains only one active ingredient, the common name of the medicinal product;
   (c)   the information necessary for correct use of the product; and
   (d)   an express and legible invitation to read carefully the instructions on the leaflet contained within the package or on the label, as the case may be.

These provisions do not apply if the advertisement relates to a relevant medicinal product which is on a promotional aid if the advertisement consists solely of the name of the product (or in the case of a homoeopathic medicinal product the scientific name of the stock) and the advertisement is solely intended as a reminder (reg.10).

Vaccination campaigns

The regulations as set out above do not apply to any advertisement which is part of a vaccination campaign relating to a relevant medicinal product provided that such a campaign has been approved by the Health Ministers (reg.11).

Sales or supplies for promotional purposes

No person who:

1   is the holder of a marketing authorisation; or
2   carries on a business which consists wholly or partly of the manufacturing, or of selling and supplying of relevant medicinal products

shall, for a promotional purpose (whether a promotional purpose of his/her own or of a third party), sell or supply relevant medicinal products to any member of the public (SI 1999 No. 267).

Advertisements for registered homoeopathic products

An advertisement relating to homoeopathic medicinal products may not mention any specific therapeutic indications and may only contain the following details:

1   the scientific name of the stock(s) followed by the degree of dilution, making use of the pharmacopoeia symbols used in relation to the homoeopathic procedure described for that stock(s);
2   the name and address of the holder of the certificate of registration and, where different, the name and address of the manufacturer;
3   the method of administration and, if necessary, the route;
4   the expiry date of the product stating the month and year;
5   the pharmaceutical form;
6   the contents of the sales presentation;
7   any special storage precautions;
8   any special warnings;
9   the manufacturer's batch number;
10   the registration number allotted by the licensing authority preceded by the letters *HR* in capital letters (reg.22);
11   the words *homoeopathic product without approved therapeutic indications*; and
12   a warning advising the user to consult a doctor if the symptoms persist during the use of the product.

Monitoring of advertising

Monitoring of advertising is governed by the Medicines (Monitoring of Advertising) Regulations 1994 (SI 1994 No.1933, as amended by SI 1999 No.267). However, the existing voluntary control under the Medicines Act is encouraged and the existing Codes of Advertising Practice administered by the Association of the British Pharmaceutical Industry (for Prescription Only Medicines) and by the Proprietary Association of Great Britain (for over-the-counter medicines) will continue.

Complaints, in the first instance, will be referred to the appropriate self-regulatory body, but the Minister has the power of civil injunction. A person holding a marketing authorisation will be required to issue corrective statements if their advertising is found to be in breach of the regulations.

In the amending regulations (SI 1999 No.267), a schedule has been introduced relating to the scrutiny of certain published or proposed advertisements. The schedule gives the Health Ministers powers for determining whether or not certain advertisements, proposed or published, breach the advertising regulations. There is an opportunity for representations to be made to an Independent Review Panel before the Health Ministers determine the case and breaches of notices issued by the Health Ministers create an offence. Details of the operation of the Review Panel are available from the MHRA.

Prohibition of representations

No representation may be made by a commercially interested party which is likely to lead to the use of a medicinal product or, where relevant, any other substance or article for any of the diseases for which advertisements are prohibited (see p. 58) if the representation:

1   is made in connection with the sale or supply, or offer for sale or supply, of that product, substance or article;
2   is made to any person for the purpose of inducing him/her to purchase from a retailer that product, substance or article; or
3   is made, in connection with medicinal products, to the patient of a doctor or dentist for the purpose of inducing him/her to request the doctor or dentist to prescribe medicinal products of that description.

The prohibition on representations does not apply to any representation:

(a)   made by a pharmacist who sells or supplies a medicinal product when dispensing a prescription given by a doctor or dentist, or when using his/her own judgment as to the treatment required by a person, i.e. counter prescribing; or
(b)   made by a state registered chiropodist (see p. 106) in relation to a medicinal product which s/he supplied to his/her patient for the purpose of treatment by being administered to the surface of the foot; or
(c)   made by a registered nurse or certified midwife to a patient in relation to a medicinal product.

Exceptions for labels and leaflets

None of the prohibitions, restrictions and requirements imposed by the regulations applies to any labelled container or package of a medicinal product or any other substance or article or any leaflet supplied with such product where that product is prepared or dispensed with a view to administration to a person in accordance with the prescription of a doctor or dentist (SI 1978 No.41).

The prohibitions on advertising imposed under the current regulations do not apply to labelled containers or packages of medicinal products or to leaflets supplied, or intended to be supplied, with medicinal products which:

1   are herbal remedies which are not restricted under the Herbal Remedies Order (SI 1977 No.2130) (see p. 131); or
2   are homoeopathic preparations with licences of right; or

3   are 'counter prescribed' by a pharmacist in a registered pharmacy (see p. 41).

These exceptions are subject to the condition that certain words or phrases are not included in labels or leaflets except in so far as it is necessary to explain the contraindications or precautions or the action to be taken in the event of overdosage of the medicinal products. The words and phrases are:

- amenorrhoea
- angina
- atherosclerosis
- erysipelas
- gallstones
- multiple sclerosis
- osteoarthritis
- phlebitis
- thrombosis
- ulcer (except when used in the phrase 'aphthous ulcer' or 'mouth ulcer').

There is a further condition for herbal, biochemic and anthroposophic remedies, namely that every container and package of these medicinal products must be labelled with appropriate particulars and warning thus:

(a)   *A herbal remedy for (name of disease)*, or as appropriate, *A biochemic remedy for*, or *An anthroposophic remedy for;*

(b)   *Warning. If you think you have (name of disease, as above) consult a registered medical practitioner before taking this product. If you are already receiving treatment, tell your doctor that you are also taking this product.*

The name of the product may be used in the warning instead of the words *this product* and the warning must be within a rectangle within which there shall be no other matter of any kind.

Summary

- Regulations prohibit advertisements for medicinal products for the treatment, prevention or diagnosis of certain diseases to the public. These include cardiovascular diseases, diabetes mellitus, malignant diseases, psychiatric diseases, etc.
- The regulations prohibit the advertising to the public of Controlled Drugs and Prescription Only Medicines.
- Requirements as to the information on medicinal products which has to be given to persons qualified to prescribe or supply medicines includes essential information compatible with the SPC. This may be given by

way of written information accompanying promotions, or by promotion by medical representatives.

- A limited number only of free samples may be supplied to a person qualified to prescribe relevant medicinal products. The samples may only be supplied in response to a written request and suppliers must maintain an adequate system of control.

- No person who is the holder of a marketing authorisation or who carries on a business which consists of the manufacturing, selling or supplying of medicinal products shall, for promotional purposes, sell or supply medicinal products to any member of the public.

- Hospitality given to persons qualified to prescribe or supply medicines must be reasonable in level and subordinate to the main objective of meetings held for scientific or professional purposes. No person may supply or promise any gift, pecuniary advantage or benefit in kind unless it is inexpensive and relevant to the practice of medicine or pharmacy.

- Monitoring of advertising is to be undertaken by self-regulatory bodies but there are also legal provisions involving the Health Ministers.

Further reading

Association of the British Pharmaceutical Industry (ABPI) (2003–2004) *Compendium of Summaries of Product Characteristics*. Datapharm Publications, London.

MHRA *Advertising and Promotion of Medicines in the UK*. Medicines and Health Care Regulatory Authority Updating Service, London.

MHRA (May/June 1999) *MAIL 113*. Medicines and Health Care Regulatory Authority Updating Service, London.

PAGB 2004 *Best Practice Guidelines*. Proprietary Association of Great Britain, London.

CHAPTER FIVE

Medicines Act 1968

Retail pharmacy businesses

A *retail pharmacy business* means a business (not being a professional practice carried on by a practitioner) which consists of or includes the retail sale of medicinal products other than medicinal products on a General Sale List (whether medicinal products on such a list are sold in the course of that business or not) (s.132). Such a business may, subject to certain conditions, lawfully be conducted by (s.69):

1   a pharmacist, or a partnership where each partner is a pharmacist, or, in Scotland, a partnership where one or more partners is a pharmacist; or

2   a body corporate where the business so far as concerns the keeping, preparing and dispensing of medicinal products, other than medicinal products on a General Sale List, is under the management of a super-intendent who is a pharmacist, and who does not act in a similar capacity for any other body corporate. A statement in writing signed by him/her, and signed on behalf of the body corporate, specifying his/her name and stating whether or not s/he is a member of the board, must have been sent to the registrar [s.71(2)]; or

3   a representative of a deceased, bankrupt or mentally ill pharmacist, whose name, together with the names and address of the representative, has been notified to the registrar [s.72(2)].

The *certain conditions* are that at all premises where the business is carried on and medicinal products, other than medicinal products on a General Sale List, are sold by retail, and:

(a)   the business, so far as concerns the retail sale at those premises of medicinal products (whether they are on a General Sale List or not), or the supply at those premises of such products in circumstances corresponding to retail sale, is under the personal control of a pharmacist; and

(b)   the pharmacist's name and certificate of registration under the Pharmacy Act 1954 are conspicuously exhibited (ss.70–72).

The effect is that, in a pharmacy business, personal control must be exercised by a pharmacist over the sale or supply of all medicinal products including those in a General Sale List. (The meaning of *personal control* has been considered by the High Court and the Statutory Committee; see Chapters 24 and 27.)

Where the business is owned by a partnership, one or more of the partners (or, in Scotland, one or more of the pharmacist partners) may be in personal control. In either case, and in the case of a proprietor pharmacist, some other pharmacist may be in personal control (s.70).

A retail pharmacy business owned by a body corporate may be under the personal control of the superintendent, or of a manager or assistant who is a pharmacist subject to the superintendent's directions (s.71). In relation to a body corporate, *the board* means the body of persons controlling the body corporate by whatever name called (s.69).

The owner of a pharmacy business who complies with appropriate conditions described above is a *person lawfully conducting a retail pharmacy business*. Registration of the premises, which is dealt with below, is not one of these conditions. Nevertheless, such registration is essential, as the retail activities controlled under the Medicines Act 1968 and the Poisons Act 1972 must take place at *registered pharmacies*.

Representatives of pharmacists

There are some situations in which the retail pharmacy business of a pharmacist may lawfully be conducted by his/her representatives subject to the conditions already set out and the further conditions described here. The meaning of *representatives* differs according to the circumstances as follows (s.72).

1   In relation to a pharmacist who has died, 'representative' means his/her executor or administrator and, for a period of three months from the date of his/her death, if s/he has died leaving no executor who is entitled and willing to carry on the business, includes any person beneficially interested in his/her estate. The representative of a deceased pharmacist may carry on the business for a period of up to five years from the date

of his/her death. Should s/he cease to be a representative before the expiry of five years, on completing the distribution of the deceased pharmacist's estate, his/her authority lawfully to carry on the pharmacy business would also come to an end.

2   Where a pharmacist is adjudged bankrupt or, in Scotland, sequestration of his/her estate is awarded, the trustee in bankruptcy or in the sequestration is the pharmacist's representative. S/he may carry on the pharmacist's business for a period of three years from the date on which s/he is adjudged bankrupt or the date of the award of sequestration, as the case may be.

3   Where a pharmacist enters into a composition or scheme or deed of arrangement with his/her creditors, or in Scotland makes a trust deed for behoof of his/her creditors, or a composition contract, then the trustee appointed under any such arrangement is the pharmacist's representative. S/he may carry on the business for a period of three years from the date on which s/he became entitled to do so.

4   Where a receiver is appointed for a pharmacist under Part VIII of the Mental Health Act 1959 or, in Scotland, a curator bonis or judicial factor is appointed for him/her on the grounds that s/he suffers from some mental disorder, or in Northern Ireland a committee, receiver or guardian is appointed in his/her case under the Lunacy Regulation (Ireland) Act 1871, then that person is the pharmacist's representative. S/he may carry on the business for three years from the date of his/her appointment.

A person lawfully conducting a retail pharmacy business as the representative of a pharmacist may take or use in connection with that business any title, emblem or description which the pharmacist him/herself could have used [s.78(8)] (see pp.69–70).

The Health Ministers may, by order, add to, revoke or vary any of these conditions relating to the carrying on of retail pharmacy business, or provide for alternative or modified conditions. Such an order must receive the approval of each House of Parliament (s.73).

Registration of pharmacy premises

The *registrar* is the Registrar of the Royal Pharmaceutical Society of Great Britain or, where appropriate, the Pharmaceutical Society of Northern Ireland (s.69). It is the registrar's duty to keep the register of pharmacy premises and, subject to the provisions described later, to enter in the register, on payment of the prescribed fee, any premises in respect of which application is made [s.75(1)]. A document purporting to be a certificate signed by the registrar and stating that, on a specified date, specified premises were, or were not, entered in the register shall be admissible in any proceedings as evidence (and, in

Scotland, shall be sufficient evidence) that those premises were, or were not, entered in the register on that date [s.76(7)].

Registered pharmacy means premises entered for the time being in the register [s.74(1)]. Where a business which concerns the retail sale or supply of medicinal products is carried on in one or more separate or distinct parts of a building, each part is taken to be separate premises [s.69(2)]. A departmental store, for example, might have a department which is a registered pharmacy and a separate department (which is not a pharmacy) where General Sale List medicines are sold.

Registration of pharmacy premises must be effected in a prescribed manner [s.75(2) and SI 1973 No.1822 as amended]. An application must be in writing and be given or sent to the registrar with the prescribed fee. It must be made and signed by or on behalf of the person carrying on, or who intends to carry on, a retail pharmacy business at the premises to which the application relates. A separate application must be made in respect of each premises and each application must contain, or be accompanied by, the following particulars.

1   The name of the person carrying on, or intending to carry on, a retail pharmacy business and his/her private residential address. In the case of a partnership, the names and such addresses of all the partners must be given. In the case of a body corporate, the registered name and address of the registered office of the body must be given. Where a business is being carried on by a representative of a pharmacist and the business is under the personal control of a pharmacist, the name of the pharmacist in personal control and the number of his/her certificate of registration must be given.

2   The business name where a person or a partnership or body corporate is carrying on or intends to carry on such a business under a business name which is different from the name of the person or of the partners or of the corporate body.

3   The name of the pharmacist or, if more than one, the names of all the pharmacists under whose personal control the business is, or is to be, carried on at all the premises to which the application relates, and in the case of a body corporate the name of the superintendent under whose management the business is, or is to be, carried on, and the number of the certificate of each such pharmacist and, as the case may be, superintendent.

4   The full postal address of the premises to which the application relates.

5   Where the application for registration relates to premises in respect of which there has been a change of ownership of the business, the name and address of the immediate former owner of that business and the date of such change of ownership.

6   The date or intended date of the commencement of the business.

7   A brief description of the premises including the internal layout of the premises as regards the areas where medicinal products are or are

intended to be sold or supplied, prepared, dispensed or stored together with:

(a)   a statement showing whether or not there are arrangements so as to enable supervision to be exercised by a pharmacist of any dispensing and sale of medicinal products at one and the same time; and

(b)   a sketch plan, drawn to scale, showing the areas and the layouts to which this paragraph relates.

The registrar must notify the appropriate Ministers (in England and Wales, the Minister of Health; in Northern Ireland, the Minister of Health and Social Services; in Scotland, the Secretary of State) whenever an application is made. S/he may not enter the premises in the register until two months from that date, unless the Minister otherwise consents [s.75(3)]. Premises are not to be entered in the register unless the registrar is reasonably satisfied that the applicant is a person lawfully conducting a retail pharmacy business or will be so at the time of commencement of business [s.75(7)].

If it appears to the Minister that in a material respect the premises do not comply with the requirements of section 66 regulations (see p. 71), s/he must within the two-month period serve on the applicant a notice stating his/her reasons for proposing to certify that the premises are unsuitable for registration. A copy of the notice must be served on the registrar, who may not then enter the premises in the register unless the Minister, after hearing the applicant, directs otherwise [s.75(4)]. An applicant may, within 28 days of receiving a notice from the Minister, submit written representations or seek to be heard by a person appointed by the Minister. Following this procedure the Minister must either:

1   send to the registrar a certificate that the premises are unsuitable for registration and notify the applicant that s/he has done so, stating his/her reasons if so requested; or

2   notify the applicant and the registrar that s/he has determined not to issue a certificate and the registrar must forthwith enter the premises in the register [s.75(5) and (6)].

Change of ownership

Where a change occurs in the ownership of a registered pharmacy, the registration becomes void at the end of the period of 28 days from the date on which the change occurs. If it occurs on the death of the person carrying on the business, that is on the death of a pharmacist owner or, in the case of a partnership, one of the partners, the period is three months from the date of the death [s.76(3)].

When the registration of pharmacy premises becomes void following a change of ownership, an application for restoration to the register may be made by the new owner. The registrar must restore the premises to the register if s/he is reasonably satisfied that the new owner is a person lawfully conducting a retail pharmacy business or will be so at the time s/he commences business at the premises. A fee equal to a retention fee must be paid by the new owner, but only if the retention fee for the year has not already been paid [s.76(5)]. No description of the premises or sketch plan need be submitted.

Premises retention fees

A *retention fee* is payable annually in respect of any premises entered in the register for each year subsequent to the year in which they were registered [s.76(1)]. In this context, *year* means a period of 12 months beginning on such date as the Council (i.e. the Council of the Royal Pharmaceutical Society) may from time to time determine [s.74(3)]. The Council has decided that the registration year shall commence on the first day of January.

In January each year, every person who carries on a retail pharmacy business must send to the registrar a list of all premises at which his/her business, so far as it consists of the retail sale of medicinal products, is carried on. S/he must also state the name of the pharmacist in charge of each pharmacy. This means, in effect, that the owner of a pharmacy or pharmacies must inform the registrar each January of all the addresses of businesses where s/he sells medicinal products of any kind, and pay retention fees in respect of those which are registered pharmacies (s.77).

The Council may direct the registrar to remove any premises from the register if the person carrying on the retail pharmacy business fails to pay a retention fee within two months from the date on which a demand for it has been made to him/her in the prescribed manner. If, before the end of the year, or whatever period is permitted by the Council in any particular case, the retention fee is paid, together with any prescribed sum by way of penalty, the registrar must restore the premises to the register. If the Council so directs, the restoration shall be deemed to have had effect as from the date on which the premises were removed from the register [s.76(2)]. (For Northern Ireland, any reference to the Council in this section should be construed as a reference to the Minister of Health and Social Services for Northern Ireland.)

The Health Ministers are responsible for making any regulations relating to the registration of pharmacies [s.76(6)]. Any fees received by the registrar may be used for the purposes of the Royal Pharmaceutical Society [s.76(8)].

Titles, descriptions and emblems

No person may, in connection with any business, use any title, description or emblem likely to suggest that s/he possesses any qualification with respect to the sale, manufacture or assembly of medicinal products which s/he does not in fact possess; or that any person employed in the business possesses any such qualification which that person does not in fact possess [s.78(6)].

Furthermore, the use of certain titles and descriptions is specifically restricted as follows [s.78(3)].

1   The description *pharmacy* may only be used in respect of a registered pharmacy or the pharmaceutical department of a hospital or a health centre. It may not be used in connection with any business, other than a pharmacy, which consists of or includes the retail sale of any goods, or the supply of any goods in circumstances corresponding to retail sale [s.78(4)]. Its use in connection with a business carried on at any premises shall be taken as likely to suggest that the person carrying on the business (where that person is not a body corporate) is a pharmacist, and that any other person under whose personal control the business (so far as concerns the retail sale of medicinal products or the supply of such products in circumstances corresponding to retail sale) is carried on at those premises, is also a pharmacist.

2   The titles *Pharmaceutical Chemist, Pharmaceutist, Pharmacist, Member of the Pharmaceutical Society* or *Fellow of the Pharmaceutical Society* may only be taken or used by pharmacists [s.78(5)]. These titles may not be used at any premises connected with a business which includes the retail sale or supply of any goods unless those premises are a registered pharmacy or a hospital or health centre [s.78(5)].

3   The titles *Chemist and Druggist, Druggist, Dispensing Chemist* or *Dispensing Druggist* may only be taken or used by a person lawfully conducting a retail pharmacy business [s.78(2)]. The taking or using of the title *Chemist* is also restricted to a person lawfully conducting a retail pharmacy business, but only in connection with the sale of any goods by retail or the supply of any goods in circumstances corresponding to retail sale [s.78(2)].

4   Where the person lawfully conducting the retail pharmacy business is a body corporate, these titles may only be used if the pharmacist who is superintendent is also a member of the board of the body corporate.

None of these titles may be used at any premises connected with a business which includes the retail sale or supply of any goods unless those premises are a registered pharmacy [s.78(3)].

The Health Ministers may by order, and after consultation with the Council of the Pharmaceutical Society, impose further restrictions or requirements with respect to the use of titles, descriptions and emblems. The Ministers may also provide that existing restrictions shall cease to have effect or be subject to specified exceptions. Regulations for these purposes must be approved by resolution of each House of Parliament (s.79).

Accommodation, storage, records, equipment, etc.

The appropriate Ministers have wide powers under the Act (s.66) to make regulations with respect to any of the following matters, although at the time this book closed for press such regulations had been made only in relation to 9 and 10 below (see p. 93):

1. the manner in which, or persons under whose supervision, medicinal products may be prepared or may be dispensed;
2. the amount of space to be provided in any premises for preparing or dispensing medicinal products, the separation of any such space from the remainder of the premises and the facilities to be provided in any premises for such persons;
3. the amount of space to be provided in any premises for the sale or supply of medicinal products;
4. the accommodation (including the amount of space) to be provided in any premises for members of the public to whom medicinal products are sold or supplied or for whom medicinal products are being prepared or assembled;
5. the amount of space to be provided in any premises for the storage of medicinal products;
6. the safekeeping of medicinal products;
7. the disposal of medicinal products which have become unusable or otherwise unwanted;
8. precautions to be observed before medicinal products are sold or supplied;
9. the keeping of records relating to the sale or supply of medicinal products;
10. the supply of medicinal products distributed as samples;
11. sanitation, cleanliness, temperature, humidity or other factors relating to the risks of deterioration or contamination in connection with the manufacture, storage, transportation, sale or supply of medicinal products; and
12. the construction, location and the use of automatic machines for the sale of medicinal products.

The Ministers can also prescribe requirements in respect of:

(a) the construction, layout, drainage, equipment, maintenance, ventilation, lighting and water supply of premises at or from which medicinal products are manufactured, stored, transported, sold or supplied;
(b) the disposal of refuse at or from any such premises; and
(c) any apparatus, equipment, furnishings or utensils used at any such premises.

Disqualification of retail pharmacy owner

It is an offence to contravene any of the regulations made under section 66 (s.67). Any person who is convicted of such an offence may, by order of the court, be disqualified from using the premises concerned for the purposes of a retail pharmacy business for a period not exceeding two years (s.68).

Summary

- Retail businesses which sell medicines not on a General Sale List must be registered as pharmacies. They may be owned by a pharmacist, a partnership, a body corporate or a representative of a deceased pharmacist.
- Detailed requirements relating to the premises, together with a fee, must be forwarded to the Royal Pharmaceutical Society in order for registration to take place.
- Certain titles may only be used by pharmacists, e.g. *pharmacist, pharmaceutical chemist, Member of the Pharmaceutical Society.*
- A body corporate may use the title *dispensing chemist, chemist and druggist* or *chemist* only if the superintendent is a member of the board, otherwise the body corporate may only use the title *pharmacy* in connection with its pharmacy premises.
- Ministers, by way of regulations, may impose a large range of conditions relating to premises from which medicines are sold.

CHAPTER SIX

Medicines Act 1968

Pharmacy Medicines

Part III of the Act is concerned with the regulation of dealings with medicinal products. The basic principle, set out in section 52, is that medicinal products may be sold or supplied by retail only from registered pharmacies, unless they are products included in a General Sale List (Chapter 7) or subject to some other exemption under the Act.

Section 52 provides that medicinal products, which are not included in a General Sale List, shall not be sold, offered or exposed for sale by retail, or supplied in circumstances corresponding to retail sale by any person in the course of a business carried on by him/her unless:

1 that person is, in respect of that business, a person lawfully conducting a retail pharmacy business;
2 the product is sold, offered or exposed for sale, or supplied on premises which are a registered pharmacy; and
3 that person, or, if the transaction is carried out on his/her behalf by another person, then that other person is, or acts under the supervision of, a pharmacist.

NB A retail pharmacy business must be under the personal control of a pharmacist so far as it concerns the sale of medicinal products including products on a General Sale List (ss.70–72). The meaning of *supervision* and *personal control* have been considered by the High Court and the Statutory Committee (Chapters 24 and 27).

Selling by retail or retail sale includes all those sales which do not fall within the definition of selling by way of wholesale dealing [s.131(3)]. Supplying in circumstances corresponding to retail sale has a comparable meaning [s.131(4)]. Retail sale or supply, therefore, constitutes all those sales or supplies of medicinal products made in the course of a business to a person who buys (or receives) them for the purpose other than that of (a) selling or supplying them or (b) administering them or causing them to be administered to one or more human beings in the course of a business carried on by him/her.

The requirements of section 52 apply to sales and supplies made in 'the course of a business'. The provision of services under the NHS is treated as the carrying on of a business [s.131(5)]. However, the dispensing of a medicinal product on a NHS prescription is not a sale but a 'supply in circumstances corresponding to retail sale' (*Appleby* v. *Sleep* [1968] 2 All ER 265; see p. 400).

Pharmacy Medicine defined

Certain medicinal products may only be sold or supplied from pharmacies in accordance with a prescription given by an appropriate practitioner. These products, called Prescription Only Medicines (POMs) are specified in a Prescription Only Order (SI 1997 No.1830, as amended) (see p. 86). Any medicinal product which is not a Prescription Only Medicine or a medicinal product on a General Sale List is a *Pharmacy Medicine* (P) (SI 1980 No.1924, as amended). There is no definitive list of Pharmacy Medicines, as the total in the class cannot be determined. It comprises all those medicines which are not in a Prescription Only List or a General Sale List and includes all medicines made in a pharmacy for retail sale under the exemptions from licensing granted to retail pharmacists (see p. 41).

Some General Sale List medicines, when presented in packs exceeding specified quantities, may only be sold or supplied from pharmacies. They are designated Pharmacy Medicines (SI 1980 No.1923, as amended) although there is no legal requirement for supervision by a pharmacist (see p. 79).

Some Prescription Only Medicine when presented in packs **not** exceeding specified quantities, may be sold or supplied from pharmacies (see pp. 86–87).

Exemptions in cases involving another's default

The restrictions imposed by section 52 of the Act shall not apply to the sale, offer or exposure for sale or supply of a medicinal product by a person who, having exercised all due diligence, believes on reasonable grounds that the product is a medicinal product on a General Sale List or subject to a temporary exemption but which due to the act or default of another person is not such a medicinal product, if and so long as the conditions applying to the sale of medicinal products on a General Sale List are fulfilled (SI 1980 No.1924) (see Chapter 7).

Temporary exemptions

Where the product licence, or a variation of a product licence, provides for the sale or supply of a medicinal product without the supervision of a pharmacist, it may be sold under General Sale List conditions despite the fact that it is not included in the current General Sale List. This temporary exemption is for two years from the date of the grant of the licence, or for one year from the date of a variation in a licence (SI 1980 No.1924). It appears that the General Sale List should be updated each year.

The conditions under which General Sale List medicines may be sold are described in Chapter 7.

Collection and delivery arrangements: exemption

A *collection and delivery arrangement* means any arrangement whereby a person is enabled to take or send a prescription given by a doctor or dentist to premises other than a registered pharmacy and to collect or have collected on his/her behalf from such premises a medicinal product prepared or dispensed in accordance with such prescription at a registered pharmacy by or under the supervision of a pharmacist if such premises at which the medicinal product is supplied are capable of being closed so as to exclude the public (SI 1978 No.1421).

When an arrangement of this kind is used by a person lawfully conducting a retail pharmacy business, the supply of dispensed medicines for human use at the non-pharmacy premises without the supervision of a pharmacist is rendered lawful by an exemption provided in SI 1978 No.1421.

Summary

- Pharmacy Medicines comprise all medicinal products which are not on the General Sale List, are not on the Prescription Only List or are exempt in some form or other from the latter.
- The legislation requires that retail sales or supplies of Pharmacy Medicines have to be made by a person conducting a retail pharmacy business, at a registered pharmacy, and by, or under the supervision of, a pharmacist.

- The conditions under which Pharmacy Medicines must be sold do not apply where there is a collection and delivery arrangement in place.

Further reading

Medicines, Ethics and Practice (published annually) The Royal Pharmaceutical Society of Great Britain, London.

CHAPTER SEVEN

Medicines Act 1968

General Sale Medicines

General Sale Medicines are those which in the opinion of the appropriate Minister can with reasonable safety be sold or supplied otherwise than by or under the supervision of a pharmacist (s.51). Medicines for human use are listed in SI 1984 No.769, as amended. Veterinary drugs are listed in SI 1984 No.768, as amended.

Conditions applying to retail sale or supply

Medicinal products on a General Sale List may only be sold by retail, offered or exposed for sale by retail or supplied in circumstances corresponding to retail sale either at registered pharmacies or in circumstances where the following conditions are fulfilled.

1   The place at which the medicinal product (unless it is a veterinary drug) is sold, offered, exposed or supplied, must be premises at which the person carrying on the business in question is the occupier and which s/he is able to close so as to exclude the public. (NB As veterinary drugs are specifically exempted [s.53(2)] they may be sold from stalls and vans. Similarly, the restriction as to premises does not apply to foods and cosmetics that are medicinal products (SI 1980 No.1924).)

2   The medicinal product must have been made up for sale in a container elsewhere than at the place at which it is sold, offered, exposed for sale

or supplied, and the container must not have been opened since the product was made up for sale in it.

3   The business, so far as concerns the sale or supply of medicinal products, must be carried on in accordance with such conditions as may be prescribed (s.53).

General Sale List Medicines for human use

The classes of medicinal product on general sale for administration to human beings are set out SI 1984 No.769, as amended by SI 2002 No.933. Appended to each of Schedules 1 and 2 are two lists of products: Table A (those for internal and external use) and Table B (those for external use only). Where a product contains a substance listed in one of the tables, it must satisfy any stated specification as to maximum strength (ms), use, pharmaceutical form, or route of administration. Similarly, products for internal use (Table A) must satisfy any specification as to maximum dose (md) or maximum daily dose (mdd). Containers and packages must be labelled with the required information given in the specification. The classes of medicinal product on general sale for administration to human beings include the following.

1   Medicinal products in respect of which a marketing authorisation has been granted, which in the marketing authorisation are classified as General Sale List medicines.
2   Medicinal products in respect of which no marketing authorisation has been granted, other than products subject to a licence of right which fall within a class specified in Schedule 1 of the regulations.
3   Medicinal products which are products the subject of a licence of right and which fall within a class specified in Schedule 2 of the regulations.
4   Licence of right products containing one or more of the following:

   (a)   haemoglobin or the following parts of animals, namely bone, brain, genitals, horn, prostate and spleen but not extracts from such parts;
   (b)   glycerine extracts of bone marrow;
   (c)   bovine blood derivatives;
   (d)   substances of vegetable origin and extracts of such substances used in the UK as food.

5   Aqueous and alcoholic extracts, spirits, syrups and liquid suspensions derived from the substances in 1 above.
6   Excipients (that is substances which do not contribute directly to the pharmacological action of the medicinal product otherwise than by regulation of the release of the active ingredient).
7   Medicinal products for human use which are for sale or supply, either for oral administration as food or external use as a cosmetic, other than products which are eye drops, eye ointments or which contain either:

(a) vitamin A, vitamin A acetate, and vitamin A palmitate with a maximum daily dose equivalent to more than 7500 iu Vitamin A or 2250 micrograms retinol; or

(b) vitamin D with a maximum daily dose of more than 400 iu antirachitic activity.

General sale list medicines for animal use

The medicinal products permitted for general sale as veterinary medicines are set out in Schedule 1 to SI 1984 No.768 as follows.

1   Those listed in Table A (substances for internal and external use) or Table B (substances for external use only). Where a product contains an ingredient which is listed in Table A or B, it must comply with specifications in the table as to maximum strength, maximum dose, maximum daily dose, use, pharmaceutical form or route of administration and be labelled accordingly.

2   Excipients.

3   Substances of animal origin (including extracts of such substances) used in the UK as a human or animal food.

4   Substances of vegetable origin (including extracts and residues of such substances) used in the UK as a human or animal food.

5   Grit in veterinary drugs for birds.

Automatic machines

Medicinal products which are on a General Sale List (other than veterinary drugs) may be sold from automatic machines. Such machines must be located in premises which the occupier is able to close so as to exclude the public (s.66 and SI 1980 No.1923).

Retail pack sizes of certain products

Limits are imposed on the pack sizes of certain General Sale List products when they are sold or supplied by retail from businesses other than pharmacies. If sold outside the limits laid down, the medicinal products concerned are classed as Pharmacy Medicine or Prescription Only Medicines. There are limits for general sale for the following products.

Aloxiprin

Medicines for human use containing aloxiprin may only be presented for sale in separate and individual containers or packages containing not more than (a) 30 tablets (effervescent tablets), (b) 16 capsules or tablets (non-effervescent), and (c) 10 sachets (powders or granules) (s.53) (SI 1980 No.1923, as amended).

Aspirin and paracetamol

Medicines for human use containing aspirin or paracetamol may only be presented for sale in separate and individual containers or packages containing not more than (a) 16 capsules or tablets (non-effervescent) (SI 1999 No.644), (b) 10 sachets (powder or granules), (c) 30 tablets containing not more than 325 mg (effervescent tablets), or (d) 20 tablets where the amount of aspirin exceeds 325 mg but does not exceed 500 mg (effervescent tablets) (SI 1994 No.2411).

In the case of tablets that are not effervescent, are enteric coated and contain aspirin only, the amount of aspirin in each tablet must not exceed 75 mg and the package contain not more than 28 tablets (SI 2001 No.3849).

Effervescent, in relation to a tablet, means containing not less than 75 per cent by weight of the tablet of ingredients included wholly or mainly for the purpose of releasing carbon dioxide when the tablet is dissolved or dispersed in water.

In the case of liquid preparations of paracetamol:

(a)   which are intended for persons over 12 years, not more than 160 ml; and
(b)   which are intended for persons less than 12 years, individual doses of not more than 5 ml and no greater quantity than 20 doses (SI 1997 No.2045).

Bisacodyl

Tablets for human use containing bisacodyl may only be presented for sale in a separate and individual container or package containing not more than 10 tablets (s.53) (SI 1990 No.1124).

Ibuprofen

Medicines for human use containing ibuprofen may only be presented in the following forms (SI 2001 No 4111).

1   In the case of tablets, capsules, powder or granules for internal use for the treatment of rheumatic or muscular pain, backache, neuralgia, migraine, dental pain, dysmenorrhoea, feverishness, or symptoms of colds and influenza, with ms 200 mg, md 400 mg and mdd 1200 mg in individual containers or packages containing not more than 16 tablets or capsules for use for adults and children over 12 years.
2   In liquid preparations for internal use, ms 2% for the treatment of rheumatic and muscle pain, headache, dental pain, feverishness or

symptoms of colds and influenza for use in children under 12 years at ms 200 mg and mdd 800 mg.

3   In the case of liquid preparations, the individual unit doses must not exceed 5 ml each and a maximum of 20 unit doses.

4   If for external use, ms 5 per cent, md 125 mg, mdd 500 mg and individual container package containing not more than 2.5 g for rheumatic pain, muscular aches and pains, swellings such as sprains, sprains and sports injuries.

Clotrimazole

A medicinal product for topical use containing clotrimazole may only be presented for sale in separate and individual containers or packages containing not more than 500 mg clotrimazole (SI 1995 No.3215).

Sodium picosulphate

Medicines for human use containing sodium picosulphate may only be presented for sale in separate and individual containers or packages containing not more than 60 ml (SI 1997 No.2045).

Loperamide hydrochloride

Medicines for human use containing loperamide hydrochloride may only be presented for sale in separate and individual containers or packages containing not more than six tablets or capsules (SI 1997 No.2045).

Mepyramine maleate

Medicines for human use containing mepyramine maleate may only be presented for sale in separate and individual containers or packages containing not more than 20 g with a maximum strength of 2 per cent for the symptomatic relief of insect stings and bites and nettle stings, in adults and in children aged 2 years and over (SI 2000 No.1070).

Ranitidine hydrochloride

Medicines for human use containing ranitidine hydrochloride may only be presented for sale in ms 75 mg tablet form in separate and individual containers or packages containing not more than 12 tablets (SI 1999 No.2510).

Cetirizine hydrochloride

Cetirizine hydrochloride may only be presented for sale in ms 10 mg tablet form for the symptomatic relief of perennial rhinitis, seasonal allergic rhinitis and idiopathic chronic urticaria in adults and children aged 12 years and over, in a individual container or package containing not more than seven tablets (SI 2001 No.4111).

Loratadine

Loratadine may only be presented for sale in ms 10 mg tablet form for the symptomatic relief of perennial rhinitis, seasonal allergic rhinitis and idiopathic chronic urticaria in adults and children aged 12 years and over, in an individual container or package containing not more than seven tablets (SI 2001 No.4111).

Veterinary medicines

For veterinary drugs, the quantities permitted in individual containers or packages are listed in Table 7.1. Packs containing more than these quantities may only be sold or supplied from pharmacies and must be labelled 'P' (SI 1981 No.1791).

Table 7.1   Quantities permitted in individual containers or packages for veterinary drugs

Drug	Quantity
Aminonitrothiazole	100 ml solution or 50 capsules
Aspirin	25 tablets or 25 sachets of powder
Bromhexine hydrochloride	20 g
Paracetamol	25 tablets
Phenylephrine hydrochloride	15 ml
Potassium chlorate	30 ml

Products not to be on general sale

The General Sale List Orders relating to medicinal products for human use (SI 1984 No.769) and for veterinary drugs (SI 1984 No.768) specify certain classes of product which are not to be on general sale.

1   Medicinal products for human use or veterinary drugs promoted, recommended, or marketed:

    (a)   for use as eye drops or eye ointments;

    (b)   for administration by parenteral injection; or

    (c)   for use as anthelmintics, except veterinary drugs consisting or containing dichlorophen, diethylcarbamazine citrate, piperazine adipate, piperazine calcium adipate, piperazine citrate, piperazine dihydrochloride, piperazine hydrate or piperazine phosphate.

2   Veterinary drugs promoted, recommended or marketed for the internal treatment of ringworms.
3   Medicines for human use promoted, recommended or marketed:
   (a)   for use as enemas (SI 1985 No.1540);
   (b)   for use wholly or mainly for irrigation of wounds or of the bladder, vagina or rectum (SI 1985 No.1540); or
   (c)   for administration wholly or mainly to children being a preparation of aloxiprin or aspirin (SI 1987 No.910).

Summary

- Medicines which in the opinion of the Minister can with reasonable safety be sold other than by or under the supervision of a pharmacist are listed as General Sale List medicines for both human and animal use. They may only be sold from closable premises and in their original packs.
- Certain medicines may be sold other than by or under the supervision of a pharmacist subject to certain pack sizes. These include aspirin, aloxiprin, bisacodyl, ibuprofen, topical clotrimazole and ranitidine hydrochloride.
- Certain medicines cannot be on general sale. These include eye drops and ointments, most anthelmintics, parenteral medicines, those medicines promoted as enemas or for use as irrigations, and aspirin for children.

Further reading

Medicines, Ethics and Practice (published annually) The Royal Pharmaceutical Society of Great Britain, London.

CHAPTER EIGHT

Medicines Act 1968

Prescription Only Medicines

A Prescription Only Medicine (POM) means a medicinal product which may only be sold or supplied by retail in accordance with a prescription given by *an appropriate practitioner* (s.58).

For the purposes of SI 1997 No.1830 – which lists Prescription Only Medicines for human use – doctors, dentists, veterinary surgeons and veterinary practitioners are designated as appropriate practitioners. For the purposes of SI 1991 No.1392 – which lists Prescription Only Medicine which are for animal use – veterinary surgeons and veterinary practitioners only are described as appropriate practitioners.

The Medicinal Products: Prescription by Nurses etc. Act 1992 amended the Medicines Act 1968 and provided that registered nurses, midwives and health visitors who are of such a description and who comply with certain conditions are considered to be appropriate practitioners. A *district nurse/ health visitor prescriber* and an *extended formulary prescriber* are defined and are classed as appropriate practitioners. The medicines which they may prescribe are listed in schedules to the regulations (SI 1997 No.1830 and SI 2002 No.549).

A *first level nurse* means a person registered in Sub-Part 1 of the Nurses Part of the professional register.

A *district nurse/health visitor prescriber* means:

1   a person who is first level nurse or registered midwife; and

2   against whose name in the professional register there is an annotation that he is qualified to order drugs, medicines and appliances from the *Nurse Prescribers' Formulary for District Nurses and Health Visitors Appendix* to the current edition of the *British National Formulary*.

An *extended formulary nurse prescriber* means:

1   a person who is first level nurse or registered midwife; and
2   against whose name is recorded in the professional register an annotation signifying that he is qualified to order drugs, medicines and appliances from the Extended Formulary.

The *Extended Formulary* means the *Nurse Prescribers' Extended Formulary Appendix* in the current edition of the *British National Formulary*.
NB The regulations described in this chapter use 'he' for male or female practitioners.

An extended formulary nurse prescriber may give a prescription for a medicinal product listed in the Schedule 3A to the regulations (SI 2002 No.549) or if that medicinal product is for parental administration may administer the product or give directions for the administration of the product. If the schedule specifies as to the use, route of administration or pharmaceutical form, then it must be administered in accordance with those specific conditions. The latter conditions need not be complied with if the extended nurse prescriber is also a supplementary prescriber and is acting in accordance with the terms of a clinical management plan (SI 2003 No.696).

In 2003, a *supplementary prescriber* was added to the list of appropriate practitioners by the Health and Social Care Act 2001. A supplementary prescriber may give a prescription for a medicinal product listed in article 3A to the regulations or if that medicinal product is for parental administration may administer the product or give directions for the administration of the product in accordance with the terms of a clinical management plan (SI 2003 No.696). Particulars to be contained in a clinical management plan are set out in the regulations. A supplementary prescriber means:

1   a first level nurse;
2   a pharmacist;
3   a registered midwife; or
4   a chiropodist, podiatrist, physiotherapist, radiographer (SI 2005 No. 765).

against whose name is recorded in the relevant statutory register an annotation signifying that he is qualified to order drugs, medicines and appliances as a supplementary prescriber.

The specified conditions for extended formulary nurse prescribers and supplementary prescribers do not apply in relation to administration of medicines where it is in accordance with the directions of another person who is an appropriate practitioner.

Prescription Only Medicines for human use

The criteria to be applied in specifying which medicinal products are to be Prescription Only Medicine are laid down in regulations (SI 2002 No.549) implementing Council Directive 2001/83/EEC (the Human Medicines Directive) and Council Directive 2001/82/EEC (the Veterinary Medicines Directives).

The Prescription Only Medicine which are not for animal use are listed in SI 1997 No.1830, as amended by SI 2002 No.549 and SI 2003 No.696. Unless exempt, they are as follows.

1   Medicinal products in respect of which a marketing authorisation has been granted, which in the marketing authorisation are classified as being Prescription Only Medicines.
2   Medicinal products in respect of which no marketing authorisation has been granted, consisting of or containing a substance in Schedule 1 to the regulations.
3   Medicinal products that are Controlled Drugs unless a marketing authorisation has been granted in respect of that medicinal product in which the product is classified as being a Pharmacy Only or on a General Sale List (see Exempted Controlled Drugs p. 88).
4   Medicinal products for human use classified as subject to medical prescription granted by marketing authorisations under Council Regulation 2309/93.
5   Medicinal products that are for parenteral administration whether or not they include any substance included in the Prescription Only Medicines List. (*Parenteral administration* means administration by breach of the skin or mucous membrane.)
6   Cyanogenetic substances other than preparations for external use.
7   Medicinal products that on administration emit radiation, or contain or generate any substance which emits radiation, in order that radiation may be used.
8   Medicinal products in respect of which a marketing authorisation has been granted consisting of or containing aloxiprin, aspirin or paracetamol in the form of non-effervescent tablets or capsules which in the marketing authorisation are as being Pharmacy Only or General Sale List medicines (SI 2003 No.696).

Exemptions from Prescription Only Medicines List

1 Medicinal products exempt owing to conditions

A medicinal product is exempt if it is listed in Column 1 of Schedule 1 and there is:

(a)   an entry in Columns 2, 3, 4 or 5 of that Schedule which contains a condition and that condition is satisfied; or

(b)   there is more than one such condition which applies where that substance is used in that product and each of those conditions are satisfied.

The conditions are that the medicinal product is:

(i)   a particular strength;
(ii)   a particular pharmaceutical form;
(iii) has the route of administration specified in the schedule; and
(iv)   in or from containers or packages labelled to show doses not exceeding the maximum dose (md), or the maximum daily doses (mdd), or both, as specified in the schedule.

All these exempted medicinal products will be Pharmacy Medicines. The *maximum strength* means either:

(a)   the maximum quantity of a substance by weight or volume contained in a dosage unit of a medicinal product; or
(b)   the maximum percentage of a Prescription Only Medicine substance contained in a medicinal product calculated in terms of weight in weight (w/w), weight in volume (w/v), volume in weight (v/w) or volume in volume (v/v) and, if the maximum percentage calculated in those ways differ, the higher or highest percentage.

The *maximum dose* means the maximum quantity of a substance contained in the amount of a medicinal product for internal use which it is recommended should be taken or administered at any one time.

The *maximum daily dose* means the maximum quantity of a substance contained in the amount of a medicinal product which it is recommended should be taken or administered in any period of 24 hours.

2 Retail pack sizes of certain products

Some Prescription Only Medicine when presented in packs **not** exceeding specified quantities may only be sold or supplied from pharmacies. These are:

(a)   *aspirin* where if the pack size for non-effervescent tablets or capsules does not exceed 32 and the ms 500 mg then the product is a Pharmacy Medicine; the total quantity sold to a person at any one time must not exceed 100;
(b)   *aspirin* where if the pack size for non-effervescent tablets or capsules does not exceed 100 and the ms 75 mg, then the product is a Pharmacy Medicine;
(c)   *paracetamol* where if the pack size for non-effervescent tablets or capsules does not exceed 32 and the ms 120 mg (for children under 12 years) or ms 500 mg (for adults or children over 12 years) then the product is a Pharmacy Medicine; the total quantity sold to a person at any one time must not exceed 100 (SI 1997 No.2044).

Aspirin and paracetamol in preparations other than non-effervescent tablets and capsules are also Pharmacy Medicines.

3 High-dilution products

There is an exemption for high-diluted products diluted to at least one part per million (6×). These now include certain high-diluted products which are not for parenteral administration and include aconite, arsenic trioxide, *Belladonna* herb, *Ignatia* bean and *Strychnos nux vomica* seeds (SI 2003 No.696).

4 Exempted controlled drugs

Maximum strengths are specified in Part 2 of Schedule 1 to the Prescription Only Order for certain Controlled Drugs. A medicinal product containing only one of those substances not in excess of the maximum strength is a Pharmacy Medicine, provided it is not a veterinary medicinal product and does not contain any other substances at a strength which would render the product a Prescription Only Medicine, and it is sold, supplied or administered:

Table 8.1   Exempted Controlled Drugs

Substance	Maximum strength	Maximum dose
Codeine, its salts	Equivalent of 1.5% codeine monohydrate base	Equivalent of 20 mg codeine monohydrate base
Dihydrocodeine, its salt	Equivalent of 1.5% dihydrocodeine base	Equivalent of 10 mg dihydrocodeine base
Ethylmorphine, its salts	Equivalent of 0.2% ethylmorphine base	Equivalent of 7.5 mg ethylmorphine base
Morphine, its salts		
Liquid	Equivalent of 0.02% anhydrous morphine base	Equivalent of 3 mg anhydrous morphine base
Solid	Equivalent of 0.04% and 300 micrograms anhydrous morphine base	Equivalent of 3 mg anhydrous morphine base
Medicinal opium		
Liquid	Equivalent of 0.02% anhydrous morphine base	Equivalent of 3 mg anhydrous morphine base
Solid	Equivalent of 0.04% anhydrous morphine base	Equivalent of 3 mg anhydrous morphine base
Pholcodine, its salts	Equivalent of 1.5% of pholcodine monohydrate base	Equivalent of 20 mg pholcodine monohydrate base

(a)   in the pharmaceutical form specified in the order; and
(b)   in or from containers or packages labelled to show a dose not exceeding a maximum dose as specified in the order.

That exemption applies to the six Controlled Drugs (Table 8.1). Subject to the limitations as to maximum strength, maximum dosage and pharmaceutical form shown, they are Pharmacy Medicines.

Prescription Only Medicines for animal use

Prescription Only Medicine products for animal use are listed in SI 1991 No.1392. They are as follows.

1   Those veterinary medicinal products containing one or more substances listed in Part I of Schedule 1 to the Order. Maximum strengths are shown in the schedule for certain substances. A veterinary medicinal product containing such a substance at or below the maximum strength and complying with any other specification in the schedule as to use, pharmaceutical form or route of administration is not a Prescription Only Medicine.
2   Veterinary medicinal products that are Controlled Drugs.
3   Veterinary medicinal products for parenteral administration. But any parenteral preparation which contains a substance in Schedule 2 to the Order is not a Prescription Only Medicine provided that substance does not exceed any specified maximum strength and the preparation is sold or supplied for the purpose stated in the schedule. These are:

- lidocaine (lignocaine)
- lidocaine hydrochloride
- procaine hydrochloride

4   Medicinal products which are veterinary medicinal products by reason of their having been sold or supplied for the administration to animals and which prior to such sale or supply were Prescription Only Medicines as defined in the Prescription Only Medicines (Human Use) Order (SI 1997 No.1830).

New medicinal products

Where a marketing authorisation has been issued in respect of a new medicinal product restricting it to Prescription Only Medicine use, that restriction will normally apply for five years from the date of the granting of the licence. Normally, it is intended that the Prescription Only Order will be updated to include the product before the expiry of the five-year period.

Administration of Prescription Only Medicines

The Act provides that no person shall administer a Prescription Only Medicine otherwise than to him/herself, unless s/he is a practitioner or is acting in accordance with the direction of a practitioner [s.58(2)(b)]. However, certain injectable products may be administered by way of parenteral injection to human beings for the purpose of saving life in an emergency. They are set out in Table 8.2.

Table 8.2   Injectable products which may be administered by way of parenteral injection to human beings for the purpose of saving life in an emergency

Epinephrine (adrenaline) injection (1 in 1000)
Atropine sulphate injection
Atropine sulphate and obidoxime injection
Atropine sulphate and pralidoxime chloride injection
Atropine sulphate, pralidoxime mesilate and avizalone injection
Cobalt edetate injection
Chlorpheniramine injection
Dextrose injection strong BPC
Diphenhydramine injection
Glucagon injection
Hydrocortisone injection
Mepyramine injection
Pralidoxime mesilate injection
Pralidoxime chloride injection
Promethazine hydrochloride injection
Snake venom antiserum
Sodium thiosulphate injection
Sodium nitrite injection
Sterile pralidoxime

Radioactive medicinal products

Radioactive substance means any substance that contains one or more radionuclides of which the activity or concentration cannot be disregarded as far as radiation protection is concerned (SI 1978 No.1006).

Only a doctor or dentist holding an appropriate certificate issued by the Health Minister or a person acting under the directions of such a doctor or dentist may lawfully administer a *radioactive medicinal product*, that is a medicinal product which is, which contains or which generates a radioactive substance and which is, contains or generates that substance in order, when administered, to utilise the radiation emitted therefrom. Certain other conditions are laid down in the regulations (SI 1978 No.1006, amended by SI 1995 No.2147).

Smallpox vaccine

The restrictions imposed by the Medicines Act do not apply to the administration of smallpox vaccine for the purposes of providing protection in the event of a suspected or confirmed case of smallpox where the vaccine is administered to members of, or persons working for, Her Majesty's forces (SI 2004 No.2693). The vaccines must be supplied by, or on behalf of, the Secretary of State, Scottish Ministers, the National Assembly of Wales, the Department of Health, Social Services and Public Safety or an NHS Body.

An *NHS Body* means the Common Services Agency, a Strategic Health Authority, Health Authority or Special Health Authority, a Primary Care Trust, a Local Health Board, a NHS Trust or a NHS Foundation Trust.

Prescriptions

A Prescription Only Medicine may only be sold or supplied in accordance with a prescription given by a practitioner [s.58(a)]. To meet that requirement, certain conditions must be satisfied (SI 2005 No. 765), as given below. The prescription:

(a) shall be signed in ink with his/her own name by the appropriate practitioner giving it;

(b) shall, without prejudice to subparagraph (a), be written in ink or otherwise so as to be indelible, unless it is a health prescription which is not for a Controlled Drug specified in Schedule 1, 2 or 3 to the Misuse of Drugs Regulations, in which case it may be written by means of carbon paper or similar material;

(c) shall contain the following particulars:

    (i) the address of the appropriate practitioner giving it;

    (ii) the appropriate date (see below);

    (iii) such particulars as indicate whether the practitioner giving it is a doctor, a dentist, supplementary prescriber, district nurse/health visitor or extended formulary nurse prescriber, a veterinary surgeon or a veterinary practitioner;

    (iv) where the practitioner giving it is a doctor, dentist, supplementary prescriber, or district nurse/health visitor or extended formulary nurse prescriber, the name, address and the age, if under 12, of the person for whose treatment it is given; and

    (v) where the practitioner giving it is a veterinary surgeon or a veterinary practitioner, the name and address of the person to whom the Prescription Only Medicine is to be delivered and a declaration that it is for an animal or herd under his/her care;

(d) shall not be dispensed after the end of the period of six months from the appropriate date, unless it is a repeatable prescription in which case it shall not be dispensed for the first time after the end of that period nor otherwise than in accordance with the direction contained in the repeatable prescription;

(e)   in the case of a repeatable prescription that does not specify the number of times it may be dispensed, shall not be dispensed on more than two occasions unless it is a prescription for oral contraceptives in which case it may be dispensed six times before the end of the period of six months from the appropriate date.

Repeatable prescription means a prescription which contains a direction that it may be dispensed more than once.

Health prescription means a prescription issued by a doctor, dentist, supplementary prescriber, district nurse/health visitor prescriber or extended formulary nurse prescriber under or by virtue of:

1   in England and Wales, the National Health Service Act 1977;
2   in Scotland, the National Health Service (Scotland) Act 1978; and
3   in Northern Ireland, the Health and Personal Social Services (Northern Ireland) Order 1972.

The *appropriate date* is the date on which the prescription was signed by the practitioner, or, in the case of a health prescription only, the date indicated by him/her as being the date before which it shall not be dispensed. Where a health prescription bears both dates, the later of those dates is the appropriate one.

Due diligence clause

Where a prescription given by an appropriate practitioner does not fulfill a required condition, the sale or supply is not rendered unlawful if the person making the sale or supply, having exercised all due diligence, believes on reasonable grounds that that condition is fulfilled in relation to that sale or supply.

This due diligence clause also applies to the supply made by a pharmacist in accordance with a prescription given by another pharmacist, a registered nurse or a registered midwife *who is not a appropriate practitioner* where the pharmacist believes that that person is such a practitioner (SI 2003 No.696).

Forgeries

Similarly, the sale or supply by a pharmacist is not rendered unlawful if made against a forged prescription provided the pharmacist has exercised all due diligence and believes on reasonable grounds that the prescription is genuine.

Pharmacy records

Every person lawfully conducting a retail pharmacy business is required to keep a record in respect of every sale or supply of a Prescription Only Medicine, unless:

1   it is a sale or supply in pursuance of a health prescription or a prescription for oral contraceptives;
2   a separate record of the sale or supply is made in accordance with regulation 19 of the Misuse of Drugs Regulations (see Chapter 17, p. 207) or regulation 19 of the Misuse of Drugs (Northern Ireland) Regulations 1974;
3   the sale or supply is to a person employed or engaged in connection with a scheme for testing the quality and checking the amount of drugs and appliances supplied under the National Health Service legislation of England and Wales, or Scotland, or Northern Ireland;
3   in Scotland, the sale or supply is to a doctor of drugs or appliances which, under the National Health Service, the doctor is entitled or required to supply; or
5   in Northern Ireland, the sale or supply is in response to an order for a doctor of medicinal products which are drugs required by him/her under the National Health Service for immediate administration or in other similar cases (SI 1980 No.1923).

For records of wholesale transactions in Prescription Only Medicine, see Chapter 10.

An entry must be a written or computerised record kept for the purpose in respect of each sale or supply (SI 1997 No.1831). The entry must be made on the day the sale or supply takes place or, if that is not reasonably practicable, on the following day.

For an emergency supply made on the undertaking of a doctor, district nurse/health visitor, extended formulary nurse prescriber or supplementary prescriber to furnish a prescription within 72 hours, the recording of (a) the date of the prescription and (b) the date on which the prescription is received may be made on the day that the prescription is received (SI 1980 No.1923).

Particulars of prescriptions to be recorded

The particulars to be recorded in the case of a sale or supply of a Prescription Only Medicine in pursuance of a prescription are:

1   the date on which the medicine was sold or supplied;
2   the name, quantity and, except where it is apparent from the name, the pharmaceutical form and strength of the medicine;

3   the date on the prescription and the name and address of the practitioner giving it; and
4   the name and address of the person for whom or for whose animal, as the case may be, the medicine was prescribed.

For second and subsequent supplies made on a repeat prescription, it is sufficient to record the date of supply and a reference to the entry in the register relating to the first supply. Additional particulars must be recorded in the case of emergency supplies to patients (see below).

Preservation of pharmacy records

The Prescription Only Record must be preserved by the owner of the retail pharmacy business for a period of two years from the date of the last entry in the record. A prescription must be retained for two years from the date on which the Prescription Only Medicine was sold or supplied, or, for a repeat prescription, the date on which the medicine was supplied for the last time (see also Chapter 17).

Labelling of dispensed medicines

See page 161.

Exemptions for hospitals, clinics, etc.

The restrictions imposed by the Medicines Act do not apply to the sale or supply of a Prescription Only Medicine in the course of the business of a hospital where the medicine is sold or supplied for the purpose of being administered (whether in the hospital or elsewhere) to a particular person in accordance with directions satisfying the following conditions The directions should:

1   be in writing;
2   relate to the particular person to whom the medicine is to be administered; and
3   be given by a person (other than a veterinary surgeon or veterinary practitioner) who is an appropriate practitioner in relation to that medicine.

Such directions may be given by an extended formulary nurse prescriber or supplementary prescriber *only* where s/he complies with any condition as to the cases or circumstances in which s/he may give a prescription for that medicine, as if the directions were a prescription. The exemption applies not withstanding the written directions do not satisfy the requirements for a prescription given (SI 2004 No.2) (see p. 91).

Exemptions for persons conducting retail pharmacy businesses

In the Act, and in the orders made under the Act, there are specific exemptions for persons lawfully conducting retail pharmacy businesses from the conditions or restrictions on the retail sale and supply of Prescription Only Medicine (SI 1997 No.1830) and from the supply and administration of Prescription Only Medicine (SI 2000 No.1917). Exemptions from control for other persons are to be found in Chapter 9.

In an emergency, a person lawfully conducting a retail pharmacy business can sell or supply a Prescription Only Medicine if and so long as certain conditions are satisfied. There are two kinds of emergency supply (those made at the request of a doctor or supplementary prescriber, and those made at the request of a patient) and different conditions apply to them.

Exemption for emergency supply made at the request of a doctor or supplementary prescriber

The conditions that apply are:

1   that the pharmacist by or under whose supervision the Prescription Only Medicine is to be sold or supplied is satisfied that the sale or supply has been requested by a doctor, supplementary prescriber, district nurse/health visitor or extended formulary nurse prescriber who by reason of an emergency is unable to furnish a prescription immediately;
2   that that doctor, supplementary prescriber, district nurse/health visitor or extended formulary nurse prescriber has undertaken to furnish the person lawfully conducting the retail pharmacy business with a prescription within 72 hours;
3   that the Prescription Only Medicine is sold or supplied in accordance with the directions of the doctor, supplementary prescriber, district nurse/health visitor or extended formulary nurse prescriber requesting it;
4   that the Prescription Only Medicine is not a Controlled Drug specified in Schedule 1, 2, or 3 to the Misuse of Drugs Regulations (Appendix 11);
5   that an entry is made in the Prescription Only Register (see above) stating:

   (a)   the date on which the medicine was sold or supplied;
   (b)   the name, quantity and, except where it is apparent from the name, the pharmaceutical form and strength of the medicine;
   (c)   the name and address of the person for whom the Prescription Only Medicine was supplied;
   (d)   the date on which the prescription was received and the name and address of the practitioner giving it; and
   (e)   the date on the prescription (SI 1997 No.1830 as amended).

Exemption for emergency supply made at the request of a patient

The conditions that apply are:

1   that the pharmacist by or under whose supervision the Prescription Only Medicine is to be sold or supplied has interviewed the person requesting the medicine and has satisfied him/herself:

  (a)   that there is an immediate need for the Prescription Only Medicine requested to be sold or supplied and that it is impracticable in the circumstances to obtain a prescription without undue delay;

  (b)   that treatment with the Prescription Only Medicine requested has on a previous occasion been prescribed by a doctor, supplementary prescriber, district nurse/health visitor or extended formulary nurse prescriber for the person requesting it; and

  (c)   as to the dose which in the circumstances it would be appropriate for that person to take;

2   that no greater quantity of the Prescription Only Medicine in question than will provide five days' treatment is sold or supplied except that there may be sold or supplied, where the medicine in question is:

  (a)   a preparation of insulin, an aerosol dispenser for the relief of asthma, an ointment or cream which has been made up for sale in a container elsewhere than at the place of sale or supply, the smallest pack that the pharmacist has available for sale or supply;

  (b)   an oral contraceptive in a quantity sufficient for a full cycle; or

  (c)   an antibiotic for oral administration in liquid form, the smallest quantity that will provide a full course of treatment;

3   that the pharmacist by or under whose supervision the medicine is sold or supplied ensures that an entry in the Prescription Only Register is made (see above) stating:

  (a)   the date on which the Prescription Only Medicine was sold or supplied;

  (b)   the name, quantity and, except where it is apparent from the name, the pharmaceutical form and strength of the medicine;

  (c)   the name and address of the person requiring the medicine; and

  (d)   the nature of the emergency;

4   that the container or package of the medicine is labelled with:

  (a)   the date on which the Prescription Only Medicine was sold or supplied;

  (b)   the name, quantity and, except where it is apparent from the name, the pharmaceutical form and strength of the Prescription Only Medicine;

  (c)   the name of the person requiring the Prescription Only Medicine;

(d)   the name and address of the registered pharmacy from which the Prescription Only Medicine was sold or supplied; and

(e)   the words 'Emergency Supply'.

5   that the Prescription Only Medicine:

(a)   is not a Controlled Drug specified in Schedule 1, 2 or 3 to the Misuse of Drugs Regulations (see Appendix 9); or

(b)   does not contain one or more of the substances in Table 8.3.

Table 8.3 Substances one or more of which may *not* be contained in a Prescription Only Medicine supplied at the request of a patient (SI 1997 No.1830, as amended)

Ammonium bromide	Methohexital (methohexitone) sodium
Calcium bromide	Pemoline
Calcium bromidolactobionate	Piracetam
Embutramide	Potassium bromide
Fencamfamin hydrochloride	Prolintane hydrochloride
Fluanisone	Sodium bromide
Hexobarbital (hexobarbitone)	Strychnine hydrochloride
Hexobarbital (hexobarbitone) sodium	Tacrine hydrochloride
Hydrobromic acid	Thiopental (thiopentone) sodium
Meclofenoxate hydrochloride	

An emergency sale or supply is permitted of a Prescription Only Medicine which consists of or contains phenobarbital or phenobarbital sodium provided that it is for use in the treatment of epilepsy and does not contain any of the other substances listed above or any substances in Schedule 1, 2 or 3 to the Misuse of Drugs Regulations.

Exemption for persons conducting retail pharmacies under a Patient Group Direction

A *Patient Group Direction* (PGD) (SI 2000 No.1917 as amended) means:

1   a written direction relating to the supply and administration of a description or class of Prescription Only Medicines; or

2   a written direction relating to the administration of a description or class of Prescription Only Medicines, and which in either case of 1 or 2:

(a)   is signed by a doctor or dentist, and by a pharmacist, and

(b)   relates to supply and administration, or to administration only, to persons generally (subject to any exclusions which may be set out in the Direction).

The restrictions on retail sale, supply or administration of Prescription Only Medicine do not apply to the supply or administration of any such medicine by a person lawfully conducting a retail pharmacy business where the medicine is supplied or is administered, by such a person subject to an arrangement made with one of the following:

(a) Common Services Agency;
(b) a Strategic Health Authority, health authority, a Special Health Authority;
(c) a NHS Trust, or NHS Foundation Trust;
(d) a Primary Care Trust;
(e   in England, Wales or Scotland, an independent hospital, an independent clinic, an independent medical agency and, in Northern Ireland a nursing home;
(f) health professionals who assist the provision of healthcare on behalf of the police in the UK or a prison service; or
(g) Her Majesty's forces;

where the medicine is supplied for the purpose of being administered, or is administered, to a particular person in accordance with a PGD and where the following conditions are satisfied.

1   The PGD relates to the supply, or the administration, of a description or class of Prescription Only Medicine by a person lawfully conducting a retail pharmacy business who supplies or administers such a medicine.
2   The PGD has effect at the time at which the medicine is supplied or is administered.
3   The PGD contains the particulars specified in Schedule 7 to the Regulations (see Appendix 6). If the PGD is for administration only, any restrictions on quantity may be omitted.
4   The PGD is signed on behalf of the authority with whom an arrangement is made:

- for authorities (a) to (d), usually by a doctor (or dentist) *and* a pharmacist
- for authority (e), by or on behalf of the relevant provider or if there is a relevant manager for the establishment, the relevant manager
- for a force under (f), by or on behalf of the person designated for that force or service (e.g chief constable, prison governor or prison management board in Scotland or Northern Ireland
- for (g), the Surgeon General or Medical Director General or chief executive at the Ministry of Defence.

5   At the time at which the medicine is supplied or administered, the medicine has a marketing authorisation or a homoeopathic certificate of registration (SI 2000 No.1917, as amended).
6   Where the medicine is administered by the person lawfully conducting a retail pharmacy business, the individual who administers the medicine belongs to one of the classes specified in the Order (see Appendix 8) and is designated in writing on behalf of the body with which an arrangement has been made (added by SI 2000 No.2899).

NB As far as pharmacies are concerned, there is no provision to use a PGD to permit the supply or administration of Pharmacy Medicines and General Sale List medicines.

Exemptions from Prescription Only for certain persons, including supply under Patient Group Directions

See Chapter 9.

Electronic prescriptions

An Order was made in 2001 permitting NHS prescriptions which were issued as part of three pilot schemes on the use of electronic prescriptions to be signed and transferred by electronic means provided certain conditions were met. One of the conditions was that the prescription had to be created and transferred to the person by whom it is dispensed as an electronic communication. The prescription must have been issued by a doctor, under the National Health Service Act, as part of the performance of personal medical services in connection with a pilot scheme and dispensed lawfully by a person lawfully conducting a retail pharmacy business (SI 2001 No.2889).

The pilots ended in 2003. At the time of writing new legislation has been proposed to put in place a permanent provision suitable for enabling electronic prescriptions across the UK. It is proposed to use the definition set out in the Electronic Signatures Regulations SI 2002 No.318, which states that the *advanced electronic signature* means an electronic signature which is:

- uniquely linked to the signatory
- capable of identifying the signatory
- created using means that the signatory can maintain under his/her control
- linked to the data to which it relates in such a manner that any subsequent change of the data is detectable.

As from April 2005, except for prescriptions for Controlled Drugs or from a veterinarian, a prescription may alternatively be electronically written and signed with an advanced electronic signature (SI 2005 No.765).

Summary

- Practitioners for the purpose of prescribing Prescription Only Medicine are doctors, dentists and veterinary surgeons. Certain nurses are also appropriate nurse practitioners and may prescribe medicines from a limited list.

- Certain medicines are Prescription Only by description or class including Controlled Drugs (some are exempt by maximum strength or maximum dose), parenteral drugs and cyanogenetic substances.
- Certain Prescription Only Medicine are exempt, dependent on strength, daily dosage, specified condition for use, etc. (e.g. cimetidine).
- Certain Prescription Only Medicine may be administered in an emergency [e.g. adrenaline (epinephrine) injection].
- Detailed prescription requirements are laid down including name and address of patient, signature and address of doctor, date, age of patient if under 12 years, etc.
- Detailed record requirements are imposed for Prescription Only Medicine except those on a health prescription or oral contraceptives.
- Prescription Only Medicines, except Controlled Drugs, may be supplied at the request of a doctor, supplementary prescriber, district nurse/health visitor or extended formulary nurse prescriber who by reason of any emergency is unable to furnish a prescription immediately.
- Prescription Only Medicines, except Controlled Drugs, may be supplied at the request of a patient if the pharmacist has interviewed the patient, is satisfied that there is an immediate need, that it is impracticable to obtain a prescription without undue delay and that the medicine has been prescribed before by a doctor, supplementary prescriber, district nurse/health visitor or extended formulary nurse prescriber. Detailed quantity, labelling and record conditions apply.
- Under certain conditions Prescription Only Medicine may be supplied under Patient Group Directions.

Further reading

Medicines, Ethics and Practice (published annually) The Royal Pharmaceutical Society of Great Britain, London. (Lists of Prescription Only Medicines are included.)

CHAPTER NINE

Medicines Act 1968

Retail sale and supply:

exemptions from controls for

other persons

In the Act, and in orders made under the Act, there are specified exemptions for certain classes of person from the conditions or restrictions on retail sale and/or supply which apply to medicines on a General Sale List (s.53), Pharmacy Medicines (s.52) and Prescription Only Medicines (s.58). Exemption from the restriction on the administration of Prescription Only Medicines for parenteral use is also conferred on certain persons (SI 1997 No.1830, as amended).

The classes of person and the bodies exempted, the medicinal products to which the exemptions apply and the conditions (if any) which attach to the retail sale, supply or administration by these exempted persons are described in this chapter.

The sale of a Prescription Only Medicine or a Pharmacy Medicine to any of these persons in accordance with the exemptions granted to them is a sale by way of wholesale dealing (SI 1980 No.1923, amended by SI 2000 No.1918). The persons who may engage in wholesale dealing, the extent to which it may be carried on at retail pharmacy businesses and the records to be kept in respect of wholesale transactions are described in Chapter 10.

Hospitals and health centres

The restrictions on the sale, offer for sale or supply of any medicinal products (not being Prescription Only Medicine) do not apply when the sale, offer for sale or supply is in the course of the business of a hospital or health centre for the purpose of being administered (whether in the hospital or health centre or elsewhere) in accordance with the directions of a doctor or dentist (s.55).

The restrictions on the sale, offer for sale or supply of any other medicinal products (not being Prescription Only Medicines) do not apply when the sale, offer for sale or supply is in the course of the business of a hospital or health centre for the purpose of being administered (whether in the hospital or health centre or elsewhere) to a particular person in accordance with the written directions of a supplementary prescriber or a nurse prescriber relating to that person (SI 2004 No.1).

National Health Service bodies: medicines supplied under Patient Group Direction

The following exceptions to the restrictions on retail sale or supply apply to NHS bodies supplying under a Patient Group Direction (PGD; see p. 97). In these, an *excepted person* means a doctor, dentist or person lawfully conducting a retail pharmacy.

1   The restrictions on retail sale or supply of Prescription Only Medicines do not apply to the supply of any such medicine by:

  (a)   the Common Services Agency;
  (b)   a Strategic Health Authority, health authority or Special Health Authority;
  (c)   a NHS Trust or NHS Foundation Trust;
  (d)   a Primary Care Trust; or
  (e)   a person, other than an excepted person, subject to an arrangement made with one of the bodies in (a) to (d) above for the supply of Prescription Only Medicines where the medicine is supplied for the purpose of being administered to a particular person in accordance with the written directions of a doctor or dentist relating to that person. The written directions need not satisfy the requirements for a prescription given in the Prescription Only Order (SI 2000 No.1917).

2   The restrictions on retail sale or supply of Prescription Only Medicines do not apply to the supply, or as the case may be, the administration of any such medicine by:

  (a)   the Common Services Agency;
  (b)   a Strategic Health Authority, health authority or Special Health Authority;
  (c)   a NHS Trust or NHS Foundation Trust;
  (d)   a Primary Care Trust; or

(e)   a person, other than an excepted person, subject to an arrangement made with one of the persons in (a) to (d) above for the supply or the administration of Prescription Only Medicines where the medicine is supplied for the purpose of being administered, or as the case may be, is administered, to a particular person in accordance with a PGD and where the following conditions are satisfied:

   (i)   the PGD relates to the supply, or the administration, of a description or class of Prescription Only Medicine by the person who supplies or administers a Prescription Only Medicine;

   (ii)   the PGD has effect at the time at which the medicine is supplied or is administered;

   (iii) the PGD contains the particulars specified in the regulations (see Appendix 6); if the PGD is for administration only any restrictions on quantity may be omitted;

   (iv)   the PGD is signed on behalf of the person specified in (a) to (d) above (the *authorising person*) by a doctor (or dentist) *and* a pharmacist;

   (v)   the individual who supplies or administers the medicine belongs to a class of health professionals (Schedule 7) (see Appendix 6) and is designated in writing on behalf of the authorising body for the purpose of supply or administration under the PGD;

   (vi)   at the time at which the medicine is supplied or administered, the medicine has a marketing authorisation or a homoeopathic certificate of registration (SI 2000 No.1917).

NB The particulars required in the PGD (iii) and the list of designated health professionals (v) are set out in Appendix 6.

Similar provisions apply to permit the supply or administration of Pharmacy Medicines and General Sale List medicines by means of PGDs (SI 2000 No.1919).

Doctors, dentists and veterinarians

The restrictions on retail sale or supply do not apply to the sale, offer for sale or supply of any medicinal products (ss.55 and 58):

1   by a doctor or dentist to a patient of his/hers, or to a person under whose care such a patient is; or

2   by a veterinary surgeon or veterinary practitioner for administration by him/her or under his/her direction to an animal or herd under his/her care.

For interpretation of *patient of his/hers* see Chapter 27.

Unorthodox practitioners

Persons who at 11 February 1982 were customarily administering medicinal products to human beings by parenteral administration in the course of a business in the field of osteopathy, naturopathy, acupuncture or other similar field (except chiropody) may *administer* Prescription Only Medicines which are only so classified because they are for parenteral use and provided they do not contain an ingredient which would otherwise make them Prescription Only. The person administering the medicine must, at the request of the person to whom it is to be administered, use his/her own judgment as to the treatment required (SI 1997 No.1830).

Midwives

Sale or supply

The restrictions on retail sale or supply do not apply to the supply or sale (but not offer for sale) of certain medicinal products by a registered midwife in the course of his/her professional practice.

The medicinal products to which this exemption applies (SI 1997 No.1830) are:

1 all medicinal products that are not Prescription Only Medicines;
2 Prescription Only Medicines containing any of the following substances but no other Prescription Only Medicine:

- chloral hydrate
- ergometrine maleate (only when contained in a medicinal product which is not for parenteral administration)
- pentazocine hydrochloride
- phytomenadione (SI 1998 No.2081)
- triclofos sodium.

Administration

Registered midwives may also administer parenterally in the course of their professional practice Prescription Only Medicines containing any of the following substances (SI 1997 No.1830 as amended):

- diamorphine (SI 2004 No.2)
- ergometrine maleate
- lidocaine
- lidocaine hydrochloride
- morphine (SI 2004 No.2)
- naloxone hydrochloride
- oxytocin, natural and synthetic
- pentazocine lactate

- pethidine hydrochloride
- phytomenadione
- promazine hydrochloride.

Additionally lidocaine, lidocaine hydrochoride and promazine hydrochloride may only be administered by a midwife while attending a woman in childbirth.

Midwives may also supply or administer Prescription Only Medicines, Pharmacy Medicines, and General Sale List medicines under PGDs (see p. 109).

Registered nurses

The restrictions on retail supply or sale do not apply to the supply or sale (but not offer for sale) by a registered nurse in the course of his/her professional practice of any medicinal product specified in an order made by the Health Ministers (s.55). No such order has yet been made. Registered nurse does not include enrolled nurses (see p. 84).

Nurse practitioners may prescribe, but not sell or supply, a limited list of Prescription Only Medicines (see p. 84).

Registered nurses may also supply or administer Prescription Only Medicines, Pharmacy Medicines, and General Sale List medicines under PGDs (see p. 109).

Ophthalmic opticians

The restrictions on retail supply or sale do not apply to the sale or supply of certain medicinal products (those in 3 and 4 below) by registered ophthalmic opticians provided they are only in the course of their professional practice and only in an emergency.

The medicinal products to which this exemption applies are:

1   all medicinal products on a General Sale List;
2   all Pharmacy Medicines;
3   Prescription Only Medicines that are either:

   (a)   eye drops containing not more than 0.5 per cent chloramphenicol; or
   (b)   eye ointments containing not more than 1.0 per cent chloramphenicol;

4   Medicines which are Prescription Only by reason only that they contain any of the following substances:

   - atropine sulphate
   - bethanecol chloride
   - carbachol

- cyclopentolate hydrochloride
- homatropine hydrobromide
- naphazoline hydrochloride
- naphazoline nitrate
- physostigmine salicylate
- physostigmine sulphate
- pilocarpine hydrochloride
- pilocarpine nitrate
- tropicamide.

Supplies of these Prescription Only Medicines may be obtained by opticians for use in their practice from a retail pharmacy business subject to the presentation of an order signed by a registered ophthalmic optician (SI 1997 No.1830).

Ophthalmic opticians may also *purchase* for use in their practice (but not for sale or supply) medicines which are prescription only by reason only that they contain any one or more of the following substances (SI 1980 No.1923):

- amethocaine (tetracaine) hydrochloride
- framycetin sulphate
- lidocaine hydrochloride
- oxybuprocaine hydrochloride
- proxymetacaine hydrochloride
- thymoxamine hydrochloride.

Registered ophthalmic opticians may also supply or administer Prescription Only Medicines, Pharmacy Medicines and General Sale List medicines under PGDs (see p. 109).

Chiropodists

Sale or supply

The restrictions on retail sale or supply do not apply to the sale or supply of certain medicinal products by state registered chiropodists provided:

1   the sale or supply is made in the course of their professional practice; and
2   the product has been made up for sale or supply in a container elsewhere than at the place at which it is sold or supplied.

The medicinal products to which this exemption applies are:

1   medicinal products for external human use that are on a General Sale List; and
2   any of the following Pharmacy Medicines for external use only: ointment of heparinoid and hyaluronidase, potassium permanganate crystals

or solution, and products containing, as their only active ingredients any of the following substances, at a strength, in the case of each substance, not exceeding that specified in relation to that substance (SI 1982 No.27):

- 9.0 per cent borotannic complex
- 10.0 per cent buclosamide
- 3.0 per cent chlorquinaldol
- 1.0 per cent clotrimazole
- 10.0 per cent crotamiton
- 5.0 per cent diamthazole hydrochloride
- 1.0 per cent econazole nitrate
- 1.0 per cent fenticlor
- 10.0 per cent glutaraldehyde
- 0.4 per cent hydrargaphen
- 2.0 per cent mepyramine maleate
- 2.0 per cent miconazole nitrate
- 2.0 per cent phenoxypropan-2-ol
- 20.0 per cent podophyllum resin
- 10.0 per cent polynoxylin
- 70.0 per cent pyrogallol
- 70.0 per cent salicylic acid
- 0.1 per cent thiomersal
- ibuprofen; other than preparations of ibuprofen which are Prescription Only Medicines and in an amount sufficient for three days' treatment where the md is 400 mg, the mdd 1200 mg and the maximum pack is 3600 mg (SI 1998 No.107).

Registered chiropodists who hold a certificate of competence in the use of the following Prescription Only Medicines, issued by or with the approval of the Chiropodists Board, may sell or supply any one of the following substances in the course of their professional practice:

- co-dydramol 10/500 tablets: the quantity sold or supplied to a person at any one time not to exceed an amount sufficient for three days' treatment to a maximum of 24 tablets
- amorolfine HCl cream: the maximum strength of amorolfine not to exceed 0.25 per cent (w/w)
- amorolfine HCl lacquer: the maximum strength of amorolfine not to exceed 5 per cent (w/v)
- topical hydrocortisone: the maximum strength of hydrocortisone in the medicinal product not to exceed 1 per cent (w/w).

The medicinal product must have been be made up for sale or supply in a container elsewhere than at a place at which it is sold (SI 1998 No.107).

Administration

Registered chiropodists who hold a certificate of competence in the use of analgesics issued by or with the approval of the Chiropodists Board may administer parenterally in the course of their professional practice Prescription Only Medicines containing any one of the following substances (SI 1998 No.108):

- bupivacaine hydrochloride
- bupivacaine hydrochloride with adrenaline (epinephrine) where the maximum strength of the adrenaline (epinephrine) does not exceed 1 mg in 200 ml bupivacaine hydrochloride
- lidocaine hydrochloride
- lidocaine hydrochloride with adrenaline (epinephrine) where the maximum strength of the adrenaline (epinephrine) does not exceed 1 mg in 200 ml lidocaine hydrochloride
- mepivacaine hydrochoride (SI 1998 No.2081)
- prilocaine hydrochloride.

Registered chiropodists may also supply or administer Prescription Only Medicines, Pharmacy Medicines, and General Sale List medicines under PGDs (see p. 109).

Ambulance paramedics

Persons who hold a certificate of proficiency in ambulance paramedic skills issued by, or with the approval of, the Secretary of State may parenterally administer (but not sell or supply) the following Prescription Only Medicines (SI 2004 No 1189):

1   diazepam 5 mg per ml emulsion for injection;
2   succinylated gelatin (modified fluid gelatin) 4 per cent intravenous infusion;
3   medicines containing ergometrine maleate 500 micrograms per ml with oxytocin 5 iu per ml but no other active ingredient
4   Prescription Only Medicines containing one or more of the following substances, but no other active ingredient:

   - adrenaline (epinephrine) acid tartrate
   - amiodarone
   - anhydrous glucose
   - benzylpenicillin
   - bretylium tosylate
   - compound sodium lactate intravenous infusion (Hartmann's solution)
   - ergometrine maleate
   - furosemide (frusemide)

- glucose
- heparin sodium
- lidocaine hydrochloride
- metoclopramide
- morphine sulphate
- nalbuphine hydrochloride
- naloxone hydrochloride
- polygeline
- reteplase (SI 2004 No. 1189)
- sodium bicarbonate
- sodium chloride
- streptokinase
- tenecteplase.

The administration may only be for the immediate, necessary treatment of sick or injured persons. In the case of a Prescription Only Medicine containing heparin sodium, it may only be used for cannula flushing (SI 1997 No.1830).

Individuals who hold a certificate of proficiency in ambulance paramedic skills issued by the Secretary of State or individuals who are state registered paramedics may also supply or administer Prescription Only Medicines, Pharmacy Medicines and General Sale List medicines under PGDs (see below under Health Professionals).

Health professionals: supply or administration of Prescription Only Medicines under a Patient Group Direction in order to assist doctors or dentists in providing National Health Service primary medical and dental services

Primary Medical (Dental) Services means the provision of general medical (dental) services under the National Health Service Act 1977, or the performance of personal medical (dental) services in connection with a pilot scheme under the National Health Service (Primary Care) Act 1997.

The restrictions on retail sale or supply of a medicinal product not apply to the supply by any of the following individuals, listed in Schedule 7 to the regulations (see Appendix 6). These include registered pharmacists, nurses and midwives, health visitors, ophthalmic opticians, chiropodists, ambulance paramedics, orthoptists, physiotherapists and radiographers where the individual supplies or administers a medicine in order to assist a doctor or dentist in the provision of NHS primary medical (or dental) service. The medicine is supplied in accordance with a PGD and the following conditions apply (SI 2000 No.1917). For definition of a *Patient Group Direction*, see. p. 97.

1   The PGD relates to the supply or the administration of a description or class of medicine in order to assist the doctor or dentist in question in the provision of NHS primary medical (dental) services.

2   The PGD has effect at the time at which the medicine is supplied or is administered.

3   The PGD contains the particulars specified in the regulations (see Appendix 6). If the PGD is for administration only, any restrictions on quantity may be omitted.

4   The PGD is signed by the doctor or dentist in question and, on behalf of the health authority, by a doctor *and* a pharmacist.

5   The health professional (Appendix 6) who supplies or administers the medicine is designated in writing by the doctor or dentist in question.

6   At the time at which the medicine is supplied or administered, the medicine has a marketing authorisation or a homoeopathic certificate of registration.

Similar provisions apply to permit the supply or administration of Pharmacy Medicines and General Sale List medicines by means of PGDs (SI 2000 No.1919 as amended).

Dietitians, occupational therapists, orthotists and prosthetists, and speech and language therapists were added by SI 2004 No 1190.

Independent hospitals, clinics and agencies: supply of medicines under a Patient Group Direction

The restrictions on the supply of a medicinal product do not apply in the course of a business of an independent hospital, independent clinic or independent medical agency where the product is supplied under a PGD (see p. 97), and the following conditions apply (SI 2003 No.697).

1   The PGD relates to the supply of a description or class of medicine.

2   The PGD has effect at the time at which the medicine is supplied.

3   lThe PGD contains the particulars specified in the regulations (see Appendix 6). If the PGD is for administration only, any restrictions on quantity may be omitted.

4   The PGD is signed by the registered provider or the relevant manager.

5   The person (see Appendix 6) who supplies the medicine is designated in writing on behalf of the registered provider or relevant manager.

6   At the time at which the medicine is supplied, the medicine has a marketing authorisation or a homoeopathic certificate of registration.

For definition of a *Patient Group Direction*, see p. 97.

Police, prison and armed forces: supply of medicines under a Patient Group Direction

The restrictions on the supply of a medicinal product does not apply to the supply of a medicinal product by an individual belonging to the police, prison service or the armed forces where it is supplied for the purpose of being administered in accordance with a PGD, and the following conditions apply (SI 2003 No.697).

1 The PGD relates to the supply of a description or class of medicine.
2 The PGD has effect at the time at which the medicine is supplied.
3 The PGD contains the particulars specified in the regulations (see Appendix 6). If the PGD is for administration only any restrictions on quantity may be omitted.
4 The PGD is signed by the registered provider or the relevant manager.
5 The person (see Appendix 6) who supplies the medicine is designated in writing on behalf of the chief constable, prison governor, surgeon general, medical director general or chief executive of Ministry of Defence as the case may be.
6 At the time at which the medicine is supplied, the medicine has a marketing authorisation or a homoeopathic certificate of registration.

For definition of a *Patient Group Direction*, see. p. 97.

Persons authorised to be sold cyanide salts under the Poisons Act 1972

Pharmacists may sell amyl nitrite to such persons who would include a person or institution concerned with scientific education or research, a person who requires the article for the purpose of his/her trade or business and a person who requires the article for the purpose of enabling him/her to comply with any requirements made by or in pursuance of any enactment with respect to the medical treatment of persons employed by that person in any trade or business carried on by him/her (see also p. 114). The sale or supply must only be so far as it is necessary to enable an antidote to be available to persons at risk of cyanide poisoning (SI 1997 No.1830).

Manufacturers of products for treatment of the hair and scalp

The holder of a manufacturer's licence for a medicinal product which is for external use in the treatment of hair and scalp conditions may sell or supply the product free from the statutory restrictions or conditions applicable to retail sales provided that:

1   the licence in question contains a provision that the licence holder shall only manufacture the medicinal product for a particular person after being requested by or on behalf of that person and in that person's presence to use his/her own judgment as to the treatment required; and

2   the sale or supply is made only upon receipt of such a request.

The medicinal products to which this exemption applies are (SI 1980 No.1924):

1   medicinal products on a General Sale List which are for human external use; and

2   Pharmacy Medicines which are for external use in the treatment of hair and scalp conditions and which contain any of the following substances:

- not more than 5 per cent boric acid
- isopropyl myristate or lauryl sulphate
- not more than 0.004 per cent oestrogens
- not more than 1 per cent resorcin
- not more than 3 per cent salicylic acid
- not more than 0.2 per cent sodium pyrithione or
- zinc pyrithione.

Public analysts, sampling officers and other such persons

The restrictions on retail sale or supply do not apply to persons who sell or supply any medicinal product to any of the following:

1   a public analyst appointed under section 27 of the Food Safety Act 1990 or Article 36 of the Food (Northern Ireland) Order 1989;

2   an authorised officer within the meaning of section 5(6) of the Food Safety Act 1990;

3   a sampling officer within the meaning of Article 38(1) of the Food (Northern Ireland) Order 1989;

4   a person duly authorised by an enforcement authority under sections 111 and 112 of the Act; or

5   a sampling officer within the meaning of Schedule 3 to the Act (see p. 22).

The sale or supply is subject to the presentation of an order signed by or on behalf of the analyst, authorised officer, sampling officer or enforcement officer, as the case may be. It must state the status of the person signing it and the amount of the Prescription Only Medicine required and shall be only in connection with the exercise by those persons of their statutory functions (SI 1997 No.1830).

National Health Service drug testing

The restrictions on retail sale or supply do not apply to persons who sell or supply any medicinal product to any person employed or engaged in connection with the scheme for testing the quality and amount of the drugs, preparations and appliances supplied under the National Health Service Act 1977, the National Health Service (Scotland) Act 1978 and the Health and Personal Social Services (Northern Ireland) Order 1972 or any subordinate legislation made under those Acts or that Order (SIs 1980 No.1924 and 1983 No.1830).

The sale or supply must be for the purpose of the relevant scheme and is subject to the presentation of an order signed on behalf of the person so employed or engaged stating:

1   the status of the person signing it; and
2   the amount of the medicinal product required.

Owners and masters of ships

The restrictions on supply (but not sale) of any medicinal product do not apply when the supply is made by the owner or the master of a ship which does not carry a doctor on board as part of her complement. An owner or master may also administer Prescription Only Medicines that are for parenteral administration. The supply or administration shall be only so far as is necessary for the treatment of persons on the ship (SI 1997 No.1830).

Offshore installations

Persons employed as qualified first-aid personnel on offshore installations may:

1   supply any medicinal product; and
2   administer all parenteral Prescription Only Medicines;

only so far as is necessary for the treatment of persons on the installation (SI 1997 No.1830).

British Standards Institution

The restrictions on the retail sale or supply do not apply to persons who sell or supply any Prescription Only Medicine, any Pharmacy Medicine or any medicinal product on a General Sale List to the British Standards Institution. The British Standard Institution *itself* cannot sell, supply or administer medicinal products.

The sale or supply shall only be for the purpose of testing containers of medicinal products or determining the standards for such containers and is subject to the presentation of an order signed on behalf of the British Standards Institution stating the status of the person signing it and the amount of the medicinal product required (SIs 1980 No.1924 and 1997 No.1830).

Statutory requirements as to medical treatment

The restrictions on retail supply (but not sale) of medicinal products do not apply to supplies made by persons requiring medicinal products for the purpose of enabling them, in the course of any business carried on by them, to comply with any requirements made by or in pursuance of any enactment with respect to the medical treatment of employees. The exemption extends to the Prescription Only Medicines and the Pharmacy Medicines specified in the relevant enactment and to medicinal products on a General Sale List.

The supply shall be:

1   for the purpose of enabling them to comply with any requirements made by or in pursuance of any such enactment; and
2   subject to such conditions and in such circumstances as may be specified in the relevant enactments (SIs 1980 No.1924 and 1997 No.1830).

Licences and group authorities

The restrictions on the supply of Prescription Only Medicines do not apply to persons authorised by licences granted under regulation 5 of the Misuse of Drugs Regulations 1973 to supply the Controlled Drugs specified in the licence.

The supply shall be subject to such conditions and in such circumstances and to such an extent as may be specified in the licence.

Similarly, the restrictions on the administration of Prescription Only Medicines do not apply to persons who are authorised as members of a group by group authority granted under regulations 8(3) or 9(3) of the Misuse of Drugs Regulations 1985. The exemption is limited to the administration of Controlled Drugs that are specified in the group authority and is subject to such conditions and in such circumstances and to such an extent as may be specified in the group authority (SI 1997 No.1830).

Royal National Lifeboat Institution

The restrictions on the retail supply of any medicinal product do not apply to supply by the Royal National Lifeboat Institution or certificated first-aiders of the Institution. The supply of any Prescription Only Medicine shall be only so far as it is necessary for the treatment of sick or injured persons in the exercise of the functions of the Institution (SI 1997 No.1830).

British Red Cross Society and other such organisations

The restrictions on the retail supply of Pharmacy Medicines and all medicinal products on a General Sale List (but *not* Prescription Only Medicines) do not apply to supply by the bodies specified below and their certificated first-aid and certificated nursing members. In all cases, the supply shall be only so far as it is necessary for the treatment of sick or injured persons. The bodies concerned are:

- British Red Cross Society
- St John Ambulance Association and Brigade
- St Andrew's Ambulance Association
- Order of Malta Ambulance Corps (SI 1980 No.1924).

Dental schemes

Pharmacy Medicines that are for use in the prevention of dental caries and consist of or contain sodium fluoride (see below) may be supplied, in the course of 'pre-school dental schemes', by health authorities and, in the course of 'school dental schemes', by persons carrying on the business of a school providing full-time education.

A *pre-school dental scheme* means a scheme supervised by a doctor or dentist in which medicinal products are supplied to parents or guardians of children under five for use by such children for the purpose of preventing dental caries. The supplies must be made by a registered nurse or an enrolled nurse.

A *school dental scheme* means a scheme supervised by a doctor or dentist in which medicinal products are supplied at a school to pupils of that school for the purpose of preventing dental caries. A supply may also be made to a child under 16 years of age with the consent of the parent or guardian of that child (SI 1980 No.1924).

NB The following are the Pharmacy Medicines affected:

1   preparations of sodium fluoride for use in the prevention of dental caries in the form of:

    (a)   tablets or drops (maximum daily dose 2.2 mg);

    (b)   mouth rinses containing not more than 0.2 per cent (other than those for daily use);

    (c)   mouth rinses for daily use (containing not more than 0.05 per cent); or

    (d)   dentifrices containing not more than 0.33 per cent.

Other medicinal products containing sodium fluoride are Prescription Only Medicines and may not be sold, supplied or administered.

Occupational health schemes

Pharmacy Medicines and Prescription Only Medicines may be supplied by a person operating an *occupational health scheme*, that is a scheme in which persons, in the course of a business carried on by them, provide facilities for their employees for the treatment or prevention of disease.

The supply must be made in the course of the scheme. The medicinal products may be supplied to the person operating the scheme in response to an order in writing signed by a doctor, a registered nurse or an enrolled nurse.

The individual supplying or administering the medicines in the course of the scheme, if not a doctor, must be:

1   a registered nurse or an enrolled nurse; and
2   where the medicinal product in question is a Prescription Only Medicine, acting in accordance with the written instructions of a doctor as to the circumstances in which Prescription Only Medicines of the description in question are to be used in the course of the occupational health scheme (SIs 1980 No.1924 and 1997 No.1830).

Aircraft commanders

The commander of an aircraft or the operator, that is the person for the time being having the management of the aircraft, may supply certain medicinal products but only so far as is necessary for the immediate treatment of sick or injured persons on the aircraft. S/he may supply any medicinal products on a General Sale List, any Pharmacy Medicine and Prescription Only Medicines which are *not* for parenteral administration and which have been sold or supplied to him/her in response to an order in writing signed by a doctor. The supply of those Prescription Only Medicines by the commander or operator shall be in accordance with the written instructions of a doctor as to the circumstances in which Prescription Only Medicines of the description in question are to be used on the aircraft (SIs 1980 No.1924 and 1997 No.1830).

In addition, the commander or operator of an aircraft may administer Prescription Only Medicines for parenteral use which have been sold or supplied to him/her in response to an order in writing signed by a doctor. The administration shall be only so far as is necessary for the immediate treatment of a sick or injured person on the aircraft and shall be in accordance with the written instructions of a doctor as to the circumstances in which Prescription Only Medicines of the description in question are to be used on the aircraft (SI 1997 No.1830).

Universities, higher education institutions or institutions concerned with research

The restrictions on retail sale or supply do not apply to persons selling or supplying any medicinal product to a university, an institution concerned with higher education or an institution concerned with research but only for the purposes of the education or research with which the institution is concerned. The sale or supply is subject to the presentation of an order signed by the principal of the institution with education or research or the appropriate head of department in charge of a specified course of research (SIs 1980 No.1924 and 1997 No.1830). The order must state:

1   the name of the institution for which the medicinal product is required;
2   the purpose for which it is required; and
3   the total quantity required.

Sales by licence holders

The restrictions on sale or supply do not apply to holders of marketing authorisations and holders of manufacturing licences who sell or supply medicinal products referred to in the licences to pharmacists so as to enable them to prepare an entry relating to the medicinal product in question in a tablet or capsule identification guide or similar publication. No greater quantity than is reasonably necessary for that purpose may be supplied (SI 1997 No.1830).

Veterinary drugs

The exemptions which apply to the retail sale or supply of certain veterinary drugs are dealt with in Chapter 13.

Foot and mouth disease vaccine

Specified government officers and other persons including contractors, volunteers and employees are exempt from the general restrictions of the Medicines Act in relation to Pharmacy Only and Prescription Only Medicines in certain conditions (SI 2004 No.2779). Those conditions are when they supply foot and mouth disease (FMD) vaccine as part of the Government's responses to an outbreak in the UK of foot and mouth disease and complying with specified EU measures laid down in Council Directive 2003/85/EC.

Summary

- Doctors and dentists may sell or supply all medicines to their own patients.
- Veterinary practitioners and veterinary surgeons may sell or supply all medicines for administration by them, or under their direction to an animal or herd under their care.
- For the purposes of their professional practice, midwives have a list of medicines which can be sold or supplied by them and another list of medicines which they may administer.
- In the course of their professional practice, and only in an emergency, ophthalmic opticians have a list of medicines which they may sell or supply to their patients. They may also purchase for use in their practice, but not for sale or supply, a limited list of Prescription Only Medicines.
- In the course of their professional practice, chiropodists may sell or supply to their patients any General Sale List medicine for external use and a limited list of Pharmacy Medicines. Chiropodists holding a certificate of competence in the use of analgesics may administer, in their practice, a named list of parenteral analgesics.
- Persons who hold a certificate of proficiency in ambulance paramedic skills may parenterally administer certain medicines for the immediate, necessary treatment of the sick or injured.
- Other categories of activities also have limited lists of medicines which they may sell or supply. These include dental and occupational health schemes, owners and masters of ships, offshore installations, the Royal National Lifeboat Institution, public analysts, aircraft commanders, universities and the British Red Cross.
- NHS bodies and certain health professionals can supply medicines under PGDs. These include registered nurses and midwives, registered health visitors, registered ophthalmic opticians, state registered chiropodists, state registered ambulance paramedics and registered orthoptists, physiotherapists and radiographers.
- Independent hospitals, clinics and medical agencies together with the police service, prison service and Her Majesty's armed forces can supply and administer under PGDs.

CHAPTER TEN

Medicines Act 1968

Wholesale dealing

Regulations (SI 1980 No.1923, as amended) made under the Act (s.61) control the sale of medicinal products by way of wholesale dealing: that is, the sale of medicinal products to a person for the purpose of (a) selling or supplying them or (b) administering them to human beings in the course of a business (see p. 36). Sales of medicinal products by way of wholesale dealing can be made as set out below by:

1 the holder of a marketing authorisation; or
2 a person carrying on a business which consists (wholly or partly) of manufacturing medicinal products or of selling them by way of wholesale dealing. The sales must be made in the course of the business. [Retail pharmacy owners, who are not licensed as wholesalers, may sell by way of wholesale dealing provided the sales constitute no more than an inconsiderable part of the business (see p. 42).]

A person making sales by way of wholesale dealing

A person making sales by way of wholesale dealing must possess a wholesale dealer's licence (p. 36). Such sales must be from a specified place and the licence holder must fulfil the following (SI 1993 No.833).

119

1   Keep records, which may be in the form of invoices or on computer or in any other form, giving the following information in respect of such products which have been received or despatched:

(a)   the date of receipt and of despatch;
(b)   the name of the products;
(c)   the quantity of the products received or despatched; and
(d)   the name and address of the person from whom, or to whom, the products are sold or supplied as appropriate.

2   Have at all times at his/her disposal the services of a person – a *responsible person* – who possesses in the opinion of the licensing authority:

(a)   knowledge of the activities to be carried out and of the procedures to be performed under the licence; and
(b)   experience in those activities and procedures which is adequate for those purposes.

The functions of the responsible person shall be to ensure that the conditions under which the licence has been granted have been, and are being, complied with and that the quality of the products is maintained in accordance with the requirements of the appropriate marketing authorisation.

3   Obtain supplies of medicinal products only from:

(a)   any person who is the holder of a manufacturer's licence or a wholesale dealer's licence which relates to those products; or
(b)   any person who holds an authorisation granted by the competent authority of a member state other than the UK authorising the manufacture of such products or the distribution by way of wholesale dealing of such products.

4   Institute an emergency plan which ensures effective implementation of any recall from the market.

Pharmacy Medicines by wholesale dealing

Pharmacy Medicines may be sold by way of wholesale dealing to (SI 1980 No.1923, as amended):

1   practitioners;
2   any person lawfully conducting a retail pharmacy business;
3   authorities or persons carrying on the business of an independent hospital, independent clinic, or independent medical agency or a hospital or health centre which is not an independent hospital or clinic (SI 2003 No.698);
4   holders of wholesale dealer's licences, or persons to whom the requirements to hold a wholesale dealer's licence do not apply by virtue of an exemption conferred by or under the Act;

5 Ministers of the Crown and government departments and officers thereof;

6 a NHS Trust established under the National Health Service and Community Care Act 1990 or the National Health Service (Scotland) Act 1978;

7 the Common Services Agency in Scotland;

8 any person who requires Pharmacy Medicines for the purpose of administering them to human beings in the course of a business where the medicines are for the purpose of being so administered;

9 any person who may sell or supply in circumstances corresponding to retail sale Pharmacy Medicines as specified in an exemption order (SI 1980 No.1924, as amended) (see Chapter 9) or certain herbal remedies (s.56 and SI 1977 No.2130) (see Chapter 12), or veterinary drugs (see Chapter 13); or

10 a person other than an exempted person who carries on a business consisting (wholly or partly) of the supply or administration of medicinal products for the purpose of assisting the provision of healthcare by or on behalf of the police force in the UK, a prison service or her Majesty's forces (SI 2003/698).

Prescription Only Medicines by wholesale dealing

Prescription Only Medicines may be sold by way of wholesale dealing to the same persons and authorities as in 1, 2, 3, 4, 5, 6 and 7 as for Pharmacy Medicines above, plus:

11 any person who is the subject of an exemption in Schedule 3 to the Prescription Only Order (SI 1997 No.1830) but only in respect of the medicinal products covered by the exemption (see Chapter 9);

12 registered ophthalmic opticians: there are certain Prescription Only Medicines which opticians are entitled to supply to their patients or use in their practice (see p. 105);

13 any person selling or supplying by retail, or administering, unit preparations of Prescription Only Medicines (other than Controlled Drugs) diluted to one part in a million (6×) having been requested by or on behalf of the particular person and in that person's presence to use their own judgment as to the treatment required (see also Homoeopathic Medicines, Chapter 11).

Wholesale sales from a pharmacy

A pharmacist may supply medicines by way of wholesale dealing provided that the sales constitute no more than an inconsiderable part of the business carried on at that pharmacy [s.10(7)] (see also p. 36). This figure is generally accepted as not more than 5 per cent of the turnover in medicinal products; above that figure, a wholesale dealer's licence would be required.

If the pharmacist does not possess a wholesale dealer's licence, then the only records required to be kept are a copy of the order or invoice relating to the supply, or alternatively an entry made in the Prescription Only Register by the owner of the retail pharmacy business (SI 1980 No.1923). Orders or invoices (and all orders required as a condition in connection with any exempted sale of a Prescription Only Medicine; see Chapter 9) must be kept for two years from the date of the sale or supply.

If the pharmacist does possess a wholesale dealer's licence, then all the provisions of such a possession apply (see above).

Wholesaling of veterinary products

See Chapter 13.

Summary

*   Normally, a person who sells medicines by way of wholesale dealing requires a wholesale dealer's licence, which requires special premises, records to be kept and the appointment of a responsible person whose functions are to ensure that the conditions of the licence are being complied with and that the quality of the products is maintained in accordance with the requirements of the appropriate marketing authorisation.
*   A pharmacist may supply medicines by way of wholesale dealing (e.g. to a doctor) provided the sales constitute no more than an inconsiderable part of the business carried on at that pharmacy [s.10(7)] (see also p. 36). This value is generally accepted as not more than 5 per cent of the turnover in medicinal products.

CHAPTER ELEVEN

Medicines Act 1968

Sale and supply of

homoeopathic medicines

Most homoeopathic medicines for human use are subject to licensing procedures but, provided certain conditions are met, a simplified system of certification is permitted under regulations made under EC Council Directive 2001/83/EEC (p. 31). A similar scheme is in force regarding registration of veterinary homoeopathic medicines under EC Council Directive 2001/82/EEC (p. 34).

Medicinal products at high dilutions (homoeopathic medicines)

Medicinal products at high dilutions are prepared from '*unit preparations*', which is defined as 'a preparation, including a mother tincture, prepared by a process of solution, extraction or trituration with a view to being diluted tenfold or one hundredfold, either once or repeatedly, in an inert diluent, and then used either in this diluted form or, where applicable, by impregnating tablets, granules, powders or other inert substances' (SI 1997 No.1830 as amended).

Homoeopathic medicines for human use: licensing

See page 31.

Homoeopathic medicines for which General Sale is permitted

If the seller complies with the conditions which apply to the sale or supply of products in the General Sale List (s.53) (see p. 77), then s/he may sell by retail, offer or expose for sale or supply certain medicinal products which consist of one or more unit preparations diluted to the extent specified and for the use specified but not any Controlled Drug or product for parenteral administration (SI 1980 No.1924).

Products for internal or external use

Products for internal or external use include:

1   any substance where the unit preparation has been diluted to at least one part in a million million (6c);
2   any substance in Part II of Schedule 2 to the Pharmacy and General Sale Exemption Order (SI 1980 No.1924), where the unit preparation has been diluted to at least one part in a million (6×) (see Table 11.1);

Table 11.1   Substances in Part II of Schedule 2 to SI 1980 No.1924 where the unit preparation has been diluted to at least one part in a million (6×)

Adonis vernalis	Bismuth subgallate
Agaricus bulbosus	Bismuth subnitrate
Agaricus muscarius	Boletus laricis
Agnus castus	Bovista
Ailanthus glandulosa	Cade oil
Alum	Calcium fluoride
Amethyst	Cantharis
Ammonium iodide	Carduus marianus
Amygdalae amarae	Cedar wood oil
Apatite	Cerium oxalicum
Apocynum androsaemifolium	Chalcocite
Apocynum cannabinum	Chalcopyrite
Argentite	Chelidonium majus
Argentum chloride	Chenopodium oil
Argentum iodide	Colocynthis
Arnica	Convallaria majalis
Artemisia cina	Copper silicate, Nat.
Aspidium anthelmintica	Crotalus horridus
Aspidium filix-mas	Cucumis melo
Aurum sulphide	Cucurbita
Balsamum copaivae	Datura stramonium
Balsamum peruvianum	Derris
Barium citrate	Diamond
Barium sulphate	Ephedra vulgaris
Bismuth metal	Ferric acetate

Table 11.1 contd

Ferrous iodide	Platinum chloride
Ferrous oxalate	Potassium hydroxide
Ferrous sulphide	Potassium silicate
Formic acid	Pyrethrum
Gall	Pyrolusite
Gelsemium sempervirens	Ranunculus acris
Gneiss	Ranunculus bulbosus
Granatum (pomegranate bark)	Ranunculus flammula
Hamamelis virginiana	Ranunculus repens
Hepar sulphuris	Ranunculus sceleratus
Hyoscyamus niger	Rhodium oxynitrate
Iris florentine	Rhododendron chrysanthemum
Jaborandi	Rhus toxicodendron
Juniperus sabina	Salicylic acid
Kaolinite	Scrophularia aquatica
Lachnanthes tinctoria	Sodium aluminium chloride
Lapis albus	Sodium aurochloride
Lycopodium	Sodium hypochlorite
Magnesium	Sodium nitrate
Magnesium acetate	Squill
Magnesium chloride	Stannum metal
Magnetite	Staphisagria
Manganese acetate	Sulphur iodide
Nicotiana tabacum	Tamus communis
Nicotiana tabacum oil	Tannic acid
Oleander	Terebinthinae oleum
Opuntia vulgaris	Theridion
Oxalic acid	Topaz
Petroleum	Uric acid
Phellandrium aquaticum	Zinc hypophosphite
Pix liquida	Zinc isovalerate
Platinum	

3   any substance in Table A of Schedule 2 to the General Sale List Order (ingredients of licences of right) (SI 1984 No.769), where the unit preparation has been diluted to at least one part in ten (1×); or

4   any substance in Part III of Schedule 2 to the Pharmacy and General Sale Exemption Order (SI 1980 No.1924), where the unit preparation has been diluted to at least one part in ten (1×) (see Table 11.2).

Table 11.2 Substances in Part III of Schedule 2 to SI 1980 No.1924, where the unit preparation has been diluted to at least one part in ten (1×)

Abies excelsa	Agate
Abies nigra	Alisma plantago aquatica
Abies nobilis	Alstonia scholaris
Acalypha indica	Aluminium

Table 11.2 contd

Amber (succinum)
Ambra grisea
Ammonium phosphate
Angostura vera
Anthoxanthum
Apis mellifera
Aqua marina
Aqua mellis
Aralia racemosa
Aranea diadema
Arum maculatum
Arum triphyllum
Asarum
Asperula odorata
Astacus fluviatilis
Auric chloride
Badiaga
Beech (Fagus sylvestris)
Bellis perennis
Berberis aquifolium
Borago officinalis
Butyric acid
Calcium metal
Calcium chloride
Calcium oxide
Calcium sulphate
Castoreum
Ceanothus americanus
Cedron
Cerato (Ceratostigma willmottiana)
Cherry plum (Prunus cerasifera)
Chestnut, red and sweet
Cholesterinum
Chrysolite
Cistus canadensis
Clematis erecta
Conchae vera
Conchiolinum
Corallium rubrum
Crab apple
Crocus sativus
Erbium
Erigeron canadense
Fuligo
Genista tinctoria
Geum urbanum
Glycogen
Gnaphalium leontropodium
Gold

Gorse (Ulex europocus)
Graphites
Gratiola officinalis
Gymnocladus (American coffee tree)
Haematoxylon campechianum
Hecla lava (Ash from Mount Hecla)
Hedeoma pulegioidies
Hedera helix
Heliotrope
Heracleum spondylium
Herniaria
Hornbeam (Carpinus betulus)
Iberis amara
Impatiens
Iris germanica
Iris pseudacorus
Jacaranda procera
Jatropha curcas
Juncus communis
Justicia adhatoda
Lamium album
Laurocerasus
Laurus nobilis oil
Ledum palustre
Lilium tigrinum
Lonicera caprifolium
Lysimachia vulgaris
Magnesium phosphate
Magnesite
Magnolia
Marum verum
Melilotus officinalis
Menispermum canadense
Mephitis putorius
Mercurialis perennis
Mimulus (Mimullis guttatus)
Moschus
Myrica gale
Myrtus communis
Ocimum basilicum
Olive
Oxalis acetosella
Pangamic acid
Paullinia cupana
Penthorum sedoides
Pollen (mixed)
Polygonatum multiflorum
Polygonum aviculare
Polypodium vulgare

Table 11.2 contd

Primula vulgaris	Silphium laciniatum
Prunella vulgaris	Sodium benzoate
Ptelea trifoliata	Spongia marina
Ratanhia	Star of Bethlehem (Ornithogalum
Robinia pseudoacacia	umbellatum)
Rubia tinctorum	Ulmus campestris
Rumex acetosella	Vine
Sal marina	Walnut (Juglerus regia)
Sarcolactic acid	Water violet (Hottonia palustris)
Sarracenia purpurea	Wild oat
Scleranthus (Scleranthus annus)	Wild rose
Silica	

Products for external use only

Products for external use only include:

1   any substance in Table B of Schedule 2 to the General Sale List Order (ingredients of licences of right) (SI 1984 No.769) where the unit preparation has been diluted to at least one part in ten (1×); and

2   any substance in Part IV of Schedule 2 to the Pharmacy and General Sale Exemption Order (SI 1980 No.1924), where the unit preparation has been diluted to at least one in part in ten (1×) (see Table 11.3).

Table 11.3   Products for external use only listed in Part IV of Schedule 2 to SI 1980 No.1924 where the unit preparation has been diluted to at least one part in ten (1×)

Adonis vernalis	Barium citrate
Agaricus bulbosus	Barium sulphate
Agaricus muscarius	Bismuth metal
Agnus castus	Bismuth subgallate
Ailanthus glandulosa	Bismuth subnitrite
Alum	Boletus laricus
Amethyst	Bovista
Ammonium iodide	Cade oil
Amygdalae amarae	Calcium fluoride
Apatite	Carduus marianus
Apocynum androsaemifolium	Cedar wood oil
Apocynum cannabinum	Cerium oxalicum
Argentite	Chalcocite
Argentum chloride	Chalcopyrite
Argentum iodide	Chelidonium majus
Artemisia cina	Chenopodium oil
Aspidium anthelmintica	Colocynthis
Aspidium filix-mas	Convallaria majalis
Aurum sulphide	Copper silicate, Nat.
Balsamum copaivae	Crotalus horridus
Balsamum peruvianum	Cucumis melo

Table 11.3 contd

Cucurbita
Datura stramonium
Derris
Diamond
Ephedra vulgaris
Ferric acetate
Ferrous iodide
Ferrous oxalate
Ferrous sulphide
Formic acid
Gall
Gelsemium sempervirens
Gneiss
Hamamelis virginiana
Hepar sulfuris
Hyoscyamus niger
Iris florentine
Jaborandi
Juniperus sabina
Kaolinite
Lachmanthus tinctoria
Lapis albus
Lycopodium
Magnesium
Magnesium acetate
Magnesium chloride
Magnetite
Manganese acetate
Nicotiana tabacum
Nicotiana tabacum oil
Oleander
Opuntia vulgaris
Oxalic acid

Petroleum
Phellandrium aquaticum
Pix liquida
Platinum
Platinum chloride
Potassium hydroxide
Potassium silicate
Pyrethrum
Pyrolusite
Ranunculus acris
Ranunculus bulbosus
Ranunculus flammula
Ranunculus repens
Ranunculus sceleratus
Rhodium oxynitrate
Rhododendron chrysanthemum
Rhus toxicodendron
Salicylic acid
Scrophularia aquatica
Sodium aluminium chloride
Sodium aurochloride
Sodium hypochlorite
Sodium nitrate
Squill
Stannum metal
Sulphur iodide
Tannic acid
Terebinthinae oleum
Topaz
Uric acid
Zinc hypophosphite
Zinc isovalerate

Homoeopathic medicines for treatment according to the judgment of the seller

If the person selling the product is requested by or on behalf of a particular person and in that person's presence to use their own judgment as to the treatment required, then they may sell by retail, offer or expose for sale or supply certain medicinal products (other than excluded products) which are registered or consist solely of one or more unit preparations diluted to the extent specified and for the use specified. The substances to which this exemption applies and which are subject to section 53 of the Act (see p. 77) are listed below.

Products for internal or external use

Products for internal or external use include:

1   any substance, where the unit preparation has been diluted to at least one part in a million (6×);
2   any substance listed in Part I of Schedule 2 to the Pharmacy and General Sale Exemption Order (SI 1980 No.1924) where the unit preparation has been diluted to at least one part in a thousand (3×) (see Table 11.4);
3   any substance in Table A of Schedule 2 to the General Sale List Order (SI 1984 No.769) (ingredients of licence of right products), where the unit preparation has been diluted to at least one part in ten (1×);
4   any substance in Part III of Schedule 2 to the Pharmacy and General Sale Exemptions Order (SI 1980 No.1924), where the unit preparation has been diluted to at least one part in ten (1×) (the substances are listed above, in Tables 11.1–11.3); and
5   any *registered* homoeopathic medicinal product for human use other than an excluded product (SI 1998 No.2368).

Table 11.4 Substances listed in Part I of Schedule 2 to SI 1980 No.1924, where the unit preparation has been diluted to at least one part in a thousand (3×)

Agaricus muscarius	Chenopodium oil
Ailanthus glandulosa	Cina
Apocynum cannabinum	Colocynthis
Aurum iodatum	Convallaria majalis
Belladonna	Gelsemium sempervirens
Bismuth subgallate	Hyoscyamus niger
Bryonia alba dioica	Lycopodium
Calcium fluoride	Manganese acetate
Cantharis	Ranunculus bulbosus
Cerium oxalicum	Terebinthinae oleum
Chelidonium majus	

Excluded products include Controlled Drugs, Prescription Only Medicines and any in a class specified in Schedule 3 of the main order (SI 1984 No.769), that is, medicines for use as anthelmintics, for parenteral administration or for use as eye drops or eye ointments.

Products for external use only

The substances and unit dilutions for external use are the same as those for homoeopathic medicines for which General Sale is permitted.

Homoeopathic medicines for animal use

See page 34.

Summary

- Most homoeopathic medicines are on the General Sale List and may be sold from any retail shop which is closable to the public.
- Certain listed homoeopathic medicines may be sold if the seller is requested by a customer to use the seller's own judgment as to the treatment required. There are certain excluded categories.

Further reading

MHRA *MAL Advisory Leaflets*. Medicines and Health Care Regulatory Authority, London.

CHAPTER TWELVE

Medicines Act 1968

Herbal remedies

In March 2004, the EU issued the Directive on Traditional Herbal Medicinal Products (2004/24/EC) to regulate herbal products. Member states must have a simplified registration scheme in force by October 2005. In October 2004, a newly formed Committee for Herbal Products was set up in advance of the new regulations. It is anticipated that herbal medicines will be placed into two categories. One category will have simplified marketing authorisations, the composition declared together with contraindications and guidance for use, have patient leaflets and comprehensive labelling and will probably be Prescription Only Medicines or Pharmacy Medicines. The second category will be those without monographs, with little evidence of efficacy and will be General Sale List provided they have been on the market in the EU for 39 years. The Directive is based on long-standing use of the product and no clinical trial evidence will be required. All herbal products now on the market can remain so for seven years.

Under the present law, a *herbal remedy* is a medicinal product consisting of a substance produced by subjecting a plant or plants to drying, crushing or any other process, or of a mixture whose sole ingredients are two or more substances so produced, or of a mixture whose sole ingredients are one or more substances so produced and water or some other inert substance (s.132).

Exemption from licensing

Subject to the limitations described in this chapter, herbal remedies are exempted from licensing requirements by section 12 of the Act, which describes remedies of two kinds.

1   Any herbal remedy which is manufactured or assembled on premises of which the person carrying on the business is the occupier and which s/he is able to close so as to exclude the public, and the person carrying on the business sells or supplies the remedy for administration to a particular person after being requested by or on behalf of that person and in that person's presence to use his/her own judgment as to the treatment required. (For convenience these can be described as 'herbal practitioner's remedies', although that term is not used in the statute.)

2   Any herbal remedy where the process to which the plant or plants are subjected in producing the remedy consists only of drying, crushing or comminuting, and the remedy is, or is to be, sold or supplied:

(a)   under a designation which only specifies the plant or plants and the process and does not apply any other name to the remedy; and

(b)   without any written recommendation (whether by means of a labelled container or package or a leaflet or in any other way) as to the use of the remedy. See also page 62.

Exemptions from controls on retail sale

There is an exemption for herbal remedies in section 56 of the Act from the restrictions on retail sale and supply of medicinal products in sections 52 and 53 (see Chapters 6 and 7). The exemption, which extends to both classes 1 and 2 described above, applies to anything done at premises of which the person carrying on the business in question is the occupier and which s/he is able to close so as to exclude the public (s.56).

   This general exemption is modified by the Herbal Remedies Order (SI 1977 No.2130) so that there is no exemption (except as below) from the restriction on retail sale or supply for herbal remedies:

1   that are not on the General Sale List;
2   that are not exempted from licensing as in 2 above; or
3   that are exempted from licensing as in 2 above but contain one or more of the substances listed in Part I or Part II of the Schedule to the Order (see Exemption of 'Herbal Practitioners', below).

The effect of this is that any shopkeeper can sell:

(a)   any herbal remedy on the General Sale List; or

(b) any herbal remedy which is exempted from licensing as in 1 above, except those in Part I and Part II of the schedule.

Further exemption for shopkeepers

The order further modifies the controls on retail sale so that any person can, subject to certain conditions, sell or supply by retail any herbal remedy included under 1, 2 or 3 above where the process to which the plant or plants are subjected consists of drying, crushing or comminuting with or without any subsequent process of tabletting, pill-making, compressing or diluting with water but not any other process.

The conditions are that:

4 the herbal remedy does not contain a substance listed in Part I or Part II of the Schedule (see below);

5 the seller (or supplier) of the herbal remedy either:

(a) has notified the enforcement authority in the UK in writing that s/he is selling or supplying or intending to sell or supply herbal remedies included in 1, 2 or 3 in the section above on Exemptions from Controls on Retail Sale, which are prepared by the limited processes described in the opening paragraph of this chapter; or

(b) has a manufacturer's licence granted under Part II of the Act in respect of that remedy.

Exemption of 'herbal practitioners'

In addition to the exemptions already described, the order (SI 1977 No.2130) provides further exemptions for herbal remedies, prepared by any process, from the controls on retail sale or supply provided:

1 the herbal remedy concerned does not contain:

(a) any substance included in Part I of the Schedule to the order; or

(b) any substance in Part III of the order, except for internal remedies, when sold or supplied in or from containers or packages labelled to show a dosage not exceeding that specified, or for external remedies, when sold or supplied with the strength of the substance not exceeding the percentage specified.

2 the person selling or supplying the herbal remedy (a *herbal practitioner*):

(a) has been requested by or on behalf of a particular person and in that person's presence to use his/her own judgment as to the treatment required; and

(b)   has notified the enforcement authority in writing that s/he is selling or supplying or intends to sell or supply from the premises specified in the notice herbal remedies as in 1, 2 or 3 in the section above on Exemptions from Controls on Retail Sale.

A person (herbal practitioner) selling or supplying herbal remedies, to which the exemption described in this section applies, may be required to furnish to the enforcement authority a list of the substances contained in those herbal remedies. The exemption will not apply if the herbal practitioner fails to furnish the list within the time specified in the notice served upon him/her by the enforcement authority.

Enforcement authority

The term *enforcement authority* includes the Secretaries of State and the Royal Pharmaceutical Society of Great Britain.

Schedule to the Herbal Remedies Order

The Schedule to the Medicines (Retail Sale or Supply of Herbal Remedies) Order 1977 (SI 1977 No.2130) is in three parts, reflecting the different degrees of control over the retail sale or supply of the substances in each part.

Part I

The substances in this part (see Table 12.1) may only be sold by retail at registered pharmacies and by or under the supervision of a pharmacist.

Table 12.1   Substances in Part I of the schedule to SI 1977 No.2130

Common name	Botanical name
Areca	*Areca catechu*
Canadian hemp	*Apocynum cannabinum*
Catha	*Catha edulis*
Chenopodium	*Chenopodium ambrosioides* var. *anthelminticum*
Crotalaria fulva	*Crotalaria berberoana*
Crotalaria spect.	*Crotalaria spectabilis*
Cucurbita	*Cucurbita maxima*
Duboisia	*Duboisia leichardtii, D. myoporoides*
Elaterium	*Ecballium elaterium*
Embelia	*Embelia ribes, E. robusta*
Erysimum	*Erysimum canescens*
Holarrhena	*Holarrhena antidysenterica*
Kamala	*Mallotus philippinensis*

Table 12.1 contd

Kousso	*Brayera anthelmintica*
Male fern	*Dryopteris filix mas*
Mistletoe berry	*Viscum album*
Poison ivy	*Rhus radicans*
Pomegranate bark	*Punica granatum*
Santonica	*Artemisia cina*
Savin	*Juniperus sabina*
Scopolia	*Scopolia carniolica, S. japonica*
Stavesacre seeds	*Delphinium staphisagria*
Strophanthus	*Strophanthus courmonti, S. emini, S. gratus, S. hispidus, S. kombe, S. nicholsoni, S. sarmentosus*
Slippery elm bark (whole or unpowdered)	*Ulmus fulva, U. rubra*
Yohimbe bark	*Pausinystalia yohimbe*

Part II

The list of substances in this part is the same as that in Part III. They may only be sold by retail from registered pharmacies and by or under the supervision of a pharmacist except when the conditions under Part III are met (see below).

Part III

Persons who comply with the requirements set out on page 133 (commonly known as *herbal practitioners*) can sell or supply by retail herbal remedies containing any of the substances listed in Table 12.2 subject to the maximum dosages and strengths indicated.

Table 12.2   Substances in Part III of the Schedule to SI 1977 No.2130

Common name	Column 1 Substance Botanical name	Column 2 Maximum dose (md) and maximum daily dose (mdd)	Column 3 Percentage
Aconite	*Aconitum balrourii* *A. chasmanthum* *A. deinorrhizum* *A. lycoctonum* *A. napellus* *A. spicatum* *A. stoerkianum* *A. uncinatum* var. *japonicum*		1.3%
Adoni vernalis	*Adonis vernalis*	100 mg (md) 300 mg (mdd)	

Table 12.2 contd

Belladonna herb	*Atropa acuminata*	150 mg (mdd)	
	Atropa belladonna	50 mg (md)	
Belladonna root	*Atropa acuminata*	90 mg (mdd)	
	Atropa belladonna	30 mg (md)	
Celandine	*Chelidonium majus*	2 g (md)	
		6 g (mdd)	
Cinchona bark	*Cinchona calisaya*	250 mg (md)	
	C. ledgerana	750 mg (mdd)	
	C. micrantha		
	C. officinalis		
	C. succirubra		
Colchicum corm	*Colchicum autumnale*	100 mg (md)	
		300 mg (mdd)	
Conium leaf	*Conium maculatum*		7%
Conium fruits	*Conium maculatum*		7%
Convallaria	*Convallaria majalis*	150 mg (md)	
		450 mg (mdd)	
Ephedra	*Ephedra distachya*		
	E. equisetina		
	E. gerardiana	1800 mg (mdd)	
	E. sinica		
Gelsemium	*Gelsemium sempervirens*	25 mg (md)	
		75 mg (mdd)	
Hyoscyamus	*Hyoscyamus albus*	300 mg (mdd)	
	H. muticus		
	H. niger	100 mg (md)	
Jaborandi	*Pilocarpus jaborandi*		5%
	P. microphyllus		
Lobelia	*Lobelia inflata*	200 mg (md)	
		600 mg (mdd)	
Poison Oak	*Rhus toxicodendron*		10%
Quebracho	*Aspidosperma*	50 mg (md)	
	quebrachoblanco	150 mg (mdd)	
Ragwort	*Senecio jacobaea*		10%
Stramonium	*Datura innoxia*	150 mg (mdd)	
	D. stramonium	50 mg (md)	

Banned herbal remedies

Aristolochia

The various forms of *Aristolochia* were made Prescription Only Medicines on 13 January 1997. Since then the sale, supply and importation of medicinal products consisting or containing a plant belonging to the species of the genus *Aristolochia* or belonging to any of the species *Akebia quinata*, *Akebia trifoliata*, *Clematis armandi*, *Clematis montana*, *Cocculus laurifolius*, *Cocculus orbiculatus*, *Cocculus trilobus* and *Stephania tetrandra*, consisting of or containing an extract from such a plant, are prohibited. The ban was extended on 16 June 2000 (SI 2000 No.1368).

Mu Tong and Fangji

The sale, supply and importation of medicinal products is prohibited where, at the time of the sale, supply or importation, the label on the container or package, or any document accompanying the product, indicates in any language that the product consists of or contains Mu Tong or Fangji or that the product consists of or contains *Akebia quinata*, *Akebia trifoliata*, *Clematis armandi*, *Clematis montana*, *Cocculus laurifolius*, *Cocculus orbiculatus*, *Cocculus trilobus* and *Stephania tetrandra*, or an extract from such a plant.

The prohibitions relating to *Aristolochia*, Mu Tong and Fangji do not apply to the importation from EU or EEA states, to the importation made by or on behalf of food and medicines enforcement agencies or to products which possess a marketing authorisation or a homoeopathic certificate of registration (SI 2000 No.1368).

Kava-kava

The order prohibits the sale, supply and importation of any medicinal product for human use which consists or contains a plant or part of a plant belonging to the species *Piper methysticum* (known as kava-kava) or an extract from such a plant.

The prohibition relating to *Piper methysticum* does not apply to the importation from the states of the EEA or originates outside an EEA state but in free circulation in member states and being, or is to be exported to, an EEA state other than the UK (SI 2002 No.3170).

Summary

- Ordinary shopkeepers can sell herbal remedies on the General Sale List and herbal remedies which are merely dried, crushed or comminuted without any written recommendation, but not those in the Schedule to the Order.
- Shopkeepers who have a manufacturer's licence, or choose to notify the enforcement authority, can sell dried, crushed and comminuted herbs which have also been subjected to certain other limited processes, but not those in the Schedule to the Order.
- Herbal practitioners can sell herbal remedies of the kind described above which shopkeepers can sell and also those remedies containing substances in and subject to the requirements of Part III of the Schedule to the Order.
- Herbal remedies containing substances in Part I or Part II of the Schedule to the Order may only be sold from pharmacies.
- Certain herbals have been banned, e.g. *Aristolochia*, Mu Tong and Fangji, and *Piper methysticum* (kava kava).

Further reading

Barnes J., Anderson L. A. and Phillipson J. D. (2002) *Herbal Medicines*, 2nd edn. Pharmaceutical Press, London.

CHAPTER THIRTEEN

Medicines Act 1968

Veterinary medicinal products: exemptions from controls

At the time of going to press there are proposals to consolidate and amend the UK regulations in regard to animal medicines. New Veterinary Medicines Regulations 2005 are expected (October) which will replace all the provisions relating to veterinary medicinal products under the Medicines Act 1968 and the existing SIs. At present the provisions that follow apply.

A *veterinary medicinal product* under Directive 2001/82/EC amended by Directive 2004/28/EC (together known as the 'amending directive') means:

- any substance or combination of substances presented as having properties for treating or preventing disease in animals, or,
- any substances or combination of substances which may be used in, or administered to, animals with a view either to restoring, correcting, or modifying physiological functions by exerting pharmacological, immunological or metabolic action, or by making a medical diagnosis.

No change is anticipated to this definition.

Classes of veterinary medicinal product

All medicinal products, whether for administration to human beings or veterinary medicinal products, fall into one of three categories:

1   those on a General Sale List;
2   those on a Prescription Only Medicines List; or
3   those not included in either the Prescription Only List or the General
      Sale List; when for administration to human beings these are termed
      Pharmacy Medicines and are for sale only in pharmacies.

The requirements of the Medicines Act and the restrictions it imposes on the
retail sale or supply of these categories of medicinal products have been fully
explained in Chapters 6–8.

Orders made under the Act provide some exemptions for certain classes of
person from the restrictions on retail sale or supply of veterinary medicinal
products. Sales made by these persons are exempted retail sales. Sales made to
them are sales by way of wholesale dealing (see Chapter 10).

The extent of the various exemptions and the conditions, if any, attached to
them are dealt with in this chapter.

Table 13.1   Proposed classes of veterinary medicine in the new regulations

Class	Description
POM V	Prescription Only Medicines prescribed by a veterinarian; supplied only by a veterinarian or a pharmacist
POM-VPM	Prescription Only Medicines prescribed by a veterinarian, pharmacist or merchant; supplied only by a veterinarian, a pharmacist or a merchant
NFA-VPM	Non-food animal medicine prescribed by a veterinarian, supplied only by a veterinarian, a pharmacist or merchant
AVM-GSL	Authorised veterinary medicine (General Sale List); no supply restrictions

In the proposed regulations the classes of veterinary medicine will
change. It is proposed that there will be four classes (Table 13.1).
Records of prescriptions must be kept for five years and retailers will
have to audit stock annually. There will also be a new definition of
'animal', namely 'all animals other than man and includes birds, reptiles,
fish, molluscs, crustacea and bees'.

Record keeping for Prescription Only veterinary products

Any veterinary surgeons, pharmacists or merchants must keep a record if they
sell veterinary medicinal products by retail intended for administration to
animals whose flesh or products are intended for human consumption and/or
in respect of which a withdrawal period must be observed.

Similarly any person who sells any other veterinary medicinal products by retail intended for administration to such animals, unless the products are on a General Sale List, must keep records.

For each incoming and outgoing transaction a record must be kept of the:

1   date of transaction;
2   precise identity of the product sold;
3   manufacturer's batch number;
4   quantity received or supplied;
5   name and address of supplier or recipient; and
6   if there is a prescription, the name and address of the prescribing veterinarian (where relevant) and a copy of the prescription.

All records must be durable but may be kept by electronic means. They must be kept for three (proposed five) years and be made available on request to any person having a duty of enforcement. The Royal Pharmaceutical Society has the duty to enforce concurrently with the Ministers in England and Scotland and the National Assembly for Wales (SI 2000 No.7).

The new proposals maintain the same record requirements other than the need to retain for five years rather than three.

Record keeping by wholesalers

A registered wholesaler must keep detailed records of all incoming and outgoing sales including disposal for at least three years. These must include:

1   date of transaction;
2   precise identity of the product sold;
3   manufacturer's batch number;
4   expiry date;
5   quantity received or supplied; and
6   name and address of supplier or recipient.

Veterinary surgeons and practitioners

The restrictions on retail sale or supply do not apply to the sale, offer for sale or supply of any medicinal product by a veterinary surgeon or practitioner for administration by him/her or under his/her direction to an animal or herd under his/her care (ss.55 and 58). Furthermore, the restrictions on retail sale or supply do not apply to any person who sells any medicinal product to a veterinary surgeon or practitioner (SIs 1980 No.1924 and 1991 No.1392).

Poultry vaccine suppliers

Persons providing a poultry vaccination service may sell a poultry vaccine if its name and authorisation number appear on a list kept by the Minister of Agriculture, Fisheries and Food in accordance with Article 3 of the Exemption Order (SI 1998 No.1044) and which, if or when for parenteral administration, is a Prescription Only Medicine. However, such sales or supplies may only be made to a person who has charge of animals for the purpose of and in the course of carrying on a business, whether as his/her sole business activity or as a substantial part of his/her business activities (SI 1991 No.1392).

Similarly, the restrictions on retail sale or supply do not apply to a person who sells or supplies any of those vaccines to a person providing a poultry vaccination service, subject to the presentation of an order signed by the purchaser stating the amount of the vaccines required (SIs 1980 No.1924 and 1991 No.1392).

Exempted veterinary medicinal products: sale or supply

The Medicines (Exemptions for Merchants in Veterinary Drugs) Order 1998 (SI 1998 No.1044, as amended) permits certain licensed medicinal products (known as PML medicinal products) which are not on a General Sale List to be sold or supplied by retail by:

1   the holders of marketing authorisations;
2   a specially authorised person, that is, a person specially authorised either, by a direction of the licensing authority, to assemble the veterinary drug otherwise than in accordance with the manufacturer's licence or, by the marketing authorisation, to sell the drug under the alternative name specified in the licence/authorisation; or
3   by certain categories of dealer.

NB Veterinarians and pharmacists are permitted to sell PML products.

The order applies to any veterinary drug whose name and authorisation number appears on a list kept by DEFRA. The explanatory note to the SI states that this list will be open for inspection at the office of the Veterinary Medicines Directorate, Woodham Lane, Addlestone, Surrey KT15 3NB and copies will be made publicly available and published in a regular bulletin.

Two classes of dealer are described in the order.

1   *Agricultural merchants* who may sell any veterinary medicinal products listed by the Minister subject to certain conditions (see below).
2   *Saddlers* who may sell any veterinary medicinal product listed by the Minister which is a horse wormer, dog wormer or cat wormer.

In these classes, an *agricultural merchant* means a person who carries on a business involving in whole or in part the sale of agricultural requisites, being things used for soil cultivation or keeping of animals for production of food or game, equipment for collecting produce from animals kept for production of food, things for the maintenance of that equipment, and protective clothing. A *saddler* means a person carrying on a business involving in whole or in part the sale of saddlery requisites, being products and equipment and things for the maintenance of that equipment, for keeping of horses or ponies, and including human clothing for that purpose.

Restrictions on sale or supply of veterinary medicinal products and horse wormers listed by the Minister

The sale of listed veterinary medicinal products and wormers by merchants and saddlers is subject to the certain conditions.

Registration requirements

Registration requirements are set out in SI 1998 No.1044, made under the Medicines Act 1968, as amended by the Animal Health and Welfare Act 1984. The *register* is maintained by the Royal Pharmaceutical Society of Great Britain, which is also responsible for inspection and enforcement. In Northern Ireland, the register is kept by the Department of Health and Social Services for Northern Ireland.

An agricultural merchant or saddler is subject to conditions in respect of inclusion and retention on the register, namely s/he must:

1   Register his/her name and details of all premises where s/he sells or stores veterinary medicinal products.
2   Give details for each premises of the name and qualifications of a person nominated to be a suitably qualified person for the premises.
3   Pay the appropriate fee for each set of premises.
4   Pay a retention fee annually in respect of each premises and notify any change in particulars as soon as possible. Failure to pay the retention fees leads to removal from the register and the payment of higher fees to have the premises restored to the register.
5   Be a fit and proper person to sell such veterinary drugs.

In addition:

6   All premises used for sale or storage must be suitable for the purpose, and premises to be used for sale, which may include a stall of a permanent nature at a market or agricultural showground, must be capable of being closed so as to exclude the public. Any alteration to premises which affect their suitability must be notified to the registration authority.
7   Any proposed permanent change to the suitably qualified person nominated must be notified to the registration authority.

Conditions of sale

The conditions of sale which must be complied with by an agricultural merchant or a saddler are that:

1   The premises at which sales of veterinary drugs are made must be occupied by him/her and under his/her control at all times when the premises are open for business, and s/he must store those products in a part of the premises partitioned off or otherwise separated from the rest of the premises and to which the public have no access.

2   The suitably qualified person nominated and notified or, in his/her temporary absence, an alternative suitably qualified person, shall authorise each sale of veterinary drugs.

3   Only exempted veterinary drugs listed by the Minister may be sold.

4   Each veterinary drug sold must be in the container in which it was made up for sale by the manufacturer or assembler, which has not been opened since then, and must bear the manufacturer's label, which has not been altered, and not be sold after the date of expiry indicated on its label.

5   The sale is not by self-service methods.

6   If the product is a cat wormer, a dog wormer or a horse wormer, the sale to is to a person whom s/he knows or has reasonable cause to believe has in his/her charge a cat if it is a cat wormer, a dog if it is a dog wormer or a horse or pony if it is a horse wormer and will use the product for the treatment of the animal concerned.

7   S/he must keep records (see below).

Additional conditions to be complied with by an agricultural merchant are:

8   If the product is *not* a cat wormer, dog wormer, or horse wormer, the sale to is to a person whom s/he knows or has reasonable cause to believe has animals under his/her control for the purpose of, and in the course of, carrying on a business either as his/her sole business activity or as a part of his/her business activities. NB This does not extend to a business wholly or mainly concerned with sales to the owners of pet animals. The keeping of animals as pets or the keeping of poultry, etc. for the sole use of the owner or his/her family or to give away is not 'carrying on a business'.

9   If the product is an organophosphate sheep dip or if the product is a sheep dip not intended for export, the sale is made to a person whom the seller knows, or has reasonable cause to believe, is the holder, or the employer of or a person acting on behalf of the holder, of a Certificate of Competence, and the agricultural merchant keeps a record of the certificate number for three years from the date of the sale.

Certificate of Competence means a Certificate of Competence in the Safe Use of Sheep Dips issued by the National Proficiency Tests Council or by that Council and the Department of Agriculture in Northern Ireland showing that parts 1 and 2 of the assessment have been satisfactorily completed.

Records

For each incoming and outgoing transaction, an agricultural merchant or a saddler must keep the following records:

1   the date of the transaction;
2   the identity of the products;
3   the manufacturer's batch number;
4   the quantity received or supplied; and
5   the name and address of the supplier or recipient.

At least once a year, a detailed audit of all transactions has to be carried out and recorded, with incomings and outgoings reconciled with those held in stock and any discrepancies recorded.

All records shall be durable, but may be kept by electronic means, and shall be kept for a period of three years from the date of the transaction or audit and made available to the registration authority or any person authorised by the enforcement authority (SI 1998 No.1044).

Code of good practice

There is a code of good practice for the sale and supply of animal medicines prepared by the Animal Medicines Training Regulatory Authority, which sets out the standards that agricultural merchants and saddlers dealing with animal medicines are expected to meet. The code has no legal status but supplements the principal legal requirements with other provisions relating to personnel, sale and storage arrangements and standards of premises.

Labelling requirements for veterinary medicinal products

See Chapter 15.

Prescriptions

A prescription for a Prescription Only Medicine must comply with the requirements given on page 91. In addition, it must carry a declaration by the veterinarian giving it that the medicine is prescribed for an animal or herd under his/her care (SI 1997 No.1830).

Summary

*   Veterinary surgeons and practitioners may sell or supply any medicinal product for administration by them, or under their direction, to an animal or herd under their care.

- There is a class of veterinary medicines known as Medicines Listed by the Minister, which may be sold by pharmacists or veterinarians and by registered agricultural merchants and registered saddlers.
- When sold by an agricultural merchant or saddler, specific conditions apply to the sale and detailed records have to be kept.
- There is a code of practice for agricultural merchants and for saddlers.

Further reading

Kayne S. and Jepson M. (2004) *Veterinary Pharmacy.* Pharmaceutical Press, London.

MAVIS (published regularly) *Advisory Leaflets.* Veterinary Medicines Directorate, Addlestone, UK.

Rules Governing Medicinal Products in the European Union, vol. 5: *Pharmaceutical Legislation, Veterinary Medicinal Products.* The Stationery Office, London.

CHAPTER FOURTEEN

Medicines Act 1968

Prohibitions for protection of

the purchaser

A prohibition, either total or limited in some way, on the sale, supply or importation of specified classes of medicinal product or of particular medicinal products may be imposed by order of the appropriate Ministers if it appears to them necessary to do so in the interest of safety. Before making such an order, the Ministers are required to consult the appropriate committee (or the Medicines Commission) and to consider representations made by other organisations who have been consulted. These requirements may be waived if, in the opinion of the Ministers, it is essential to make the order with immediate effect to avoid serious danger to health, whether of human beings or of animals. An order made without consultation is effective for three months only but may be renewed (s.62).

Any person who, otherwise than for performing or exercising a statutory duty or power, is in possession of such a medicinal product, knowing or having reasonable cause to suspect that it was sold, supplied or imported in contravention of the order is guilty of an offence (s.67) (see also p. 21).

Section 62 orders

Bal Chivan Chamcho

The sale, supply, or importation of Bal Chivan Chamcho is prohibited. It is a baby tonic in the form of a dark brown aromatic solid substance affixed to a spoon-shaped metal appliance (SI 1977 No.670, as amended). The prohibition does not apply to importation from a member state of the EU or if it originated in a state within the EEA. Neither does the prohibition apply to the sale or supply to a public analyst, a sampling officer or a person duly authorised by an enforcement authority under the Act.

Three other section 62 banning orders have been made in relation to herbal medicines (see pp. 136 and 137).

Non-medicinal antimicrobial substances

There are a number of antimicrobial substances which have medicinal and non-medicinal uses (e.g. sulfanilamide, streptomycin and certain other antibiotics). For medicinal purposes, they are classed as Prescription Only Medicines. When used for non-medicinal purposes, they are also within the control of the Medicines Act by virtue of an order made under section 105 (p. 17). Further orders under section 62 (SIs 1977 No.2131 and 1992 No.2684) prohibit the sale or supply of these substances when used for non-medicinal purposes except for certain purposes. The list of substances and the exceptions to the prohibition on sale are set out in Appendices 1 and 2.

Stilbenes and thyrostatic substances

Regulations (SI 1982 No.626) made under the European Communities Act 1972 prohibit the administration to farm animals of stilbenes and thyrostatic substances or of medicinal products or animal feeding stuffs containing them. Administration is not prohibited if prior steps are taken to ensure that the animals and their products are unavailable for animal or human consumption.

Chloroform

The sale or supply of medicinal products for human use which consist of or contain chloroform is prohibited (SI 1979 No.382) subject to the following exceptions. A sale or supply made:

1   by a doctor or dentist to a patient of his/hers, where the medicinal product has been specially prepared by that doctor or dentist for administration to that particular patient; or

2   by a doctor or dentist who has specially prepared the medicinal product at the request of another doctor or dentist for administration to a particular patient of that other doctor or dentist; or

3   from a pharmacy or hospital where the medicinal product has been specially prepared in accordance with a prescription given by a doctor or dentist for a particular patient; or

4   to a hospital, a doctor or a dentist for use as an anaesthetic; or

5   to a person who buys it for the purpose of reselling it to a hospital, a doctor or a dentist for use as an anaesthetic;

6   where the medicinal product contains chloroform in a proportion of not more than 0.5 per cent (w/w) or (v/v); or

7   where the medicinal product is solely for use in dental surgery; or

8   where the medicinal product is solely for use by being applied to the external surface of the body which for the purpose of this order does not include any part of the mouth, teeth or mucous membranes; or

9   where the medicinal product is for export; or

10   where the medicinal product is sold for use as an ingredient in the preparation of a substance or article in a pharmacy, a hospital or by a doctor or dentist.

For the purposes of sale or supply (but not of importation) of medicines for human use, the exemption limits for chloroform given in the Prescription Only List and General Sale List Orders are overridden by this order. The practical effect is that only products falling within 6 and 8 above may be sold by retail to the general public. But for the purposes of record keeping, the exemption levels in the Prescription Only Order still apply, so that records are required to be kept only of sales or supplies of products for internal use which contain more than 5 per cent chloroform (w/w) or (v/v) as appropriate.

Adulteration of medicinal products

It is an offence (s.63):

1   to add any substance to, or abstract any substance from, a medicinal product so as to affect injuriously the composition of the product, with intent that the product shall be sold or supplied in that state; or

2   to sell or supply, or offer or expose for sale or supply, or have in possession for the purpose of sale or supply, any medicinal product whose composition has been injuriously affected by the addition or abstraction of any substance.

It is also an offence to sell (or supply on a practitioner's prescription) to the prejudice of the purchaser (or patient) any medicinal product which is not of the nature or quality demanded by the purchaser (or specified in the prescription) (s.64).

There is no offence if the medicinal product contains some extraneous matter, the presence of which is proved to be an inevitable consequence of the process of manufacture, nor is it an offence where:

1   a substance has been added to, or abstracted from, the medicinal product which did not injuriously affect the composition of the product and was not carried out fraudulently; and

2 the product was sold having attached to it, or to a container or package in which it was sold, a conspicuous notice of adequate size and legibly printed specifying the substance added or abstracted.

False or misleading advertisements or representations

An advertisement or representation (whether it contains an accurate statement of the composition of medicinal products of the description or not) is taken to be false or misleading if (but only if) it falsely describes the medicinal products to which it relates or is likely to mislead as to the nature or quality of medicinal products of that description or as to their uses or effects (s.93).

A document, advertisement or representation is taken to be likely to mislead as to the uses or effects of medicinal products of a particular description if it is likely to mislead as to any of the following matters [s.130(10)]:

1 any purposes for which medicinal products of that description can with reasonably safety be used;
2 any purposes for which such products cannot be so used; or
3 any effects which such products when used (or when used in any particular way referred to in the document, advertisement or representation) produce or are intended to produce.

Medicinal products are 'of the same description' if (but only if) they are manufactured to the same specifications and they are, or are to be, sold, supplied, imported or exported in the same pharmaceutical form [s.130(8)].

The purposes for which medicinal products of any description may be recommended for use are limited to those specified in the licence relating to them. Any recommendation that they may be used for purposes other than those specified is an *unauthorised recommendation* [s.93(1) and (10)].

Any commercially interested party, or other person acting at that party's request or with their consent, who issues or causes to be issued a false or misleading advertisement or one containing an unauthorised recommendation relating to medicinal products of any description is guilty of an offence (s.93). It is also an offence [s.93(3)] to make, in the course of a relevant business, a false or misleading representation or one which amounts to an unauthorised recommendation:

1 in connection with the sale or offer for sale of a medicinal product;
2 to a practitioner, or to a patient or a client, for the purpose of inducing the practitioner to prescribe medicinal products of a particular description; or
3 to a person for the purpose of inducing him/her to purchase medicinal products of a particular description from a retailer.

A *relevant business* is one which consists of or includes the sale or supply of medicinal products [s.92(4)].

Summary

- The sale or supply of some medicinal products is either prohibited (e.g. Bal Chivan Chamcho) or prohibited subject to exceptions (e.g. stilbenes and thyrostatic substances, non-medicinal antimicrobial agents and chloroform).
- It is an offence to adulterate, by way of addition or abstraction, a medicinal product, or to sell, supply or possess an adulterated product.
- It is an offence to sell or supply to the prejudice of the purchaser (or patient) any medicinal product which is not of the nature or quality demanded by the purchaser (or specified on a prescription).
- An advertisement is false or misleading if it falsely describes the medicinal product to which it relates or is likely to mislead as to the nature and quality of the product or to its use.

CHAPTER FIFTEEN

Medicines Act 1968

Containers, packages and identification

There are detailed labelling requirements for relevant medicinal products for human use which include such features as additional warning labels or specific labels for certain products.

Regulations and penalties

Regulations may be made as the appropriate Ministers consider expedient or necessary for promoting the safety of medicinal products and for securing (a) that such products are correctly described and readily identifiable and (b) that any appropriate warning or information or instruction is given, and that false or other misleading information is not given. These regulations may apply to:

1 the labelling of containers [s.85(1)];
2 the labelling of packages [s.85(1)];
3 the display of distinctive marks on containers and packages [s.85(1)];
4 leaflets [s.86(1)];
5 colour or shape [s.88(1)];
6 distinctive marks to be displayed on such products [s.88(1)]; and
7 information to be displayed on automatic machines (s.89).

For the same purposes and also for preserving the quality of the products, regulations may prohibit the sale of medicinal products in containers which do not comply with specified requirements, in particular as to the strength, shape or pattern of the containers or of the materials of which they are made (s.87).

It is an offence for any person in the course of a business carried on by him/ her to sell or supply, or have in their possession for the purpose of sale or supply, any medicinal product or any leaflet relating to medicinal products in such circumstances as to contravene any requirements which may be imposed by these regulations [ss.85(3) and 86(2)].

The sale of a medicinal product without it being enclosed in a container is regarded as a contravention of the regulations concerning the labelling of containers [s.85(4)].

It is an offence for any person in the course of a business carried on by him/ her to supply a product to which the provisions of Council Directive 2001/83/EC applies, unless:

1   a leaflet is enclosed in, or supplied with, the container or package; or
2   the container or package itself contains the particulars which a leaflet relating to the product is required by the regulations to contain and does so in the manner required (SI 1994 No.276).

It is also an offence for a person in the course of a business carried on by him/ her to sell or supply or have in their possession for the purpose of sale or supply a medicinal product in a container or package which is labelled or marked in such a way, or supplied with a leaflet so that the container, package or leaflet falsely describes the product, or is likely to mislead as to the nature or quality of the product or as to its uses or the effects of medicinal products of that description [ss.85(5) and 86(3)].

Any person contravening the labelling regulations (see below) is liable on summary conviction to a fine of up to £5000 and, on conviction or indictment, to a fine or to imprisonment for a term not exceeding two years or to both.

Definitions

The terms defined here are those used in the Act and regulations in connection with labelling which are not explained elsewhere in the text.

Appropriate non-proprietary name means, briefly:

1   the international non-proprietary name (INN);
2   any name, or abbreviation or suitable inversion of such name, at the head of a monograph in a 'specified publication' (see below);
3   where the product is not described in a monograph, the British approved name; or

4   where there is no monograph name, British approved name or INN, the accepted scientific name or other name descriptive of the true nature of the product (SI 1976 No.1726, as amended by SI 2002 No 236).

Appropriate quantitative particulars means the quantity of each active ingredient (or that part of the active molecule responsible for the therapeutic or pharmacological activity) identified by its appropriate INN and expressed in terms of weight, volume, capacity or for certain products, in units of activity or as a percentage.

The quantity to be shown is:

1   the quantity in each dosage unit (for pastilles and lozenges only, it can be shown as a percentage);
2   if there is no dosage unit, the quantity of each active ingredient in the container; or
3   if the product contains any active ingredient which cannot be definitively characterised, the quantity of the ingredient present in the highest proportion other than diluents, excipients, etc.

The quantity of antimicrobial preservative added to a biological medicinal product must be stated. That applies to antigens, toxins, antitoxins, sera, antisera and vaccines.

The quantity can be expressed in terms of the dilution of the unit preparation for a *homoeopathic product* (that is, a product prepared in accordance with the methods of homoeopathic medicine or similar system which is sold or supplied as a homoeopathic product and is so described by the person who sells or supplies it) (SI 1976 No.1726, as amended by SI 2002 No 236).

Strength in relation to a relevant medicinal product means the content of active ingredient in that product expressed quantitatively per dosage unit, per unit volume or by weight, according to the dosage form.

Dosage unit means:

1   where the medicinal product is in the form of a tablet or capsule or is an article in some other similar pharmaceutical form, that tablet, capsule or other similar article; or
2   where the medicinal product is not in the form of aforesaid that quantity of the medicinal product which is used as the unit by reference to which the dose of the medicinal product is measured (SI 1976 No.1726, as amended by SI 2002 No 236).

Quantity means, where the quantity is not the exact quantity, the quantity which is as near the exact quantity as is reasonably practicable or which differs from the exact quantity only to such extent as is reasonably necessary in the circumstances having regard to the nature of the medicinal product in question (SI 1976 No.1726, as amended by SI 2002 No 236).

A *container*, in relation to a medicinal product, means the bottle, jar, box, packet or other receptacle which contains or is to contain it, not being a capsule, cachet or other article in which the product is or is to be administered; where any such receptacle is or is to be contained in another such receptacle, it includes the inner receptacle but not the outer (s.132).

It should be noted that a capsule, cachet or other article in which a medicinal product is to be administered is not normally a container, but if the capsule etc., is not to be administered, then it is a container.

A *package*, in relation to any medicinal products, means any box, packet or other article in which one or more containers of the products are to be enclosed, and where any such box, package or other article is or is to be itself enclosed in one or more other boxes, packets or other articles, includes each of the boxes, packets or other articles in question (s.132).

In effect, the inner receptacle which actually contains the medicinal products is a container, every outer receptacle is a package.

Labelling, in relation to a container or package of medicinal products, means affixing to or otherwise displaying on it a notice describing or otherwise relating to the contents (s.132).

Expiry date means the date after which, or the month and year after the end of which, the medicinal product should not be used or the date before which or the month and year before the beginning of which, the medicinal product should be used (SI 1977 No.996).

External use means:

1   in relation to medicinal products for use by being administered to human beings, application to the skin, hair, teeth, mucosa of the mouth, throat, nose, ear, eye, vagina or anal canal;
2   in relation to veterinary drugs, application to the skin, hair, fur, feathers, scales, hoof, horn, ear, eye, mouth, or mucosa of the throat or prepuce;

in either case when a local action only is necessary and extensive systemic absorption is unlikely to occur; references to *medicinal products for external use* shall be read accordingly, except that in relation to 1 above the references shall not include throat sprays, throat pastilles, throat lozenges, throat tablets, nasal sprays, nasal inhalations or teething preparations (SI 1997 No.1830, as amended).

Proprietary medicinal product means a ready-prepared medicinal product placed on the market in the UK under a special name and in a special pack (SI 1992 No.604).

Ready-made veterinary drug means a ready-prepared veterinary drug placed on the market in the UK in a pharmaceutical form in which it may be used without further processing, not being a drug placed on the market under a special name and in a special pack.

Specified publication means the *European Pharmacopoeia*, the *British Pharmacopoeia*, the *British Pharmaceutical Codex*, the *British Veterinary Codex* (or other official compendia which may in the future be produced under the Medicines Act) and the list of British approved names (Medicines Act, s.100).

Labelling regulations

The regulations apply at all stages of distribution, except where otherwise stated. Medicinal products which are Controlled Drugs must also be labelled in accordance with the Misuse of Drugs Regulations 1985 (see p. 206).

Regulations implementing Council Directive 2001/83/EC have been issued dealing with *relevant medicinal products* (SI 1992 No.3273, as amended) (see the definition, below). Regulations dealing with homoeopathic medicinal products (SI 1994 No.104) have also been issued.

Labelling of relevant medicinal products

Relevant medicinal product means a product to which the provisions of Council Directive 2001/83/EC applies in respect of which a marketing authorisation is granted or renewed. Thus, all medicinal products for human use are included except those prepared on the basis of magistral (see p. 16) or official formula, those intended for research or development trials, or intermediate products intended for further processing.

General labelling provisions for relevant medicinal products for human use

All labelling of containers and packages must be:

1   legible;
2   comprehensible;
3   indelible; and
4   either in the English language only or in English and in one or more other languages provided that the same particulars appear in all the languages used.

Where the holder of a marketing authorisation for a relevant medicinal product proposes to alter the labelling relating to it in any respect, s/he must notify the licensing authority and, unless the licensing authority has notified him/her that it does not approve the alterations, s/he may, after a period of 90 days from the date of notification by him/her, supply the product with the altered labelling (SI 1992 No.3273, as amended).

Standard labelling requirements for relevant medicinal products for human use

The standard requirements for the labelling of containers and packages of relevant medicinal products are set out in Council Directive 2001/83/EC and

SI 1992 No.3273, as amended. There are modifications for small containers and blister packs (see p. 158). The standard requirements are as follows.

1   The name of the medicinal product, followed by the common name where the medicinal product contains only one active ingredient and if its name is an invented name; where a medicinal product is available in several pharmaceutical forms and/or several strengths, the pharmaceutical form and/or strength (baby, child or adult as appropriate) must be included in the name of the medicinal product. (*Common name* means the international non-proprietary name or, if one does not exist, the usual common name. *Strength* in this context means: the suitability of the product for a baby, child or adult.)

2   A statement of the active ingredients expressed qualitatively and quantitatively per dosage unit or according to the form of administration for a given volume or weight, using their common names.

3   The pharmaceutical form of the product and the contents by weight, by volume or by number of doses of the product.

4   A list of those excipients known to have a recognised action or effect and included in the guidelines published in pursuant to Article 12. However, if the product is injectable or a topical or eye preparation, all excipients must be stated.

5   The method and, if necessary, the route of administration.

6   A special warning that the medicinal product must be stored out of the reach of children.

7   Any special warning if this is necessary for the medicinal product concerned.

8   The expiry date in clear terms (month/year).

9   Special storage precautions, if any.

10   Special precautions for disposal of unused medicinal products, if appropriate, or waste materials derived from such products.

11   The name and address of the holder of the marketing authorisation.

12   The marketing authorisation number.

13   The manufacturer's batch number.

14   In the case of self-medication, instructions on the use of the medicinal product.

The outer packaging may be labelled to show symbols or pictograms designed to clarify certain information mentioned in 1 to 14 above and other information compatible with the summary of product characteristics which is useful for health education, to the exclusion of any element of a promotional nature.

In addition, member states of the EU may require certain additional labelling such as the price of the product, the reimbursement conditions, and the classification [e.g. Prescription Only Medicine (POM)].

Summary of product characteristics means the information required to accompany any application for a marketing authorisation under Council Directive 2001/83.EC (see also p. 411).

Small containers for relevant medicinal products for human use

Where the container of a relevant medicinal product is *not* a blister pack but is too small to include all the standard particulars for relevant medicinal products, it must be labelled with:

1   the name of the medicinal product as laid down in standard labelling (see p. 156);
2   the contents of the product by weight, by volume or by unit
3   the method, and if necessary the route, of administration;
4   the expiry date; and
5   the batch number.

Blister packs for relevant medicinal products for human use

Where the container of a relevant medicinal product is a blister pack and is enclosed within a package which complies with the standard labelling (see above), the container must be labelled with:

1   the name of the medicinal product as laid down in standard labelling (see p. 156);
2   the expiry date;
3   the name of the holder of the marketing authorisation; and
4   the batch number.

Standard labelling requirements for containers and packages for radiopharmaceuticals for human use

Containers and packages for radiopharmaceuticals must be labelled with the standard particulars for relevant medicinal products (p. 156) together with the following additional particulars:

1   the container and package must be labelled in accordance with the current edition of the Regulations for the Safe Transport of Radioactive Materials;
2   the labelling on the shielding must explain in full the codings used on the vial and shall indicate where necessary, for a given time and date, the amount of radioactivity per dose or per vial and the number of capsules, or for liquids the number of millilitres in the container; and
3   the vial shall be labelled to show:

   (a)   the name or code of the medicinal product, including the name or chemical symbol of the radionuclide;

(b)   the international symbol for radioactivity;
(c)   the name of the manufacturer; and
(d)   the amount of radioactivity as specified in 2 above.

Labelling of relevant General Sale List medicinal products

All relevant medicinal products for human use on a General Sale List when sold or supplied by retail must be labelled as follows (SI 1994 No.3144, Sch.5 as amended). If the product contains:

1   aloxiprin, aspirin or paracetamol, with the words *If symptoms persist, consult your doctor* and, except where the product is for external use only, the recommended dosage; in addition the following words must appear on the container and package *Do not give to children under 16 years, unless on the advice of a doctor* (SI 2003/1618);

2   aloxiprin, with the words *Contains an aspirin derivative*;

3   aspirin, except where the product is for external use only or where the name of the product includes the word *aspirin* and appears on the container or package, the words *Contains aspirin*;

4   paracetamol, except where the name of the product includes the word *paracetamol* and appears on the container or package, the words *Contains paracetamol*;

5   paracetamol, the words *Do not exceed the stated dose* (these words must appear adjacent to either the directions for use or the recommended dosage);

6   paracetamol, unless it is wholly or mainly intended for children who are 12 years old or younger (i.e. is a product for children 12 and over), the words *Do not take with any other paracetamol containing products* and

  (a)   if a package leaflet accompanying the product displays the words *Immediate medical advice should be sought in the event of over-dose, even if you feel well, because of the risk of delayed, serious liver damage* the words *Immediate medical advice should be sought in the case of overdose, even if you feel well* must be added to the label; or

  (b)   if no package leaflet accompanies the product or the package leaflet does not display the words *Immediate medical advice should be sought in the event of overdose, even if you feel well, because of the risk of delayed, serious liver damage* then those words must be added to the label (SI 1998 No.3105).

7   paracetamol and is wholly or mainly intended for children who are 12 years old or younger, the words *Do not give with any other paracetamol containing products* and

(a) if a package leaflet accompanying the product displays the words *Immediate medical advice should be sought in the event of overdose, even if the child seems well, because of the risk of delayed, serious liver damage* the words *Immediate medical advice should be sought in the case of overdose, even if the child seems well* must be added to the label; or

(b) if no package leaflet accompanies the product or the package leaflet does not display the words *Immediate medical advice should be sought in the event of overdose, even if the child seems well, because of the risk of delayed, serious liver damage* then those words must be added to the label (SI 1998 No.3105).

Where more than one of the phrases in 2, 3 and 4 above apply they may be combined, for example, *Contains aspirin, an aspirin derivative and paracetamol*. Those phrases must be within a rectangle in which there is no other matter and must be in a prominent position.

On those General Sale List medicines which are subject to pack size provisions (see p.79), the larger pack sizes must be labelled with a 'P' within a rectangle in which there is no other matter.

Labelling of relevant medicinal products for pharmacy sale only

All medicinal products for pharmacy sale only when sold or supplied by retail must be labelled as follows (SI 1994 No.3144, Sch.5, as amended SI 2002 No.236).

1 With the capital letter 'P' in a rectangle containing no other matter. This also applies:

(a) to sales of Pharmacy Medicines by way of wholesale dealing; and

(b) to General Sale List Medicines in pack sizes restricted to pharmacy sale (SI 1994 No.3144, as amended SI 2002 No.236).

2 If containing aspirin, aloxiprin or paracetamol, in the manner described above for medicinal products on a General Sale List.

3 If for human use and exempt from Prescription Only control by reason of the proportion or level in such a product of the Prescription Only substance, with the words *Warning. Do not exceed the stated dose*. (This does not apply to products for external use or products containing any of the substances set out in 5 below.)

4 If for the treatment of asthma or other conditions associated with bronchial spasm or contains ephedrine or any of its salts, with the words *Warning. Asthmatics should consult their doctor before using this product*. (This does not apply to products for external use.)

5 If the product contains an antihistamine or any of its salts or molecular compounds, with the words *Warning. May cause drowsiness. If affected*

do not drive or operate machinery. Avoid alcoholic drink. (This does not apply to products for external use or where the marketing authorisation contains no warning to the sedating effect of the product in use.)

6   If the product is an embrocation, liniment, lotion, liquid antiseptic or other liquid preparation or gel and is for external application, with the words *For external use only*.

7   If the product contains hexachlorophane, either with the words *Not to be used for babies* or a warning that the product is not to be administered except on medical advice to a child under two years.

The relevant warning phrase or phrases described under Labelling of Relevant General Sale List Medicinal Products and Labelling of Relevant Medicinal Products for Pharmacy Sale Only above must be in a rectangle within which there is no other matter. That does not apply to the phrases *Do not exceed the stated dose* or *If symptoms persist consult your doctor* on the labels or products for human use required to be labelled because of their aspirin, aloxiprin, or paracetamol content.

Labelling of relevant Prescription Only Medicinal products

The container and package of every medicinal product included in a Prescription Only List must be labelled to show:

1   The letters 'POM' in capital letters within a rectangle within which there shall be no other matter of any kind. That requirement applies to wholesale transactions (which include sales to doctors or dentists) but does not apply to dispensed medicines.

2   If the product is an embrocation, liniment, lotion, liquid antiseptic or other liquid preparation or gel and is for external application, with the words *For external use only*.

3   If the product contains hexachlorophane, either with the words *Not to be used for babies* or a warning that the product is not to be administered except on medical advice to a child under two years.

Labelling of relevant dispensed medicinal products

The standard labelling requirements do not apply to dispensed medicines.

A *dispensed relevant medicinal product* means a relevant medicinal product prepared or dispensed in accordance with a prescription given by a practitioner.

The container of a dispensed relevant medicinal product must be labelled to show the following particulars:

1   the name of the person to whom the medicine is to be administered;

2   the name and address of the person who sells or supplies the relevant medicinal product;
3   the date of dispensing; and
4   where the product has been prescribed by a practitioner such of the following particulars as s/he may request:

(a)   the name of the product or its common name;
(b)   directions for use of the product; and
(c)   precautions relating to the use of the product; or

where a pharmacist, in the exercise of his/her professional skill and judgment, is of the opinion that any of such particulars are inappropriate and has taken all reasonable steps to consult with the practitioner and has been unable to do so, particulars of a same kind as those requested by the practitioner which the pharmacist considers appropriate;

5   the words *Keep out of the reach of children* or words of direction bearing a similar meaning;
6   the phrase *For external use only* if the product is not on a General Sale List and is an embrocation, liniment, lotion, liquid antiseptic or other liquid preparation or gel and is for external use only.

A container need not be labelled if it is enclosed in a package which is labelled with the required particulars.

Labelling of medicinal products exempt from product marketing authorisations

The following classes of medicinal product, exempt from marketing authorisations (product licences) by various orders made under the Medicines Act, are subject to modified labelling requirements.

Foods and cosmetics

Certain medicinal products which are foods are exempt from marketing authorisations (product licences) by the Foods and Cosmetics Order (SI 1971 No.1410), and the labelling particulars (see above) which apply to these products are:

1   name of product (container and package);
2   description of pharmaceutical form (package only);
3   appropriate quantitative particulars (container only);
4   quantity (container and package);
5   any special handling and storage requirements (container and package); and
6   expiry date (container only).

The labels of the container and of the package must also bear the name and address of the manufacturer or the person responsible for its composition or the person who first sells or supplies it as a medicinal product.

These labelling requirements do not apply to any product which is subject to the Labelling of Food Regulations. There are no labelling requirements for cosmetics.

Special and transitional cases

'Special' dispensing and manufacturing services provided by manufacturers for practitioners, pharmacists and others are the subject of two orders (SIs 1971 No.1450 and 1972 No.1200) under the Medicines Act, which provide exemptions from marketing authorisations (see Chapter 3). These orders also extend to certain other special cases. The label of the container of medicinal products affected, and the packages immediately enclosing them, must show the following labelling particulars:

1   name of the product;
2   pharmaceutical form (package only);
3   appropriate quantitative particulars;
4   quantity;
5   any special handling and storage requirements;
6   batch reference; and
7   manufacturer's licence number, or name and address.

The package must also bear the name and address of the manufacturer, or of the person responsible for the composition of the product, or of the person who first sells or supplies it as a medicinal product.

Other exempt medicinal products

Apart from the orders mentioned under Foods and Cosmetics and Special and Transitional Cases above, the Medicines Act provides other exemptions from marketing authorisation (product licence) requirements for certain medicinal products.

The following requirements apply, for example, to medicinal products which are prepared in a registered pharmacy for retail sale from that pharmacy and which are not advertised. (Such products are familiarly known as 'chemist's nostrums'.)

The label of the container of such a medicinal product and the package immediately enclosing it must show the following labelling particulars:

1   name of the product;
2   pharmaceutical form (package only);
3   appropriate quantitative particulars;
4   quantity;
5   directions for use;

6   any special handling and storage requirements; and
7   expiry date (if relevant).

The label of the container and the package must also show the name and address of the seller.

Ingredient medicinal products

The label of the container and of the package of ingredients which are to be used in the preparation of medicinal products must show the following labelling particulars:

1   name of the product (i.e. ingredient);
2   pharmaceutical form;
3   appropriate quantitative particulars;
4   quantity;
5   any special handling and storage requirements;
6   expiry date (if relevant);
7   marketing authorisation number (or the name and address of the holder of the marketing authorisation);
8   batch reference;
9   manufacturer's licence number, or name and address; and
10   particulars required by the marketing authorisation.

Contract manufacture or assembly

Where a medicinal product is supplied solely for the purpose of assembly and the supply is between persons concerned in the manufacture or assembly of the product, the package immediately enclosing the container must be labelled to show:

1   name of the product;
2   name and address of the person supplying the product;
3   marketing authorisation number (if any); and
4   batch reference.

The person taken to be concerned in the manufacture or assembly of a medicinal product is (a) the marketing authorisation holder or, if there is no authorisation, the person responsible for the composition of the product, or (b) the person who manufactures or assembles the product to the order of the authorisation holder etc. or to the order of the Crown.

Those are the only requirements which apply to stocks held in the manufacturing process.

Delivery and storage

The labelling particulars required for delivery and storage must appear on the outer package, that is to say the package enclosing the package immediately enclosing the container. The required labelling particulars are:

1   any special handling and storage particulars;
2   the expiry date of the product; and
3   the manufacturer's batch number.

Clinical trials

Where a medicinal product is for administration in a clinical trial, the labelling on the container and package must sufficiently identify the clinical trial, the product (if more than one product is supplied in the course of the trial) and such designation as will identify the person to whom the product is to be administered. It must also show the name and address of the premises where the clinical trial is to be carried out (or the name and address of the product licence holder) and particulars required to be stated on the labels by the product licence or clinical trial certificate.

Standard labelling requirements for containers and packages of homoeopathic products for human use

All containers and packages for homoeopathic products must be labelled clearly and make reference to their homoeopathic nature by clear use of the words *homoeopathic medicinal product*. In addition they must carry the following particulars and no others (SI 1994 No.104):

1   the scientific name of the stock or stocks followed by the degree of dilution, making use of the symbols of the pharmacopoeia used in relation to the homoeopathic manufacturing procedure described therein for that stock or stocks;
2   the name and address of the holder of the certificate of registration and, where different, the name and address of the manufacturer;
3   the method of administration and, if necessary, route;
4   the expiry date of the product in clear terms, stating the month and year;
5   the pharmaceutical form;
6   the contents of the sales representation;

7   any special storage precautions;
8   any special warning necessary for the product concerned;
9   the manufacturer's batch number;
10   the registration number allocated by the licensing authority preceded by the letters 'HR' in capital letters;
11   the words *homoeopathic medicinal product without approved therapeutic indications*; and
12   a warning advising the user to consult a doctor if the symptoms persist during the use of the product.

Surgical materials

Certain surgical materials (for example, ligatures and sutures) are medicinal products by virtue of the Medicines (Surgical Materials) Order 1971 (SI 1971 No.1267). The label of the container of such a product and the package immediately enclosing it must show the following labelling particulars:

1   name of the product;
2   description of the pharmaceutical form;
3   directions for use;
4   contra-indications, warnings and precautions (if any);
5   any special handling and storage requirements;
6   expiry date where relevant;
7   name and address of the holder of the marketing authorisation;
8   marketing authorisation number;
9   batch reference;
10   manufacturer's licence number, or name and address;
11   particulars required by the marketing authorisation (product licence).

The label must also show the nature and origin of the article or substance and the quantity of the product in the container expressed in terms of weight or volume or length.

Labelling of animal medicines

Animal medicines which possessed product licences prior to 1 January 1995 are subject to the same general and standard labelling requirements as medicinal products for human use (see p. 156).

All medicinal products for animal use obtaining new marketing authorisations or having their licences renewed have to comply with the provisions of the Marketing Authorisations for Veterinary Medicinal Products Regulations 1994 (SI 1994 No.3142, reg.6). These regulations implement Council Directive 81/851/EEC, as amended.

It is an offence not to label animal medicines under the new regulations. The regulations require the following information to appear in legible characters on the containers and outer packages:

1   the name of the veterinary medicinal product;
2   a statement of the active ingredients expressed qualitatively and quantitatively per dosage unit or according to the form of administration for a given volume or weight, using the international non-proprietary name or where none exists the usual non-proprietary name;
3   manufacturer's batch number;
4   marketing authorisation number;
5   name and address or registered business address of the person responsible for marketing and of the manufacturer if different;
6   the species of animal for which the product is intended together with the method and route of administration;
7   the withdrawal period, even if nil, in the case of products administered to food-producing animals;
8   the expiry date in plain language;
9   special storage precautions, if any;
10 special precautions for disposal of unused product or waste material;
11 any special precautions relating to use or other particulars essential for safety or health protection;
12 the words *For animal treatment only*;
13 the words *Store out of the reach of children*; and
14 the indications 'POM', 'P', 'PML' or 'GSL' in a box in which there is no other written material.

Labelling small containers for animal medicinal products

For containers such as ampoules, the information required is:

1   the name of the veterinary medicinal product;
2   quantity of the active ingredients;
3   manufacturer's batch number;
4   route of administration;
5   the expiry date in plain language; and
6   the words *For animal treatment only*.

Sales by agricultural merchants and saddlers

Exempted veterinary drugs must be labelled in accordance with the principal labelling regulations (see p. 156), as amended and with the additional labelling requirements in SI 1977 No.2168.

The containers and the immediately enclosed package of an exempted veterinary drug, when sold or supplied by retail, must be labelled.

1   'PML' (Schs.1 and 2) or 'POM' (Sch.3), as appropriate. The letters must be in capitals within which there shall be no other matter of any kind. (NB For wholesale transactions, the letters need only appear on the immediately enclosing package.)

2   If containing hexachlorophane and for oral administration for the prevention or treatment of liver fluke disease in cattle, with a warning that it is not for use in lactating cattle, and also, if for liver fluke disease in sheep or cattle, with a warning that protective clothing must be worn when the product is being administered.

3   If containing aloxiprin, with the words *Unsuitable for cats* and *Contains an aspirin derivative*.

4   If containing aspirin, with the words *Unsuitable for cats* and *Contains aspirin*. (*Contains aspirin* may be omitted where the word *aspirin* is included in the name of the product.)

5   If containing salicylamide, with the words *Unsuitable for cats*.

In 3, 4 and 5 the special *Unsuitable for cats* words must be within a rectangle within which there shall be no other matter.

Labelling of medicinal tests on animals

The labelling requirements of containers and packages of a medicinal product or medicated feeding stuff for medicinal tests on animals are set out in separate regulations (SI 1988 No.1009) and are briefly as follows. (The general provisions as to the English language, indelibility and legibility apply.)

1   Designations to identify the animal test.

2   Where there is more than one medicinal product or medicated feeding stuff in the course of a test, such designation to identify each medicinal product or excepted medicated feeding stuff.

3   Quantity.

4   Purpose for which to be used, the species and the directions for use including dosage and any warning statements.

5   Requirements (if any) for incorporation in animal feeding stuffs.

6   Any special handling and storage requirements.

7   Expiry date.

8   Any other particulars required by the licence or certificate.

9   In the case of small-sized labels, the statement that a leaflet of instructions is supplied with each product.

10   The words *For animal test use only*.

Where any container is of a size which makes it impracticable to be labelled to show all the particulars above, it must be labelled with items 1, 2, 7 and 8, and a leaflet containing all the particulars must be supplied with the product and delivered to the purchaser.

Leaflets

Medicinal products which are relevant medicinal products for human use

All leaflets included in the package or container of any relevant medicinal product (see p. 156) must comply with section 7(1) of SI 1994 No.3144 and contain the particulars as set out in Council Directive 92/27/EEC.

All particulars must be drawn up in accordance:

1   with the summary of product characteristics (see p. 411), if there is one;
2   if there is no summary of product characteristics, with the data sheet, if there is one; or
3   if there is no summary of product characteristics and no data sheet, with the information which would be required to accompany an application for a product licence under Council Directive 2001/83/EC.

The particulars must be written in clear and understandable terms for the patient and be clearly legible in the language of the member state where the product was placed on the market. Other languages may be used provided that the same particulars appear in all the languages used.

The particulars which must be included are:

1   For identification of the medicinal product:

   (a)   the name of the product, followed by the common name if the product contains only one active ingredient and if its name is an invented name; where a medicinal product is available in several pharmaceutical forms and/or several strengths, the pharmaceutical form and/or strength (for example, baby, child, adult) must be included in the name of the product;

   (b)   a full statement of the active ingredients and excipients expressed qualitatively and a statement of the active ingredients expressed quantitatively, using their common names, in the case of each presentation of the medicinal product;

   (c)   the pharmaceutical form and the contents by weight, by volume or by number of doses of the product, in the case of each presentation of the product;

   (d)   the pharmaco-therapeutic group, or type of activity in terms easily comprehensible for the patient; and

   (e)   the name and address of the holder of the marketing authorisation and of the manufacturer.

2   The therapeutic indications.

3   A list of information which is necessary before taking the medicinal product, as follows:

(a)   contra-indications;
(b)   appropriate precautions for use;
(c)   forms of interaction with other medicinal products and other forms of interaction (e.g. with alcohol, tobacco and foodstuffs) which may affect the action of the medicinal product; and
(d)   special warnings, which:

  (i) take into account the particular condition of certain categories of users (e.g. children, pregnant or breastfeeding women, the elderly, and persons with specific pathological conditions);
  (ii) mention, if appropriate, potential effects on the ability to drive vehicles or operate machinery; and
  (iii) give details of those excipients, knowledge of which is important for the safe and effective use of the medicinal product.

4   The necessary and usual instructions for proper use, in particular:

(a)   dosage;
(b)   method and, if necessary, route of administration;
(c)   the frequency of administration, specifying if necessary, the time at which the medicinal product may or must be administered;

and, where the nature of the product makes it appropriate:

(d)   the duration of treatment, where it should be limited;
(e)   the action to be taken in the case of an overdose (e.g. symptoms and emergency procedures);
(f)   the course of action to be taken where one or more doses have not been taken; and
(g)   indication, if necessary, of the risk of withdrawal effects.

5   A description of the undesirable effects which can occur with normal use of the medicinal product and, if necessary, the action to be taken in such a case, together with an express invitation to the patient to communicate any undesirable effect which is not mentioned in the leaflet to his/her doctor or pharmacist.

6   A reference to the expiry date indicated on the label with:

(a)   a warning against using the product after this date;
(b)   where appropriate, special storage precautions; and
(c)   if necessary, a warning against certain visible signs of deterioration.

7   The date upon which the leaflet was last revised.

The licensing authority may decide that certain therapeutic indications need not be included in a leaflet where the dissemination of such information might have serious disadvantages for the patient.

A leaflet for a relevant medicinal product may include:

1   a symbol or pictogram designed to clarify the particulars set out in 1 to 7 above; and
2   other information compatible with the summary of product characteristics which is useful for health education, to the exclusion of any element of a promotional nature.

Paracetamol

Where a package leaflet is included in the packaging of a relevant medicinal product containing paracetamol, unless the product is wholly or mainly intended for children who are 12 years old or younger (i.e. where the product is intended for children 12 and over), the leaflet shall display the words *Immediate medical advice should be sought in the event of overdose, even if you feel well, because of the risk of delayed, serious liver damage.*

Where a package leaflet is included in the packaging of a relevant medicinal product containing paracetamol, and the product is wholly or mainly intended for children who are 12 years old **or younger,** the leaflet shall display the words *Immediate medical advice should be sought in the event of overdose, even if the child seems well, because of the risk of delayed, serious liver damage* (SI 1998 No.3105).

Aspirin

Where in accordance with the relevant Community provisions a package leaflet is included in the packaging of a relevant medicinal product containing aspirin or aloxiprin, the leaflet must display the words '*There is a possible association between aspirin and Reye's syndrome when given to children. Reye's syndrome is a very rare disease, which can be fatal. For this reason aspirin should not be given to children aged under 16 years, unless on the advice of a doctor*' (SI 2003 No.1618).

Radiopharmaceuticals and radiopharmaceutical-associated products

A leaflet enclosed with a radiopharmaceutical or radiopharmaceutical-associated products must in addition to containing particulars required in the regulations (SI 1994 No.3144) contain:

1   details of any precautions to be taken by the user and the patient during the preparation and administration of the product; and
2   details of any special precautions to be taken in respect of the disposal of the container and its unused contents.

Homoeopathic medicinal products

Any leaflet enclosed in or supplied with the packaging of a homoeopathic product which is placed on the market in accordance with a certificate of registration must bear the words *homoeopathic medicinal product*. In addition the leaflet must carry the following particulars and no others (SI 1994 No.104):

1 the scientific name of the stock or stocks followed by the degree of dilution, making use of the symbols of the pharmacopoeia used in relation to the homoeopathic manufacturing procedure described therein for that stock or stocks;

2 the name and address of the holder of the certificate of registration and, where different, the name and address of the manufacturer;

3 the method of administration and, if necessary, route;

4 the expiry date of the product in clear terms, stating the month and year;

5 the pharmaceutical form;

6 the contents of the sales representation;

7 any special storage precautions;

8 any special warning necessary for the product concerned;

9 the manufacturer's batch number;

10 the registration number allocated by the licensing authority preceded by the letters 'HR' in capital letters;

11 the words *homoeopathic medicinal product without approved therapeutic indications*; and

12 a warning advising the user to consult a doctor if the symptoms persist during the use of the product.

Animal medicines

Leaflets supplied with proprietary veterinary drugs or ready-made veterinary drugs must contain the particulars set out in the regulations (SI 1983 No.1727, as amended). The requirements are similar to those for human relevant medicinal products (see above) and include 1 to 3 and 5 to 7 inclusive, with the substitution of the words 'proprietary veterinary drug' or 'ready-made veterinary drug' for the words 'proprietary medicinal product'. Numbers 4, 8, and 9 are substituted by the following:

4 the species of animal for which the proprietary veterinary drug or ready-made veterinary drug is intended, the dosage for each species, the method and route of administration and, if necessary, advice on correct administration;

8 the name and address of the holder of the product licence which relates to the proprietary veterinary drug or ready-made veterinary drug, and, if different therefrom, the name and address of the person responsible for the composition of the drug;

9   the withdrawal period specified in the product licence before an animal which has been treated with the proprietary veterinary drug or ready-made veterinary drug is slaughtered for the production of food and before products derived from such an animal are used as food.

Relevant animal medicines

See page 166.

Child safety regulations

It is an offence to sell or supply relevant medicinal products otherwise than in containers that are both opaque or dark tinted and are child resistant [Medicines (Child Safety) Regulations SI 2003 No.2317].

For the purpose of these regulations, *relevant medicinal products* means medicinal products for human use consisting of or containing aspirin, paracetamol or more than 24 mg elemental iron which are in the form of tablets, capsules, pills, lozenges, pastilles, suppositories or oral liquids, except for

1   effervescent tablets containing not more than 25% of aspirin or paracetamol by weight;
2   medicinal products in sachets or other sealed containers which hold only one unit of dose;
3   medicinal products that are not intended for retail sale by a retail pharmacy or supplied in pursuance of a prescription; and
4   for export.

Containers that are not-reclosable are child resistant if they have been evaluated in accordance and comply with

1   British Standard BS 8404 published by the British Standard Institution on 21 December 2001; or
2   any equivalent or higher specification for non-reclosable child-resistant packaging recognised for use in the EEA.

Containers that are reclosable are child resistant if they have been evaluated in accordance and comply with

1   British Standard BS 28317 published by the British Standard Institution on 15 February 1993; or
2   any equivalent or higher specification for reclosable child-resistant packaging recognised for use in the EEA.

The regulations do not apply to products which are (a) for export or not intended for retail sale; (b) sold or supplied from a registered pharmacy under the supervision of a pharmacist on the prescription of a practitioner (which are subject to voluntary controls under the Society's Code of Ethics) or at the request of a person (not a child) who specifically request the non-use of a child-resistant container; (c) sold or supplied by a doctor or dentist to a patient of his/hers or to the patient's carer or to another prescriber for a particular patient; or (d) sold or supplied for administration in accordance with the directions of a prescriber at a hospital or health centre.

These products, for aspirin and paracetamol, when for administration exclusively to children must be white and the contents of each container or pack of unit packages must not exceed 25. This does not apply to the sale or supply of a medicinal product containing either paracetamol in oral liquid dosage form or more than 24 mg elemenal iron.

Transitional arrangements: these regulations do not apply to those products in respect of which a UK licence was granted before 1 October 2003, were placed on the market before 1 October 2005 and their shelf life has not expired.

Use of fluted bottles

A liquid medicinal product which is for external use (for definition see p. 155) must be sold or supplied in a bottle the outer surface of which is fluted vertically with ribs or grooves recognisable by touch if the product contains any of the substances listed below (SI 1978 No.40). This requirement applies to the following substances subject to the exemptions shown:

- aconite, alkaloids of
- adrenaline (epinephrine); its salts
- amino-alcohols esterified with benzoic acid, phenylacetic acid, phenyl-propionic acid, cinnamic acid or the derivatives of these acids; their salts
- p-aminobenzenesulphonamide; its salts; derivatives of
- p-aminobenzenesulphonamide having any of the hydrogen atoms of the p-amino group or of the sulphonamide group substituted by another radical; their salts
- p-aminobenzoic acid; esters of; their salts
- ammonia except in medicinal products containing less than 5 per cent weight in weight of ammonia
- arsenical substances, the following; arsenic sulphides, arsenates; arsenites; halides of arsenic; oxides of arsenic; organic compounds of arsenic
- atropine; its salts
- cantharidin; cantharidates
- carbachol
- chloral; its addition and its condensation products other than alpha-chloralose; their molecular compounds
- chloroform except in medicinal products containing less than 1 per cent volume in volume of chloroform
- cocaine; its salts

- creosote obtained from wood except in medicinal products containing less than 50 per cent volume in volume of creosote obtained from wood
- croton, oil of
- demecarium bromide
- dyflos
- ecothiopate iodide
- ephedrine, it salts, except in medicinal products containing less than the equivalent of 1 per cent weight in volume of ephedrine
- ethylmorphine; its salts
- homatropine; its salts
- hydrofluoric acid; alkali metal bifluorides; potassium fluoride; sodium fluoride; sodium silicofluoride: except in mouth washes containing not more than 0.05 per cent weight in volume of sodium fluoride
- hyoscine; its salts
- hyoscyamine; its salts
- lead acetates except in medicinal products containing lead acetates equivalent to not more than 2.2 per cent weight in volume of lead calculated as elemental lead
- mercury, oxides of; nitrates of mercury; mercuric ammonium chloride; mercuric chloride; mercuric iodide, potassium mercuric iodide; organic compounds of mercury; mercuric oxycyanide; mercuric thiocyanate: except in medicinal products containing not more than 0.01 per cent weight in volume of sodium ethylmercurithiosalicylate as a preservative
- nitric acid except in medicinal products containing less than 9 per cent weight in weight of nitric acid
- opium
- phenols (any member of the series of phenols of which the first member is phenol and of which the molecular composition varies from member to member by one atom of carbon and two atoms of hydrogen); compounds of phenol with a metal except in:

  — medicinal products containing one or more of the following: butylated hydroxytoluene, carvacrol, creosote obtained from coal tar, essential oils in which phenols occur naturally, tar (coal or wood, crude or refined), tert-butylcresol, p-tert-butyl-phenol, p-tert-pentylphenol, p-(1,1,3,3-tetraethylbutyl) phenol, thymol
  — mouth washes containing less than 2.5 per cent weight in volume phenols
  — any liquid disinfectant or antiseptics not containing phenol and containing less than 2.5 per cent weight in volume of other phenols
  — other medicinal products containing less than 1 per cent weight in volume of phenols

- physostigmine; its salts

- picric acid except in medicinal products containing less than 5 per cent weight in volume of picric acid
- pilocarpine; its salts except in medicinal products containing less than the equivalent of 0.025 per cent weight in volume of pilocarpine
- podophyllum resin except in medicinal products containing not more than 1.5 per cent weight in weight of podophyllum resin
- solanaceous alkaloids not otherwise included in the schedule.

Other exceptions to fluted bottle requirements

The fluted bottle requirements do not apply where:

1   medicinal products are contained in bottles with a capacity greater than 1.14 litres;
2   a medicinal product is a Prescription Only Medicine containing a listed substance (fluted bottle requirements do apply to dispensed medicinal products or any other retail sale or supply);
3   medicinal products are packed for export for use solely outside the UK;
4   medicinal products are sold or supplied solely for the purpose of scientific education, research or analysis;
5   eye or ear drops are sold or supplied in a plastic container; or
6   where the product licence, clinical trial certificate or animal test certificate otherwise provides.

Summary

- There are detailed labelling requirements for relevant medicinal products for human use which includes all medicines which have been granted, or had renewed, marketing authorisations (product licences) since January 1994. These do not include those medicines dispensed against a prescription or official formula, or for research or trials.
- There are specific labelling requirements for relevant medicinal products for human use containing aloxiprin, aspirin and paracetamol, and additional requirements for Prescription Only Medicines.
- There are additional warning labels for paracetamol.
- There are modified labelling provisions for relevant medicinal products for human use which are in small containers, blister packs, homoeopathic products and for radiopharmaceuticals.
- Abbreviated labelling provisions exist for medicines dispensed against a prescription given by a practitioner.
- There are separate labelling requirements for ingredients, food and cosmetics, contract manufacture and assembly, chemist's nostrums, import and export, surgical materials, clinical trials, animal medicines, animal tests and animal feeding stuffs.

- Every container or package of relevant medicinal products must contain a patient leaflet. Detailed requirements exist for the contents of these leaflets.
- Similar requirements exist for leaflets for animal medicines.
- Special leaflets provisions exist for homoeopathic medicinal products.
- Special requirements apply to the sale of medicinal products in unit-dose form which contain aspirin or paracetamol. These products must be packed in child-resistant containers, i.e. opaque reclosable resistant containers or bubble/blister packs.
- There is a list of liquid medicinal products which are for external use which must be sold in bottles the outer surface of which is fluted with ribs or grooves recognisable by touch. These 'fluted' bottle requirements do not apply where medicinal products are contained in bottles greater than 1.14 litres, for export, for analysis or clinical trial, or which are eye or ear drops.

CHAPTER SIXTEEN

Medicines Act 1968

Pharmacopoeias and other publications

European Pharmacopoeia

The *European Pharmacopoeia* is published under the direction of the Council of Europe (Partial Agreement) in accordance with the Convention on the Elaboration of a European Pharmacopoeia held in 1964.

In 1973, the standards in the *European Pharmacopoeia*, together with any amendments or alterations published in the *Gazette*, took precedence over the standards in other publications. The Health Ministers may publish amendments to the *British Pharmacopoeia* when necessary to give effect to the Convention but, should a difference exist at any time between the two pharmacopoeias, the standard of the *European Pharmacopoeia* would prevail (s.102).

A name is taken to be an approved synonym for a name at the head of a monograph in the *European Pharmacopoeia*, if, by a notice published in the *Gazette* and not subsequently withdrawn, it is declared to be approved by the Medicines Commission as a synonym for that name [s.65(8)].

British Pharmacopoeia, compendia and other publications

Until 1970, the *British Pharmacopoeia* was compiled by the General Medical Council under the Medical Act 1956 when the copyright was assigned to Her

Majesty (Medicines Act, s.98). A committee set up under section 4 of the Act, known as the British Pharmacopoeia Commission, has been established to prepare new editions of the *British Pharmacopoeia* and any amendments to such editions.

The *British Pharmacopoeia* comprises *relevant information*, i.e. information consisting of descriptions of, standards for, or notes or other matters relating to:

1   substances and articles (whether medicinal products or not) which are or may be used in the practice of medicine (other than veterinary medicine), surgery other than veterinary surgery, dentistry and midwifery; and

2   substances and articles used in the manufacture of substances and articles listed under 1.

In addition to the *British Pharmacopoeia*, compendia containing other relevant information may be published (s.99). Information relating to substances and articles used in veterinary medicine and surgery (whether veterinary drugs or not) is published in a separate compendium, the *British Pharmacopoeia (Veterinary)*.

The British Pharmacopoeia Commission is authorised to prepare lists of suitable names (British Approved Names) for substances and articles for placing at the head of monographs in the *British Pharmacopoeia* or in the compendia (s.100 and SI 1970 No.1256). The publication of any such lists supersedes any previously published list.

If the Medicines Commission so recommends, the *British Pharmacopoeia*, the compendia and the lists of names must be published and made available for sale to the public by the appropriate Ministers. Every copy must specify the date from which it is to take effect, and notice must be given in the *Gazette* not less than 21 days before that date (s.102). The Agriculture Ministers are responsible for the veterinary publication and the Health Ministers for the others (s.99).

Apart from the *British Pharmacopoeia* and the compendia, other publications containing relevant information may be prepared at the discretion of the Medicines Commission (s.101). These may be journals published periodically and made available to the public.

British Pharmaceutical Codex *and* British Veterinary Codex

The *British Pharmaceutical Codex*, prepared and published by the Royal Pharmaceutical Society of Great Britain, first appeared in 1907. Successive editions were published, the last being in 1973. The requirements for drugs and dressings in the *British Pharmaceutical Codex* have provided legally recognised standards which continue to be official standards under the Medicines Act. No analytical standards have been given in any codex published by the Royal Pharmaceutical Society of Great Britain since 1973.

The *British Veterinary Codex*, also prepared and published by the Royal Pharmaceutical Society, has similarly provided standards for medicines in veterinary use, which are now official standards under the Medicines Act.

The Medicines Commission has recommended that there should be only one source of published standard for medicines, namely the *British Pharmacopoeia*.

Compliance with official standards

It is unlawful for any person, in the course of a business carried on by him/her, (a) to sell a medicinal product which has been demanded by the purchaser by, or by express reference to, a particular name; or (b) to sell or supply a medicinal product in pursuance of a prescription given by a practitioner in which the product required is described by, or by express reference, to a particular name; or (c) to sell or supply a medicinal product which, in the course of the business, has been offered or exposed for sale by, or by express reference to, a particular name; if that name is at the head of the relevant monograph in a specified publication, or is an approved synonym for such a name, and the product does not comply with the standard specified in that monograph (ss.65 and 67).

It is also an offence if the name in question is the name of an active ingredient of the product and, in so far as the product consists of that ingredient, it does not comply with the standard specified.

The publications to which these requirements extend are the *European Pharmacopoeia*, the *British Pharmacopoeia*, the *British Pharmaceutical Codex*, the *British Veterinary Codex* and any compendium published under Part VII of the Act.

For the purpose of complying with official standards, the *relevant monograph* is ascertained as follows.

1   If a particular edition of a particular publication is specified together with the name of the medicinal product, then the *relevant monograph* is (a) the monograph (if any) headed by that name in that edition of the publication; or (b) if there is no such monograph in that edition, the *appropriate current monograph* (if any) headed by that name.

2   If a particular publication, but not a particular edition, is specified, together with the name of the medicinal product, then the *relevant monograph* is (a) the monograph (if any) headed by that name in the current edition of the specified publication; or (b) if there is no such monograph in the current edition of the publication *the appropriate current monograph* headed by that name; or (c) if there is no *appropriate current monograph*, then the monograph headed by that name in the latest edition of the specified publication which contained a monograph so headed.

3   If no publication is specified together with the name of the medicinal product, the *relevant monograph* is *the appropriate current monograph*, if any [s.65(4)].

Appropriate current monograph, in relation to a particular name, means the monograph (if any) headed by that name, or by a name for which it is an approved synonym, in the current edition of: (a) the *European Pharmacopoeia*; or (b) the *British Pharmacopoeia*; or (c) a compendium published under section 99 of the Act; or (d) the *British Pharmaceutical Codex* or the *British Veterinary Codex,* taken in that order of precedence.

Current means current at the time when the medicinal product in question is demanded, described in a prescription or offered or exposed for sale; and the current edition of a publication is the one in force at that time, together with any amendments, alterations or deletions. If the reference is to an edition previous to the current edition, it must be taken as it was immediately before the time when it was superseded by a subsequent edition of that publication. Any monograph shall be construed in accordance with any general monograph, notice, appendix, note or other explanatory material applicable to the monograph which is contained in the relevant edition of the publication [s.65(5) and (6)].

Specifications in licences

When reference is made in a licence or certificate (Part II of the Act) to a publication specified in the Act, but no particular edition is mentioned, then it is to be construed as the current edition, that is, with any amendment, alteration or deletion made up to the date of issue of the licence or certificate (s.103). The publications specified are those mentioned above, that is the *European Pharmacopoeia*, the *British Pharmacopoeia*, the *British Pharmaceutical Codex*, the *British Veterinary Codex*, and compendia prepared under section 99 of the Act, and the lists of names prepared under section 100 of the Act, together with the *British National Formulary* and the *Dental Practitioners' Formulary.*

These two formularies are published jointly by the British Medical Association and the Royal Pharmaceutical Society of Great Britain. The *British National Formulary* is a standard formulary, with notes on drugs and other information for medical practitioners and pharmacists, which is recognised for use in the NHS. The *Dental Practitioners' Formulary* similarly provides standard formulae, notes and information relating to dental treatment pharmacopoeias and other publications.

Summary

• The *British Pharmacopoeia* comprises descriptions and standards for substances and articles which may be used in medicine other than veterinary medicine together with substances and articles used in the manufacture of medicinal products.

- The *European Pharmacopoeia*, where appropriate, takes precedence over the standards in other publications.
- It is an offence to sell, supply or dispense a medicinal product of a particular name if that name is at the head of a monograph in a pharmacopoeia and the product does not comply with the standard specified in that monograph.

CHAPTER SEVENTEEN

Misuse of Drugs Act 1971

During 2004, information has been received in several reports of the Shipman Report that will undoubtedly lead to new regulations concerning the supply and control of Controlled Drugs. It is not anticipated that any consultations to alter the distribution of such drugs will be published until mid 2005 and subsequent legislation be implemented until the end of 2005. In the meanwhile the following is the current law.

The Misuse of Drugs Act 1971 came into operation on 1 July 1973 [SI 1973 No.795 (C.20)]. It consolidates and extends previous legislation and controls the export, import, production, supply and possession of dangerous or otherwise harmful drugs. The Act is also designed to deal with the control and treatment of addicts and to promote education and research relating to drug dependence. It extends to Northern Ireland (s.38).

In relation to drugs the Act is largely restrictive in its terms, although it does provide for licences to be issued for importation and exportation (s.3). Apart from that, the general effect is to render unlawful all activities in the drugs that are controlled under the Act, except as provided in the regulations made under the Act. The extent to which these regulations relax the restrictions is dealt with later in this chapter.

Advisory Council on Misuse of Drugs

The *Advisory Council* (s.1) was formally established from 1 February 1972 [SI 1971 No.2120 (C.57)] replacing the former Advisory Committee on Drug Dependence, which had no statutory authority. It advises the Ministers, that is, the Secretary of State for the Home Department, and the Ministers responsible for Health and Education in England, Wales, Scotland and Northern Ireland.

The Council consists of not fewer than 20 members appointed by the Secretary of State after consultation with such organisations as s/he considers appropriate, including at least one person appearing to the Secretary of State to have wide and recent experience in each of the following:

1   the practice of medicine (other than veterinary medicine);
2   the practice of dentistry;
3   the practice of veterinary medicine;
4   the practice of pharmacy;
5   the pharmaceutical industry; or
6   chemistry other than pharmaceutical chemistry;

together with persons appearing to the Secretary of State to have wide and recent experience of social problems connected with the misuse of drugs (Sch.1 to the Act). The Secretary of State appoints one of the members of the Advisory Council to be chairman of the Council, and the Council may appoint committees and include on them persons who are not members of the Council.

The Council is required to keep under review the situation in the UK with respect to drugs which are being, or appear to them likely to be, misused (s.1). If it considers that misuse could cause harmful effects which might constitute a social problem, it has a duty to advise the Ministers on the action to be taken. In particular it must advise on measures:

1   to restrict the availability of such drugs or to supervise the arrangements for their supply;
2   to enable persons affected by the misuse of such drugs to obtain proper advice, and to secure the provision of proper facilities and services for the treatment, rehabilitation and aftercare of such persons;
3   to promote co-operation between the various professional and community services which, in the opinion of the Council, have a part to play in dealing with social problems connected with the misuse of such drugs;
4   to educate the public (and in particular the young) in the dangers of abusing such drugs, and to give publicity to those dangers; and
5   to promote research into, or otherwise to obtain information about, any matter which in the opinion of the Council is of relevance for the purpose of preventing the misuse of such drugs or dealing with any social problem connected with their misuse. The Secretary of State has authority to conduct or assist in conducting such research (s.32).

The Advisory Council also has a duty to advise on any matter relating to drug dependence or misuse of drugs which any of the Ministers may refer to it. In particular, the Council is required to advise the Secretary of State on communications relating to the control of any dangerous or otherwise harmful drug received from any authority established under a treaty, convention or other agreement to which HM Government is a party. Before any regulations are made under the Act, the Advisory Council must be consulted [s.31(3)].

Class A, Class B and Class C drugs

The drugs subject to control are listed in Schedule 2 to the Act and the term *Controlled Drug* means any substance or product so listed. The schedule is divided into three parts or classes largely on the basis of decreasing order of harmfulness: Part I (Class A), Part II (Class B) and Part III (Class C). This division into three classes is solely for the purpose of determining penalties for offences under the Act (s.25) (Appendix 8).

Changes may be made to the list of Controlled Drugs subject to consultation with the Advisory Council. Amendment is made by an Order in Council, which must be approved by an affirmative resolution of each House of Parliament (s.2).

It should be noted that the classification of Controlled Drugs for purposes of the regimes of control which must be applied to drugs when used for lawful purposes appears in the schedules to the Misuse of Drugs Regulations 2001. This classification is of importance to practitioners and pharmacists in their daily work and is set out in Appendix 9.

Restrictions and exemptions

The importation or exportation of Controlled Drugs is prohibited, except in accordance with a licence issued by the Secretary of State or when permitted by regulations (s.3). Certain activities are specifically declared to be unlawful:

1   producing a Controlled Drug (s.4);
2   supplying or offering to supply a Controlled Drug to another person (s.4);
3   possessing a Controlled Drug (s.5); or
4   cultivating any plant of the genus *Cannabis* (s.6).

Producing a Controlled Drug means producing it by manufacture, cultivation or any other method, and *supplying* includes distribution (s.37). For the purposes of the Act the things which a person has in his/her possession are taken to include anything subject to his/her control which is in the custody of another (s.37). *Cannabis* (except in the expression *cannabis resin*) means any plant of the genus *Cannabis* or any part of any such plant (by whatever name designated) except that it does not include cannabis resin or any of the following products after separation from the rest of the plant, namely (Criminal Law Act 1977, s.52):

1   mature stalk of any such plant;
2   fibre produced from mature stalk of any such plant; and
3   seed of any such plant.

Exemptions from these controls may be authorised by the Secretary of State. S/he may:

1   by regulations, exempt any specified Controlled Drug from any of the restrictions on import, export, production, supply or possession (s.7);
2   by regulations, make it lawful for persons to produce, supply or possess Controlled Drugs to the extent which s/he thinks fit (s.7); or
3   permit by licence or other authority any of the activities in 2 and prescribe any conditions to be complied with (s.7).

The Secretary of State must exercise his/her powers to make regulations so as to secure appropriate exemptions for the possession, supply, manufacture or compounding of Controlled Drugs by practitioners, pharmacists and persons lawfully conducting retail pharmacy businesses, and for prescribing and administration by practitioners (s.7). The term *practitioner* (except in the expression veterinary practitioner) means a doctor, dentist, veterinary practitioner or veterinary surgeon (s.37).

If the Secretary of State considers that it is in the public interest for a drug to be used only for the purposes of research or other special purposes, s/he may make an order to that effect. It is then unlawful for a practitioner, pharmacist or a person lawfully conducting a retail pharmacy business to do anything in relation to that drug except under licence. In this connection *doing* things includes having things in one's possession. When making an order of this kind, the Secretary of State must act on the recommendation of the Advisory Council or after consulting that Council (s.7). Licence fees are prescribed in SI 1986 No.416, as amended.

The 2001 Regulations (SI 2001 No.3998) list 'exempted' products, which means a preparation or other product consists of one or more parts any of which contains a Controlled Drug where:

1   the preparation or other product is not designed for administration of the Controlled Drug to a human being or animal;
2   the Controlled Drug in any component part is packaged in such a form or in combination with other active or inert substances in such a manner that it cannot be recovered by readily applicable means or in a yield which constitutes a risk to health; or
3   no one component part of the product or combination contains more than 1 mg of the Controlled Drug or 1 microgram in the case of lysergide or any other N-alkyl derivative of lysergamide.

Other exemptions will apply, for example to *in vitro* diagnostic devices or kits used by laboratories for the detection of drugs of misuse or for clinical diagnosis, or other products containing very small quantities of Controlled Drugs (e.g. radioactive research compounds). The provisions of the Act will apply to the possession of a stock of Controlled Drugs for the purpose of producing kits and other exempted products. The safe custody regulations will also apply to any stock of Schedule 1 and 2 Controlled Drugs and stocks of buprenorphine, diethylpropion, flunitrazepam and temazepam held for the propose of manufacture of the exempted products.

Supply of articles for administering or preparing Controlled Drugs

The following persons:

- a practitioner;
- a pharmacist; and
- a person employed or engaged in the lawful provision of drug treatment services and acting in their capacity as such

may supply or offer to supply the following articles:

- a swab;
- utensils for the preparation of a controlled drug;
- citric acid;
- a filter; and
- ampoules of water for injection

only when supplied or offered for supply in accordance with the Medicines Act and its regulations.

Provisions for preventing misuse

The Secretary of State may make such regulations as appear to him/her necessary or expedient for preventing the misuse of Controlled Drugs (s.10). In particular s/he may make provisions that:

1   require precautions to be taken for the safe custody of Controlled Drugs;
2   impose requirements as to the documentation of transactions involving Controlled Drugs, and require copies of documents relating to such transactions to be furnished to the prescribed authority;

3   require the keeping of records and the furnishing of information with respect to Controlled Drugs and in such circumstances and in such manner as may be prescribed;

4   provide for the inspection of any precautions taken or records kept in pursuance of regulations under this section;

5   relate to the packaging and labelling of Controlled Drugs;

6   regulate the transport of Controlled Drugs and the methods used for destroying or otherwise disposing of such drugs when no longer required;

7   regulate the issue of prescriptions containing Controlled Drugs and the supply of Controlled Drugs on prescriptions, and require persons issuing or dispensing prescriptions containing such drugs to furnish to the prescribed authority such information relating to those prescriptions as may be prescribed;

8   require any doctor who attends a person who, s/he considers or has reasonable grounds to suspect, is addicted (within the meaning of the regulations) to Controlled Drugs of any description to furnish to the pre-scribed authority such particulars with respect to that person as may be prescribed; and

9   prohibit any doctor from administering, supplying and authorising the administration and supply to persons so addicted, and from prescribing for such persons, such Controlled Drugs as may be prescribed, except and in accordance with the terms of a licence issued by the Secretary of State in pursuance of the regulations.

In addition to making regulations about safe custody, the Secretary of State may also, by notice in writing, require the occupier of any premises where Controlled Drugs are kept to take further precautions as specified in the notice (s.11).

Information concerning misuse

Doctors, pharmacists and persons lawfully conducting retail pharmacy busi-nesses in any area may be called upon to give particulars of the quantities of any dangerous or otherwise harmful drugs (not necessarily controlled under the Act) which have been prescribed, administered or supplied over a particu-lar period of time. The Secretary of State may call for this information if it appears to him/her that a social problem exists in that area caused by a drug or drugs.

A notice in writing may be served on the persons concerned specifying the period, and requiring particulars of the drug to be furnished in such a manner and within such time as set out in the notice. Pharmacists may be required to give the names and addresses of the prescribing doctors but may not be required to identify the patients concerned. It is an offence to fail, without reasonable excuse, to give the information required or to give false information (s.17).

Prohibition on possession, prescribing and supply

Directions following convictions

Where a pharmacist or practitioner has been guilty of any offence under the Act or any offence under the Customs and Excise Act 1952 or the Customs and Excise Management Act 1979 relating to the unlawful importation or exportation of Controlled Drugs, the Secretary of State may make a direction in respect of him/her. If s/he is a practitioner, the direction will prohibit him/her from having in his/her possession, prescribing, administering, manufacturing, compounding and supplying, and from authorising the administration and supply of, the Controlled Drugs specified in the direction. If s/he is a pharmacist, the direction will prohibit him/her from having in his/her possession, manufacturing, compounding and supplying and from supervising and controlling the manufacture, compounding and supply of the Controlled Drugs specified in the direction (s.12).

A copy of any such direction given by the Secretary of State must be served on the person to whom it applies and notice of it must be published in the London, Edinburgh and Belfast *Gazettes*. A direction takes effect when a copy has been served on the person concerned and it is then an offence for him/her to contravene it. The Secretary of State may cancel or suspend any direction which s/he has given. S/he may also bring a suspended direction into force again by cancelling its suspension (ss.12, 13 and 16).

Conviction for an offence under the Act committed by a pharmacist or other person who is a director, officer or employee of a body corporate carrying on a retail pharmacy business renders that body liable to disqualification under Part IV of the Medicines Act 1968 (s.80) and consequent removal of its premises from the register of pharmacies (Chapter 22).

Prohibitions affecting doctors

If a doctor contravenes the regulations relating to notification of addicts or the prescribing of Controlled Drugs for addicts, s/he does not commit any offence under the Act. The Secretary of State may, however, make a direction prohibiting him/her from prescribing, administering or supplying or authorising the administration or supply of the Controlled Drugs specified in the direction. The doctor commits an offence if s/he contravenes that direction (s.13).

Irresponsible prescribing

If the Secretary of State is of the opinion that a practitioner has been prescribing, administering or supplying, or authorising the administration or supply of, any Controlled Drugs in an irresponsible manner, s/he may give a direction in respect of the practitioner concerned prohibiting him/her from prescribing, administering and supplying or authorising the administration and supply of the Controlled Drugs specified in the direction (s.13).

Tribunals, advisory bodies and professional panels

Before s/he gives a direction prohibiting a doctor or other practitioner from prescribing, administering or supplying Controlled Drugs, the Secretary of State must, except when the direction is based on a conviction, follow the procedure set out in the Act (ss.14, 15 and 16). S/he must refer the case to a *tribunal* consisting of four members of the practitioner's profession and with a lawyer as chairman (Sch.3). The procedure to be followed before tribunals is in SI 1974 No.85 (L.1) and, for Scotland, SI 1975 No.459 (s.59). If, as a result of the tribunal's finding that the practitioner has been responsible for the contravention or conduct alleged, the Secretary of State then proposes to make a direction, the practitioner must be informed and given the opportunity to make representations in writing within 28 days. If the practitioner so does, then the case must be referred to an *advisory body* of three appointed persons, one being a member of the practitioner's profession. After receiving the advice of that body, the Secretary of State may (a) advise that no further proceedings be taken; (b) refer the case back to the same, or another, tribunal; or (c) give a direction under section 13 as described above (s.14).

In a case of irresponsible prescribing, if the Secretary of State considers circumstances require that a direction be given with the minimum of delay, s/he may refer the matter to a *professional panel* consisting of three members of the practitioner's profession appointed by the Secretary of State. The panel must afford the practitioner an opportunity to appear before it and, after considering the circumstances of the case, must report to the Secretary of State whether or not it believes there are reasonable grounds for thinking that there has been conduct as alleged. If the panel considers there are such grounds, the Secretary of State may give a direction at once which is effective for a period of six weeks. S/he must also refer the case at once to a tribunal, in accordance with the procedures outlined above. The period of operation of the temporary direction may be extended from time to time by a further 28 days if the tribunal consents. After the tribunal, or the advisory body as appropriate, has considered the case, the Secretary of State may, if s/he thinks fit, make a permanent direction, if that is the advice given to him/her. If no such direction is given, the temporary prohibition will cease (s.15).

Offences, penalties and enforcement

Schedule 4 to the Act is a tabulated summary of offences under the Act and the penalties applicable to them. The level of penalty for offences which concern a Controlled Drug varies according to the class (A, B or C) into which the drug falls, the generally more harmful drugs attracting greater penalties.

The occupier or manager of any premises commits an offence if s/he knowingly permits or suffers any of the following to take place on the premises:

1   producing or supplying, or attempting to produce or supply, or offering to supply any Controlled Drug in contravention of the Act;
2   preparing opium for smoking; or
3   smoking cannabis, cannabis resin or prepared opium (s.8).

It is an offence for any person to:

1   smoke or otherwise use prepared opium;
2   frequent a place used for the purpose of opium smoking; or
3   have in his/her possession:

(a)   any pipes or other utensils made or adapted for use in connection with the smoking of opium, being pipes or utensils which have been used by him/her or with his/her knowledge and permission in that connection or which s/he intends to use or permit others to use in that connection; or
(b)   any utensils which have been used by him/her or with his/her knowledge and permission in connection with the preparation of opium for smoking (s.9).

Other offences are described in some detail in Schedule 4. Those relating to contravention of regulations or of conditions of any licence, or of directions relating to safe custody of Controlled Drugs, are of special concern to practising pharmacists (ss.11 and 18).

A person commits an offence if in the UK s/he assists in or induces the commission in any place outside the UK of an offence punishable under the provisions of a corresponding law in force in that place (s.20).

Corresponding law means a law stated, in a certificate purporting to be issued by or on behalf of the Government of a country outside the UK, to be a law providing for the control and regulation in that country of the production, supply, use, export and import of:

1   drugs and other substances in accordance with the provisions of the Single Convention on Narcotic Drugs signed at New York on 30 March 1961; or
2   dangerous or otherwise harmful drugs in pursuance of any treaty, convention or other agreement or arrangement to which the government of that country and of the UK are parties (ss.20 and 36).

The unlawful import and export of Controlled Drugs is an offence under the Customs and Excise Management Act 1979, which provides penalties for improper importation or exportation or for fraudulent evasion of any prohibition or restriction affecting Controlled Drugs.

Attempting to commit an offence under any provision of the Act or inciting or attempting to incite another to commit such an offence are also offences. They attract the same penalty as the substantive offences (ss.19 and 25).

Where any offence under the Act committed by a body corporate is proved to have been committed with the consent or connivance of, or to be attributable to any neglect on the part of, any director, manager, secretary or other similar officer of the body corporate, or any person purporting to act in any such capacity, s/he, as well as the body corporate, is guilty of the offence and is liable to be proceeded against accordingly (s.21).

Proof that the accused neither knew of nor suspected, nor had reason to suspect, the existence of some fact which it is necessary for the prosecution to prove is a defence in connection with the offences of production, supply or possession of Controlled Drugs, cultivation of cannabis or possession of opium pipes and utensils. When it is necessary, in connection with any offence, to prove that a substance or product is a Controlled Drug, the accused may prove that s/he believed it to be a different Controlled Drug. This, in itself, will not constitute a defence unless there could have been no offence had the drug been of that description (s.28).

It is also a defence for a person accused of unlawful possession of a Controlled Drug to prove that s/he took possession of it to prevent another person committing an offence, and that s/he took steps to destroy it as soon as possible, or that s/he took possession of the drug to hand it over to some authorised person as soon as possible (s.5).

A constable, or other person authorised by the Secretary of State, has power to enter any premises used for the production and supply of Controlled Drugs and inspect books and documents and any stocks of drugs. An inspector of the Royal Pharmaceutical Society of Great Britain is authorised by the Secretary of State to inspect books and documents. It is an offence to conceal any such books, documents or stock.

A constable may also, on the authority of a warrant, enter any premises named in the warrant, by force if necessary, and search them and any person found therein, seizing any Controlled Drug or any document relevant to the transaction if s/he has reasonable grounds to consider that an offence under the Act has been committed (s.23).

A constable may arrest a person who has committed an offence under the Act, or whom s/he suspects has committed an offence, if that person's name and address are unknown to him/her or cannot be ascertained, or if s/he suspects the name and address are false, or if s/he has reasonable cause to think that the person may abscond unless arrested (s.24). S/he may detain for the purposes of search any person whom s/he has reasonable grounds to suspect is in unlawful possession of a Controlled Drug. S/he may also stop and search any vehicle or vessel for the same reason and may seize anything which appears to be evidence of an offence under the Act (s.23).

It is an offence intentionally to obstruct a person exercising their powers of examination or search. Failure to produce any book or document without reasonable excuse is also an offence, and proof of the reasonableness of the excuse rests with the person offering it as a defence (s.23).

Upon a conviction, anything relating to the offence may be forfeited and destroyed or otherwise dealt with by order of the court, subject to any person claiming to be the owner showing cause why the order should not be made (s.27). The Drug Trafficking Offences Act 1986 provides for the confiscation of the proceeds of drug trafficking received by convicted persons.

Scheduled substances: precursors

Scheduled substances means those substances which are useful for the manufacture of Controlled Drugs.

Council Regulation 90/3677/EEC controls the import, export, recording and labelling of scheduled substances and the power to enter business premises to obtain evidence of irregularities. Records must be kept for two years. It also requires member states to adopt measures to enable them to obtain information on any orders for, or activities in, scheduled substances. There is a list of scheduled substances.

The EC regulation was implemented by the Criminal Justice (International Co-operation) Act 1990 (s.12), which created the offences of manufacturing or supplying scheduled substances knowing or suspecting they are to be used in or for the unlawful production of a Controlled Drug. Regulations made under the 1990 Act (s.13) enable the other requirements of the EC regulation to be investigated and enforced (SI 1991 No.1285, as amended).

Council Directive 92/109/EEC, which is complementary to the above EC regulation, applies to the manufacture and trade in scheduled substances within the EU and is implemented in the UK by the Controlled Drugs (Substances Useful for Manufacture) (Intra-Community Trade) Regulations SI 1993 No.2166, as amended by SI 2004 No.850. It requires the person who manufactures or trades in these substances to be licensed and restricts the persons to whom supplies may be made. The 1993 UK regulations as amended treat the provisions of Council Directive 92/109/EEC as if they were requirements of regulations made under section 13 of the 1990 Act.

Powers of the Secretary of State

The power of the Secretary of State to make regulations is exercised by statutory instruments (ss.7, 10, 22 and 31). Regulations may make provision for different cases and circumstances and for different Controlled Drugs and different classes of person. The opinion, consent or approval of a prescribed authority or of any person may also be made material to a regulation (e.g. the approval of a chief officer of police is required in connection with certain safekeeping requirements for drugs) (s.31). Any licence or other authority issued by the Secretary of State for the purposes of the Act may be made subject to such conditions as s/he thinks proper and may be modified or revoked at any time (s.30).

The application of any provision of the Act which creates an offence, and those provisions of the Customs and Excise Management Act 1979 which apply to the importation and exportation of Controlled Drugs (see p. 191), may, in prescribed cases, be excluded by regulation. Similarly, any provision of the Act or any regulation or order made under it may, by regulation, be made applicable to servants and agents of the Crown (s.22).

Most of the regulations are designed to render lawful various activities in connection with Controlled Drugs which would otherwise be unlawful under the Act. For example, they are necessary to enable doctors, pharmacists and others to prescribe, administer, manufacture, compound or supply Controlled Drugs as appropriate to their particular capacities. They also govern such matters as the safekeeping of Controlled Drugs and their destruction, the notification of addicts and the supply of Controlled Drugs to addicts.

Regimes of control

The drugs controlled under the Act are classified in the Misuse of Drugs Regulations 2001 (SI 2001 No.3998, as amended) into five schedules in descending order of control, the most stringent controls applying to drugs in Schedule 1. All the schedules are set out fully in Appendix 9 and the controls applying to each are outlined below.

Schedule 1

Schedule 1 lists Controlled Drugs which may not be used for medicinal purposes, their production and possession being limited, in the public interest, to purposes of research or other special purposes. Certain limited classes of person have a general authority to possess these drugs in the course of their duties, e.g. constables, carriers, etc. (reg.6). Other persons may only produce, supply or possess the drugs within the authority of a licence issued by the Secretary of State. The requirements of the Misuse of Drugs Regulations relating to (a) documentation, (b) keeping of records, (c) preservation of records, (d) supply on prescription, (e) marking of containers and (f) procedure for destruction, apply in full to these drugs in Schedule 1.

Schedule 2

Schedule 2 includes the opiates (such as diamorphine (heroin), morphine and methadone) and the major stimulants (such as the amphetamines). A licence is needed to import or export drugs in this schedule, but they may be manufactured or compounded by a practitioner, a pharmacist, a person lawfully conducting a retail pharmacy business acting in their capacity as such or a person holding an appropriate licence. A pharmacist may supply a Schedule 2 drug to a patient (or the owner of an animal) only on the authority of a prescription in the required form issued by an appropriate practitioner (rcgs.15 and 16).

The drugs may only be administered to a patient by a doctor or dentist, or by any person acting in accordance with the directions of a doctor or dentist (reg.7). Requirements as to safe custody in pharmacies and control over destruction apply to these drugs, and the provisions relating to the marking of containers and the keeping of records must also be observed (regs.18 and 19). A list of persons who may lawfully possess or supply them is given on page 197.

Schedule 3

Schedule 3 includes the barbiturates [except secobarbital (quinalbarbitone), which is a Schedule 2 Controlled Drug] and a number of minor stimulant drugs, such as benzfetamine (benzphetamine) and other drugs which are not thought likely to be so harmful when misused as the drugs in Schedule 2. The controls which apply to Schedule 2 also apply to drugs in this schedule, except that:

1   they may also be manufactured by persons authorised in writing by the Secretary of State;
2   there is a difference in the classes of person who may possess and supply them;
3   the requirements as to destruction do not apply to retail dealers; and
4   entries in the Register of Controlled Drugs need not be made in respect of these drugs but invoices or like records must be kept for a period of two years (see p. 207).

Schedule 4, Part I

Part I of Schedule 4 contains the benzodiazepine tranquillisers. The restrictions applicable to Schedule 3 drugs apply to them with the relaxations as for Schedule 4, Part I drugs at 1, 2, 3, 4 and 5 above. There is no restriction on imports and exports.

Schedule 4, Part II

Part II of Schedule 4 contains the anabolic and androgenic steroids and derivatives, together with an adrenoceptor stimulant and polypeptide hormones. The restrictions applicable to Schedule 3 drugs apply to them with the following relaxations:

1   there is no restriction on the possession of any Schedule 4, Part II drug when contained in a medicinal product;
2   prescription and labelling requirements under the Misuse of Drugs Act do not apply, but the provisions of the Medicines Act do apply;

3   records need not be kept by retailers;
4   destruction requirements apply only to importers, exporters and manu-
      facturers;
5   there are no safe custody requirements;
6   there is no restriction on imports or exports *provided* they are imported
      or exported:

   (a)   in the form of a medicinal product; *and*
   (b)   by a person for administration to him/herself.

Schedule 5

Schedule 5 specifies those preparations of certain Controlled Drugs for which
there is only negligible risk of abuse. There is no restriction on the import,
export, possession or administration of these preparations, and safe custody
requirements do not apply to them. A practitioner or pharmacist, acting in
his/her capacity as such, or a person holding an appropriate licence, may
manufacture or compound any of them.

   No record in the Register of Controlled Drugs need be made in respect of
Schedule 3, 4 or 5 drugs obtained by a retail dealer but the invoice, or a copy
of it, must be kept for two years. Producers and wholesale dealers must retain
invoices of quantities obtained and supplied [reg.24(1)]. No authority is
required to destroy these drugs, and there are no special labelling requirements, though Medicines Act labelling requirements apply. A *retail dealer* is
defined as a person lawfully conducting a retail pharmacy business or a
pharmacist engaged in supplying drugs to the public at a NHS health centre.

Poppy straw

Poppy straw, which includes poppy heads, is listed as a Controlled Drug in
Schedule 2 to the Act, where it is defined as 'all parts, except the seeds, of the
opium poppy, after mowing'. It is not included in any of the schedules to the
regulations. Although a licence is required to import or export poppy straw,
its production, possession and supply are free from control (reg.4). *Concentrate of poppy straw,* which means the material produced when poppy straw
has entered into a process for the concentration of its alkaloids, is included in
Schedule 1 to the regulations to which apply the stringent controls described
above.

Import and export

Controlled Drugs may only be imported or exported in accordance with the
terms and conditions of a licence issued by the Secretary of State (s.3 of the
Act) but drugs in Schedules 4 (Part II) and 5 are exempted from this

requirement (reg.4). Drugs in Schedule 4 Part I are subject to certain restrictions (see p. 195). Unlawful import or export is an offence under the Customs and Excise Management Act 1979 (see p. 191).

The 2001 regulations include the exemption for drugs included in Part II of Schedule 4 in the form of medicinal products that were imported or exported by any person for administration to him/herself.

Possession and supply

It is unlawful for any person to be in possession of a Controlled Drug unless:

1   s/he holds an appropriate licence from or is registered by the Secretary of State (reg.10);
2   s/he is a member of a class specified in the regulations and is acting in his/her capacity as a member of that class (regs.6 and 10); or
3   the regulations provide that possession of that drug or group of drugs is not unlawful.

Possession of poppy straw or drugs in Schedule 5 and medicinal products in Schedule 4 are not controlled (reg.4).

The classes of person who may possess or supply Controlled Drugs are given in Table 17.1, with an indication of the range of drugs they may possess and/or supply. A person authorised to supply may supply only those persons authorised to possess, and such supply is subject to any provisions of the Medicines Act 1968 which apply to the drug being supplied.

Table 17.1   Possession and supply of Controlled Drugs

	Class of person	Possession	Supply
1	A person holding an appropriate licence from the Home Office	S1 S2 S3 S4 S5	S1 S2 S3 S4 S5
2	A constable when acting in the course of his/her duty	S1 S2 S3 S4 S5	S1 S2 S3 S4 S5
3	A person engaged in the business of a carrier when acting in the course of that business	S1 S2 S3 S4 S5	S1 S2 S3 S4 S5
4	A person engaged in the business of a postal operator when acting in the course of that business (SI 2003 No.1653)	S1 S2 S3 S4 S5	S1 S2 S3 S4 S5
5	An officer of Customs and Excise when acting in the course of his/her duty as such	S1 S2 S3 S4 S5	S1 S2 S3 S4 S5

6 A person engaged in the work of any laboratory to which the drug has been sent for forensic examination when acting in the course of his/her duty as a person so engaged [The supply of any Controlled Drug by any person in categories 1–6 above may only be to a person who may lawfully possess that drug]	S1 S2 S3 S4 S5	S1 S2 S3 S4 S5
7 A person engaged in conveying the drug to a person authorised by the regulations to have it in his/her possession (see under Requisitions p. 203)	S1 S2 S3 S4 S5	S1 S2 S3 S4 S5
8 A person possessing a drug for administration in accordance with the directions of a practitioner (for example, on a prescription) [The Home Office take the view that it is unlawful for a doctor to possess a Controlled Drug on the strength of a prescription issued by him/herself and naming him/herself as patient (*Pharm J* 8 October 1977 p. 328)]	S2 S3 S4 S5	
9 A person authorised under a group authority	S2 S3 S4 S5	S2 S3 S4 S5
10 A practitioner	S2 S3 S4 S5	S2 S3 S4 S5
11 A pharmacist	S2 S3 S4 S5	S2 S3 S4 S5
12 A person lawfully conducting a retail pharmacy business	S2 S3 S4 S5	S2 S3 S4 S5
13 The person in charge or acting person in charge of a hospital or nursing home, which is wholly or mainly maintained by a public authority out of public funds or by a charity or by voluntary subscriptions (cf. 24 below) may not supply if there is a pharmacist responsible for dispensing and supply of drugs	S2 S3 S4 S5	S2 S3 S4 S5
14 The sister or acting sister for the time being in charge of a ward, theatre or other department in a hospital or nursing home as in 13, in the case of drugs supplied to him/her by a person responsible for the dispensing and supply of medicines at the hospital or nursing home (cf. 25 below). *Sister or acting sister* includes any male nurse occupying a similar position. Supply subject to direction by doctor or dentist	S2 S3 S4 S5	S2 S3 S4 S5

15 A person who is in charge of a laboratory, the recognised activities of which consist in, or include, the conduct of scientific education or research and which is attached to a university, university college or a hospital as described in 13 or to any other institution approved for the purpose by the Secretary of State (cf. 26 below)

S2 S3 S4 S5   S2 S3 S4 S5

16 A public analyst appointed under section 89 of the Food and Drugs Act 1955 or section 27 of the Food and Drugs (Scotland) Act 1956

S2 S3 S4 S5   S2 S3 S4 S5

17 A sampling officer within the meaning of the Food and Drugs Act 1955 or the Food and Drugs (Scotland) Act 1956

S2 S3 S4 S5   S2 S3 S4 S5

18 A sampling officer within the meaning of Schedule 3 to the Medicines Act 1968

S2 S3 S4 S5   S2 S3 S4 S5

19 A person employed or engaged in connection with a scheme for testing the quality or amount of the drugs, preparations and appliances supplied under the National Health Service Act 1946 or the National Health Service (Scotland) Act 1947 and the regulations made thereunder

S2 S3 S4 S5   S2 S3 S4 S5

20 A person authorised by the Royal Pharmaceutical Society of Great Britain for the purposes of sections 108 and 109 of the Medicines Act 1968

S2 S3 S4 S5   S2 S3 S4 S5

21 The owner or master of a ship (which is not carrying a doctor) for the purposes of complying with the Health and Safety at Work, etc. Act 1974 or the Merchant Shipping Acts. *Master of ship* includes every person (except a pilot) having command or charge of any ship

S2 S3 S4 S5   S2 S3 S4 S5

22 The master of a foreign ship in port in Great Britain possessing drugs as necessary for the equipment of his ship and authorised by the local medical officer of health

S2 S3 S4 S5

23 The installation manager of an offshore   S2 S3 S4 S5   S2 S3 S4 S5
    installation possessing drugs for the pur-
    pose of compliance with the Health and
    Safety at Work etc. Act 1974, or the Min-
    eral Workings (Off-Shore Installations) Act
    1971. S/he may supply to (a) any person
    who may lawfully supply the drug; (b) any
    person on the installation whether
    employed there or not; (c) any constable
    for destruction

24 The person in charge or acting person in   S3 S4 S5   S3 S4 S5
    charge of a hospital or nursing home (cf.
    13 above). May not supply if there is a
    pharmacist responsible for dispensing and
    supply of drugs

25 The sister or acting sister for the time being   S3 S4 S5   S3 S4 S5
    in charge of a ward, theatre or other
    department in a hospital or nursing home
    in the case of drugs supplied to him/her by
    a person responsible for the dispensing and
    supply of medicines at the hospital or nurs-
    ing home (cf. 14 above). Supply subject to
    direction by doctor or dentist

26 A person in charge of a laboratory the   S3 S4 S5   S3 S4 S5
    recognised activities of which consist in, or
    include, the conduct of scientific education
    or research (cf. 15 above)

27 A person whose name is entered in a regis-   S3 S4 S5   S3 S4
    ter maintained by the Home Office relating
    to Schedule 3 drugs

28 A person authorised in writing by the Sec-   S5   S5
    retary of State

29 Registered practising midwives (see below   see below   see below
    for supply to midwives and administration)
    [reg.11]. Any Controlled Drug s/he may
    lawfully administer under the Medicines
    Act Regulations

30 A person licensed under the Wildlife and   S2 S3   S2 S3
    Countryside Act 1981

31 A registered nurse (SI 2003 No.2429)	A registered nurse may posses in accordance with a Patient Group Direction any drug specified in Schedule 4 and 5 to a person who can lawfully possess that drug except anabolic steroids or any preparation for injection	A registered nurse may supply in accordance with a Patient Group Direction any drug specified in Schedule 4 and 5 to a person who can lawfully possess that drug except anabolic steroids or any preparation for injection
32 A registered nurse (SI 2003 No.2429)	A registered nurse may possess in accordance with a Patient Group Direction diamorphine for the treatment of cardiac pain to a person admitted as a patient to a coronary care unit or an accident and emergency department of a hospital	A registered nurse may supply in accordance with a Patient Group Direction diamorphine for the treatment of cardiac pain to a person admitted as a patient to a coronary care unit or an accident and emergency department of a hospital
33 Extended formulary nurse prescriber (SI 2003 No.2429)	Only diazepam, lorazepam and midazolam for use in palliative care plus codeine phosphate, dihydrocodeine tartrate or co-phenotrope	Only diazepam, lorazepam and midazolam for use in palliative care plus codeine phosphate, dihydrocodeine tartrate or co-phenotrope

There are several other general authorities for possession and supply.

1 Any person who is lawfully in possession of a Controlled Drug may supply that drug to the person from whom s/he obtained it.

2 Any person who is in possession of a Schedule 2, 3, 4 or 5 drug which has been supplied for him/her by, or on the prescription of, a practitioner may supply that drug to any doctor, dentist or pharmacist *for the purpose of destruction*.

3   Any person who is in lawful possession of a Schedule 2, 3, 4 or 5 drug which has been supplied by, or on the prescription of, a veterinary surgeon or veterinary practitioner for the treatment of animals may supply that drug to any veterinary surgeon, veterinary practitioner or pharmacist *for the purpose of destruction.*

4   Any of the following persons may supply or administer a specified controlled drug under a Patient Group Direction

  • a person who holds a certificate of proficiency in ambulance paramedic skills issued by, or with the approval of, the Secretary of State or a person who is a state registered paramedic;
  • a registered health visitor;
  • a registered midwife;
  • a registered ophthalmic optician;
  • a state registered chiropodist;
  • a person who is registered in the register of orthoptists under the Health Professions Council;
  • a person who is registered in the register of physiotherapists under the Health Professions Council; or
  • a person who is registered in the register of radiographers under the Health Professions Council.

Midwives and pethidine

A registered midwife who has, in accordance with the Nurses, Midwives and Health Visitors Act 1997, notified to the local supervising authority his/her intention to practise may, as far as is necessary for the practice of his/her profession or employment as a midwife, possess and administer any Controlled Drug which the Medicines Act 1968 permits him/her to administer. Supplies may only be made to him/her, or possessed by him/her, on the authority of a *midwife's supply order,* that is, an order in writing specifying the name and occupation of the midwife obtaining the Controlled Drug, the purpose for which it is required and the total quantity to be obtained (reg.11). It must be signed by the *appropriate medical officer,* which means:

1   a doctor who is for the time being authorised in writing for the purpose of regulation 11 by the local supervising authority for the region or area in which the Controlled Drug was, or is to be, obtained; or

2   a person appointed by that authority to exercise supervision over certified midwives within their area, e.g. a non-medical supervisor of midwives.

A midwife may surrender any stocks of Controlled Drugs in his/her possession which are no longer required by him/her to a doctor falling within category 1 above (reg.11) or to the person from whom s/he obtained them (reg.6).

The midwife must, on each occasion on which s/he obtains a supply of a Controlled Drug, enter in a book kept by him/her solely for this purpose: (a)

the date and (b) the name and address of the person from whom the drug was obtained; the amount obtained; and the form in which it was obtained. When administering any Controlled Drug to a patient, s/he must enter in the same book as soon as practicable the name and address of the patient, the amount administered and the form in which it was administered (reg.21).

A midwife's supply order must be retained for two years by the pharmacist who supplies the Controlled Drug and s/he must make an appropriate entry in his/her Controlled Drugs register (regs.19 and 22).

Requisitions

A requisition in writing must be obtained by a supplier before s/he delivers any Controlled Drug except those in Schedules 4 and 5, poppy straw or any drug in Schedule 3 contained in or comprising a preparation which (a) is required for use as a buffering agent in chemical analysis, (b) has present both a substance in the schedule and a salt of that substance, and (c) is pre-mixed in a kit [reg.14(7)]. A *supplier*, in this context, means any person who is not a practitioner supplying such a Controlled Drug, otherwise than on prescription, or by way of administration, to any of the following *recipients*:

1 a practitioner;
2 the person in charge or acting person in charge of a hospital or nursing home;
3 a person who is in charge of a laboratory;
4 the owner of a ship, or the master of a ship which does not carry a doctor among the seamen employed in it;
5 the installation manager of an off-shore installation; or
6 the master of a foreign ship in a port in Great Britain [reg.14(4)].

The requisition must be signed by the recipient; must state his/her name, address and profession or occupation; and must specify the total quantity of the drug and the purpose for which it is required. A *wholesale dealer*, that is a person who carries on the business of selling drugs to persons who buy to sell again, when supplying a pharmacist does not require a requisition. The supplier must be reasonably satisfied that the signature is that of the person purporting to have signed the requisition and that s/he is engaged in the profession or occupation stated [reg.14(2)].

Where a supplier, who is not a practitioner, supplies a Controlled Drug for which a requisition is required, s/he may not supply it to any person sent on behalf of the recipient to collect the drug unless that person (a) is authorised to have the drug in his/her possession otherwise than as a messenger; or (b) produces to the supplier a statement in writing signed by the recipient to the effect that s/he is empowered by the recipient to receive the drug on his/her behalf, and the supplier is reasonably satisfied that the document is a genuine document [reg.14(1)].

Where a recipient is a practitioner who represents that s/he urgently requires a Controlled Drug for the purpose of his/her profession, the supplier, if s/he is reasonably satisfied that the practitioner requires the drug and is by reason of some emergency unable to furnish a written requisition, may deliver the drug on an undertaking by the practitioner to furnish a written requisition within the next 24 hours. Failure to do so is an offence on the part of the practitioner [reg.14(2)].

A requisition furnished by the master of a foreign ship must contain a statement signed by the proper officer of the port health authority or, in Scotland, the Medical Officer designated under section 14 of the National Health Service (Scotland) Act 1978 by the Health Board within whose jurisdiction the ship is that the quantity of drug to be supplied is the quantity necessary for the equipment of the ship [reg.14(5)].

A requisition furnished by the matron or acting matron of a hospital or nursing home must also be signed by a doctor or a dentist employed or engaged in that hospital or nursing home [reg.14(5)].

A *sister* or *acting sister* for the time being in charge of any ward, theatre or other department of a hospital or nursing home who obtains a supply of a Controlled Drug from the person responsible for dispensing and supplying medicines at that hospital or nursing home must furnish a requisition in writing signed by him/her which specifies the total quantity of the drug required. S/he must retain a copy or note of the requisition. The person responsible for the dispensing and supply of medicines must mark the requisition in such a manner as to show that it has been complied with and must retain the requisition in the dispensary [reg.14(6)].

Prescriptions for Controlled Drugs

Prescription means a prescription used by a doctor for the medical treatment of a single individual, by a dentist for the dental treatment of a single individual, or by a veterinary surgeon or veterinary practitioner for the purposes of animal treatment.

No prescription requirements are laid down for any Controlled Drug in Schedules 4 or 5 to the regulations. Neither are there any prescription requirements for the drug temazepam. In the case of other Controlled Drugs (i.e. those in Schedules 2 and 3), a prescription must not be issued unless it complies with the following requirements:

1   it must be in ink or otherwise indelible and be signed by the person issuing it with their usual signature and dated by them (it is unlikely that a carbon copy, even one bearing an original signature, would be sufficient to satisfy the indelibility requirement);

2   except in the case of a health prescription, it must specify the address of the person issuing it;

3   it must have written thereon, if issued by a dentist, the words *for dental treatment only* and, if issued by a veterinary surgeon or a veterinary

practitioner, a declaration that the Controlled Drug prescribed is for an animal under his/her care;

4   it must specify, in the handwriting of the person issuing it, the name and address of the person for whose treatment it is issued or, if it is issued by a veterinary surgeon or veterinary practitioner, the name and address of the person to whom the Controlled Drug prescribed is to be delivered;

5   it must specify, in the handwriting of the person issuing it, the dose to be taken and

(a)   in the case of a prescription containing a Controlled Drug which is a preparation, it must specify the form and, where appropriate, the strength of the preparation, and either the total quantity (in both words and figures) of the preparation or the number (in both words and figures) of dosage units, as appropriate, to be supplied;

(b)   in any other case, it must specify the total quantity (in both words and figures) of the Controlled Drug to be supplied;

6   in the case of a prescription for a total quantity intended to be dispensed by instalments, it must contain a direction specifying the amount of the instalments of the total amount which must be dispensed and the intervals to be observed when dispensing [reg.15(1)].

The requirement that the particulars in 4 and 5 above must be in the prescriber's own handwriting does not apply to a prescription containing no drug other than (a) phenobarbital, (b) phenobarbital sodium or (c) a preparation containing either of those drugs. The requirement can also be waived by the Secretary of State in relation to a prescription issued by a prescriber approved for this purpose either personally or as a member of class. This latter exemption is used to facilitate the issue of prescriptions from treatment centres for drug addiction [reg.15(2)].

A prescription issued for the treatment of a patient in a hospital or nursing home and written on the patient's bed card or case sheet need not specify the address of the patient [reg.15(3)].

When a drug is administered from stock held in the ward, the prescription requirements do not apply.

A Controlled Drug, except those in Schedules 4 and 5 must not be supplied by any person on a prescription:

1   unless the prescription complies with the provisions set out above;

2   unless the prescriber's address on the prescription is within the UK;

3   unless the supplier is either acquainted with the prescriber's signature, and has no reason to suppose that it is not genuine, or has taken reasonably sufficient steps to satisfy him/herself that it is genuine;

4   before the date specified on the prescription; or

5   later than 13 weeks after the date specified on the prescription unless it is an instalment prescription (see below).[Reg 16].

Prescriptions (other than those for drugs in Schs.4 or 5) which contain a direction that specified instalments of the total amount may be supplied at stated intervals must not be supplied otherwise than in accordance with the directions:

1   the first instalment must be supplied not later than 13 weeks after the date specified in the prescription;
2   the prescription must be marked with the date at the time when each instalment is supplied;
3   the prescription must be retained for two years after the supply of the last instalment; and
4   repeat prescriptions as such are not provided for, in that the total quantity of drug prescribed must be stated on the prescription [regs.16(4) and 23(3)].

A person supplying temazepam in accordance with an electronic prescription shall at the time of supply enter on the form by electronic means the date on which the drug was supplied [16(3) of the 2001 Regulations].

Nothing in the regulations relating to prescriptions (regs.15 and 16) has effect in relation to prescriptions issued for the purposes of a scheme for testing the quality and amount of the drugs, preparations and appliances supplied under the NHS, or to any prescriptions issued to sampling officers under the Food and Drugs (Scotland) Act 1956 or the Medicines Act 1968 (reg.17).

A person is not in lawful possession of a drug if s/he obtained it on a prescription which s/he obtained from the prescriber (a) by making a false statement or declaration or (b) by not disclosing to the doctor that s/he was being supplied with a Controlled Drug by or on the prescription of another doctor [reg.10(2)].

Marking of containers

The container in which a Controlled Drug, other than a preparation, is supplied must be plainly marked with the amount of drug contained in it. If the drug is a preparation made up into tablets, capsules or other dosage units, the container must be marked with the amount of Controlled Drug(s) in each dosage unit and the number of dosage units in it. For any other kind of preparation, the container must be marked with the total amount of the preparation in it and the percentage of Controlled Drug(s) in the preparation [reg.18(1)]. These requirements do not apply to (a) poppy straw; (b) Controlled Drugs in Schedules 4 and 5; (c) Controlled Drugs supplied on the prescription of a practitioner or for administration in a clinical trial or a medicinal test on animals; or (d) any Schedule 3 drug in a preparation used as a buffering agent in chemical analysis, or which has present in it both a substance in that schedule and a salt of that substance or is pre-mixed in a kit [reg.18(2), as amended].

Registers and records

An entry in a Register of Controlled Drugs must be made in respect of every quantity of any drug in Schedules 1 and 2 which is obtained or supplied (whether by way of administration or otherwise) (Figs 17.1 and 17.2). This requirement applies to any person authorised to supply those drugs except a sister or acting sister for the time being in charge of a ward, theatre or other department in a hospital or nursing home, or a person licensed to supply by the Secretary of State if the licence does not require a register to be kept (reg.19). A pharmacist or practitioner need not record any prescribed drug

Figure 17.1 Entries to be made in case of obtaining Controlled Drugs

Date on which supply received	NAME	ADDRESS	Amount obtained	Form in which obtained
	Of person or firm from whom obtained			

Figure 17.2 Entries to be made in case of supply of Controlled Drugs

Date on which transaction was effected	NAME	ADDRESS	Particulars as to licence or authority of person or firm supplied to be in possession	Amount supplied	Form in which supplied
	Of person or firm supplied				

returned to him/her for destruction. Entries in the register must be made in chronological sequence in the form specified in Schedule 6 to the regulations, as illustrated. *Register* means a bound book and does not include any form of loose-leaf register or card index.

A separate register or separate part of the register must be used in respect of each class of drugs, but the salts of any drug or any stereoisomeric form of the drug may be classed with the drug. Dexamphetamine, for example, may be entered under amphetamine, but a separate part of the register is required for methylamphetamine. Separate sections can be used, if desired, in respect of different drugs or different strengths of a drug falling within the same class (reg.19).

The class of drugs recorded must be specified at the head of each page of the register and entries must be made on the day of the transaction or the following day. No cancellation, obliteration or alteration of any entry may be made, and corrections must be by way of marginal notes or footnotes, which must be dated. Every entry and correction must be in ink or be otherwise indelible (reg.20).

A register must not be used for any other purpose and must be kept at the premises to which it relates. A separate register must be kept in respect of each set of premises of the business. There may only be one such register for each premises unless the Secretary of State has approved the keeping of separate registers in different departments (reg.20).

Where a supply is made to a member of the crew of a ship or a person on an off-shore installation, an entry, specifying the drug, in the official log book or installation log book is a sufficient record. These books are required to be kept under the Merchant Shipping Acts. In the case of a ship which is not required to carry an official log book, a report signed by the master of the ship is sufficient if it is delivered as soon as may be to the superintendent of a mercantile marine office.

For record keeping requirements for midwives, see page 202.

Furnishing of information

Particulars of stocks, receipts and supplies of Controlled Drugs must be furnished on request to any person authorised in writing by the Secretary of State. The register, the stocks of drugs and other relevant books and documents must also be produced if requested (reg.25). Inspectors of the Royal Pharmaceutical Society are authorised for this purpose in relation to registered pharmacies.

Those required to furnish information are:

1   practitioners;
2   wholesale dealers;
3   retail dealers;
4   persons in charge of hospitals, nursing homes or laboratories;

5   persons authorised under the Act or regulations to produce, import or export any Controlled Drug; or

6   persons authorised under regulation 9(4)(a) to supply drugs in Schedules 3 and 4.

Professional *personal records* relating to the physical or mental health of an individual are exempt.

Preservation of records

All registers and midwives' record books must be preserved for two years from the date on which the last entry is made therein. Every requisition, order or prescription (other than a health prescription) on which a Controlled Drug is supplied must be preserved for two years from the date on which the last delivery is made (reg.23).

For Controlled Drugs in Schedules 3 and 5 to the regulations, it is sufficient if every invoice is preserved for two years from the date on which it is issued. Producers and wholesalers must keep invoices in respect of Schedule 3 and 5 drugs obtained or supplied by them, and retail dealers must keep invoices in respect of the drugs they obtain. Copies of invoices (e.g. on microfilm) may be retained in place of the original document (reg.24).

Destruction of Controlled Drugs

Persons who are required to keep records in respect of Controlled Drugs in Schedules 1, 2, 3 or 4 may only destroy them in the presence of a person authorised by the Secretary of State either personally or as a member of a class. Among the classes of authorised person for this purpose are police officers, inspectors of the Home Office and of the Royal Pharmaceutical Society of Great Britain and, for stock kept in a hospital, the Regional Pharmaceutical Officer or the senior administrative officer employed on duties connected with the administration of the hospital concerned.

Particulars of the date of destruction and the quantity destroyed must be entered in the Register of Controlled Drugs and signed by the authorised person in whose presence the drug was destroyed. The authorised person may take a sample of the drug which is to be destroyed, and destruction must be carried out according to his/her directions. A pharmacist or practitioner may destroy prescribed drugs returned by a patient or the patient's representative without making any record and without the presence of an authorised person.

The master of a ship or installation manager of an off-shore installation may not destroy any surplus drugs but may dispose of them to a constable or to a person who is lawfully entitled to supply them (that is, to any pharmacist or licensed dealer who could have supplied them to him/her) (reg.26).

Addicts

There are separate regulations relating to addicts and the supply of certain Controlled Drugs to them (SI 1997 No.1001). A person is regarded as being addicted to a drug 'if, and only if, s/he has, as a result of repeated administration, become so dependent on a drug that s/he has an overpowering desire for the administration of it to be continued'. The expression drug in this context means those specified in the regulations namely:

1   cocaine, dextromoramide, diamorphine, dipipanone, hydrocodone, hydromorphone, levorphanol, methadone, morphine, opium, oxycodone, pethidine, phenazocine and piritramide;
2   any stereoisomeric form of a substance specified in paragraph 1 above, except dextrorphan;
3   any ester or ether of a substance specified in paragraph 1 or 2 above not being a substance for the time being specified in Part II of Schedule 2 to the Misuse of Drugs Act 1971 (see Appendix 9);
4   any salt of a substance specified in any of the paragraphs 1 to 3 above; or
5   any preparation or other product containing a substance or product specified in any of paragraphs 1 to 4 above.

Except for the treatment of organic injury or disease or unless s/he is licensed so to do by the Secretary of State, no doctor may administer or authorise the supply of cocaine, diamorphine or dipipanone, or the salts of any, to an addicted person.

There is provision for addicts to receive daily supplies of cocaine, heroin, dextromoramide, dipipanone, methadone and pethidine on special prescription forms [FP(10) HP] issued by drug addiction clinics. There is also provision for supplies of all Schedule 2 Controlled Drugs for the treatment of addiction to be issued by general medical practitioners on special prescription forms [FP(10) MDA or in Scotland GP10]. These are administrative arrangements made under the NHS and do not form part of the Misuse of Drugs Regulations.

Safe custody of Controlled Drugs

The regulations relating to safe custody (SI 1973 No.798, as amended) apply to all Controlled Drugs apart from the following.

1   Any drug in Schedules 4 and 5.
2   Any liquid preparations, apart from injections, which contain any of the following:

    (a)   amphetamine;
    (b)   benzphetamine (benzfetamine);
    (c)   chlorphentermine;

(d)   fenethylline (fenetylline);

(e)   mephentermine;

(f)   methaqualone;

(g)   methylamphetamine;

(h)   methylphenidate;

(i)   phendimetrazine;

(j)   phenmetrazine;

(k)   pipradol; or

(l)   any stereoisomeric form of a substance specified in (a) to (k) above; and any salt of a substance specified in (a) to (l) above.

3   Any of the following:

(a)   cathine;

(b)   ethchlorvynol;

(c)   ethinamate;

(d)   mazindol;

(e)   meprobamate;

(f)   methylphenobarbitone (methylphenobarbital);

(g)   methyprylone;

(h)   pentazocine;

(i)   phentermine;

(j)   any 5,5-disubstituted barbituric acid;

(k)   any stereoisomeric form of a substance specified in (a) to (j) above; or

(l)   any salt of a substance specified in (a) to (k) above; and any preparation or other product containing a substance or product specified in (a) to (l) above.

The premises to which the safe custody requirements apply are:

1   any premises occupied by a retail dealer (see p. 196) for the purposes of his/her business;

2   any nursing home within the meaning of Part VI of the Public Health Act 1936 or the Nursing Homes Registration (Scotland) Act 1938;

3   any residential or other establishment provided under or by virtue of section 59 of the Social Work (Scotland) Act 1968;

4   any mental nursing home within the meaning of Part III of the Mental Health Act 1959; or

5   any private hospital within the meaning of the Mental Health (Scotland) Act 1960.

The occupier and every person concerned in the management of any of these premises must ensure that all Controlled Drugs (except those mentioned above) are, so far as circumstances permit, kept in a locked safe, cabinet or room which is so constructed and maintained as to prevent unauthorised access to the drugs (see also p. 187).

This requirement does not apply in respect of any Controlled Drug which is for the time being constantly under the direct personal supervision of (a) a pharmacist in the premises of a retail dealer (e.g. when dispensing prescriptions); or (b) the person in charge of the premises or any member of his/her staff designated by him/her for the purpose in the case of other premises to which the regulations apply.

The relevant requirements which apply to safes, cabinets and rooms where Controlled Drugs are kept are in Schedule 2 to the regulations.

The owner of a pharmacy may, as an alternative, elect to apply to the police for a certificate that his/her safes, cabinets or rooms provide an adequate degree of security. Applications must be made in writing. After inspection by the police, and if the degree of security is found to be adequate, a certificate, renewable annually, may be issued. The certificate will specify conditions to be observed and may be cancelled if there is a breach of any condition, if the occupier has refused entry to a police officer, or if there has been any change of circumstances lowering the degree of security.

Quite apart from these special requirements, which affect only certain classes of premises, a person having possession of any Controlled Drug to which the safe custody regulations apply must ensure that, as far as circumstances permit, it is kept in a locked receptacle which can be opened only by him/her or by a person authorised by him/her. This requirement does not apply to a carrier in the course of his/her business, to a person engaged in the business of the Post Office when acting in the course of that business, or to a person to whom the drug has been supplied on the prescription of a practitioner for his/her own treatment or that of another person or an animal.

Summary

Table 17.2 summarises the Misuse of Drugs Regulations.

Table 17.2   Misuse of Drugs Regulations summarised

	Schedule 1	Schedule 2	Schedule 3	Schedule 4 Part I & II	Schedule 5
Administration	By licence only	To a patient by a doctor or dentist or by any person acting in accordance with the directions of a doctor or dentist	As for Schedule 2	As for Schedule 2	No restriction
Import and Export	By licence only	By licence only	By licence only	No restriction when contained in a medicinal product [Part I] No restriction [Part II]	No restriction

Possession	By licence only	See under Possession and Supply (p. 197)	See under Possession and Supply (p. 197)	No restriction	No restriction
Supply	By licence only	See under Possession and Supply (p. 197)	See under Possession and Supply (p. 197)	See under Possession and Supply (p. 197)	See under Possession and Supply (p. 197)
Emergency supply permitted	No	No	No except phenobarbital for epilepsy	Yes	Yes
Production	By licence only	Licence holders, pharmacists, practitioners and owners of pharmacies	Licence holders, authorised persons, pharmacists practitioners and owners of pharmacies	Licence holders, authorised persons, pharmacists, practitioners and owners of pharmacies	Licence holders, pharmacists, practitioners and owners of pharmacies
Prescription requirements	By licensed person only	Yes	Yes except temazepam	Do not apply	Do not apply
Hand-written	Yes	Yes	Yes except phenobarbital for epilepsy and temazepam	No	No
Records in Register	Yes	Yes	No register, but records to be kept by licensed and authorised persons. Invoices to be kept by retail dealers, wholesalers, hospitals, nursing homes and laboratories	No register, but licensed producers and authorised suppliers must keep records of imports and exports	No register, but licensed producers, wholesalers, and retail dealers must keep invoices
Labelling requirements	Yes	Yes	Yes	No	No
Destruction requirements	Yes	Yes, but do not apply to drugs returned by patients	Apply only to imports, exports, and licensed manufacturers	Apply only to imports, exports, and licensed manufacturers	Do not apply
Safe custody required	Yes	Yes (except certain liquids, quinalbarbital and temazepam) (see p. 210)	No (except temazepam buprenorphine and diethylpropion) (see p. 210)	No	No

Further reading

National Prescribing Centre (2004) *A Guide to Good Practice in the Management of Controlled Drugs in Primary Care (England),* preview edn. National Prescribing Centre, Liverpool.

CHAPTER EIGHTEEN

Poisons Act

List and rules

The Poisons Act 1972 and the rules made under it are concerned with the sale of poisons. Unlike the Medicines Act 1968, the Poisons Act does not extend to Northern Ireland.

A *poison* means a non-medicinal poison (r.2) and is defined in the Act (s.11) as a substance which is included in Part I or Part II of the Poisons List made under the Act and which is neither a medicinal product as defined under section 130 of the Medicines Act 1968 nor a substance which is treated as a medicinal product by virtue of an order made under section 104 or 105 of the Medicines Act (Chapter 2). In line with the Medicines Act, the other definitions include *the board* (s.11); this means, in relation to a body corporate, the persons controlling the body by whatever name it is called (e.g. the management committee of a co-operative society). The Act also follows the definitions of the Medicines Act for 'persons lawfully conducting a retail pharmacy business' and a 'registered pharmacy' (Chapter 5). A more restricted meaning is given to 'sale by way of wholesale dealing' in relation to poisons; this means sale to a person who buys for the purpose of selling again (see Medicines Act definition, p. 36).

Poisons Board

The Act (s.1) provides for the continuation of an advisory committee first established under the Pharmacy and Poisons Act 1933 called the Poisons

Board. It consists of at least 16 members and the Secretary of State has powers to appoint up to three additional members if s/he thinks fit. The board must include five persons appointed by the Royal Pharmaceutical Society of Great Britain, one of whom is required to be engaged in the manufacture for sale by wholesale dealing of pharmaceutical preparations. Members of the Poisons Board hold office for three years and the Secretary of State appoints one of the members as the chair. The quorum is 11 and the Board has power to appoint replacements for casual vacancies. The Board makes its own regulations as to procedure, subject to the approval of the Secretary of State (s.1).

Poisons List

The Poisons List is a list of substances treated as poisons for the purposes of the Act (s.2) and is set out in a Poisons List Order, as amended (SI 1982 No.218) (Appendix 10). After consultation with, or on the recommendations of, the Poisons Board, the Secretary of State may amend or vary this list. This list is divided into two parts.

> *Part I.* This consists of poisons the sale of which is restricted to persons lawfully conducting a retail pharmacy business (subsequently referred to as Part I poisons).
> *Part II.* This consists of poisons which may only be sold either by a person lawfully conducting a retail pharmacy business or by a person whose name is entered in a local authority's list (subsequently referred to as Part II poisons). Except where provision is made to the contrary an unqualified reference to a poison includes a substance containing that poison.

NB Some substances in the Poisons List also have medicinal uses (e.g. arsenic, strychnine). When sold as medicinal products, they are controlled under the Medicines Act 1968 (p. 15) but when sold for non-medicinal purposes they are subject to the Poisons Act 1972.

Local authorities' lists

Every local authority is obliged to keep a list of the names and business addresses of persons, *listed sellers*, who are entitled to sell Part II poisons and must enter on the list all those persons who make application. A local authority has power (a) to refuse to enter a name if, in its opinion, the person is not fit to be on the list, and (b) to remove a name for non-payment of the prescribed fee. A person aggrieved by such a decision can appeal to the Crown Court or, in Scotland, to the Sheriff (s.5).

A local authority's list, which is open to inspection without fee, must include particulars of the premises and of the names of the persons listed (Sch.9 and r.24, see p. 468).

The Act provides for the payment of reasonable fees as determined by the authority by a person making application for their name to be included on the list, and also for further annual payments of fees for having their name retained on the list [s.6(2), as amended].

If a person whose name is on a local authority's list is convicted of any offence which, in the opinion of the court, renders him/her unfit to have his/her name so listed, the court may, as part of the sentence, order his/her name to be removed and disqualified from being on the list for a specified period. Any person whose name is on a local authority list may not use in connection with his/her business any title, emblem or description reasonably calculated to suggest that s/he is entitled to sell any poisons which s/he is not entitled to sell (s.6).

Local authority means (a) in relation to England and Wales, the council of a county or London borough or the Common Council of the City of London; and (b) in relation to Scotland, the council of a region or island area [s.11(2), as amended].

Inspection and enforcement

It is the duty of the Royal Pharmaceutical Society of Great Britain to take reasonable steps by means of inspection and otherwise to enforce the provisions of the Poisons Act and its rules. To do this, the Society must appoint as many inspectors as the Privy Council may direct. Nineteen have been appointed. Only a pharmacist can be appointed as an inspector, and every such appointment is subject to the approval of the Privy Council.

An inspector appointed by the Society to ensure compliance by pharmacists and persons carrying on retail businesses has (a) power at all reasonable times to enter any registered pharmacy and (b) power to enter any premises in which s/he has reasonable cause to suspect that a breach of the law has been committed in respect of any Part I poison. Whether in a retail pharmacy business or any other premises, an inspector has power to make such examination and inquiry and do any other thing, including the taking of samples, as is necessary to ascertain that the Act and the rules are being complied with. (The Society's inspectors also have other duties under the Medicines Act 1968 and the Misuse of Drugs Act 1971; see pp. 22 and 190.)

It is the duty of every local authority, by means of inspection and otherwise, to take all reasonable steps to secure compliance with the provisions of the Act and its rules, as far as they concern Part II poisons, (a) by persons not being persons conducting a retail pharmacy business, and (b) by any persons lawfully conducting a retail pharmacy business in so far as that business is carried on at premises which are not a registered pharmacy. Each local authority must appoint inspectors for these purposes.

An inspector appointed by the Society may, with the consent of the Society, also be appointed by a local authority to be an inspector for the purposes of this section of the Act (s.9).

For the purposes of enforcement an inspector appointed by a local authority has power at all reasonable times to enter any premises on the local authority's list and any premises where s/he has reasonable cause to suspect that a breach of the law has been committed in respect of any Part II poison (s.9). An inspector appointed by a local authority has power, with the consent of the authority, to institute proceedings before a court of summary jurisdiction and to take any proceedings instituted by him/her, notwithstanding that s/he is not of counsel or a solicitor.

It is an offence for any person wilfully to delay or obstruct an inspector, to refuse to allow a sample to be taken or to fail without reasonable excuse to give any information which the Act requires him/her to give to an inspector (s.9). It is specifically provided that nothing in the Act authorises an inspector to enter or inspect the premises of a doctor, a dentist, a veterinary surgeon or a veterinary practitioner unless those premises are a shop (s.9).

A document purporting to be a certificate sent by a public analyst appointed under section 89 of the Food and Drugs Act 1955 or section 27 of the Food and Drugs (Scotland) Act 1956 or a person appointed by the Secretary of State (in Scotland the Lord Advocate) to make analyses for the purposes of the Poisons Act, is admissible in any proceedings under the Act as evidence of the matters stated therein, and either party may require the person who has signed the certificate to be called as a witness (s.8).

Penalties and legal proceedings

Any person who contravenes or fails to comply with the Act, or any of the provisions made under the Poisons Rules, is liable on summary conviction to a fine not exceeding £2500, and for continuing offences to a further fine not exceeding £200 for every day subsequent to the day on which s/he is convicted of the offence (s.8 and the Criminal Law Act 1977). For the misuse of titles (s.6) and obstruction of an inspector (s.9), the maximum fine is £500.

In the case of proceedings against a person under the Act or Rules or in connection with the sale, exposure for sale or supply of a poison effected by an employee, it is not a defence that the employee acted without the authority of the employer and any material fact known to the employee is deemed to have been known to the employer (s.8).

Information in respect of any offence under the Act or Rules must be laid within 12 months of the commission of the offence. There is an additional provision that the Secretary of State may institute proceedings within a period of three months after the date on which evidence sufficient in his/her opinion to justify a prosecution for an offence comes to his/her knowledge (s.8).

Poison rules

The Poisons Act (s.7) provides that the Secretary of State may, after consultation with or on the recommendation of the Poisons Board, make rules in respect of any of the following:

1   the sale, whether wholesale or retail, or the supply of poisons, by or to any persons or classes of person and in particular but without prejudice to the generality of the foregoing provisions:

   (a)   for regulating or restricting the sale or supply of poisons by persons whose names are entered in a local authority's list and for prohibiting the sale of any specified poison or class of poisons by any class of such persons; and
   (b)   for dispensing with or relaxing with respect to any poisons of this Act relating to the sale of poisons;

2   the storage and labelling of poisons (but see pp. 220 and 221);
3   the containers in which poisons may be sold or supplied;
4   the addition to poisons of specified ingredients for the purpose of rendering them readily distinguishable as poisons;
5   the compounding of poisons, and the supply of poisons on and in accordance with a prescription duly given by a doctor, a dentist, a veterinary surgeon or a veterinary practitioner;
6   the period for which any books required to be kept for the purpose of this Act are to be preserved;
7   the period for which any certificate for the purchase of a poison given under section 3 of the Act (see p. 468) is to remain in force; and
8   for prescribing anything which is by the Act to be prescribed by rules.

The Secretary of State may issue to the Poisons Board a direction that, before recommending rules under 1(a), 2, 3 and 4 above, the Board must first consult a body representative of persons engaged in the manufacture of poisons or preparations containing poisons.

The power to make rules or orders under the Act is exercised by Statutory Instrument. The current rules are set out in the Poison Rules 1982 (SI 1982 No.218, as amended) (Appendix 11). Apart from their general classification into Part I or Part II poisons, poisons may, in addition, be divided into classes by their inclusion in certain schedules to the Poison Rules.

There are eight schedules to the rules and they are described, briefly, below. More detailed reference is made later (see also Appendix 11).

   Schedule 1.   A list of poisons to which special restrictions apply relating to storage, conditions of sale and keeping of sales records.
   Schedule 4.   A list of articles exempted from control as poisons (r.8). It is in two groups. Group I comprises classes of article which contain poisons but are totally exempt (e.g. builders' materials). Group II lists exemptions for certain poisons when in specified articles or substances

(e.g. paraquat in pellet form containing not more than 5 per cent salts of paraquat calculated as paraquat ion).

Schedule 5. Some Part II poisons may be sold by listed sellers only in certain forms. The details are given in this schedule, which also specifies certain poisons which may be sold by a person duly authorised, in England or Wales, by the Minister of Agriculture, Fisheries and Food, only to persons engaged in the trade or business of agriculture or horticulture and for the purpose of that trade or business. In any other circumstances the sale of poisons in this schedule is restricted to pharmacies.

Schedule 8. Form of application for inclusion in local authority's list of sellers of Part II poisons.

Schedule 9. Form of the list kept by a local authority of listed sellers of Part II poisons.

Schedule 10. Form of certificate for the purchase of a poison.

Schedule 11. Form of entry to be made in poisons book on sale of a Schedule 1 poison.

Schedule 12. Restriction of sale and supply of strychnine and other substances. Forms of authority required for certain of these poisons.

NB Schedules 2, 3, 6 and 7 were deleted by the Poisons Rules (Amendment) Order 1985 (SI 1985 No.1077). Packaging and labelling of poisons is now controlled under the Chemicals (Hazard Information and Packaging) Regulations 1994, as amended (Chapter 20).

Sale and supply of poisons

General requirements

Except in certain circumstances (see Sales Exempted by the Act, p. 226) it is unlawful for a person to sell any substance which is a Part I poison unless:

1 s/he is a person lawfully conducting a retail pharmacy business;
2 the sale is effected on the premises which are a registered pharmacy; or
3 the sale is effected by or under the supervision of a pharmacist (s.3).

It is unlawful for a person to sell any substance which is a Part II poison unless:

1 s/he is a person lawfully conducting a retail pharmacy business and the sale is effected on premises which are a registered pharmacy; or
2 his/her name is entered in a local authority list in respect of the premises on which the poison is sold (s.3).

As sales of poisons must be effected on registered or listed premises, it is not lawful for sales to take place from door to door, although a sale through the post from registered or listed premises would appear to be lawful.

The conditions required for persons lawfully to conduct 'a retail pharmacy business' have been described in Chapter 5. Such persons may sell at a registered pharmacy any poison whether it is in Part I or Part II of the Poisons List. The sale of a Part I poison from retail premises must be made by or under the supervision of a registered pharmacist (s.3). Each sale, if not made by the pharmacist personally, must be effected under his/her supervision in the sense that s/he should be in a position to intervene to prevent the sale.

The opinion was expressed in the High Court (*Roberts v. Littlewoods Mail Order Stores* [1943] KB 269; see Chapter 27) that supervision could not be said to have been exercised if the pharmacist were in another part of the building from that at which the sales were effected. The sale, by a person lawfully conducting a retail pharmacy business, of a poison included in Schedule 1 (see p. 221) must be effected by or under the supervision of a pharmacist even though it may be a Part II poison (r.9).

Listed sellers may not sell any Part II poison which has, since being obtained by them, been subject to any form of manipulation, treatment or processing as a result of which the poison has been exposed and, in the case of any poison included in Schedule 1, unless the sale is effected by him/herself or by a responsible deputy (r.10).

A *responsible deputy* means a person nominated as a deputy on the listed seller's form of application or any person substituted, by notice in writing to the local authority, for the person originally nominated. Not more than two deputies can be nominated at the same time in respect of one set of premises (r.10).

A listed seller may not sell (r.10):

1   any poison included in the first column of Part A of Schedule 5 (see p. 464) unless the article or substance is in the form specified in the second column of that Part; or
2   any poison included in Part B of Schedule 5 (see p. 466) unless the purchaser is engaged in the trade or business of agriculture, horticulture or forestry and requires the poison for the purposes of that trade or business.

Containers

Rule 20 of the rules which set out provision for containers has been repealed (SI 1992 No.2293). Provision for containers which have to bear tactile danger warnings are contained in the Chemicals (Hazard Information and Packaging for Supply) Regulations 1994 (see Chapter 20).

Storage of poisons

When a poison is included in Schedule 1 (see p. 459) it must be stored in any retail shop or premises used in connection with a retail shop:

1   in a cupboard or drawer reserved solely for the storage of poisons;

2   in a part of the premises which is partitioned off or otherwise separated from the remainder of the premises and to which customers are not permitted to have access; or
3   on a shelf reserved solely for the storage of poisons and no food is kept directly under the shelf.

Schedule 1 poisons used in agriculture, horticulture or forestry must not be stored on any shelf, or in any part of the premises where food is kept, or in any cupboard or drawer unless the cupboard or drawer is reserved solely for the storage of poisons to be used in agriculture, horticulture or forestry (r.21).

Labelling of hydrogen cyanide

It is an offence to sell or supply any compressed hydrogen cyanide unless the container is labelled with the words *Warning: This container holds poisonous gas and should only be opened and used by persons having expert knowledge of the precautions to be taken in its use* (r.18). This does not apply to sale or supply of compressed hydrogen cyanide to be exported to purchasers outside the UK (r.18).

Labelling and packaging of poisons which are 'chemicals'

Substances in the Poisons List are also subject to the Chemicals (Hazard Information and Packaging for Supply) Regulations 1994, as amended and must be labelled and packed in accordance with those regulations (see Chapter 20). The provisions of the Poisons Act and rules relating to labelling, containers and storage do not apply to these substances except:

1   the special warning label for compressed hydrogen cyanide (see above); and
2   the storage requirements for poisons on retail premises (p. 220).

Schedule 1 poisons

Sales of poisons included in Schedule 1 to the Poisons Rules are subject to requirements additional to those applying to Part I and Part II poisons.

Knowledge of the seller

The purchaser of a Schedule 1 poison must be either:

1   certified in writing in the prescribed manner, by a person authorised in the Poisons Rules to give such a certificate, to be a person to whom the poison may properly be sold; or

2   known by the seller, or by a pharmacist employed by him/her at the premises where the sale is effected, to be a person to whom the poison may properly be sold (s.3).

Any householder is a person authorised to give a certificate as in 1 above (r.25). If the householder giving the certificate is not known to the seller to be a responsible person of good character, then the certificate is required to be endorsed by a police officer in charge of a police station. NB The police officer certifies that the householder, not the purchaser, is a responsible person of good character. The form of the certificate is laid down in Schedule 10 (see p. 468) and the certificate has to be retained by the seller (r.25).

For certain sales or supplies of Schedule 1 poisons, the requirement of knowledge of the purchaser by the seller is deemed to be satisfied if the purchaser is known by the person in charge of the premises in which the poison is sold, or of the department of the business in which the sale is effected, to be a person to whom the poison may properly be sold or supplied.

This relaxation applies to:

1   sales of Part II, Schedule 1 poisons made by listed sellers (r.5);
2   supplies of commercial samples of Schedule 1 poisons (r.6); and
3   sales of Schedule 1 poisons exempted under section 4 of the Act (r.6) (see also p. 223).

Records

The seller must not deliver a Schedule 1 poison until s/he has made, or caused to be made, the required entry in the Poisons Book and the purchaser has signed it (s.3). The entries must be made in the manner and form prescribed in Schedule 11 (r.26; see also p. 469). The particulars to be recorded are the:

1   date of the sale;
2   name and quantity of the poison supplied;
3   purchaser's name and address and their business trade or occupation;
4   purpose for which the poison is stated to be required;
5   date of certificate (if any); and
6   name and address of persons giving certificate (if any).

The Poisons Book must be retained for two years from the date on which the last entry was made (r.27). A signed order may be accepted in lieu of the purchaser's signature in certain circumstances (see below).

Signed orders

A person who requires a Schedule 1 poison for the purpose of their trade, business or profession may give the seller a signed order in lieu of his/her signature in the Poisons Book (r.6). The seller must obtain, before completion of the sale, the order in writing signed by the purchaser stating:

1   their name and address;
2   their trade, business or profession;
3   the purpose for which the poison is required; and
4   the total quantity of the poison to be purchased.

The seller must be reasonably satisfied that the signature is that of the person purporting to have signed the order and that that person carries on the trade, business or profession stated in the order, being one in which the poison is used. The seller must make the entry in the Poison Book before delivery. S/he must include the words *signed order* in place of the signature and add a reference number by which the order can be identified.

When a person represents that s/he urgently requires a poison for his/her trade, business or profession, the seller may, if s/he is reasonably satisfied that there is an emergency and the purchaser is unable to supply a signed order before delivery, supply the poison on an undertaking by the purchaser that the purchaser will supply a signed order within 72 hours. Failure to comply with an undertaking or the making of false statements in order to obtain Schedule 1 poisons without a signed order are contraventions of the Poison Rules (r.6).

Exemptions from Schedule 1 requirements

The requirements described above as to the knowledge of the purchaser by the seller and entry in the Poisons Book with signature of the purchaser or supplier of a signed order do not apply to:

1   the sale of poisons to be exported to purchasers outside the UK;
2   the sale of any article by its manufacturer, or by a person carrying on a business in the course of which poisons are regularly sold by way of wholesale dealing if:

(a)   the article is sold or supplied to a person carrying on a business in the course of which poisons are regularly sold or regularly used in the manufacture of other articles; and
(b)   the seller or supplier is reasonably satisfied that the purchaser requires the article for the purpose of that business (r.6);

3   the sale of nicotine, which is a Part II Schedule 1 poison, in the form of agricultural or horticultural insecticides consisting of nicotine dusts containing not more than 4 per cent (w/w) nicotine (r.5); and
4   the sale of articles containing barium carbonate or zinc phosphide and prepared for the destruction of rats or mice (r.7).

Schedule 1 poisons subject to additional restrictions (rule 12)

All the Schedule 1 poisons mentioned below are subject to additional restrictions on sale or supply. They may only be sold or supplied:

1   by way of wholesale dealing;
2   for export to purchasers outside the UK;
3   to persons or institutions concerned with scientific education or research or chemical analysis for the purpose of that education research or analysis; or
4   in the circumstances described below under the name of each particular poison.

Sodium and potassium arsenites may only be sold for the purposes of 1, 2 and 3 above.

   Strychnine may be sold:

(a)   for the purposes of 1, 2 and 3 above;
(b)   to a person producing a written authority, in the form set out in Part II of Schedule 12 (see p. 471) issued in England or Wales, by a person duly authorised by the Minister of Agriculture, Fisheries and Food or, in Scotland, by a person duly authorised by the Secretary of State, authorising the purchase for the killing of moles. The quantity must not exceed 100 grams and the sale must be made within three months of the date of the written authority; or
(c)   to an officer of the Ministry of Agriculture, Fisheries and Food (now DEFRA) or, in Scotland, of the Department of Agriculture and Fisheries, producing a written authority in the form set out in Part III of Schedule 12 (see p. 472) authorising the purchase by that officer for killing foxes in an infected area within the meaning of the Rabies (Control) Order 1974. The quantity must not exceed that stated in the authority and must be supplied within four weeks of the date of the written authority.

NB Since 1991, strychnine has also been controlled under the Control of Pesticides Regulations 1986 and may only be supplied to holders of an Authority to Purchase issued by DEFRA (in Wales by the Welsh Office Agriculture Department and in Scotland by the Department of Agriculture and Fisheries). It must be labelled in an approved manner and supplied only in the original sealed package(s) and only in units of 2 grams or multiples thereof. Quantities of more than 8 grams may only be supplied to providers of a commercial service. These conditions are *in addition* to the possession of a strychnine permit under the Poisons Rules (see p. 262).

   Fluoroacetic acid, its salts or fluoroacetamide may be sold for the purposes of 1, 2 and 3 above, or to a person producing a certificate in form 'A' or form 'B' as provided in Schedule 12 (see pp. 472 and 473). The quantity must not exceed that specified and must be sold or supplied within three months of the date on the certificate. The certificates must specify the quantity, certify that the substance is to be used as a rodenticide and identify the place where it is to be used, which may be:

(a) ships or sewers as indicated in the certificate;
(b) such drains as are identified in the certificate, being drains which are in restricted areas and wholly enclosed and to which all means of access are kept closed when not in use; or
(c) such warehouses as are identified in the certificate which are in residential dock areas and to which all means of access are kept securely locked or barred when not in use.

Only the proper officer of a local authority or port health authority may issue form 'A' to employees of the authority for the purpose of purchasing rodenticide for use in (a), (b) or (c) above, or form 'B' to persons carrying on the business of pest control for the purpose of rodenticide for use in (a) and (b) above. For the purpose of rodenticide for use in (a) and (b) above, form 'B' may also be issued by a person duly authorised in England or Wales by the Minister of Agriculture, Fisheries and Food or in Scotland by the Secretary of State.

Salts of thallium may be sold:

(a) for the purposes of 1, 2 and 3 above; or
(b) to a local authority or port health authority for the purpose of the exercise of its statutory powers;
(c) to a Government department or an officer of the Crown, for the purpose of the public service;
(d) to a person producing a written authority in the form set out in Part V of Schedule 12 (see p. 473) issued within the preceding three months, authorising the purchase of thallium sulphate for use by him/her or by the employees of the persons named in the authority for the purpose of killing rats, mice or moles in the course of the business of pest control (authorities are issued in Scotland by the Secretary of State);
(e) to a manufacturer who regularly uses them in the manufacture of articles for the purpose of his/her business; or
(f) as an ingredient in any article which is not intended for consumption by any person or animal.

The exemptions under (e) and (f) do not extend to thallium sulphate. *Port health authority* means in England or Wales the port health authority of the Port of London or a port health authority for the purposes of the Public Health Act 1936 and in Scotland a port health authority as constituted in the Public Health (Scotland) Act 1897.

Zinc phosphide may be sold:

(a) for the purposes of 1, 2 and 3 above;
(b) to a local authority for the purpose of the exercise of its statutory powers;

(c)   to a government department or an officer of the Crown, for the purpose of the public service; or

(d)   to a person, or persons, carrying on a trade or business for the purpose of that trade or business.

Calcium, potassium and sodium cyanides (r.14) may only be sold in any of the circumstances described in section 4 of the Act (see Sales Exempted by the Act, below).

Wholesale dealing

See Sales exempted by the Act, category 1 below.

Sales exempted by the Act

Section 4 of the Act exempts certain categories of sales of poisons from the provisions of the Act, except as provided by the Poisons Rules. The principal effect is that sales of poisons falling within these categories are not required to be made from pharmacies or the premises of listed sellers; for Part I poisons, the supervision of a pharmacist is not required. Except as indicated, the provisions as to labelling (p. 221), containers (p. 220) and Schedule 1 poisons (p. 221) do apply to these exempted sales (rr. 4, 6 and 2).

The exempted categories are as follows.

1   Sales of poisons by way of wholesale dealing, that is sales made to a person who buys for the purpose of selling again. NB 'Wholesale dealing' has a wider meaning in the Medicines Act 1968 (see p. 36). A wholesaler who sells a Part I poison to a shopkeeper must have reasonable grounds for believing that the purchaser is a person lawfully conducting a retail pharmacy business. If not, then the wholesaler must obtain a statement signed by the purchaser, or a person authorised by the purchaser, to the effect that the purchaser does not intend to sell the poison on any premises used for or in connection with his/her retail business (r.11).

2   Sales of poisons to be exported to purchasers outside the UK; these are exempted from the Act and rules.

3   The sale of an article to a doctor, dentist, veterinary surgeon or veterinary practitioner for the purposes of his/her profession.

4   The sale of an article for use in connection with any hospital, infirmary or dispensary or similar institution approved by an order of the Secretary of State.

5   The sale of an article by a person carrying on a business, in the course of which poisons are regularly sold either by way of wholesale dealing or for use by purchasers in their trade or business to:

(a) a government department or an officer of the Crown requiring the article for the public service, or any local authority requiring the article in connection with the exercise of any statutory powers;

(b) a person or institution concerned with scientific education or research, if the article is required for the purposes of that education or research;

(c) a person who requires the article for the purpose of enabling him/ her to comply with any requirements made by or in pursuance of any enactment with respect to the medical treatment of persons employed by that person in any trade or business carried on by him/her; or

(d) a person who requires the article for the purpose of his/her trade or business. A person can be said to be carrying on a business if s/he engages in full-time, or part-time, commercial activity with a view to profit. A sale of cyanide to a commercial fruit grower for killing wasps would be a *trade or business* sale but a sale for the same purpose to a householder for garden use would not. Sales in circumstances exempted by section 4 are the only sales of cyanides which are lawful (see p. 226) so a sale made to a householder would be unlawful.

Automatic machines

It is unlawful for a poison to be exposed for sale in, or to be offered for sale by means of, an automatic machine (s.3) (see p. 79).

Summary

- The Poisons Board advises the Secretary of State as to which substances should be in the Poisons List.
- The Poisons List is divided into two parts. Poisons in Part I may be sold only by authorised sellers of poisons (i.e. from retail pharmacies by or under the supervision of a pharmacist), whereas Part II poisons can be sold from retail pharmacies and other shopkeepers who are listed with the local authority.
- There are eight active schedules. Schedule 1 contains poisons to which special restrictions apply relating to sale, storage and the keeping of records. The seller must have special knowledge of the purchaser and record the transaction and obtain the purchaser's signature in a 'Poisons Register'. Special provisions are made for signed orders in lieu of the purchaser's signature and for storage of poisons (away from the public).
- Special conditions apply to the sale of strychnine. It may only be sold by way of wholesale, to persons or institutions concerned with education or

research, for export or to a person who has obtained a written authority from the appropriate agricultural authority in England, Scotland or Wales. The format of the written authority is set out in Schedule 12.

• Various specific additional conditions apply to sodium and potassium arsenites, fluoroacetic acid and its salts, thallium, zinc phosphide and the cyanides.

Further reading

Medicines, Ethics and Practice (published annually) The Royal Pharmaceutical Society of Great Britain, London. (Lists of poisons are included.)

CHAPTER NINETEEN

Spirits and methylated spirits

The law relating to spirits and methylated spirits is contained mainly in the Customs and Excise Management Act 1979, in the Alcoholic Liquor Duties Act 1979 and in various regulations and notices.

The term *spirits* means 'spirits of any description and includes all liquor mixed with spirits and all mixtures, compounds or preparations made with spirits but does not include methylated spirits'.

Intoxicating liquor means spirits, wine, beer, cider and any other fermented, distilled or spirituous liquor, but (apart from cider) does not include any liquor for the sale of which by wholesale no excise licence is required.

Retail sales of intoxicating liquor

Intoxicating liquor may be sold only by a person holding an appropriate justice's licence granted in England and Wales by licensing justices or in Scotland by a licensing court. The justices have an absolute discretion in the granting of such licences.

The justice's licence may be granted to authorise sales for consumption either on or off the premises. Sales of intoxicating liquor may be made only during permitted hours and these hours are usually fixed by the licensing justice. The holder of a licence requires to have painted on or affixed to his/her premises in a conspicuous place his/her name and, after the name, the word 'licensed', followed by words sufficient to express the business for which the licence is granted.

The maximum quantity of intoxicating liquor which may be sold by retail to any one person is: in the case of spirits, wine or made wine nine litres or one case; in the case of beer or cider 21 litres or two cases.

NB A licence is not required for the sale by retail of spirits made up in a medicine by a pharmacist or a sale to a trader for the purpose of that trade.

Spirits duty

Spirits and all goods containing spirits imported into the UK are liable to a customs duty, and all spirits made in the UK by a licensed distiller are liable to an excise duty (Customs and Excise Management Act 1979). Exemption from customs and excise duty exists for spirits used in making methylated spirits (see below).

A *reduced rate of duty* is payable if any person can prove to the Commissioner of Customs and Excise that s/he has used spirits, upon which the full duty has been paid, solely for the purpose of manufacturing or preparing any article recognised by the Commissioner as being used for medical or scientific purposes. This concession is granted subject to any conditions which the Commissioner may impose by means of regulations. The guidelines have been made and are contained in the Spirits Regulations 1952 (SI 1952 No.2229, as amended) (see below).

A person wishing to claim repayment of a portion of the duty must comply with the following (as set out in Part VIII of the regulations): s/he must not *receive* at his/her premises any spirits except (a) spirits accompanied by a permit or certificate, or (b) spirits which, if not required to be accompanied by a permit or certificate on removal, are accompanied by an invoice or similar document containing particulars of the spirits and the duty paid, and the name and address of the supplier (reg.63).

A claimant must *store* separately: (a) spirits recovered from spirits in respect of which s/he has or intends to make a claim; (b) any other recovered spirits; (c) any other spirits (reg.65). S/he is not allowed to mix spirits recovered from spirits, in respect of which s/he has or intends to make a claim, with any other spirits except for use in the manufacture or preparation of a medicine which is recognised as such by the Commissioners or for scientific purposes (reg.65). On each container in which s/he stores spirits or recovered spirits, the claimant must permanently and legibly mark the capacity of the container. Each container has to be stored to give convenient access to a Customs and Excise officer (reg.64).

The claimant is required to keep a *stock book* in an approved form (reg.66) and is required to make immediate entries in respect of:

1   spirits received at the premises, brought back into stock for use or recovered on the premises;

2   spirits or recovered spirits intended to be delivered from, or to be used on, the premises; or

3   any article made with spirits (reg.67).

The pharmacist both in retail and hospital is mainly concerned with spirits other than recovered spirits. Separate accounts must be kept for spirits and recovered spirits in a stock book. Specimen stock-book rulings are illustrated in Figures 19.1 and 19.2.

Figure 19.1   Spirits received

DATE	PERMIT NO.	NAME AND ADDRESS OF SUPPLIER	QUANTITY RECEIVED	STRENGTH O.P.

Figure 19.2   Spirits used or sold

REPAYMENT OF DUTY NOT CLAIMED PLUS SALES			REPAYMENT OF DUTY CLAIMED				
DATE	QUANTITY	STRENGTH	DATE	QUANTITY	STRENGTH	RECOGNISED ARTICLE MADE	
						NAME	QUANTITY

If a person uses spirits in the *manufacture or preparation of any recognised medicine* (e.g. homoeopathic medicine), entries must be made in a stock book recording:

1   all spirits received at his/her premises;

2   all spirits and mixtures brought back into stock for use in the manu-
      facture or preparation of a recognised medicinal article, being spirits or
      mixtures previously entered in the stock book as having been used and
      in respect of which s/he has in accordance with the Alcoholic Liquor
      Duties Act 1979 refunded any duty repaid;
3   all spirits delivered from his/her premises;
4   all spirits used on his/her premises, the purposes for which they are used
      and the quantities used for each purpose;
5   the name and quantity of each recognised medical article made;
6   the name and quantity of any other article made; and
7   any other use of the spirits (reg.66).

Separate particulars are required for spirits used for scientific purposes
(reg.66).

It is an offence for a claimant to cancel, obliterate or, except with the
permission of a Customs and Excise officer, alter any entry in the book
(reg.68). The book must be left on the premises while in use and for 12
months following the final entry, together with all books, invoices and other
trade documents containing any information on which entries in the book are
based. The claimant must at all reasonable times allow an officer to inspect
the book, invoices and documents, and to take extracts therefrom or make
entries in the book (reg.69). Unless the Commissioners permit otherwise, the
claimant, if not a rectifier, must take stock and balance the account of spirits
in his/her stock book at the end of each month (reg.70) or when required to
do so by an officer.

A claimant must not deliver from his/her premises or use for any purpose
other than manufacture or preparation of a recognised medicinal article or for
a scientific purpose any spirits in respect of which s/he has made or intends to
make a claim (reg.71). Claims for recovery of duty must be made on the
approval form obtainable from a Customs and Excise officer. The claim must
be signed by the claimant or a person duly authorised by the claimant and
must be made within three months of the date on which the spirits were used.
Claims cannot be made more frequently than twice a month in respect of
spirits used on any one set of premises (reg.73).

When in doubt concerning any provisions of the spirits regulations, pharmacists are advised to consult the local officer of Customs and Excise.

Methylated spirits

Methylated spirits are spirits which are mixed with other substances in
accordance with regulations made by the Commissioners under the Alcoholic
Liquor Duties Act 1979.

There are three types of methylated spirits but the pharmacist is generally
concerned only with two: mineralised methylated spirits and industrial
methylated spirits. The regulations giving particulars for the methylation

of spirit and governing the supply, receipt, sale, storage, etc. of all types of methylated spirits are to be found in the Methylated Spirits Regulations (SI 1987 No.2009), although the provisions for licensing and inspection are to be found in the Act itself. In addition, the Commissioners issue notices for guidance and these can be obtained from local Customs and Excise offices. No person may methylate, or wholesale, methylated spirits of *any type* unless they hold a licence as a methylator from the Commissioners authorising them to do so.

The local Customs and Excise officer may enter and inspect in the daytime the premises of any person authorised by the regulations to receive methylated spirits, and may inspect and examine any of the methylated spirits stored there. The local officer is empowered to take samples of methylated spirits and any goods containing methylated spirits, provided a reasonable price is paid for the sample.

It is unlawful:

1   to prepare, attempt to prepare or sell any methylated spirits for use as a beverage or mixed with a beverage;
2   to use methylated spirits in the preparation of any article capable of being used as a beverage or as a medicine for internal use;
3   to sell or possess any such article; or
4   to purify or attempt to purify any methylated spirits, or recover or attempt to recover the alcohol therein, by means of distillation, condensation or in any other manner unless permitted to do so by the Commissioners.

Nothing in the statute prevents the use of methylated spirits in the making for external use only of any article sold or supplied in accordance with regulations.

If required to do so by the Commissioners the retailer must keep an account, in a prescribed form, of his/her stock of methylated spirits (reg.27). The retailer is required to keep methylated spirits under proper control or under the control of a responsible person appointed by the retailer and held under lock or otherwise stored to the satisfaction of the local officer.

On the closure or transfer of a business, or on the death of the retailer, the stock of methylated spirits must be disposed of in an approved manner and within a reasonable time to the satisfaction of the Commissioners (reg.26).

Industrial methylated spirits

The regulations require that industrial methylated spirits must consist of 95 parts by volume of spirits together with 5 parts by volume of wood naphtha (reg.15).

A person lawfully conducting a retail pharmacy business cannot receive industrial methylated spirits for sale by him/her or for export unless s/he has made application to the proper officer in the required form which is available from the local office of Customs and Excise, and has supplied such information as may be required. The proper officer may make the certificate of authority subject to conditions (reg.25) and restrict it to the receipt of methylated spirits for certain purposes only. Pharmacists *must* comply with the conditions of the certificate. The certificate of authority may be revoked or varied for any reasonable cause at any time (reg.24). The authorised uses for which it may be sold are set out in HM Customs and Excise Notice No.474 dated March 1993.

The proper officer may authorise a pharmacist to receive industrial methylated spirits and:

1   use them to make any article approved by the proper officer;
2   dispense them, or articles made from them, on a prescription; or
3   sell or supply them, other than on a prescription, for medical or scientific purposes.

Sales of industrial methylated spirits may be made:

1   to any person authorised to receive them in any quantity not exceeding 20 litres provided that a written statement is received from the user that s/he is authorised to receive them;
2   in any quantity not exceeding 3 litres to a doctor, dentist, nurse, chiropodist, veterinary surgeon or any other person entitled by law to provide medical or veterinary services in the UK, provided that a written order signed by such a person is received;
3   of not more than 20 litres to persons outside the UK; and
4   for medical or veterinary purposes on a prescription or order of a medical practitioner, dentist or veterinary surgeon or practitioner.

Similarly, a pharmacist may supply or sell articles:

1   which have been manufactured by that pharmacist using industrial methylated spirits in accordance with the conditions imposed in the certificate of authority; or
2   which are so manufactured in accordance with the certificate of authority and are sold or supplied on a prescription.

Industrial methylated spirits must be purchased from an authorised methylator in quantities of not less than 20 litres. Alternatively, not more than 20 litres at a time can be obtained from an authorised user, e.g. a wholesale chemist.

An authorised user, such as a pharmacist, must keep records of his/her dealings with industrial spirits in accordance with any conditions imposed by the proper officer who must be allowed to inspect such records at any reasonable time. An annual return of all industrial methylated spirits received and used or supplied must be made to the proper officer on request. Records must be kept for two years.

All stocks must be kept under lock and key under the control of the pharmacist. The local Customs and Excise may require a pharmacist to comply with special storage requirements.

All bottles and other containers in which industrial methylated spirits or articles containing it are supplied must be labelled in accordance with the Chemicals (Hazard Information and Packaging for Supply) Regulations (see Chapter 20 and pp. 241–243). If supplied or dispensed for medical use it must also be labelled *For External Use, Not To Be Taken*, or words to the same effect. A specimen form of account is shown in Figure 19.3.

Figure 19.3 Specimen form of account for guidance of pharmacists when selling industrial methylated spirits otherwise than on prescription

Received or set aside as a separate stock for sale			Sold		
Date	Whence received	Quantity	Date	Whether sold on requisition or for use of a doctor etc., on written order	Quantity

Mineralised methylated spirits

The regulations require that mineralised methylated spirits must consist of 90 parts by volume of spirits together with 9.5 parts by volume of wood naphtha and 0.5 part of crude pyridine. To every 1000 litres of the mixture must be added 3.75 litres petroleum oil and not less than 1.5 g by weight of powdered aniline dye (methyl violet).

Mineralised methylated spirits can be purchased from a methylator or, in small quantities, from a wholesaler. No restrictions are placed on the retailing of mineralised methylated spirits in England and Wales. The weekend restrictions on sale were removed by the Regulatory Reform (Sunday Trading) Order 2004 (SI.2004 No.470). The local officer of Customs and Excise visits the premises to satisfy him/herself as to the suitability of the premises for the storage of mineralised methylated spirits.

Scotland: sale of mineralised methylated spirits and surgical spirits

For many years there were additional restrictions on the retail sale of methylated spirits and surgical spirits in Scotland. These included the need for sellers to register, keep records and additional labelling requirements. These restrictions were removed in 1998 by the Deregulation (Methylated Spirits Sale by Retail) (Scotland) Regulations [SI 1998 No.1602 (S.87)].

The requirements in Scotland are now similar to those in England and Wales. However it remains an offence to sell mineralised methylated spirits to a person under 14 years of age.

Summary

- The law relating to spirits and methylated spirits and the rules regarding duty on products is outlined.
- The terms *spirits* includes spirits of any description including all liquor mixed with spirits and all mixes made with spirits but not methylated spirits. *Intoxicating liquor* comprises any fermented, distilled or spirituous liquor but (apart from cider) does not include any liquor that does not require an excise licence for wholesale.
- There are three types of methylated spirits but the pharmacist is generally concerned only with two: mineralised methylated spirits and industrial methylated spirits. There are specific regulations for the methylation of spirit and governing the supply, receipt, sale, storage, etc. of all types of methylated spirits.

CHAPTER TWENTY

Dangerous substances and consumer protection

The way in which certain chemicals are classified, packaged and labelled is now controlled under the Chemical (Hazard Information and Packaging for Supply) Regulations 1994 (SI 1994 No.3247, as amended by SI 2000 No.2897). They are known collectively as the CHIP Regulations. The regulations, made under the Health and Safety at Work etc. Act 1974 and the European Communities Act 1972, implement within Great Britain the European Community Directives regulating and controlling the classification, packaging and labelling of dangerous substances (Council Directive 99/43/EEC, as amended, and Council Directive 96/769/EEC).

Chemicals classified under the CHIP Regulations as being harmful to health are also subject to control under the Control of Substances Hazardous to Health Regulations 1999 (COSHH) (see p. 244).

Definitions

Substances dangerous to supply means a substance listed in Part 1 of an approved supply list.

Approved supply list means the list approved by the Health and Safety Commission entitled *Information Approved for the Classification and Labelling of Substances and Preparations Dangerous for Supply* (6th edn) (SI 2000 No.2381).

Preparations means mixtures or solutions of two or more substances and *preparation dangerous to supply* means a preparation which is in one or more categories of danger in Schedule 1 to the CHIP Regulations 1994 (SI 1994 No.3247, as amended).

Supply, in relation to a substance or preparation, means supply by way of:

1   sale or offer for sale;
2   commercial sample; or
3   transfer from a factory, warehouse or other place of work and its curtilage to another place of work whether or not in the same ownership.

Application of the regulations and exceptions

The regulations apply to the classification, packaging and labelling of any substance or preparation which is dangerous for supply except:

1   a substance which is either:

   (a)   a medicinal product; or
   (b)   a substance specified in an order made under sections 104 or 105 of the Medicines Act 1968;

2   Controlled Drugs;
3   animal feeding stuffs;
4   cosmetic products;
5   pesticides approved under the Food and Environmental Act 1985 (NB a preparation intended for use as a pesticide is classified as dangerous to supply and must comply with the regulations unless it is approved under the 1985 Act);
6   radioactive substances;
7   substances and preparations intended for use as food;
8   substances intended for export to a country which is not a member state of the EU;
9   munitions, including fireworks;
10   waste materials;
11   substances and preparations which are dangerous by reason that they contain disease-producing microorganisms;
12   a substance transferred from a factory, warehouse or other place of work to another place of work in the same ownership and in the immediate vicinity;
13   a substance to which the Notification of New Substances Regulations 1982 apply and is labelled in accordance with such regulations; or
14   a substance imported and still under customs control.

Most of the substances controlled as dangerous substances in the approved supply list are chemicals and only a few are likely to be encountered in pharmacy. A selection of the substances taken from the approved supply list is given in Appendix 12. It comprises:

1   those dangerous substances which are also controlled by the Poisons Act 1972 (see Chapter 18); and
2   other dangerous substances which may be held in stock in a pharmacy.

A pharmacy dealing with a request for any chemical not shown in Appendix 12 should refer to the approved supply list and regulations, or seek advice from the Royal Pharmaceutical Society of Great Britain. It should be borne in mind that substances sold as medicinal products or pesticides are not subject to the labelling requirements of the CHIP Regulations 1994 (SI 1994 No.3247, as amended).

Inspection and enforcement

The provisions are enforced as if they were health and safety regulations made under the Health and Safety at Work etc. Act 1974.

Where a dangerous substance is supplied in or from a registered pharmacy the enforcing authority is the Royal Pharmaceutical Society of Great Britain. The enforcing authority in relation to supplies made in any shop, market stall or other retail outlet is the local weights and measures authority and in all other cases the Health and Safety Executive (reg.16).

Classification

Substances or preparations which are dangerous to supply have to be classified by the manufacturer. The manufacturer must decide what kind of danger the chemical presents and allocate to it a phrase describing the general nature of the risk attached to it (a *risk phrase*).

Each substance or preparation is classified in the approved list as to its category of danger.

1   *Physico-chemical properties*: explosive, extremely flammable, highly flammable or flammable, and oxidising;
2   *Health effects*: very toxic, toxic, harmful, irritant, corrosive, sensitising, carcinogenic, mutagenic and toxic for reproduction;
3   *Dangerous to the environment*.

All substances and preparations which are classified as carcinogenic, mutagenic or toxic for reproduction, together with certain solvents (e.g. chloroform and carbon tetrachloride) have to be labelled *Restricted for professional users* and thus cannot be sold to the general public.

Pharmacists will normally not have to classify dangerous substances or preparations as this will have been done by the supplier. However, if a pharmacist still produces preparations to his/her own formulation then s/he will have to classify the dangers.

Each classification of danger will carry with it indications of danger, particular risks, and safety precautions, which will be required when such substances or preparations are labelled and sold.

Indications of danger

There are ten categories of indications of danger. Each category has its own symbol, which must be in black on an orange/yellow background. The symbols (Appendix 12) are:

1   explosive: an exploding bomb;
2   extremely flammable, highly flammable: a flame;
3   very toxic, toxic: a skull and cross-bones;
4   corrosive: a hand and a piece of metal being dissolved by liquid dropping from two test tubes;
5   oxidising: a flame over a circle;
6   irritant, harmful: a St Andrew's cross; and
7   dangerous to the environment: a tree and a fish.

Indication of particular risks

Each dangerous substance or preparation is classified in the approved list as to the indications of particular risks with which the receptacle must be labelled. These include, for example: *reacts violently with water*; *irritating to the eyes*; *harmful if swallowed*; *explosive when mixed with a combustible material*; *sensitising*; *carcinogenic*, etc. (Appendix 12).

Indication of safety precautions required

Each dangerous substance or preparation is classified in the approved list as to the indication of safety precautions with which the receptacle must be labelled. These include (Appendix 12), for example: *keep out of the reach of children*; *wear suitable protective clothing*; *never add water to this product*.

Packaging

It is unlawful to supply any person with a substance or preparation dangerous to supply unless it is in a receptacle which is designed, constructed, maintained and closed so as to prevent its escape when subjected to the stresses and strains of normal handling. This does not prevent the fitting of a suitable safety device (reg.8).

When the receptacle is fitted with a replaceable closure, the latter must be so designed that the receptacle can be repeatedly reclosed without the contents escaping.

The packaging must be made of materials which are neither adversely affected by the substance nor liable in conjunction with that substance to produce another substance which is a risk to the health and safety of the public (reg.8).

Receptacle means a vessel or the innermost layer of packaging which is in contact with the substance and which is liable to be individually handled when the substance is used and includes any closure or fastener.

Package means the package in which a substance or preparation is supplied and which is liable to be individually handled during the course of the supply and includes the receptacle containing the substance or preparation and any other packaging associated with it and any pallet or other device which enables more than one receptacle containing a substance or preparation to be handled as a unit, but does not include:

1   a freight container (other than a tank container), a skip, a vehicle or other article of transport equipment; or
2   in the case of supply by way of retail, any wrapping such as a paper or plastic bag into which the package is placed when presented to the purchaser.

Child-resistant closures

Child-resistant closures must be used on certain products when sold to the general public. These substances or preparations include those that are classified as *toxic*, *very toxic*, or *corrosive* and methanol above 3 per cent (reg.12).

Tactile danger warnings

In order to aid the blind and partially sighted, a tactile danger warning (EN ISO 11683) (SI 2000 No.2381), such as a raised triangle, must be used on packaging when products classified as *harmful*, *highly flammable*, *extremely flammable*, *toxic*, *very toxic* and *corrosive* are sold to the general public (reg.12).

Labelling for supply

Labelling for supply must be in English, unless supply is to another member state of the EU, when it has to be in the language of that state. It must be clearly and indelibly marked on a part of the package reserved for that purpose and securely fixed with its entire surface in contact with the package. Where it is impracticable to attach a label in this way, because the package is an awkward shape or is too small, then it may be attached in some other appropriate manner.

The colour and nature of the markings on the label must be such that the symbols required (see below) stand out from the background so as to be readily noticeable and the wording be of such a size and spacing as to be easily read (reg.11).

The package must be labelled so that the particulars can be read horizontally when the package is set down normally (reg.11).

The dimensions of the label must be in accordance with Table 20.1.

Table 20.1   Label dimensions for supply

Capacity of package	Dimensions of label
(a) 3 litres or less	If possible at least 52 mm × 74 mm
(b) Exceeding 3 litres but not exceeding 50 litres	At least 74 mm × 105 mm
(c) Exceeding 50 litres but not exceeding 500 litres	At least 105 mm × 148 mm
(d) Exceeding 500 litres	At least 148 mm × 210 mm

Any symbol required to be shown must be printed in black on an orange/yellow background and its size, including the orange/yellow background, must be at least equal to one-tenth of the area of a label and in any case shall not be less than 100 mm^2 (reg.11).

Where because of the size of the label it is not reasonably practicable to provide safety phrases on the label, that information may be given on a separate label or on a sheet accompanying the package (reg.9).

No *dangerous substance* may be supplied unless it is in a package which clearly shows the following particulars [reg.9(2)]:

1   the name and full address and telephone number of a person in a member state who is responsible for supplying the substance, whether s/he is the importer, manufacturer, or distributor;
2   the name of the substance;
3   the following particulars:

   (a)   the indication(s) of danger and the corresponding symbol(s) (if any);
   (b)   the risk phrases (set out in full);
   (c)   the safety phrases (set out in full); and
   (d)   the EEC number and, in the case of a substance dangerous for supply which is listed in Part 1 of the approved supply list, the words *EC label* or *EEC label*;

4   certain substances which are specified in Schedule 6 to the regulations
     and which are classified as carcinogenic, mutagenic or toxic for repro-
     duction have to be labelled *Restricted for professional users.*

NB The risk and safety phrases need not be shown on packages of 125 ml or
less except if the substance is classified as *flammable, highly flammable,
oxidising* or *irritant.*

   No *dangerous preparation* may be supplied unless it is in a package which
clearly shows the following particulars [reg.9(3)]:

1   the name and full address and telephone number of a person in a
     member state who is responsible for supplying the preparation whether
     s/he is the importer, manufacturer, or distributor;
2   the trade name or other designation of the preparation;
3   the following particulars:

     (a)   the identification of the constituents of the preparation which
           result in the preparation being classified as dangerous to supply;
     (b)   the indication(s) of danger and the corresponding symbol(s)
           (if any);
     (c)   the risk phrases (set out in full);
     (d)   the safety phrases (set out in full); and
     (e)   in the case of a preparation intended for sale to the public, the
           nominal quantity;

Figure 20.1   Example of a label

Mineralised Methylated Spirits	
	Highly flammable Toxic by inhalation and if swallowed Keep locked up and out of reach of children Keep container tightly closed Keep away from sources of ignition - no smoking
	Avoid contact with skin In case of accident or if you feel unwell, seek medical advice immediately and show label where possible
EEC 250 659 6	
Tel: 0101 1111	A.N.Other MRPharmS 1 High Street Blanktown 500 ml

4   certain preparations which are specified in Schedule 6 to the regulations and which are classified as carcinogenic, mutagenic or toxic for reproduction have to be labelled *Restricted for professional users*.

Data sheets

Safety data sheets have to be provided when substances and preparations which are subject to the regulations are supplied for the first time in connection with work (e.g. a supply to a doctor for use in his/her practice, to a health centre, to factories, etc.). This is to ensure that the recipient can take any necessary precautions relating to the protection of health and safety at work and relating to the protection of the environment.

The supplier must ensure that the data sheet is kept up to date and revise it in line with any new health or safety information. A revised data sheet must be supplied to a customer who has received a supply within the last 12 months.

Data sheets do not have to be given when supplies are made to the general public for their private use.

The data sheet must contain the following headings: identification of the substance/preparation, composition/information on the product, supplier's name, hazard identification, first-aid measures, fire-fighting measures, accidental release measures, handling and storage, exposure controls and personal protection, and physical and chemical properties.

Control of Substances Hazardous to Health (COSHH) Regulations

The Control of Substances Hazardous to Health Regulations 1999 (SI 1999 No.437), made under the Health and Safety at Work Act, imposes duties on employers to protect employees and other persons who may be exposed to substances hazardous to health and imposes certain duties on employees concerning their own protection in the workplace. The regulations implement a number of European Directives and are consistent particularly with Council Directive 80/1107/EEC, which provides for protection of workers from risks related to exposure from chemical, physical and biological agents.

The regulations apply to any place of work including hospital or community pharmacies, pharmaceutical laboratories or administrative offices. They cover virtually any substance (except those subject to specific legislation such as asbestos, ionising radiation) but are particularly relevant to pesticides, chemicals, harmful microorganisms and medicines. Persons consuming medicines are not covered by the regulations.

COSHH requires that an assessment of risk is made of substances used and procedures operated in the workplace.

Risk means the likelihood of harm in the actual circumstances of use and depends on, for example, how the substance is used, who is using it, how much substance is involved, how long the exposure and what precautions are taken. A high-level hazard could arise from mishandling a low-risk substance, for example licking the fingers while handling metallic mercury. The level of hazard is usually greater following ingestion and becomes progressively less through inhalation to skin contamination as a result of leakage and spillage.

Every employer must ensure that the exposure of their employees to substances hazardous to health is either prevented or, where this is not reasonably practicable, is adequately controlled. *Substances hazardous to health* are those as defined in the CHIP Regulations 1994 (p. 237).

No employer must carry out work which is liable to expose their employees to any hazardous substance unless they have made a suitable and sufficient assessment of the risks created by that work and the steps needed to avoid risk as set out in the regulations. Where employees are exposed to risk, the employer must ensure that they are under suitable health surveillance.

Manufacturers of substances which may be hazardous to health must provide full details (e.g. labels, leaflets, data sheets, instruction manuals) of the precautions to be taken when handling the substance.

Employers must take measures to train and inform staff of the dangers, to prevent or minimise exposure where possible and, if necessary, monitor exposure and implement a health surveillance programme for all those exposed. Risk can be reduced by avoiding the substance altogether, using a safer substance or the same substance in a safer form, by enclosing the process and extracting the by-products, by improving ventilation or hygiene facilities, by instituting safer handling procedures or by introducing personal protective equipment such as gloves, masks and respirators. In cases of difficulty, advice should be sought from the local area office of the Health and Safety Executive or from the local authority environmental health officer.

Summary

- The CHIP regulations, as amended, require that all substances and preparations defined as dangerous to supply must be classified, usually by the supplier, as to the kind of danger the chemical presents and it must be allocated a phrase that describes the general nature of the risk.
- All substances and preparations defined as dangerous to supply must be supplied in packages which comply with the standards set out in the regulations including child-resistant closures and tactile warnings.
- All packages must be labelled with the appropriate symbols of danger, the relevant risk phrases and safety precautions.
- The COSHH Regulations impose duties on employers to protect employees and other persons who may be exposed to substances hazardous to health and impose certain duties on employees concerning their own protection in the workplace.

- Employers must take measures to train and inform staff of the dangers, to prevent or minimise exposure where possible and, if necessary, monitor exposure and implement a health surveillance programme for all those exposed.

Further reading

COSHH (1998) *The New Brief Guide for Employers*, IND(G 136(L) (rev). Health and Safety Executive, London.

Health and Safety Executive (2000) *The Complete Idiot's Guide to CHIP*. IND(G)181(D). HSE Books, Sudbury.

Medicines, Ethics and Practice (published annually) The Royal Pharmaceutical Society of Great Britain, London.

CHAPTER TWENTY-ONE

Miscellaneous legislation affecting pharmacy

The principal statutes concerning medicines, controlled drugs, poisons, spirits and dangerous substances have been explained in Chapters 2 to 20. There remain several enactments, and other measures, which are relevant to pharmacy. Some are of general application; others may apply only to one of the branches of pharmacy practice. This chapter comprises notes on the remaining statutes and regulations. The law outlined is that applying in England and Wales. Where the law in Scotland differs it is described (e.g. jury service).

The notes are grouped under appropriate subject headings, as follows:

- pharmacy ownership
- employment law
- retail law
- health and safety law
- controls on waste, on pesticides and controls to protect animals and birds
- merchant shipping: medical scales
- data protection and freedom of information
- jury service.

Pharmacy ownership

A full explanation has been given in Chapter 5 of the controls applied by the Medicines Act 1968 to the conduct of 'retail pharmacy businesses'. As such, a business can be owned by an individual pharmacist, a partnership of pharmacists or a body corporate (i.e. a company); it is desirable that the legal status of partnerships and companies should be understood. Only a brief explanation can be given here and any pharmacist contemplating ownership should seek legal advice.

Partnerships

A partnership is defined in the Partnership Act 1890 as the relationship which exists between persons carrying on a business in common with a view of profit. In contrast to a company (see below), a partnership, or *firm*, is simply a number of individuals each of whom has a responsibility for the affairs and the liabilities of the firm as a whole.

In England and Wales a partnership (firm) does not have a legal status of its own as does a company. This means that the private assets of each partner can be called upon to satisfy any of the firm's debts. All the partners are liable for any debts incurred by one partner acting on behalf of the firm.

In Scotland, a partnership has a status similar to that of a body corporate (i.e. it *is a legal person distinct from the partners of whom it is composed*). It is for this reason that in a partnership owning a retail pharmacy in England and Wales, all the partners must be pharmacists, whereas in a Scottish partnership only one partner need be a pharmacist (Chapter 5).

A partnership can arise in either of two ways: by express agreement or by implied agreement between two or more persons. A partnership can be implied if two or more persons work together in such a way as to fall within the definition as set out in the Act. Generally, if they share in the management of the business and share the profits, then the law will recognise them as partners.

When a partnership is formed to run a retail pharmacy, it is invariably a partnership of express agreement, and the conditions of the partnership are set out in a partnership contract or articles. The articles can be altered at any time with the consent of all the partners, whether this is express or implied. The only exception is where the articles restrict the right to vary (e.g. that no change may be made for two years).

A partnership can be formed where one of the partners may limit their responsibility for the firm's debts, leaving the other partners to share the unlimited liability. This partner is often referred to as a *sleeping partner*, as s/he takes no part in the management of the firm. Partnerships of this type are not common and are governed by the Limited Partnerships Act 1907. If a person wishes to limit their liability in this way today, they are more likely to invest in a limited company. Once again, it is stressed that before contemplating forming a partnership pharmacists should take legal advice and have any partnership contract drawn up by a solicitor.

The Limited Liability Partnership Act 2000 allowed the creation of Limited Liability Partnerships (LLPs) within England, Scotland and Wales to retain the organisational flexibility and tax treatment of a partnership but also derive benefit from the separate legal personality of a company with limited liability. LLPs must register and submit annual accounts to Companies House.

Companies

A company – or corporation aggregate – is a body of persons combined or incorporated for some common purpose. The most common example is a registered trading company, that is, a company which has been incorporated under the Companies Act 1985. This Act is a consolidation of the law relating to companies contained in a number of earlier statutes, including certain sections of the European Communities Act 1972. The notes given here can only outline the general principles of company law, with some special reference to certain aspects which particularly affect pharmacy businesses.

Incorporation as a company enables a group of people to act and to trade in the same way as an individual owner. It also enables them to trade with limited liability to the individual shareholder. Once incorporated, a company is *a legal person* and quite distinct from its members. It can own property, employ persons and be a creditor or debtor just like a human being. This is the fundamental principle of company law.

The promoters of a company must file the following documents with the Register of Companies:

1   memorandum of association;
2   articles of association;
3   list of directors and name of secretary;
4   statement of the nominal share capital;
5   notice of the address of the registered office; and
6   declaration by a solicitor or a person named in the articles as a director or secretary that all the requirements of the Companies Acts in respect of registration have been complied with.

If all the documents are in order, the registrar will issue a certificate of incorporation which is conclusive evidence that the company has been registered and that the requirements of the Act have been complied with.

There are at least three types of company: a public company, a private limited company and a private unlimited company. Most pharmacists will be concerned with the private company, whether limited or not.

A *private company* needs only one director but if there is a sole director, s/he cannot also be the company secretary. Shares and debentures in a private company cannot be offered to the public.

An *unlimited company* is one where there is no limit on the members' liability to contribute to the assets in order to satisfy the company's debts.

Memorandum of association

The memorandum of association regulates the external affairs of the company and must include five clauses, namely those relating to the name, registered office, objects, liability and capital of the company. It must be signed by each subscriber.

The name of a private limited company must end with the word *limited*. For a public limited company the last words must be *public limited company* or *plc*.

There is a general freedom of choice of the company name, but a company cannot be registered under the Act by a name which includes, otherwise than at the end of its name, the word *limited, unlimited* or *public limited company* or the Welsh equivalents (e.g. *cfyngedig*). Where *cfyngedig* is used, the fact that the company is a limited company must be stated in English and in legible characters on all official company stationery and publications, and in a notice conspicuously displayed in every place where the company's business is carried on.

No name may be used which the registrar considers offensive or which, if used, would constitute a criminal offence. In the latter category would fall a retail company which is not conducting a retail pharmacy business and which wished to use the title *chemist*.

Certain words and expressions may only be used in company or business names with the approval of the Secretary of State or other relevant body specified in regulations (SI 1981 No.1685, as amended). For the word *chemist* the Royal Pharmaceutical Society of Great Britain is the relevant body, but, when *chemist* or *chemistry* is used in an industrial sense, it is the Royal Society of Chemistry. Similarly, for the word *apothecary* the relevant body in England and Wales is the Worshipful Society of Apothecaries and in Scotland, the Royal Pharmaceutical Society of Great Britain.

Articles of association

The articles regulate the internal affairs of the company (i.e. the rights of shareholders and the manner in which the business of the company is conducted). A model set of articles is set out in regulations made under the Act. It may be used by a company as it is or adapted as required. If no articles are submitted with the application for registration, the statutory ones will apply. The articles of a company are freely alterable by special resolution, subject to certain safeguards.

The legal effect of the memorandum and articles is that they bind the company and its members as if they had been signed and sealed by each individual member and contained covenants on the part of each member to observe all the provisions of the memorandum and articles.

Directors

The first directors of a company are usually appointed in accordance with the articles; if not they are appointed by the original subscribers to the company. Subsequent appointments are usually governed by a procedure laid down in the articles. It must be stressed that a pharmacist becoming a director should be fully aware of the contents of the memorandum and articles of association of the company s/he joins. Directors must exercise their powers as directors for the benefit of the company. A director has a duty to the company to exercise such skill and care as s/he possesses. If appointed in a specific capacity calling for a particular skill (e.g. a pharmacist who is a director of a body corporate), s/he must exercise that skill in a reasonable manner for the benefit of the company. Directors are not bound to give continuing and unremitting attention to the company's affairs and are justified in trusting the officers of the company to perform their duties honestly.

A pharmacist who becomes superintendent chemist of a company will almost invariably be appointed a director, and a knowledge of the powers and duties of directors is essential. For example, if a company fails to make its annual return then the company and/or any of its officers or directors is liable to a default fine. A pharmacist who resigns as a superintendent chemist should ensure that s/he also resigns as a director. Instances have occurred where a pharmacist, some years after having resigned as a superintendent chemist, has been prosecuted for failing to make an annual return as s/he had remained a director of the company.

Business Names Act 1985

A *business name* is a name used by a business which is other than (a) for a sole trader, his/her surname; (b) for a partnership, the surnames or corporate names of all members of the partnership, or (c) for a corporate business, the names of the company concerned. Certain additions are permitted (e.g. forenames or initials).

Where a business name is used, the true name(s) and address(es) of the owner(s) must appear on all business stationery and that information must be prominently displayed at the business premises. The use of certain types of business name require the written approval of the Secretary of State and regulations may specify certain words or expressions which may only be used with the approval of a government department or some other relevant body.

Employment law

Knowledge of employment law is important to pharmacists both in their capacity as employer and as employee. Employment rights derive from two main areas: those created by Acts of Parliament (statutory employment rights) and those created by decisions of courts over time (common law rights; Chapter 1).

Statutory employment rights

Employment rights cover rights such as equal pay, sick pay, the right not to be unlawfully discriminated against on the grounds of sex or marital status, sexual orientation, race, disability, religion or belief, trade union membership, part-time or fixed term status, not to suffer a detriment for making a protected closure in the public interest ('whistle blowing') and not to be dismissed unfairly. Employees have also been granted rights to a written statement of the terms of employment, of the reasons for dismissal, minimum disciplinary procedures, to be accompanied at a disciplinary hearing, an itemised pay statement, time off for public duties, time off for antenatal care, time off for care of dependants, a minimum wage, a minimum period of notice for termination of employment, maternity leave and pay, paternity leave and pay, to request flexible working and entitlement to rest breaks and restrictions on weekly working time. This list is not exhaustive.

The rights are enforceable by employees in the Employment Tribunal. Some rights require the employee to have a qualifying period of service before they be enforced in the Employment Tribunal. The compensation that can be awarded by the tribunal is sometimes subject to a statutory minimum or a statutory cap depending on the nature of the claim. However, in other claims, the tribunal considers what is just and equitable in all the circumstances having regard to the loss sustained by the employee.

In the context of employment law, *disability* means 'a physical or mental impairment which has a substantial and long-term adverse effect on a person's ability to carry out normal day-to-day activities'. *Day-to-day activities* involve mobility; manual dexterity; physical co-ordination; ability to lift, carry or move ordinary objects; speech, hearing or eyesight; memory; or ability to concentrate, learn, understand or perceive physical danger. Thus the definition includes those with hearing or visual impairment, those with learning disabilities or mental illness and those with long-term illnesses such as severe arthritis, human immunodeficiency virus infection, multiple sclerosis and muscular dystrophy. Certain conditions are excluded, notably addiction to alcohol, nicotine or non-therapeutic drugs.

Common law rights

In the employment context, the principal common law claim is where an employee claims that the employer has acted in breach of the contract of employment. Employment Tribunals can deal with breach of contract claims where the breach has arisen or is outstanding on the termination of the employment. There is a limit of £25 000 on the awards a tribunal can make in these circumstances. Alternatively, employees can make claims either in the

County Court or High Court (Chapter 1), depending on the amount of damages claimed and other certain criteria applied by the courts.

European law

Sometimes, UK national law is in conflict with EU legislation. In these instances, the case may be referred to the European Court of Justice (Chapter 1), the decisions of which will be binding on UK courts and tribunals. Decisions of the European Court of Justice may also result in amendments to national law.

Further information on this complex and fast changing area of law can be obtained at the websites at the end of this chapter.

Vicarious liability

The term *vicarious liability* in this context signifies the liability which an employer may incur to a customer for damage caused by an employee in the course of his/her employment. This in legal terms is the relationship between *master* and *servant* and means that the 'master' cannot only order or require *what* must be done but also *how* it shall be done.

All employee pharmacists should have a contract of employment but in many areas pharmacists themselves will decided *how* a task should be performed and this will often be a matter for the pharmacist's own professional judgment. Therefore, if an employee pharmacist makes a mistake or is so careless as to cause *damage* (e.g. injury, fear, anxiety, etc.) to a patient or customer, the employer would probably be liable. However, if the act or omission fell into the realm of professional judgment, the pharmacist may also incur additional personal liability and might be accountable to the Society and/or to his/her employer to justify his/her actions. This is why pharmacists are advised to carry their own professional indemnity insurance or ensure that they practise only in an establishment which is covered by such insurance (see pp. 312 and 328 and Appendix 16).

Access to services

From October 2004, it became unlawful for businesses or organisations providing services (which includes pharmacy services) to treat disabled people less favourably than other people for a reason related to their disability. Such service providers must consider making changes to physical features that make it difficult for disabled people to use their services. In response to a Disability Rights Task Force Report, the Government intends in 2005 to introduce a new duty on the public sector to promote equality for disabled people. This means taking positive steps to encourage, identify and support people with disabilities in accessing health services – a similar duty to that placed on the education sector a few years earlier.

Retail law

All retailers are subject to controls on price, description and the safety of the goods they sell. The majority of the law in this area is enforced by the local authority, usually the trading standards department. In some cities, those duties may be shared with the local environmental health officer. The general principle of most of this law is that it makes it a criminal offence to mislead consumers as to the description, price or safety of goods and services. The majority of the criminal offences in this area are strict liability offences, coupled to a defence of due diligence. It is, therefore, vitally important that processes and procedures are in place so that a pharmacist can show that s/he took reasonable steps and precautions to check that descriptions of goods and services were accurate or that the goods s/he sold were safe. The following points should be specifically noted.

Trades Descriptions Act 1968

The Trades Descriptions Act makes it an offence to falsely describe goods or services in the course of a trade or business. The law is wide enough to cover all forms of description and it should be noted that the retailer is to some extent in double jeopardy as there is an offence for supplying goods to which a false description has been applied as well as an offence of applying a false description to goods. Particular care needs to be taken where verbal descriptions are being applied to goods, as the individual becomes personally liable for those descriptions should they subsequently prove to be inaccurate. With regard to services, it is an offence to knowingly make a false statement.

Consumer Protection Act 1987

PRODUCT LIABILITY

The Consumer Protection Act 1987 creates liability without fault on the part of the producer for damage caused by a defect in their product. Four classes of person may face liability for a defective product: the manufacturer, the importer, the person who holds themselves out as the manufacturer or, in the event of none of the former being identified, the person supplying the product to the victim. The first three groups have a primary liability; the supplier has a secondary liability based upon their inability to identify a primary producer. When medicines might be the subject of an action in the courts (there have been very few cases under the Act), the primary producer will normally be the product licence holder. The supplying pharmacist should, therefore, ensure that s/he has adequate systems and records to ensure that the licence holder or manufacturer can always be identified with some certainty. Liability probably does not arise from repackaging licensed medicines or from supplying them against a prescription, provided the source is known.

The supplying pharmacist will carry full liability for 'own branded' goods in which the pharmacy's name and address are affixed to containers of medicines made up elsewhere and not so identified. The supplying pharmacist also carries full liability when s/he prepares his/her own remedies for a patient under section 10 of the Medicines Act (see p. 41). In these circumstances, it is advisable to maintain full manufacturing records so that the producer of the ingredients can always be identified. Claims may be made for up to three years after the 'relevant date' – when the victim became aware of the facts – subject to a maximum of ten years from the date of putting the product into circulation.

PRICE CONTROL

Customers' rights on pricing are protected in two areas of consumer protection law: controls on misleading price indications and requirements to display price, and in certain circumstances unit price, in close proximity to the goods. It is an offence to give a misleading price indication and it is, therefore, important for any pharmacist involved in retailing to be aware of the Code of Practice for Traders on Price Indications. This code provides guidance to retailers on what constitutes 'misleading' and how 'offer' prices can be constructed. A second obligation is simply a requirement to display a price, in such a way that customers see it without having to ask, in close proximity to all goods available for sale. If those goods are required to be sold by weight or measure, then there is an obligation to give a unit price (cost per kilogram/ litre) as well as the actual selling price. Unit price controls do not apply to medicines. Within pharmacies, cosmetics, toiletries and food supplements are the items most likely to be affected. Unit price controls apply only in larger stores (over 280 m^2). Details of the controls are complicated and subject to change. Advice on price indications should, therefore, be sought from the local trading standards department.

SAFETY OF GOODS

Consumer protection law also creates an obligation to provide customers with goods that are safe. Any reasonably foreseeable risks arising out of the goods should have been dealt with by the manufacturer and addressed either by changing the design of the goods to make them safer or by issuing warnings or instructions that deal with the issue. Where local authorities find unsafe goods, as well as prosecuting they can also serve enforcement notices requiring that the products are removed from the marketplace.

Weights and Measures Act 1985

The Weights and Measures Act 1985 and the regulations made under it control the manner in which goods should be weighed, measured and retailed. They also control the way quality indications should be given on the packaging. The legislation lays down specific construction criteria for equipment and measures and sets down the accuracy tests that the equipment must pass if it is to be used for selling goods. The regulations also set out a detailed regime for the packaging of goods, and those pharmacists involved in packing bulk goods should consult the Code of Practice for Guidance of Packers available from the Stationery Office as well as seeking guidance from the local trading standards department. The selling of goods deficient in weight or volume is a strict liability offence but defences are available.

Competition Act 1998

The Competition Act 1998 reflects a worldwide trend to open up markets, stimulate competition and establish transparent and fair marketing arrangements. It seeks to do this by outlawing agreements between businesses and decisions taken by businesses on concerted practices that affect trade in the UK or Europe. Those decisions are not allowed to have as their object or effect the prevention, distortion or restriction of competition within the UK. An example of such a practice would be people acting together directly or indirectly to fix the purchase or selling process. The rules not only affect retailers but also trade associations or any other group of persons acting together in a way as to distort competition. The fines under the Competition Act can be very high as the maximum ceiling on the fine is 10% of company turnover.

In pharmacy, the advent of the Competition Act led to the abolition of *resale price maintenance* on the price at which medicines available over the counter could be supplied (*Pharm J* 16 August 1997 p. 236; 25 October 1997 p. 676). This Act has also affected the profession's Code of Ethics. The rules of trade associations and professional bodies are covered by the anticompetitive prohibitions in the Act, unless they are specifically exempted in Schedule 4. For historical reasons, pharmacy was not included in Schedule 4 (although some other health professions were) and the Code of Ethics for pharmacy must comply with the provisions of the Act. Prior to 2002, Codes of Ethics contained several restraints, in the public interest, on the promotion and supply of medicines. The current code has been modified to comply with the Competition Act.

Websites providing detailed information on trading and other retail law are given at the end of this chapter.

Health and Safety law

Health and Safety at Work Act 1974 and other related Acts

The Health and Safety at Work Act 1974 is extremely broad and basically sets out the requirements for a 'duty of care' for everyone in the workplace, including the protection of the health and safety of the public against the risks to health arising from work activities. It, therefore, applies to employers, employees, owners/occupiers of premises, suppliers and the self-employed. The Act provides a framework for other health and safety legislation. Detailed requirements are set out in specific regulations; an example being the Workplace (Health, Safety and Welfare) Regulations 1992 (SI 1992 No.3004). These regulations are themselves supported by an Approved Code of Practice that expands the requirements contained within individual regulations by providing detailed interpretation and guidance. Approved Codes of Practice are the main working documents for those with health and safety responsibilities.

Employers have a duty of care under the Health and Safety at Work etc. Act, together with its associated regulations, to ensure, so far as is reasonably practicable, the health, safety and welfare of employees while they are at work. The main areas covered are:

- safe plant and machinery (work equipment) and safe operating procedures
- safe use, handling and storage and transport of articles and substances
- provision of information, instruction, training and supervision
- provision and maintenance of a safe place of work with safe means of access and egress
- for an employer with more than four employees, provide a written policy for health and safety and details of the arrangements for carrying out the requirements of the policy.

Employers, including the self-employed (e.g. a locum pharmacist), and owners/occupiers have a similar duty to safeguard the health and safety of others who are not employees but who may be affected by his/her business activities. 'Others' include customers, visitors and the general public. Employees themselves also have a duty under the Act to take reasonable care for their own health and safety and for that of anyone else who may be affected by what they (employees) do or fail to do. There is also a duty to co-operate with their employer on health and safety issues.

Enforcement of health and safety requirements is undertaken by inspectors from the Health and Safety Executive for 'industrial premises' or by officers from the local authorities for 'retail premises'. Both regulatory groups have the powers to inspect, investigate cases of non-compliance, warn and issue 'improvement notices' or 'prohibition notices' as well as prosecute offenders.

It is beyond the scope of this book to provide much detail about health and safety legislation. However, it is important to raise the awareness of *risk assessment* as the basic 'tool' for identifying and managing risk. Areas where risks might arise in pharmacy practice include:

- work equipment (Provision and Use of Work Equipment Regulations)
- substances (COSHH Regulations; Chapter 20)
- manual handling (Manual Handling Operations Regulations).

To manage health and safety risks, it is necessary to identify the risks. The risk assessment process achieves this by examining the workplace itself and work activities (tasks). Hazards (things with the potential to cause harm) are noted and the associated consequences (severity) of each hazard ranked should the harm be inflicted. For each hazardous situation, the types of person at risk are also identified. An assessment is also made of the likelihood of the harm actually occurring, again ranked according to likelihood. An assessment of the risk is then made for each situation based on the equation:

Risk = Consequence × Likelihood for each category of persons at risk.

The basic principles of risk assessment are detailed in a Health and Safety Executive Approved Code of Practice 'Management of Health and Safety at Work Regulations 1999', to which reference should be made. Persons compiling risk assessments must be trained and have sufficient knowledge and experience of the process such that they are able to demonstrate their competence to the persons at risk depending upon the assessment and any regulatory inspector. Consideration should always be given to engaging suitable experts to do this work for anything other than situations where there are low consequences from workplace hazards. A key outcome of risk assessment is to require the identification and implementation of control measures to reduce risks to as low a level as is reasonably practicable. Control measures may range from hardware (e.g. guards for machinery) to procedural matters (e.g. operating procedures) to personal protective equipment (e.g. gloves/goggles). Risk can be eliminated only if a hazard is eliminated. Substituting something less hazardous (e.g. less-toxic cleaning materials) can reduce risk.

Regulatory inspectors would expect to see 'suitable and sufficient' risk assessments during any visit. It is important to review risk assessments and other health and safety arrangements periodically, or in the event of an accident or even a 'near miss', to see if the assessment and control measures are still valid and whether they can be improved to reduce risks to health and safety further. All such assessments should be discussed with employees who are 'at risk'.

Websites providing detailed information on health and safety law are given at the end of this chapter.

Environmental law

The Department for Environment, Food and Rural Affairs (DEFRA) is the government department responsible for a vast range of public services and controls such air quality, noise pollution, litter, energy and chemicals. This section provides an overview of three areas that are relevant to pharmacy practice: controls on waste, controls on pesticides and the protection of animals and birds. Much more information and detail can be found on the DEFRA website listed at the end of this chapter.

Controls on waste

The Environmental Protection Act 1990 introduced a *duty of care* which applies to all persons who import, produce, carry, keep, treat or dispose of controlled waste. This, therefore, applies to pharmacists, who necessarily handle waste or unwanted medicines in the course of their practice. An exemption is given to householders (s.26) but this is not extended to those accepting waste from a private householder, for example, when a pharmacy agrees to take back returned medicines from a patient or patient's relative. The duty of care lies on all holders of waste at every stage in its history, such that a pharmacist having held controlled waste may only pass it on to an *authorised person*, such as a registered carrier, a licensed waste manager or a waste collection or regulation authority. Further, s/he must transfer with the waste such a written description of the waste – a transfer note – as will enable others to avoid committing an offence under the Act. The removal of NHS Crown immunity in 1991 meant that all NHS and governmental incinerators had to meet the full provisions of environmental protection legislation, and a substantial number were substandard in relation to temperature of operation, load limits, smoke emission, warning systems, etc. Anyone consigning medicines or other controlled waste to hospital facilities for disposal must discharge the full duty of care as set out above.

CONTROLLED AND SPECIAL WASTE

Proposals to amend the Special Waste Regulations in England were made in July 2004 and new legislation may be expected in 2005.

At the time of going to press, the Controlled Waste Regulations 1992 (SI 1992 No.588) define *clinical waste* as, amongst other things, 'waste arising from . . .pharmaceutical or similar practice. . .' and describes clinical waste which arises from a private dwelling or residential home as household waste, as distinct from that from any other source, which becomes industrial waste. This is significant because the local waste collection authority has a duty to collect household waste, albeit for a fee, but producers of industrial waste are more likely to have to use private contractors for this purpose.

It is unlawful to deposit controlled waste in, or to keep it on, any land or knowingly cause or permit such waste to be deposited unless a waste management licence authorising the deposit is in force under the Environmental Protection Act 1990. The Water Resources Act 1991 prohibits a person from causing or knowingly permitting any noxious poisonous or polluting matter to enter any controlled inland waters.

A pharmacist whose actions give rise to controlled waste, including a decision to discard such material, is fully bound under the legislation as a producer of controlled waste and carries the corresponding duty of care, including where medicines are returned by patients. A clear interpretation as to how the code of practice should be applied to medicines returned by patients is not available. It is clearly wise to contact the local office of the Environment Agency (or equivalent in Scotland) for specific guidance on compliance with the code.

The special restrictions on the destruction of Controlled Drugs under the Misuse of Drugs Act 1971 were considered in Chapter 17. Controlled Drugs returned by patients are subject to the same considerations described above for other returned medicines and advice should be sought from the relevant environment agency. Unwanted stocks of Controlled Drugs are still subject to the requirement for witnessed destruction on the site of their production but disposal via the sewage system does not comply with the Water Resources Act. Accordingly, the practice has developed that the pharmacist will arrange with the relevant environment agency for the drugs to be subject to a process of denaturing. The resultant product and its container is then treated as a special waste.

Controlled waste includes household, industrial and commercial waste of any kind, whether conventionally thought of as polluting or not.

The Special Waste Regulations 1996 (SI 1996 No.972, as amended) made under the Act provide that waste falling within certain descriptions should be designated as *special waste* and subject to more extensive documentation than is required for non-special waste before it may be removed from premises. Most consignments of special waste require prior notice being given to the waste regulation authorities, namely the Environment Agency in England and Wales and the Scottish Environmental Protection Agency in Scotland; fees are payable.

Special waste means controlled waste containing substances listed in Schedule II to the regulations and which has specified hazardous properties (set out in the regulations) or is a Prescription Only Medicine.

The responsibility for enforcing the provisions of the Act lies with the waste regulation authorities. Local authorities have a responsibility for physical collection and disposal of controlled waste in their capacities as water collection and waste disposal authorities.

Where an offence has been committed by a body corporate and it is proved to have been committed with consent or connivance, or attributable to any neglect on the part of a director, manager, secretary or other similar officer of the body corporate, including a member concerned with management where the affairs are managed by its members (e.g. a co-operative society), then that person is also guilty of the offence. Thus, pharmacist directors of companies and, indeed, individual pharmacists could be liable under this Act for wrongful disposal, without notice, of medicinal products and non-medicinal poisons. This is particularly pertinent when a pharmacy closes down and old stocks of, for example arsenicals and mercurials, are being destroyed.

In March 1997, the Producer Responsibilities Obligations (Packaging Waste) Regulations 1997 (SI 1997 No.648) set obligations for the recovery and recycling of packaging waste. From 1 January 2000, businesses handling more than 50 tonnes of packaging waste per year and with a turnover of more than £1m must comply. A 'shared producer responsibility' may be adopted whereby each part of the supply chain undertakes a share of the recovery targets. Businesses must register with the Environment Agency or its Scottish equivalent, pay a fee, provide data on the packaging passing through their business and certify that they reached their targets each year. Special waste packaging, which includes packaging immediately in contact with Prescription Only Medicines, is not covered by the regulations but must be included in the calculations. (An article on the practical implications for pharmacy practice appeared in *Pharm J* 2 August 1997 p.186.)

The Carriage of Dangerous Goods (Classification, Packaging and Labelling) Regulations 1996 (SI 1996 No.2092) require carriers of what is termed *healthcare waste* under proposed Health and Safety Executive guidelines to use new containers for such waste and different containers for *healthcare risk waste*, which may include pharmaceutical waste. Carriers can be expected to pass on these new requirements to their customers and expect the latter to change their methods as to how they separate, pack and label their waste.

Controls on pesticides

The Food and Environment Protection Act 1985 is concerned, amongst other matters, with the reduction of pollution of the environment by pesticides. Subject to certain exemptions, the Control of Pesticide Regulations 1986 (SI 1986 No.1510, as amended) prohibit the advertisement, sale, supply, storage and use of pesticides unless in accordance with an approval and consent given by DEFRA. Any breach of the regulations may result in seizure and disposal of the offending pesticide and any material treated with it, and an order for remedial action.

Pesticide is defined as 'products used for the control of rats and mice, flies and other garden pests, cyanide, strychnine, wood and masonry treatments, and pesticides used in public health maintenance'. Additional restrictions are placed on *pesticides approved for agricultural use*. These apply to all crop protection products such as herbicides, fungicides and insecticides, plus some soil sterilants and fumigants. The regulations and consents are supplemented by two codes of practice: one dealing with sale, supply and storage, and the other covering use.

Failure on the part of any person to follow the guidance given in the codes does not of itself render that person liable to proceedings, but such failure is admissible in evidence in any criminal proceedings brought under the Act.

Anyone stocking in excess of 200 litres or 200 kg of *pesticides approved for agricultural use* must comply with parts of the code dealing with the physical construction, design and maintenance of sites used for the storage of any pesticide. A person in charge of a store or a salesperson who advises on the use of these products must be in possession of the appropriate Ministry certificate.

Anyone offering a commercial service for the use of pesticides must possess ministry certification, and any persons using pesticides must be instructed as to such matters as storage and transport on the farm, application techniques and disposal and record keeping.

The effect of all these provisions is to impose the following obligations upon anyone selling, supplying or storing pesticides.

1   They and their staff must be provided with such instructions and guidance as is necessary to enable them to be competent for the duties they are called upon to perform.
2   All reasonable precautions must be taken, especially with regard to storage and transport, to protect the health of human beings and creatures, and to safeguard the environment.
3   The pesticide must be sold or supplied in the container supplied by the manufacturer of the pesticide and under the label approved by the Ministry.

STRYCHNINE

Under pesticides legislation, strychnine must be labelled with an approved label, supplied in original containers and supplied only to holders of an authority to purchase issued by DEFRA (England), a person authorised by the Scottish Ministers (Scotland) or a person authorised by the National Assembly for Wales (Wales). The authority should be retained by the users, but the supplying pharmacist is not required to see it (see also p. 224).

Controls to protect animals and birds

ANIMALS IN RESEARCH

The Animal (Scientific Procedures) Act 1986 makes provision for the protection of animals used for experimental or scientific procedures. A *protected animal* for the purposes of the Act means *any living vertebrate other than a human*. Any experimental or other scientific procedure applied to a protected animal which may have the effect of causing that animal pain, suffering, distress or lasting harm is known as a *regulated procedure*. The Act provides for a system of (a) personal licences, (b) project licences and (c) scientific establishment licences. Before issuing any licence, the Secretary of State must consult one of the inspectors appointed under the Act (s.9). The breeding and sale of animals for experimental purposes is also controlled.

The Act specifies the type of programmes for which project licences may be issued including, amongst other things, the prevention, diagnosis or treatment of disease; certain educational purposes; and forensic enquiries. Projects may only be carried out by licensed persons on licensed scientific establishments. The Act deals specifically with humane methods of killing experimental animals. The Animals Procedures Committee has the duty of advising the Secretary of State on matters concerned with the Act. S/he may consult the Committee on the question of licences and on the preparation of codes of practice.

WILD ANIMALS AND FARM LIVESTOCK

Where under the Animal (Cruel Poisons) Act 1962, the Secretary of State has specified that a poison cannot be used for destroying animals without causing undue suffering and that other suitable methods of destroying them exist, s/he may, by regulations, prohibit or restrict the use of that poison for destroying animals or animals of a particular description.

Regulations have been made (SI 1963 No.1278) which prohibit the use of yellow phosphorus and red squill for the destruction of animals. The regulations also prohibit the use of strychnine for killing any animals except moles. The supply of these substances for prohibited purposes could constitute aiding and abetting an offence under the Act.

NB Where the Minister believes or suspects that rabies exists in any area, s/he may by an order made under the Rabies Act 1974 declare that area to be an *infected area* for purposes connected with the control and eradication of that disease. S/he may also take steps to secure destruction of foxes in an *infected area* and an officer of DEFRA and any person authorised in writing by the Minister may enter any land for the purpose of carrying out such destruction. Where the Minister exercises this power, methods of destruction may be used (e.g. the use of strychnine) which would apart from these provisions be unlawful [Rabies (Control) Order 1974 (SI 1974 No.2212)]. For restrictions on the sale of strychnine under poisons legislation, see Chapter 17.

The Protection of Animals Act 1911 provides that it is unlawful wilfully to administer, or cause or procure to be administered, to any animal a poisonous or injurious drug or substance. Similarly, it is unlawful to sell or offer or expose for sale any grain or seed which has been rendered poisonous except for *bona fide* use in agriculture. It is also an offence to place upon any land or in any building any poison or any fluid or edible matter (not being seed or grain) which has been rendered poisonous.

It is a defence to prove that the poison was placed for the purpose of destroying insects and other invertebrates where it is found necessary in the interest of public health or agriculture, or to preserve other animals, and that adequate precautions have been taken to prevent injury to dogs, cats, other domestic animals and wild birds [Protection of Animals (Amendment) Act 1927].

A defence also exists where a person uses poisonous gas in a rabbit hole or places in a rabbit hole a substance which by evaporation or any contact with moisture generates poisonous gas [e.g. Cymag (Prevention of Damage by Rabbits Act 1939]. These defences are not valid where the poison concerned is prohibited by the Animal (Cruel Poisons) Act 1962 (see above). It is also a defence under the Wildlife and Countryside Act 1981 to prove that what was done was performed in accordance with a licence granted under that Act.

In relation to wildlife, the Wildlife and Countryside Act 1981 prohibits certain methods of killing or taking of wild birds and wild animals including the laying of 'any poisonous, poisoned or stupefying substance'. The prohibition does not apply to anything done under or in accordance with the terms of a licence granted by the appropriate authority. The appropriate authority varies according to the purpose of the licence (e.g. if the licence is issued for the purpose of preventing the spread of disease, then the appropriate authority is the Agriculture Minister). Such a licence may be issued by Agriculture Ministers for the killing or taking of certain wild birds (e.g. feral pigeons, house sparrows, etc.), using the chemical alpha-chloralose. Alpha-chloralose can be sold to local authorities and to *bona fide* pest control companies who have had issued to them by the Agriculture Minister a licence which allows them to compound and use their own bait. Farmers have been known to make approaches to pharmacists for supplies of alpha-chloralose; although the pharmacist may lawfully supply this chemical under poison legislation, a supply made for the purpose of stupefying birds could be an offence under the Wildlife and Countryside Act 1981. Pharmacists receiving requests for alpha-chloralose or stupefying bait should, before supplying, contact the Royal Pharmaceutical Society of Great Britain for further details.

Merchant shipping: medical scales

The Merchant Shipping and Fishing Vessels (Medical Stores) Regulations 1995 (SI 1995 No.1802, as amended), implement Council Directive 92/29/EEC and make for the minimum safety and health requirements for improved medical treatment so far as the Directive relates to the carriage of medicines and other medical stores. They cover the carrying of appropriate medical stores on board ships, including fishing vessels. A *ship* in this context means a UK ship other than pleasure vessels used for non-commercial purposes and not manned by professional crews and ships employed in inland navigation.

The master of any ship which does not carry a doctor is required to make arrangements for securing medical attention on board ship to be given by himself or by some other person appointed by him/her for the purpose. There are minimum requirements for the medicines and medical stores to be carried before a ship may put to sea and the *scale of medicines* to be carried depends upon whether or not there is a duly qualified medical practitioner in the ship's complement.

The various scales are provided for in the 1995 regulations and in Merchant Shipping Notices M.1607 and M.1608. The regulations also specify requirements for the packaging, labelling, and storage of medicines and other medical items (e.g. disinfectants).

The containers must be labelled amongst other things, with:

1 the name of the medicine, in English, as indicated in the respective scale;
2 the expiry date, where appropriate;
3 any storage requirements;

4   name and address of supplier, product licence number and batch number; and
5   any further information required by the notices.

The containers of capsules and tablets must be capable of reclosure so as to prevent the ingress of moisture.

A ship in the UK may be detained if a person empowered under the Act to inspect the medical stores is not satisfied that the required stores are being carried.

Orders made under the Misuse of Drugs Act 1971 and the Medicines Act 1968 permit the owner or master of a ship which does not carry a doctor as part of its complement to obtain certain Controlled Drugs (see p. 199) and any other Prescription Only Medicines (see p. 113) which are necessary for the treatment of persons on the ship. The medical scales issued under the Merchant Shipping Act are minimum requirements only.

Data protection and freedom of information

Data Protection Act 1998

The Data Protection Act 1998 regulates the 'processing' of 'personal data'. *Personal data* means any information whereby a living individual can be identified. *Processing* means virtually any activity such as obtaining, recording or holding the data; carrying out operations or sets of operations on the data; organisation, adaptation or alteration of the data; retrieval; consultation or use of the data; and alignment, combination, blocking, erasure or destruction of the data. Unlike the earlier Act of 1984, which applied only to 'computerised' data, the 1998 Act additionally covers paper records and filing systems and, indeed, any storage system structured so that data relating to a living individual can be retrieved.

The person to whom the data relates is called the *data subject*. The person who determines how and for what purposes the personal data is processed is called the *data controller*; anyone else who actually processes the data is called a *data processor* (s.1). The 1998 Act also imposes additional controls on *sensitive personal data*, which includes any information, including opinion, relating to the physical or mental health or condition of the data subject (s.2).

The Act is administered by the Information Commissioner (formerly Data Protection Registrar, then Commissioner) who maintains a register of *registrable particulars* notified by data controllers, who pay an annual fee (s.18). Data controllers must comply with the eight *data protection principles* set out in the Act (Sch.1). These principles have the force of law. Briefly, the principles require that personal data shall be:

1   obtained and processed fairly and lawfully and shall not be processed at all unless certain conditions are met (see below);

2   obtained and processed for, or in ways compatible with, one or more lawful purpose;

3   adequate, relevant and not excessive in relation to that purpose or purposes;

4   accurate and kept up to date;

5   kept for no longer than necessary;

6   processed in accordance with the rights of data subjects under the Act (see below);

7   protected against unauthorised or unlawful processing and against accidental loss, destruction or damage; and

8   not transferred (with certain exceptions) outside the EEA unless the recipient country operates the same controls on data protection as applies within the EEA.

The Information Commissioner may refuse to register notification if s/he considers that these principles will be contravened (s.22). Processing personal data without notification is a criminal offence (s.21).

The Act imposes conditions which must be met even before processing of personal data can be contemplated (see principle 1 above). Generally, no personal data may be processed at all unless either the data subject has given consent or one of a series of other conditions has been met. These include 'the need to pursue the legitimate interests of the controller' *provided* these are not prejudicial to the interests of the data subject (Sch.2). This condition should be applicable to all uses of personal data in pharmacy practice. In addition, where the data is also *sensitive* personal data, either *explicit consent* must be obtained from the data subject or such consent may not be needed if the processing is 'necessary for medical purposes and is undertaken by:

1   a health professional, or

2   a person who in the circumstances owes a duty of confidentiality which is equivalent to that which would arise if that person were a health professional.'

Medical purposes includes the purposes of preventative medicine, medical diagnosis, medical research, the provision of care and treatment and the management of healthcare services (Sch.3).

Therefore, virtually all personal data used in pharmacy practice are 'sensitive' but 'explicit consent' (which implies a written explanation, a consent form and a decision freely made in appreciation of all its consequences) is not deemed necessary for patient medication records at least, provided all personnel who may process such data are bound by the health professional's duty of confidentiality. The definition of *health professional* in the Act includes pharmacists (s.69).

The Act sets out explicit rights of data subjects and others (see principle 6 above). Data controllers must, on receipt of a written request accompanied by a fee:

1   inform the data subject if personal data are being processed;
2   give data subjects a description of the data which are being processed, for what purposes and to whom the data will be disclosed; and
3   provide data subjects with that information in an intelligible form within 40 days of the request (s.7).

Data subjects also have a right to prevent processing of their data for marketing purposes (s.11) and to be notified if 'automated' decisions are taken in relation to, for example, work performance, creditworthiness, reliability or conduct (s.12). Rights are also conferred to allow data subjects to claim compensation from the data controller for failure to comply with any of the requirements of the Act or to fail to rectify, block, erase or destroy any inaccurate data (s.14).

There are exemptions allowing the data controller to exclude information relating to an individual other than the data subject, to allow some latitude where provision of copy records is very difficult or impossible to achieve, to protect trade secrets (s.8) and to withhold data if they are likely to cause substantial damage or distress to the data subject or any other person (s.10). Regulations made under section 7 also allow data controllers to decline to disclose data if this would be likely to cause serious harm to the physical or mental health or condition of the data subject or any other person. Information should not normally be disclosed without data subject consent unless it has been established that the data subject is incapable of managing his/her own affairs and the person requesting disclosure has been appointed by a court to manage those affairs (SI 2000 No.413).

Parents, guardians or carers may seek disclosure of information about data subjects other than themselves for whom they undertake parental or carer responsibility. If the data subject is a child or anyone else who is likely to understand fully his or her rights to confidentiality, then consent should be established if at all possible. The maximum fee for arranging access to automated health records is £10, although £50 is the maximum if paper records are included (SI 2000 No.191).

A further condition for the processing (which includes disclosure) of sensitive personal data is in accordance with circumstances specified by the Secretary of State (para.10, Sch.3 of the Act). This could, therefore, include disclosure where it is necessary for the prevention or detection of crime or for protecting the public against dishonesty, malpractice, incompetence or mis-management where seeking the consent of the data subject would prejudice those purposes (SI 2000 No.417).

Additional controls (SI 2003 No. 2426) over the processing of personal data electronically introduced two new rules for email marketing: all market-ing messages must disclose the sender's identity and provide a valid address for opt-out requests and unsolicited messages, and, in most circumstances, require prior consent from the recipient.

Access to health records

Most of the provisions of the Access to Health Records Act 1990 are now within the Data Protection Act 1998, but the 1990 Act continues to provide that a personal representative of a deceased person or anyone who has a claim arising out of a patient's death can also claim access to 'sensitive personal data' maintained in health records.

Generally speaking, the requirements of data protection legislation do not apply to any information which relates to a data subject who has died (but see above) nor to data which have been 'anonymised' (i.e. has been detached from any details or any links whatsoever which could identify a living individual). A series of legal cases have been brought to clarify the limits on the use of anonymised data when derived from patient medication records held by community pharmacists. Details are given in Chapter 27 (p. 401).

Freedom of Information Act 2000

The Freedom of Information Act 2000 seeks to promote the openness and accountability of public authorities. Whereas the Data Protection Act is concerned to protect the privacy of individuals and their personal data, the Freedom of Information Act gives people the right to seek information from public authorities about how they carry out their duties, why they make the decisions they do and how they spend public money. Public authorities would include NHS Trusts and Primary Care Trusts. Such Trusts must adopt and maintain a publication scheme, setting out details of information it will routinely make available, how the information can be obtained and whether there is any charge for it. From January 2005, each Trust must comply, normally within 28 days, with requests for the information that it holds unless an exemption from disclosure applies. Exemptions include personal data covered by the Data Protection Act (see above), information provided to the public authority in confidence and some limited protection from disclosure which may jeopardise commercial interests.

Jury service

All persons normally resident in the UK and aged between 18 and 70 who are registered as parliamentary or local government electors are, with very few exceptions, liable for jury service. Schedule 33 (under s.321 of the Criminal Justice Act 2003) sets out the exemptions, which are broadly: persons who are mentally disordered; persons who are or have been subject to certain detention, custody, prison or court martial sentences; and, as a discretionary exemption, persons who are needed for military service at the material time.

Pharmacists have no occupational exemption. Details of what jury service entails and the payment and expenses arrangements can be found on the Court Service website at the end of this chapter.

In Scotland, pharmacists may be eligible for exemption from jury service. Exemption is not automatic and the pharmacist who wishes to be excused must give written notice to the clerk of the court from whom the citation is received, indicating his/her right and desire to be so excused. Details can be found on the Scottish Courts website at the end of the chapter.

Summary

- This chapter outlines enactments and other measures which can be relevant to pharmacy. Some are of general application and others may apply only to one of the branches of pharmacy practice.
- The law covering being an owner, an employer or an employee is outlined as is the law relating to running a retail business and health and safety issues.
- There are controls on disposal of waste, on supply of pesticides and to protect animals and birds.
- The carriage of appropriate medical stores on board ships to fulfil minimum safety and health requirements for medical treatment where a ship does not carry a doctor is covered by scales that specify the medicines to be included.
- Data protection and freedom of information legislation covers virtually all personal data used in pharmacy practice. Under the legislation, health professionals, including pharmacists, have a duty of confidentiality.

Further reading

Websites

Department of Trade and Industry: http://www.dti.gov.uk
Advisory, Conciliation and Arbitration Service: http://www.acas.gov.uk
Commission for Racial Equality: http://www.cre.gov.uk
Equal Opportunities Commission: http://www.eoc.org.uk
Disability Rights Commission: http://www.drc.org.uk
Trading Standards Departments: http://www.tradingstandards.gov.uk
Office of Fair Trading: http://www.oft.gov.uk
Consumer Regulations Website: http://www.crw.gov.uk
Health and Safety Executive: http://www.hse.gov.uk
Local Authority Circulars Subject Index: http://www.hse.gov.uk/lau/lacs/index.htm
Department for Environment, Food and Rural Affairs: http://www.defra.gov.uk
Pesticides Safety Directorate: http://www.pesticides.gov.uk/home.asp
Office of the Information Commissioner: http://www.informationcommissioner.gov.uk/
Jury Service: http://www.courtservice.gov.uk
Jury service in Scotland: http://www.scotcourts.gov.uk

CHAPTER TWENTY-TWO

The Royal Pharmaceutical Society of Great Britain

The Royal Pharmaceutical Society of Great Britain (referred to as the Society) is a unique body with three distinct, and occasionally conflicting, functions. Firstly, like the General Medical Council (GMC; see Chapter 25), the Society is a regulatory and disciplinary body and has statutory powers to exercise professional discipline (Chapter 24). Secondly, like the British Medical Association, it is also a representative body, influencing and developing pharmacy policy with government and others. However, because it is also a regulatory body, the Society can only represent pharmacy and pharmacists' interests as a whole, not on an individual basis. Thirdly, the Society has law enforcement powers under various sections of the Medicines Act 1968 and the Animal Health and Welfare Act 1984 (Chapter 2) and the Poisons Act 1972 (Chapter 18).

In June 1999, the Government passed the Health Act 1999, which provided powers to amend NHS law and change ('modernise') the regulation of health professions and health professionals. The NHS changes are now more or less complete (Chapter 26).

Because of the complex roles of the Society, the consequences of implementing the 1999 Act for the Society's constitution, its professional conduct role, its disciplinary role and the bye-laws (Appendix 14) were not complete at the time of going to press. The major vehicle for these changes is a section 60 Order under the 1999 Health Act. The areas covered by these changes are expected to include the constitution and powers of the Council and its committees, registration of pharmacists and premises, education, continuing professional development, fitness to practise and disciplinary matters. Consultation on these proposed changes are expected in August 2005. (See also Appendix 13.)

In addition, the Society had sought a new Charter (an authority directly from the monarch to take certain powers) to clarify the remit of its representational role. The Queen has now approved this *2004 Charter*. The *2004 Charter* is a 'new' charter although legally it is a supplemental charter since it retains the incorporation aspect of the 1843 Charter while replacing all the provisions of the 1953 Charter. The full text of the *2004 Charter* appears on the Society's website (also see p. 283) and came into force on 7 December 2004. As part of the process, the terminology for the Society's regulatory powers will be clarified: *rules* will be made under the new section 60 legislation and *regulations* will be made under the Charter. The making of section 60 rules would be part of statutory consultation process, common to all government legislation. All new regulations, being Charter derived, would be published to the membership of the Society and approved by the Privy Council before coming into force.

External to the Society's activities, Part 2 of the NHS Reform and Health Care Professionals Act 2002 (see also Chapter 26) provided power to set up an over-arching body to investigate and report on the performance of, and recommend changes to, a range of healthcare regulatory bodies, including the Society. The statutory title of this body is the Council for the Regulation of Health Care Professionals, but it prefers to be called the Council for Health Care Regulatory Excellence (CHRE). The CHRE has powers 'to formulate principles relating to good professional self-regulation and to encourage regulatory bodies to conform to them' (s.25) so it takes a keen interest in the constitution and powers of the Society. The CHRE is also empowered to receive details of all the decisions of the Society's disciplinary cases (Chapter 24) and it may then, if it considers that any decision is 'unduly lenient' or 'should not have been made' and 'that it would be desirable for the protection of members of the public' (s.29), refer the case to the Appeal Court. The CHRE consulted in July 2004 on procedures under section 27 of the 2002 Act to oblige professional regulators to change or make new rules (*Pharm J* 31 July 2004 p. 141). CHRE noted a need for cross-notification between regulators when a practitioner is removed from a professional register and suggested that greater control may be needed to manage the rise of corporate ownership within pharmacy (*Pharm J* 14 August 2004 p. 237).

The Royal Pharmaceutical Society of Great Britain is the professional body for pharmacy; it was founded in 1841 and incorporated by Royal Charter in 1843. A Supplemental Charter was granted in 1953. These Charters are revoked by the Supplemental Charter of 2004 (see above) except in so far as the 1843 Charter incorporated the Society, authorised it to have a common seal and to sue and be sued. The main objects (in short) of the current Supplemental Charter are:

1   to advance knowledge of, and education in, pharmacy and its application;
2   to safeguard, maintain the honour and promote the interests of the members in their exercise of the profession of pharmacy;
3   to promote and protect the health and well-being of the public; and
4   to maintain and develop the science and practice of pharmacy.

The Charter also provides powers to:

1   promote public understanding of pharmacy;
2   maintain any charitable or benevolent trusts for distressed members or dependants or students of the Society;
3   to undertake any functions designed to maintain fitness to practise;
4   to undertake any function relating to the control and licensing of premises used in connection with pharmacy;
5   to maintain registers of members;
6   to maintain registers of premises;
7   to fix fees for any non-statutory services provided by the Society;
8   to set and enforce standards of education and to hold examinations;
9   to award fellowships and other distinctions;
10   to establish and maintain museum collections;
11   to undertake, encourage, fund or commission research and its publication;
12   to co-operate with other relevant bodies and authorities;
13   to engage and pay staff and run pension schemes;
14   to acquire, dispose or mortgage property;
15   to take out liability insurance for the Society;
17   to indemnify members of Council in respect of any liability arising from the performance of their duties in good faith;
18   to receive income, legacies or gifts and to borrow money;
19   to invest money;
20   to carry on trade in furtherance of Charter objects;
21   to do anything else lawful to promote the attainment of the Charter objects; and
22   to set terms of office for Council members.

The Charter goes on to control how the income and property of the Society may be used, to limit membership of the Society to registered pharmacists in Great Britain, to require an Annual General Meeting to be held, to make arrangements to recognise the devolved powers and responsibilities for health in Scotland and Wales and to establish the branch structure for members of the Society. Control, direction and management of the policies and affairs of the Society are vested in the Council, whose constitution is as follows:

1   seventeen elected registered pharmacists, of which one place each is reserved for members from Scotland and Wales;
2   one registered pharmacist appointed by the universities (schools of pharmacy);
3   two pharmacy technicians; and
4   ten persons appointed by the Privy Council.

No places on the Council are to be reserved for sectoral pharmacy practice representation. The election and appointment processes are laid down in the Charter regulations. The Council may then exercise all powers and functions of the Society except where a Special Resolution is required. The Council itself is subject to a Code of Governance and a conduct panel. Council members can be suspended or removed from office following breach of this code. Transcripts of recent Council meetings are available on the Society's website; from 2005 this will be extended to agendas and other relevant papers.

The Supplemental Charter gives the Council power to make regulations for all or any of the purposes for which regulations may, by the express provisions of the Charter, be made, and such other regulations as seem to the Council to be necessary for the management and regulation of the affairs and property of the Society and its chartered objects. The former bye-laws (Appendix 14) will remain in force until they are superseded by Charter regulations. Regulations will not come into force unless they have been published to the members for a period of 60 days, approved by Special Resolution if required and approved by the Privy Council. No regulation may exceed the powers laid down in the Charter or Pharmacy Acts or otherwise be in conflict with the laws of the land. The extent of the Society's powers under its Royal Charter and its powers and duties under the Pharmacy Acts have been considered by the High Court in *Jenkin* v. *Pharmaceutical Society of Great Britain* [1921] 1 Ch 392 and by the House of Lords in *Pharmaceutical Society of Great Britain* v. *Dickson* [1968] 2 All ER 686 (see p. 287 and Chapter 27).

The Charter requires that there shall be a president, who is a registered pharmacist, and other officers as laid down by regulations. Although many of the powers of the Society are contained in the *2004 Charter*, additional powers and duties have been conferred and/or imposed by various Acts of Parliament. One of the principal duties under statute is that the Council of the Society must appoint 'a fit and proper person' as registrar (Pharmacy Act 1954, s.1). It is the duty of the registrar to maintain the Register of Pharmaceutical Chemists under the Pharmacy Act 1954 (s.2) and the Register of Premises (registered pharmacies) under the Medicines Act 1968 (s.75).

Organisation

The Council has full power to manage the Society's affairs but needs a Special Resolution to amend, add to or revoke any of the Supplemental Charter provisions. A Special Resolution means a resolution of the Council confirmed, in accordance with regulations, either at a duly convened general meeting of members of the Society by not less than a two-thirds majority of the votes of the members present (or by proxy), or by ballot of the membership. The Council has a duty to manage the Society's affairs and, subject to the provision of the regulations, has power to regulate the conduct of proceedings at meetings of the Council and its committees and subcommittees. The Society operates through seven directorates. Those primarily relevant here are Education and Registration, Practice and Quality Improvement, and Fitness to Practise and Legal Affairs.

The Council exercises its powers through a number of committees, three of which are particularly relevant to this book, namely the Law and Ethics Committee, the Infringements Committee, and the Animal Medicines Committee (these may change during 2005). The Law and Ethics Committee deals with policy matters involving professional conduct and the legal aspects of the Society's affairs. It is responsible for the interpretation of the Code of Ethics (see Chapter 23 and Appendix 16) and for advising the Council on any question of professional conduct that may arise. The Infringements Committee considers alleged breaches of the legislation which the Society enforces (e.g. the Medicines Act 1968 and the Poisons Act 1972) and alleged infringements of standards of professional conduct. The Animal Medicines Committee deals with registration matters concerning agricultural merchants and saddlers, infringements of the relevant Codes of Practice and policy.

> The management of the Scottish and Welsh Executives was under review at the time of writing as part of the measures to implement the Health Act 1999. The following account is, therefore, likely to change considerably. Readers are advised to refer to the Society's website for the current position.

The bye-laws currently provide that the Society has a Scottish Department governed by the Scottish Executive acting under the authority of the Council. The president and vice-president of the Society and such members of the Council as are resident in Scotland are ex-officio members of the Scottish Executive; the others are elected annually by the members of the Society resident in Scotland. The Executive elects from among its members a chairman and vice-chairman. The chairman has charge of the funds voted for the use of the department, and the Executive reports to the Council of the Society in London. The Society's Council appoints a resident secretary of the Scottish Department, based in Scotland.

The Society has a Welsh Executive responsible under the authority of the Council for the implementation of its policies in Wales. The president and vice-president of the Society and such members of Council as are resident in Wales are ex-officio members of the Welsh Executive; the others are elected from and by the members of the Society resident in Wales. The Executive elects from among its members a chairman and vice-chairman. The Council appoints a resident secretary of the Welsh Executive, based in Wales.

Branches and regions

In 1922, the Council of the Society set up branches throughout Great Britain. These, with their own officers, function at local level and at present number 136. They organise local meetings of members and pharmacy students on topics of common interest and provide a medium for members to take an active part in the Society's affairs. In 1968, the Society set up a regional organisation in England and Wales, each region being based on a school of pharmacy. In 1975, the boundaries were revised to become coterminous with the then regions of the NHS and one of the resulting Society regions has two schools of pharmacy within its boundaries. The regions are intended to supplement the branch structure and help the smaller branches. In addition, the regions are intended to improve communication between the Council and the membership.

Membership groups

The Council has authority under the bye-laws to establish and determine the constitution of special groups of members based on the nature of their occupation or special interests. The function of any such group must be the discussion of matters of a professional and technical character of common interest to the members of the group.

In 1965, an Agricultural and Veterinary Pharmacy Group was established to promote the study of agricultural and veterinary pharmacy. Membership is open to any pharmacist engaged in 'the preparation and supply of agricultural chemicals, veterinary medicines and allied products'.

An Industrial Pharmacists Group was formed in 1972 for all those members engaged within the pharmaceutical industry. In 1975, a Hospital Pharmacists Group and in 1990 an Academic Group were also formed. In 1995, a Community Pharmacists Group was formed to consider issues relating to community pharmacy and to work to promote knowledge and standards of practice in this field. During 1999, the Society consulted on the future of special interest groups and a number of new groups and changes to existing groups, particularly in relation to primary care practice, were proposed (*Pharm J* 2 October 1999 p. 517). These proposals are now likely to be taken together with consultation on the changes needed to implement the Health Act 1999.

Membership and registration

The membership of the Society consists of members and fellows. Membership is restricted to those persons registered as pharmaceutical chemists under the Pharmacy Act 1954. Every person registered as a pharmaceutical chemist pays an annual retention fee and is a member of the Society. If s/he ceases to be registered, s/he ceases to be a member. In 2004, power was secured through the bye-laws (I 3rd Schedule) to annotate the register with 'sp' to denote those members who have qualified as a supplementary prescriber (Chapter 7). In 2005, the letters 'P' or 'NP' will denote whether the member is 'practising' or 'non-practising' (see also under retention fees, below).

Fellows of the Society (who are also members) can be divided into several categories.

1   All members registered as pharmaceutical chemists on or before 1 February 1951 were designated as fellows. Until the Pharmacy Act 1953 came into force, there were two qualifications. The Chemist and Druggist examination led to the basic qualification and membership of the Society. Those who took a further examination (the 'Major') after a further year's study were known as pharmaceutical chemists. The Registers of Chemists and Druggists and of Pharmaceutical Chemists were merged following the 1953 Act, which was later replaced by the Pharmacy Act 1954. All chemists and druggists were then designated pharmaceutical chemists and those pharmaceutical chemists who had passed the old 'Major' examination were then, on application, designated as fellows.

2   Members of not less than five years' standing who have made outstanding original contributions to the advancement of pharmaceutical knowledge, or who have attained exceptional proficiency in a subject embraced by or related to the practice of pharmacy, may be designated as fellows by the Council.

3   A member of not less than 12 years' standing (formerly 20, changed in August 2002) who has made outstanding original contributions to the advancement of pharmaceutical knowledge, or who has obtained distinction in the science, practice, profession or history of pharmacy, may be designated as a fellow by a panel of fellows appointed by the Council for that purpose.

Members designated as fellows only remain so designated as long as they remain members. Both designated fellows and ordinary members are registered pharmaceutical chemists and they pay the same annual retention fee. From 2005, fellows will be indicated in the register with the letter 'F'.

Persons who have rendered distinguished service to the Society or to pharmacy can be elected honorary members. A person who is nominated by the Privy Council to serve as a member of the Society's Council is an honorary member while holding that position. The Council also has power to elect as honorary fellows such persons as scientific workers who have distinguished themselves in any branch of knowledge which embraces the educational objects of the Society, or other persons eminent in national life. Honorary members and Honorary fellows are not registered pharmacists.

Registration as a pharmaceutical chemist

The Pharmacy Act 1954 (s.4) and the bye-laws provide that any person who has obtained a degree in pharmacy at one of the UK universities approved by the Council or passed the Pharmaceutical Chemist Qualifying examination shall be registered as a Pharmaceutical Chemist provided that s/he has attained the age of 21 years; has paid the prescribed registration fee; has produced to the registrar of the Society evidence that s/he is of good character and in good health, both physically and mentally; and has produced to the registrar of the Society a declaration that subsequent to passing the final degree examination the applicant has satisfactorily performed, under the direct personal supervision of a pharmacist and as his/her sole pupil, a course of training of not less than one year in one or more of the following:

1   a community pharmacy approved for the purpose by the Council;
2   the pharmaceutical department of a hospital or similar institution, approved by the Council for the purpose;
3   a pharmaceutical industrial establishment approved by the Council for the purpose; and
4   a school of pharmacy.

At least 26 weeks must be spent in a community or hospital pharmacy. The person concerned must also pass a registration examination after completing their course of training.

Full details of the requirements for such pre-registration training and the examination are given in section XX of the bye-laws (Appendix 14).

Recognition of pharmaceutical qualifications by the European Union

An Order made under the European Communities Act 1972 (SI 1987 No.2202) amended the Pharmacy Act 1954 to give effect to the Council Directives 85/432/EEC and 85/433/EEC relating to the mutual recognition of diplomas, to the right of establishment of pharmacists and to their freedom to provide pharmaceutical services. The Royal Pharmaceutical Society of Great Britain and the Pharmaceutical Society of Northern Ireland are the competent authorities for certifying matters relating to the registration of pharmacists in Great Britain and Northern Ireland, respectively. Section XIX of the bye-laws (Appendix 14) sets out the full registration requirements.

Any pharmacist who is a national, or is entitled to be treated no less favourably than a national (SI 1996 No.1405), of a member state in the EEA (which includes the European Community, EU and the European Free Trade Association Areas) and has a recognised qualification awarded in a member state, or has acquired rights under the Directives, has the right to be registered as a pharmacist in the UK. Before registration, such a pharmacist must produce to the registrar evidence that s/he is of good character and in good health, both mentally and physically. Pharmacists from all member states have the right of establishment, although they cannot be in personal control of a pharmacy which has been open for less than three years.

A European Directive, 2002/0061, is likely to be adopted in 2005 to require EEA nationals who move to another member state to 'have a knowledge of languages necessary for practising the profession in the host member state'. In May 2004, the EU was expanded to include 25 member states (Chapter 1).

Reciprocal registration

The bye-laws provide that the Council may by resolution enter into reciprocal agreements with a pharmaceutical authority that is empowered to grant certificates of qualification to practise pharmacy in any states outside the UK. At present such reciprocal agreements exist with Northern Ireland; New Zealand; in Australia with New South Wales, Queensland, South Australia, Victoria, Western Australia and Tasmania; and in South Africa for persons registered in South Africa before 31 March 1968. The Council agreed in October 2003 to end the reciprocal arrangements with Australia and New Zealand and this will take effect from 30 June 2006 (*Pharm J* 23 April 2005 p. 495). For Northern Ireland, the provision for reciprocity is to be found in the Pharmacy Act 1954.

Under these reciprocal arrangements, registration as a pharmaceutical chemist in the UK may take place without examination provided the applicant is resident in the UK, can produce evidence of their identity, can prove that s/he has passed a qualifying examination specified in the reciprocal agreement and can prove that s/he is registered and is in good standing with the pharmaceutical registration authority of the state concerned (Appendix 14).

A person who has been granted a certificate of qualification in an Australian state or in New Zealand after 31 March 1968, must also:

1   produce a certificate from the registrar of the Pharmacy Board concerned that s/he has completed, normally within their jurisdiction, a period of one year's employment in pharmacy as a registered pharmacist;

2   produce evidence satisfactory to the Council that s/he has completed in Great Britain a period of four weeks' employment in a pharmacy under the direct personal control and supervision of a pharmacist registered in Great Britain; and

3   produce a declaration in accordance with the Statutory Declarations Act 1835 that s/he has studied the laws governing the practice of pharmacy and the sale of medicines and poisons in Great Britain.

All applicants for reciprocal registration are required to pay a registration fee.

Recognition by adjudication

A person with a degree or diploma in pharmacy granted by a university or body outside the UK which is not covered by reciprocal arrangements may nevertheless apply for registration in Great Britain. S/he must produce evidence that s/he holds a degree or diploma in pharmacy granted by a university or body of comparable academic status in a country outside the UK, that s/he is registered or qualified to be registered in that country and is of good character and in good health, both mentally and physically. S/he must then satisfy an adjudicating committee appointed by the Council of the Society as to the content and standard of the course and examination in pharmacy that s/he has taken, and as to his/her knowledge of pharmacy as practised in the UK.

If English is not his/her mother tongue, s/he must demonstrate his/her knowledge of the English language. S/he may also be required by the adjudicating committee to take certain examinations and s/he must complete a period of employment in the practice of pharmacy in Great Britain under conditions laid down by the committee. Two certificates of character satisfactory to the Council and given by British subjects must be submitted. If these conditions are complied with, the Council may, by resolution, authorise registration of the applicant as a pharmaceutical chemist in Great Britain on payment of a registration fee (Appendix 14).

Registration without examination

The Council has power under the Pharmacy Act 1954 (s.4) to make bye-laws providing for registration of persons who satisfy the Council that they have sufficient skill and knowledge to practise and who are either persons registered as pharmaceutical chemists of Northern Ireland, qualified military dispensers or certified assistants to apothecaries under the Apothecaries Act 1815. However, this power has not been fully exercised and the bye-laws do not provide either for the registration of qualified military dispensers or of certified assistants to apothecaries. Northern Ireland pharmacists can register under the reciprocal arrangements (see above).

The Register and registration certificates

Until the implementation of the section 60 Order, the registrar is obliged under the Pharmacy Act 1954 (s.2) to publish annually a Register of Pharmaceutical Chemists in the form prescribed in section XXI of the bye-laws (Appendix 14).

The Act places a duty on the Council to issue on the demand of any registered pharmaceutical chemist, without fee, a certificate of registration signed by the registrar and countersigned by either the president of the Society or two members of the Council (s.5).

A further certificate may be issued to a person to whom a certificate has already been issued if that person satisfies the registrar that the original has been lost or destroyed. The fee prescribed in the bye-laws for the supply of such a further certificate must be paid.

A certificate of registration is admissible as evidence that the person named thereon is a registered pharmaceutical chemist. Similar provisions as to evidence apply to the printed *Annual Register of Pharmaceutical Chemists* (s.6).

Annual retention fees

In addition to the initial registration fee, a pharmacist must also pay an annual retention fee as prescribed in the bye-laws in order to retain his/her name on the register. The fee structure from 2005 relates to the mandatory requirement for evidence of continuing professional development (CPD; see Chapter 23). The register is in two parts: practising members and non-practising members. 'Practising pharmacist' is defined as 'a member who undertakes any work in, or gives advice in relation to, the science of medicines or the practice of pharmacy or healthcare' (marked in the register with a letter 'P'); 'non-practising pharmacist' is defined as 'a member who does not engage in pharmacy practice, is not involved in patient care and does not work in or give advice in relation to, the science of medicines or the practice of pharmacy or healthcare' (marked with the letters 'NP'; bye-law XXI 3rd Schedule). Practising pharmacists will have to provide evidence of their CPD to be retained on the register.

The registrar is empowered to send a demand for a fee by registered post or recorded delivery addressed to the pharmacist at his/her address on the register. If a pharmacist does not pay his/her fee within two months of having received such a demand, the registrar must inform the Council and the Council may direct the registrar to remove the name of the pharmacist from the register. If, before the expiry of the year or such longer period as the Council may allow, the fee plus an additional sum by way of penalty is paid, the registrar has a duty to restore the name to the register (Pharmacy Act 1954, s.12).

Students

In 1978, the Society formed a section of the Society entitled 'The British Pharmaceutical Students Association', membership of which was open to all pharmaceutical students. Membership is also open to those members of the

Society who have been registered initially for not more than 12 months. The Association, which is jointly financed by the Society, is recognised by the Council to be the representative body for the students. The Association is administered, in accordance with its constitution, by an elected Executive.

Health problems

During the early 1990s, the Society set up a scheme to assist pharmacists who have alcohol, drug or stress-related problems. This is now in two parts: the Listening Friends Scheme and the Pharmacists Health Support Scheme. Both provide telephone support and referral facilities for pharmacists who are under stress and/or need help to manage dependence on alcohol or drugs. In this way, the Society has sought to discharge its benevolent support role for pharmacists as well as its duties to protect the public from pharmacists who transgress through dependence and other problems.

Regulation of support staff

Since 1996, the Society has required pharmacists to ensure that all staff whose work in the pharmacy regularly includes the sale of medicines have completed a course covering the knowledge syllabus of the chemist counter assistant unit of the Scottish/National Vocational Qualification (S/NVQ) level 2 in retail operations ('Medicines Counter Assistant' qualification) or be completing such a course. From January 2005, the Society requires pharmacists to ensure that dispensing or pharmacy assistants – essentially those staff involved in the assembly of prescriptions – have completed a Pharmacy Services S/NVQ level 2 qualification or be completing such a course. An exempting 'grandparent' clause for existing experienced staff engaged in this work was available throughout 2004. Also from January 2005, the Society will be implementing a voluntary registration scheme for a further tier of support staff: pharmacy technicians. Pharmacy technicians will be expected to hold or be undertaking an appropriate S/NVQ level 3 qualification. A Code of Ethics, fitness to practise procedures and other guidance for pharmacy technicians were published at the end of 2004 (*Pharm J* 4 September 2004 pp. 329–330). Statutory powers to underpin this aspect of the Society's registration activities will be incorporated in the anticipated section 60 Order under the 1999 Health Act.

Summary

* The Society derives its powers from two Royal Charters, 1843 and 2004, and the Pharmacy Act 1954.

- The Society exercises its powers principally through bye-laws, which cover the management of the Society and the achievement of the Charter objects.
- The Council comprises 17 elected registered pharmacists, one registered pharmacist appointed by the Schools of Pharmacy, two pharmacy technicians and 10 persons appointed by the Privy Council.
- A president and other officers of the Council must be appointed annually; the Council also appoints a registrar to maintain the registers of pharmacists and pharmacies.
- The committees of Council which are concerned with law and ethical matters are the Law and Ethics Committee, the Infringements Committee and the Animal Medicines Committee.
- Members of the Society are assigned to 136 geographical branches, falling within 12 regions – not the same as the NHS regions (Chapter 26).
- There are membership groups for pharmacists in agricultural and veterinary, hospital, industrial and community pharmacy practice.
- The bye-laws specify requirements for pre-registration training, registration and retention on the registers and make provisions for fellowship and honorary membership of the Society.
- The bye-laws allow, subject to detailed conditions, for admission to the register of pharmacists from other countries.
- Arrangements for regulation of support staff will be completed following the implementation of a section 60 Order under the Health Act 1999.
- The Society has a section for membership of students.
- The Society runs a help-line for pharmacists with alcohol, drug or stress-related problems.

Further reading

Bellingham, C. (2003) Modernisation: how pharmacists are regulated and represented elsewhere. *Pharm J* 271: 539.

Hawksworth, G. (2003) What the Society does for its members. *Pharm J* 271: 187.

Hawksworth, G. (2004) Why pharmacists can be confident about the future. *Pharm J* 272: 260.

Leviseur, N. (2002) Which takes precedence? The Society's Charter or Section 60? *Pharm J* 269: 653.

Mason, P. (2004) As the European Union expands, what are the implications for pharmacy? *Pharm J* 272: 537.

Robinson, A. (2003) A unique service for pharmacists in Wales. *Pharm J* 271: 564.

Stone, L. (2003) Registration of overseas pharmacists. *Pharm J* 271: 563.

Thomson, D. (2003) What the Society does for its members in Scotland. *Pharm J* 271: 306.

Other articles on the work of the Society: http://www.pjonline.com→ noticeboard→ Guide to the Society

Websites

Council for the Regulation of Health Professionals: http://www.crhp.org.uk
Association of Pharmacy Technicians UK: http://www.aptuk.org
The Royal Pharmaceutical Society of Great Britain site carries information on all the functions and organisation of the Society, how it assures pharmacists' competence and fitness to practise, its services to members and continuing news about pharmacy policy and practice: http://www.rpsgb.org.uk. A selection of useful routes (not exclusive) to key documents mentioned in this chapter is given below as at August 2004:

- current position on the reform process: 'modernisation': About the Society→ Fit for the Future
- section 60 Order: About the Society→ Fit for the Future
- Charter: About the Society→ History and Regulations→ charter
- bye-laws: About the Society→ History and Regulations→ byelaws
- the Council, its governance and meeting transcripts: About the Society→ The Council
- staff structure and directorates: About the Society→ Staff Structure
- complaints and investigation procedures: Home→ Making a Complaint (right screen link)
- regions and branches: About the Society→ Branches and Regions
- membership groups: About the Society→ Membership Groups
- registration of overseas and reciprocity agreement pharmacists: registration→ Overseas
- registration fees: About the Society→ Registration→ Fees
- support for pharmacists: About the Society→ Support
- regulation of support staff: Registration→ Technicians or Home→ Pharmacy Support Staff (right screen link).

CHAPTER TWENTY-THREE

Professional conduct

In June 1999, the Government passed the Health Act 1999 which provided powers in section 60 to change the regulation of health professions and health professionals and to amend NHS law. The consequences of implementing this Act were not complete at the time of going to press and may affect the scope and operation of the Society's powers to enforce standards of professional conduct. Where possible, an indication of probable changes is given. Reference to the Society's website should be made for the current position.

The term 'profession' was formerly applied only to the church, the law and medicine – the three 'learned' professions. The meaning of the term is now broader, as is apparent from the definition in the *Oxford English Dictionary*: 'a vocation in which a professed knowledge of some department of learning is used in its application to the affairs of others, or in the practice of an art founded upon it'. In modern usage, it seems that almost all occupations that require some measure of intellectual training can be described as professions.

However, an organised profession requires more than the mere existence of an intellectual discipline. The essence of professionalism is the relationship of trust which exists between the practitioner and the person who receives his/ her advice or services. The recipient, relying entirely on the knowledge of the practitioner, must be able to have complete trust in his/her services and the impartiality of his/her advice. It follows that there must be an established minimum standard of knowledge for practitioners, and that there must be agreement amongst them about standards of behaviour in their professional work. This means that there must be a body which determines the standard of education and establishes the code of conduct, and that this body must be representative of practitioners and be subject to their collective control.

The profession of pharmacy

If the characteristics described are accepted as the elements of a profession, then pharmacy meets the essential requirements, which are four in number.

An intellectual discipline and a standard of knowledge. Pharmacy is of ancient origin. In Great Britain, it was never clearly separated from medicine until the formation of the Pharmaceutical Society of Great Britain in 1841. Membership of the Society was, from the first, by examination, but it was not until the Pharmacy Act 1868 that all newcomers to the profession who wished to practise were required to pass a qualifying examination, whether or not they intended to become members of the Society. Today a university degree in pharmacy followed by a period of practical training is required before registration as a pharmaceutical chemist (Chapter 22).

A representative body of practitioners. The representative body of the profession is the Royal Pharmaceutical Society of Great Britain. The Council of the Society is elected by the members and its functions include control over educational standards for pharmaceutical chemists. It also guides the profession in establishing and interpreting a code of conduct. All registered pharmaceutical chemists are, by statute, members of the Society (Chapter 22). *Pharmacist* means a registered pharmaceutical chemist (Medicines Act 1968, s.132).

Standards of conduct. There are accepted standards of conduct known throughout the profession. Many of these are expressed in the Code of Ethics, a document which represents the collective views of members of the Society and which has been approved at a general meeting of members. The Council of the Society, through its Law and Ethics Committee and its Infringements Committee (proposed to be reconstituted as the Investigating Committee), interprets the Code and gives guidance on any matter concerning professional conduct. The disciplinary committee of the Society – the Statutory Committee – takes into account the Code of Ethics when considering complaints of misconduct but is not bound by it (see p. 303, Chapter 24).

Service and advice. Pharmacists have traditionally been mainly concerned with the supply to the public of medicines, either in response to a prescription or other authority or sold over the counter. In these supplies, the pharmacist should give whatever advice is necessary in the interest of the patient or customer. Increasingly, pharmacists are also concerned with the provision of services specifically to improve the management and use of medicines, usually accompanied by advice or recommendations, intervention and support for patients and fellow health professionals.

The existence of a body of independent private practitioners has been held to be essential if an occupation is truly to be regarded as a profession. The argument is that only the relationship between an independent practitioner and his/her client is a fully professional one, and an employed practitioner must inevitably be subject to external pressures, either consciously or unconsciously, according to the conditions of his/her employment. No pharmacist, whether employed in public service or in the service of a body corporate engaged in retail pharmacy, would accept that his/her standards or his/her judgment are in any way affected by the fact that s/he is an employee. Indeed, some might argue that a pharmacist in public service is free from some of the commercial pressures which may influence the judgment of the independent practitioner. Even so, there is some force in the argument that the existence of a number of independent practitioners is indispensable for the full development of the profession.

Trade and profession

There is a deep-rooted feeling that trading and professional activities are incompatible. Yet what is the difference between making a living from selling one's professional services and making a living from the buying and selling of goods? The professional person might have some difficulty in explaining his/her objections to commerce without casting doubts on the integrity of the tradesperson. Although there is an element of snobbery in it, there is undoubtedly a difference between the trading outlook and the professional outlook. The tradesperson, however honest, is principally concerned with the profitability of his/her business. His/her main object is to achieve as large a financial return as possible. S/he holds his/her customers to be the best judges of what they want and s/he seeks to satisfy their demands. The old common law maxim applicable to trade was *let the buyer beware*.

Professional people working in their special field of knowledge where their advice is crucial must often be the judges of what is best for their clients or customers, although patients are increasingly encouraged to take part in and exercise choice over healthcare decisions. If professionals do this according to the standards of their profession, then the advice they give must, at times, be to the practitioners' own financial disadvantage. It is recognition of this essential trust by the public which confers any special status the professional person may have.

Some pharmacists, such as those who work in hospitals or in teaching, do not engage in trade, although within the context of the NHS (Chapter 26) they are increasingly involved in marketing their services and operating within budgets and business constraints similar to those applied in retailing. However, the majority of pharmacists in retail pharmacy businesses practise pharmacy in a trading environment. In addition to the supply of medicines and the provision of other professional services, they sell many other goods. Theirs is a *trading profession*, a description applied by Lord Wilberforce in the *Dickson* case (see below and Chapter 27).

Not surprisingly, pharmacists are often misunderstood in their attempts to apply professional principles in a commercial world. If it is hard for the proprietor pharmacist, it is even harder for the employed superintendent pharmacist of a company or other body corporate which is controlled by non-pharmacist directors or shareholders. The fact that the control of the pharmacy is given by statute to the pharmacist is sometimes found irksome to the owners, and the restrictions pharmacists place on ordinary commercial practices because of their profession are not understood. For this reason, the Society has found it necessary to incorporate statements setting out the personal responsibilities of a superintendent pharmacist in the Code of Ethics and Standards (Appendix 16).

The *Dickson* case

The conflict between professional and commercial methods in pharmacy has its origin in the economic need for most pharmacists to engage in ordinary trade as well as pharmacy, together with the fact that any corporate body which complies with certain requirements has the legal right to establish a retail pharmacy business (Chapter 5). As might be expected, the Royal Pharmaceutical Society of Great Britain, as the professional body, has throughout its history resisted any pressures of the commercial world that have appeared to be adverse to the profession. The *Dickson* case is the most recent example of a clash of this kind.

For a fuller understanding of the events leading to the case, it is necessary to read the Report on the General Practice of Pharmacy published by the Society in 1963 (*Pharm J* 20 April 1963). Whether or not one agrees with the recommendations in the report, it is a succinct review of the state of retail pharmacy at that time. The report was adopted by the Council and accepted by a meeting of branch representatives of the Society. It was suggested in paragraph 19 of the report that it was undesirable for non-professional business to predominate in a pharmacy, and that the extension of this kind of business in pharmacies should be controlled. An attempt to incorporate this principle into the then Statement upon Matters of Professional Conduct was challenged and led to the *Dickson* case, which is discussed in some detail in Chapter 27.

The Society was unable during the hearing of this case to satisfy the courts, on the evidence presented, that the professional side of a pharmacy business was adversely affected by other activities. As it was not shown that the public suffered any harm, the proposed restraints were held to be unjustified, and an injunction was granted preventing the proposed addition to the Statement Upon Matters of Professional Conduct. The House of Lords upheld the decision of the lower courts.

In the course of the case, the practice of pharmacy in Great Britain was subjected to searching examination and discussion, with the result that the judgment brought clarity to a situation which had tended to become uncertain. It was made plain that the Society could make rules affecting the non-professional as well as the professional activities of pharmacists, but only if the rules could be shown to be in the interest of the public and the profession. The following extracts illustrate the point.

> The restraints upon professional men are justifiable in law for they are not only necessary in the interests of the profession but of the public who trust to the peculiarly high standing and integrity of a profession to serve it well.
>
> (Lord Upjohn)

> I have no doubt that there could be some trading activities which it would be undesirable for pharmacists to undertake in conjunction with their professional activities as pharmacists.
>
> (Lord Morris)

> I have no doubt that it would be within the competence of the Society as a body concerned for the honour and well-being of those engaged in the profession of pharmacy, to lay down rules concerning non-professional (as well as professional) activities to professional standards and behaviour. But that would have to be proved. In agreement with the Court of Appeal, I do not think that it was proved in this case. It will normally be for a profession itself to decide in regard to its standards and its codes of behaviour and the mere fact that certain rules are laid down which are severely restrictive will not warrant attack upon them if the interests of members and in the public interest such rules are reasonable.
>
> (Lord Morris)

The thrust of the above arguments is reinforced by the adoption of competition law (Chapter 21), which now limits the extent to which the Society can impose ethical constraints on the promotion and supply of medicines (see Society's website).

Professional ethics and law

Ethics is the science of morals, or moral philosophy. The principles, written or unwritten, which are accepted in any profession as the basis for proper behaviour are the ethics of the profession. Rules of law and rules of ethics are commonly held to differ because law is enforced by the state while ethical rules are only morally binding. However, law and ethics are not opposites. The law itself has a basis in ethics; in general it reflects the moral standards of the community. Criminal law comprises those rules of conduct which the community (through Parliament) has decided must be observed on pain of a penalty, such as a fine or imprisonment. Criminal law, therefore, includes the Medicines, Poisons and Misuse of Drugs Acts, where transgression may result in prosecution.

Other parliamentary legislation creates administrative law, which gives power to public bodies to regulate certain activities carried out on behalf of the public. The NHS Terms of Service is an example. A breach may result in an administrative sanction following investigation under the NHS complaints procedures (Chapter 26).

Moral obligations are also recognised by the state through common law, which essentially enshrines certain duties which individuals owe to one another. Breach of these duties may result in action through the civil law courts to seek compensation for a 'civil wrong'. The most familiar of these is probably an action alleging negligence on the part of a health practitioner. Negligence is just one of a range of *torts* or civil wrongs and is discussed in more detail later in this chapter (see p. 292). Other torts which might arise in pharmacy practice are breach of confidentiality and defamation.

Pharmacists, as they become integrated into the healthcare team, will increasingly come into possession of sensitive information and will be expected to observe strict confidentiality over the use and disclosure of such information and refrain from using it in ways which may lower the standing of the subject in the eyes of the community (i.e. defamation).

However, the state does not attempt to enforce every rule of social behaviour, nor does it interfere in those matters which are by common consent left to the consciences of individuals (e.g. religious observance) and in those standards which are agreed amongst a profession provided they can be seen to be necessary for the further protection of the public.

Code of Ethics

Ever since the foundation of the Society in 1841, there has been concern about the need to maintain and improve standards of conduct in pharmacy. The advantage of having a written code was recognised, but nothing positive emerged until the changes made by the Pharmacy and Poisons Act 1933 gave the Society wider authority, including the power to take disciplinary action and to remove names from the Register of Pharmaceutical Chemists (see p. 300).

A proposal for a code of ethics made by the Teesside branch of the Society in 1937 was widely discussed, but it was found difficult to strike the right balance between a general description of good behaviour and the expression of specified principles in clear-cut terms. The document which was finally accepted by the profession was the first attempt at a written code. An amended version of this 'Statement upon Matters of Professional Conduct' was later published in *Pharmaceutical Journal* (17 June 1944).

Other amendments led to the publication of revised versions in 1953, 1964, 1970, 1984, 1992 and 2002. In each case, a revised code was presented to the membership for approval and ratification at the Annual General Meetings in May.

The Code of Ethics now comprises:

> *Part 1.* Pharmacists' ethics including the key responsibilities of a pharmacist;
> *Part 2.* Standards of professional performance; and
> *Part 3.* Service specifications.

Disreputable behaviour, a breach of professional responsibility or requirement identified in the Code of Ethics could form the basis of a complaint of misconduct. The Council and the Statutory Committee, in considering whether or not action should follow, take into consideration the circumstances of an individual case and do not regard themselves as being limited to those matters which are mentioned in the Code of Ethics.

For ease of reference a brief overview of the Code of Ethics is given below. The full text appears in Appendix 16 and on the Society's website.

Part 1: pharmacists' ethics

Part 1 covers an outline of the process of ethical decision making, the exercise of professional judgment and the key responsibilities of a pharmacist as, briefly, being knowledgeable, competent and up to date in his/her field of practice, respectful of and sensitive to patients' rights and needs, and behaving with integrity and probity.

Part 2: standards of professional performance

Section A: personal responsibilities
This part is divided into three subsections: A1, which relates to those pharmacists providing professional services; A2, which relates to pharmacists who own a pharmacy, superintendent pharmacists and pharmacist managers in hospitals or other fields of practice; and A3, covering pre-registration tutors and pharmacists supervising pre-registration trainees.

Section B: professional competence
Section B covers the process of continuing professional development (CPD), evidence of the undertaking of a minimum of 30 hours per year of such development, the provision of information and advice to patients, the public and prescribers and responding to adverse drug reactions. A mandatory requirement for practising pharmacists to undertake CPD came into force in January 2005 [for details see Practice Guidance in the current *Medicines, Ethics and Practice Guide* (Further Reading) and the education section of the Society's website).

SECTION C: CONFIDENTIALITY

Section C covers detailed requirements for protection of information acquired in the course of pharmacy practice and the safeguards which must be exercised over disclosure. (See also the requirements of data protection legislation, Chapter 21 p. 265.)

Part 3: service specifications

Part 3 opens with five general principles of clinical governance which should be addressed when innovating or developing professional services. Specifications are then given for 23 specific services as follows:

1 publicity, promotion and information;
2 stock;
3 pharmacy premises and facilities;
4 supply of prescribed medicines;
5 patient medication records;
6 repeat medication services;
7 prescription collection services;
8 delivery services;
9 on-line pharmacy services;
10 sales of Pharmacy Medicines;
11 the supply of emergency hormonal contraception as a Pharmacy Medicine;
12 complementary medicines and therapies;
13 healthcare information and advice;
14 diagnostic testing and health screening;
15 emergencies;
16 collection and disposal of pharmaceutical waste;
17 advisory services to nursing and residential homes;
18 domiciliary oxygen services;
19 services to drug misusers;
20 needle and syringe exchange schemes;
21 extemporaneous preparation/compounding;
22 aseptic dispensing from non-licensed units; and
23 Patient Group Directions.

Practice guidance and council statements

The Council of the Society also issues practice guidance to supplement the service specifications or to support good practice. From time to time, such guidance is published in the *Pharmaceutical Journal*, often in the form of Law and Ethics Bulletins. The Council also publishes a consolidated version of the Code of Ethics and supplementary statements and advice on practice, once a year in *Medicines, Ethics and Practice*. The profession is asked to endorse these additions and amendments at the Annual General Meeting held in May every year. Further guidance may be found in a series of fact sheets covering questions of law and ethics interpretation.

Clinical governance

Since 1999, following publication of the Government's white paper *A First Class Service*, the concept of clinical governance has been applied to all healthcare provision, especially by those within or contracted to the NHS (Chapter 26). The concept essentially makes all health professionals and their staff accountable for their standards of patient care. Clinical governance requires a continuous commitment to measuring and improving those standards. As the quality of patient care to be expected becomes more transparent, then the expectations of 'a reasonably competent practitioner' as used in determining negligence and Statutory Committee cases will become higher. The Society's guidance on clinical governance can be found in the 'practice' section of its website and in the Practice Guidance section of the *Medicines, Ethics and Practice Guide*.

Continuing professional development

Instituting CPD is a key responsibility for all pharmacists on the Register (Code of Ethics Part 2: A1b) and the facilitation of CPD is a key responsibility for those who manage or supervise pharmacists (Part 2: A.2h). Mandatory CPD will become effective during 2005. Fuller details of the Society's requirements may be found in the Practice Guidance section of the *Medicines, Ethics and Practice Guide* and on the Society's website. Failure to undertake and document participation in CPD could jeopardise the registration status of a pharmacist and be considered a breach of duty of care in both professional disciplinary cases and litigation.

Professional discipline and negligence

The inability of a pharmacist to carry out his/her duties because of a mental or physical disability does not normally amount to misconduct. Whether or not actions arising solely out of mere incompetence can be regarded as misconduct is doubtful, although the Statutory Committee could consider such cases (Chapter 24). Certainly, in most cases considered by the Statutory Committee (Chapter 24), there has always been some additional factor such as an indifference to the consequence of errors which amounts to a dereliction of duty.

A pharmacist is not normally likely to find him/herself charged with misconduct merely because s/he has made one mistake, although in 1985 one pharmacist was so charged before the Statutory Committee and was found guilty of misconduct and reprimanded (see p. 317 and *Pharm J* 11 May 1985 p. 600).

Until 2000, a pharmacist was also unlikely to be charged with criminal sanctions in respect of a dispensing error. However, this position may change following charges of manslaughter brought that year against a pharmacist and a pre-registration graduate who failed to prevent a fatal dispensing error when preparing a mixture for an infant. The mixture was erroneously compounded using concentrated instead of double-strength chloroform water. When the case came to court, the Crown prosecution service agreed to drop the charges of manslaughter and to substitute prosecutions under section 64 of the Medicines Act (see Chapter 2 p. 21) for supplying a medicine not of the nature and quality demanded (*Pharm J* 4 March 2000 p. 356; 11 March 2000 pp. 389–392; 18 March 2000 p. 427).

A Corporate Killing Bill is currently (May 2005) progressing through Parliament and could pave the way for manslaughter charges to be laid against managers and directors of large companies, as well as 'front-line' employees, if death occurs through major failures in management arrangements, such as staffing, training or resources.

A pharmacist is more likely, however, to be faced with an action for negligence in the civil courts. The essence of the tort of negligence is that there is on the part of the defendant a legal *duty of care* which s/he has failed to meet, as a result of which the plaintiff has suffered damage. The duty to take care was described in the case of *Donoghue* v. *Stephenson* [1932] AC 562 at 580 thus:

> You must take reasonable care to avoid acts or omissions which you can reasonably foresee would be likely to injure your neighbour. Who, then, in law is my neighbour? The answer seems to be. . .persons who are so closely and directly affected by my act that I ought reasonably to have them in contemplation as being so affected when I am directing my mind to the acts or omissions which are called in question.

The law imposes a duty to take care in a variety of circumstances. As sellers of goods, retail pharmacists have a duty to take reasonable care to warn customers of any potential dangers arising from them. Quite apart from this general duty on all vendors of goods, there is a special relationship between pharmacists and their customers in respect of transactions involving pharmaceutical knowledge. Reliance is placed upon the special skill and knowledge of the pharmacist when selling, dispensing or prescribing medicinal products. The law would expect him/her to exercise that degree of competence which the average member of the profession is required to possess. This is known as the 'duty of care' (see also Practice Guidance in *Medicines, Ethics and Practice Guide*).

A pharmacist occupying a special position in any branch of pharmacy would be expected to have a degree of ability commensurate with that position. Pharmacists consistently, and with good reason, press for recognition as experts upon drugs and medicines, and for the right to take a greater part in the health services. Every right has its correlative duty, and pharmacists, as they achieve greater recognition, must expect the law to require from them a higher degree of skill. It is probable that they will as a consequence be more liable to actions for professional negligence.

Three High Court decisions illustrate this point well. A woman who suffered gangrene in both feet, requiring extensive surgery, as a result of receiving an overdose of Migril (ergotamine tartrate, cyclizine hydrochloride and caffeine citrate) prescribed for migraine was awarded £100 000 damages (*Pharm J* 20 February 1982 p. 205). The owner of the pharmacy, who admitted negligence, was held liable for 45 per cent of the damages awarded. The judge, Mr Justice Stuart-Smith, in making the award said that the pharmacist owed a duty to the patient to ensure that drugs were correctly prescribed and that the pharmacist should have spotted the doctor's error and queried the prescription with the prescriber.

It is clear from the judgment that a pharmacist must not be deterred in querying prescriptions with the prescriber by any adverse response on the part of the prescriber, who may resent his/her decisions being questioned. The legal and professional responsibility of the pharmacist to verify and question prescriptions has been highlighted and established by this case.

In another case in 1988, a patient had gone to his doctor for his regular prescription for inhalers and tablets. At the same time, he was prescribed Amoxil (amoxicillin) for a chest infection. When he took the prescription to the pharmacy, the pharmacist misread Amoxil as Daonil (glibenclamide) and the patient suffered irreversible brain damage.

Mr Justice Auld in awarding £139 000 damages (75 per cent against the pharmacist; 25 per cent against the doctor) said that even assuming that the prescription was unclear, the pharmacist should have been alerted to the fact that Daonil was being recommended in the wrong dosage and quantity. He should also have noticed that the man who collected the drugs did not claim exemption from paying for the Daonil, although diabetics were entitled to free drugs. It was not enough for pharmacists to blindly dispense drugs without giving thought to what they were doing. Giving the decision in the High Court, Mr Justice Auld held that a doctor had a duty to his/her patient to write a prescription sufficiently legibly so as to reduce the likelihood of its being misread by a busy or careless pharmacist. But the pharmacist, in turn, was under a duty to give some thought to the prescriptions s/he was dispensing. If there was an ambiguity in the prescription, s/he should not dispense a drug without first satisfying him/herself that it was the correct one (*Pharm J* 26 March 1988 p. 404).

That apportioned liability is now an accepted principle in dispensing negligence cases was much more recently demonstrated in a settlement in the High Court in Manchester on 28 February 2000. The claim arose from a negligently written prescription, in November 1999, for Epilim (sodium valproate) 500 mg tablets where the strength, and hence the dosage and administration instructions, were incorrect. The pharmacy's professional indemnity insurer agreed to pay 25 per cent of the settlement (£225 000 plus costs) for the pharmacist's failure to detect and correct the error. The prescribing doctor was held liable for the remaining 75 per cent of the compensation paid to the patient (*Chemist and Druggist* 4 March 2000 p. 5).

Summary

- Pharmacy is regarded as a profession because its members must belong to a professional body which determines their standard of education and establishes a code of conduct – the Code of Ethics.
- Most pharmacists are engaged in trading in goods as well as the provision of services and advice; this has led to the development of detailed guidance on how to avoid conflict between these two areas.
- The *Dickson* case established that the Society could make rules affecting the non-professional as well as the professional activities of pharmacists, but only if the rules could be shown to be in the interest of the public and the profession.
- Pharmacists' activities are subject to criminal law, administrative law, civil law and the Society's Code of Ethics.
- The Code of Ethics comprises statements on pharmacists' ethics and key responsibilities, standards of professional performance and service standards.
- The Code is supplemented by guidance and practice advice published in the *Pharmaceutical Journal* and the Society's annual *Medicines, Ethics and Practice Guide*.
- Several cases now demonstrate the duty of care owed by pharmacists to their clients.

Further reading

Medicines, Ethics and Practice (published annually) The Royal Pharmaceutical Society of Great Britain, London.
Appelbe G. E. (1995) Pharmacy: profession or trade. *Irish Pharmacy J* October: 289.
Barber N. and O'Neill, R. (1999) Suggestions for a new code of ethics. *Pharm J* 262: 923–925.
Brazier M. (1992) *Medicine, Patients and the Law*, 2nd edn. Penguin Books, London.
Carey D. (1998) *Medical Negligence Litigation*. CLT Professional Publishing, Birmingham.
Gillon R. (ed.) (1994) *Health Care Ethics*. Wiley, Chichester.
Mason J. K. and McCall Smith R. A. (1994) *Law and Medical Ethics*, 5th edn. Butterworths, London.
Smith M. and Strauss, S. (eds) (1991) *Pharmacy Ethics*. Pharmaceutical Products Press, New York. (Covers American pharmacy practice but still relevant.)
Weinstein B. (1996) *Ethical Issues in Pharmacy*. Applied Therapeutics, Vancouver.
Wingfield J. (1990) Pharmacy and advertising: the pendulum swings. *Pharm J* 246: 542.

Websites

The Royal Pharmaceutical Society of Great Britain site carries information on all the functions and organisation of the Society, how it assures pharmacists' competence and fitness to practice, its services to members and continuing news about pharmacy policy and practice: http://www.rpsgb.org.uk

A selection of useful routes (not exclusive) to key documents mentioned in this chapter is given below as at August 2004:

- current issue of *Medicines, Ethics and Practice Guide*: Law and Ethics→ Law
- Code of Ethics, practice guidance: Law and Ethics→ Ethics
- law and ethics fact sheets: Law and Ethics→ Fact sheets
- clinical governance: Practice→ Clinical Governance
- continuing professional development: Education→ Continuing Professional Development

CHAPTER TWENTY-FOUR

The Statutory Committee of the Royal Pharmaceutical Society

In June 1999, the Government passed the Health Act 1999 which provided powers in section 60 to change the regulation of health professions and health professionals and to amend the NHS. The consequences of implementing this section were not complete at the time of going to press and may affect the constitution, powers and operation of the Statutory Committee. Changes will be incorporated into a section 60 Order, an outline of which appears in Appendix 13. Reference to the Society's website should be made for the current position.

Part 2 of the NHS Reform and Health Care Professionals Act 2002 (see also Chapters 22 and 26) provided power to set up an over-arching body, the Council for the Regulation of Health Care Professionals, now known as the Council for Health Care Regulatory Excellence (CHRE), to investigate and report on the performance of, and recommend changes to, a range of healthcare regulatory bodies, including the Society. The CHRE is empowered to receive details of all the decisions of the Society's disciplinary cases and it may then, if it considers that any decision is 'unduly lenient' or 'should not have been made' and 'that it would be desirable for the protection of members of the public' (s29), refer the case to the Appeal Court.

The following account of the Statutory Committee will be subject to changes (including a name change to the Disciplinary Committee) as set out in the section 60 Order.

The Statutory Committee (referred to below as the Committee) of the Royal Pharmaceutical Society of Great Britain exercises the disciplinary powers of the Society. The provisions relating to pharmacists are to be found in the Pharmacy Act 1954 (ss.7 and 8) and the constitution of the Committee appears in the first schedule to that Act. The provisions relating to bodies corporate are in the Medicines Act 1968 (ss.80 to 83).

Constitution

The Committee comprises a chairman and five members. The chairman is appointed by the Privy Council and has to be a person *having practical legal experience*. In practice, the Committee has always had as its chairman an eminent member of the legal profession.

The five members are appointed by the Council of the Society. They need not all necessarily be pharmacists, although one must be a pharmacist resident in Scotland. However, it has always been the practice to appoint as members of the Committee pharmacists of wide experience. A lay member was appointed to the Committee for the first time in 1998 (*Pharm J* 27 June 1998 p. 942). A member of the staff of the Society normally acts as secretary of the Committee.

The quorum of the Committee is three, one of whom must be the chairman. The Committee makes decisions by a majority vote of its members present and where necessary the chairman has a casting vote. A decision to remove a name from the register, however, can be taken only with the consent of the chairman. The Committee has power to make its own regulations as to procedure, but they must be approved by the Privy Council (Appendix 15). These regulations are subject to change under the proposed section 60 Order (see Appendix 13).

Procedure

The secretary of the Committee must submit a report to the chairman whenever s/he receives information from which it appears that:

1   any of the following *persons* has been convicted of a criminal offence or has been guilty of misconduct (Pharmacy Act 1954, s.8):

   (a)   a registered pharmaceutical chemist or a person employed by him/her in his/her business;
   (b)   a member of the board or an officer or an employee of a body corporate which is carrying on a retail pharmacy business;
   (c)   a representative (see Chapter 4) or an employee of a representative in a retail pharmacy business;
   (d)   a person applying for registration as a pharmaceutical chemist; or

(e)   a person whose name has been removed from the register under section 12(1) of the Pharmacy Act 1954, or a business employee of such a person.

2   a *body corporate* which is carrying on a retail pharmacy business has been convicted of an offence under the Pharmacy Acts, the Misuse of Drugs Act 1971 or the Medicines Act 1968.

It will be noted that for *corporate bodies* only offences under the Pharmacy Acts, the Medicines Act 1968 and the Misuse of Drugs Act 1971 need be reported to the Statutory Committee; but for any of the *persons* listed from (a) to (e) above, *any* criminal offence is relevant.

The chairman can deal with the information received from the secretary in any of the following ways.

1   If s/he considers that the case is not within the jurisdiction of the Committee, that the complaint is frivolous or that because of lapse of time or other circumstances that complaint may properly be disregarded, s/he must decide that the case will not proceed further.
2   If s/he considers that the conviction or misconduct alleged is not serious or is for any other reason of such a character that the matter can be disposed of without any inquiry, s/he can, after consultation orally or by letter with the other members of the Statutory Committee, decide that the case shall not proceed further. S/he may, however, direct the secretary to send a reprimand to the person affected and caution that person as to their future conduct.
3   In any other case, s/he must direct the secretary to take steps for an inquiry to be held. The procedure for an inquiry is specified in the regulations of the Committee (Appendix 15). A notice of the charge must be sent to the affected person at least 28 days before the hearing takes place. The hearing must open in public and must continue in public unless the Committee otherwise directs.

In 1999, the chairman clarified three circumstances in which a hearing might be in private: where there was evidence involving a person's medical history, especially if it was intimate; where there was evidence involving a young child; and where the evidence involved serious allegations against a third party who was unaware of the allegation and unable to rebut it (*Pharm J* 4 September 1999 p. 347).

At the hearing, a statement of the case against the person affected is given first, usually by a solicitor representing the body or person who has made the complaint. Then the person affected, or their counsel or solicitor, replies to the charges. Evidence may be received by the Committee orally, in a written or signed statement, or by means of a statutory declaration.

Witnesses may be examined and cross-examined at the hearing. A Crown Court subpoena can be issued to ensure attendance of witnesses, but there is no power to administer oaths or to deal with contempt of court.

The chairman must announce in public the decision of the Committee. If the decision, or any part of it, is postponed, the chairman must announce such postponement and state the terms, if any, on which it is made. The secretary must then communicate the decision of the Committee in writing to the person affected.

Information covering the notices of inquiry, timetable of meetings and directions made by the Statutory Committee can be found on the Society's website. Short reports summarising the decisions are reported from time to time in the *Pharmaceutical Journal* and full decisions, 'determinations', became available on the Society's website from January 2005. Transcripts of cases are not yet available electronically but can be obtained on request from the Society.

Jurisdiction

The Committee's authority, as will have been seen, extends to five classes of person and to corporate bodies.

In a case affecting a *registered pharmaceutical chemist*, the Committee can adopt one of the following courses (proposals for change appear in Appendix 13):

1   direct that no further action be taken;
2   give an admonishment or caution as to the pharmaceutical chemist's future conduct;
3   postpone their decision generally or on approved terms; or
4   direct that the registrar remove the pharmaceutical chemist's name from the register; such a direction requires the consent of the chairman.

In a case of a person applying to be registered, the Committee can direct that the person's name shall not be registered or shall not be registered until the Committee otherwise directs. Although this last power is most usually exercised following removal of a pharmacist's name from the register, it can also be invoked when considering an initial application for registration (see below).

A person aggrieved by a direction of the Committee may at any time within three months appeal to the High Court. A direction for removal from the register does not take effect until three months after the giving of notice of the direction or, if there is an appeal to the High Court, until the appeal is determined or withdrawn.

In a case affecting a *body corporate* the Committee may decide to:

1   take no further action;
2   admonish or caution;
3   adjourn a hearing for a set amount of time, usually 12 months;

4   direct the registrar to remove from the register all those premises at which the body corporate carries on a retail pharmacy business, or such of them as may be specified; or

5   direct that the body corporate be disqualified for the purposes of the Medicines Act 1968 (i.e. be unable to conduct retail pharmacy businesses); if a direction is given to disqualify, then the Committee must direct the registrar to remove from the register all those premises at which the body corporate carries on a retail pharmacy business.

A direction under 4 or 5 may, if the Committee thinks fit, be given so as to have effect for a limited period.

Sanctions can also be applied against a body corporate if any member of the board, or any officer or person employed by that body, has committed an offence or has been guilty of misconduct, and if the offence or misconduct is such as in the opinion of the Statutory Committee renders him/her, or would if s/he were a pharmacist have rendered him/her, unfit to be on the register.

The words *in the opinion of the Statutory Committee* in the Pharmacy Act 1954 (s.8) leave the Committee completely unfettered in its discretion. It is not bound by its previous decisions. Further, as it is a Committee of the Royal Pharmaceutical Society and not of the Council of the Society, it is completely independent of the Council, even though the Council appoints all the Committee members except the chairman. A number of references to the Committee's independent status were made in the case of *Pharmaceutical Society of Great Britain* v. *Dickson* (p. 393).

Inquiries following criminal convictions

So far as pharmacists are concerned, the Committee has jurisdiction in all cases of criminal conviction, whether they arise from offences under the Medicines Act or from offences of a general nature (e.g. theft). The jurisdiction was challenged in 1979 when it was argued before, and accepted by, the Committee that the facts leading to the imposition by the courts of conditional discharge orders could not be adduced before the Committee (*Pharm J* 24 March 1979 p. 245). The Society applied successfully to the Divisional Court for the decision to be quashed (*R* v. *Statutory Committee and Others, ex parte the Pharmaceutical Society of Great Britain* [1981] All ER 805; *Pharm J* 15 November 1980 p. 272).

From time to time, various chairmen have stressed that the directions given by the Committee are not given by way of punishment. For example, in 1953, one chairman said:

> . . .a man who had already suffered punishment had to come before the Committee not for the purpose of considering additional punishment but for the purpose of considering whether in the interests of the public it was right that he should remain on the Register.

> (*Pharm J* 10 October 1953 p. 297)

In 1990, the chairman said:

> Parliament set up this Committee for the purposes of taking care of three dimensions. . .the protection of the public, next comes the honour and dignity of the profession and the third dimension is the best interest of the pharmacist.
>
> *(Pharm J* 14 April 1990 p. 488)

In the past, the majority of Statutory Committee inquiries arose following criminal convictions relating to pharmaceutical matters such as lack of supervision. In more recent years, inquiries have more often followed convictions for theft or fraud. Inquiries are also held relating to other criminal offences, not all of which are connected with a pharmacist's professional work, for example motoring offences, theft, receiving stolen goods, forgery, indecent assault and other sexual offences, offences against the Misuse of Drugs Act or the Food and Drugs Act, procuring abortion, firearms offences and labelling offences under the Medicines Act 1968.

In a case in which a pharmacist had been convicted of firearms offences, the chairman said:

> . . .ought a professional man, such as a pharmacist, who has been convicted of an offence of this character be allowed to remain on the Register? The test is whether the offence of which the accused pharmacist stands convicted is an offence which, in the opinion of the Committee, rendered him unfit to have his name on the Register. So we are not really concerned with the particular motive or behaviour of the particular man. We are concerned with the nature of the offence of which he has been convicted.
>
> *(Pharm J* 15 April 1972 p. 344)

This view was confirmed in 1982 in the appeal case *Re Harari* (see p. 327), involving an unlawful eviction. Since then, pharmacists have appeared before the Committee for trading unlawfully in written-off cars (*Pharm J* 20 April 1985 p. 511), making false statements to collect insurance monies (*Pharm J* 7 August 1993 p. 189), making untrue endorsements on passport applications (*Pharm J* 13 December 1997 p. 965), impersonating a general practitioner (*Pharm J* 29 June 1991 p. 811), paedophilia (*Pharm J* 15 August 1998 p. 234), false imprisonment and assault (*Pharm J* 27 November 1999 p. 853), breaching the terms of a community service order (*Pharm J* 2 November 2002 p. 660), possession and distribution of indecent photographs (*Pharm J* 21/28 December 2002 p. 891), indecent assault (*Pharm J* 24 July 2004 p. 130) and the sending of offensive letters to the editor of the *Pharmaceutical Journal* (*Pharm J* 22 February 2003 p. 285).

Most Statutory Committee cases, however, deal directly with a pharmacist's professional and legal responsibilities and are related to his/her professional work.

The jurisdiction of the Committee also applies to offences committed outside the UK [e.g. drug offences committed in Canada (*Pharm J* 1 December 1984 p. 695) and convictions under Jersey's state law (*Pharm J* 3 December 1988 p. 727)]. Moreover, there is no time limit which removes the possibility of inquiry; in 1999, a pharmacist was removed from the register by the

Committee in relation to child abuse offences which were committed 20 years previously (*Pharm J* 10 July 1999 p. 51).

Inquiries following allegations of misconduct

In 1947 the chairman made clear the jurisdiction of the Committee in relation to allegations of misconduct:

> The jurisdiction is not limited to acts which constitute criminal offences. Indeed, in a very large number of cases we are not considering criminality but conduct which pharmacists ought not to pursue.
>
> (*Pharm J* 26 July 1947 p. 60)

Nearly all the complaints to the Committee alleging professional misconduct are made by the Council of the Society but there have been exceptions. In the 'Care Chemist' case (*Pharm J* 16 November 1974 p. 473 and 14 December 1974 p. 575), the 'Boots Scribbling Diary' case (*Pharm J* 11 February 1978 p. 126) and the 'Boots Times Advertisement' case (*Pharm J* 4 January 1992 p. 13), the complainants were individual members of the Society and not the Council. Although the Committee deals with allegations of professional misconduct, the question of what is good conduct for a professional person is a matter for the profession itself (Chapter 23). Nevertheless, one Statutory Committee chairman said in an address to students in 1953:

> With regard to the Code of Ethics, the actual decision as to what conduct is misconduct which justified removal from the register is one which can be made only by the Statutory Committee, and the Committee is not bound by any code formulated by the Pharmaceutical Society.
>
> (*Pharm J* 4 April 1953 p. 238)

While this is strictly true, the Committee has in practice used as a guideline the Code of Ethics, issued by the Council of the Society and amended from time to time (Chapter 23), as reflecting standards of professional practice.

Support for this view may be found in a 1987 case when the chairman began his judgment thus:

> . . .it is well known that this Committee is not bound by the Code. . .but nevertheless [it represents] in clear terms the views of the most senior members of the profession and they have been approved by the profession as a whole, they are expressed in terms which are easy to understand and this Committee attaches great importance to them.
>
> (*Pharm J* 21 November 1987 p. 633)

Notwithstanding the above, there is no specific reference in any Code of Ethics suggesting that it is wrong to be in charge of a pharmacy when drunk or to make a dispensing error. Such things are self-evident and implicit in the duty of pharmacists to have in mind at all times their responsibilities to the general public, although many of these responsibilities have now been made explicit in the Code of Ethics (Appendix 16).

Applications for restoration to the register

Applications for restoration to the register are also considered by the Committee (see Appendix 14). Such an application is considered in private unless the chairman grants a specific application for a public hearing. It must be supported by a statutory declaration made by the applicant, and also by at least two certificates as to the applicant's identity and good character. One of the certificates must be given by a registered pharmaceutical chemist; the other can be given by a registered pharmaceutical chemist, a Justice of the Peace, a fully registered medical practitioner or a legally qualified holder of a judicial office (reg.31). The secretary must notify the applicant in writing of the Committee's decision.

If the High Court has dismissed an appeal against a decision that a name be removed from the register, then a direction of the Committee authorising restoration cannot take effect unless it is approved by the Privy Council.

The Committee has always placed public safety and the reputation of the profession as its prime concerns and has limited scope for dealing with the rehabilitation of an offending pharmacist. To address this need, the Society proposed the creation of a Health Committee in 1998 and introduced the Sick Pharmacists Schemes in the early 1990s (see p. 281). Six years after the original proposal, the Chairman noted that, albeit reluctantly, the Statutory Committee had to act as a Health Committee in the meantime (*Pharm J* 26 June 2004 p. 823). So the Committee has played this part by imposing certain conditions on the respondent pharmacist before consideration will be given to an application for restoration to the register. For example, a pharmacist who had a 'history of heavy and chaotic drinking' was strongly recommended to continue to receive counselling and support, to produce a report on his conduct, a psychiatric assessment and a clear prognosis of his ability to refrain from excessive consumption of alcohol before restoration to the register might be considered (*Pharm J* 3 July 2004 p. 33). In a similar case, the conditions included submission to blood tests to ensure freedom from alcohol or drugs and an agreement to work only in situations where the pharmacist was not in sole charge of the pharmacy at any time (*Pharm J* 24 April 2004 p. 525).

Restoration to the register generally depends upon some evidence of rehabilitation (*Pharm J* 14 February 2004 p. 201) or commitment to improved practice (*Pharm J* 22 February 2003 p. 286). Applications may be rejected if there is little evidence of 'genuine regret' for wrongdoing (*Pharm J* 5 April 2003 p. 494) or substantially less that two years has elapsed from the 'striking off' order (*Pharm J* 8 November 2003 p. 660). Initial applications to register can also be blocked. A pre-registration graduate who had convictions for actual bodily harm, failed to surrender to custody and who attempted to deceive the Society in regard to details about his pre-registration training was refused admittance to the register on the grounds that:

. . .the Register should only be entered upon by persons of good character.

(*Pharm J* 20 July 1996 p.91).

Similarly, admittance was refused in the case of an overseas pharmacist involved in a benefit fraud (*Pharm J* 24 June 2000 p. 947) and again in 2001 (*Pharm J* 24 March 2001 p. 386). Conversely, a case involving the provision of untruthful information about pre-registration training, but lacking in evidence of an intention to deceive, resulted in eventual permission to seek registration (*Pharm J* 6 September 1997 p. 367).

Statutory Committee cases

Analysis of the work of the Statutory Committee taken from Appelbe's doctoral thesis in 1992 showed that 75 per cent of all convictions leading to reference to the Statutory Committee fell into five clearly defined areas: supervision, theft of cash, theft of drugs, unlawful sale of Prescription Only Medicines and Controlled Drug offences. Cases involving lack of supervision are now rare. Cases involving misconduct also largely fall into five categories: unsatisfactory conduct, unsatisfactory premises, excessive or uncontrolled supply of substances of abuse, dispensing mistakes and advertising. Although an inordinate amount of the Committee's time has been spent on this last topic, it has only once resulted in the erasure of a pharmacist's name, and that was associated with other aspects of misconduct (*Pharm J* 14 October 1972 p. 373). No cases related to advertising have been brought in recent years. Some cases have bridged both conviction and misconduct, such as drink-driving offences linked to erratic behaviour in the pharmacy. It has been necessary to be selective over the cases quoted; interested readers will find earlier examples in previous editions of this work. What follows is a selection of cases exemplifying the kinds of activity or behaviour which have resulted in sanctions by the Statutory Committee.

Supervision

The Committee has always been concerned with cases which involve the lack of supervision of the sale of Pharmacy Medicines and of dispensing. The cases illustrate the Committee's attitude to supervision. For example in a case in 1971, the chairman, referring to large departmentalised pharmacies, said:

> . . .it is vitally important to ensure that the drug counter and the dispensary are adequately covered by a qualified pharmacist at all times of the day with a real 100% cover.
>
> (*Pharm J* 23 January 1971 p. 72)

Much more recently in a case of unsupervised sales, the chairman stated that:

> . . .to be on the shop floor looking after the public was essential to the pharmacist's role.
>
> (*Pharm J* 30 August 1997 p. 322)

In the following year, the Committee removed a pharmacist from the register for attempting to supervise by telephone from 19 miles away (*Pharm J* 2 May 1998 p. 625).

Permanent or temporary absence is equally culpable. Late arrival in the pharmacy on three occasions led to pharmacist being reprimanded (*Pharm J* 22 January 2000 p. 128). A locum pharmacist who failed to fulfil his engagement was reprimanded in the following terms:

> We can point out that the sale of these medicines without any supervision by a pharmacist is a matter that is not only serious, but the cause of great possible and potential danger to the public.
>
> (*Pharm J* 25 May 1985 p. 662)

Failure on the part of a pharmacist proprietor, about to holiday in New Zealand, to act when he knew that a locum had cancelled a booking led to the unsupervised dispensing of over 200 prescriptions and an unknown number of unsupervised sales before the inspector intervened. The pharmacist was removed from the register (*Pharm J* 1 February 1997 p. 166). Erasure in a very similar case, arising when the proprietor was on holiday in India, followed failure to arrange adequate locum cover in his absence (*Pharm J* 3 June 2000 p. 840).

Inquiries have resulted from attempts to run two pharmacies with only one pharmacist, to do without the services of a pharmacist at quiet times like Saturday afternoons (*Pharm J* 26 June 1999 p. 915), Sundays (see below) or Bank Holidays (*Pharm J* 18 February 1995 p. 221) or to leave businesses in the charge of a range of unqualified persons. In 1990, a pharmacist had paid a visit to his 'other shop' following which the chairman commented:

> . . .The fact that dispensing is left to the hands of experienced staff we will not receive as mitigation. Such staff should never be regarded as a substitute for what the Act requires. . .
>
> (*Pharm J* 18 August 1990 p. 220)

Later the same year, a pharmacy had had no regular pharmacist for seven months and sales of Pharmacy Medicines were in the hands of a 15-year-old girl. The company owning both pharmacies was disqualified following the chairman's general statement:

> The signal we send out to the profession is, 'if you cannot get proper cover then the pharmacy has to be closed'. . .There are no half measures.
>
> (*Pharm J* 29 September 1990 p. 436)

In two cases in 1991, the chairman was even more forceful:

> Parliament does not offer a choice, such as 'I would like to run this pharmacy without proper cover, because it helps those around and in the district'. There is no alternative – the pharmacy has to close and that is the end of the matter.
>
> (*Pharm J* 19 January 1991 p. 89)

and, following an attempt to operate a partial service on a Sunday:

> . . .a point arose as to whether or not the shop was open. . .A sale can take place whether the premises are open or not. . .it is the opinion of the Committee that the shop was willing to take casual trade. . .and customers would be dealt with. . .as and when they came in.
>
> *(Pharm J* 27 July 1991 p. 136)

The reasons for the Committee's position are clear:

> . . .medicines can be ill-used, ill-advisedly, by members of the public when they are uninstructed by a pharmacist. . .Sales have to be under the supervision of a pharmacist, not for any fanciful notion, but because the law requires it for the safety of the public.
>
> *(Pharm J* 17 August 1991 p. 224)

In 1994, the chairman felt it necessary to issue a general warning to the profession:

> . . .pharmacists need to be particularly alert towards certain categories of unqualified persons whose standing may lead them into usurping the pharmacist's role. . .One is employers; another is long service employees whose over familiarity with practices in the pharmacy may lead them to transgress; and the third category. . .is the unqualified relative.
>
> *(Pharm J* 29 January 1994 p. 154)

The chairman went on to say that the subject of supervision should be routinely discussed from time to time with such individuals to ensure the meaning of the prohibition on their activities was *brought home and fully understood.*

To the above list should be added the dispensing assistant (*Pharm J* 3 May 1997 p. 622) and the pre-registration graduate, who does not assume the privileges or responsibilities of a pharmacist either in the sale of Pharmacy Medicines (*Pharm J* 8 October 1994 p. 496) or in dispensing (*Pharm J* 17 May 1997 p. 697) until registration. In the last case, the chairman said:

> It is very important indeed to make sure that those persons you leave behind know precisely what they can do and what they cannot do. . .ultimately the pharmacist is there to serve the public safely. The pharmacist should not put the public at risk for the sake of his own private profit.
>
> *(Pharm J* 17 May 1997 p. 697)

Cases before the Committee almost exclusively reflect situations where the pharmacist was simply not present, rather than any failure to ensure supervisory procedures were carried out.

Theft of money and deception

Cases of theft or deception are always treated by the Committee very seriously on the grounds that the pharmacist is in a position of trust, both in relation to his/her employer and the NHS.

In one case the chairman said:

> It is just one more incident of a tale so often told of a man who falls from his earlier position of honour because, he says, he has got into financial difficulties and in that process he lets down those who have trusted him, not only his employers but his wife and children as well and, of course his profession. . .insofar as professional conduct is concerned this Committee has no doubt at all that he was guilty of gross professional misconduct.
>
> (*Pharm J* 24 January 1987 p. 108)

In 1998, a pharmacist who drew cheques to purchase goods on stolen cheque books and cards was described as demonstrating:

> . . .disgusting behaviour. . .he himself does the very thing that he is on the lookout to stop other people doing. . .[and shows]. . .irresponsibility, a cavalier attitude and a lack of sensitivity towards other persons.
>
> (*Pharm J* 25 July 1998 p. 118)

The theft by an employee of a substantial sum accumulated through 'air miles' by over-purchasing dispensary stock paid for by the employer was considered a very serious breach of trust towards Mr X's employer and the pharmacist's name was erased from the register (*Pharm J* 9 January 1999 p. 47).

Repeatedly, the Committee's decisions reflect the view that pharmacists who breach their position of trust in such a way are unfit to be on the register:

> Honesty, integrity and honourable behaviour are at the core of all professional people . . .dishonesty and professionalism never go together. Secondly [a feature of this case] is a breach of trust. Mr X has been placed. . .in a position of trust as the manager. . .How does he repay that trust? He repays it by acting dishonestly. . .Our conclusion is that there [is] no place for a pharmacist who behaves like this on the Register. . .
>
> (*Pharm J* 22 May 1993 p. 704)

Theft of money from the NHS by deception has frequently led to erasures: for example where a pharmacist had made false claims for rota payments and false endorsements relating to non-resident claims and pack sizes (*Pharm J* 7 March 1987 p. 312); where false declarations of exemption were made when submitting prescriptions for payment (*Pharm J* 24 November 1990 p. 702); for falsely claiming urgent dispensing fees on non-urgent prescriptions (*Pharm J* 5 March 1994 p. 323); falsely claiming extemporaneous fees (*Pharm J* 10 June 2000 p. 876); making false endorsements (*Pharm J* 3 June 2000 p. 841); claiming for prescriptions not dispensed (*Pharm J* 22 January 2000 p. 128); and withholding low-cost prescriptions and keeping the difference between the prescription charge and the actual cost price of the medicines (*Pharm J* 3 July 2004 p. 34). A reprimand was administered for substituting medicines on a prescription without the prescriber's consent (*Pharm J* 31 October 1998 p. 698) and for falsified claims for emergency contraception supply (*Pharm J* 29 November, 2003 p. 759).

Theft by deception from employers (*Pharm J* 18 November 2000 p. 751), (*Pharm J* 7 July 2001 p. 32) or wholesalers (*Pharm J* 8 December 2001 p. 834) have led to reprimands or striking off. An attempt to deceive the

Society by forging a certificate of professional indemnity resulted in erasure from the register (*Pharm J* 4 December 1999 p. 896).

Theft and unlawful consumption or supply of drugs

In 1984, the chairman commented on the potential danger to the public of a pharmacist who consumes or is addicted to drugs:

> He became so irrational that not only did he steal from his employers but also deceived his friend. . .This illustrates the dangers inherent in addiction in the case of a pharmacist upon whom the lives and the well-being of his customers or patients may depend. . .
>
> (*Pharm J* 24 March 1984 p.358)

In 1993 on the public danger which results from the pharmacist's efforts to disguise the theft of Controlled Drugs:

> It involved substitution of Epsom salts in three tubs (formerly containing cocaine), which could have jeopardised the comfort and assistance that cocaine may have given to other patients. . .
>
> (*Pharm J* 10 July 1993 p.58)

Again in 1995, in a case where the pharmacist had stolen diamorphine, replaced it with tragacanth powder and abused the stolen diamorphine himself:

> . . .three years of dispensing in a pharmacy while taking diamorphine, with its euphoric and distorting effects, and while there was no-one to check him, correct him or monitor him, meant that there was the chance of a mistake.
>
> (*Pharm J* 19 August 1995 p.246)

Such activities clearly bring the profession into disrepute and represent a breach of trust and potential risk to the public. Nevertheless, such cases continue to arise: for example, theft and consumption of amoxicillin, salbutamol, ephedrine and Sudafed (paracetamol and pseudoephedrine hydrochloride) (*Pharm J* 14 December 2002 p. 870), Equagesic (meprobamate, ethoheptazine citrate and aspirin) (*Pharm J* 14 December 2002 p. 871), temazepam (*Pharm J* 22 February 2003 p. 285), Ritalin (methylphenidate) and Dexedrine (dexamfetamine sulphate) (*Pharm J* 8 November 2003 p. 661), dihydrocodeine tablets (*Pharm J* 3/10 January 2004 p. 38) and 'ecstasy' (methylenedioxymethamfetamine) and cocaine (*Pharm J* 14 February 2004 p. 201).

Sometimes the theft is for the purpose of illegal supplies to others: for example illegal import of steroids at the employer's expense and supply to gymnasiums (*Pharm J* 18 November 2000 p. 750), theft of medicines for illegal sale (*Pharm J* 21 April 2001 p. 534), illegal sales of Rohypnol (flunitrazepam) and Distalgesic (co-proxamol) (*Pharm J* 1 November 2003 p. 629) and theft of several thousand bottles of glycerin and rosewater for export to Nigeria (*Pharm J* 6 July 2002 p. 38). The advent of medicines for erectile dysfunction, with restrictions on prescribing within the NHS, led to a series of cases concerning illegal supplies of Viagra (sildenafil) to individual patients

(*Pharm J* 23 February 2003 p. 265; 7 September 2002 p. 343; 2 November 2002 p. 659; and 7 December 2002 p. 829).

A persistent 'misuse' of medicines involves the use of steroid creams for 'skin lightening'. Investigation by the media resulted in a complaint leading to erasures for pharmacists who unlawfully made supplies of Dermovate (clobetasol) without prescription in 1997 (*Pharm J* 12 July 1997 p. 57) and, following convictions, again in 2000 (*Pharm J* 19 February 2000 pp. 290–291).

Controlled drugs

The majority of convictions relating to Controlled Drugs have related to inadequate record keeping (e.g. *Pharm J* 30 June 2001 p. 885; 5 April 2003 p. 495). The importance of keeping proper records was summed up in a case in 1990 when the chairman listed four important reasons.

> One is that it is essential to know where dangerous drugs are. [Secondly], where one is dealing with a drug commonly supplied to addicts, one is playing with fire if records are not kept. Such people, in order to feed their habit, frequently lie, sell part of the drugs they are given, horde drugs and forge prescriptions. . .it is. . .extremely important that records are kept right up to date, scrupulously and accurately. [Thirdly]. . .it is for the greater protection of the pharmacist himself that he keeps records in that fashion. . .his records would help to avoid any false accusations being made against him. . .[Fourthly] Controlled Drugs have to be locked away. . .sometimes those cabinets are broken into and the drugs stolen. It therefore becomes very, very important for the proper authorities to know precisely what had been in the cabinet before the commencement of their enquiries.
>
> (*Pharm J* 4 August 1990 p. 158)

Commenting that the Committee was growing weary of repeating the following injunction, the chairman said:

> Pharmacists across the country should recognise how close they would come to imperilling their careers if they fail to do what the law requires, and fail to keep the registers. . .up to date, and make the entries on the day, or the next day
>
> (*Pharm J* 24 April 2004 p. 526)

Not all inquiries relate to the keeping of registers. Convictions for possession of cannabis resulted in an erasure from the register of a practising pharmacist (*Pharm J* 19 August 2000 p. 262) but a reprimand for a graduate who had offended shortly before registration (*Pharm J* 20/27 December 2003 p. 850).

Disposal of dangerous waste

Implementation of environmental protection laws has led to a number of convictions of pharmacists. In 1987, a pharmacist entrusted some 20 plastic sacks of trade and domestic waste to an outside contractor. These contained a small number of Prescription Only Medicines, which eventually surfaced on the waste ground where the contractor had illegally dumped the sacks (*Pharm J* 27 June 1987 p. 798). The following year, a pharmacist was reprimanded following a conviction for herself placing sacks of unwanted medicines in a skip at a local authority tip (*Pharm J* 23 July 1988 p. 128).

Reprimands followed in three later cases. A pharmacist had cleared out stock from a pharmacy he had just acquired and caused sacks containing Prescription Only Medicines and Controlled Drugs to be left in a skip outside the premises. The chairman concluded that the pharmacist had made no enquiries at all about what the refuse sacks contained and added:

> . . .by that carelessness, led the public to be exposed to dangerous substances.
> (*Pharm J* 2 February 1991 p. 154)

Two years later, irresponsible dumping by a pharmacist of waste containing potassium dichromate and other dangerous material caused a fire in the dustcart that attempted disposal (*Pharm J* 9 January 1993 p. 50); more recently, a pharmacist simply left sacks of obsolete medicines in the garden of his old house (*Pharm J* 22 January 2000 p. 129).

Other notable cases have concerned supply of dangerous chemicals and irregularities surrounding parallel imports. None of these has recurred since 1997 and the interested reader is referred to earlier editions of *Pharmacy Law and Ethics* for details.

Unsatisfactory conduct

Until the 1990s, cases which could be classified under this heading would principally be situations where a pharmacist's personal or professional conduct was compromised by alcoholism. Today, transgressions which reflect lack of professional competence or application of proper standards for whatever reason have become more common and they frequently arise from a *course of conduct* rather than a single event.

The Committee has taken a strong line with pharmacists who have been found incapable of carrying out their duties as a pharmacist through the influence of alcohol and has used its limited powers to introduce measures which approximate to both suspension from the register and the imposition of conditions before readmission (proposals to change this situation are in Appendix 13).

For example, in 1999, after ordering the removal of her name from the register, the chairman said:

> [this case] gives rise to a clear indication that she has a drink problem, is going to be a danger if she works in a pharmacy. . .we regard alcoholism. . .as an illness which needs treatment. . .there is a scheme available in this profession which will extend help to her if she is willing to receive it.

He directed that Mrs X would not be restored to the register until she could show that she had been free from alcohol abuse for at least 12 months, supported by references to that effect from psychiatrists, doctors and others who knew her (*Pharm J* 30 January 1999 p. 153).

This last case arose from driving convictions, which can sometimes lead to erasure (*Pharm J* 20 September 2003 p. 388), reprimand (*Pharm J* 18 August

2001 p. 246), admonition (*Pharm J* 27 November 1999 p. 854) or no further action (*Pharm J* 25 August 2001 p. 277) depending on the circumstances.

The discretion exercised by the Statutory Committee is now subject to review and intervention by the CHRE (see above). The first instance of such intervention occurred at the end of 2004 when the CHRE required additional conditions to be met before a former pharmacist convicted of drink-driving could be considered for restoration to the register (*Pharm J*. 18/25 December 2004 p. 895).

A range of sanctions have been administered for other forms of unsatisfactory conduct, which generally include *failure to adopt safe practices*. In the first case of its kind, a pharmacist was erased from the register principally for failure to maintain his professional indemnity insurance cover for a period of at least 40 months. In this case, the chairman was also critical of how long it took the Society's Council to bring the complaint forward, pointing out that it would have been dreadful to imagine 'an uninsured patient' having a claim for personal injuries and uncovering that the Society knew all about it (*Pharm J* 17 May 1997 p. 698; see also p. 269 and Table 24.1 on p. 330). In a second case, involving failure to maintain routine paperwork and the controlled drugs register as well, a pharmacist was removed from the register after practising for at least five years without professional indemnity insurance (*Pharm J* 16 February 2002 pp. 227–228). Lack of safety can also involve taking on too much work (*Pharm J* 7 September 2002 p. 344), knowingly dispensing a prescribed overdose (*Pharm J* 20 September 2003 p. 386) and putting patients at risk by failing to meet appropriate standards for aseptic manufacture of cytotoxic preparations (*Pharm J* 14 December 2002 p. 870).

Pharmacists have been removed from the register for other unsafe practices such as using an open and unlocked Controlled Drugs cabinet, the presence of unlabelled pre-packs on the dispensary shelves, the presence of plastic measures containing unidentified tablets recovered from monitored dosage system trays and an intention to re-use tablets of which the pharmacist had no knowledge of either batch number or expiry date (*Pharm J* 8 January 2000 p. 52). A reprimand was given to a pharmacist who removed expiry dates from medicines (*Pharm J* 20 September 2003 p. 387) but such behaviour led to an erasure, in another case, when accompanied by the re-use of patients' returned medicines and deliberate 'popping' of tablets from their original blister packaging (*Pharm J* 22 August 1998 p. 264).

Following three reprimands at earlier hearings, a pharmacist was erased for *failure to achieve proper standards*, namely failure to produce evidence of professional indemnity insurance cover, trading as a pharmacy when the premises were not registered, re-use of patient returned medicines, sale of restricted medicines in the absence of a pharmacist, lack of personal control, poor physical standards of the premises (such as stock stored in the toilet area, heavily frosted refrigerator and no segregation of waste medicines) and unacceptable practices in relation to handling medicines (such as handling tablets with bare hands and preparing food in a room used for dispensing) (*Pharm J* 27 November 1999 p. 852). Such standards might also include faulty systems for supplies of medicines to a hospice (*Pharm J* 16 June 2001 p. 813), inadequate record keeping and medicines storage (*Pharm J* 23 February 2002 p. 266) or regularly dispensing unsigned prescriptions (*Pharm J* 8 May 2004 p. 590). A reprimand was given to a pharmacist who had claimed for items not dispensed and allowed himself to be duped into giving credit to a bogus doctor (*Pharm J* 10 June 2000 p. 876) and to a pharmacist who kept a stock of blank prescription forms to fill in on behalf of prescribers (*Pharm J* 26 June 1999 p. 914); when this last practice was linked to deliberate sale of blank forms to drug misusers, the pharmacist's name was erased from the register (*Pharm J* 24 June 2000 p. 947).

An erasure also followed a case of *pharmaceutical incompetence* where the supply of medicines to residential homes was so chaotic that monthly requests were being made for prescriptions which bore amounts for two and three months' duration; some patients were supplied with two years' supply of medicines in six months; prescriptions had been requested for a deceased patient and 30 outstanding prescriptions had never been dispensed (*Pharm J* 17 May 1997 p. 597).

Inappropriate behaviour, including rudeness and aggression to patients, resulted in a reprimand (*Pharm J* 7 December 2002 p. 830) although refusal to accept warnings from the Council's Infringements Committee about the handling of a patient's complaint subsequently resulted in no further action (*Pharm J* 24 April 2004 p. 525). Other 'irregularities' in professional practice which have resulted in Statutory Committee cases have included working full-time for three years while paying a part-time retention fee (*Pharm J* 3/10 January 2004 p. 37), continuing to work as a pharmacist after being struck-off (*Pharm J* 29 November 2003 p. 758) or having not paid the current retention fee (*Pharm J* 21/28 December 2002 p. 891) and a locum 'storming out' of a pharmacy, thus obliging it to be closed for three days (*Pharm J* 3/10 January 2004 p. 37).

Unsatisfactory state of pharmacy premises

Allegations about pharmacists conducting pharmacies in such a state as to be a potential hazard to the public are now relatively rare. This follows enforcement of the Guide to Good Dispensing Practice, which in 1979 set minimum environmental standards for pharmacies as part of the Code of Ethics. These were incorporated into a more rigorous set of Standards of Practice in the 1992 Code of Ethics and now appear in rather less detail in standard 3 of the service specifications in the current Code of Ethics, with some accompanying practice guidance.

However, the Committee continues to deal with a few cases where the conditions are still unacceptable. For example, in 1993, a pharmacist was reprimanded for conditions in his pharmacy described as:

> . . .the floor covering [was] dirty and split, constituting a hazard to the public. . .the shelves [were] dirty and dusty. There had been insufficient work surfaces, and these had

been cluttered, leaving little usable space. The sink had been dirty and the surfaces around it had been cluttered with old medicine bottles and rubbish.

On a later date:

> The refrigerator was dirty, had no maximum/minimum thermometer and water was running out of the bottom. Some of the stock was found to be wet.
>
> *(Pharm J* 31 July 1993 p. 162)

In a 1994 case, similar conditions led to the dispensing of a mixture containing the remains of insects and a consequent reprimand for the pharmacist (*Pharm J* 17 June 1995 p. 840), and in 1997 a pharmacist's name was erased for allowing the pharmacy to be contaminated with food debris and to be poorly maintained (*Pharm J* 2 August 1997 p. 195).

Excessive or uncontrolled supplies of substances of abuse

The fact that the sale of certain substances is not unlawful does not permit the pharmacist to abrogate his professional responsibility as custodian of the nation's medicines, nor to ignore his specialised knowledge of chemicals and other harmful material. The names of many pharmacists have been erased from the register in connection with selling excessive quantities of medicines likely to be abused or for being unable to account, other than by way of sale, for large discrepancies between the amount of such medicines purchased and supplies made on prescription. A complaint of misconduct commonly follows irresponsible supply of abused medicines such as those containing codeine, morphine, methadone, ephedrine, cyclizine and antihistamines or anabolic steroids.

The distinctions between what is and is not considered to be irresponsible can be fine. In the 1980s, the chairman made it clear that a pharmacist should not supply adjuvants such as cyclizine to drug misusers saying:

> . . .he dealt with these potentially dangerous medicines (cyclizine), knowing them to be dangerous, with complete recklessness and a complete disregard for the health of those to whom he supplied.
>
> *(Pharm J* 9 January 1988 p. 62; see also *Pharm J* 25 July 1987 p. 104)

Commenting on a more recent case, involving the supply, over a six-month period, of 39 000 Valoid tablets to a single customer, the chairman commented:

> It was startling to the point of disbelief if he did not know that Valoid was [cyclizine]. . .[the pharmacist] had demonstrated a complete lack of expertise, the public had been put at risk, no check had been made on the customer or on the use of the tablets, and no warning had been given.
>
> *(Pharm J* September 2, 2000 p. 326)

However in June 2000, steps were underway to include the provision of another adjuvant, citric acid, as part of the support services for drug misusers, at least in Scotland (*Pharm J* 24 June 2000 p. 950).

Five cases involving the supply of hundreds of litres of codeine linctus in the Glasgow area were considered by the Committee between 1987 and 1989. In defence, the pharmacists often gave as the explanation for supplying such large quantities that they were trying to help the addict. The chairman rejected this argument in round terms:

> . . .in the existing climate which appertains to drug abuse these days, we think it would be a dereliction of our duty to take a charitable view of the wilful, deliberate omission to take action, which was carried out over the period in question to his own profit and to the detriment, the serious detriment, of members of the public.
>
> (*Pharm J* 10 March 1990 p. 307)

In a later case, involving failure to account satisfactorily for 725 g ephedrine hydrochloride powder, 59.5 litres ephedrine hydrochloride elixir, 541.5 litres Phensedyl linctus, 1857.9 litres codeine linctus, 9432 tablets of codeine phosphate 30 mg and 5600 tablets of codeine phosphate 60 mg, the chairman declared that the pharmacist's duty of care could not be avoided even under duress and added:

> Even if those threats were made, which we do not accept, we were invited. . .to consider the balance of the Code of Ethics. . .and. . .the law. . .against the threat of violence to himself, to his children and to his livelihood. . .and, upon striking that balance, to determine that what he did was right and the only alternative a professional man could follow. We emphatically reject that suggestion and anything approaching that. A professional man does not see things in that way at all. It is not a question of balance. A professional man does not act illegally, neither does he deliberately act in a flagrant breach of the Code. . .What he does is to face up to threats and temptations as part of his professional responsibilities.

The chairman continued:

> It is no way for a professional man to behave, to feed secretly the addiction of drug addicts, having given in to the temptation of supplying their demands, and to allow seepage of drugs of abuse and addiction onto the street where they can be absorbed into the black market and into the wrong hands. . .We have decided. . .that Mr X, by behaving in such an utterly irresponsible way, must reasonably expect that he may have forfeited forever his right to practise as a pharmacist.
>
> (*Pharm J* 28 September 1991 p. 445)

Despite these clear warnings, two pharmacists were removed from the register in 1999 for making excessive sales of codeine linctus (*Pharm J* 30 January 1999 p. 152) and similarly in relation to kaolin and morphine mixture (*Pharm J* 10 July 1999 p. 50). Regarding supply of more than the authorised instalment amount of methadone to two addicts, the chairman commented that the Committee wished it to be crystal clear that it could never be a legitimate excuse to plead intimidation in such circumstances. Pharmacies known as a 'soft touch' would attract ever greater numbers of drug abusers.

> If they (pharmacists) give way to intimidation. . .the whole arrangement will collapse
>
> (*Pharm J* 21 April 2001 p. 534)

The dangers of too close a relationship with drug misusers was dramatically demonstrated in a case where a pharmacist had allowed her pharmacy to be used by a substantial number of recreational drug users, giving rise to drug dealing on the premises, brawls and the dumping of used needles and syringes in the vicinity. The pharmacy had been christened a 'drug den' and 'Smack Street' by local residents and had attracted drug users far beyond the local population; in short, it was 'a honey pot for illicit trading in drugs'. The chairman said that a pharmacist could not dispense a prescription simply because a doctor had written it and added that:

> The pharmacist is there to check, to monitor, to counsel, to use his informed judgement, to use experience, to sniff out mistakes. If one is asked to do something which is unlawful, or which is highly likely to be, then one should challenge it and confront the prescriber.
>
> (*Pharm J* 29 November 1997 p. 888)

Such sentiments are reflected in the standards 19 and 20 of the service specifications of the current Code of Ethics, together with associated practice guidance.

Dispensing mistakes

It has been rare for dispensing errors to lead to removal from the register unless there are particularly worrying circumstances. In December 1973, the Committee heard a complaint alleging that a pharmacist had made a series of dispensing mistakes over a period of three weeks. Moreover, the same pharmacist had been before the Committee two years earlier on a very similar charge. Directing erasure from the register the chairman said:

> . . .it was quite properly impressed upon us that we ought to view the whole matter cumulatively, without putting the microscope on each particular item in isolation. . .we [cannot] resist the conclusion that the cumulative effect of all these individual matters, coupled with the history of what had taken place before, amounted to misconduct. We have borne very much in mind that our prime duty is to see that the public is protected. This is an important duty, for one can hardly imagine anybody who could be more dangerous to the public than a pharmacist who is liable to make errors in dispensing what may be dangerous drugs.
>
> (*Pharm J* 5 January 1974 p. 11)

However, in a much later case, a series of dispensing errors ultimately (after a year's adjournment) resulted in a reprimand for a pharmacist who was dispensing nearly twice the national average of prescriptions without dispensing assistance and in the knowledge that he had impaired eyesight. The chairman commented that Mr X should have backed up his practice with protocols and double-checks so that even if he had blurred vision, mistakes were picked up. He added

> Pharmacists must not act without safety nets.
>
> (*Pharm J* 5 June 1999 p. 804)

Later the same year, another pharmacist was reprimanded for making dispensing errors while being grossly overworked (*Pharm J* 21 August 1999 p. 270).

Confirmation that a single dispensing error *could* constitute misconduct arose in a 1985 case and was later confirmed by the High Court (see p. 331). A patient was prescribed by his doctor pethidine in the form of a 'Brompton' mixture. The doctor intended the mixture of 50 mg pethidine per 1 ml to be diluted to 15 ml. The mixture dispensed was not diluted to 15 ml and was in fact 15 times the strength intended by the doctor. The patient died, death being from pethidine poisoning (*Pharm J* 11 May 1985 p. 600). Any error which results in death, notwithstanding that all errors could possibly lead to death, is likely to be referred to inquiry by the Committee.

Any error which demonstrates lack of competence is also likely to result in an inquiry. In 1992, a pharmacist who did not understand the difference between Oramorph Concentrate and Oramorph Solution supplied a medicine which was ten times as strong as it should have been. The patient survived but the pharmacist was erased from the register (*Pharm J* 6 June 1992 p. 746).

A case in 1998 provided the opportunity for the chairman to give advice on what to do, or rather what not to do, when a dispensing mistake is discovered. A pharmacist discovered that a supply of atenolol had inadvertently been given to the wrong patient but did nothing active to try and remedy the mistake. The chairman did not accept that the pharmacist could simply expect the patient to realise the mistake and return to the pharmacy. In fact it took 28 days before the wrong recipient of the atenolol was identified. Listing all the things that could have been done when a mistake is discovered, the chairman said:

> Forget personal dignity and reputation. The patient comes first. If it needs to be disclosed to the whole world that one has made a mistake, so be it. . .Let the profession know that this particular pharmacist. . .sat on her hands and waited for the tablets to turn up. Pharmacists should not do that; they should get on the rooftop and shout.
>
> (*Pharm J* 27 February 1999 p. 288)

Since 1999, an increasing number of inquiries into dispensing errors have been considered by the Committee but erasures have been rare. In such cases, it is fair to say that there are usually some aggravating circumstances pertaining to the pharmacist, such as looking unkempt 'as if he (the pharmacist) had been sleeping rough', talking to himself, failing to answer questions, appearing confused and falling asleep in the dispensary (*Pharm J* 16 June 2001 p. 812). In two further cases, the pharmacists demonstrated failure to respond to a postponed hearing pending a change in employment (*Pharm J* 24 August 2002 p. 264) or to take advice or heed warnings (*Pharm J* 2 November 2002 p. 658). Even where the consequences have been hospitalisation of a child (*Pharm J* 11 August 2001 p. 211) or death of an infant, actions have varied. No action was taken against the pre-registration graduate who actually prepared the prescription in the former (*Pharm J* 11 August 2001 p. 212) and the pharmacist who supervised the preparation in the latter was reprimanded (*Pharm J* 16 February 2002 p. 228).

Advertising

In the past, many cases of alleged professional misconduct in relation to advertising came before the Committee. Most notable were the cases involving the Boots organisation, all of which related to the advertising of professional services, in particular the advertising of dispensing (*Pharm J* 4 June 1949 p. 411; 8 July 1950 p. 26; 16 May 1959 p. 361), the 'Scribbling Diary' case in 1977 (*Pharm J* 11 February 1978 p. 126) and *The Times* newspaper advertisement for their monitored dosage system (*Pharm J* 4 January 1992 p. 13), together with the 'Care Chemist' campaign launched by Independent Chemists Marketing Ltd, a company sponsored by the National Pharmaceutical Union (as it then was) (*Pharm J* 16 November 1974 p. 473; 14 December 1974 p. 575). A full account of these cases appears in earlier editions of *Pharmacy Law and Ethics*.

The provision of information (i.e. advertising, about professional services) is now positively encouraged by the Code of Ethics as being in the public interest. However, it should not be thought that there are *no* limits on the form that such advertising may take. Such material must now meet standard 1 of the service specifications in the current Code of Ethics (see Appendix 16). Moreover, the series of cases involving Boots demonstrates the paramount importance of the superintendent pharmacist in controlling the professional activities of a corporate body which owns retail pharmacy businesses.

Responsibility of the superintendent pharmacist

In 1971, the Committee considered the responsibility of a superintendent pharmacist particularly in circumstances where the effective proprietors of the business are not pharmacists. The relevant section of the decision reads:

> The proper course if it were necessary for him to absent himself would have been to close the business. In that it is the superintendent pharmacist's responsibility to control the whole of the running of the pharmacy, it is for him to say if the business is to be closed and it is for nobody else to say that. I make that remark because there was some suggestion that his better judgement was overborne by the proprietors of the business; but I do want him and indeed any other superintendent pharmacist to whom my words may come, to appreciate that it is the superintendent pharmacist's responsibility and nobody else's. He is responsible for the whole of the conduct of the pharmacy. The Committee is left in no doubt that his behaviour did in the circumstances amount to gross misconduct on the part of Mr X.
>
> (*Pharm J* 30 January 1971 p. 107)

Conflicts with employers still arise. In 1995, the Committee ordered the removal from the register of a superintendent pharmacist whose conduct had appalled the Committee. The non-pharmacist sole director of the company which owned the pharmacy was also arraigned. The Committee heard that the director had insisted that the superintendent pharmacist should only work for four of the eight hours a day that the pharmacy was open and that no other pharmacist had been present at other times. When the Society's inspectors made test purchases to demonstrate the absence of a pharmacist, the superintendent could not return to the unsupervised pharmacy because he was employed on a regular basis at another pharmacy.

Making reference to the Code of Ethics at that time (Guidance to Principle 6 1992), *The superintendent may carry total responsibility if, as a result of his neglect or inactivity, a director is permitted to exercise functions which are the superintendent pharmacist's own responsibility*, the chairman said:

> [the superintendent pharmacist should have been] obliged to resign. He cannot lend his name to an operation to be carried on in the pharmacy in flagrant defiance of either the law or the ethics of the profession. . .It is the superintendent pharmacist who must insist on things being done as he wishes and as he requires, being informed pharmaceutically as to what is right and proper. . .The employer should not be. . .allowed to do [just] what he wishes. A superintendent pharmacist should be firm and robust with his employer and exercise his own professional integrity and insist. . .that things are done properly.
>
> (*Pharm J* 25 February 1995 p. 255)

In a case involving a young female pharmacist, the chairman said she had been unable to stand up to the pressure put on her by a non-pharmacist director who was effectively in day-to-day control of the business. For two or three years, the pharmacy had been run without a pharmacist between 3.00 p.m. and 6.00 p.m. on Saturday afternoons and Ms X ought to have known such a thing was happening because it was 'her job to find out'. The chairman set out a very clear summary of the duties of a superintendent:

> A superintendent pharmacist. . .was in charge of seeing that the premises were run in a proper manner – legally, pharmaceutically and ethically. A superintendent pharmacist had to insist on things being done properly even when they may be contrary to the company's interests. Furthermore. . .a superintendent pharmacist had to take responsibility for any acts or omissions by the company or its directors which were within the scope of the superintendent's responsibilities.

Noting that Ms X became superintendent at the age of 23 or 24, the chairman commented that it was 'simply outrageous' for the *Pharmaceutical Journal* to have accepted an advertisement for a superintendent which included the words 'suitable for a newly qualified pharmacist'. Given the responsibilities set out above, the chairman considered that, having entered the role at 'a young age and in a vulnerable frame of mind', the fact that the non-pharmacist director had run the pharmacy since 1981 was pertinent to the case (*Pharm J* 23 August 1997 p. 283). In the accompanying editorial, the Editor did not agree and also questioned the fairness of the judgment in which the name of the pharmacist was erased from the register but the employing company was only reprimanded.

In more recent cases, superintendents have been erased for allowing two pharmacies to operate without a pharmacist in personal control (*Pharm J* 19 August 2000 p. 261) (see also the next section) and reprimanded for failing to notify the Society of their resignation (*Pharm J* 24 March 2001 p. 385), for failing to prevent returned medicines from being re-dispensed (*Pharm J* 24 March 2001 p. 385), failing to prevent excessive sales of codeine linctus (*Pharm J* 9 June 2001 p. 781) and failure to ensure that a pharmacist was present at a late-opening pharmacy (*Pharm J* 2 November 2002 p. 660).

An example of the *right* approach by a superintendent pharmacist, and indeed by a locum pharmacist, can be found in a case reported in 2000 in which a locum went to lunch and returned to find that the director, a former pharmacist struck off three years earlier, had dispensed seven prescriptions in her absence. She immediately closed the premises, contacted the superintendent and took steps to trace all the patients involved. Several dispensing errors had been made by the non-pharmacist director.

The superintendent pharmacist contacted the Society, told the non-pharmacist to leave the premises and ordered the locks on the pharmacy to be changed. The chairman congratulated the superintendent for acting in a way that was a model for all superintendent pharmacists (*Pharm J* 24 June 2000 p. 948).

Personal control of a pharmacy

The Medicines Act 1968 (s.71) requires that in respect of each set of premises the business must, as concerned the retail sale of drugs, be under the *personal control* of a pharmacist. The requirement that medicinal products not on the General Sale List must be *supervised* by the pharmacist is an additional provision. The more general requirement of personal control by the pharmacist extends to all medicinal products, including those on the General Sale List.

A case in 1966 concerned a pharmacist who had made a habit of not arriving before 10 a.m. each morning although the pharmacy opened at 9 a.m. In that case the chairman said:

> . . .to leave his pharmacy unattended from 9 a.m. till 10 a.m. every morning is in itself a breach of the regulations, and if he persists in doing that another complaint will be made against him which may not be treated so leniently.
>
> (*Pharm J* 2 April 1966 p. 311)

A complaint was made to the Committee in 1970 alleging that a pharmacist had not been complying with the Pharmacy and Poisons Act 1933 in that he had left his premises on several occasions for long periods without a pharmacist in personal control. There was no question of sales of poisons having been made as the pharmacist had put them into the dispensary and the dispensary had been locked in his absence.

In giving the Committee's decision, the chairman discussed the matter of personal control as follows:

> It must be plain that a question of degree is involved. I would not for my part say that the pharmacist ceased to be in personal control of his premises because he slipped out for a few minutes even if he went down the street to make some purchases in some other shops. At the other end of the scale, it is equally clear that a pharmacist cannot claim to be in personal control of the premises if he has exercised what may be described as

remote control and has put in only an occasional appearance. Somewhere between these two extremes a line has to be drawn. I think it is probably fair to say that the question is whether the attendance of the pharmacist at the premises is such as to give him substantial personal control over the business for a substantial part of the time. Wherever the line is drawn this much I think, is clear – Mr. X fell on the wrong side of it. . .If a pharmacist wishes to carry on while making absences of that sort then either, as I see it, he must obtain the services of a locum pharmacist to take his place and to act for him in his absence, or the premises must be closed. . .

(Pharm J 12 September 1970 p. 286)

In 1982 the Committee considered a case where a company conducted a pharmacy for substantial periods of each week when there was no pharmacist on the premises. Sales of General Sale List medicines had taken place in the absence of the pharmacist and it was alleged that when these were made the business was not under the personal control of a pharmacist. The super-intendent pharmacist maintained that despite these facts he was capable of being reached by telephone and, therefore, the conduct of the business was under his personal control. In giving the decision of the Committee the chairman said:

. . .it will come as no surprise to the persons in this matter. . .that we do not propose to try and lay down strict lines which have got to be toed to achieve personal control. . .We have considered the facts of this matter. We are faced with a deliberate course of conduct involving the absence of a pharmacist for substantial periods of each day, one to one and a half hours during the week days and anything up to six hours over the weekend. . .it was pointed out to us that the pharmacist who did attend during those periods in the evening and at the weekend was a man who unfortunately had no appreciation that General Sale List medicines needed the control of a pharmacist. . .we. . .have come to the conclusion that in our view such a course of control of this pharmacy could not amount to its being under the personal control of a pharmacist during the relevant periods. In the circumstances it means that the business was not being run as a retail business in accordance with the Acts.

(Pharm J 4 December 1982 p. 664)

The Committee had little difficulty in determining that the facts amounted to misconduct and issued a reprimand to the pharmacist.

Further support for the view that a pharmacy cannot simply revert to behaving as though it were a *drugstore* when the pharmacist is absent comes in a case in 1994. Two pharmacists allowed their pharmacy to be open on Saturday afternoons without a pharmacist present for a period of about three years and, more recently, on Thursday afternoons as well. Quoting sections 69 and 70 of the Medicines Act 1968 (on personal control of pharmacies), the chairman looked at the mischief which the Act sought to avoid:

Any premises which sold more than just GSL medicines was holding itself out as a specialist in medicinal products. It was only to be expected that such specialist premises – i.e. a pharmacy – would be under a pharmacist's personal control and that what was done there impliedly had his approval whatever the range of products involved.

At one point, one of the pharmacists had been in the USA and the other not on the premises and there was no procedure whereby either could be contacted. Commenting further the chairman said:

What could be more fundamental in exercising personal control than to make yourself available should you be needed and so instruct the staff so that they know how to contact you?

The Committee regarded as totally misconceived the defence that if pharmacists could be away for a lunchtime period then in some way this clothed their absence for three or four hours with legitimacy. Such practices neither conformed with the spirit of the Act nor protected the public. Nor were they fair to the public. This was an irresponsible way of carrying on a business, which was far removed from personal control. Describing the reprimands as *lenient*, the chairman issued a warning to the profession that:

> . . .on future occasions, if they turn out to be as bad as this [we could] disqualify a company. . .from trading.
>
> *(Pharm J* 3 September 1994 p. 308)

Despite these precedents, a pharmacist was reprimanded in 1997 for 'a pattern of. . .turning up at 10.00 a.m. or later' when the shop opened at 9.00 a.m. *(Pharm J* 1 February 1997 p. 166). In later cases, a pharmacist was reprimanded for allowing his pharmacy to be open on several successive Saturdays without a pharmacist *(Pharm J* 18 November 2000 p. 751) and a pharmacist was erased from the register for repeatedly leaving her pharmacy open during normal working hours without a pharmacist being present *(Pharm J* 5 April 2003 p. 494).

In relation to a case reported in 2002 *(Pharm J* 2 November 2002 p. 660), the Chairman of the Statutory Committee provided a liberal interpretation of the meaning of 'personal control' *(Pharm J* 7 August 2004 p. 203). However, a later *Law and Ethics Bulletin (Pharm J* 28 August 2004 p. 298) reiterated that for the lawful conduct of a registered retail pharmacy business, a pharmacist should be in personal control.

'Quackery' or unprofessional claims

Two cases of an unprecedented nature came before the Committee in the late 1990s. In the first, a five-day inquiry resulted in an unusual order to the superintendent of Signalysis Ltd, a company which provided 'Spagyrik Therapy'. Adjourning the case till later that year, the superintendent was advised that she would be reprimanded if she had resigned from the company by that time; if not, her name would be removed from the register. An order was also made immediately to remove from the register all the premises at which the company conducted a retail pharmacy business.

Spagyrik Therapy was said to consist of a treatment of the patient's own body fluids in such a way that they became the remedy for that patient. Such activity was not accepted as a therapy either by the MHRA or the Centre for Complementary Health Studies at the University of Exeter. Conducting such activity from registered pharmacy premises under the supervision of a pharmacist might lead potential customers to believe that the therapy enjoyed some recognition within the profession, which it did not (*Pharm J* 16 August 1997 p. 250).

The following year, a pharmacist who had made misleading and unprofessional claims for products which were not licensed medicines was reprimanded by the Committee. Despite a warning from the Society, the pharmacist had continued to lend her name to advertising material from a company called NutriHealth Ltd which suggested that certain products could be 'fat eliminators', could reduce mood swings, reduce cholesterol, relieve symptoms of poor bowel function, reduce risk of bowel cancer and many similar medicinal claims. The Committee was impressed by the pharmacist's sincerity but said she had overstepped the mark.

> This profession has won the reputation that if it says something then it really is true. . .and these claims from a pharmacist are likely to be believed totally. . .We should be very careful when we appeal to the public's greed and vanity. . .
>
> (*Pharm J* 24 October 1998 p. 663)

Appeals against decisions

It has been explained that a direction for erasure from the register does not take effect until the expiration of three months from the giving of notice of such a direction. During that three months, a person who is aggrieved by a direction of the Committee has a right of appeal against that direction to the Queen's Bench Division of the High Court. This right is provided for pharmacists in the Pharmacy Act 1954 (s.10) and for bodies corporate in the Medicines Act 1968 (s.82). A High Court decision is final and there is no further right of appeal.

The number of appeals against a direction for erasure heard by the High Court since the Statutory Committee was established in 1933 has been relatively small. Those establishing major points of principle are set out in some detail below.

Appeals establishing major points of principle

RE LAWSON

The first appeal from a decision of the Statutory Committee was heard in the King's Bench Divisional Court in February 1941 before the Lord Chief Justice (Viscount Caldicote) and Mr Justice Humphreys (see also p. 396).

The Council of the Pharmaceutical Society had complained to the Statutory Committee that the appellant, a member of the Society, had distributed to a member or members of the public, and without invitation or request, a printed pamphlet of an objectionable or indecent nature and that he had been guilty of such misconduct as could render him unfit to be on the register. The pamphlet had consisted of an advertisement for certain drugs which were described as 'Hormonal Treatment for Impotence and Sexual Debility in Men, and Frigidity and Apathy in Women'. In giving the decision of the Committee in 1940 the chairman had said:

> The second rule in the Statement on Matters of Professional Conduct is that advertisements of medicines should not be issued to the public referring to sexual weakness. Quite clearly, this pamphlet issued by a man who is on the Register contravenes that rule of professional conduct which ought to guide its members. Even if such a rule did not exist we should have had no hesitation in saying that for a chemist to issue this pamphlet broadcast to members of the public is misconduct which renders him unfit to be on the Register of Pharmacists.

There were several grounds of appeal and each was considered unfounded. One of the main grounds was that the offence was not of sufficient gravity as to justify removal of a name from the register. In dismissing the appeal, both judges commented on the weight which should be placed on decisions of the Statutory Committee. The Lord Chief Justice said:

> Arguments have been addressed to us that that decision was a harsh one, and that, having regard to similar publications which have been going on for a number of years of which the appellant was well aware and of which the Council must be taken to be aware also, it was a very harsh measure that the appellant's name should have been removed from the Register. As to that matter, I observe that the intention of the Act seems to me to make, as one might say, the Council of the Pharmaceutical Society, as representing the profession as it has been called, masters in their own house. They were to have a Statutory Committee composed of members of the Society,* and the Statutory Committee was to undertake such inquiries as have been conducted in this case and to give such directions as have been given in this case so as to maintain, and perhaps improve, the standard of the members of the Society as the members of a respectable and honourable profession. Although I do not say for a moment that the mere fact that the Statutory Committee have come to this decision that it is right to remove the appellant's name from the Register is conclusive, if they have evidence upon which they may act I say that the opinion is entitled to the greatest possible respect, because they know what is the standard of requirement of the profession to which they belong and which, as I read the Act of Parliament, they are directed to take into consideration. One cannot shut one's eyes to the fact, which indeed was mentioned by learned counsel on behalf of the appellant in opening this case, that the Act of 1933 was intended, as I think he said in substance, to elevate this business into the status of a profession which is to be part managed and controlled by members of the Society to which all persons carrying on the business or exercising the profession must belong. While I agree with the decision to remove the appellant's name from the Register, I go further and say that the view which the Statutory Committee have formed they themselves, being members of the Society, is one which should carry, and does carry, great weight with me in the decision which I have formed.

Mr Justice Humphreys said:

> There are various powers given to the Statutory Committee, one of which we are told in certain cases they do exercise. It is the power of reserving their judgement for a time and giving the person against whom the allegation is made an opportunity of mending his ways, and then inquiring after the lapse of time, and hearing evidence as to what has happened since their original decision. That is a very useful power, and one which they exercise, although it is for the Statutory Committee to decide in which cases they should exercise that power, and in what cases they should decide that the penalty stated by the

---

* This is not strictly true (see p. 298).

Act should be imposed. For my own part I should be very loath indeed to interfere seeing that I am not a pharmaceutical chemist, and cannot be as well acquainted with the ethics and proper way of carrying on business by such a person as the members of this Statutory Committee are. I should be extremely loath to interfere with their discretion in the matter, assuming I had power to do so.

(Pharm J 22 February 1941 p. 60; report and leading article)

The appeal was dismissed with costs.

RE SIMS

This was an appeal from a decision of the Statutory Committee, which had directed that a pharmacist's name be removed from the register following a conviction for the unlawful sale of drugs (Dexedrine tablets). The appeal was dismissed. The Lord Chief Justice (Lord Parker), sitting with Mr Justice Ashworth and Mr Justice McKenna, said:

> It will be seen therefore that, so far as the present case is concerned, it had to be shown that he had been guilty of a criminal offence. That was shown. The Statutory Committee had then to be satisfied that the criminal offence was of a kind that rendered the convicted person unfit to have his name on the Register. That they so found, and there is no challenge to their finding. Thirdly, they have had to inquire into the matter and having reached that conclusion, to decide whether it was a case in which they should direct the Registrar to remove the chemist's name. It is only against their decision to remove the appellant's name that he now appeals. . .As I conceive it the principle upon which this Court can act is this, that only in a very extreme case would they interfere with the penalty which the professional body concerned has inflicted for a very good reason, that it is the intention of Parliament that they should be the judges of the case because they are the people who can judge best the need for a particularly drastic penalty in the circumstances prevailing. The matter was dealt with on that basis in the case of the Statutory Committee under the Pharmacy and Poisons Act 1933 in the case *Re Lawson* [1941] 57 TLR 315 (p. 146) and words to the same effect were used by Lord Goddard in connection with the Disciplinary Committee of the Law Society in the case *Re a Solicitor* [1956] 3 AFR 516. Lord Goddard there said at p. 517: 'If a matter were one of professional misconduct, it would take a very strong case to induce this Court to interfere with the sentence passed by the disciplinary committee, as obviously the disciplinary committee are the best possible people for weighing the seriousness of professional misconduct'.

(Pharm J 3 February 1962 p. 89)

RE LEVY AND PHARMACEUTICS (M/C) LTD

Disciplinary proceedings in this case had originally begun in March 1966 following a prosecution against the company under the Pharmacy and Poisons Act 1933 for sales of poisons not under the supervision of a pharmacist. The Committee had adjourned the case until April 1966 to allow the defendant to attend. At that hearing, judgment had been postponed for 12 months. In May 1967, the defendant had not appeared and the Committee had adjourned the case further until November 1967.

Immediately before the November hearing, the company had again been prosecuted for a similar offence. At the Statutory Committee hearing, the name of the pharmacist had been ordered to be erased from the register and a direction had been made that the company ceased to be an authorised seller of poisons for a period of 12 months.

The appeal was heard before the Lord Chief Justice (Lord Parker), who sat with Mr Justice Waller and Mr Justice Fisher. Lord Parker commented:

> It is not the nature of the offence, but the fact that it disclosed a casual attitude, also indicated by the fact that he did not appear before the Committee. The Statutory Committee in April 1966 gave what was in effect a conditional discharge. They decided not to sentence him in any way, but the chairman gave him a pretty severe warning. The Committee had adjourned the matter for 12 months and instructed an inspector to make visits to the premises. He then had a clear warning of what would happen if he did anything of the sort again. Unfortunately in November 1967 the company had been fined over the sale of Veganin. Mr. Levy had come before the Committee a month later, where it had been pointed out to him that he had had his chance, and the Committee had made their direction. . .It is equally clear that this Statutory Committee has been put in charge and entrusted with the affairs of the profession and this court would rarely interfere. This seems to me to be a case in which the Committee were almost forced to act as they did as a result of this man being given a conditional discharge and getting into trouble again. So far as sentence was concerned, the Committee had only two alternatives. One was to do nothing and give a conditional discharge and the other was to direct removal from the Register . . .In this case they decided, after postponing the matter time and time again to give him every chance, to strike his name off.
>
> (*Pharm J* 25 May 1968 p. 615)

The appeal was dismissed.

RE EYRE

In October 1975, the Committee had directed the removal of the name of a pharmacist from the register following his conviction on 21 offences involving the forging of documents purporting to be NHS prescriptions with intent to defraud. The basis of the offences was that the pharmacist had used blank both signed and unsigned NHS prescription forms which had been left with him by doctors to make entries for medicines not supplied by him in order to obtain payment from the NHS. This he had claimed had been done with the agreement of several local doctors. It was alleged that the doctor would come into the pharmacy and obtain toothpaste, toiletries and other goods such as contraceptives and would charge them up to an account which was later satisfied by means of the bogus prescriptions.

The pharmacist had appealed against the direction of the Committee and in the High Court Mr Justice Croom-Johnson sitting with the Lord Chief Justice (Lord Widgery) and Mr Justice May said in dismissing the appeal:

> The effect of all this was that really the people who seemed to get the most financial benefit out of this course of conduct were the doctors concerned, and there was some profit but not a great deal of profit which came to Mr. X. This court has to consider whether the Statutory Committee was justifiably to come to the conclusion which it did. It is quite clear that it considered that the convictions at the Central Criminal Court in this fashion were of a nature as to render the appellant unfit to have his name on the Register. The committee had to consider this fact that, although little profit was accruing to Mr. X what was being done was that the standing of the pharmaceutical profession as a whole was being gravely affected by the fact that the National Health Service was being defrauded systematically over a period of several years, and that the defrauding was being made possible by Mr X in his capacity as a pharmaceutical chemist facilitating the doctors in getting their money and their goods in this way. He was, in other words,

consenting to be used as a tool for the fraud on the National Health Service even though it may be that he was not actually getting much of the money into his own pocket. He also of course had a motive in assisting the doctors in this way because he was afraid that if he did not fall in with what they wanted him to do they could do, as it were, financial damage to his practice.

This court, although it has power to review the decision of statutory committees and statutory bodies which control the discipline of the various professions, such as this, is loath to interfere with those decisions unless it is clear that the decision which was come to was a wrong one. For my part I am quite unable to say on the facts of this case, by Mr X going in for a course of conduct over a number of years in this way and in a way which makes the National Health Service wide open to frauds of this kind if they are practised by anything, that in coming to the conclusion that it did that the Statutory Committee was wrong. In those circumstances I should be in favour of dismissing this appeal.

(Pharm J 24 July 1976 p. 69)

RE FLETCHER AND LUCAS

In September 1976, the Committee had directed that the names of the two appellants be removed from the register following allegations of excessive sales of amyl nitrite *(Pharm J* 6 November 1976 p. 430).

The appeal was heard before the Lord Chief Justice (Lord Widgery), sitting with Mr Justice Milmo and Mr Justice Tudor Evans, Mr Justice Milmo giving judgment said:

Basically what was being alleged against the appellants was [that they] were selling to the public large quantities of Amyl Nitrite ampoules knowing, or deliberately shutting their eyes to two facts (1) that the bulk of these were being sold to people who were going to use them for an improper purpose and, (2) that such use could be injurious to health. . .The first ground [of appeal] is that the Committee misdirected itself on the burden of proof. . .I find that contention is without substance. . .It is said as a second ground that there is no evidence that either of the appellants had himself made a sale to any purchaser. . .In my judgment there was abundant evidence. . .to find that very substantial quantities of this drug were being sold to individual members of the public in the full knowledge of the appellants that the persons in question were going to use the drugs so supplied for an improper purpose. . .The third ground is what has been described as the 'Martindale' point. . .The appellants now complain that this textbook was introduced into the case in the judgment without reference to the defence. . .I cannot see that there would be any valid objection to their [the Committee] refreshing, or confirming, their professional knowledge and experience by reference to a standard textbook, but it is apparent from the judgment that in the present case they went very much further. The reference to the difficulty and anxiety which they experience satisfies me that this particular point was not covered by their professional knowledge and that they were driven to extraneous sources to acquire the knowledge which they lacked. In the result they reached a decision on the strength of evidence which had not been adduced at the hearing. . .for this reason I would allow the appeal.

(Pharm J July 1978 p. 93)

RE HARARI

In this case, the pharmacist had appeared before the Statutory Committee after being convicted of offences which had no connection with his professional work. They included assault, motor offences and convictions under the Protection from Eviction Act 1977. A direction was given for the erasure of his name from the register and he appealed.

In dismissing the appeal Lord Justice May, sitting with Mr Justice Stephen Brown, said:

> . . .in the course of that enquiry witnesses were called to speak to the facts which had given rise to the convictions. . .He [Mr Harari] submits that the Statutory Committee in following that procedure effectively re-presented the prosecution material that was before the criminal courts by which he was convicted. . .In my judgment it is quite clear from the decision of this court in *Shutt and Others* ([1981] 2 All ER 805, p. 241). . .that the Statutory Committee was entirely correct in the procedure which they followed . . .Indeed the circumstances in which the chemist came to be convicted, and so give rise to the enquiry, are matters which the Statutory Committee must have available to it in a way in which it can be, if necessary, challenged by the chemist. That is not to say however that the fact that the chemist was convicted of the offences alleged can itself be challenged. . .the Divisional Court has made it quite clear in these and other cases that it is loath to interfere with decisions of domestic tribunals of this nature unless it is clear that they are decisions that are wrong. . .it is the tribunals themselves who actually see the witnesses involved, and even more importantly, in addition to the legally qualified chairman, comprise members of the relevant profession who have specialist knowledge of and opinions on the issues raised in these sort of disciplinary hearings. Consequently this court should not lightly disturb any such decision.

Dealing with the question of the severity of the penalty his Lordship continued:

> Mr Harari stresses that the conduct, of which complaint was made, related in no way to his activity, experience or business as a pharmaceutical chemist. But I am sure that Mr Harari would be the first person, upon cool reflection when this matter is completed, to accept that it is not only conduct directly related to pharmacy and pharmacists of which the Statutory Committee is entitled and should properly take cognisance. When one is dealing with the activities of professional men and women it must be realised that there can be conduct on their part which although in no way directly referable to their profession, nevertheless, in the view of right minded members of that profession, renders them unsuitable to continue to be members of the profession. . .Once again the decisions of this court in other cases relating to pharmaceutical chemists and, indeed other professional bodies, have made it clear that the principle that it will only interfere where the tribunal below has clearly gone wrong applies with greater force in relation to any penalties imposed by the domestic tribunal than to the actual decision on the merits. That must follow from the professional composition of the Statutory Committee, who have to decide on the suitability of the particular defendant before them to continue to carry on practising as a pharmaceutical chemist.
>
> *(Pharm J* 1 May 1982 p. 509)

RE WHITECHURCH

In 1997, the Statutory Committee considered the case of a pharmacist who had failed to maintain professional indemnity insurance contrary to the Society's Code of Ethics (see p. 289). It was alleged that this conduct demonstrated a lack of professional responsibility which could have had serious consequences for members of the public using his pharmacy and any locum pharmacists working there. The Committee found the alleged misconduct proved and directed that the pharmacist's name be removed from the register (*Pharm J* May 1997 p. 698). The pharmacist appealed to the High Court on the basis (1) that he was partially insured and (2) that the penalty was too severe.

In dismissing the appeal, Mr Justice Schiemann, sitting with Mr Justice Mitchell, said in relation to the first leg of the appeal:

> . . .the insurance which he had was manifestly not designed to cover a pharmacist's liability to the public arising out of his activities as a pharmacist with the heavy obligations for those imposed. . .[and] the Committee clearly regarded his failure to insure himself promptly, once the matter was drawn to his attention, as significant misconduct. . .in my judgment they were right to do so.

On the second ground for appeal Mr Justice Schiemann said:

> The right approach for this Court. . .is set out in the case of *Alnazir Thobani* v. *The Royal Pharmaceutical Society of Great Britain* in January 1990. In that case Watkins LG said 'the function of this Court when reviewing a sentence of the Society, as has been said on many previous occasions, is not to impose its own view in substitution for a view taken by the Committee unless it comes to the conclusion that the decision of the Committee was plainly wrong or unless of course the Committee has, in reaching its conclusion, misdirected itself'. Having read all the material before the Committee and now before me I am convinced that the penalty, which they imposed on the material before them, was amply justified and this Court should not interfere with it.
>
> (*Whitechurch* v. *Royal Pharmaceutical Society of Great Britain* (1998) 41 BLMR 46, QB)

RE KORSNER

In 1998, the Committee considered the case of a pharmacist who arranged for patients of a private doctor to go on the list of a NHS doctor as well (see also p. 249). When patients received a private prescription, they would take it to the pharmacist, who would let them have the drugs but would not receive payment from the patients. The pharmacist would then send to the NHS doctor a list of medicines for which NHS prescriptions were required for that patient and would then add further items to the prescriptions to compensate for the NHS charges he had not received. The pharmacist was also making declarations of exemption from NHS charges on behalf of these patients.

The Committee directed that Mr Korsner's name be removed from the register (*Pharm J* 24 January 1998 p. 116). Mr Korsner appealed on the grounds that he was prejudiced by a failure to give him a fair hearing and to observe minimum standards of procedural fairness. This was said to be because he had not had the chance to agree, or not, to the submission of certain statements submitted to the Statutory Committee.

Declining to make a finding on this point, Lord Justice Brooke, in dismissing the appeal, said that even if the evidence in the disputed statements was put to one side there was ample evidence on which the Committee was entitled to make the findings that it did (*Pharm J* 30 January 1999 p. 147; 27 February 1999 p. 277).

However, the judges criticised the Society's procedures, saying that the regulations under which they operated, contained in a 1978 Order in Council, bore a 'rather dated air' and needed modernising, especially in the light of the Human Rights Act 1998 (brought into force October 2000). Thus the need for change to the constitution and operation of the Statutory Committee is recognised by the High Court (see Appendix 17).

Other appeals

For completeness the other appeals are listed in Table 24.1, together with the type of 'offence' which led to erasure and whether the appeal by the pharmacist was successful or not.

Table 24.1 Other appeals

Case	Result
Re Zygmunt (Chemists) Ltd (*Pharm J* 4 April 1966 p. 324)	Appeal won
Conviction/Pharmacy and Poison Act 1933	
Re Robinson (*Pharm J* 19 April 1975 p. 19)	Appeal lost
Conviction/Misuse of Drugs Act 1971	
Re Jobson (*Pharm J* 22 November 1980 p. 589)	Appeal lost
Conviction/Misuse of Drugs Act 1971	
Re Rajabali (*Pharm J* 7 February 1981 p. 136)	Appeal lost
Misconduct/Excessive sale of drugs liable to misuse	
Re Kuperberg (*Pharm J* 29 January 1983 p. 97)	Appeal lost
Misconduct/Excessive sale of drugs liable to misuse	
Re Riley (*Pharm J* 2 March 1985 p. 282)	Appeal won
Conviction/Theft Act 1968	
Re Tenbrook Ltd (*Pharm J* 13 July 1985 p. 61)	Appeal lost
Conviction/Medicines Act 1968	
Re Leach (unreported, July 1985)	Appeal lost
Conviction/Misuse of Drugs Act 1971	
Re Patel (unreported, January 1986)	Appeal lost
Conviction/Medicines Act 1968	
Re Sowood (*Pharm J* 6 December 1986 p. 754)	Appeal lost
Conviction/Medicines Act 1968	
Re Smith (*Pharm J* 3 January 1987 p. 17)	Appeal lost
Misconduct/under influence of drink	
Re Singh (*Pharm J* 28 March 1987 p. 416)	Appeal lost
Convictions/Misuse of Drugs Act 1971 and others	
Re Parkin (*Pharm J* 2 April 1988 p. 451)	Appeal lost
Misconduct/unsatisfactory pharmacy premises	
Re Shah (*Pharm J* 7 May 1988 p. 607)	Appeal won
Conviction/Theft Act 1968	
Re Sabir (*Pharm J* 19 November 1988 p. 665)	Appeal lost
Conviction/Misuse of Drugs Act 1971	
Re Thobani (*Pharm J* 3 February 1990 p. 122)	Appeal lost
Offences/Theft Act 1968	
Re Kansal (*Pharm J* 27 July 1996 p. 111)	Appeal lost
Offences of dishonesty	
Re Mistry (unreported)	Appeal lost
Forged certificate of professional indemnity	
Re Chanins (*Pharm J* 28 May 2005 p. 636)	Appeal lost
Offensive, abusive and threatening behaviour	

- The Committee uses, but is not bound by, the Code of Ethics when considering whether there has been such misconduct as renders a pharmacist unfit to be on the register.
- Examples of cases have been given under the headings: supervision; theft; theft and unlawful possession or supply of drugs; controlled drugs; disposal of dangerous waste; unsatisfactory conduct; unsatisfactory state of pharmacy premises; excessive or uncontrolled supplies of substances of abuse; dispensing mistakes; advertising; responsibility of the superintendent pharmacist; personal control of a pharmacy; and quackery.
- Appeals establishing major points of principle are discussed: *Re Lawson*; *Re Sims*; *Re Levy and Pharmaceutics (M/C) Ltd*; *Re Eyre*; *Re Fletcher and Lucas*; *Re Harari, Re Whitechurch*; and *Re Korsner*. A summary of all others is given.
- Three judicial reviews are discussed where the Committee's decisions were not considered to be subject to appeal.

Further reading

Appelbe G. E. and Harrison I. H. (1993) The Statutory Committee: convictions. *Pharm J* 253: 565.

Appelbe G. E. and Harrison I. H. (1994) The Statutory Committee: major misconduct. *Pharm J* 254: 22.

Appelbe G. E. and Harrison I. H. (1994) The Statutory Committee: advertising and sundry misconduct. *Pharm J* 254: 56.

Appelbe G. E. and Harrison I. H. (1994) The Statutory Committee. *Pharm J* 255: 197.

Soothill K. and Sharp D. (2000) Discipline and punishment: reflections on the disciplinary procedures of the Royal Pharmaceutical Society. *Pharm J* 264: 266–267.

Wingfield J. (1990) Misconduct and the pharmacist, Parts 1 and 2. *Pharm J* 247: 531, 572.

Websites

The Royal Pharmaceutical Society of Great Britain site carries information on all the functions and organisation of the Society, how it assures pharmacists' competence and fitness to practice, its services to members and continuing news about pharmacy policy and practice: http://www.rpsgb.org.uk. A route (not exclusive) to the key documents mentioned in this chapter is given below as at August 2004.

- Statutory Committee: About the Society→ Fitness to Practise or Law and Ethics→ Statutory Committee.

Judicial review

A reprimand is not considered to be a direction against which there is a right of appeal (see p. 300); hence a pharmacist reprimanded by the Statutory Committee seeking redress may only do so by way of the legal remedy of judicial review.

In December 1982, a company, its superintendent pharmacist and a pharmacist manager in charge of one of the company's pharmacies applied by way of judicial review in the High Court to have reprimands, which each had received, quashed. The reprimands had been administered by the Statutory Committee (*Pharm J* 15 May 1982 p. 557) following an advertising feature which had appeared in a local newspaper. Mr Justice Woolf, in quashing the reprimands, said that it was not disputed that the feature had contravened the Society's guidelines on advertising or that the company had been a party to the advertising appearing, but the company had argued that it had done its best to prevent the feature appearing in the form it did and, therefore, had done everything to prevent the guidelines being broken. If the company's account of what happened was accepted by the Statutory Committee, then it could not have found them guilty of misconduct. It appeared that the Statutory Committee disbelieved the pharmacists' account when it came to its decision, but Mr Justice Woolf said that there was absolutely no evidence to indicate that the superintendent's account was incorrect and, therefore, the reprimand in his case was unjustified. Because the decision in the case of the superintendent was clearly wrong, the whole decision was unsafe and the reprimands against all the applicants were set aside (*Pharm J* 1 and 8 January 1983 p. 13).

In 1986 another pharmacist, Mr Sokoh, applied to the High Court for judicial review following a reprimand which had been administered to him by the Statutory Committee. The case concerned the dispensing of a 'Brompton mixture' and the facts are summarised on page 317. Counsel for Mr S. argued that the decision was wrong and that the Committee had failed to direct itself that a single considered exercise of professional judgment, without more, even if wrong, could not amount to professional misconduct. Professional misconduct, he said, involved an act or omission deserving of moral condemnation by the profession. His Lordship rejected the submission that misconduct necessarily carried moral censure, commenting that *misconduct* meant no more than incorrect or erroneous conduct of any kind of a serious nature. As to the submission that the Committee failed to direct itself, that one error could not constitute misconduct, Mr Justice Webster said:

> One error is in my judgment, as a matter of law, capable of constituting misconduct if it is sufficiently serious, though whether it in fact constitutes misconduct or misconduct such as to render the person unfit to be on the Register must depend on the precise evidence taken as a whole and on the Committee's view of that evidence.

In discussing the Court's primary function in judicial review, Mr Justice Webster, in dismissing the application, said:

If in [the Court's] judgment conduct occurred which was capable of constituting misconduct then in the absence of a material misdirection or a decision which no reasonable Committee could reach if it had properly directed itself [the Court] cannot interfere with the Committee's findings.

(Pharm J 13 December 1986 p. 797)

A unique situation arose in January 1996 when the Statutory Committee failed to reach a unanimous judgment. The case involved a Council complaint against Boots The Chemists Ltd and its superintendent in relation to two collection and delivery services in rural areas formerly served by dispensing doctors, namely Durrington in Wiltshire and Winterton in South Humberside. The Council had decided in June 1993 that a pharmacy operating a prescription collection and delivery service should discontinue such a service if a new pharmacy opened in the area, although this decision appeared only in the monthly report of Council and was not promulgated as a new ethical requirement. Both services had been initiated at the request of local general practitioners and residents after NHS contracts had been awarded to new pharmacies in the villages. In the case of Durrington, the residents arranged for the collection of the prescriptions, the return of the dispensed medicines and undertook the transport themselves. Boots argued that these services were patient driven and widened choice and that the Council's position was a restraint of trade. The Council argued that the continuance of a collection and delivery service in these circumstances could deprive patients of a full pharmaceutical service, in particular the absence of direct face-to-face contact between patient or carer and the pharmacist. The hearing lasted two days and judgment was deferred *(Pharm J* 21 October 1995 p. 533; 28 October 1995 p. 571).

When judgment was given, the majority of the Committee (in this case three pharmacists) found misconduct proved but decided that it was not serious enough to warrant any further action. The chairman, a Queen's Counsel, gave a dissenting judgment. Almost the full text of the majority decision was reported in *Pharmaceutical Journal* (20 January 1996 pp. 89–93) and this should be referred to for a full account of the reasoning of the pharmacists on the Committee. The dissenting decision of the chairman was somewhat truncated and the best understanding of his reasoning may be obtained from the two passages below, which did not appear in the *Pharmaceutical Journal* report but appear in the transcript.

> It is simply not right to say that Boots' activities could deprive local people of a full pharmaceutical service. The villagers are deprived of nothing. It really is impossible to describe as serious misconduct the provision of a doctor approved delivery and collection service which the patient chose to use, rather than use the village pharmacy. In fact what Boots were providing was an **additional** service and not one that compelled the patients to take their service in substitution for the village pharmacy.
>
> It is very disturbing to read the statements of mature witnesses who as patients are exasperated by the notion that is implicit in the Society's case that the choice of where they are to obtain their dispensing services is not theirs to make. Some of the patients' views are expressed with vehemence and I would have thought it unwise not to have

proper regard to what patients really feel. . .In these days of consumer choice I am not at all surprised that Boots feel that they should respond if it is lawfully possible to do what their patients actually want.

On this basis, Boots applied for judicial review. As reported in *Pharmaceutical Journal* (14 February 1997), the High Court quashed the finding of misconduct and said that the Committee's decision-making process had been 'fundamentally tainted'. The Court did not attempt to adjudicate on whether the Council's position on collection and delivery services was correct but considered that the finding of misconduct had not been justified on the evidence. In further (unreported) comments, Justice Ognall said the pharmacist members of the Committee should have heeded more closely the admonitions which appeared in the judgment of the legally qualified chairman. The test was the same as in Sokoh (above), that 'misconduct can be any incorrect or erroneous conduct *provided it is of a serious nature*'. He held that the pharmacist members of the Committee had failed to address whether the undoubted knowing and continuing breach of the promulgated policy was of such quality as to constitute serious misconduct.

Since this case, medicines have become available over the Internet and the Society has taken steps to produce guidelines for pharmacies which wish to undertake such a service (Appendix 16). These aim to provide a measure of protection where the patient elects not to seek face-to-face contact but to exercise more fully their right to choice as a consumer.

Summary

- The Statutory Committee exercises the disciplinary powers of the Society.
- Its constitution, procedures, jurisdiction and sanctions are laid down in regulations made under the Pharmacy Act 1954.
- The Committee comprises a legally experienced chairman and five members who have until very recently all been pharmacists.
- The Committee may discipline pharmacists, pharmacists' representatives and employees of pharmacy businesses and persons applying for admission or restoration to the Register of Pharmaceutical Chemists.
- When making their decisions, the Committee may take no action, admonish or caution (usually a reprimand), postpone their decision or direct erasure of a pharmacist's name from the register. Additionally, for a company, the Committee may disqualify it from conducting retail pharmacies or remove any or all of their premises from the register.
- The Committee may consider all convictions against pharmacists; for pharmacy businesses, its jurisdiction is limited to those Acts relating to Pharmacy, Poisons, Medicines, and Misuse of Drugs.
- The Committee's jurisdiction extends to offences committed outside the UK and is not subject to any time limits.

CHAPTER TWENTY-FIVE

Organisation of other professions

In June 1999, the Government enacted the Health Act 1999 which provided powers to change by order the regulation of health professions and health professionals. Many changes have since been made to the statutory regulations applying to the medical, dental, nursing and midwifery professions together with changes regulating to the smaller healthcare professions.

Various classes of professional person are mentioned in the statutes relating to poisons, medicinal products and Controlled Drugs. Pharmacists are principally concerned with supplies made to, or to the order of, medical practitioners, veterinary surgeons, dentists and nurse prescribers, and some knowledge of the statutory registration requirements of these and other related professions is desirable.

The medical profession

The Acts at present regulating the medical profession are the Medical Act 1983 as amended by Order (SI 2002 No.3135) and the Medical (Professional Performance) Act 1995.

The General Medical Council

The General Medical Council (GMC), which is the sole registering authority in the UK, was established by the Medical Act 1858. Its main objective is to protect, promote and maintain the health and safety of the public. The GMC shall consist of no more than 35 members. At present there are 19 elected members from the profession, two appointed members (one from the universities and one from the medical colleges), and 14 nominated (lay) members, the number of elected members exceeding the number of appointed and nominated members (SI 2002 No.3136). The quorum is 25.

The nominated or lay members, the majority of whom must be without any registerable medical qualification, are nominated by the Privy Council. The electoral scheme for elected members is made by the GMC with the approval of the Privy Council.

The Act provides for four constituencies:

1   England, the Channel Islands, and the Isle of Man;
2   Wales;
3   Scotland; and
4   Northern Ireland.

There is provision for any of the constituencies to be divided into two or more separate constituencies. The persons qualified to elect members for any constituency are those resident in the constituency for which the election is held and who are registered medical practitioners. The universities and other bodies which appoint members to the GMC are designated in an Order in Council. Persons who are fully registered, provisionally registered or registered with limited registration are eligible for election (subject to certain restrictions for those with limited registration). The term of office for a member is four years. The GMC has power to regulate medical education and to provide advice for members of the medical profession on standards of professional conduct or on medical ethics.

The GMC must establish and maintain a system for the declaration and registration of the private interests of its members and must publish such interests in a register.

The GMC must have following Committees (SI 2002 No.3135):

1   The Education Committee
2   One or more Interim Orders Panels
3   One or more Registration Decisions Panels
4   One or more Registration Appeals Panels
5   The Investigation Committee
6   One or more Fitness to Practice Panels.

The register and registration

The registrar of the GMC is appointed under Schedule 1 to the 1983 Act but the procedures for registration and the maintenance of the registers are dealt with in Part IV of the Act and the regulations made thereunder. There are two registers: the *Register of Medical Practitioners* and the *Register of Medical Practitioners with Limited Registration*. The former includes the names of those doctors who are *fully registered*, that is, those with UK qualifications and those doctors who hold primary European qualifications and who are nationals of a EEA member state,

Where a person satisfies the registrar that s/he holds an acceptable overseas qualification other than a primary European one and that s/he is an eligible specialist, of good character and knowledge of English, the registrar may direct that s/he be registered as a fully registered medical practitioner (s.21A).

The registrar must publish the Register of Medical Practitioners and the Register of Medical Practitioners with Limited Registration (s.34)(SI 2002 No.2135). The register must contain each practitioner's qualifications, whether he has a licence to practise and other such directions as the Council may direct. Practitioners must pay registration fees and annual retention fees.

Appeals are provided for persons whom the registrar has decided shall not be registered as a fully registered medical practitioner. The person concerned may appeal to the Registration Appeals Panel (see below) (Schedule 3A). A further appeal is possible against a decision of the Registration Appeals Panel to a County Court or in Scotland to the sheriff. Costs may be awarded.

Any reference (however expressed) to a person registered under the Medical Act or as a medical practitioner means a fully registered person registered under the 1983 Act. A prescription for a Controlled Drug or a Prescription Only Medicine may lawfully be dispensed even though the prescriber's name is in the Overseas List.

Section 60 of the Medicines Act 1968 provides that specified medicinal products may be prescribed only by a practitioner who holds a certificate issued for that purpose from the appropriate Minister (Chapter 9) and a licence from the Secretary of State is required in respect of certain Controlled Drugs (Chapter 17). Apart from these restrictions, there is no limitation on the prescribing of a fully registered practitioner, unless s/he is the subject of a direction by the Secretary of State under the Misuse of Drugs Act 1971 in respect of named Controlled Drugs (Chapter 17).

Only fully registered persons may hold certain appointments as physicians, surgeons or other medical officers (e.g. in the naval, military or air services or in the prison service), or recover in any court of law any charge made for medical or surgical advice or attendance. A certificate required by law to be from a physician, surgeon, licentiate in medicine and surgery, or other medical practitioner, is not valid unless the person signing it is fully registered.

Any person who wilfully and falsely pretends to be or takes or uses the name or title of physician, doctor of medicine, licentiate in medicine and surgery, bachelor of medicine, surgeon, general practitioner (GP) or apothecary, or any name, title, addition or description implying that s/he is registered under any provision of the 1983 Act, or that s/he is recognised by law as such, commits an offence (s.49). Nothing in the Act prejudices or in any way affects the lawful occupation, trade or business of chemists and druggists, or of dentists, so far as they extend to selling, compounding and dispensing of medicines (s.54).

VISITING EEC PRACTITIONERS LIST

An applicant can also be registered as a *visiting EEC practitioner*, although s/he may render medical services temporarily without first being registered. The registrar is required to enter the names of such practitioners on a list of visiting EEC practitioners, which forms part of the Register of Medical Practitioners (s.18). Visiting EEC practitioners will be issued with certificates of registration by the GMC.

Pharmacists may lawfully supply Prescription Only Medicines and Controlled Drugs (Chapter 17) against a prescription issued by a visiting practitioner only if that practitioner is in fact registered in the UK in accordance with the Act.

PROVISIONAL REGISTRATION

A person who holds a qualification which entitles him/her to be registered but has not completed the requirements as to experience is entitled to be provisionally registered. While s/he is completing these requirements, s/he is deemed to be fully registered so far as is necessary to enable him/her to be engaged in employment in a resident medical capacity in one or more approved hospitals or institutions, but not further (s.15).

The effect is that s/he may issue prescriptions for Controlled Drugs or for Prescription Only Medicines only if required to do so as part of his/her duties in that resident medical post. S/he may not order or prescribe such drugs or medicinal products in any other circumstances (e.g. for his/her own use or for the use of his/her own private patients).

LIMITED REGISTRATION

There is also provision in the Act (ss.22–25) for the limited registration of practitioners having *acceptable overseas qualifications* (i.e. qualifications granted outside the UK) which are accepted by the GMC as furnishing a sufficient guarantee of possession of the knowledge and skill required for the practise of medicine under the supervision of a fully registered medical practitioner. An applicant for limited registration must, in addition to holding an acceptable overseas qualification:

1   satisfy the registrar that s/he has been selected for employment in the British Isles as a medical practitioner in one or more approved hospitals or institutions;
2   that s/he has the necessary knowledge of English;
3   that s/he is of good character; and
4   that s/he has the knowledge and skill and has acquired the experience which is necessary for practise as a medical practitioner appropriate in his/her case.

A direction for limited registration is for a specified period only; the total aggregate period in which limited registration is permitted is five years, except for doctors who have held temporary registration. In relation to employment covered by his/her limited registration and to things done or omitted to be done in the course of it, and to any other thing incidental to his/her work in that employment which may not lawfully or validly be done except by a fully registered person, a doctor holding limited registration is treated as being fully registered, but not otherwise (s.22).

S/he may, therefore, only issue prescriptions for Controlled Drugs and Prescription Only Medicines in connection with employment to which his/her limited registration relates. The names of practitioners with limited registration are not included in any published register. Any enquiries about such practitioners should be made to The Registrar, General Medical Council, 24 Gosfield Street, London W1P 8BP.

Voluntary erasure from the register

Provisions have been made for a doctor to request that his name be removed from, and following voluntary erasure subsequently restored to, the register. The registrar shall remove the name unless he is aware that any proceedings are pending or have been started against the doctor (SI 2003 No.1341).

Licence to practise

The GMC has to make regulations with respect to the grant, refusal to grant and the withdrawal of a licence to practise by a licensing authority and for the revalidation of medical practitioners continuation to remain registered. There is an appeals procedure to the Registration Appeals Panel and subsequently to the county court, or, in Scotland, the sheriff.

The *licensing authority* means the registrar, the Registration Decisions Panel, or such other committee the Council may prescribe.

Revalidation means evaluation of a medical practitioner's fitness to practise.

If a person who does not have a licence to practise holds himself out as having such a licence or engages in any conduct calculated to suggest he has such a licence then he is liable on summary conviction to a fine.

The Education Committee

The composition of the Education Committee shall be such as the GMC may think fit. The Committee has to determine the extent of the knowledge and skill required for the granting of primary UK medical qualifications and secure that the instruction in universities is sufficient to equip students with such skill and knowledge. It has to determine and maintain the standard of proficiency required from students and determine patterns of experience which may be recognised as suitable for giving to those engaged in the practical training of students.

Professional conduct and fitness to practise

The functions of the GMC in respect of professional conduct and fitness to practise are performed by the following committees:

1   an Investigation Committee;
2   one or more Fitness to Practise Panels; and
3   an Interim Orders Panel.

These committees are constituted as provided by the GMC by rules made under the Medical Act 1983 (Amendment) Order 2002 No.3135.

The Council has the power to provide advice for members of the medical profession on matters of standards of professional conduct, standards of professional performance and medical ethics. The GMC makes rules for the each of these committees with respect to referral of complaints to these panels and for the procedure and evidence to be followed before the committee or the panels (Schedule 4 of SI No.3135).

In May 2004, the GMC published a document on changes it has made to its procedures when dealing with complaints. This is available on the GMC website (see Further Reading).

INVESTIGATION COMMITTEE

Where an allegation is made against a registered medical practitioner to the effect that his/her fitness to practise is impaired, then the Investigation Committee shall investigate the allegation and decide whether or not the matter should be considered by a Fitness to Practise Panel.

A person's fitness to practise is regarded as 'impaired' by reason only of:

- misconduct;
- deficient professional performance;
- a conviction or caution in the British Isles for a criminal offence or a conviction elsewhere for an offence which, if committed in England and Wales, would constitute a criminal offence;
- adverse physical or mental health;
- a determination by a body in the UK responsible for the regulation of a health or social care profession to the effect that his/her fitness to practise as a member of that profession is impaired.

The Investigation Committee may:

1   refer the matter to a Fitness to Practise Panel for its consideration;
2   refer the matter to a Fitness to Practise Panel or an Interim Orders Panel for their consideration to issue an order for interim suspension or interim conditional registration;
3   decide that an allegation ought not to be considered under (1) or (2) but to issue a warning letter itself; or
4   decide that an allegation ought not to be considered under (1) or (2) but to take no further notice.

In any of the circumstances above, the registrar is informed and s/he, in turn, serves notification of the facts on the person who is subject to the allegation.

Rules made under Schedule 4 of the Act may make provision for the registrar or any other officer of the Council to exercise the functions of the Investigation Committee either generally or in relation to such cases as may be specified in the rules.

FITNESS TO PRACTISE PANEL

Where any registered person's fitness to practise is found to be impaired by a Fitness to Practise Panel, the Panel may:

1   except in a health case, direct that the person's name shall be erased from the register;
2   direct that his/her registration shall be suspended during a period not exceeding 12 months, as may be specified in the direction; or
3   direct that his/her registration shall be conditional on his/her compliance, during a period not exceeding three years as may be specified in the direction, with such requirements so specified as the Panel thinks fit to impose for the protection of the public or in his/her interest.

Where the Fitness to Practise Panel finds the person's fitness to practise is not impaired, it may nevertheless give him/her a warning letter regarding his/her future conduct or performance. During a period of suspension, the suspension can be extended or converted to an erasure.

In a health case, a Fitness to Practise Panel may extend a suspension indefinitely where the initial period of suspension has lasted two years. In these cases, there are provisions for review either after two years has elapsed or at the person's request. After review, a Fitness to Practise Panel may confirm its direction or direct that the suspension be terminated.

All directions are appealable within 28 days of the direction being given; appeals are to the relevant court.

The *relevant court* means in Scotland the Court of Session; in Northern Ireland the High Court of Justice in Northern Ireland; in any other case means the High Court of Justice in England and Wales.

When a name has been erased from the register, a Fitness to Practise Panel may, if it thinks fit, direct that his/her name be restored but no application for restoration may be made before the expiration of five years from the date of erasure.

THE INTERIM ORDERS PANEL

The Interim Orders Panel was established under the Medical Act 1983 (Amendment) Order 2002 (SI 2002 No.3135). Where the Interim Orders Panel or a Fitness to Practise Panel is satisfied that it is necessary for the protection of the public, or in the interests of the doctor, for registration of the doctor to be suspended, or made subject to conditions, the Panel may make an order suspending registration for up to 18 months or one that registration may continue conditional on compliance during a period not exceeding 18 months, with such requirements as the Panel think fit.

The Panel must review the order within six months of the order being made and every three months subsequently as long as the order remains in force or where new evidence becomes available.

The Panel may revoke the order or any condition, or vary any condition, if it is satisfied that to do so is necessary for the protection of, or in the interest of, the public or the doctor and can replace it with an interim suspension order for the remainder of the term. The Council may apply to the courts for any order to be extended and the courts may further extend an order for up to 12 months.

Disclosure of information

Regulations give power to persons authorised by the Council to require disclosure of information that would assist them in carrying out their functions in respect to fitness to practise and professional conduct.

In addition, the Council is obliged to notify specified persons when formal proceedings are initiated against a doctor in respect of his/her fitness to practise or professional conduct where they consider it in the public interest so to do. Those specified persons include the Secretary of State, Scottish Ministers, the National Assembly of Wales and any person in the UK who the Council is aware that the doctor concerned is employed by in any area of medicine (SI 2002 No.3135).

The veterinary profession

Under a proposed major agricultural plan, the Veterinary Medicines Directorate is to undertake a review of the provisions of the Veterinary Surgeons Act 1966. A consultation paper has been produced. No further details were available at the time of going to press.

The Council of the Royal College of Veterinary Surgeons

The Veterinary Surgeons Act 1966 is the principal statute dealing with the management of the veterinary profession in relation to registration, education and professional conduct. The Council of the Royal College of Veterinary Surgeons, the controlling body, includes 24 persons elected by the members, four appointed by the Privy Council and two appointed by each university in the UK that grants a veterinary degree recognised by the Privy Council. Degrees of Irish universities are also recognised by the Privy Council.

Veterinary surgery means the art and science of veterinary surgery and medicine and includes the diagnosis of diseases in, and injuries to, animals, including tests performed on animals for diagnostic purposes; the giving of advice based upon such diagnosis; the medical or surgical treatment of animals; and the performance of surgical operations on animals (s.27).

The Register of Veterinary Surgeons

The registrar of the college, who is appointed by the Council of the Royal College, maintains the register. It is published as often as the Council thinks fit, but in any year in which a full register is not produced, alterations to it must be published instead (s.9). It comprises four lists (s.2).

1   The *General List* of persons entitled to be registered as graduates in veterinary surgery of universities recognised by the Privy Council (s.3) or as students of other universities who have passed the examinations held by the Royal College of Veterinary Surgeons (s.4) or persons from the EU who hold recognised European qualifications (s.5a).

2   The *Commonwealth List* of persons entitled to be registered as holding some Commonwealth qualification (s.6).

3   The *Foreign List* of persons entitled to be registered as holding some foreign qualification (s.6).

4   The *Temporary List* of persons registered to practise veterinary surgery temporarily, subject to such restrictions as to place and circumstances as the Council of the Royal College may specify (e.g. persons who have passed the examinations for a degree but have not yet formally graduated, or the holders of Commonwealth or foreign qualifications not otherwise registerable). It is not lawful for a temporarily registered person to practise except in accordance with the restrictions specified in the Council's direction.

The details required for registration, and the powers to register and de-register members is set out in the Veterinary Surgeons and Veterinary Practitioners (Registration) Regulations Order of Council 2003 No.3342.

An applicant for registration on lists 2 and 3 must satisfy the Council that s/he has the requisite knowledge and skill to practise veterinary surgery in the UK.

In addition to these lists, there is the *Supplementary Register* (first established under the Veterinary Surgeons Act 1948) of persons known as *veterinary practitioners*. The 1948 Act restricted the practice of veterinary surgery by unqualified persons as from 30 July 1949. Those persons whose principal means of livelihood, for seven out of ten years before that date, had been the diagnosing of diseases of animals were included in the Supplementary Register. Certain licensed employees of societies and institutions providing free treatment for animals were also transferred to the Supplementary Register under the 1966 Act but are subject to such restrictions as the Council of the Royal College may impose.

Professional discipline

Names may be removed from the register for crimes or 'disgraceful conduct in any professional respect'. There is a preliminary investigation committee and a disciplinary committee. The disciplinary procedure is similar to that of the medical profession and there is provision for suspension of registration as well as complete removal from the register (ss.15 and 17). Appeals against a direction are made to the Privy Council.

Restrictions on practice and use of titles

No one may practise, or hold themselves out as practising, or being prepared to practise, veterinary surgery unless they are registered as a veterinary surgeon or are in the supplementary register as a veterinary practitioner (s.19). It is an offence for an unregistered person to use the titles 'veterinary surgeon' or 'veterinary practitioner' or any name, title, addition or description implying that s/he is qualified to practise veterinary surgery (s.20).

The Act provides some limited exceptions for students of veterinary surgery, for medical practitioners and dentists in certain circumstances, and for the carrying out of minor treatment in terms of exemption orders made under the Act. Examples include orders allowing treatment by physiotherapists at veterinarians' request, blood sampling for the brucellosis eradication scheme, vaccinations of poultry against certain diseases and the use of epidural anaesthesia (SIs 1973 No.308; 1982 No.1267; 1983 No.6, as amended; and 1990 No.2217).

Exemption is also provided in Schedule 3 to the Act, as amended by SI 1988 No.526 for the following treatments and operations to be given or carried out by unqualified persons:

1   Any minor medical treatment given to an animal by its owner, by another member of a household of which the owner is a member, or by a person in the employment of the owner.
2   Anything given, otherwise than for the reward, to an animal used in agriculture, as defined in the Agriculture Act 1947, by the owner of the animal or by a person engaged or employed in caring for animals so used.
3   The rendering in an emergency of first-aid for the purpose of saving life or relieving pain.
4   The performance by any person aged 18 or more of any of the following operations:
    (a)   castration of a male animal or caponising of an animal, whether by chemical means or otherwise (except the castration of a horse, pony, ass or mule; of a bull, boar or goat which has reached the age of two months; or of a ram which has reached the age of three months; the spaying of a cat or dog);
    (b)   the docking of the tail of a lamb;

(c) the amputation of the dew claws of a dog before its eyes are open; or

(d) the disbudding of a calf subject to certain conditions.

5 Any medical treatment or minor surgery (not involving entry into the body cavity) to a companion animal by a veterinary nurse provided the animal is under the care of a veterinary surgeon, the treatment is carried out under his/her direction and the veterinary surgeon is the employer, or acting on behalf of the employer, of the nurse (SI 1991 No.1412).

6 Any medical treatment or any minor surgery (not involving entry into the body cavity) to any animal by a veterinary nurse if the following conditions are complied with:

(a) the animal is for the time being under the care of a veterinarian and any treatment or minor surgery is carried out under his direction;

(b) the veterinarian is the employer or acting on behalf of the employer of the veterinary nurse; or

(c) the veterinarian directing the treatment or minor surgery is satisfied that the veterinary nurse is qualified to carry out the treatment or surgery (SI 2002 No.1479).

The dental profession

The General Dental Council

The practice of dentistry is controlled by the Dentists Act 1984 through the General Dental Council, whose constitution, as amended (SI 2002 No.1625), comprises 15 registered dentists, four dental auxiliaries, and 10 lay members appointed by the Privy Council. The functions in respect of education, registration and discipline are similar to those of the GMC.

The practice of dentistry is deemed to include the performance of any such operation and the giving of such treatment, advice or attendance as is usually performed or given by dentists, and any person who performs any operations or gives any treatment, advice or attendance on or to any person as preparatory to or for the purpose of or in connection with the fitting, insertion or fixing of dentures, artificial teeth or other dental appliances is deemed to have practised dentistry within the meaning of the Act (s.37).

The Dentists Register

The Dentists Register is required to be published each year (s.22). It is kept by the registrar appointed by the General Dental Council in the manner prescribed by the Council's regulations (ss.14 and 19). The following are entitled to be registered:

1   any person who is a graduate or licentiate in dentistry of a dental authority;
2   any person who is a national of a EU member state and holds an appropriate European diploma; and
3   any person who holds a recognised overseas diploma.

An applicant must satisfy the registrar as to his/her identity, good character and good physical and mental health. An overseas applicant under item 3 above must also satisfy the registrar that s/he has the necessary skill and knowledge, and a knowledge of English which, in the interests of him/herself and patients, is necessary for the practice of dentistry in the UK.

The holder of a recognised overseas diploma may, without meeting any additional requirements, be temporarily registered in the Dentists Register for a specified period for the purpose of practising dentistry in a specified hospital or institution. The register must include a note of the restriction.

The names of all dentists who are entitled to practise are, therefore, included in the published register and there is no provisional registration as is the case with the medical profession. It is not lawful for a temporarily registered dentist to practise except as indicated in the register.

Serious professional misconduct or conviction in the UK for a criminal offence may lead to removal of a dentist from the register. There is a Preliminary Proceedings Committee and a Disciplinary Committee. The disciplinary procedure closely resembles that of the medical profession.

Titles and descriptions

Only registered dentists and medical practitioners may use the titles dentist, dental surgeon or dental practitioner. It is an offence for other persons to use such titles. Similarly, no person, including a medical practitioner, may use the term *registered dentist* unless s/he is so registered (s.39). Dentists, however, have no legal right or title to be registered under the Medical Act 1983 and may not assume any title implying a right to practise medicine or general surgery (s.7).

The practice of dentistry is restricted to registered dentists and medical practitioners (s.38). It is no longer lawful for a pharmaceutical chemist to extract a tooth in the case of emergency.

The business of dentistry

A person is treated as carrying on the business of dentistry if, and only if, s/he or a partnership of which s/he is a member receives payment for services rendered in the course of the practice of dentistry by him/her or by a partner of his/hers, or by an employee of his/hers or of the partnership (s.40). A lay person cannot employ dentists for the purpose of carrying on a business of dentistry (s.41) but there is an exception for individuals who were carrying on the business of dentistry on 21 July 1955. That was the date of the introduction into Parliament of the Bill for the Dentists Act 1956, which was subsequently absorbed into the Dentists Act 1984. Bodies corporate which were in the business of dentistry on that date are also exempted if the majority of the directors are dentists and all the operating staff are dentists or dental auxiliaries.

The Act provides for the establishment of classes of dental auxiliary and for regulations, made by the General Dental Council, to prescribe qualifications for such auxiliaries and the dental work they undertake. The General Dental Council may entrust to the Dental Auxiliaries Committee all matters relating to ancillary dental services, including enforcement of standards of conduct (Part V of the Act).

Nurse, midwives and health visitors

The Nurses, Midwives and Heath Visitors Act 1977 was replaced on 12 February 2002 by the Nursing and Midwifery Order 2001. This Order, which applies in the UK, establishes a body corporate to be known as the Nursing and Midwifery Council. The objective of the Council is to safeguard the health and well-being of persons using or needing the services of registered nurses and midwives.

The Nursing and Midwifery Council

The Nursing and Midwifery Council comprises 12 elected registrant members, 12 elected alternate members, who attend in the absence of the corresponding elected registrant member, and 11 lay members appointed by the Privy Council. There must be at least one registrant member and one alternate member from each part of the Nursing and Midwifery Register and at least one member from each of the national constituences for each part of the register.

There are four statutory committees of the Council:

1   the Investigating Committee;
2   the Conduct and Competence Committee;
3   the Health Committee; and
4   the Midwifery Committee.

The Council must ensure that the standards of training meet any EU obligations of the UK and, by means of rules, establish the standards of education and training necessary to achieve standards of proficiency and the requirements for admission to, and continued participation in, such education and training, which may include requirements as to good health and good character for registration. The rules may also make provision for further training to be available to persons already registered.

The Council has power to provide advice to the professions on standards of professional conduct and has done so, for example the *Code of Professional*

Conduct for the Nurse, Midwife and Health Visitor. The principal functions of the Council are to establish standards of education, training, conduct and performance for nurses and midwives and to ensure the maintaintenance of those standards. It is required, in the discharge of its functions, to have a proper regard for the interests of all groups within the professions, including those with minority representation. The powers and procedures of the Council are laid down in Part I of Schedule I to the Nursing and Midwifery Order 2001.

The register

The Council is required to establish and maintain, on a proposal from the Council, a register of qualified health professionals and must from time to time establish standards of proficiency necessary to be admitted to the different parts of the register, being standards it considers necessary for safe and effective practice. It must also prescribe requirements to be met as to evidence of good health and good character in order to satisfy the registrar that an applicant is capable of safe and effective practice as a registrant under the relevant part of the register. Before prescribing these standards and subsequently publishing them, the Council must consult the Conduct and Competence Committee.

The register is divided into such parts as the Privy Council determine, on a proposal from the Council, each part having a designated title indicative of different qualifications and different kinds of education or training; a registrant is entitled to use the title corresponding to that part of the register. The register may contain the recording in Welsh of titles, qualifications and other entries in respect of those registrants whose registered address is in Wales, together with their competence in a field of practice or at a particular level of practice.

The Council may make rules as to the format of the register, method of entries and erasures and the payment of fees. The Council must make the register available for inspection by members of the public and must publish the register in such a manner and at such times as it considers appropriate.

A person may be registered if s/he holds an approved qualification within the past five years and satisfies the registrar as to any additional education required, that s/he is capable of safe and effective practice as a nurse or midwife and that s/he has paid the prescribed fee.

On renewing registration, a nurse or midwife must satisfy the registrar as to his/her initial registration particulars and that s/he has met any prescribed requirements for continuing professional development within the prescribed time; where s/he has not practised or has practised for less than the prescribed period, a nurse or midwife must satisfy the registrar that s/he has met such requirements as to additional education and training or experience as the Council may specify.

Fitness to practise

The Council must establish and keep under review the standards of conduct, performance and ethics expected of registrants and give them guidance on these matters. It must also establish and keep under review effective arrangements to protect the public from persons whose fitness to practise is impaired. The Council has to make rules governing the procedure of the three Practice Committees.

When any allegation is made against a registrant that his/her fitness is impaired by reason of misconduct, lack of competence, a conviction or by way of physical or mental health, the Council must refer it to the Investigating Committee.

The Investigating Committee

The Investigating Committee comprises a chairman and deputy chairman plus three other members and has a quorum of three, which must include the chairman or deputy chairman (SI 2003 No.1738). Where the Investigating Committee considers there is a case to answer, it must undertake mediation, refer the case to screeners for them to undertake mediation or refer the case to the Health Committee or to the Conduct and Competence Committee. In order to protect the public, in the public interest or in the interest of the registrant, the Investigating Committee may make an interim order suspending the registrant's registration for not more than 18 months ('interim suspension order') or make an order imposing conditions with which the registrant must comply ('interim conditions of practice order'). There is an appeal procedure to a County Court or Sheriff (in Scotland).

The Conduct and Competence Committee

The Conduct and Competence Committee comprises a chairman and deputy chairman plus six other members and has a quorum of three, which must include the chairman or deputy chairman (SI 2003 No.1738). Where the Conduct and Competence Committee considers there is a case to answer, it must either undertake mediation itself or refer the case to screeners for them to undertake mediation. Alternatively, it may order the person's name to be struck of the register ('striking off order'), suspend registration (a 'suspension order'), issue a caution ('caution order') or impose conditions for practice (a 'conditions of practice order'). Appeals are to the High Court or Court of Session (in Scotland) or High Court in Northern Ireland.

The Health Committee

The Health Committee comprises a chairman and deputy chairman plus two other members and has a quorum of three, which must include the chairman or deputy chairman (SI 2003 No.1738). The Health Committee has the same powers, and appeal procedures, as the Conduct and Competence Committee.

MIDWIFERY COMMITTEE

The majority of the members of the Midwifery Committee must be practising midwives and the chairman a member of the Council. The Midwifery Committee advises the Council on matters affecting midwifery and the Council must consult the Committee in matters affecting midwifery. The Council shall determine by rules the circumstances and procedures by means of which a midwife may be suspended from practice and any courses of instruction required to be attended by midwives. Rules may also require midwives to give notice of their intention to practise to a local supervising authority for the area in which they intend to practise. Each local supervising authority must exercise general supervision over midwives practising in their area and report back to the Council where it appears that any midwife's fitness to practise as a midwife is impaired.

Offences by unqualified persons

Except in a case of sudden or urgent necessity, or a person undergoing training with a view to becoming a midwife or doctor, it is an offence for any person other than a registered midwife or a registered medical practitioner to attend a woman in childbirth.

It is also an offence for any person, with intent to deceive, falsely to represent him/herself to be registered or to possess qualifications in nursing or midwifery. The deception may be expressly or by implication or by the assumption of any title, name or description or by any other kind of conduct.

Opticians

In April 2004, the Department of Health issued a document entitled *The Reform of the General Optical Council: A Paper for Consultation* together with a draft Opticians Act Amendment Order. Further details are awaited.

The Opticians Act 1989 is the statute which regulates the practice of opticians and the conduct by bodies corporate of their business as opticians.

General Optical Council

The General Optical Council, established under the Act (s.1), has the general function of promoting high standards of professional education and professional conduct among opticians. Its members include elected representatives of ophthalmic opticians and dispensing opticians, together with medical practitioners nominated by the College of Ophthalmologists, persons nominated by the Privy Council and the examining bodies, including the British College of

Optometrists. The Council must appoint an Education Committee (s.2), and a Companies Committee to advise on matters relating to bodies corporate (s.3). The Council has an Investigation Committee (s.4) and a Disciplinary Committee (s.5). The Council has power to approve institutions for the purpose of training opticians and to approve of qualifications (s.12).

Registers of opticians

The Council is required to maintain two registers (s.7) of *ophthalmic opticians*: namely, those engaged in the testing of sight and the fitting and supply of optical appliances and those engaged in the testing of sight only. In addition, the Council must maintain a register of *dispensing opticians*: persons who are engaged in the fitting and supply of optical appliances.

Those persons entitled to be included in any of the health service ophthalmic lists at the time of establishment of the General Optical Council in 1959 were entitled to be registered, as also were other persons who in 1961 satisfied the Council as to their qualifications. Subsequently, only applicants holding qualifications approved or recognised by the Council could be accepted for inclusion in the appropriate register (s.8).

The register must be published by the Council (s.11). The Council is also required to maintain and publish lists of bodies corporate carrying on businesses as ophthalmic opticians or carrying on businesses as dispensing opticians (s.9). A body corporate is entitled to be included in any of the following circumstances:

1   if the majority of its directors are registered opticians;
2   if it was included in one of the NHS ophthalmic lists on 20 November 1957;
3   if the greater part of its business consists of activities other than the testing of sight and the fitting and supply of optical appliances; or
4   if it is a society registered under the Industrial and Provident Societies Act 1965.

In 3 and 4, the business of testing sight or the fitting or supply of optical appliances must be under the management of a registered ophthalmic optician or a registered optician as is appropriate.

Professional discipline

The General Optical Council has an Investigating Committee (s.4) and a Disciplinary Committee (s.5) to deal with any disciplinary case. The Disciplinary Committee may direct the removal of a name from the register or list (s.17). The name of a registered optician may be suspended or removed from the register following a conviction in the UK for any criminal offence or following a judgment of the Disciplinary Committee that s/he has been guilty of serious professional misconduct. A financial penalty can also be imposed, either on its own or together with a suspension or erasure. The name of an enrolled body corporate may be removed following a conviction of the body corporate for an offence under the Act; aiding, abetting, counselling or inciting another person to commit an offence; or following a finding of the Disciplinary Committee that the conditions for enrolment of the body corporate are no longer satisfied.

The Disciplinary Committee may also direct the suspension or erasure of a name from the list or register on grounds of fraud or error (s.19); for a contravention of any rule of the Council made under section 31 (e.g. advertising); or for carrying on a practice or business without the supervision of a registered ophthalmic or dispensing optician, as appropriate (s.17).

Offences under the Opticians Act 1989

Subject to certain exceptions, it is unlawful for any person who is not a registered medical practitioner or registered ophthalmic optician to test the sight of another person (s.24). It is also unlawful to sell any optical appliance, that is an appliance designed to correct, remedy or relieve a defect of sight, unless the sale is effected by or under the supervision of a registered medical practitioner or a registered optician (s.27). This does not apply to certain types of sale (e.g. sales to an optician, to medical practitioners, to hospitals or to government departments); neither does it apply to the sale to a person over 16 of 'reading glasses', subject to limitation on spherical power, to correct presbyopia (s.27). It is a defence to prove that an appliance was sold as an antique.

The Sale of Optical Appliances Order of Council 1984 (SI 1984 No.1778), which is applicable to the new Act, also exempts from the supervision requirements the sale of spectacles provided such sales are made against a prescription written by a registered medical practitioner or registered optician. The exemption does not apply to the sale or supply of contact lenses or spectacles for those aged under 16 years.

It is an offence for any person or body corporate to use any of the titles ophthalmic optician, dispensing optician, registered optician or ancillary optician if that person is not registered or, in the case of a body corporate, enrolled. It is also an offence to use any name, title, addition or description falsely implying registration or enrolment (s.28).

Healthcare and associated professions

The Professions Supplementary to Medicines Act 1960 was replaced on 12 February 2002 by the Health Professions Order 2001 (SI 2002 N0.254). This Order, which applies in the UK, establishes a body corporate to be known as the Health Professions Council. The objective of the Council is to safeguard the health and well-being of persons using or needing the services of health professionals.

The Order provides a regulatory system for a number of smaller health professions: arts therapists, chiropodists, clinical scientists, dieticians, medical laboratory technicians, occupational therapists, orthoptists, paramedics, physiotherapists, prosthetists and orthotists, radiographers, and speech and language therapists.

In July 2004 several changes were made. Firstly, *operating department practitioners* became the thirteenth member of the smaller professions. Secondly, *chiropodists* changed their name to *chiropodists and podiatrists* and *medical laboratory technicians* became *biomedical scientists* (SI 2004 No.2033).

The Health Professions Council

The Health Professions Council now comprises 13 elected registrant members, 13 elected alternate members, who attend in the absence of the corresponding elected registrant member, and 12 lay members appointed by the Privy Council (SI 2002 No.254, as amended by SI 2004 No.2033). There are four committees of the Council:

1   the Investigating Committee;
2   the Conduct and Competence Committee;
3   the Health Committee; and
4   the Education and Training Committee.

The registers

The Council is required to establish and maintain, on a proposal from the Council, a register of qualified health professionals and must from time to time establish standards of proficiency necessary to be admitted to the different parts of the register, being standards it considers necessary for safe and effective practice. It must also prescribe requirements to be met as to evidence of good health and good character in order to satisfy the registrar that an applicant is capable of safe and effective practice as a registrant under the relevant part of the register. Before prescribing these standards and subsequently publishing them, the Council must consult the Conduct and Competence Committee.

The Register shall be divided into such parts as the Privy Council determines, on a proposal from the Council, each part having a designated title indicative of different qualifications and different kinds of education or training; a registrant is entitled to use the title corresponding to that part of the register. The register may contain the recording in Welsh of titles, qualifications and other entries in respect of those registrants whose registered address is in Wales; it also contains possession of qualifications and competence in a field of practice or at a particular level of practice.

The Council may make rules as to the format of the register, method of entries and erasures and the payment of fees. The Council must make the register available for inspection by members of the public and must publish the register in such a manner and at such times as it considers appropriate.

A person may be registered if s/he holds an approved qualification within the past five years and satisfies the registrar as to any additional education required, that s/he is capable of safe and effective practice as a health professional, and that s/he has paid the prescribed fee.

On renewing registration, a health professional must satisfy the Education and Training Committee as to his/her initial registration particulars and satisfy that Committee that s/he has met any prescribed requirements for continuing professional development within the prescribed time. Where s/he has not practised, or has practised for less than the prescribed period, s/he must satisfy the Committee that s/he has met such requirements as to additional education and training or experience as the Council may specify.

The Education and Training Committee

The Council must establish the standards of education and training necessary to achieve standards of proficiency and the requirements for admission to, and continued participation in, such education and training, which may include requirements as to good health and good character for registration. The rules may also make provision for further training to be available to persons already registered.

The Committee must take appropriate steps to satisfy itself that those standards and requirements are met and advise the Council on the performance of the Council's functions in relation to standards and proficiency.

Fitness to Practise Committees

The Council must establish and keep under review the standards of conduct, performance and ethics expected of registrants and give them guidance on these matters. It must also establish and keep under review effective arrangements to protect the public from persons whose fitness to practise is impaired. The Council has to make rules governing the procedure of the three Practice Committees and must consult the Conduct and Competence Committee before establishing any standards. The Council must appoint a chairman for each of its Practice Committees and may appoint another member of the committee to act as deputy chairman in the chairman's absence.

When any allegation is made against a registrant that his/her fitness is impaired by reason of misconduct, lack of competence, a conviction or by way of physical or mental health, then the Council must refer it to the Investigating Committee.

THE INVESTIGATING COMMITTEE

The Investigating Committee comprises a chairman and possibly a deputy chairman and not less than nine members and has a quorum of five, which must include the chairman (SI 2003 No.1209). Where the Investigating

Committee considers there is a case to answer, it must undertake mediation, refer the case to screeners for them to undertake mediation, refer the case to the Health Committee or refer the case to the Conduct and Competence Committee. In order to protect the public, in the public interest or in the interest of the registrant, the Investigating Committee may make an interim order suspending the registrant's registration for not more than 18 months ('interim suspension order') or make an order imposing conditions with which the registrant must comply ('interim conditions of practice order'). There is an appeal procedure to a County Court or Sheriff (in Scotland).

THE CONDUCT AND COMPETENCE COMMITTEE
The Conduct and Competence Committee comprises a chairman plus other members and has a quorum of five. A member, appointed as deputy chairman, may act in the chairman's absence (SI 2003 No.1209). Where the Conduct and Competence Committee considers there is a case to answer, it must either undertake mediation itself or refer the case to screeners for them to undertake mediation. Alternatively, it may order the person's name to be struck of the register ('striking off order'), suspend registration (a 'suspension order'), issue a caution ('caution order') or impose conditions for practise (a 'conditions of practise order'). Appeals are to the High Court or Court of Session (in Scotland) or High Court in Northern Ireland.

THE HEALTH COMMITTEE
The Health Committee, dealing with mental or physical matters, has a similar constitution, powers and procedures as the Conduct and Competence Committee.

Titles and descriptions

A registered person is entitled to use the title state registered (e.g. state registered dietician and similarly for the other professions). It is an offence for any person to take or use, alone or in conjunction with other words, the title state registered, state or registered [e.g. state registered chiropodist, state chiropodist or registered chiropodist (and similarly for the other professions)] if s/he is not so registered, or to take or use any name, title, addition or description falsely implying, or otherwise to pretend, that his/her name is on a register established under the Act (s.6).

Only registered persons may be employed by health authorities within the NHS unless they were employed in their specific capacity prior to the registration requirements applying to their profession. Apart from these restrictions, there is no prohibition on practice by unregistered persons.

Hearing aid supply

The main Hearing Aid Council Act 1968 was amended by the Hearing Aid Council (Amendment) Act 1989. The Hearing Aid Council has the general function of securing adequate standards of competence and conduct among persons engaged in dispensing hearing aids. It is required to draw up standards of competence for dispensers of hearing aids and codes of trade practice for adoption by such dispensers and by persons employing them (s.1). The Hearing Aid Extension Act 1975 extended the Act to Northern Ireland.

The Council is appointed partly from persons representing persons registered under the Act and partly from persons representing the interests of persons with impaired hearing. The Council is required to maintain for public inspection a register of dispensers of hearing aids, and a register of persons (including bodies corporate) employing such dispensers (s.2).

A *dispenser of hearing aids* means an individual who conducts or seeks to conduct 'oral negotiations' with a view to effecting the supply of a hearing aid, whether by him/her or another, to or for the use of a person with impaired hearing. An *employer of dispensers* includes any person who enters into any arrangement with an individual whereby that individual undertakes for reward or anticipation of reward to act as a dispenser with a view to promoting the supply of hearing aids by that person (s.14).

Professional discipline

The Hearing Aid Council must also establish an Investigating Committee (s.5) and a Disciplinary Committee (s.6) comparable with those under the Professions Supplementary to Medicine Act 1960. A registered person may have his/her name suspended or removed from the register for any criminal conviction or if judged by the Disciplinary Committee to be guilty of serious misconduct in connection with the dispensing of hearing aids or the training of persons to act as dispensers of hearing aids (s.7, as amended by the 1989 Act). A financial penalty may also be imposed. Appeals against a direction lie to the High Court. It is an offence for any person whose name is not in the appropriate register to act as a dispenser of hearing aids or to employ such a dispenser.

The Council for the Regulation of Health Care Professionals

Under the National Health Service and Health Care Professions Act 2002, the Government has established the Council for the Regulation of Health Care Professionals. Now known as CRHE, the Council is intended to promote the interests of patients and other members of the public in relation to the performance by the regulatory bodies of health professionals including the medical, dental, nursing, optical, chiropractic and osteopathic councils plus the Pharmaceutical Societies of Great Britain and Northern Ireland.

The Council may investigate, and report on the performance by each regulatory body of its functions, and recommend to such a body changes to the way in which it performs its functions. It may refer to the High Court those bodies whose disciplinary committees appear to be too lenient in dealing with the public's complaints against health professionals.

Further reading

Appelbe G.E. and Harrison I. (1994) Professional self-regulation: pharmacy and the other health professions. *Pharm J* 254: 679.
Gray C. (2002) How the other professions are responding to the drivers for change. *Pharm J*. 268: 154–155.

Websites

General Dental Council: http://www.gdc-uk.org/
General Medical Council: http://www.gmc-uk.org/
General Optical Council: http://www.optical.org/
Health Professions Council: http://www.hpc-uk.org/
Nursing and Midwifery Council: http://www.gnmc-uk.org/nmc/main/home.html
Royal College of Veterinary Surgeons: http://www.rcvs.org.uk

CHAPTER TWENTY-SIX

National Health Service law and management

The National Health Service Act 1946 made it the duty of the Minister of Health (now the Secretary of State for Health) in England, and the Secretary of State for Wales (SI 1968 No.1699):

> to promote the establishment in England and Wales of a comprehensive health service designed to secure improvement in the physical and mental health of the people of England and Wales and the prevention, diagnosis and treatment of illness. . .
>
> (s.1)

For that purpose, a number of services specified in the Act were to be provided. Generally, they were to be free of charge unless otherwise expressly provided in the Act (s.1). In Scotland, a similar health service was established by the National Health Service (Scotland) Act 1947, the Minister responsible being the Secretary of State for Scotland. Following the implementation of the 1946 Act in July 1948, the NHS was organised into three distinct parts, which were managed and financed separately. These were the hospital service, the local health authority service (community health services) and the general practitioner (GP) service (which included the doctors and the chemists). The service was reorganised into a single management structure in England and Wales by the National Health Service Reorganisation Act 1973 (now revoked) and in Scotland by the National Health Service (Scotland) Act 1978.

In 1977, the provisions of the 1946 Act and most of the provisions of the 1973 Act, including those affecting the pharmaceutical service, were consolidated into the National Health Service Act 1977. The principal duty set out in section 1 of the 1946 Act was repeated in the 1977 Act (s.1). Under the 1997 Act, the NHS was essentially split into two different systems. The first (Part I services) relates to the provision of healthcare in hospital and those provided in the community by district nurses, midwives, health visitors and the schools services. The second group (Part II services) could be called the 'NHS in the High Street' comprising services from GPs, dentists, optometrists and pharmacists. Each of these is in contract with the NHS according to the relevant national contract and Terms of Service. Part II services are often called Family Health Practitioner Services.

Overall, the Secretary of State or the appropriate ministers are required to provide, to such an extent as they believe necessary to meet reasonable requirements:

1   hospital accommodation;
2   other accommodation for the purpose of any service provided under the Act;
3   medical, dental, nursing and ambulance services;
4   facilities for the care of expectant and nursing mothers and young children;
5   facilities for the prevention of illness, the care of persons suffering from illness and the aftercare of persons who have suffered from illness;
6   services for the diagnosis and treatment of illness; and
7   a family planning service.

The Secretary of State or Ministers are also required to appoint Health Service Commissioners to investigate complaints about the operation of the service (s.106). The remit of the Health Service Commissioner (Ombudsman) was extended in April 1996 to include clinical matters and complaints involving practitioners (see p. 377). In 1999, the first complaint involving a dispensing error by a community pharmacist was investigated by the Health Service Ombudsman (*Chemist and Druggist* 3 July 1999 p. 5).

The organisation of the National Health Service

The NHS is highly sensitive to political change and the advent of a Labour Government in 1997 changed the tenor of the service from a competitive internal market (see 1990 Act below) of purchasers and providers to one of co-operation and partnership. This was not a complete change, however, since the Government's aim was to 'keep what works and discard what fails'. Thus, the legislative framework is complicated by retention of parts of earlier (pre-Labour) legislation overlaid by the new. Moreover, in 1999, power to manage health matters in Scotland and Wales passed to the Scottish Parliament and the Welsh Assembly, respectively. This means that the operation of the NHS in the three countries is now diverging and each jurisdiction is developing its own body of NHS legislation and management guidance. The account below, therefore, applies primarily to England; later sections in this chapter point to differences which are apparent in Wales and Scotland. In addition to statute law, the Secretary of State is empowered to make further 'directions' to the health service which have the force of law, and a substantial body of strategic direction, circulars, guidance and instruction is set out in 'white papers' and similar policy documents.

National Health Service and Community Care Act 1990

The 1990 Act paved the way for the creation of an internal market by transforming the then district health authorities into purchasers with power to use contracts or service agreements with providers, including those in the private sector [Private Finance Initiative (PFI)]. It enabled the setting up of self-governing Trusts (mostly hospitals) and GP fundholders as providers and removed Crown immunity (see Chapter 1) from hospital premises, so allowing equal competition with other providers. GP fundholders were abolished by the 1999 Health Act.

A Trust is an NHS body which is permitted, initially by individual orders made under the 1990 Act, to assume responsibility for the ownership and management of hospitals and certain other facilities, such as ambulance or local community health services. Under the 1999 Health Act (see below), this approach is extended to primary healthcare services. A Trust is run by a board, which may engage its own staff and set their rates of pay and may borrow capital and dispose of assets. However, this freedom is constrained in that the staff remain NHS employees and the premises remain NHS property. Moreover, the Secretary of State may require that certain services are provided (e.g. accident and emergency facilities), regardless of the wishes of the Trust Board. NHS Trusts are essentially **providers** of healthcare; their services are **commissioned** principally by Primary Care Trusts (PCTs).

National Health Service (Primary Care) Act 1997

The National Health Service (Primary Care) Act 1997 introduced a new option for the delivery of two of the family health services, namely, those from GPs and dentists. In addition to the national contracts for general medical services and for general dental services, schemes known as personal medical services and personal dental services were put in place with individual health authorities (now Primary Care Trusts). Originally set up as 'pilots' using Part I NHS funding, the 1997 Act makes provision for these schemes to be permanent. This Act also added the definition of a 'health service body' into the 1977 National Health Service Act; a provision brought into force in 2002 to advance the modernisation of the NHS (SI 2002 No. 1616).

Health Act 1999

The Health Act 1999 gave the powers needed by the Government to deliver its plans for managing the NHS. These plans were set out in 1998 in a series of white papers and consultation documents: in England, *The New NHS* (Cm.3807), *A First Class Service* (*Health Service Circular* 1998/113) and *Partnership in Action* (published by Department of Health September 1998) together with companion documents for Wales and Scotland. The 1999 Act made ten major changes:

1   abolition of GP fundholding;
2   enabling the establishment of PCTs in England and Wales and NHS Trusts in Scotland;
3   amending the NHS and Community Care Act to change the purposes and financing of NHS Trusts;
4   introduction of a statutory duty of quality on NHS bodies and services (*clinical governance*);
5   creation of the Commission for Health Improvement to monitor and improve the quality of healthcare;
6   introduction of a requirement for family health practitioners to hold approved indemnity cover;
7   introduction of a statutory duty of co-operation within the NHS and between authorities in England and Wales;
8   introduction of measures to control fraud;
9   enabling powers to set maximum prices for medicines supplied to the NHS; and
10 enabling powers to regulate healthcare professions.

Thus the 1999 Act has a profound effect on the way pharmacy interacts with the NHS by creating a powerful local focus for health services in the PCT and by requiring a commitment to quality and co-operation in achieving health improvement for local populations. Measures to control costs, tackle fraud and overhaul the self-regulation of health professionals also have an impact on pharmacy.

Modernising the National Health Service

In July 2000, the Government published a further blueprint for the NHS in England, *The NHS Plan* (Cm.4818-1), setting out proposals for a number of changes significant to pharmacy. This plan signalled an intention to 'shift away from (pharmacies) being paid mainly for dispensing of individual prescriptions towards rewarding overall service'. In September 2000, further details, including a significant number of potential changes to NHS legislation, were clarified in a government document setting out a strategy for pharmacy in England entitled *Pharmacy in the Future: Implementing the NHS Plan. A Programme for Pharmacy*. In July 2003, the Department of Health issued *A Vision for Pharmacy in the New NHS,* which set out 10 key roles for pharmacists and the NHS. In June 2004, the *NHS Improvement Plan* set out priorities for development until 2008, including the institution of repeat dispensing services as a fundamental part of the community pharmacy contract, revising the criteria for the awarding of contracts, extending electronic transmission of prescriptions, facilitating transfer of more medicines from Prescription Only Medicines to Pharmacy Medicines and developing the public health role of community pharmacists. These four policy documents, together with many more addressing other aspects of the NHS,* describe a major programme of change for pharmacy, most notably a complete reform of the NHS community pharmacy contract (see p. 373 and Appendix 17).

> These changes were not complete at the time of going to press but are likely to commence from April 2005. In October 2004 the Department of Health announced its intention to move towards GP practice-based commissioning, while recognising that some services would remain better commissioned at the PCT level or even wider for certain specialised services.

Health and Social Care Act 2001

The Health and Social Care Act 2001 paved the way to introduce much of the modernisation programme. It enabled legislation in the following areas:

* facilitation of repeat dispensing arrangements for Prescription Only Medicines (implemented by SI 2003 No.1084);
* changes to the particulars which must appear on a prescription for a Prescription Only Medicine to allow 'electronic signatures' (see p. 99);
* changes to the awarding of contracts to dispense NHS prescriptions to include virtual e-pharmacies operating over the Internet, to recognise patient demand in major retail developments and 'one-stop primary care centres' for out-of-hours dispensing;

---

* Examples of policy documents in England, all issued by the Department of Health on www.dh.gov.uk , include:
Tackling Health Inequalities. Consultation on a Plan for Delivery. February 2001
Shifting the Balance of Power; Securing Delivery. July 2001
Modernising Regulation in the Health Professions. Consultation Document. August 2001
Involving Patients and the Public in Healthcare: A Discussion Document. September 2001
Reforming the NHS Complaints Procedure: A Listening Document. September 2001
Shifting the Balance of Power: The Next Steps. January 2002
Pharmacy Workforce in the New NHS. September 2002
Overview and Scrutiny of Health: Guidance. July 2003
Building on the Best. Choice, Responsiveness and Equity in the NHS. December 2003
Building a Safer NHS for Patients. January 2004
Standards for Better Health. July 2004
Practice Based Commissioning: Engaging Practices in Commissioning. October 2004

- changes to existing NHS contracts for dispensing to include clinical quality, speed and efficiency, standards of premises and private consultation areas, record keeping and information, continuing professional development and clinical governance;
- introduction of an alternative contract for Local Pharmaceutical Services to include dispensing along with medicines management, health promotion, and disease prevention components;
- inclusion of pharmacists (s.63) in the growing groups of health practitioners who are able to authorise a prescription for a Prescription Only Medicine (see independent and supplementary prescribing: Chapters 8 and 9).

National Health Service Reform and Health Care Professions Act 2002

The NHS Reform and Health Care Professions Act 2002 abolished the health authorities (established under the Health Authorities Act 1995) as the commissioners and planners of Part II Family Health Services and passed their responsibilities to the PCTs (established by the Health Act 1999). Thus the responsibilities for the NHS dispensing contract passed to PCTs. At the same time, this Act established Strategic Health Authorities to co-ordinate, monitor and performance manage the Trusts in their management of NHS services within their geographical areas. The Act strengthened the scope of the 'duty of quality' and the role of the Commission for Health Improvement in the 1999 Act and established arrangements for patient involvement in the NHS. This Act also established the Council for the Regulation of Health Care Professionals [it prefers to be called the Council for Health Care Regulatory Excellence (CHRE); see Chapters 22, 24 and 25] to oversee and regulate the activities of a range of healthcare regulatory bodies, including the Royal Pharmaceutical Society of Great Britain.

Health and Social Care (Community Health and Standards) Act 2003

The Health and Social Care (Community Health and Standards) Act 2003 allowed the creation of NHS Foundation Trusts (see below). It also changed the Commission for Health Improvement to the Commission for Health Care Audit and Inspection (now called the Health Care Commission) and established the Commission for Social Care Inspection. Both of these bodies include the services provided by pharmacists in their audit regimes. The Act also consolidated so-called 'pilot' arrangements for personal medical services and general medical services (see under NHS (Primary Care) Act 1997 above) into a new 'general medical services contract', implemented in April 2004.

The National Health Service Act 1977, the National Health Service and Community Care Act 1990, the National Health Service (Primary Care) Act 1997, the Health Act 1999, the Health and Social Care Acts of 2001 and 2003 and the NHS Reform Act and Health Care Professions Act 2002 all now form the legal basis for the NHS in England and Wales, plus further enactments post-1999 which apply to Wales only. The National Health Service (Scotland) Act 1978 together with the relevant parts of the pre-1999 legislation covers Scotland, to which should now be added its own post-1999 Scottish enactments.

National Health Service structure in Great Britain

Like the legislation that underpins it, the structure of the NHS undergoes constant change. Reference should be made to the Department of Health website for the latest position in England. Although the structures and titles vary significantly in England, Wales and Scotland, all have organisations that plan and commission local health services and deliver family health practitioner services, plus organisations that provide secondary (mostly hospital) care. Simple summaries and national links can be found on the NHS UK Gateway.

England

THE DEPARTMENT OF HEALTH

The Department of Health has six ministers (the most senior is called the Secretary of State for Health) who work with a board of eight members to manage Department of Health business and priorities (Fig. 26.1). Department of Health business is managed in three business groups: delivery, standards and quality and strategy and business development. Key national clinical priorities, such as cancer and cancer networks, mental health, older people's services or diabetes are led by National Clinical Directors (often termed 'czars' by the media). In addition, there are five Heads of Professions, including a Chief Pharmaceutical Officer. The Department of Health works with a wide range of agencies and independent bodies to deliver its objectives: executive agencies such as the Medicines and Health Care products Regulatory Agency (see Chapter 2 *et seq.*), Special Health Authorities such as the Prescription Pricing Authority or the National Patient Safety Agency, and commissions and tribunals such as the Health Care Commission and the Family Health Services Appeal Authority. These so-called 'arm's length bodies' are constantly evolving. A review in July 2004 reconfigured their functions into four areas: regulation, standards, public welfare and central services. The intention is to reduce the total from 38 to 20 such bodies by 2008.

STRATEGIC HEALTH AUTHORITIES

England is split into 28 strategic health authorities to develop plans for improving health services in their local areas and to make sure that their local

Figure 26.1 NHS structure in England

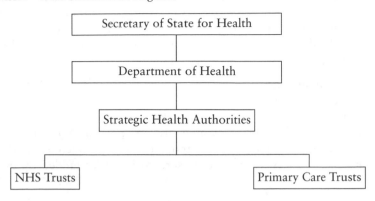

NHS organisations are performing well. Secondary legislation under the NHS Reform and Health Care Professions Act replaces the legislation concerning the former health authorities, amends or revokes earlier statutes on PCTs and sets out in detail the apportionment of powers and responsibilities between strategic health authorities and PCTs (SI 2002 No. 2375 and amendments)

TRUSTS
There are several types of Trust taking legal responsibility for running particular health services in particular localities. The most familiar perhaps are Acute Trusts, which essentially manage hospitals delivering secondary or NHS Part I healthcare. Some Acute Trusts are regional or national centres for more specialised (tertiary) care or are attached to universities and train health professionals (Teaching Trusts). Acute Trusts may also provide community healthcare through clinics and outpatient services, although these are increasingly being transferred to PCTs. Since April 2004, some Trusts have become Foundation Trusts with greater financial and operational freedom and are accountable to the Independent Regulator of NHS Foundation Trusts (known as the Monitor). There are also Ambulance Trusts providing emergency access to healthcare and Mental Health Trusts, often working closely with local council social services, to provide health and social care for people with mental health problems.

Some 300 PCTs receive 75% of the budget for NHS Part II healthcare and increasingly commission and deliver the majority of healthcare in a community. Statutory instruments under the Health Act have formalised the membership, procedure and administration arrangements for PCTs, the composition of their executive committees and their functions (SI 2000 No.89, as amended, with Directions). Although the statutory input of pharmacists to local health planning, lost in 1990, has not been formally replaced, the composition of the PCT executive committee is now covered by 'directions' [The PCT Executive Committees (Membership) Directions 2003] made under the authority of the Secretary of State for Health. These provide explicit authority for local community pharmacists to be eligible for inclusion on the

Committee. PCTs commission services from other Trusts and from NHS Direct (see below), award NHS dispensing contracts, administer the relevant conditions (the Terms of Service, see below), operate statutory disciplinary arrangements and make arrangements for persons in the PCT locality to be supplied with 'pharmaceutical services', namely:

1   proper and sufficient drugs and medicines and listed appliances which are ordered for those persons by a medical practitioner in pursuance of his/her functions in the Health Service;
2   listed drugs and medicines which are ordered for those persons by a dental or nurse practitioner in pursuance of such functions; and
3   such other services as may be prescribed by order (added by the 1990 Act).

The pharmaceutical services are provided by community pharmacists, or their employers, who are under contract to the local PCT and are legally known as *pharmacy* or *chemist contractors* or simply *chemists*.

A small number of Care Trusts have also been established to deliver social care, mental healthcare and primary healthcare in a given locality.

NHS Direct, National Health Service walk-in centres
NHS Direct was established in 1999 as a directly funded Department of Health body; in 2004, it became a Special Health Authority (SI 2004 No. 569). The service provides 24 hour nurse-led telephone help on health matters plus an online website and digital TV service, publishes a self-help guide and provides interactive Information Point terminals in public places such as surgeries, pharmacies, accident and emergency departments, libraries and post offices. Since 2004, PCTs have received funding to commission the telephone and other core services and many will integrate their out-of-hours arrangements with NHS Direct support.

A number of pilot NHS walk-in centres were established during 1999 and 2000. Again led by nurses, these aim to improve access to primary healthcare services. Legally they are equivalent to NHS hospital outpatient units so supplies of medicines and collection of prescription charges may be made on the spot to patients who use the centres. If appropriately trained, nurse prescribers in walk-in centres may also issue NHS prescriptions for products in the nurse prescribers' formulary (see p. 85) (SIs 2000 No.121; 2000 No.122). Most NHS walk-in centres also supply a range of medicines under Patient Group Directions (see Chapters 8 and 9).

Managed National Health Services and the private sector
The term 'managed service' generally implies services paid for 'out of the public purse', that is through the payment of taxes to the state. In that sense, pharmacists who work within PCTs, NHS Trusts (mostly hospitals but see above), most prison health services and health services for the armed forces are working in the managed sector. Increasingly, pharmacists working for GP practices are subject to NHS management. By contrast, pharmacists in

community practice are employed privately but their NHS services are subject to NHS management arrangements. The private sector (such as private hospitals run by a range of insurers and provident societies or nursing homes run by commercial agencies) is financed by shareholders and by direct payments from the service users.

Boundaries between these sectors, at least in the provision of health services, have become increasingly blurred, and management and measurement of the quality of these services is converging. Since April 1991 (removal of Crown immunity; Chapter 1), the major statutes concerning medicines (including Controlled Drugs) and related matters now apply to NHS hospitals as well to hospitals and nursing homes that are privately owned. Prison services, whether state or privately run, are expected to comply with UK law as far as is practicable as are military health services, even when operating overseas. In addition, it is now relatively common for an NHS Trust to register the hospital dispensary or pharmacy department with the Royal Pharmaceutical Society as a *registered pharmacy* (see Chapter 5), thus enabling it to engage in over-the-counter sales and a limited amount of wholesale dealing (licence exempted; Chapter 10).

Trusts and other public bodies are legally responsible for the activities they manage. Litigation against them is increasing and it is important that pharmacists employed in these sectors of pharmacy understand not only the legislation but also the criteria against which accepted standards of care may be judged. The common law principles of negligence (pp. 6 and 293) and professional responsibility apply to pharmacists in the managed sector and they should be aware of the differences between managerial responsibility (master/servant relationship) and professional obligations.

NATIONAL HEALTH SERVICE DIRECTIONS
In addition to the requirements of primary statutes and subsidiary legislation (such as the Misuse of Drugs Act 1971 and the regulations made under it), power is also given to the Secretary of State for Health (and occasionally to Strategic Health Authorities) to make additional 'directions'. They must be in writing and cite the relevant powers being used. They have the force of law so that a breach is a breach of statutory duty but are applicable only to the managed service. The vast majority of such directions have been addressed to PCTs to set up, amend and regulate their functions and powers regarding the contracted family health services; others have applied to NHS Trusts and their complaints procedures or provisions on delayed discharge.

CIRCULARS AND OFFICIAL PUBLICATIONS
The NHS is an enormous bureaucracy and vast quantities of communication are sent from the Department of Health to Trusts and other NHS bodies giving guidance and instruction on how they should carry out their work. This guidance may incorporate, for example, interpretation of statute law within the managed service, policy directions, reports of studies into matters of NHS importance, changes to financial arrangements or simply information on

current topics of importance. Mechanisms include a weekly *Chief Executive's Bulletin*, a numbered series of *Health Service Circulars*, updates from the Chief Medical Officer or other heads of professions and letters to chief executives and non-executive directors of NHS bodies. Similar arrangements prevail to manage the NHS services in Wales and Scotland, but the names and form may vary. A detailed account of these internal communications is outside the scope of this book but interested readers are referred to the websites listed at the end of this chapter.

CLINICAL GOVERNANCE

Introduced by the Health Act 1999 and strengthened by subsequent National Health Service Acts, the concept of clinical governance is now embedded in a wide range of mechanisms for maintaining the competence of health professionals and ensuring the quality of health services provided both within the NHS and in the private sector. The scope of clinical governance is too wide to encompass here but brief details are given below of arrangements for audit and inspection, patient safety and public involvement where they are likely to have an impact on pharmacists employed by, or providing services to, the NHS.

In the first few years of the 21st century, measures have been implemented to reform, tighten and rationalise initially the processes of hospital (NHS Trust) inspection and then to extend the standards to PCTs and to voluntary and private healthcare. Initially the Commission for Health Improvement implemented a programme of improvement in the NHS and the National Care Standards Commission worked along similar lines in the voluntary and private health sectors. Using powers under the Health and Social Care (Community Health and Standards) Act 2003, two new bodies took over these functions for England and Wales in April 2004. The former was replaced by the Commission for Health Care Audit and Inspection – now known as the Health Care Commission – and its functions were extended to include the audit activities of the Audit Commission, the registration and inspection of private and voluntary hospitals (formerly carried out by the National Care Standards Commission) and provision of an independent assessment of complaints relating to healthcare. In turn, the National Care Standards Commission was replaced by the Commission for Social Care Inspection, thus losing overview of healthcare to the Health Care Commission while expanding its remit to include complaints relating to local authority social services and other aspects of the efficiency and effectiveness of social care. The Health Care Commission is now the lead body for healthcare inspection and audit and, from August 2004, is adapting the Controls Assurance Standards developed for NHS hospital Trusts (see below) for wider use.

CONTROLS ASSURANCE STANDARDS

One component of clinical governance is the implementation of organisational risk management. In the managed service, this is effected through Controls

Assurance Standards, developed by the Controls Assurance Standards Unit. The unit published these standards annually, together with the reporting mechanisms that were part of the performance targets reviewed by Commission for Health Improvement. All NHS Trusts were required, in 2000, to have completed a baseline self-assessment of compliance with these standards, 'together with a prioritised action plan with clearly assigned responsibilities'.* In version 4 (October 2003), there were 21 standards covering a wide range of activities such as catering and food hygiene, fire safety, infection control and records management. Several are of direct relevance to pharmacists, in particular those related to medicines management, governance, health and safety, information management and technology (information governance), managing of purchase and supply, professional advice and services, and risk management. Within each area is a statement encapsulating the overall goal – the standard – followed by a series of criteria itemising the components that will contribute to achievement of that standard.

Boxes 26.1 and 26.2 set out the detail of the Standard for medicines management as an example. The standard includes a comprehensive list of those legal authorities, reports, circulars, internal instructions and professional requirements that underpin each criterion.

Under powers introduced by the 2003 Health and Social Care Act, a simplified regime of controls and performance targets (*Standards for Better Health*) passed responsibility for the development of future quality standards in healthcare to the Health Care Commission, supported by the successor to Controls Assurance Standards Unit, the Health Care Standards Unit. *Standards for Better Health* adopts a common framework for all matters related to performance as follows:

Standards are a means of describing the level of quality that healthcare organisations are expected to meet or aspire to. The performance of an organisation can be assessed against this level of quality.

Quality requirements will be established through the National Service Frameworks. They describe the care which clinicians and others will use to guide their practice.

Criteria are ways of demonstrating compliance with, and performance relevant to, a standard. They establish specific, objective expectations, drawing on such evidence and indicators as the Health Care Commission may establish.

Targets refer to defined levels of performance that are being aimed for, often with numerical and time dimensions. The purpose of a target is to provide incentives for improvement in the specific area covered by the target over a particular time frame.

Benchmarks are used as comparators to compare performance between similar organisations or systems.

---

* Dean B. (2001) Controls assurance: implications for pharmacists. *Pharmacy in Practice* April: 89–90

Box 26.1 Example of a Controls Assurance Standard: Medicines Management

Standard

The organisation handles medicines safely and securely, in accordance with legislative requirements and best practice

Overview of standard and key references

Includes, for example, the Duthie Report, relevant Health Service Circulars and Executive Letters, links to legislation websites, white papers, published reports with appropriate weblinks

Criterion 1: Board level responsibility for the safe and secure handling of medicines is clearly defined and there are clear lines of accountability throughout the organisation, leading to the Board

Criterion 2: Suitable controls are in place, which ensure that the principles of the Duthie Report are met

Criterion 3: Medicines are stored in a safe and secure manner

Criterion 4: The organisation conforms to Regulation 5 (1) of the NHS (Charges for Drugs and Appliances) Regulations 2000 (as amended)

Criterion 5: Unlicensed aseptic dispensing in hospital pharmacies complies with EL (97) 52, and licensable activities are covered by a manufacturing 'specials' licence

Criterion 6: Prescription, supply and administration conform to the requirements of the relevant legislation. Prescription, supply and administration of medicines is undertaken only by appropriately qualified, competent staff

Criterion 7: The prescribing, supply, administration, safe custody and destruction of controlled drugs complies with appropriate legislation

Criterion 8: All medicines no longer required are destroyed or otherwise disposed of in accordance with safety, legal and environmental requirements

Criterion 9: The supply of medicines for clinical trials is undertaken in accordance with relevant legislation and best practice guidelines

Criterion 10: The organisation reports adverse incidents involving medicinal products and devices to the relevant agency, and appropriately manages any subsequent required action

Criterion 11: Supervision of pharmaceutical dispensing processes is undertaken in accordance with relevant legislation and professional standards

Criterion 12: The risk management process contained within the risk management standard is applied to the safe and secure handling of medicines

Criterion 13: All healthcare staff involved with medicines undertake continuing professional development to ensure that there are safe and secure handling processes in place

Criterion 14: The organisation, through the Chief Pharmacist, has access to up-to-date legislation and guidance relating to the safe and secure handling of medicines

contd

Box 26.1 *continued*

Criterion 15: Adequate resources support the safe and secure handling of medicines

Criterion 16: Key indicators capable of showing improvements in the safe and secure handling of medicines and the management of associated risk are used at all levels of the organisation, including the Board, and the efficacy and usefulness of the indicators are reviewed regularly

Criterion 17: The system in place for the safe and secure handling of medicines, including risk management arrangements, is monitored and reviewed by management and the Board in order to make improvements to the system

Criterion 18: The Board seeks independent assurance that an appropriate and effective system for the safe and secure handling of medicines is in place and that the necessary level of controls and monitoring are being implemented

---

Rev 04 (October 2003) Crown copyright.

The standards are organised into seven 'domains': safety, clinical and cost effectiveness, governance, patient focus, accessible and responsive care, care environment and amenities, and public health.

PATIENT SAFETY

In 2001, the National Patient Safety Agency was established to develop and deliver a programme for healthcare providers to improve the safety and quality of care through reporting, analysing and learning from adverse incidents involving NHS patients. This process is now well advanced with anonymous reporting of patient safety incidents to the agency from NHS Trusts.

PATIENT AND PUBLIC INVOLVEMENT

The 2003 Health and Social Care Act set up the Commission for Patient and Public Involvement in Health; it was established in January 2003 but it is set to be abolished following the Arm's Length Bodies review in July 2004 (see above p. 364). In addition, local groups initially called Patient and Public Involvement Forums, later just Patient Forums, have been established in each Trust to 'watch over the quality of local healthcare'. In relation to complaints (and general advice), each Trust has been required since September 2003 to set up a Patients Advice and Liaison Service (PALS) which, in turn, makes use of an Independent Complaints Advocacy Service. The latter aims to secure consistent national standards and performance indicators for the handling of complaints.

PRISON HEALTH SERVICES

The Home Office generally administers prisons and the Home Office used to purchase health services within prisons from a variety of NHS and private providers. From April 2004, responsibility for healthcare services transfers

Box 26.2   Details of a single criterion: Criterion 1

Criterion 1: Board level responsibility for the safe and secure handling of medicines is clearly defined and there are clear lines of accountability throughout the organisation, leading to the Board.

Information

Source

- NHS Executive (1999) Clinical Governance in the New NHS. HSC 1999/065 1999
- NHS Executive (1999) Governance in the New NHS. Controls Assurance Statements 1999/2000 Risk Management and Organisational Controls. HSC 1999/123 1999
- Standards Australia (1999) Risk Management AS/NZS 4360: 1999 Standards Association of Australia, Strathfield NSW

Guidance

The Chief Executive of the organisation has the overall statutory responsibility for the safe and secure handling of medicines. The Chief Pharmacist should be responsible for ensuring that systems are in place to appropriately address all aspects of safe and secure handling of medicines and report directly to the Chief Executive for this purpose across the whole of the organisation. The organisation's commitment to the safe and secure handling of medicines should be clearly signalled.

Clear lines of accountability for the Safe and Secure Handling of Medicines throughout the organisation should be established; these should define the relationships between the Trust Board, the Risk Management Committee, Clinical Governance Committee, Pharmacy services and other relevant groups.

Examples of Verification

- Accountability arrangements chart
- Minutes of the Risk Management Committee
- Board minutes
- A strategy for medicines use, within the organisation, has been approved by the Board, reviewed and reported annually
- Terms of reference for any medicines management committee required
- Job description of the Chief Pharmacist

Links with other standards

All standards (generic criterion)

Rev 04 (October 2003) Crown Copyright

gradually to PCTs, a process planned to be complete by April 2006. These health services are then likely to be subject to the same legislation and clinical governance arrangements as apply to other NHS services.

HEALTH SERVICES IN THE ARMED FORCES

Health services for the armed forces are the responsibility of the Ministry of Defence. In the *Defence Health Programme for 2003–2007*, a commitment was made to ensure that the nature and quality of healthcare services provided met the specific needs of the military population to defined standards, at least to the level of those in the NHS.

CONTRACTED NATIONAL HEALTH SERVICE PHARMACEUTICAL SERVICES (COMMUNITY PHARMACY SERVICES): PROVISION OF PHARMACEUTICAL SERVICES

At the time of going to press (January 2005), the arrangements for the provision of NHS pharmaceutical services (or the community pharmacy contract) were undergoing a radical revision. Key proposals are to change the procedures for approving applications for inclusion in the pharmaceutical list and to change the content of the contract itself. The proposed revisions at this stage appear in Appendix 17 and are expected to commence, in stages, from April 2005. Readers are advised to check the websites given at the end of this chapter and in Appendix 17 for details. Changes to the contract are also under review in both Wales and Scotland and will differ from England. The account below relates to the arrangements in England at the time of going to press; new arrangements are likely to build on these.

The arrangements for the provision of pharmaceutical services are in the National Health Service (Pharmaceutical Services) Regulations 1992 (SI 1992 No.662). These incorporate, among other things, provisions to enable any person to receive such drugs, medicines and appliances as are ordered and include the terms of service for chemists. (The term 'chemist' is mainly historic, but as it is included in the regulations, the term will be used throughout this section. It is understood that the new contractual framework may use the term 'pharmacy' if this can readily be amended with the other legislative changes.)

Each PCT is required to prepare a list, a pharmaceutical list of the names and addresses together with the services provided, of all those chemists who have undertaken to provide pharmaceutical services in the area (reg.4). Any chemist who wishes to be included in the list must apply to the PCT in the prescribed form. Other than for a minor relocation of an existing pharmacy, or the transfer of ownership, the application is only granted if the PCT is satisfied that a service is necessary or it is desirable to grant the application in order to provide in its locality adequate pharmaceutical services (reg.4) (proposals for change appear in Appendix 17). The PCT must remove from the list the name of any chemist who has died or has ceased to be a chemist. Provision is made for representatives of a deceased chemist who comply with the provisions of the Medicines Act (s.71) (Chapter 5) and who agree to be bound by the terms of service to remain on the list (reg.17). If a chemist fails to provide pharmaceutical services over a period of six months, the PCT may remove the chemist's name from the list. The chemist must, however, be given 28 days' notice of the intention, and s/he must be given the opportunity to make representations. In addition, the Local Pharmaceutical Committee must be consulted (reg.17).

THE *DRUG TARIFF*

The *Drug Tariff*, compiled and published by the Secretary of State, includes (reg.18):

1   the list of appliances approved by the Secretary of State;
2   the list of chemical reagents approved by the Secretary of State;
3   the list of drugs approved by the Secretary of State;
4   the prices on the basis of which the payment for drugs and appliances ordinarily supplied is to be calculated;
5   the method of calculating the payment for drugs not mentioned in the *Drug Tariff*;
6   the method of calculating the payment for containers and medicine measures;
7   the dispensing or other fees payable in respect of the supply of drugs and appliances and other supplemental services;
8   arrangements for claiming fees, allowances and remuneration for the provision of pharmaceutical services; and
9   the method by which a claim may be made for compensation for financial loss in respect of oxygen equipment.

CHEMISTS' TERMS OF SERVICE

The basic requirements of the chemists' terms of service are set out in Schedule 2, Part II, of the 1992 Regulations as follows. A chemist must provide pharmaceutical services at the place or places of business and during the hours specified in his/her application form for contract. At each place of business, s/he is required to exhibit a notice, provided by the PCT, showing his/her hours of contract. At times when the business is not open, the contractor must exhibit, in such a manner as to be legible to the public from outside the premises, a notice listing the addresses of the other contractors in the pharmaceutical list, together with the hours of opening of their premises for the supply of medicines.

A chemist may supply pharmaceutical services only against a prescription form signed by a doctor or dentist, or a nurse prescriber (Chapters 8 and 9). Prescription is defined as a form normally supplied by a PCT (e.g. FP10 etc.). The chemist must supply any drugs except those called 'scheduled drugs' This list, introduced in 1985, is popularly known as the Black List and, as its name suggests, comprises medicines in certain categories which cannot be prescribed for supply against NHS prescriptions. The categories were originally indigestion remedies, laxatives, analgesics for mild to moderate pain, bitters and tonics, vitamins and the benzodiazepine tranquillisers and sedatives. The 'black list' is made under the National Health Service (General Medical Services Contracts) (Prescription of Drugs) Regulations 2004 (SI 2004 No.629) and the list now includes many other medicines, more recently, and subject to exceptions, so-called 'lifestyle' drugs such as Viagra (sildenafil) and Propecia (finasteride). Some of the scheduled drugs can be supplied in certain circumstances; for example, Viagra can be prescribed for men suffering from certain medical conditions. A full list of the drugs affected is also to be found in Part XVIIIA of the *Drug Tariff*.

All supplies must be made with reasonable promptness. However, when a doctor, by telephone or in writing, requests the chemist to dispense a medicine in a situation of urgency without a signed prescription, the chemist may dispense the medicine provided that the doctor is personally known to him/her and has undertaken to supply a signed prescription within 72 hours. Provision is made for the supply of some original packs, calendar packs etc., which are different in quantity from that ordered (e.g. sterile products, effervescent or hygroscopic tablets, oral contraceptives, etc.).

A chemist must supply medicines in a suitable container, which must be supplied free of charge. A suitable container for tablets or capsules means an airtight container made of glass, aluminium or rigid plastic. Cardboard containers must not be used for ointments or creams; they must be used only for foil or strip packed tablets. Eye, ear and nose drops must be supplied in a dropper bottle or with a separate dropper. When an oral liquid medicine is dispensed, a 5 ml measuring spoon or oral syringe must be provided unless the patient already possesses one.

A chemist must not give, promise or offer any person any gift or reward (whether by way of a share of or dividend on the profits of the business, or by way of discount, rebate or otherwise) as an inducement for prescriptions to be presented to a particular pharmacy.

The dispensing of medicines must be performed either by or under the direct supervision of a registered pharmaceutical chemist. The chemist must, on request of the PCT, give the name of the registered pharmaceutical chemist employed in the dispensing of medicines at any set of premises.

Subject to any regulations under the Act (s.77), no charge may be made for medicines or appliances under the NHS except those set out in the regulations. Currently most medicines (except oral contraceptives) and all trusses and appliances (except elastic hosiery and certain multiple charge items) carry a fee per item when ordered on an NHS prescription. Fees payable may be altered by regulation. All fees are collected by the chemist, who is later debited with them when his/her prescriptions are submitted for pricing.

In certain circumstances, no fees are payable, but to qualify for exemption the patient, their representative or, in the case of a young child, the parent or guardian or other representative must sign a declaration on the back of the prescription form. The patient or representative must also sign a declaration stating the amount which has been paid, if the patient is not exempt. The categories exempted from fees are of four types (full details are to be found in Part XVI of the *Drug Tariff*):

1   exemptions on age grounds;
2   holder of exemption certificate;
3   receiver of, or partner of, someone receiving state benefits; or
4   receiver of no-charge contraceptives.

AMENDMENTS TO THE CHEMISTS' TERMS OF SERVICE

The substantive 1992 Regulations have been significantly altered by almost annual amendments, the most important of which are outlined below.

In 1993, amending regulations (SI 1993 No.2451) made arrangements for the PCT to pay for additional professional services (new reg.16A), which became known as the professional allowance. This allowance depends upon the chemist dispensing a threshold number of prescriptions per month, publishing a practice leaflet, displaying health promotion leaflets as agreed between the PCT and the local pharmaceutical committees (LPCs) and, from 1996, the maintenance of patient medication records (1996 SI No 698).

Further amending regulations (SI 1995 No.644) provided for PCTs to determine the local service level requirement and rates of remuneration for out-of-hours service and professional advice to residential and nursing homes. This has to be done in consultation with LPCs. The regulations also clarified the distinction between normal opening hours and additional hours, which would fall to be negotiated locally. Normal working hours are defined as between 9 a.m. and 5.30 p.m. on working days (or 9 a.m. to 1 p.m. on early closing days: those working days when most shops in the neighbourhood are habitually closed after the hour of 1 p.m.). Working days are then further defined as 'Monday to Saturday excluding a Good Friday, Christmas Day or a bank holiday which falls on any such day' (Sch.2). Later regulations allowed PCTs to make arrangements for out-of-hours 'on-call' services from a chemist, subject to appropriate consultation and payment (SI 1999 No.696).

Further amendments to the chemists' terms of service (SI 1996 No.698) required the institution of a complaints procedure in every pharmacy, together with an obligation to give the procedure publicity and co-operate with the PCT in any investigations it may make following a complaint from a recipient of pharmaceutical services (para.10A and 10B). In 1999, as part of a concerted Government attack on fraud in the NHS, chemists were required to implement point-of-dispensing checks by asking patients or their representatives for evidence of their exemption (other than on the grounds of age) from paying prescription charges. If no such evidence is available, the chemist must endorse the prescription accordingly. Later regulations extended these arrangements to checking for evidence of exemption on the grounds of age (SI 1999 No.2563). A reward system for the detection of fraud was also introduced (*Health Service Circular* 1999/133 and SI 1999 No. 696) as was the power for responsible authorities to recover penalty fees from patients who evade charges (SI 1999 No.2794).

A series of amendments in 2001 facilitated the provision of 'electronic transmission of prescriptions' by amending the Prescription Only Medicines Order and the Terms of Service to allow the dispensing of prescriptions sent electronically and bearing electronic signatures from certain pilot sites (SIs 2001 No. 2887; No. 2888; No. 2889; No. 2890).

> These provisions have not been repealed but the Secretary of State withdrew consent at the end of the pilots. Proposals to change the law to allow prescriptions (other than controlled drugs) to be signed electronically were made in August 2004 and regulations came into force in April 2005 (see p. 99) to facilitate implementation of the new Community Pharmacy Contract (Appendix 17).

Regulations in 2002 (SI 2002 No. 551) extended the definition of nurse prescribers to include the extended formulary (independent) nurse prescribers, allowed the dispensing of their NHS prescriptions and added their formulary to the *Drug Tariff* (Part XVIIB).

In 2002, provisions for Local Pharmaceutical Services were introduced (SIs 2002 No. 888; No. 2016; No. 2861) followed by a series of internal NHS Directions in 2003. Also in 2003, the Terms of Service were amended to allow the dispensing of NHS prescriptions from supplementary nurse and pharmacist prescribers (SI 2003 No. 699) and to accommodate repeat dispensing arrangements (SI 2003 No. 1084).

The Terms of Service also include limited entry and inspection rights to members of a local Patients Forum (see below) (SI 2003 No. 2863).

DISCIPLINE COMMITTEES AND THE NATIONAL HEALTH SERVICE TRIBUNAL

Disciplinary arrangements for GPs, dentists and opticians do not now include referral to the NHS Tribunal (abolished by SI 2001No. 3744) but to the Family Health Services Appeal Authority (SI 2001 No. 3750), itself likely to be absorbed into the NHS Litigation Authority following the 'arm's length bodies review' (p. 364). The NHS Tribunal continues to have the power (SI 1996 No. 698) to suspend or declare unfit a chemist to prevent their involvement in the provision of pharmaceutical services. Moreover, arrangements are now in place to control the inclusion of GPs, dentists and opticians in the relevant practitioner lists maintained by PCTs.

Discipline (formerly Service) Committees and Tribunals under the NHS are governed by the National Health Service (Service Committees and Tribunal) Regulations 1992 (SI 1992 No.664). Amending regulations (SI 1996 No.703) required that complaints about practitioners (such as chemists) should be dealt with firstly at 'practice' (i.e. pharmacy) level and may only be considered by the health authority (as it then was) if this fails. These processes were termed Local Resolution and Independent Review, respectively. Reforms of the complaints procedures were still under consideration at the time of going to press although regulations to transfer the Independent Review stage to the Health Care Commission (2004 SI No 1768) came into force in July 2004.

Where a complaint is made by a patient, the PCT must ensure that an opportunity has been given to resolve the complaint through the above processes first. If, however, the complaint is withdrawn or abandoned by the patient and the PCT has information which it considers could amount to an allegation that a chemist has failed to comply with his/her terms of service, then disciplinary proceedings may be instituted. In such a case the PCT becomes the complainant and the matter is referred to another PCT for investigation (regs.4 and 5).

Every PCT is required to establish a Pharmaceutical Discipline Committee, which consists of a chairman, no more than three lay members appointed by the PCT and no more than three pharmacists appointed by the PCT from a list of nominees provided by the LPC. The chairman must be a solicitor or barrister appointed by the PCT and the lay members must not be, or have been, a doctor, dentist, pharmacist or optometrist (Sch.2). The PCT is also required to establish a Joint Discipline Committee consisting of a chairman as above and ten other persons, two of whom must be lay members appointed by the PCT, and two appointed by and from each of the respective professional discipline committees (Sch.2). Such a Committee would deal with matters involving, for example, a doctor and a pharmacist. When a PCT decides to refer a matter to the Pharmaceutical Discipline Committee, it must do so within 28 days of the allegation having ceased to be the subject of a complaint which is being investigated. If the matter has not been the subject of a complaint, the PCT must refer it within 13 weeks of the event which is the subject of the allegation (reg.6).

The procedure of the Pharmaceutical Discipline Committee is governed by the regulations (Sch.4). After the procedure has been followed, a report is prepared for the PCT, including details of material evidence given to it, its findings on all relevant questions of fact, its inferences, its reasons for drawing such inferences and its recommendations for action. The PCT, which must accept as conclusive the Discipline Committee's findings of facts and inferences, may determine to take the recommended action, to take no action or to take action other than that recommended in the report. In the last two cases, the PCT must give reasons for its decision. Where the PCT has determined that the chemist has failed to comply with any of his/her terms of service it may:

1   recover from the chemist an amount of money by way of deduction from his/her remuneration; or
2   warn the chemist to comply more closely with their terms of service in future.

All decisions have to be notified in writing to all parties, who have a right of appeal to the Secretary of State. The procedure for appeals is set out in the regulations (reg.9).

If the PCT, or any other person, considers that the continued inclusion of a chemist on the pharmaceutical list would be prejudicial to the efficiency of the service, it may make representations to that effect to the NHS Tribunal constituted under section 46 of the 1977 Act. The constitution of the NHS Tribunal, together with its procedure, is set out in the 1992 regulations (Part III).

LOCAL PHARMACEUTICAL COMMITTEES

The LPCs are recognised under the 1977 Act (s.44) as representative of the persons providing Part II pharmaceutical services in the locality of one or more PCTs. Those LPCs that have adopted the model constitution promulgated by the Pharmaceutical Services Negotiating Committee comprise 13 pharmacists elected or appointed by contractors in accordance with the 'Model Constitution'.

The constitution firstly sets aside places for the Company Chemists Association – a body representing nationally operating pharmacy multiples – and for any contractor providing services from more than five per cent of the premises on the pharmaceutical list or lists within the LPC area. The Company Chemists Association may then appoint members of the LPC in proportion to the number of businesses owned by association members in the LPC area, but such that the number of members appointed to the LPC does not exceed 40 per cent of the membership. A contractor owning more than five per cent of the businesses in the LPC area may appoint a member of the Committee and more in proportion to the businesses owned but not more than 40 percent of the available places. Remaining places are then filled by election from those pharmacies not already represented in this process. If a 'Co-op' business or businesses operate in the LPC area, then a further place is reserved for nomination by the Co-operative Pharmacy Technical Panel, which represents Co-op pharmacies nationally. Finally a further place is available for one pharmacist per PCT area if not represented by those already appointed or elected and a place for pharmacists engaged in providing Local Pharmaceutical Services (see above) in the area (if any).

Each Committee appoints its own secretary and the appointment has to be notified to the PCT and to the Pharmaceutical Services Negotiating Committee. The terms of office for members of the Committee is four years and the Committee has power of co-option for casual vacancies. A person ceases to be a member of the Committee if s/he ceases to be engaged in the section of the NHS which s/he represents. His/her seat must be declared vacant if s/he has been absent from three consecutive meetings of the Committee without reasonable cause.

The duties of an LPC include:

1   consultations with the PCT on such occasions and to such an extent as may be prescribed by the Secretary of State;
2   ensuring that the Committee conducts its affairs in accordance with accepted principles of good governance;

3   establishing effective liaison with other NHS bodies in the PCT(s) area;
4   appointing representatives to any body on which pharmaceutical representation is required;
5   advising any pharmacy contractor who needs help or assistance on NHS matters;
6   considering any complaint made by a pharmacy contractor against another pharmacy contractor carrying on a business in the area and involving any question of the efficiency of the pharmaceutical services;
7   making representations to the PCT and to the Pharmaceutical Services Negotiating Committee on matters of importance to pharmacy contractors;
8   making requests to the PCT(s) for such sums of money required to defray the Committee's administrative expenses from money available for remuneration of pharmacy contractors;
9   assisting in the formulations of bids for local funding;
10   ensuring transparency and equality of information and opportunity for all contractors in matters relating to the local purchasing of pharmaceutical services;
11   collaborating with the Pharmaceutical Services Negotiating Committee;
12   collaborating with other LPCs; and
13   responding to any request from a contractor for an enquiry into irregularities in the LPC's activities.

The Committee must prepare an annual report and accounts, and must circulate them to the electors in the area and to the Pharmaceutical Services Negotiating Committee.

PHARMACEUTICAL SERVICES NEGOTIATING COMMITTEE
The Pharmaceutical Services Negotiating Committee negotiates terms and conditions of service for pharmacy contractors. The Committee is composed of 31 persons as follows: 14 members elected on a regional basis from England, one member from Wales, five members from the board of the National Pharmaceutical Association, seven members from the Company Chemists Association, three members from the Association of Independent Multiple Pharmacies and one representative nominated by the Co-operative Pharmacy Technical Panel. The Pharmaceutical Services Negotiating Committee has four subcommittees concerned with contract planning; marketing and public affairs; resource development and finance; and finally strategic planning and policy. The Pharmaceutical Services Negotiating Committee has also set up the National Prescription Research Centre, which carries out either random or routine checking and special checks at the request of a contractor, of the pricing of prescriptions by the Prescription Pricing Authority.

THE PRESCRIPTION PRICING AUTHORITY
The Prescription Pricing Authority is a Special Health Authority established under the 1977 Act to calculate and make payments to pharmacy and

appliance contractors. It also produces prescribing and costs information for the NHS, administers a range of health benefits such as maternity and pre-payment exemption, certifies the checking of these exemptions, and produces the *Drug Tariff* (see below). Under the 2004 *Arm's Length Review* (see above, p. 364), the Prescription Pricing Authority will be absorbed within the remit of the NHS Business Services Authority. It consists of eight members, of whom one must be a pharmacist providing pharmaceutical services under the Act (SI 1990 No.1718).

NATIONAL HEALTH SERVICE AUDIT, INSPECTION, PATIENT SAFETY AND
PUBLIC INVOLVEMENT

As providers of NHS services, pharmacy contractors are also expected to co-operate with a range of NHS governance measures, described very briefly here. The powers of the Health Care Commission (see pp. 363 and 368) do not extend directly to pharmacy contractors but the inspection regimes for PCTs include performance targets for their management of pharmacy contractors. The Commission for Social Care Inspections also has no direct remit for pharmacy inspection but monitors the services in care homes, including the arrangements for the provision of medicines to residents. The local authority can also take an interest in the management of local health services through the Overview and Scrutiny Committees, given an additional health-care scrutiny function in 2003 (SI 2002 No. 3048). The new Community Pharmacy Contract is expected to include increased clinical governance measures, including a mandatory process of anonymous reporting of errors to the National Patient Safety Agency. Local reporting operations are in place in some PCTs but, at present, there is no legal obligation in the Terms of Service to provide such information to PCTs. Community Health Councils were abolished at the end of 2003. In their place, Patients Forums and PALS services (see above, p. 371) will assist PCTs to manage complaints about contracted NHS services.

Note that similar governance arrangements are in place in Wales and Scotland but the names of bodies, and their structure and operation, will vary.

Wales

NATIONAL HEALTH SERVICE ORGANISATION

In Wales, secondary legislation (i.e. that which is made under enabling powers set out in an Act) on health is made by the National Assembly for Wales (Fig. 26.2). The Welsh Assembly Government then executes Assembly policies; on health and social care, through NHS Wales. The Welsh Pharmaceutical Committee was set up in 2000 to provide professional advice to the National Assembly and the Government but, owing to changes in all the professional advisory structures in Wales, the membership and constitution were under review at the time of going to press. In 2000 the Welsh Pharmaceutical Committee roles were to:

- advise the First Secretary and the Assembly Minister for Health and Social Services on pharmaceutical services in Wales;
- implement an annual work programme agreed between the Director of the NHS Directorate, Chief Pharmaceutical Adviser and the Chairman on behalf of the Committee;
- receive for comment and advice, documents or issues referred to it by the National Assembly for Wales;
- bring to the attention of the First Secretary and the Assembly Minister for Health and Social Care, issues concerning the maintenance and development of health services and health issues in Wales generally;
- produce an annual report.

Figure 26.2 NHS structure in Wales

NHS Wales has three regional offices which co-ordinate and manage the performance of local health boards and NHS Trusts. At the time of writing there were 22 local health boards and 15 NHS Trusts. The local health boards share common boundaries with local government authority areas to facilitate a partnership approach to planning healthcare and social care. The local health boards commission health services and are supported by the Business Service Centre, which, amongst other functions, manages payments for pharmacy contractor services. There is a place for a pharmacist on each local health board. Responsibility for inspection and investigation of health lies with Health Inspectorate Wales, an 'arm's length body' answerable directly to the Welsh Permanent Secretary. In October 2004, NHS Wales published a proposal for a common framework of healthcare quality and safety standards across Wales. Community Health Councils represent the patient's voice in healthcare and may inspect both primary and secondary care establishments.

PHARMACY ORGANISATION

Negotiation on reimbursement and national service payments are undertaken by Community Pharmacy Wales, which is separate from but has close links to the Pharmaceutical Services Negotiating Committee (see above, p. 380). The status of Community Pharmacy Wales as a negotiating body for Welsh pharmacy contractors was legally established in April 2004; full details of its constitution and activities are available on the relevant website at the end of this chapter. Wales is also working on changes to the NHS community pharmacy contract (Appendix 17) and this is likely to differ from similar contracts in both Scotland and England. Complaints must be dealt with within a time frame determined by the relevant local authority and the prescription levies in Wales now differ from England and Scotland. Other differences will emerge in the future and readers are advised to check the websites for Community Pharmacy Wales and NHS Wales for current information.

Scotland

NATIONAL HEALTH SERVICE ORGANISATION

Scotland has had its own Parliament since July 1999 and it has powers to make primary legislation on healthcare. The NHS in Scotland has always operated separately from the service in England and Wales. Although the principal Act remains the National Health Service (Scotland) Act 1978, this has now been modified by the NHS Reform (Scotland) Act 2004. NHS Scotland policy is developed and administered through the Scottish Executive Health Department via 15 'unified' NHS Boards, thus completing the merging of purchaser/provider functions separated by the UK-wide 1990 Act (see above and Fig. 26.3). The former Acute Trusts and PCTs have become operating divisions of these NHS Boards, which have representation from the local authorities to improve management of health and social care. The functions of the NHS Boards include the planning and commissioning of healthcare services and the management of pharmacy contracts. The Scottish Health Council monitors the performance of the NHS Boards and promotes public involvement in healthcare. Former Local Health Care Co-operatives have evolved into Community Health Partnerships, which report to the NHS unified Boards and focus on planning and provision of local health services. Each Community Health Partnership has on its committee a place for a registered pharmacist whose name is included in, or who is fully or substantially employed by a person or body whose name is included in, a

Figure 26.3 NHS structure in Scotland

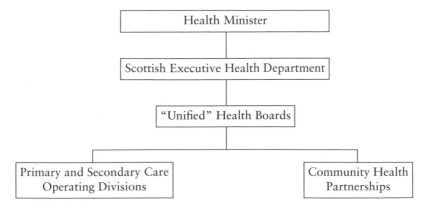

pharmaceutical list prepared by an NHS Board. Most NHS Boards have the services of a pharmacist, called variously a 'consultant' or 'specialist' in pharmaceutical public health, who provides strategic pharmacy advice to the NHS Board. In addition all NHS Boards have an *Area Pharmaceutical Committee*. These Committees comprise pharmacists who work in both the hospital and community sectors and are representative of the professionals working in the area.

The Practitioner Services Division of NHS National Services Scotland manages payments for pharmacy contractors. Responsibility for inspection and audit of healthcare lies with the NHS Quality Improvement Scotland. Local Health Councils represent the patient's voice in healthcare and may inspect both primary and secondary care establishments.

PHARMACY ORGANISATION

Practitioner Services – Pharmacy deal with payments for NHS prescriptions in Scotland, which has a separate *Drug Tariff* from England and Wales. Negotiations on reimbursement and national service payments are undertaken by the *Scottish Pharmaceutical General Council*. This comprises 42 representatives elected by the 15 Area Pharmacy Contractors Committees, together with two representatives elected by the Company Chemists Association and one elected by the Co-operative societies. In addition, there are three pharmacists appointed by the Council after consultation with the Royal Pharmaceutical Society's Scottish Executive, the Scottish Pharmaceutical Federation and the Pharmaceutical Contractors Committee in Northern Ireland. (The NHS Terms of Service adopted by the Northern Ireland chemists are, with minor amendments, those agreed in Scotland.)

Area Pharmacy Contractor Committees have been set up in each of the 15 NHS Board areas. Their functions include negotiating with their own Board the local service agreements for the chemists in the area. In addition, they establish liaison with other organisations within the NHS and elect representatives to the Scottish Pharmaceutical General Council. The committees have power to co-opt any pharmacist who in their opinion could assist the work of the committee.

The Terms of Service for chemists in Scotland are laid down in the National Health Service (Pharmaceutical Services) (Scotland) Regulations [SI 1995 No.414 (s.28), as amended; see Appendix 19]. Amendments include adoption of procedures for the handling of complaints and the establishment of discipline committees [SIs 1996 No.840 (s.95); 1996 No.938 (s.103)], the adoption of point-of-dispensing checks for evidence of exemption [SI 1998 No.3031 (s.174)] and powers to exclude from the pharmaceutical list pharmacists who are subject to fraud enquiries (SI 2004 No. 39). The NHS Community Pharmacy Contract in Scotland is also under review and the precise structure and terms are likely to differ from the NHS dispensing contracts in Wales and England (Appendix 17). Readers are advised to refer to the Scottish Pharmaceutical General Council website for current information.

Arrangements for disciplinary service committees and tribunals are now covered by SI 2004 No.38.

Summary

- The statutory framework for NHS services differs between England, Scotland and Wales, although the objectives are similar.
- The NHS is a mixed market of commissioning and provision of services by a range of health service bodies, overseen by civil service departments reporting to governments.
- NHS Trusts, mostly hospitals, provide NHS secondary care in England and Wales; in Scotland, apart from Lanarkshire, the provision of secondary care comes under the Acute Operational Division of the NHS Board.
- PCTs in England and Wales secure the provision of primary care, including pharmaceutical services, through contracts with local owners of pharmacies; in Scotland, this activity has passed to the Primary Care Operational Division of the NHS Board.
- These NHS contracts are limited in number and impose numerous conditions on the chemist, as set out in the NHS chemists' Terms of Service.
- Specifications for the amount and conditions which apply to payments under the NHS chemists' Terms of Service are set out in the *Drug Tariff*.
- Negotiations for payments take place nationally through the Pharmaceutical Services Negotiating Committee, Community Pharmacy Wales or the Scottish Pharmaceutical General Council and locally through the Local Pharmaceutical Committees or Area Pharmacy Contractor Committees.
- The public interest in the NHS is represented by Patients Forums and PALS in England, Community Health Councils in Wales and Local Health Councils in Scotland.

Further reading

Arnison, S. and Alexandra, E. (2003) Understanding the NHS in Scotland. *Pharm J* 271: 149.
Craig, G. (2003) Understanding the NHS in England. *Pharm J* 271: 121.
Merrills J. and Fisher J. (1997) *Pharmacy Law and Practice*, 2nd edn. Blackwell Scientific, Oxford.
Montgomery, J. (2002) *Health Care Law*, 3rd edn. Oxford University Press, Oxford.
Parry, P. (2003) Understanding the NHS in Wales. *Pharm J* 271: 177.

Websites

All legislation: http://www.hmso.gov.uk/stat.htm
Health Service Circulars in England: http://tap.ccta.gov.uk/doh/coin4.nsf/

NHS England (includes National Service Frameworks (NSFs): http://www.dh.gov.uk/
NHS UK gateway: http://www.nhs.uk
Checklist of important Health circulars: www.pharman.co.uk
Bower, A. Review of circulars and official publications: www.pharmj.com/Hospital/Editorial
Pharmaceutical Services Negotiating Committee: http://www.psnc.org.uk
Prescription Pricing Authority: http://www.ppa.org.uk/index.htm
Commission for Health Care Audit and Inspection (Health Commission):
      http://www.chai.org.uk
Commission for Social Care Inspection: http://csci.org.uk
National Institute for Clinical Excellence: http://www.nice.org.uk
Health Care Standards Unit: http://hcsu.org.uk
National Patient Safety Agency: http://www.npsa.nhs.uk
Commission for Patient and Public Involvement in Health: http://www.cppih.org
Prison Health Services: information on Department of Health website Ministry of Defence:
      http://www.mod.uk
NHS Scotland: http://www.show.scot.nhs.uk/
NHS Wales: http://www.wales.gov.uk/ (click on policy and information)
Community Pharmacy Wales: http://www.cpwales.org.uk
Scottish Pharmaceutical General Council: http://www.spgc.org.uk
Summary of English, Welsh and Scottish health circulars: http://www.pharman.co.uk

CHAPTER TWENTY-SEVEN

Legal decisions affecting pharmacy

The decisions in important cases in the courts which have directly affected pharmacy are brought together in this chapter. Although Acts of Parliament take precedence over all other law, the meaning of any statute is subject to interpretation by the courts. Consequently, most of the cases outlined here are about the meaning of terms, or of individual words, used in the statutes. Some arise from the application of a statute in particular circumstances. A few are concerned with general principles. *Jenkin* v. *The Pharmaceutical Society* and *The Pharmaceutical Society* v. *Dickson* deal with the extent of the Society's powers under its Charter; the authority of the Statutory Committee is considered in *Re Lawson*; while *The Pharmaceutical Society* v. *Boots Cash Chemists (Southern) Ltd* has a bearing on the law of contract.

The cases are set out individually, or in groups, under headings which indicate the subject or the point at issue. Where appropriate, some explanatory comment is added. Table 27.1 lists the cases together with references to the pages on which the relevant points at issue are explained.

Table 27.1 Decisions in important cases in the courts which have directly affected pharmacy

Topic	Cases	Discussed on page
Meaning of *acting in accordance with the directions of a practitioner*	Roberts v. Coombs (1949)	389
Meaning of *by a doctor or dentist to a patient of his*	*Pharmaceutical Society* v. *Wright* (1981)	390
Meaning of *person*	*Pharmaceutical Society* v. *L & P Supply Association Ltd* (1880)	390
Meaning of *personal control*	*Hygienic Stores Ltd* v. *Coombes* (1937)	391
Powers of the Royal Pharmaceutical Society	*Jenkin* v. *Pharmaceutical Society of Great Britain* (1921)	392
	Pharmaceutical Society v. *Dickson* (1968)	393
The meaning of *poison*	Three cases under the Pharmacy Act 1868	394
Meaning of *sale by way of wholesale dealing*	Oxford v. Sanger (1964)	395
Meaning of *shop*	Greenwood v. Whelan (1966)	395
Functions of the Statutory Committee	Re Lawson (1941)	396
Meaning of *supervision*	*Roberts* v. *Littlewoods Mail Order Stores Ltd* (1943)	396
	Pharmaceutical Society v. *Boots Cash Chemists (Southern) Ltd* (1953)	397
	R v. *Family Health Services Appeal Authority, ex parte Elmfield Drugs Ltd, Selles Dispensing Chemists Ltd, E Moss (Chemists) Ltd* (1998)	397
Use of titles and descriptions	*Norris* v. *Weeks* (1970)	398
Meaning of *a sample* under the Medicines Act 1968	Mistry v. Norris (1985)	399
Sale of Prescription Only Medicine: offence of strict liability	*Pharmaceutical Society* v. *Storkwain Ltd* (1986)	399

Table 27.1 *contd*

Topic	Cases	Discussed on page
Is dispensing a medicine on a National Health Service prescription a *sale*?	*Appleby* v. *Sleep* (1968)	400
Importation of medicinal products from the European Community	R v. *Royal Pharmaceutical Society of Great Britain, ex parte Association of Pharmaceutical Importers and others* (1989)	400
Sale of prescription data: breach of confidentiality?	R v. *Department of Health, ex parte Source Informatics Ltd* (2000)	401

The meaning of 'acting in accordance with the directions of a practitioner'

Roberts v. Coombs *(1949)*

The Penicillin Act 1947 reads:

> . . .no person shall sell or otherwise supply any substance to which this Act applies or any preparation of which any such substance is an ingredient or part unless (a) he is a duly qualified medical practitioner, a registered dental practitioner or a registered veterinary surgeon, or a person acting in accordance with the directions of any such practitioner or surgeon, and the substance or preparation is sold or supplied for the purposes of treatment by or in accordance with the directions of that practitioner or surgeon; or (b) he is a registered pharmacist or an authorised seller of poisons, and the substance or preparation is sold or supplied under the authority of a prescription signed and dated by any such practitioner or surgeon as aforesaid.

A shopkeeper, who was not an authorised seller, sold penicillin ointment to customers who presented prescriptions signed and dated by a medical practitioner. The shopkeeper was charged with selling ointment containing penicillin contrary to section 1(1) of the Act as he was not one of the qualified persons mentioned in that subsection. The magistrates dismissed the summonses on the grounds that, although the shopkeeper was not a practitioner, he was a person acting in accordance with the directions of a duly qualified medical practitioner.

On appeal to the High Court it was held that *a person acting in accordance with any such practitioner or surgeon* was a person in the employment of a doctor or in some way actually under the direct orders of the doctor. A prescription signed and dated by a medical practitioner could be made up only by a registered pharmacist or an authorised seller of poisons.
[1949] 2 All ER 37; *Pharm J* 14 May 1949 p. 356.

Comment. The Penicillin Act 1947 was later replaced by the Therapeutic Substances Act 1956. The wording was subsequently retained in section 58(2)(b) of the Medicines Act 1968, which also repealed the 1956 Act.

The meaning of 'by a doctor or dentist to a patient of his' under the Medicines Act 1968

Pharmaceutical Society v. Wright *(1981)*

The Medicines Act requires that no person shall sell a Prescription Only Medicine except in accordance with a prescription given by an appropriate practitioner. However, the Act provides that this provision does not apply to the sale or supply of a medicinal product to a patient of his/hers by a doctor or dentist who is an appropriate practitioner.

Once a week, Dr Wright ran a slimming clinic and those attending were given a medicinal product which was on the Prescription Only List. Many of the persons attending the clinic were patients of other doctors in the town and only attended the clinic, which was supervised by a nurse, for slimming purposes. The issue turned upon whether or not there was a doctor/patient relationship between the attendees and Dr Wright.

Mr Justice Bingham said:

> . . .if a doctor acting as such, treats or gives advice to a person and assumes responsibility for that treatment or advice, that person may very well be his patient. . .in determining whether the relationship does exist it is not. . .of primary importance whether the person is a patient of another doctor as well nor whether the treatment or advice is given by the doctor's staff under his supervision rather than the doctor himself. Nor. . .whether the relationship is a short-lived or long-lived. Nor. . .need it be of primary importance whether the doctor takes less care in giving the advice or treatment than he should. . .

(1981) Unreported.

Comment. In dismissing the appeal brought by the Society, Lord Donaldson, who sat with Mr Justice Bingham, said that it was for the Society to prove there was no doctor/patient relationship not for Dr Wright to prove there was.

The meaning of 'person'

Pharmaceutical Society of Great Britain v. London and Provincial Supply Association Ltd *(1880)*

The Pharmacy Act 1868 (s.1) provided:

> From and after 31 December, 1868 it shall be unlawful for any person to sell or keep open shop for retailing. . .poisons. . .unless such person shall be a pharmaceutical chemist, a chemist and druggist. . .and be registered under this Act. . .

Section 15 provided penalties for offences under section 1.

A company had sold poisons by retail from its shop. The Society took legal proceedings against the company, contending that a body corporate was a 'person' in law and that section 1 applied to it. The High Court had supported that view but the Court of Appeal had not.

On appeal to the House of Lords, it was held that in the context of the Act the word *person* in sections 1 and 15 meant a natural person and did not include a body corporate.
5 App. Cases 857; *Pharm J* 31 July 1880 p. 83.

Comment. This decision enabled a company to keep open shop for the sale of poisons provided the other conditions in the Act were met. The Poisons and Pharmacy Act 1908 and subsequent statutes took account of the decision and required a body corporate to appoint a superintendent to conduct and manage the keeping, retailing and dispensing of poisons.

The meaning of 'personal control'

Hygienic Stores Ltd *v.* Coombes *(1937)*

The Pharmacy and Poisons Act 1933 (s.9) reads:

> A body corporate carrying on a business which comprises the retail sale of drugs shall be an authorised seller of poisons if the following conditions are complied with: (a) the business must, so far as concerns the keeping, retailing, dispensing and compounding of poisons, be under the management of a superintendent who must be a registered pharmacist. . .and; (b) in each set of premises the business must, so far as concerns the retail sale of drugs, if not under the personal control of the superintendent, be carried on subject to the direction of the superintendent, under the personal control of a manager or assistant who is a registered pharmacist.

Section 18(1) provided, amongst other things, that it is unlawful for any person to sell poisons in Part I of the Poisons List unless s/he is an authorised seller of poisons.

A company carried on retail business at 16 shops. At three of the shops, pharmacists were employed, but at one of these the pharmacist did not attend full time. At the other 13 shops, where there were no pharmacists, proprietary medicines and some non-poisonous drugs were sold. The company was prosecuted under section 18(1) of the Act in respect of the sale of Part I poisons at two of the pharmacies. The magistrates found the case proved in that the company was not an authorised seller of poisons. The medicines sold at the 13 shops were drugs. There were no pharmacists in personal control of those shops, and at one of the pharmacies there was a pharmacist present only for part of the time the business was open. Consequently, the company did not fulfil the requirements for an authorised seller of poisons laid down in section 9. On appeal to the High Court, the magistrates' decision was upheld and the appeal by the company dismissed.
[1938] 1 All ER 63; *Pharm J* 18 December 1937 p. 664.

Comment. The Pharmacy and Poisons Act 1933 (s.9) has been replaced by the Medicines Act 1968 (s.71) (Chapter 5). The requirements for bodies corporate remains unchanged. The meaning of *personal control* has also been considered by the Statutory Committee of the Royal Pharmaceutical Society (Chapter 24).

The powers of the Royal Pharmaceutical Society

Jenkin v. Pharmaceutical Society of Great Britain (1921)

The Society's Charter of Incorporation 1843 had, as one of its objects, *the protection of those who carry on the business of chemists and druggists.*

In 1919, the Council of the Society took part in promoting an Industrial Council for the drug trade. The objects of the proposed body included, among others, the regulation of wages, hours and working conditions, and of production and employment. Mr Jenkin, who was a member of the Society and, prior to the case, a member of the Council of the Society, sought an injunction in the High Court (Chancery Division) to prevent the Society from sponsoring the Industrial Council on the grounds that the functions proposed were not within the scope of the Society's powers.

It was held by the Court that a member was entitled to obtain an injunction restraining the commission of acts outside the scope of the Charter. The Society could not carry on a business of general insurance, even though limited to members, as it would not benefit members as a whole. Nor could it legalise by its Charter a combination in restraint of trade and so convert itself into a trade union as defined in the Trade Union Act 1876 (s.16).

The Court declared that it was not within the power or purposes of the Society to take part in, or expend any of its funds in the formation, establishment, maintenance or work of, the Industrial Council, or to undertake or perform the following matters:

1 to regulate the hours of business of members of the Society;
2 to regulate the wages and conditions of employment as between masters and their employees who were members of the Society;
3 to regulate the prices at which members should sell their goods; or
4 to insure and to effect insurance of members of the Society against errors, neglect and misconduct of employees, and against fire, burglary, damage to plate glass and generally against insurable risks.

[1921] 1 Ch 392; *Pharm J* 23 October 1920 p. 386; *Pharm J* 30 October 1920 p. 405.

Comment. As a result of this decision a separate body, the Retail Pharmacists' Union (later called the National Pharmaceutical Association), was established to carry out various functions including those denied to the Society. No action was taken by the Society to carry on any of the other activities which had been proposed for the Industrial Council and which had not been declared to be outside the Society's powers. They were:

1 the provision and maintenance of an employment register and a register of unsatisfactory employees;
2 the auditing of accounts, the collection of debts and the taking of stock for its members;

3   the provision and supply of information to the commercial standing of persons and firms with whom members of the Society wish to transact business; and
4   the provision of legal advice to members.

In the Supplemental Charter of 1953 (Chapter 22), the objects of the Society were amended. The wording 'the protection of those who carry on the business of chemists and druggists' was replaced by 'to maintain the honour and safeguard and promote the interests of the members in the exercise of the profession of pharmacy'.

In the *Dickson* case (see below), reference was made to the decision in the *Jenkin* case to the change of emphasis in the chartered objects of the Society from *business* to *profession*.

Pharmaceutical Society of Great Britain v. Dickson (1968)

This was an appeal by the Society to the House of Lords against an Order of the Court of Appeal ([1967] All ER 558; *Pharm J* 4 February 1967 p. 113), which upheld a judgment of the High Court (Chancery Division) ([1966] 3 All ER 404; *Pharm J* 2 July 1966 p. 22).

The background to the case was as follows. Arising out of a recommendation of the Report on the General Practice of Pharmacy (*Pharm J* 20 April 1963), a motion was put to the Annual General Meeting of the Pharmaceutical Society in 1965 in the following terms:

New pharmacies should be situated only in premises which are physically distinct, and should be devoted solely to:

(i)   professional services, as defined,
(ii) non-professional services, as defined. . .and
(iii) such other services as may be approved by the Council; and the range of services as may be approved by the Council; and the range of services in existing pharmacies, or in pharmacy departments of larger establishments should not be extended beyond the present limits except as approved by the Council.

Owing to the large attendance at the Annual General Meeting, no vote could be taken and a Special General Meeting to consider the recommendation was held at the Royal Albert Hall on 25 July 1965. Mr R. C. M. Dickson (a director of Boots Pure Drug Co. Ltd) sought an injunction to restrain the holding of the meeting. He also claimed that the motion:

1   was outside the scope of the Society's powers; and
2   if implemented, would be a restraint upon trade.

Application for an injunction was refused by the High Court, an undertaking being given by the Society that the motion would not be made effective until after the judgment in the action to determine whether or not the object of the motion was within the Society's powers. At the Albert Hall meeting, a motion supporting the recommendation was passed by 5020 votes to 1336.

The order of the High Court declared:

> That it is not within the powers, purposes or objects of the Pharmaceutical Society of Great Britain. . .to enforce or carry out or attempt to enforce or carry out the provisions of the motion. . .on the ground that the said provisions are in restraint of trade.

The Court of Appeal dismissed an appeal by the Society against the order. On further appeal to the House of Lords, the order given by the High Court was affirmed. It was held that:

1   The proposed restriction, although intended to be binding in honour only, might be a basis for disciplinary action. The Courts had the power and the duty to determine its validity.
2   It was not within the powers or purposes of the Society to control selling activities which did not interfere with the proper performance of professional pharmaceutical duties. The only relevant object in the Society's Charter was 'To maintain the honour and safeguard and protect the interests of the members in their exercise of the profession of pharmacy', and the proposed rules of conduct had too slender a connection or link with that object.
3   The proposed restrictions were beyond the powers of the Society as they were in restraint of trade and had not been shown to be reasonable.

[1968] 2 All ER 686; *Pharm J* 1 June 1968 p. 651.

Comment. This decision did not affect the Society's powers to regulate professional conduct in pharmacy (Chapter 23).

The meaning of 'poison'

Three cases under the Pharmacy Act 1868

The meaning of *poison* was the subject of three cases brought under the Pharmacy Act 1868: *Pharmaceutical Society of Great Britain* v. *Piper and Co.* ([1893] 1 QB 686; *Pharm J* 11 February 1893 p. 656; *Pharm J* 18 February 1893 p. 669), *Pharmaceutical Society of Great Britain* v. *Delve* ([1893] 1 QB 71; *Pharm J* 4 November 1893 p. 378) and *Pharmaceutical Society of Great Britain* v. *Armson* ([1894] 2 QB 720; *Pharm J* 28 April 1894 p. 902).

Comment. These three cases concerned the interpretation of certain sections of the Pharmacy Act 1868 (now repealed). The principal point at issue was the meaning of the word *poison* as used in the Act. It was held by the High Court that a compound containing a poison, as well as the actual poison, was subject to the Act.

The meaning of 'sale by way of wholesale dealing'

Oxford v. Sanger *(1964)*

The Pharmacy and Poisons Act 1933 (s.18) provided that poisons in Part I of the Poisons List could be lawfully sold only by authorised sellers of poisons. An exemption from this requirement was given in section 20(1) of the Act in respect of sales of poisons by way of wholesale dealing. Section 29 defined *sale by way of wholesale dealing* as 'sale to a person who buys for the purposes of selling again'.

Sanger Ltd (wholesalers) had on five occasions sold Part I poisons to a retail shopkeeper, who had subsequently sold the poisons (tablets) to the public by retail. The shopkeeper was not an authorised seller of poisons.

The wholesaler was charged with selling Part I poisons contrary to section 18 of the Act. It was contended for the prosecution that the company could not claim the benefit of the exemption for wholesale dealing as the poison had been sold to a shopkeeper who could not lawfully sell again. The magistrate dismissed the information, and an appeal to the High Court against that decision was also dismissed.

It was held in the High Court that the word *lawfully* could not be read into the definition of *wholesale dealing*. Section 20 did not lay any duty upon a wholesaler to ascertain that the retailer to whom he sold was lawfully entitled to resell. If it was desired to control wholesalers, it could and must be done by rule.

[1965] 1 All ER 96; *Pharm J* 12 December 1964 p. 599.

Comment. Rule 11 of the Poisons Rules made under the Poisons Act 1972 now requires wholesalers who sell Part I poisons to be satisfied that their shopkeeper customers who order such poisons are authorised sellers of poisons, or that they do not intend to sell the poisons by way of retail trade. The Medicines Act 1968 (s.61) provides for similar regulations to be made in respect of medicinal products (SI 1980 No.1923).

The meaning of 'shop'

Greenwood v. Whelan *(1966)*

[1967] All ER 294; *Pharm J* 3 December 1966 p. 575.

Comment. This case turned on the meaning of the word *shop* in the Pharmacy and Medicines Act 1941. In *Greenwood* v. *Whelan*, the Lord Chief Justice, referring to the Shops Act 1950, pointed out that retail trade or business could be carried out in three different ways: firstly from a shop, secondly, from a place that is not a shop (e.g. a stall), and thirdly from a barrow or itinerant van, in a way where there is no fixed place. The stall in that case, notwithstanding the regularity of the business, the permanence of the site and the type of the structure was a *place not being a shop*. The 1941 Act was repealed by the Medicines Act 1968, which now refers to *premises* not *shops* (s.53). Medicinal products may only be sold from premises which the occupier can 'close so as to exclude the public' (Chapter 7).

Functions of the Statutory Committee

Re Lawson *(1941)*

Mr Lawson's appeal against the direction of the Statutory Committee of the Pharmaceutical Society of Great Britain that his name should be removed from the Register of Pharmaceutical Chemists was dismissed. Extracts from this judgment and other appeal cases are given in Chapter 24.
[1941] 57 LT 315; *Pharm J* 22 February 1941 p. 60.

The meaning of 'supervision'

Roberts *v.* Littlewoods Mail Order Stores Ltd *(1943)*

The Pharmacy and Poisons Act 1933 (s.18) provided: '. . .it shall not be lawful for a person to sell any poison in Part I of the Poisons List unless. . .the sale is effected by, or under the supervision of, a registered pharmacist.' Similar wording is now in the Medicines Act (s.52) (Chapter 6).

A sale of a Part I poison was made at the company's pharmacy to one of the Society's inspectors while the sole pharmacist was in a stockroom upstairs and unaware that the sale was being made by an unqualified assistant. The magistrates found that the sale, though not effected by the pharmacist, was effected sufficiently under his supervision. His actual presence was not reasonably required.

The decision was reversed in the High Court, where it was held that the sale had not been supervised. Lord Caldecote said:

> . . .the man who was upstairs might have been a person who was exercising personal control of a business, but I do not think that, while he was upstairs and therefore absent, he could be a person who was supervising a particular sale. It has been suggested that a man can supervise a sale without being bodily present. I do not accept that contention. . .each individual sale must be, not necessarily effected by the qualified person, but something which is shown by the evidence to be under his supervision in the sense that he must be aware of what is going on at the counter, and in a position to supervise or superintend the activities of the young woman by whom each individual sale is effected.

[1943] 1 All ER 271; *Pharm J* 30 January 1943 p.38.

Pharmaceutical Society of Great Britain v. Boots Cash Chemists (Southern) Ltd *(1953)*

This was a case arising under the Pharmacy and Poisons Act 1933 (s.18) (see also *Roberts* v. *Littlewoods Mail Order Stores Ltd*, above). It was an appeal by the Pharmaceutical Society against a judgment of the Lord Chief Justice in the High Court.

A Boots pharmacy was arranged on a 'self-service' system. A customer could select goods, including Part I poisons, from the shelves, place them in a wire basket and take them to the cash desk. Before the cashier accepted payment, a pharmacist at the cash desk could, if he thought fit, prevent a sale. It was suggested by the Society that a purchase was completed when a customer took an article and put it in the basket so that the pharmacist could not later intervene. That suggestion had not been accepted in the High Court by the Lord Chief Justice, who had said that self-service was no different from the normal transactions in a shop. He had continued:

> . . .the mere fact that a customer picks up a bottle of medicine from the shelves in this case does not amount to an acceptance of an offer to sell. It is an offer by the customer to buy. . .By using the words the sale is effected by, or under the supervision of, a registered pharmacist, it seems to me the sale might be effected by somebody not a pharmacist. If it be under the supervision of a pharmacist, the pharmacist can say: 'You cannot have that. That contains poison'. In this case I decide. . .that there is no sale until the buyer's offer to buy is accepted by the acceptance of the money, and that takes place under the supervision of a pharmacist. . .

The Court of Appeal upheld this decision and dismissed the appeal by the Society.

[1953] 1 All ER 482; *Pharm J* 14 February 1953 p. 115.

R v. Family Health Services Appeal Authority, ex parte Elmfield Drugs Ltd, Selles Dispensing Chemists Ltd, and E Moss (Chemists) Ltd *(1998)*

The pharmacy companies appealed against a judicial review judgment that three health authorities were correct in allowing dispensing contracts to doctors who intended to delegate dispensing of medicines to their staff. The case was based on the wording of section 55(1)(a) of the Medicines Act 1968 which reads:

> The restrictions imposed by s.52 (supervision) do not apply to the sale or offer for sale of a medicinal product:
>
> (a)   *by a doctor or dentist to a patient of his.* . .

The companies contended that the words meant that the exemption for a doctor required the doctor to sell or supply the medicinal product **personally** and did not authorise him to delegate the sale or supply to another person. The state maintained that applying the general principles of agency and the normal principles of construction there was no requirement for the doctor to hand over medicines to his patients personally.

At the earlier hearing for judicial review, the companies failed to convince the judges of their argument and Mr J. Owen said:

> I have no hesitation in finding that if Parliament had intended doctors to be guilty of an offence in the factual situation described by the pharmacists it would have said so.
>
> (*Pharm J* 18 October 1997 p. 634).

In dismissing the appeal Mr L. J. Stuart-Smith said:

> Whatever the reason I can see no basis for imposing a far stricter regime on doctors who *ex hypothesi* have prescribed or ordered medicine for their patients, by requiring them not merely to supervise the supply, as in the case of pharmacists, but actually to perform the mechanical act of delivery in person.

The judge agreed with counsel for the respondents that the solution to the problem was to be found in the general principles of agency and the ordinary principles of statutory construction. i.e. '. . .*prima facie what a person can do himself he can do by an agent.*

Pharm J 1 August 1998 p. 146; *The Times* 16 September 1998.

Comment. The judge said that if he had ruled in favour of the pharmacy companies he would have been making doctors criminals. It would have been criminalising something that has been widely adopted, particularly in rural areas, for many years.

Use of titles and descriptions

Norris *v.* Weeks *(1970)*

The Pharmacy Act 1954 (s.19) reads: 'it shall not be lawful for any person, unless he is a registered pharmaceutical chemist. . .(b) to take or use, in connection with the sale of goods by retail, the title of chemist'.

A notice, about 1 ft by 2.5 ft wide was displayed at Mr Weeks' drug store over goods intended for retail sale. It bore the wording on three lines, *Wyn's/Chemist/Sundries*. The word 'chemist' was in larger script than the other words and in a different colour. The magistrate dismissed a summons under section 19(1)(b) on the ground that, having regard to the articles displayed, the word *chemist* was merely descriptive of the type of goods sold.

The High Court dismissed an appeal against this decision. It was held that an offence is committed only if a person asserts that they are a chemist or takes to themselves the title 'chemist'. It could not be said that an offence is committed whenever the word 'chemist' appears.

Pharm J 14 March 1970 p. 268; *The Times* 6 March 1970.

Meaning of *a sample*

Mistry *v.* Norris *(1985)*

This case concerned the sale of a bottle of medicine containing phenobarbital (phenobarbitone) without the authority of a prescription issued by a medical practitioner, as required by the Medicines Act 1968 (s.58). The appellant argued that, as the sale had been made to an enforcement officer under the Act, it was a sample subject to section 112. Therefore, the evidence of analysis of the contents of the medicine was not admissible as the mixture had not been divided and a portion left with the appellant, in accordance with the sampling requirements under the Act.

The appeal was dismissed by the High Court. It was held that the inspector was not acting as a sampling officer but making an ordinary purchase as any member of the public has the right to do.
The Times 16 October 1985 p. 27.

Sale of Prescription Only Medicines: offence of strict liability

Pharmaceutical Society of Great Britain *v.* Storkwain Ltd *(1986)*

Section 58 of the Medicines Act 1968 provides for orders to be made specifying those medicinal products which may only be sold by retail in accordance with the prescription of an appropriate practitioner. Storkwain Ltd supplied quantities of Physeptone (methadone) ampoules, Ritalin (methylphenidate) tablets and Valium (diazepam) tablets, all of which are Prescription Only Medicines, on the authority of two 'prescriptions' which were, in fact, forgeries. In 1984, the Pharmaceutical Society prosecuted the company for unlawfully selling those medicines contrary to section 58(2)(a) of the Act. It was submitted for Storkwain Ltd that they were unaware that the 'prescriptions' were not genuine. In the absence of any guilty knowledge (*mens rea*) of the forgeries on the part of the company, the magistrates dismissed the charges. The Society successfully appealed to the Court of Appeal, who held that an offence under section 58(2)(a) was one of strict liability and directed the magistrates to convict.

On further appeal by Storkwain Ltd, the House of Lords confirmed the decision of the Court of Appeal. It was held that guilty knowledge (*mens rea*) was a required ingredient of offences under certain sections of the Act, but section 58 was not one of those sections. That view was supported by the construction of sections 58(4) and 58(5) and by section 121. The wording of the Prescriptions Only Order also conformed with that construction of the statute. An offence under section 58(2)(a) was, therefore, one of strict liability.
[1986] 2 All ER 635; *Pharm J* 28 June 1986 p. 829.

Is dispensing a medicine on a National Health Service prescription a 'sale'?

Appleby v. Sleep (1968)

A woman obtained a National Health Service prescription for Penidural (benzathine benzylpenicillin) syrup and took it to the pharmacy for dispensing. A few days later, she found a sliver of glass in the medicine. The pharmacy was charged with selling a medicine not of the quality demanded under the Food and Drugs Act 1955. The magistrates dismissed the case and ruled there was no *sale*. The Executive Council appealed to the High Court.

In dismissing the appeal Lord Parker CJ said that:

> In *Pfizer Corporation* v. *Ministry of Health* [1965] AC 512 it was held that there was no *sale* of a medicine to a person presenting a National Health Service prescription and that was clearly the case because, even if there was a prescription charge, the patient was not paying for the medicine itself. The sole question was whether the contract between the pharmacy and the Executive Council was a contract of sale. A chemist. . .undertook to perform services. . .for those services he was remunerated by the Executive Council . . .not only a sum to cover the basic price of the medicine but for his general services. . .the property did not pass to the Executive Council and it was not a contract of sale. . .

[1968] 2 All ER 265.

Comment. The provisions of the Food and Drugs Act 1955 as they applied to medicines have since been replaced by similar provisions in the Medicines Act 1968 (s.64) (see p. 21).

Importation of medicinal products from the European Community

R v. Royal Pharmaceutical Society of Great Britain, ex parte Association of Pharmaceutical Importers and Others (1989)

The Society had adopted a provision in its Code of Ethics which, amongst other things, prohibited a pharmacist from substituting, except in an emergency, any other medicine for the medicine specifically ordered on a prescription, even if s/he believed that the quality and therapeutic effect were identical. In 1986, the Society had published a statement to the effect that this rule applied to imported medicines as well as to UK-licensed medicines. The Association of Pharmaceutical Importers, who represented companies who were involved in importing medicines from the EU, maintained that the Society's rule infringed the provisions of the Treaty of Rome on the basis that its effect was to impose a quantitative restriction on their importing medicines – *parallel imports* – from the Community.

The European Court of Justice held that in the absence of any Community legislation regulating the doctor/pharmacist relationship, and in particular the doctor's freedom to prescribe any medicine s/he chose, it was for each member state to decide, within the limits of the Treaty, the degree to which they wish to protect the health of their people and how that was to be achieved. It was said that there was no evidence that the Society's rule went beyond what was necessary to achieve the objective, which was to leave the entire responsibility for the treatment of the patient in the hands of the doctor treating him/her. It followed, therefore, that the rule could also be justified under the Treaty on the grounds of the protection of public health.

[1989] 2 All ER 758; *Pharm J* 27 May 1989 p. 613.

Sale of prescription data: breach of confidentiality?

R v. Department of Health, ex parte Source Informatics Ltd (2000)

Source Informatics Ltd proposed a scheme whereby after they, Source Informatics, had obtained the prescribers' consent, pharmacists, for a fee, would supply anonymised information contained on NHS prescriptions for the purposes of market research. The Department of Health in a policy document entitled *The Protection and Use of Patient Information* had made clear that under common law and the Data Protection Act principles the general rule was that information given in confidence may not be disclosed without the consent of the provider of the information (i.e. doctor or pharmacist). It also stated that anonymisation, with or without aggregation, did not remove the duty of confidence towards patients who are the subject of the data, namely details on their prescriptions written by the doctor and dispensed by the pharmacist. The High Court ([1999] 4 All ER 185) agreed with the Department of Health. The Court of Appeal on judicial review reversed the decision and Mr L. J. Simon Brown said:

> . . .the patient has no proprietorial claim to the prescription form or to the information it contains. . .[he has] no right to control its use provided only and always that his privacy is not put at risk. . .

He concluded by saying:

> Participation in Source's scheme by doctors and the pharmacists would not in my judgment expose them to any serious risk of successful breach of confidence proceedings by a patient.

The Times 18 January 2000.

Comment. This case was not appealed and it would seem that the Data Protection Act does not normally cover data which have been anonymised (i.e. detached from any details which could identify a living individual).

Further reading

Dale and Appelbe's Pharmacy Law and Ethics. Pharmaceutical Press, London.
(Other pharmaceutical cases of historical interest are outlined in earlier editions.)

Medicines Act 1968

Medicinal products

Various articles and substances are treated as medicinal products (see Chapter 2) by virtue of orders made under the Act, as follows.

Section 104(1) Orders

Orders made under section 104(1) of the Act can extend the application of specified provisions of the Act to articles and substances which are not medicinal products as defined in section 130 of the Act but which are manufactured, sold, supplied, imported or exported for use wholly or partly for a medical purpose. Two orders under this section are still extant:

1   *The Medicines (Radioactive Substances) Order 1978 (SI 1978 No.1004)* extends the application of the provisions relating to the holding of licences to the following articles and substances:

    (a)   Interstitial and intracavity appliances (other than nuclear powered cardiac pacemakers) which contain or are to contain a radioactive substance sealed in a container (otherwise than solely for the purpose of storage, transport or disposal) or bonded solely within material and including the immediate container or bonding that are designed to be inserted into the human body or body cavities.

    (b)   Surface applicators, that is to say plates, plaques and ophthalmic applicators which contain or are to contain a radioactive substance sealed in a container (otherwise than solely for the purpose of storage, transport or disposal) or bonded solely within material and including the immediate container or bonding that is designed to be brought into contact with the human body.

(c)   Any apparatus capable of administering neutrons to human beings when the neutrons are administered in order to generate a radioactive substance in the person to whom they are administered for the purpose of diagnosis or research.

(d)   Other substances or articles (not being an instrument, apparatus or appliance) which consist of or contain or generate a radioactive substance and which:

(i)   consist of or contain or generate that substance in order, when administered, to utilise the radiation emitted therefrom; and

(ii)   are manufactured, sold or supplied for use wholly or mainly by being administered to one or more human beings solely by way of a test for ascertaining what effects it has when so administered.

The meaning of *administer* in relation to any apparatus in paragraph (c) above is modified to include the exposure of the body or any part of the body to the neutrons issued by the apparatus. The order also enables regulations to be made under section 60 prohibiting sale, supply and administration except by certain practitioners (see p. 90).

2   *The Medicines (Cyanogenetic Substances) Order 1984 (SI 1984 No.187)* extends to *cyanogenetic substances* the application of those provisions of the Act relating to dealings with products (including sale, supply or importation), the packaging and promotion of products and miscellaneous and supplementary provisions. Licensing requirements are not applied. *Cyanogenetic substances* means preparations which:

(a)   are presented for sale or supply under the name of, or as containing, amygdalin, laetrile or vitamin B_{17}; or

(b)   contain more than 0.1 per cent by weight of any substance having the formula either α-cyanobenzyl-6-Oβ-D-glucopyrosol-D-glucopyranoside or α-cyanobenzyl-6-Oβ-D-glucopyranosiduronic acid.

Section 105(1)(a) Orders

Orders made under section 105(1)(a) of the Act extend the application of specified provisions of the Act to certain substances which are not medicinal products but which are used in the manufacture of medicinal products. Two orders under this section have been made.

1   *The Medicines (Control of Substances for Manufacture) Order 1971 (SI 1971 No.1200)* controls the substances set out below. The terms used are defined in detail in Schedule 2 (not here reproduced). The order makes those substances subject to certain provisions of the Act concerning the holding of licences and certificates; the regulation of dealings; offences and penalties; labelling, leaflets and containers; and certain miscellaneous matters. The substances affected, and the circumstances in which they are affected, are as follows:

(a)   When manufactured, assembled, sold, supplied, imported or exported for use as an ingredient in a medicinal product *for parenteral injection* into human beings or animals, the following:

amphotericin B, bacitracin, capreomycin, colistin, erythromycin, gentamicin, heparin, hyaluronidase, kanamycin, neomycin, nystatin (added by SI 1985 No.1403), penicillin, polymyxin B, preparations of the pituitary (posterior lobe), streptomycin, the lincomycins, the rifamycins, the tetracyclines, vancomycin, viomycin.

(b)   When manufactured, assembled, sold, supplied, imported or exported for use as an ingredient in a medicinal product which is to be administered to human beings or animals by means *other than parenteral injection*, the following:

gentamicin,* neomycin,* nystatin,* oxytetracycline, tetracycline. (*added by SI 1985 No.1403).

(c)   When manufactured, assembled, sold, supplied, imported or exported for use as ingredients of *dextran injection* for human or animal use, the following:

dextrans.

(d)   When manufactured, assembled, sold, supplied, imported or exported for use as an ingredient in a *medicinal product for human or animal use,* the following:

antigens, antisera, antitoxins, chorionic gonadotrophin, corticotrophin, follicle-stimulating hormone, insulin, sera, streptodornase, streptokinase, toxins, vaccines.

(e)   When manufactured, assembled, sold, supplied, imported or exported for use as an ingredient in a medicinal product *for human use,* the following:

preparations of blood.

(f)   When manufactured, assembled, sold, supplied, imported or exported for use as an ingredient in a medicinal product *for administration to animals,* the following:

plasma; any substances wholly or partly derived from animals not being substances specifically mentioned in any of the above paragraphs.

Section 105(1)(b) and (2) Orders

Orders made under section 105(1)(b) and (2) of the Act extend the application of specified provisions of the Act to substances which, if used without proper safeguards, are capable of causing damage to the health of the community or of causing danger to the health of animals generally or of one or more species of animals. One order has been made under this section:

The Medicines (Extension to Antimicrobial Substances) Order 1973 (SI 1973 No.367) extends certain specified provisions of the Act concerning such matters as the holding of licences; the provision of information; the commission of offences; the prohibition of sale, supply or importation; and the promotion of sales to the following classes of substance:

Substances which are not medicinal products, which are or contain:

1   any of the substances commonly known as *antibiotics* being:

(a)   substances synthesised by bacteria, fungi or protozoa which have antimicrobial properties, and derivatives of such substances possessing such properties;
(b)   substances which are synthesised in any other way and are identical with any substances described in sub-paragraph (a) of this paragraph;
(c)   any salt of any of the substances described in sub-paragraphs (a) and (b) of this paragraph;

2   any other substances *which possess antigenic properties* similar to the antigenic properties of any of the substances described in paragraph 1 above;
3   sulphanilamide (being *p*-aminobenzene sulphonamide) or any derivative of sulphanilamide which possesses antimicrobial properties, and any salt of any such substance; or
4   any derivative of the *nitrofurans* which possesses antimicrobial properties, and any salt of any such derivative.

APPENDIX TWO

Medicines Act 1968

Prohibition of non-medicinal

antimicrobial substances

Antimicrobial substances were brought within the control of the Act by an order under section 105 (see Appendix 1).

The Medicines (Prohibition of Non-Medicinal Antimicrobial Substances) Order 1977 (SI 1977 No.2131) prohibits, subject to certain exceptions, the sale or supply of the antimicrobial substances set out below. The prohibition applies whether or not the substance is contained in any other substance or article, unless it is a medicinal product or an animal feeding stuff.

Prohibited substances: Part I

Amphomycin	Furazolidone	Oleandomycin
Bacitracin	Fusidic acid	Paromomycin
Candicidin	Griseofulvin	Spectinomycin
Capreomycin	Hachimycin	Spiramycin
Chloramphenicol	Nalidixic acid	Tylosin
Cycloserine	Nitrofurantoin	Vancomycin
Erythromycin	Nitrofurazone	Viomycin
Framycetin	Novobiocin	Virginiamycin.
Furaltadone	Nystatin	

NB In this Part:

(a)   a reference to any substance, other than furaltadone, shall be construed as a reference to the substance for which such name is shown in the current edition of the list of names prepared and published under section 100 of the Act; and

(b)   *furaltadone* means (6)-5-morpholino-methyl-3-(5-nitrofurylideneamino)-2-oxazolidine.

Part 2	
Class of substance	Meaning
Amphotericins	Antimicrobial substances or mixtures of such substances produced by *Streptomyces nodosus*
Cephalosporins	Antimicrobial substances containing in their chemical structure a fused dihydrothiazine β-lactam nucleus
Gentamicins	Any antimicrobial basic substance or mixture of such substances produced by the strain *Micromonospora purpurea* which on 1 September 1967 was numbered NRRL 2953 in the culture collection of the Northern Utilisation Research and Development Branch of the United States Department of Agriculture
Kanamycins	Any antimicrobial substance or mixture of such substances produced by *Streptomyces kanamyceticus*
Lincomycins	Antimicrobial substances produced by *Streptomyces lincolnensis* (var. *lincolnensis*). These substances are the basic amides of hygric acid or of a substituted hygric acid with 6-amino-6,8-dideoxy-1-thiogalacto-octopyranose or with substituted 6-amino-6,8-dideoxy-1-thiogalacto-octopyranose
Neomycins	Antimicrobial substances or mixtures of such substances produced by *Streptomyces fradiae* which are complex organic bases and which yield on hydrolysis with mineral acids the base neamine
Penicillins	Any antimicrobial acid which contains in its structure a fused thiazolidine β-lactam nucleus
Polymyxins	Any antimicrobial substance produced by any strain of *Bacillus polymyxa*
Rifamycins	A group of related antimicrobial macrolactams produced by the growth of *Streptomyces mediterranei* and containing the chemical structure of 11-acetoxy-7,9,15-trihydroxy-13-methoxy-2,6,8,10,12-penta-methyl-pentadeca-2,4,14-trienoic acid amide attached by the nitrogen atom and by the oxygen atom in the 15-position respectively to the 7- and 2-positions of a 5,6,9-trioxygenated 2,4-dimethyl-1-oxonaphtho-(2,1-β)-furan
Ristocetins	Antimicrobial substances produced by a strain of a *Nocardia* species referred to as *Nocardia lurida*
Streptomycins	Any antimicrobial complex organic base or mixture of such bases produced by *Streptomyces griseus* which: (a) yields on hydrolysis with mineral acids the base streptidine (meso-1-3-diguanidocyclohexane-2,4,5,6-tetraol); and (b) yields on hydrolysis by a 4 per cent solution of sodium hydroxide the substance maltol (3-hydroxy-2-methyl-8-pyrone)
Sulphanilamide	Sulphanilamide being *p*-aminobenzenesulphonamide, having any of the hydrogen atoms of either or both nitrogen atoms substituted by an equal number of univalent atoms or radicals
Tetracyclines	Antimicrobial bases which contain the chemical structure naphthacene-2-carboxamide, hydrogenated to any extent and having each of the positions 1, 3, 10, 11, 12 and 12a substituted by a hydroxyl or an oxo group

Permitted sales or supplies

Sale or supply of prohibited substances is permitted in the circumstances described below:

(a)   Where a sale by way of wholesale dealing is made to:

  (i)   a veterinary surgeon or veterinary practitioner;
  (ii)   a person lawfully conducting a retail pharmacy business;
  (iii)   a holder of a manufacturer's licence granted under Part II of the Act; or
  (iv)   a person carrying on the business of selling by way of wholesale dealing.

(b)   Where the sale or supply is to any of the following:

  (i)   a public analyst appointed under section 89 of the Food and Drugs Act 1955, section 27 of the Food and Drugs (Scotland) Act 1956 or section 31 of the Food and Drugs Act (Northern Ireland) 1958;
  (ii)   an agricultural analyst appointed under section 67 of the Agriculture Act 1970;
  (iii)   a person duly authorised by an enforcement authority under sections 111 and 112 of the Act;
  (iv)   a sampling officer within the meaning of Schedule 3 to the Act; or
  (v)   universities, other institutions concerned with higher education or institutions concerned with research.

(c)   Griseofulvin. When sold or supplied in a fungicide for horticultural purposes and containing other ingredients in such a quantity as to render the product unfit for any medicinal purpose and unpalatable to such a degree as to prevent consumption by human beings.

(d)   Streptomycins as for griseofulvin plus when used, sold or supplied for use as a preservative in a product used in the artificial breeding of animals.

(e)   Sulphanilamide. When, as the derivative sulphaquinoxaline (not exceeding 0.5 per cent), it is sold or supplied in a product for the destruction of rats or mice, or for the manufacture of such a product. The product must also contain warfarin, or its sodium or triethanolamine derivative.

(f)   Sulphonamide. When, as the derivative methyl-4-aminobenzenesulphonyl carbamate, it is sold or supplied for use in the manufacture of herbicides, or contained in a product used as a herbicide for agricultural, horticultural or forestry purposes or for use in or near water or on uncultivated land.

(g)   Amphotericins, gentamicins, kanamycins, lincomycins, nystatin, tylosin, penicillins, and spectinomycin when used, sold or supplied for use as a preservative in a product used in the artificial breeding of animals.

Medicines Act 1968

Applications for marketing

authorisations

Relevant medicinal products for human use

Council Directive 2001/83/EC together with the Medicines for Human Use (Marketing Authorisations, etc.) Regulations 1994 (SI 1994 No.3144, as amended by SI 2002 No.236) prescribe the form and manner in which applications for marketing authorisations for medicinal products for human use are to be made. These provisions also apply to medicinal products consisting of vaccines, toxins and/or sera and allergens together with radio-pharmaceuticals and blood products.

Applications for marketing authorisations for relevant medicinal products for human use

Any application must be made in writing, signed by or on behalf of the applicant and be accompanied by any fee which may be payable. Twenty-six copies of the application shall be supplied to the licensing authority in English. Where any material has been translated from another language, then a copy in the original language must be supplied.

An application shall indicate what legal category the medicinal product falls into namely Prescription Only, Pharmacy Only, or General Sale.

An application for a marketing authorisation shall be accompanied by the following particulars and documents.

1   The name or corporate name of and the permanent address of the person responsible for placing the product on the market and, where applicable, the name and address of the manufacturer.
2   The name of the medicinal product (brand name, or common name) together with a trade mark or name of manufacturer, or scientific name together with a trade mark or name of manufacturer.

3   The qualitative and quantitative particulars of all the constituents of the product in usual terminology, but excluding empirical chemical formulae, with the mention of the international non-proprietary name recommended by the World Health Organization where such a name exists.

4   A brief description of the method of preparation.

5   Particulars of the therapeutic indications, contra-indications and side-effects.

6   Posology, pharmaceutical form, method and route of administration and expected shelf-life. If applicable, the reasons for any precautionary and safety measures to be taken for the storage of the medicinal product, its administration to patients and for the disposal of waste products, together with an indication of any potential risks presented by the product for the environment.

7   Description of the control methods employed by the manufacturer – qualitative and quantitative analysis of the constituents and of the finished product; special tests, e.g. sterility tests, tests for the presence of pyrogenic substances and for the presence of heavy metals; stability tests; biological and toxicity tests; and controls carried out at an intermediate stage of the manufacturing process.

8   Results of:

(a)   physico-chemical, biological or microbiological tests;
(b)   pharmacological and toxicological tests; and
(c)   clinical trials.

However, and without prejudice to the law relating to the protection of industrial and commercial property:

(a)   The applicant shall not be required to provide the results of pharmacological and toxicological tests or the results of clinical trials if:

   (i) either the product is essentially similar to a product authorised in the country concerned by the application and that the person responsible for the marketing of the original product has consented to the pharmacological, toxicological or clinical references contained in the file on the original medicinal product being used for the purpose of examining the application in question; or

   (ii) by detailed references to published scientific literature presented in accordance with Council Directive 2001/83/EC that the constituent(s) of the medicinal product have a well established use, with recognised efficacy and an acceptable level of safety; or

   (iii) the medicinal product is essentially similar to a product which has been authorised within the Community, in accordance with Community provisions in force for not less than six years (ten years for high technology products) and is marketed in the member state for which an application is made; this period shall be extended to ten years in the case of high technology medicinal products within the meaning of Directive 87/22/EEC (Part A of Annex) or a medicinal product within the meaning of that Directive (Part B of Annex).

   Furthermore, a member state may also extend this period to ten years by a single decision covering all products marketed on its territory where it considers this necessary in the interest of public health. Member states are at liberty not to apply the six-year period beyond the date of expiry of the patent protecting the original product. However, where the medicinal product is intended for a different therapeutic use from that of the other medicinal products marketed or to be administered by different routes or in different doses, the results of appropriate pharmacological and toxicological tests and/or of appropriate clinical trials must be provided.

(b) In the case of new medicinal products containing known constituents not hitherto used in combination for therapeutic purposes, the results of pharmacological and toxicological tests and of clinical trials relating to the combination must be provided, but it is not necessary to provide references relating to each individual constituent.

9   A summary of the product characteristics (see below), one or more mock-ups of the sales presentation of the product, together with a package leaflet where one is to be enclosed.

10   A document showing that the manufacturer is authorised in his own country to produce medicinal products.

11   Copies of any authorisation obtained in another member state or a third country to place the medicinal product on the market, together with a list of those member states in which an application for authorisation submitted in accordance with this Directive is under examination. Copies of the summary of product characteristics proposed by the applicant in accordance with this Directive (see below) or approved by the competent authorities of the member state concerned. Copies of the package leaflet proposed in accordance with Directive 2001/83/EC or approved by the competent authorities of the member state concerned. Details of any decision to refuse authorisation, whether in the Community or a third country and the reasons for such a decision.

This information must be updated on a regular basis.

NB Member states must take all appropriate measures to ensure that the documents and particulars listed in points 7 and 8 above are drawn up by experts with the necessary technical or professional qualification before they are submitted to the competent authorities.

Summary of the product characteristics

The summary of product characteristics must contain the following information:

(a) name of the medicinal product;

(b) its qualitative and quantitative composition in terms of the active ingredients and constituents of the excipient, knowledge of which is essential for proper administration of the product, the international non-proprietary names recommended by the World Heath Organization must be used where such names exist, or, failing this, the usual common name or chemical description;

(c) pharmaceutical form;

(d) pharmacological properties and, in so far as this information is useful for therapeutic purposes, pharmacokinetic particulars;

(e) clinical particulars covering:

   (i) therapeutic indications;
   (ii) posology and method of administration for adults and, where necessary, for children;
   (iii) contra-indications;
   (iv) special precautions for use;
   (v) undesirable effects (frequency and seriousness);
   (vi) interaction with other medicaments and other forms of interaction;
   (vii) use during pregnancy and lactation;
   (viii) effects on ability to drive and to use machines;
   (ix) special warnings;
   (x) overdose (covering symptoms, emergency procedures and antidotes);

(f) pharmaceutical particulars covering:

   (i) major incompatibilities;

(ii) shelf-life, when necessary after reconstitution of the product or when the container is opened for the first time;

(iii) special precautions for storage;

(iv) nature and contents of container;

(v) special precautions for disposal of unused products or waste materials derived from such products, if appropriate; and

(vi) name or style and permanent address or registered place of business of the holder of the marketing authorisation.

When the marketing authorisation has been issued, the competent authority of the member state must inform the person responsible for placing the product on the market that the summary of product characteristics has been approved. The competent authority must send a copy of the marketing authorisation together with the summary of product characteristics to the European Agency for the Evaluation of Medicinal Products.

Immunologicals, radiopharmaceuticals and blood products

The codification Council Directive 2001/83/EC now encompasses immunologicals, radio-pharmaceuticals and blood products. The documents and particulars (see Applications for marketing authorisations, above) apply but there are additional requirements for blood products; vaccines, toxins, sera, or allergen products; and radiopharmaceuticals

Blood products

1   Where the name of the product derived from human blood or human plasma is expressed, the common or scientific name of the active constituents must also be included, at least once (though they may be abbreviated in other references).

2   The statement required by Council Directive 2001/83/EC shall:

(a)   as respects quantitative composition, be expressed by mass, by international units or by units of biological activity as appropriate to the product concerned;

(b)   qualitative and quantitative particulars of constituents must include particulars relating to biological activity and qualitative and quantitative composition shall include the composition of the product expressed in terms of biological activity.

Vaccines, toxins, sera, or allergen products

1   Whenever the name of the product is expressed, the common or scientific name of the active constituents must also be included.

2   The statement required by Council Directive 2001/83/EC shall:

(a)   in respect to quantitative composition, be expressed by mass, by international units or by units of biological activity as appropriate to the product concerned;

(b)   qualitative and quantitative particulars of constituents must include particulars relating to biological activity or to protein content and qualitative and quantitative composition shall include the composition of the product expressed in terms of biological activity or of protein content.

3   The particulars must include any special precautions to be taken by persons handling the immunological product and persons administering the product to patients, together with any precautions to be taken by the patient.

Radiopharmaceuticals

Authorisations are required for generators, kits, precursor radiopharmaceuticals and industrially prepared pharmaceuticals. The particulars shall include:

(a) full details of internal radiation dosimetry;
(b) additional detailed instructions for extemporaneous preparation and quality control of such preparation and, where appropriate, maximum storage time during which any intermediate preparation such as an eluate or the ready to use pharmaceutical will conform with its specifications; and
(c) if the application is in respect of a radiopharmaceutical which is a generator:

  (i) a general description of the system together with a detailed description of the components of the system which may affect the composition or quality of the daughter nuclide preparation; and
  (ii) qualitative and quantitative particulars of the eluate or the sublimate.

An application for the issue of a clinical trial certificate

Particulars relating to the applicant, the certificate holder and the activities to which the certificate relates must include the following.

1 The name and address of the applicant, and, where the applicant is not the proposed certificate holder, the name and address of the proposed certificate holder.
2 The period for which the certificate is desired, where it is for less than two years.
3 A statement of the activities to which the certificate is to relate, and in respect of each medicinal product which is the subject of the application, whether it is one or more of the following:

  (a) to sell or supply the medicinal product for the purpose of a clinical trial;
  (b) to procure the sale or supply of the medicinal product for the purpose of a clinical trial;
  (c) to procure the manufacture or assembly of the medicinal product for sale or supply for the purpose of the clinical trial and whether or not in addition to the purpose specified in sub-paragraphs (a) or (b) of this paragraph.
  (d) to import into the United Kingdom the medicinal product for the purpose of a clinical trial.

4 Whether in respect of each medicinal product which is the subject of the application it is to be sold or supplied for the purposes of the trial:

  (a) to practitioners;
  (b) to persons engaged in providing hospital services; or
  (c) otherwise.

5 (a) The name and address of any person in the United Kingdom other than the proposed certificate holder taking part in the manufacture or assembly of each medicinal product; and
  (b) in the case of an imported medicinal product, the name and address of the manufacturer or assembler of the medicinal product in the form in which it is to be imported; and
  (c) a statement of the relevant manufacturing or assembling operations; and
  (d) the address of the place or proposed place of manufacture or assembly.

Applications for certificates of registration for homoeopathic products

An application for special, simplified registration submitted by a person responsible for placing the product on the market relates to homoeopathic medicinal products and may cover a series of homoeopathic medicinal products derived from the same homoeopathic stock or stocks.

The application must be in writing and be accompanied by the following material and information (SI 1994 No.105, as amended by SI 1998 No.574 and SI 2002 No.236).

1 The name or corporate name of and the permanent address of:

(a)   the person responsible for placing the product on the market in the United Kingdom;

(b)   the manufacturers and the sites involved in the different stages of the manufacture including the manufacturer of the finished product and the manufacturers of the homoeopathic stock or stocks; and

(c)   where relevant, the importer.

2   Details of the scientific name or other name given in a pharmacopoeia of the homoeopathic stock or stocks.

3   A statement of the various routes of administration, pharmaceutical form and degree of dilution to be registered.

4   A dossier describing how the homoeopathic stock or stocks is or are to be obtained and controlled and justifying its or their homoeopathic nature.

5   A manufacturing and control file for each pharmaceutical form and a description of the method of dilution and potentisation.

6   A copy of the manufacturer's licence or corresponding authorisation granted by a member state other that the United Kingdom in respect of the product.

7   Copies of any registrations or authorisations obtained for the same product in member states other than the United Kingdom.

8   One or more specimens of mock-ups of the sales presentation of the product to be registered.

9   Data concerning the stability of the product.

Medicinal products for animal use

The Marketing Authorisations for Veterinary Medicinal Products Regulations 1994 (SI 1994 No.3142, as amended) together with Council Directives 2001/82/EC and 2004/28/EC prescribe the form and manner in which applications for marketing authorisations for animal use are to be made. The particulars required in applications for marketing authorisations are thus:

Any application must be made in writing, and signed by or on behalf of the applicant, and be accompanied by any fee which may be payable. Four copies of the application shall be supplied to the licensing authority in English, plus a further 22 copies if requested. Where any material has been translated from another language, then a copy in the original language must be supplied.

Application for a marketing authorisation for a medicinal product for animal use

An application for a marketing authorisation shall be accompanied by the following particulars and documents.

1   The name or business name and the permanent address or registered place of business of the person responsible for placing the product on the market and, if different, of the manufacturer(s) involved and of the sites of manufacture.

2   The name of the veterinary medicinal product (brand name, non-proprietary name), with or without trade mark or name of manufacturer, or scientific name or formula with or without a trade mark or name of the manufacturer.

3   The qualitative and quantitative particulars of all the constituents of the product using the usual terminology, but not empirical chemical formulae, also giving the international non-proprietary name recommended by the World Health Organization where such a name exists.

4   A description of the method of preparation.

5   Therapeutic indications, contra-indications and side-effects.

6   Dosage for the various species of animal for which the product is intended, its pharmaceutical form, method and route of administration and proposed shelf life.

7   If applicable, the reasons for any precautionary and safety measures to be taken when the product is stored, when it is administered to animals and when the waste therefrom is disposed of, together with an indication of any potential risks the product might pose to the environment and the health of humans, animals and plants.

8   Indication of the withdrawal period necessary between the last administration of the product to animals under normal conditions of use and the production of foodstuffs from such animals in order to ensure that such foodstuffs do not contain residues in quantities in excess of the maximum limits laid down. Where necessary, the applicant must propose and justify a tolerance level for residues which may be accepted in foodstuffs without risk for the consumer, together with routine analysis methods which could be used by the competent authorities to trace residues.

9   Description of the control testing methods employed by the manufacturer – qualitative and quantitative analysis of the constituents and of the finished product; special tests, e.g. sterility tests, tests for the presence of pyrogens, for the presence of heavy metals; stability tests; biological and toxicity tests; and tests on intermediate products.

10   Results of:

(a)   physico-chemical, biological or microbiological tests;
(b)   pharmacological and toxicological tests;
(c)   clinical trials.

However, and without prejudice to the law relating to the protection of industrial and commercial property:

(a)   The applicant shall not be required to provide the results of pharmacological and toxicological tests or the results of clinical trials if:

(i)   either the product is essentially similar to a product authorised in the country concerned by the application and that the person responsible for the marketing of the original product has agreed to the pharmacological, toxicological or clinical references contained in the file on the original medicinal product may be used for the purpose of examining the application in question; or

(ii)   by detailed references to the scientific literature presented in accordance with the second paragraph of Directive 2001/82/EC that the constituent(s) of the medicinal product have a well-established medicinal use, with recognised efficacy and an acceptable level of safety; or

(iii)   the veterinary medicinal product is essentially similar to a product which has been authorised within the Community, in accordance with Community provisions in force for not less than six years and is marketed in the member state for which an application is made; this period shall be extended to ten years in the case of high technology medicinal products within the meaning of Directive 87/22/EEC (Part A of Annex) or a medicinal product within the meaning of that Directive (Part B of Annex).

Furthermore a member state may also extend this period to ten years by a single decision covering all products marketed on its territory where it considers this necessary in the interest of public health. Member states are at liberty not to apply the six-year period beyond the date of expiry of the patent protecting the original product.

(b)   In the case of new medicinal products containing known constituents not hitherto used in combination for therapeutic purposes, the results of pharmacological and toxicological tests and of clinical trials relating to the combination must be provided, but it is not necessary to provide references relating to each individual constituent.

11   A summary of the product characteristics, one or more mock-ups of the sales presentation of the product, together with a package leaflet where one is to be enclosed.

12   A document showing that the manufacturer is authorised in his own country to produce medicinal products.

13   Any authorisation to place the relevant product on the market obtained in another member state or in a third country together with a list of those countries to which an application for authorisation to place the product on the market has been made and explanation of the reasons for which the member state or third country has refused to grant authorisation for the product concerned.

NB Member states must take all appropriate measures to ensure that the documents and particulars listed in points 8, 9 and 10 are drawn up by experts with the necessary technical or professional qualification before they are submitted to the competent authorities.

The summary of product characteristics is similar to that for human medicinal products (see p. 411) with the added requirement as to the target species and withdrawal periods.

Medicines Act 1968

Prescribed conditions for

manufacturers' undertakings

In dealing with applications for licences for the importation of medicinal products, the licensing authority may require the production of an undertaking to comply with prescribed conditions. Those conditions are in the schedule to the Medicines (Manufacturers' Undertakings for Imported Products) Regulations 1977 (SI 1977 No.1038, as amended by SI 1992 No.2845), and are set out below.

For the purpose of these regulations *medicinal product* includes a relevant medicinal product within the meaning of the Medicines for Human Use (Marketing Authorisations etc.) Regulations 1994 (SI 1994 No.3144, as amended by SI 2002 No.236).

1   The manufacturer shall provide and maintain such staff, premises, and plant as are necessary for the carrying out in accordance with the relevant product licences of such stages of the manufacture and assembly of the medicinal products to which the relevant product licences relate as are undertaken by him.

2   The manufacturer shall provide and maintain such staff, premises, equipment and facilities for the handling, storage and distribution of the medicinal products to which the relevant product licences relate which he handles, stores or distributes as are necessary to avoid deterioration of the medicinal products.

2A   In relation to medicinal products for human use, the manufacturer shall provide and maintain a designated quality control department having authority in relation to quality control and being independent of all other departments.

3   The manufacturer shall conduct all manufacture and assembly operations in such a way as to ensure that the medicinal products to which the relevant product licences relate conform with the standards of strength, quality and purity applicable to them under the relevant product licences.

3A   In relation to medicinal products for human use, the manufacturer shall maintain an effective pharmaceutical quality assurance system involving the active participation of the management and personnel of the different services involved.

4   Where animals are used in the production of any medicinal product and the relevant product licences contain provisions relating to them, the manufacturer shall arrange for the animals to be housed in premises of such a nature and to be managed in such a way as will facilitate compliance with such provisions.

5   The manufacturer shall make such adequate and suitable arrangements as are necessary for carrying out in accordance with the relevant product licences any tests of the strength, quality or purity of the medicinal products to which the licences relate.

6   The manufacturer shall inform the holder of the relevant product licences of any material alteration in the premises or plant used in connection with the manufacture or assembly of the medicinal products to which the relevant product licences relate or in the operations for which such premises or plant are used and of any change, since the granting of the relevant product licences, in respect of any person:

(a)   responsible for supervising the production operations; or
(b)   responsible for quality control of the medicinal products to which the relevant product licences relate; or
(c)   in charge of the animals from which are derived any substance used in the production of the medicinal products to which the relevant product licences relate; or
(d)   responsible for the culture of any living tissues used in the manufacture of the medicinal products to which the relevant product licences relate.

7   The manufacturer shall keep readily available for inspection by a person authorised by the licensing authority durable records of the details of manufacture and assembly of each batch of every medicinal product to which each relevant product licence relates and of the tests carried out thereon in such a form that the records will be easily identifiable from the number of the batch as shown in each container in which the medicinal product is exported from the country where it has been manufactured or assembled; the manufacturer shall permit the person authorised to take copies of or make extracts from such records. Such records shall not be destroyed:

(a)   in relation to medicinal products for human use, for a period of five years from the date of release of the relevant batch, or for a period of one year after the expiry date of the relevant batch, which ever expires later;
(b)   in any other case.

7A   In relation to medicinal products for human use to which a product licence relates, the manufacturer shall keep readily available for examination by a person authorised by the licensing authority, samples of:

(a)   each batch of finished products for at least a period of one year after their expiry date; and
(b)   starting materials (other than solvents, gases or water) for at least a period of two years after release of the medicinal product of which the relevant starting materials formed part;

except where the manufacturer is authorised by the licensing authority to destroy such samples earlier.

7B   (1) The manufacturer shall implement a system for recording and reviewing complaints in relation to medicinal products for human use to which a product licence relates together with an effective system for recalling promptly and at any time the medicinal products in the distribution network.

(2) The manufacturer shall record and investigate all complaints described in sub-paragraph (1) of this paragraph and shall immediately inform the licensing authority of any defect which could result in a recall from sale, supply or exportation or is an abnormal restriction on such sale, supply or exportation.

8   The manufacturer shall inform the holder of the relevant product licence of any material change since the date upon which such licence was granted in respect of:

(a)   the facilities and equipment available at each of the premises of the manufacturer for carrying out any stage of the manufacture or assembly of the medicinal products to which the relevant product licences relate; or

(b)   the facilities and equipment available in each of the premises of the manufacturer for the storage of the medicinal products to which the relevant product licences relate on, and distribution of the products from or between, such premises; or

(c)   any manufacturing operations, not being operations in relation to the medicinal products to which the relevant product licences relate, which are carried on by the manufacturer on or near any of the premises on which such medicinal products are manufactured or assembled and the substances or articles in respect of which such operations are carried on; or

(d)   the arrangements for the identification and storage of materials and ingredients before and during manufacture of the medicinal products to which the relevant product licences relate and the arrangements for the storage of the medicinal products after they have been manufactured or assembled; or

(e)   the arrangements for ensuring a satisfactory turnover of stocks of medicinal products to which the relevant product licences relate; or

(f)   the arrangements for maintaining production records and records of analytical and other testing procedures applied in the course of manufacture or assembly of the medicinal products to which the relevant product licences relate; or

(g)   the arrangements for keeping reference samples of materials used in the manufacture of any medicinal products to which the relevant product licences relate and reference samples of such medicinal products.

APPENDIX FIVE

Medicines Act 1968
Standard provisions and obligations for marketing authorisations

The standard provisions and obligations relating to marketing authorisations for human medicines are set out in Council Directive 2001/83/EC and in SI 1994 No.3144, as amended by SI 2002 No.236.

Definitions

Allergen product   means any product which is intended to identify or induce a specific acquired alteration in the immunological response to an allergising agent.

Expiry date   means the date after which the medicinal product should not be used.

Good manufacturing practice   means the part of quality assurance which ensures that medicinal products are consistently produced and controlled to the quality standards appropriate to their intended use, the principles and guidelines of which are specified in Chapter II of Commission Directive 91/356/EEC.

Relevant period   means the period of five years from the date of certification of the relevant batch referred to in paragraph 16(3)(b) of Schedule 2 to the Regulations or the period of one year from the expiry date of the relevant batch, whichever expires later.

Adverse reaction   means a reaction which is harmful and unintended and which occurs at doses normally used in humans for the prophylaxis, diagnosis or treatment of disease or the modification of physiological function.

Serious adverse reaction   means an adverse reaction which is fatal, life threatening, disabling, incapacitating, or which results in or prolongs hospitalisation.

Unexpected adverse reaction   means an adverse reaction which is not mentioned in the summary of product characteristics.

Serious unexpected adverse reaction   means an adverse reaction which is both serious and unexpected.

Obligations on holders of marketing authorisations for relevant medicinal products for human use

The licensing authority in this context can mean either the member state competent authority (e.g. the Medicines Control Agency in the UK, or the European Agency for the Evaluation of Medicinal Products in the EU).

1   The person responsible for placing the product on the market must inform the Licensing Authority of any new information which might entail the amendment of the particulars and documents referred to in his application for a marketing authorisation or in the summary of product characteristics (Appendix 3). In particular, he must inform the Licensing Authority, the Commission and the member states of any prohibition or restriction imposed by a competent authority of any country in which the medicinal product is placed on the market and any other new information which might influence the evaluation of the benefits and risks of the medicinal product concerned (Regulation 2309/93/EEC).

2   The holder of a marketing authorisation shall comply with all the obligations which relate to him by virtue of the relevant Community provisions including in particular obligations relating to providing or updating information, making changes, to applying to vary the authorisation, to pharmacovigilance, and to labels and package leaflets (SI 1994 No.3144, as amended).

3   The holder of a marketing authorisation shall maintain a record of reports of which he is aware of suspected adverse effects in accordance with the relevant Community provisions, which shall be open to inspection by a person authorised by the Licensing Authority, who may take copies of the record and, if the Licensing Authority so directs, the authorisation holder shall furnish the Licensing Authority with a copy of any such reports of which he has a record or of which he is or subsequently becomes aware (SI 1994 No.3144, as amended).

4   The holder of a marketing authorisation shall keep such documents as will facilitate the withdrawal or recall from sale or supply any relevant medicinal product to which the authorisation relates (SI 1994 No.3144, as amended).

5   The person responsible for placing the product on the market must notify the Licensing Authority forthwith of any action taken by him to suspend the marketing of a product, or withdraw a product from the market, together with the reasons for such action if the latter concerns the efficacy of the product or the protection of public health.

6   The person responsible for placing the product on the market must, in respect of methods of production and control take account of technical and scientific progress and make any amendments that may be required to enable the product to be manufactured and checked by means of generally accepted scientific methods. These changes shall be subject to approval of the Licensing Authority (Regulation 2309/93/EEC).

7   In exceptional circumstances a marketing authorisation may be granted subject to certain specific obligations to be reviewed annually including:

(a)   the carrying out of further studies following the granting of the authorisation;

(b)   the notification of adverse reactions to the medicinal product (Directive 2001/83/EC).

8   The person responsible for placing the product on the market must have permanently and continuously at his disposal an appropriately qualified person responsible for pharmacovigilance. That qualified person shall be responsible for:

(a)   the establishment and maintenance of a system which ensures that information about all suspected adverse reactions which are reported to the personnel of the company, and to medical representatives, is collected and evaluated and collated so that it may be accessed at a single point within the Community;

(b)   the preparation of the reports for the competent authorities in accordance with the requirements of Regulation 93/2309/EEC;

(c)   ensuring that any request from the competent authorities for the provision of additional information necessary for the evaluation of the benefits and risks afforded by a medicinal product is answered fully and promptly, including the provision of information about the volume of sales or prescriptions of the medicinal product concerned (Regulation 2309/93/EEC).

9   The person responsible for placing the product on the market shall be required to record and to report all suspected serious adverse reactions, which are brought to his attention by a health care professional, to the Licensing Authority immediately and in any case within 15 days of their receipt at the latest (Regulation 2309/93/EEC).

10   The person responsible for placing the product on the market must be required to maintain detailed records of all other suspected adverse reactions which are reported to him by a health care professional. These records shall be submitted to the competent authorities immediately upon request or at least every six months during the first two years following authorisation and once a year for the following three years. Thereafter the records shall be submitted every five years together with the renewal of the authorisation or immediately upon request. They shall be accompanied by a scientific evaluation (Regulation 2309/93/EEC).

Additional obligations for holders of marketing authorisations relating to blood products and immunological medicinal products

Blood products

1   The holder of a marketing authorisation shall take all necessary measures to ensure that the manufacturing and purifying processes used in the preparation of blood products to which the licence relates:

(a)   are properly validated;

(b)   attain batch-to-batch consistency;

(c)   guarantee, in so far as the state of technology permits, the absence of specific viral contamination;

and shall take all necessary measures to ensure that appropriate records relating to relevant control measures are:

(i) signed by the qualified person referred to in paragraph 16 of Schedule 2 to these Regulations;

(ii) kept for the relevant period; and

(iii) if so requested, submitted to the competent authority.

2   The manufacturer shall notify the competent authority of the method or methods used to reduce or eliminate pathogenic viruses liable to be transmitted by blood products.

Immunological products

3 The holder of a marketing authorisation shall take all necessary measures to ensure that the processes used in the production of vaccines, toxins, sera or allergen products to which the licence relates:

(a) are properly validated; and
(b) attain batch-to-batch consistency;
and shall take all necessary measures to ensure that appropriate records relating to control measures are:

    (i) signed by the qualified person referred to in paragraph 16 of Schedule 2 to these Regulations;
    (ii) kept for the relevant period; and
    (iii) if so requested by the Licensing Authority, submitted to the Licensing Authority.

Standard provisions for clinical trials

The provisions are in the Medicines (Standard Provisions for Licences and Certificates) Regulations 1971 (SI 1971 No.972, as amended).

1 The certificate holder shall forthwith report to the Licensing Authority any change in his name and address and in any address at which there is carried on a business to which the clinical trial certificate relates.

2 The certificate holder shall forthwith inform the Licensing Authority of any information received by him that casts doubt on the continued validity of the data which was submitted with, or in connection with, the application for the clinical trial certificate for the purpose of being taken into account in assessing the safety, quality or efficacy of any medicinal products to which the certificate relates for the purpose for which the certificate holder proposed that it may be used.

3 The certificate holder shall forthwith inform the Licensing Authority of any decision to discontinue the trial of any medicinal product to which the certificate relates and shall state the reason for the decision.

4 The clinical trial in respect of which the clinical trial certificate has been issued shall be carried out in accordance with the outline of the clinical trial contained in the application for that certificate subject to any changes thereto which the Licensing Authority may from time to time approve.

5 (1) The medicinal product to which the clinical trial certificate relates shall be administered only by or under the direction of a doctor or dentist named in the application for that certificate or by or under the direction of a doctor or dentist approved by the Licensing Authority for this purpose.

(2) Where the medicinal product to which the clinical trial certificate relates is to be administered by or under the direction of a doctor or dentist who has not been named in the application for the certificate or where it is intended that there shall be a change of the doctor or dentist so named, the certificate holder shall seek the approval of the Licensing Authority and for this purpose shall notify the Licensing Authority in writing of the name, address and qualifications of the doctor or dentist in question.

(3) In the event of any doctor or dentist ceasing to participate in the clinical trial in respect of which the clinical trial certificate has been issued, the certificate holder shall as soon as is reasonably possible inform the Licensing Authority and shall give the reason for such cessation.

6 Before any administration of the medicinal product to which the clinical trial certificate relates takes place, the certificate holder shall communicate the provisions of that certificate to each and every doctor or dentist who, in the course of the clinical

trial in respect of which that certificate has been issued, is to administer or to direct the administration of that medicinal product.

Standard provisions for animal test certificates

The provisions are in the Medicines (Standard Provisions for Licences and Certificates) Regulations 1971 (SI 1971 No.972, as amended).

1   The certificate holder shall forthwith report to the Licensing Authority any change in his name and address and in any address at which there is carried on a business to which the animal test certificate relates.

2   The certificate holder shall forthwith inform the Licensing Authority of any proposed change in the arrangements for the supervision of the performance of the medicinal test on animals to which the certificate relates.

3   The certificate holder shall forthwith furnish the Licensing Authority with any information received by him that casts doubt on the continued validity of the data which was submitted with, or in connection with, the application for the animal test certificate for the purpose of being taken into account in assessing the safety, quality or efficacy of any medicinal product to which the certificate relates for the purpose for which the certificate holder proposed that it may be used.

4   The certificate holder shall maintain a record of any report received by him of adverse effects in any animal or animals associated in the report with the use of any medicinal product to which the certificate relates, which shall be open to inspection by a person authorised by the Licensing Authority, who may take copies thereof, and the certificate holder, unless requested by the Licensing Authority not to do so, shall forthwith furnish the Licensing Authority with a copy of any such reports that have been received by him.

5   The certificate holder shall keep readily available for inspection by a person authorised by the Licensing Authority durable records of his arrangements:

(a)   for procuring the sale, supply, manufacture, assembly or importation of any medicinal product to which the certificate relates; and

(b)   for obtaining materials for the purpose of the manufacture or assembly by him, or on his behalf, of any medicinal product to which the certificate relates; and

(c)   for tests to be carried out on the materials used for manufacture or assembly of any medicinal products and on any medicinal products to which the certificate relates;

and shall permit the person authorised to take copies or to make extracts from such records. Such records shall not, without the consent of the Licensing Authority, be destroyed for a period of one year from the date of the expiry of the last certificate for the medicinal test on animals to which such records relate.

6   The certificate holder shall forthwith notify the Licensing Authority of any decision to discontinue the test of any medicinal product to which the certificate relates and shall inform the Licensing Authority of the reason for the decision.

7   The medicinal test on animals in respect of which the animal test certificate has been issued shall be carried out in accordance with the outline of the medicine test on animals contained in the application for that certificate subject to any changes thereto which the Licensing Authority may from time to time approve.

8   (1) The medicinal product to which the animal test certificate relates shall be administered only by, or under the direction of, the person named in the application for that certificate as the person to whom it was proposed that the medicinal test on animals should be carried out by or under the direction of such other person approved by the Licensing Authority for this purpose.

(2) Where the medicinal product to which the animal test certificate relates is to be administered by, or under the direction of, a person who has not been named in the application for that certificate or where it is intended that there shall be a change of the person so named, the certificate holder shall seek the approval of the Licensing Authority and for this purpose shall notify the Licensing Authority in writing of the name, address and qualifications of the person in question.

(3) In the event of any such named or approved person ceasing to participate in the medicinal test on animals in respect of which the animal test certificate has been issued, the certificate holder shall as soon as is reasonably possible inform the Licensing Authority and shall give the reason for such cessation.

9   (1) The medicinal test on animals in respect of which the animal test certificate has been issued shall be carried out only at the location specified in the application for that certificate.

(2) Where the medicinal test on animals to which the animal test certificate relates is to be carried out at a location that has not been specified in the application or where it is intended that there shall be a change in the location so specified, the certificate holder shall seek the approval of the Licensing Authority and for this purpose shall notify the Licensing Authority in writing of the location in question.

10   Before any administration of the medicinal product to which the animal test certificate relates takes place, the certificate holder shall arrange that the particulars relating to the administration of that medicinal product together with any relevant safety precautions be communicated to each and every person who, in the course of the medicinal test on animals in respect of which that certificate has been issued, is to administer or to direct the administration of that medicinal product.

Standard provisions for a manufacturer's licence for medicinal products for human use

The standard provisions for a manufacturer's licence are laid down in Council Directive 2001/83/EC. Commission Directive 2003/94/EC lays down the principles and guidelines of *good manufacturing practice,* which is applicable to all activities that require a licence under Council Directive 2001/83/EC. The provisions are as follows.

1   The licence holder shall provide and maintain such staff, premises and plant as are necessary for the carrying out in accordance with his licence and the relevant product licences of such stages of the manufacture and assembly of the medicinal products as are undertaken by him, and he shall not carry out any such manufacture or assembly except at the premises specified in his manufacturer's licence.

2   The licence holder shall provide and maintain such staff, premises, equipment and facilities for the handling, storage and distribution of the medicinal products which he handles, stores or distributes under his licence as are necessary to avoid deterioration of the medicinal products and he shall not use for such purposes premises other than those specified in the licence or which may be approved from time to time by the Licensing Authority.

3   The licence holder shall conduct all manufacture and assembly operations in such a way as to ensure that the medicinal products conform with the standards of strength, quality and purity applicable to them under the relevant product licences and, in relation to medicinal products for human use, shall conduct all such operations in accordance with the principles and guidelines of good manufacturing practice.

3A   The licence holder shall, in relation to medicinal products for human use, establish and implement an effective pharmaceutical quality assurance system involving the active participation of management and personnel of the different services involved.

4   The licence holder, where animals are used in the production of any medicinal products and the relevant product licences contain provisions relating to them, shall

arrange for the animals to be housed in premises of such a nature and to be managed in such a way as will facilitate compliance with such provisions.

5   The licence holder, in relation to medicinal products other than for human use, shall either:

(a)   provide and maintain such staff, premises and plant as are necessary for carrying out in accordance with the relevant product licences any tests of the strength, quality or purity of the medicinal products that he manufactures under his manufacturer's licence as required by those product licences, and when animals are used for such tests they shall be suitably housed and managed; or

(b)   make arrangements with a person approved by the Licensing Authority for such tests to be carried out in accordance with the relevant product licences on his behalf by that person.

5A   (1) The licence holder shall, in relation to medicinal products for human use:

(a)   provide and maintain a designated quality control department having authority in relation to quality control and being independent from all other departments in the exercise of that authority; and

(b)   place the quality control department under the authority of the person notified to the Licensing Authority in accordance with paragraph 7(2) of Schedule 1 to the Medicines (Applications for Manufacturer's and Wholesale Dealer's Licences) Regulations 1971 as being responsible for quality control.

(2) Subject to 5B of this Schedule, the licence holder shall, in order to support the quality control department, provide and maintain such staff, premises and plant as are necessary for carrying out:

(a)   such tests of the strength, quality and purity of the medicinal products which he manufactures for human use under the manufacturer's licence as are required by the relevant product licences; and

(b)   any tests or controls which relate to the conditions of production and in-process controls.

(3) Any animals used for the tests referred to in sub-paragraph (2) of this paragraph shall be suitably housed and managed.

(4) The licence holder shall ensure that the quality control department, in determining whether finished medicinal products for human use are to be released for sale or distribution, takes into account, in addition to analytical results:

(a)   the conditions of production;

(b)   the results of in-process controls;

(c)   the examination of production documents;

(d)   the conformity of products to the specification in the relevant product licence.

5B   A licence holder need not himself provide and maintain staff, premises and plant as are necessary for carrying out such tests as are specified in paragraph 5A(2) of this Schedule provided that he makes arrangements with a person approved by the Licensing Authority to carry out such tests on his behalf in accordance with paragraph 5A(2) and (3) of this Schedule.

6   The licence holder shall provide such information as may be requested by the Licensing Authority for the purposes of the Act, about the products currently being manufactured or assembled under his licence and of the operations being carried out in relation to such manufacture and assembly.

7   The licence holder shall inform the Licensing Authority before making any material alteration in the premises or plant used under his licence, or in the operations for which they are used, and he shall inform the Licensing Authority of any change that he proposes to make in any personnel named in his licence as respectively:

(a)   responsible for supervising the production operations; or

(b)   responsible for quality control of the medicinal products being manufactured or assembled including the person named as the qualified person for the purposes of paragraphs 16 or 17, as the case may be, of this Part of this Schedule; or

(c)   in charge of the animals from which are derived any substances used in the production of the medicinal products being manufactured or assembled; or

(d)   responsible for the culture of any living tissues used in the manufacture of the medicinal products being manufactured or assembled.

8   The licence holder shall keep readily available for inspection by a person authorised by the Licensing Authority durable records of the details of manufacture and assembly of each batch of every medicinal product being manufactured or assembled under his licence and of the tests carried out thereon, including any register or other record referred to in paragraph 16(3)(b) or 17(3)(b), as the case may be, of this Schedule, in such a form that the records will be easily identifiable from the number of the batch as shown on each container in which the medicinal product is sold, supplied or exported, and he shall permit the person authorised to take copies or make extracts from such records. Such records shall not be destroyed without the consent of the Licensing Authority:

(a)   in relation to a medicinal product for human use, for the relevant period;

(b)   in any other case, for a period of five years from the date when the manufacture or assembly of the relevant batch occurred.

8A   The licence holder shall keep readily available for examination by a person authorised by the Licensing Authority, samples of each batch of finished medicinal products for human use manufactured or assembled under his licence for at least a period of one year from their expiry date and shall retain samples of starting materials (other than solvents, gases or water) for at least a period of two years from the date of the release of the relevant batch of which the relevant starting materials formed part, except where the licence holder is authorised by the Licensing Authority to destroy any such sample earlier.

8B   The licence holder shall make suitable arrangements to ensure that any record or sample referred to in paragraph 8 or 8A above relating to a medicinal product for human use is retained for the relevant period.

9   The licence holder shall, in relation to medicinal products other than for human use, keep such documents as will facilitate the withdrawal or recall from sale, supply or exportation of any such medicinal products to which the licence relates.

9A   (1) The manufacturer shall implement a system for recording and reviewing complaints in relation to medicinal products for human use manufactured or assembled under his licence, together with an effective system for recalling promptly and at any time such medicinal products in the distribution network.

(2) The manufacturer shall record and investigate all complaints described in sub-paragraph (1) of this paragraph and shall immediately inform the Licensing Authority of any defect which could result in a recall from sale, supply or exportation or in an abnormal restriction on such sale, supply or exportation.

10   Where the licence holder has been informed by the Licensing Authority that any batch of any medicinal product to which his licence relates has been found not to conform as regards strength, quality or purity with the specification of the relevant product or with the provisions of the Act or of any regulations under the Act that are applicable to the medicinal product, he shall, if so directed, withhold such batch from sale, supply or exportation, so far as may be reasonably practicable, for such a period not exceeding six weeks as may be specified by the Licensing Authority.

11 The licence holder shall ensure that any tests for determining conformity with the standards and specifications applying to any particular product used in the manufacture shall, except so far as the conditions of the relevant product licence may otherwise provide, be applied to samples taken from the medicinal product after all manufacturing processes have been completed, or at such earlier stage in the manufacture as may be approved by the Licensing Authority.

12 (1) The licence holder who is not the holder of a product licence in respect of the medicinal product to which the manufacturer's licence relates shall comply with any provisions of such a product licence that relates to the sale of that medicinal product and shall, by means of a label or otherwise, communicate the particulars of such provisions as relate to mode of sale, or restrictions as to sale, to any person to whom the licence holder sells or supplies that medicinal product.

(2) Where the manufacturer's licence relates to the assembly of a medicinal product, and the licence holder sells or supplies that medicinal product at such a stage of assembly that does not fully comply with the provisions of the relevant product licence that relates to labelling, that licence holder shall communicate the particulars of those provisions to the person to whom that medicinal product has been so sold or supplied.

13 Where in his application for a manufacturer's licence the licence holder had specified a general classification of medicinal products in respect of which that licence was required or had given particulars of manufacturing operations and of substances or articles in accordance with paragraph 6 of Schedule 1 to the Medicines (Applications for Manufacturer's and Wholesale Dealer's Licences) Regulations 1971 and there has been, or it is proposed that there shall be, a change in such general classification or such particulars, the licence holder shall forthwith notify the Licensing Authority in writing of such change or proposed change.

14 Where the manufacturer's licence relates to the assembly of a medicinal product and that medicinal product is not manufactured by the licence holder, and where particulars as to the name and address of the manufacturer of, or of the person who imports, that medicinal product have been given by the licence holder to the Licensing Authority, the licence holder shall forthwith notify the Licensing Authority in writing of any changes in such particulars.

15 The licence holder, for the purpose of enabling the Licensing Authority to ascertain whether there are any grounds for suspending, revoking or varying any licence or certificate granted or issued under Part II of the Act, shall permit, and provide all necessary facilities to enable, any person duly authorised in writing by the Licensing Authority, on production if required of his credentials, to carry out such inspection or to take such samples or copies, in relation to things belonging to, or any business carried on by, the licence holder, as such person would have the right to carry out or take under the Act for the purpose of verifying any statement contained in an application for a licence or certificate.

16 (1) Subject to sub-paragraph (5) below, the licence holder shall at all times have at his disposal the services of a person who as respects qualification and experience satisfies the provisions of Articles 23 and 24 of the Second Council Directive, to carry out the functions specified in sub-paragraph (3) below (*qualified person*). For the purposes of this paragraph, but without prejudice to sub-paragraph (4) below, the licence holder may regard a person as satisfying the provisions of the said Article 24 as respects formal qualifications if he produces evidence that he is a member of the Royal Pharmaceutical Society or of the Royal Society of Chemistry or of such other body as may appear to the Licensing Authority to be an appropriate body for the purpose, and that he is regarded by the body of which he is a member as so satisfying those provisions.

(2) The licence holder shall at all times provide and maintain such staff, premises, equipment and facilities as will enable the qualified person who is at his disposal to carry out the said functions.

(3) The functions to be carried out by the qualified person shall be as follows:

(a)   to ensure that each batch of the medicinal product to which the licence relates has been manufactured or assembled and checked in compliance with the provisions of the Act and regulations made thereunder, the provisions of the licence and the provisions of the product licence which relates to the product;

(aa)   where there is in relation to the product which has been manufactured or assembled, a certificate of registration, to ensure that each batch of the product has been manufactured or assembled and checked in compliance with that certificate and the provisions of the Medicines (Homoeopathic Medicinal Products for Human Use) Regulations 1994;

(b)   to certify in a register, or other record appropriate for the purpose, whether each production batch of the medicinal product to which the licence relates satisfies the requirements set out in (a) or, as the case may be, (aa) above and to ensure that such register or other record is regularly maintained, in particular that the appropriate entries in such register or other record are made as soon as practicable after each such batch has been manufactured.

(4) Where, after giving the licence holder and the person acting as a qualified person the opportunity of making representations to them (orally or in writing), the Licensing Authority are of the opinion that the person so acting does not satisfy the provisions of the said Articles 23 and 24 of the Second Council Directive as respects qualifications and experience, or that he is failing to carry out the functions specified in sub-paragraph (3) above, and have notified the licence holder accordingly in writing, the licence holder shall not permit that person to act as a qualified person so long as the said notification has not been withdrawn by the Licensing Authority.

(5) The provisions of this paragraph shall not apply in relation to veterinary drugs.

(6) The provisions of this paragraph shall also not apply where the licence relates to manufacturing activity which:

(a)   is limited to medicinal products to which Article 2 of the Medicines (Exemption from Licences) (Special and Transitional Cases) Order 1971 as amended applies, and consists solely of mixing together medicinal products and ingredients, other than active ingredients, on premises of which the licence holder is the occupier and which he is able to close so as to exclude the public; or

(b)   is limited to assembly only, where all the products to be assembled are for sale or supply in the course of a business and are supplied, without any recommendation, for the purpose of administration to a particular person after the licence holder has been requested by or on behalf of that person, and in that person's presence, to use his judgement as to the treatment required.

(7) The provisions of this paragraph shall not have effect until 22 November 1977 in relation to a licence which has been granted before the coming into operation of these Regulations.

Standard provisions for manufacturer's licences relating to vaccines for human use (SI 1971 No.972, Part I, Schedule 4, as amended)

1   Revoked by SI 1992 No. 2846.

2   The licence holder shall provide separate premises or separate parts of premises for the activities specified in the following sub-paragraphs, namely:

(a)   the production and the testing involved in the production of cell cultures for use in the production of vaccine;

(b)   the production and the testing involved in the production of vaccine prepared from viruses; and

(c)   the production and the testing involved in the production of vaccine prepared from micro-organisms or detoxified microbial toxins;

and shall ensure that only persons necessary to each activity as aforesaid shall have access to the separate premises or separate parts of premises provided for that activity.

3   The licence holder shall ensure that any procedure which, in the course of any of the activities specified in the preceding paragraph, involves or might involve:

(a)   the presence of transmissible agents; or

(b)   the use of cell cultures, animal tissues or micro-organisms, other than those from which the vaccine is produced;

shall not be carried out in the separate premises or separate parts of premises as aforesaid.

4   The licence holder shall ensure that no person who has been in contact with transmissible agents or experimental animals other than those connected with the vaccine being produced in the separate premises or separate parts of premises as aforesaid shall enter those premises or separate parts of premises on the same day that the contact as aforesaid has been made.

5   Before an animal is used in the production of vaccine the licence holder shall take all reasonable steps to ensure that it is free from disease and to this end shall keep the animal in quarantine and under observation for such period as the Licensing Authority may direct.

6   (1) The licence holder shall ensure that animals used in the production of vaccine are isolated and shall provide separate premises (not being the premises or parts of premises referred to in paragraph 2 above) for this purpose.

(2) The licence holder shall ensure that only persons engaged in the production and testing of vaccine or in the maintenance of animals or premises shall have access to the separate premises in which the animals are isolated.

7   The licence holder shall provide a special room capable of being washed and disinfected in the separate premises referred to in paragraph 6 above for the purpose of:

(a)   the inoculation of animals; and

(b)   the collection of material to be used in the preparation of vaccine.

8   Without prejudice to any other requirements to keep records, where vaccines contain or might contain micro-organisms or microbial toxins the licence holder shall keep a durable record, readily available for inspection by a person authorised by the Licensing Authority, of the origin, properties and characteristics of the cell cultures used in the production of those vaccines and shall ensure that the said record is not destroyed for a period of five years from the date when the relevant production occurred.

Standard provisions for manufacturer's licences relating to smallpox (SI 1971 No.972, Part II, Schedule 4, as amended)

1   (1) The licence holder shall ensure that animals used in the production of smallpox vaccine:

(a)   shall only be inoculated on a part of the skin that has been depilated and cleansed and which cannot be soiled by urine or faeces; and

(b)   are kept under observation for 28 days after the collection of the vaccinal material.

(2) Should any animal during the 28 days as aforesaid be found to be suffering from any infection other than vaccinia or show serious or persistent signs of ill health, vaccinal material obtained from that animal shall not be used in the production of smallpox vaccine.

2   Where it is necessary for an animal which has been inoculated as aforesaid to be killed, the licence holder shall ensure that:

(a)   the vaccinal material is collected immediately after the animal has been killed;

(b)   if the Licensing Authority so direct, a post-mortem examination of the carcass of the animal is made by a person with experience of the diseases of the particular animal so killed;

(c)   a durable record of the examination is kept readily available for inspection by a person authorised by the Licensing Authority;

(d)   the said record is not destroyed for a period of five years from the date when the animal was killed; and

(e)   where the examination indicates that the animal was suffering from diseases other than vaccinia, no vaccinal material obtained from that animal shall be used in the production of smallpox vaccine.

Standard provisions for manufacturer's licences relating to BCG vaccine (SI 1971 No.972, Part III, Schedule 4, as amended)

1   The licence holder shall provide separate premises or separate parts of premises for the production of BCG vaccine and shall ensure that only persons necessary to the production and testing of that vaccine shall have access to those separate premises or separate parts of premises.

2   The licence holder shall ensure that any procedure which involves or might involve:

(a)   the presence of transmissible agents other than BCG; or

(b)   the use of microbial cultures other than BCG, shall not be carried out in the separate premises or separate parts of premises referred to in paragraph 1 of this Part of this Schedule.

3   The licence holder shall ensure that all media, glassware and other apparatus issued in the production of BCG vaccine shall be kept and prepared for use in the separate premises or separate parts of premises referred to in paragraph 1 of this Part of this Schedule.

4   The licence holder shall not permit animals to be in the separate premises or separate parts of premises referred to in paragraph 1 of this Part of this Schedule and where it is necessary to use animals for testing BCG vaccine, the tests shall not be carried out in those separate premises or separate parts of premises.

5   (1) The licence holder shall arrange for all persons engaged in the production of BCG vaccine to be examined clinically by a doctor and where appropriate, radiologically and bacteriologically, at least every twelve months and whenever such a person shows signs of ill health.

(2) The licence holder shall ensure (as far as sub-paragraph (c) below is concerned, in so far as is reasonably practicable), that persons falling within the following descriptions shall not engage in the production of BCG vaccine, that is to say:

(a)   persons examined as aforesaid who are found to be suffering from active or potentially active tuberculosis lesions;

(b)   persons who show a negative reaction when tested with tuberculin; or

(c)   persons who are in close contact with a person who is suffering from any active form of tuberculosis.

(3) If on examination as aforesaid a person engaged in the production of BCG vaccine is found to be suffering from active or potentially active tuberculosis lesions, then, after that person has been removed from the separate premises or separate parts of premises referred to in paragraph 1 of this Part of this Schedule, the licence holder shall make arrangements for those separate premises or separate parts of premises and all equipment used in the production of BCG vaccine to be treated in such a manner as to remove the risk of contamination of the vaccine and shall cease to use any unsealed cultures of BCG and all current preparations of BCG vaccine which may have become contaminated with other *Mycobacterium tuberculosis* organisms.

6   The licence holder shall ensure that no person who has been in contact with transmissible agents other than BCG vaccine shall enter the separate premises or separate parts of premises referred to in paragraph 1 of this Part of this Schedule on the same day that the contact as aforesaid has been made.

Standard provisions for manufacturer's licences relating to toxins (SI 1971 No.972, Part IV, Schedule 4, as amended)

1   Revoked by SI 1992 No.2846.
2   The licence holder shall provide separate premises or separate parts of premises for the production and the testing involved in the production of toxins and shall ensure that only persons necessary to the production and testing of toxins (or related toxoids) shall have access to the separate premises or separate parts of premises as aforesaid.
3   The licence holder shall ensure that any procedure which in the course of the production and testing referred to in the previous paragraph involves or might involve the presence of micro-organisms, plants or animals other than those from which the toxins are to be produced, shall not be carried out in the separate premises or separate parts of premises as aforesaid.

Standard provisions for manufacturer's licences relating to sera (SI 1971 No.972, Part V, Schedule 4, as amended)

1   Revoked by SI 1992 No.2846.
2   The licence holder shall ensure that blood used in the production of any serum shall only be collected from living animals in separate premises which:

(a)   are used for no other purpose;
(b)   have impervious walls and floors; and
(c)   are capable of being washed and chemically disinfected.

3   The licence holder shall ensure that an adequate system of manure removal is in operation in the separate premises referred to in paragraph 2 of this Part of this Schedule.
4   Before an animal is used in the production of any serum, the licence holder shall take all reasonable steps to ensure that it is free from disease and to this end shall keep the animal in quarantine and under observation for such period as the Licensing Authority may direct.
5   The licence holder shall notify the Licensing Authority if any animal which has been used in the production of any serum is found to be suffering from an infection other than an infection produced by living organisms against which it is being immunised or shows serious or persistent signs of ill health not attributable to the process of immunisation and shall withhold any serum obtained from that animal from sale,

supply or exportation until he has obtained the consent of the Licensing Authority in writing to its release.

6   The licence holder shall notify the Licensing Authority if any post-mortem examination on any animal indicates that any other animals used in the production of any serum are or are likely to be unhealthy, and the licence holder shall not use those animals for the production of any serum until either he has obtained the consent of the Licensing Authority in writing or has complied with any requirements the Licensing Authority may consider necessary in the interest of safety.

7   The licence holder shall ensure that laboratories in which any serum is processed are separate from premises in which animals are housed.

8   The licence holder shall provide such number of sterilisers as are necessary for the sterilisation of all glassware and other apparatus used in the production of sera as aforesaid.

9   Without prejudice to any other requirements to keep records, the licence holder shall keep the following durable records relating to the production of sera readily available for inspection by a person authorised by the Licensing Authority and shall ensure that the said record is not destroyed for a period of five years from the date when the relevant production occurred:

(a)   as to the cultures used:

(i)   the source from which the culture was obtained;

(ii)   the nature of the material from which the culture was isolated;
(iii)   the date of the isolation; and
(iv)   evidence of the identity and specificity of the culture;

(b)   as to the procedure used in the immunising of animals:

(i)   the method of preparing the culture or antigen used for immunisation;
(ii)   the dosage and methods employed in administering the culture or antigen;
(iii)   the time in the course of immunisation at which blood is withdrawn for preparation of the serum;

(c)   the results of any tests which may have been applied to the serum to determine its content of specific antibodies or its specific therapeutic potency.

Standard provisions for a wholesale dealer's licence (Council Directive 92/25/EEC and SI 1971 No.972, Schedule 3, as amended)

1   The licence holder shall provide and maintain such staff, premises, equipment and facilities for the handling, storage and distribution of the medicinal products which he handles, stores or distributes under his licence, as are necessary to avoid deterioration of the medicinal products and he shall not use for such purposes premises other than those specified in the licence or which may be approved from time to time by the Licensing Authority.

2   The licence holder shall provide such information as may be requested by the Licensing Authority concerning the type and quantity of any medicinal product which he currently handles, stores or distributes.

3   The licence holder shall inform the Licensing Authority of any proposed structural alterations to, or discontinuance of use of, premises to which the licence relates or premises which have been approved from time to time by the Licensing Authority.

4   The licence holder shall keep such documents relating to his transactions by way of the sale of medicinal products to which the licence relates as will facilitate the withdrawal or recall from sale or exportation of such products.

4A   Where the licence relates to products to which Council Directive 2001/83/EC apply, the licence holder shall institute an emergency plan which ensures effective implementation of any recall from the market which is either:

(a)   ordered by the Licence Authority or the competent authority of a member state other than the United Kingdom; or
(b)   carried out in co-operation with the manufacturer or the holder of the product licence or of the marketing authorisations granted by the competent authority of a member state other than the United Kingdom in respect of the products.

4B   (1) Where the licence relates to products to which Council Directive 2001/83/EC apply, the licence holder shall keep records, which may be in the form of invoices or on computer or in any other form giving the following information in respect of such products which have been received or despatched:

(a)   the date of receipt and of despatch;
(b)   the name of the medicinal products;
(c)   the quantity of the medicinal products received or despatched;
(d)   the name and address of the person from whom or to whom the products are sold or supplied as appropriate.

NB The licence holder may only sell medicinal products to persons who hold authorisations or who are entitled to sell to the public. The licence holder may only purchase from a person who possesses an authorisation.

(2) The record referred to in sub-paragraph (1) above shall be made available for inspection by any person duly authorised in writing by the Licensing Authority for a period of five years after the date of receipt or despatch.

5   Where the licence holder has been informed by the Licensing Authority or by the holder of the product licence that any batch of any medicinal product to which the wholesale dealer's licence relates has been found not to conform as regards strength, quality or purity with the specification of that product or with the provisions of the Act or of any regulations under the Act that are applicable to the medicinal product, he shall, if so directed, withhold such batch from sale or exportation, so far as may be reasonably practicable, for such period not exceeding six weeks as may be specified by the Licensing Authority.

6   (1) Subject to the provisions of sub-paragraph (2) of this paragraph, no medicinal product to which the wholesale dealer's licence relates shall be sold or offered for sale by way of wholesale dealing by virtue of that licence unless there has been granted in respect of that medicinal product a product licence or certificate of registration which is for the time being in force and any sale or offer for sale shall be in conformity with the provisions of such product licence or certificate of registration.

(2) The provisions of the preceding sub-paragraph of this paragraph shall not apply where:

(a)   by virtue of any provisions of the Act or of any order made thereunder, the sale (other than sale by way of wholesale dealing) of the medicinal product to which the wholesale dealer's licence relates is not subject to the restrictions imposed by section 7(2) of the Act; or
(b)   the sale or offer for sale by way of wholesale dealing is of a medicinal product the dealings in which, at the time of its acquisition by the licence holder, were not subject to the said restrictions imposed by section 7(2) of the Act; or
(c)   at the time of such sale or offer for sale, the licence holder does not know, or could not by reasonable diligence and care have known, that such sale or offer for sale is of a medicinal product, or believes, on reasonable grounds, that the provisions of sub-paragraph (2)(a) or (2)(b) of this paragraph apply in relation to such sale or offer for sale.

7   The licence holder, for the purpose of enabling the Licensing Authority to ascertain whether there are any grounds for suspending, revoking or varying any licence or certificate granted or issued under Part II of the Act, shall permit and provide all necessary facilities to enable any person duly authorised in writing by the Licensing Authority, on production if required of his credentials, to carry out such inspection or to take samples or copies, in relation to things belonging to, or any business carried on by, the licence holder, as such person would have the right to carry out or take under the Act for the purpose of verifying any statement contained in an application for a licence or certificate.

7A   (1) Where the licence relates to products to which Council Directive 2001/83/EC apply, the licence holder shall at all times have at his disposal the services of a person (in this paragraph called a *responsible person*) who possesses in the opinion of the Licensing Authority:

(a)   knowledge of the activities to be carried out and of the procedures to be performed under the licence which is adequate for performing the functions of the responsible person; and

(b)   experience in those activities and procedures which is adequate for those purposes.

(2) The functions of the responsible person shall be to ensure that the conditions under which the licence has been granted have been, and are being, complied with and that the quality of the products is maintained in accordance with the requirements of the appropriate product licence.

(3) The provisions of sub-paragraphs (5) and (6) of paragraph 8 of this Schedule shall apply in relation to a responsible person as they apply to a qualified person within the meaning of that paragraph but as though the references to:

(a)   the provisions of Articles 23 and 24 of the Second Council Directive as respects qualifications and experience were to the provisions of sub-paragraph (1) and (2) of this paragraph; and

(b)   sub-paragraph (3) of paragraph 8 were to sub-paragraph (2) of this paragraph.

7B   (1)   Where the licence relates to products to which Chapters II to V of the 1965 Directive apply, the licence holder shall obtain supplies of such products only from:

(a)   any person who is the holder of a manufacturer's licence or a wholesale dealer's licence which relates to those products; or

(b)   any person who holds an authorisation granted by the competent authority of a member state other than the United Kingdom authorising the manufacture of such products or the distribution by way of wholesale dealing of such products.

7C   (1) Where the licence relates to products to which Council Directive 2001/83/EC apply, the licence holder shall distribute them by way of wholesale dealing only to:

(a)   the holder of a wholesale dealer's licence which relates to those products;

(b)   the holder of an authorisation granted by the competent authority of a member state other than the United Kingdom authorising the supply of such products by way of wholesale distribution; or

(c)   any person who may lawfully sell those products by retail or may lawfully supply them in circumstances corresponding to retail sale; or,

(d)   any person who may lawfully administer those products.

(2) where supply is made pursuant to paragraph (1)(c) above, the licence holder shall enclose with the products a document which makes it possible to ascertain:

(a)   the date on which the transaction took place;

(b)   the name and pharmaceutical form of the products;

(c)   the quantity of the products supplied;

(d)   the names and addresses of the persons from whom the products were supplied.

8   (1) Subject to sub-paragraphs (7), (7A) and (8) below, where the licence relates to imported proprietary products the licence holder shall at all times have at his disposal the services of a person who as respects qualifications and experience satisfies the provisions of Articles 23 and 24 of the Second Council Directive to carry out the functions specified in sub-paragraph (3) below (*qualified person*). For the purposes of this paragraph, but without prejudice to sub-paragraph (6) below, the licence holder may regard a person as satisfying the provisions of the said Article 24 as respects formal qualifications if he produces evidence that he is a member of the Royal Pharmaceutical Society or of the Royal Society of Chemistry or of such other body as may appear to the Licensing Authority to be an appropriate body for the purpose, and that he is regarded by the body of which he is a member as so satisfying those provisions.

(2) The licence holder shall at all times provide and maintain staff, premises, equipment and facilities as will enable the qualified person who is at his disposal to carry out the said functions.

(3) The functions to be carried out by the qualified person shall be as follows:

(a)   to ensure that each production batch of any imported proprietary product to which the licence relates has undergone a full qualitative analysis, a quantitative analysis of at least all the active ingredients and all other tests or checks necessary to ensure that the quality of the product imported satisfies the requirements of the product licence which relates to the product; or

(aa)   where there is in relation to the imported proprietary product, a certificate of registration, to ensure that each batch of the product has been tested in accordance with the manufacturing and control file submitted with the application for that certificate;

(b)   to certify in a register or other record appropriate for the purpose whether each batch of the imported proprietary product to which the licence relates satisfies the requirements set out in (a) or (as the case may be) (aa) above and to ensure that such register or other record is regularly maintained.

Provided that the above functions shall be deemed to be carried out in respect of a batch which had entered the territory of another member state prior to its importation if there is available evidence in writing, signed by a person carrying out the functions of a qualified person in that member state, that the batch in question satisfies the requirements set out in (a) above.

(4) The licence holder shall keep the said register or other record readily available for inspection by a person authorised by the Licensing Authority and such register or other record shall not be destroyed for a period of five years from the date of the certification referred to in sub-paragraph (3)(b) above.

(5) The licence holder shall notify the Licensing Authority of the name and address and degrees, diplomas or qualifications and experience of the person who will carry out the functions of a qualified person and shall notify the Licensing Authority of any change as to the qualified person and shall not permit any person to act as a qualified person except the person named in his licence as the qualified person for the purposes of this paragraph or, subject to the provisions of paragraph (6) below, any other such person whose name is notified to the Licensing Authority.

(6) Where, after giving the licence holder and the person acting as a qualified person the opportunity of making representations to them (orally or in writing), the Licensing Authority are of the opinion that the person so acting does not satisfy the provisions of the said Articles 23 and 24 of the Second Council Directive as respects qualifications and experience, or that he is failing to carry out the functions specified in sub-paragraph (3) above, and have notified the licence holder accordingly

in writing, the licence holder shall not permit that person to act as a qualified person so long as the said notification has not been withdrawn by the Licensing Authority.

(7) The provisions of this paragraph shall not apply where the imported proprietary product that is to be sold or offered for sale or in any other way distributed has been in the possession of a person in the course of his business who is the holder of a wholesale dealer's licence which relates to imported proprietary products of the same description in circumstances by virtue of which that licence holder is required to comply with the provisions of this paragraph.

(7A) The provisions of this paragraph shall also not apply where the imported proprietary product is an exempt imported product.

(8) The provisions of this paragraph shall also not apply where the licence holder handles the imported proprietary product:

(a) in the course of the provision of facilities solely for the transport of the medicinal product; or

(b) in the course of a business carried on by him as an import agent where he imports the medicinal product solely to the order of another person who intends, in the course of a business carried on by him, to sell, or offer for sale the medicinal product by way of wholesale dealing or in any other way intends to distribute the medicinal product.

(9) The provisions of this paragraph shall not have effect until 22 November 1977 in relation to a licence which has been granted before the coming into operation of these regulations.

8A (1) Where the licence relates to imported proprietary products, the licence holder shall in relation to medicinal products for human use:

(a) ensure that all manufacture and assembly operations have been carried out by a duly authorised manufacturer or assembler and that the products have been manufactured or assembled in accordance with the principles and guidelines of good manufacturing practice;

(b) keep readily available for examination by a person authorised by the Licensing Authority, samples of each batch of finished medicinal products for at least one year after their expiry date except where the licence holder is authorised by the Licensing Authority to destroy any such samples earlier;

(c) implement a system for recording and reviewing complaints relating to the medicinal products to which his licence relates, together with an effective system for recalling promptly and at any time any such medicinal product in the distribution network; and

(d) record and investigate all such and immediately inform the Licensing Authority of any defect which could result in a recall from sale, supply or exportation or is an abnormal restriction on such sale, supply or exportation.

8B (1) Where the licence relates to exempted imported products, the licence holder shall only sell or supply such products in response to a bona fide unsolicited order to fulfil special needs, formulated in accordance with the specification of a doctor or dentist and for use by his individual patients on his direct personal responsibility and where the provisions set out in sub-paragraphs (2) to (9) are complied with.

(2) No later than 28 days prior to each importation of an exempted imported product, the licence holder shall give written notice to the Licensing Authority stating his intention to import that medicinal product and stating the following particulars:

(a) the name of the medicinal product, being the brand name or the common name, or the scientific name, and any name, if different, under which the medicinal product is to be sold or supplied in the United Kingdom;

(b) any trademark or name of the manufacturer of the medicinal product;

(c) in respect of each active constituent of the medicinal product, any international non-proprietary or British approved name or monograph name or where that constituent does not have an international non-proprietary name, a British approved name or monograph name, the accepted scientific name or any other name descriptive of the true nature of the constituent;

(d)   the quantity of the medicinal product which is to be imported which shall not exceed the quantity specified in sub-paragraph (6); and

(e)   the name and address of the manufacturer or assembler of that medicinal product in the form in which it is to be imported and, if the person who will supply that medicinal product for importation is not the manufacturer or imported, the name and address of such supplier.

(3) Subject to sub-paragraph (4), the licence holder shall not import the exempt imported product if, before the end of 28 days from the date on which the Licensing Authority sends or gives the licence holder an acknowledgement in writing by the Licensing Authority that they have received the notice referred to in sub-paragraph (2) above, the Licensing Authority have notified him in writing that the product should not be imported.

(4) The licence holder may import the exempted imported product referred to in the notice where he has been notified in writing by the Licensing Authority before the end of the 28 day period referred to in sub-paragraph (3), that the exempted import product may be imported.

(5) Where the licence holder sell or supplies exempted imported product he shall in addition to those records mentioned in 4B of this Schedule make and maintain written records relating to:

(a)   the batch number of the batch of the product from which the sale or supply was made; and

(b)   details of any adverse reaction to the product sold or supplied of which he becomes aware.

(6) Where the licence holder shall import no more on anyone occasion than such an amount as is sufficient for 25 single administrations, or 25 courses of treatment where the amount imported is sufficient for a maximum of three months' treatment and on any such occasion shall not import more than the quantity notified to the Licensing Authority under sub-paragraph (2)(d).

(7) the licence holder shall inform the Licensing Authority forthwith of any matter coming to his attention which might reasonably cause the Licensing Authority to believe that the medicinal product can no longer be regarded either as a product which can safely be administered to human beings or as a product which is of satisfactory quality for such administration.

(8) The licence holder shall not issue an advertisement, catalogue, price list or circular relating to the exempted imported product or make any representations in respect of that product.

(9) The licence holder shall cease importing or supplying an exempt imported product if he has received a notice in writing from the Licensing Authority directing that, as from a date specified in that notice, a particular product or class of products shall no longer be imported or supplied.

(10) In this paragraph:

British approved name means the name which appears in the current edition of the list prepared by the appropriate body in accordance with section 100 of the Act and published by the Ministers on the recommendation of the Medicines Commission and *current* in this definition means current at the time the notice is sent to the Licensing Authority.

Common name means the international non-proprietary name or, if one does not exist, the usual common name.

International non-proprietary name means the name which has been selected by the World Health Organization as a recommended international non-proprietary name and in respect of which the Director-General of the World Health Organization has given notice to that effect in the *World Health Organization Chronicle*.

Monograph name means the name or approved synonym which appears at the head of a monograph in the current edition of the *British Pharmacopoeia*, the *British Pharmaceutical Codex*, the *European Pharmacopoeia* or a foreign or international compendium of standards and *current* in this definition means current at the time the notice is sent to the Licensing Authority.

APPENDIX SIX

Medicines Act 1968

Patient Group Directions (PGD)

Schedule 7 to the Regulations

(SI 2000 No.1917 as amended)

Classes of individual by whom Prescription Only Medicines may be supplied or administered

Pharmacists
Registered nurses
Registered midwives
Registered health visitors
Registered ophthalmic opticians
Registered chiropodists
Registered orthoptists
Registered physiotherapists
Registered radiographers
Registered paramedics or individuals who hold a certificate of proficiency in ambulance paramedic skills issued by or with the approval of, the Secretary of State or state registered paramedics
Registered dieticians (SI 2004 No.1189)
Registered occupational therapists (SI 2004 No.1189)
Registered orthotists and prosthetists (SI 2004 No.1189)
Registered speech and language therapists (SI 2004 No.1189).

Particulars to be included in a Patient Group Direction

(a)   the period during which the Direction shall have effect;
(b)   the description or class of Prescription Only Medicine to which the Direction applies;

(c)   whether there are any restrictions on the quantity of medicine which may be supplied on any one occasion, and, if so, what restrictions;

(d)   the clinical situations which Prescription Only Medicines of that description or class may be used to treat;

(e)   the clinical criteria under which the person shall be eligible for treatment;

(f)   whether any class is excluded from treatment under the Direction and, if so what class of person;

(g)   whether there are any circumstances in which further advice should be sought from a doctor or dentist and if so what circumstances;

(h)   the pharmaceutical form or forms in which Prescription Only Medicines of that class or description are to be administered;

(i)   the strength, or maximum strength, at which Prescription Only Medicines of that description or class are to be administered;

(j)   the applicable dosage or maximum dosage;

(k)   the route of administration;

(l)   the frequency of administration;

(m)   any minimum or maximum period of administration applicable to Prescription Only Medicines of that description or class;

(n)   whether there are any relevant warnings to note and, if so, what warnings;

(o)   whether there is any follow up action to be taken in any circumstances and, if so, what action and in what circumstances;

(p)   arrangements for referral for medical advice;

(q)   details of the records to be kept of the supply, or the administration, of medicines under the Direction.

Medicines Act 1968

Veterinary drugs: pharmacy

and merchants list

The Medicines (Exemptions for Merchants in Veterinary Drugs) Order 1998 (SI 1998 No.1044, as amended) permits the retail sale of certain categories of veterinary drugs which are listed by the Minister. This list is open to inspection at the office of the Veterinary Medicines directorate and copies will be publicly available and published regularly (Chapter 13). The Minister's list includes such products specified only by their product licence number and name.

The vast majority of pharmacies do not regularly handle these listed medicines which are used in the commercial husbandry of livestock. For the convenience of pharmacists, the details of the listed cat, dog and horse wormers are set out below. They are all permitted licensed medicinal products (PML).

Veterinary drugs saleable by pharmacists, merchants and saddlers

Cat and dog wormers	
Marketing authorisation No.	Name of product
Vm 00010/4113	Bayer Dog Wormer Tablets
Vm 00010/4115	Bayer Multi-Worm for Dogs
Vm 00715/4071	Bob Martins Easy to use Wormer Granules
Vm 00010/4102	Drontal Puppy Suspension
Vm 11188/4003	Granofen Wormer for Cats and Dogs
Vm 15476/4059	Panacur Pet Paste
Vm 11990/4014	Zerofen 22% Granules for Cats and Dogs

Horse wormers

Marketing authorisation No.	Name of product
Vm 00057/4131	Equitac
Vm 0025/4069	Eqvalan Paste for Horses and Donkeys
Vm 00242/4038	Furexel
Vm 0844/4207	Multiwurma
Vm 0286/4039	Oxfendazole Horse Paste
Vm 15476/4060	Panacur Equine Guard
Vm 15476/4053	Panacur Paste
Vm 00086/4158	Panacur 22% Granules Horse Wormer
Vm 15476/4009	Panacur 10% Suspension
Vm 12597/4013	Pyratape-P Horse Wormer
Vm 00057/4060	Strongid-P Granules
Vm 00057/4062	Strongid-P Paste
Vm 05869/4151	Systamex Horse Paste Wormer
Vm 00242/4013	Telmin
Vm 00242/4026	Telmin B
Vm 00242/4014	Telmin Paste
Vm 00015/4052	Verdisol
Vm 11990/4017	Zerofen 22% Equine Granules

Misuse of Drugs Act 1971

Controlled Drugs classified for level of penalties

Schedule 2 to the Act classifies Controlled Drugs into three lists (Class A, Class B, and Class C) for the purpose of the level of penalties for offences under the Act. The penalties are given in Schedule 3 (not reproduced here).

Since the Act came into force, numerous additions have been made, by Orders, to the original list of drugs in Schedule 2. In this appendix, a date shown against any drug indicates the year it was added to the list.

For the Schedules to the Misuse of Drugs Regulations, which classify Controlled Drugs according to the relevant regimes of control, see Appendix 9.

Schedule 2

Part I: Class A drugs

1   (a)   The following substances and products, namely:

Acetorphine
Alfentanil (1984)
Allylprodine
Alphacetylmethadol
Alphameprodine
Alphamethadol
Alphaprodine
Anileridine
Benzethidine
Benzylmorphine
  (3-benzylmorphine)

Betacetylmethadol
Betameprodine
Betamethadol
Betaprodine
Bezitramide
4-Bromo-2,5-dimethoxy-
  α-methylphenethylamine (1975)
Bufotenine
Carfentanil (1986)
Clonitazene
Coca leaf

Cocaine

4-Cyano-2-dimethylamino-4,4-diphenylbutane

4-Cyano-1-methyl-4-phenylpiperidine

Desomorphine

Dextromoramide

Diamorphine

Diampromide

Diethylthiambutene

N,N-Diethyltryptamine

Difenoxin (1-(3-cyano-3,3-diphenylpropyl)-4-phenylpiperidine-4-carboxylic acid) (1975)

Dihydrocodeinone O-carboxymethyloxime

Dihydroetorphine

Dihydromorphine

Dimenoxadole

Dimepheptanol

Dimethylthiambutene

2,5-Dimethoxy-α,4-dimethylphenethylamine

N,N-Dimethyltryptamine

Dioxaphetyl butyrate

Diphenoxylate

Dipipanone

Drotebanol (3,4-dimethoxy-17-methylmorphinan-6-β,14-diol) (1973)

Ecgonine, and any derivative of ecgonine which is convertible to ecgonine or to cocaine

Ethylmethylthiambutene

Eticyclidine (1984)

Etonitazene

Etorphine

Etoxeridine

Etryptamine (1998)

Fentanyl

Furethidine

Hydromorphinol

Hydromorphone

Hydroxypethidine

N-Hydroxy-tenamphetamine (1990)

Isomethadone

Ketobemidone

Levomethorphan

Levomoramide

Levophenacylmorphan

Levorphanol

Lofentanil (1986)

Lysergamide

Lysergide and other N-alkyl derivatives of lysergamide

Mescaline

Metazocine

Methadone

Methadyl acetate

Methyldesorphine

Methyldihydromorphine (6-methyldihydromorphine)

4-Methylaminorex (1990)

2-Methyl-3-morpholino-1,1-diphenylpropanecarboxylic acid

1-Methyl-4-phenylpiperidine-4-carboxylic acid

Metopon

Morpheridine

Morphine

Morphine methobromide, morphine N-oxide and other pentavalent nitrogen morphine derivatives

Myrophine

Nicomorphine (3,6-dinicotinoyl-morphine)

Noracymethadol

Norlevorphanol

Normethadone

Normorphine

Norpipanone

Opium, whether raw, prepared or medicinal

Oxycodone

Oxymorphone

Pethidine

Phenadoxone

Phenampromide

Phenazocine

Phencyclidine (1979)

4-Phenylpiperidine-4-carboxylic acid ethyl ester

Phenomorphan

Phenoperidine

Piminodine

Piritramide

Poppy-straw and concentrate of poppy-straw

Proheptazine

Properidine (1-methyl-4-phenylpiperidine-4-carboxylic acid isopropyl ester)

Psilocin

Racemethorphan

Racemoramide

Racemorphan

Remifentanil

Rolicyclidine (1984)   Thebaine
Sufentanil (1983)   Tilidate (1983)
Tenocyclidine (1984)   Trimeperidine;
Thebacon

(b)   any compound (not being a compound for the time being specified in sub-paragraph (a) above) structurally derived from tryptamine or from a ring-hydroxy tryptamine by substitution at the nitrogen atom of the side-chain with one or more alkyl substituents but no other substituent [sub-paragraph added by SI 1977 No.1243];

(c)   addition of thirty-six phenethylamine derivatives;

(d)   any compound (not being methoxyphenamine or a compound for the time being specified in sub-paragraph (a) above) structurally derived from phenethylamine, an N-alkylphenethylamine, α-methylphenethylamine, an N-alkyl-α-methylphenethylamine, α-ethylphenethylamine, or an N-alkyl-α-ethylphenethylamine by substitution in the ring to any extent with alkyl, alkoxy, alkylenedioxy or halide substituents, whether or not further substituted in the ring by one or more other univalent substituents [sub-paragraph added by SI 1977 No.1243];

(e)   any compound (not being a compound for the time being specified in sub-paragraph (a) above) structurally derived from fentanyl by modification in any of the following ways, that is to say:

(i)   by replacement of the phenyl portion of the phenethyl group by any heteromonocycle whether or not further substituted in the heterocycle;

(ii)   by substitution in the phenethyl group with alkyl, alkenyl, alkoxy, hydroxy, halogeno, haloalkyl, amino or nitro groups;

(iii)   by substitution in the piperidine ring with alkyl or alkenyl groups;

(iv)   by substitution in the aniline ring with alkyl, alkoxy, alkylenedioxy, halogeno or haloalkyl groups;

(v)   by substitution at the 4-position of the piperidine ring with any alkoxycarbonyl or alkoxyalkyl or acyloxy group;

(vi)   by replacement of the N-propionyl group by another acyl group [sub-paragraph added by SI 1986 No.2230];

(f)   any compound (not being a compound for the time being specified in sub-paragraph (a) above) structurally derived from pethidine by modification in any of the following ways, that is to say:

(i)   by replacement of the 1-methyl group by an acyl or alkyl group, whether or not unsaturated, benzyl or phenethyl group, whether or not further substituted;

(ii)   by substitution in the piperidine ring with alkyl or alkenyl groups or with a propano bridge, whether or not further substituted;

(iii)   by substitution in the 4-phenyl ring with alkyl, alkoxy, aryloxy, halogeno or haloalkyl groups;

(iv)   by replacement of the 4-ethoxycarbonyl by any other alkoxycarbonyl or any alkoxyalkyl or acyloxy group;

(v)   by formation of an N-oxide or of a quaternary base [sub-paragraph added by SI 1986 No.2230].

2   Any stereoisomeric form of a substance for the time being specified in paragraph 1 above not being dextromethorphan or dextrorphan.

3   Any ester or ether of a substance for the time being specified in paragraph 1 or 2 above, not being a substance for the time being specified in Part II of this Schedule.

4   Any salt of a substance for the time being specified in any of paragraphs 1 to 3 above.

5   Any preparation or other product containing a substance or product for the time being specified in any of paragraphs 1 to 4 above.

Part II: Class B drugs

1   (a)   The following substances and products, namely:

Acetyldihydrocodeine	Methylphenobarbitone
Amphetamine	[methylphenobarbital] (1984)
Codeine	Nicocodine
Dihydrocodeine	Nicodicodine
Ethylmorphine (3-ethylmorphine)	(6-nicotinoyldihydrocodeine) (1973)
Glutethimide (1985)	Norcodeine
Lefetamine (1986)	Pentazocine (1985)
Mecloqualone (1984)	Phenmetrazine
Methaqualone (1984)	Pholcodine
Methcathinone (1998)	Propiram
Methylamphetamine	Zipeprol (1998);
Methylphenidate	

(b)   any 5,5-disubstituted barbituric acid.

2   Any stereoisomeric form of a substance for the time being specified in paragraph 1 of this Part of this Schedule.

3   Any salt of a substance for the time being specified in paragraph 1 or 2 of this Part of this Schedule.

4   Any preparation or other product containing a substance or product for the time being specified in any of paragraphs 1 to 3 of this Part of this Schedule, not being a preparation falling within paragraph 6 of Part I of this Schedule.

Part III: Class C drugs

1   (a)   The following substances, namely:

Alprazolam	Estazolam (1985)
Aminorex (1998)	Ethchlorvynol
Benzphetamine [benzfetamine]	Ethinamate (1985)
Bromazepam (1985)	Ethyl loflazepate (1985)
Brotizolam (1998)	N-Ethylamfetamine
Camazepam (1985)	Fencamfamin (1986)
Cannabinol (2003)	Fenethylline (1986)
Cannabinol derivatives (2003)	Fenproporex (1986)
Cannabis and cannabis resin	Fludiazepam (1985)
(2003)	Flunitrazepam (1985)
Cathine (1986)	Flurazepam (1985)
Cathinone (1986)	Halazepam (1985)
Chlordiazepoxide (1985)	Haloxazolam (1985)
Clorphentermine	4-Hydroxyl-*n*-butyril acid (2003)
Clobazam (1985)	Ketazolam
Clonazepam (1985)	Loprazolam (1985)
Clorazepic acid (1985)	Lorazepam (1985)
Clotiazepam (1985)	Lormetazepam (1985)
Cloxazolam (1985)	Mazindol (1985)
Delorazepam (1985)	Medazepam (1985)
Dextropropoxyphene (1983)	Mefenorex (1985)
Diazepam (1985)	Mephentermine
Diethylpropion (1984)	Meprobamate (1985)

Mesocarb (1998)
Methyprylone (1985)
Midazolam (1990)
Nimetazepam (1985)
Nitrazepam (1985)
Nordazepam (1985)
Oxazepam (1985)
Oxazolam (1985)
Pemoline (1989)
Phendimetrazine

Phentermine (1985)
Pinazepam (1985)
Pipradol
Prazepam (1985)
Pyrovalerone (1986)
Temazepam (1985)
Tetrazepam (1985)
Triazolam (1985)
Zolpidem.

2   Any stereoisomeric form of a substance for the time being specified in paragraph 1 of this Part of this Schedule, not being phenylpropanolamine.

3   Any salt of a substance for the time being specified in paragraph 1 or 2 of this Part of this Schedule.

4   Any preparation or other product containing a substance for the time being specified in any of paragraphs 1 to 3 of this Part of this Schedule, Part IV.

5   The following substances:

4-Androstene-3,17-dione
5-Androstene-3,17-diol
Atamestane
Bolandiol
Bolazine
Boldenone
Bolenol
Calusterone
4-Chloromethandienone
Clostebol
Drostanolone
Enestebol
Epitiostanol
Ethyloestrenol [ethylestrenol]
Fluoxymesterone
Formebolone
Furazabol
Mesbolone
Mestanolone
Mesterolone
Methandienone
Methandriol
Methenolone [metenolone]
Methyltestosterone

Metribolone
Mibolerone
Nandrolone
19-Nor-4-androstene-3,17-dione
19-Nor-4-androstene-3,17-diol
Norboletone
Norclostebol
Norethandrolone
Ovandrotone
Oxabolone
Oxandrolone
Oxymesterone
Oxymetholone
Prasterone
Propetandrol
Quinbolone
Roxibolone
Silandrone
Stanozolol
Stenbolone
Testosterone
Thiomesterone
Trenbolone.

6   Any compound (not being trilostane or a compound for the time being specified in paragraph 5 above) structurally derived from 17-hydroxyandrostan-3-one or from 17-hydroxy-estran-3-one by modification in any of the following ways:

(a)   by further substitution at position 17 by a methyl or ethyl group;

(b)   by substitution to any extent at one or more positions 1, 2, 4, 6, 7, 9, 11, or 16, but at no other position;

(c)   by unsaturation in the carbocyclic ring system to any extent, provided that there are no more than two ethylenic bonds in any one carbocyclic ring;

(d)   by fusion of ring A with a heterocyclic system.

7   Any substance which is an ester or ether (or, where more than one hydroxyl function is available, both an ester and an ether) of a substance specified in paragraph 5 above or described in paragraph 6 above.

8	Chorionic gonadotrophin (HCG)	Somatrem
	Somatotropin	Non-human chorionic gonadotrophin
	Clenbuterol	Somatropin.

Meaning of certain expressions used in this schedule

For the purposes of this schedule, the following expressions (which are not among those defined in section 37(1) of this Act) have the meanings assigned to them below.

cannabinol derivatives   means the following substances, except where contained in cannabis or cannabis resin, namely tetrahydro derivatives of cannabinol and 3-alkyl homologues of cannabinol or of its tetrahydro derivatives;

coca leaf   means the leaf of any plant of the genus *Erythroxylon* from whose leaves cocaine can be extracted either directly or by chemical transformation;

concentrate of poppy straw   means the material produced when poppy straw has entered into a process for the concentration of its alkaloids;

medicinal opium   means raw opium which has undergone the process necessary to adapt it for medicinal use in accordance with the requirements of the *British Pharmacopoeia*, whether it is in the form of powder or is granulated or is in any other form, and whether it is or is not mixed with neutral substances;

poppy straw   means all parts, except the seeds, of the opium poppy, after mowing;

raw opium   includes powdered or granulated opium but does not include medicinal opium.

APPENDIX NINE

Misuse of Drugs Regulations 2001 (as amended)

Classification of Controlled Drugs for regimes of control

The five Schedules of Controlled Drugs appended to the Misuse of Drugs Regulations 2001 (SI 1985 No.3998, as amended) are reproduced in this appendix. It should be used in conjunction with Chapter 17 and the tabulated summary on pages 212–213 at the end of that chapter. They provide a full explanation of the regulations, and how they affect the drugs in the various Schedules.

Schedule 1

Controlled Drugs subject to the requirements of Regulations 14, 15, 16, 18, 19, 20, 23, 26 and 27

1   The following substances and products, namely:

    (a)   4-Bromo-2,5-dimethoxy-α-methylphenethylamine
            Bufotenine
            Cannabinol: not being dronebenol or its stereoisomers
            Cannabinol derivatives
            Cannabis and cannabis resin
            Cathinone
            Coca leaf
            Concentrate of poppy straw
            N,N-Diethyltryptamine

2,5-Dimethoxy-α,4-dimethylphenethylamine
N,N-Dimethyltryptamine
Eticyclidine
Etryptamine (1998)
N-Hydroxy-tenamphetamine
Lysergamide
Lysergide and other N-alkyl derivatives of lysergamide
Mescaline
Methcathinone (1998)
4-Methylaminorex
Psilocin
Raw opium
Rolicyclidine
Tenocyclidine

(b)   any compound (not being a compound for the time being specified in sub-paragraph (a) above) structurally derived from tryptamine or from a ring-hydroxy tryptamine by substitution at the nitrogen atom of the side-chain with one or more alkyl substituents but no other substituents;

(c)   there is a list of 36 phenethylamine derivatives.

(d)   any compound (not being methoxyphenamine or a compound for the time being specified in sub-paragraph (a) above) structurally derived from phenethylamine, an N-alkylphenethylamine, α-methylphenethylamine, an N-alkyl-α-methylphenethylamine, α-ethylphenethylamine, or an N-alkyl-α-ethylphenethylamine by substitution in the ring to any extent with alkyl, alkoxy, alkylenedioxy or halide substituents, whether or not further substituted in the ring by one or more other univalent substituents;

(e)   any compound (not being a compound for the time being specified in Schedule 2) structurally derived from fentanyl by modification in any of the following ways, that is to say:

(i)   by replacement of the phenyl portion of the phenethyl group by any heteromonocycle whether or not further substituted in the heterocycle;

(ii)   by substitution in the phenethyl group with alkyl, alkenyl, alkoxy, hydroxy, halogeno, haloalkyl, amino or nitro groups;

(iii)   by substitution in the piperidine ring with alkyl or alkenyl groups;

(iv)   by substitution in the aniline ring with alkyl, alkoxy, alkylenedioxy, halogeno or haloalkyl groups;

(v)   by substitution at the 4-position of the piperidine ring with any alkoxycarbonyl or alkoxyalkyl or acyloxy group;

(vi)   by replacement of the N-propionyl group by another acyl group.

(f)   any compound (not being a compound for the time being specified in Schedule 2) structurally derived from pethidine by modification in any of the following ways, that is to say:

(i)   by replacement of the 1-methyl group by an acyl or alkyl group, whether or not unsaturated, benzyl or phenethyl group, whether or not further substituted;

(ii)   by substitution in the piperidine ring with alkyl or alkenyl groups or with a propano bridge, whether or not further substituted;

(iii)   by substitution in the 4-phenyl ring with alkyl, alkoxy, aryloxy, halogeno or haloalkyl groups;

(iv)   by replacement of the 4-ethoxycarbonyl by any other alkoxycarbonyl or any alkoxyalkyl or acyloxy group;

(v)   by formation of an N-oxide or of a quaternary base.

2   Any stereoisomeric form of a substance specified in paragraph 1.

3   Any ester or ether of a substance specified in paragraph 1 or 2.
4   Any salt of a substance specified in any of paragraphs 1 to 3.
5   Any preparation or other product containing a substance or product specified in any
      of paragraphs 1 to 4, not being a preparation specified in Schedule 5.

Schedule 2

Controlled Drugs subject to the requirements of Regulations 14, 15, 16, 18, 19, 20, 21, 23,
26 and 27.

1   The following substances and products, namely:

Acetorphine
Alfentanil
Allylprodine
Alphacetylmethadol
Alphameprodine
Alphamethadol
Alphaprodine
Anileridine
Benzethidine
Benzylmorphine (3-benzylmorphine)
Betacetylmethadol
Betameprodine
Betamethadol
Betaprodine
Bezitramide
Carfentanil
Clonitazene
Cocaine
4-Cyano-2-dimethylamino-
    4,4-diphenylbutane
4-Cyano-1-methyl-4-phenylpiperidine
Desomorphine
Dextromoramide
Diamorphine
Diampromide
Diethylthiambutene
Difenoxin
Dihydrocodeinone O-
    carboxymethyloxine
Dihydroetorphine
Dihydromorphine
Dimenoxadole
Dimepheptanol
Dimethylthiambutene
Dioxaphetyl butyrate
Diphenoxylate
Dipipanone
Dronabinol
Drotebanol
Ecgonine, and any derivative of
    ecgonine which is convertible to
    ecgonine or to cocaine
Ethylmethylthiambutene
Etonitazene

Etorphine
Etoxeridine
Fentanyl
Furethidine
Hydrocodone
Hydromorphinol
Hydromorphone
Hydroxypethidine
Isomethadone
Ketobemidone
Levomethorphan
Levomoramide
Levophenacylmorphan
Levorphanol
Lofentanil
Medicinal opium
Metazocine
Methadone
Methadyl acetate
Methyldesorphine
Methyldihydromorphine
    (6-methyldihydromorphine)
2-Methyl-3-morpholino-
    1,1-diphenylpropanecarboxylic acid
1-Methyl-4-phenylpiperidine-
    4-carboxylic acid
Metopon
Morpheridine
Morphine
Morphine methobromide, morphine N-
    oxide and other pentavalent nitrogen
    morphine derivatives
Myrophine
Nicomorphine
Noracymethadol
Norlevorphanol
Normethadone
Normorphine
Norpipanone
Oxycodone
Oxymorphone
Pethidine
Phenadoxone
Phenampromide

Phenazocine
Phencyclidine
Phenomorphan
Phenoperidine
4-Phenylpiperidine-4-carboxylic acid
   ethyl ester
Piminodine
Piritramide
Proheptazine
Properidine
Quinalbarbitone [secobarbital]

Racemethorphan
Racemoramide
Racemorphan
Remifentanil
Sufentanil
Thebacon
Thebaine
Tilidate
Trimeperidine
Zipeprol.

2   Any stereoisomeric form of a substance specified in paragraph 1 not being dextromethorphan or dextrorphan.

3   Any ester or ether of a substance specified in paragraph 1 or 2, not being a substance specified in paragraph 6.

4   Any salt of a substance specified in any of paragraphs 1 to 3.

5   Any preparation or other product containing a substance or product specified in any of paragraphs 1 to 4, not being a preparation specified in Schedule 5.

6   The following substances and products, namely:

Acetyldihydrocodeine
Amphetamine
Codeine
Dextropropoxyphene
Dihydrocodeine
Ethylmorphine (3-ethylmorphine)
Fenethylline
Glutethamide
Lefetamine
Mecloqualone
Methaqualone

Methylamphetamine
Methylphenidate
Nicocodine
Nicodicodine
   (6-nicotinoyldihydrocodeine)
Norcodeine
Phenmetrazine
Pholcodine
Propiram
Quinalbarbitone [secobarbital].

7   Any stereoisomeric form of a substance specified in paragraph 6.

8   Any salt of a substance specified in paragraph 6 or 7.

9   Any preparation or other product containing a substance or product specified in any of paragraphs 6 to 8, not being a preparation specified in Schedule 5.

Schedule 3

Controlled Drugs subject to the requirements of Regulations 14, 15, 16, 18, 22, 23, 24, 26 and 27

1   The following substances, namely:

(a)   Benzphetamine [benzfetamine]
    Buprenorphine
    Cathine
    Chlorphentermine
    Diethylpropion
    Ethchlorvynol
    Ethinamate
    Flunitrazepam (1998)
    Mazindol
    Mephentermine

    Meprobamate
    Methylphenobarbitone
       [methylphenobarbital]
    Methyprylone
    Pentazocine
    Phendimetrazine
    Phentermine
    Pipradrol
    Temazepam

(b)   any 5,5- disubstituted barbituric acid, not being quinalbarbitone [secobarbital].

2   Any stereoisomeric form of a substance specified in paragraph 1, not being phenylpropanolamine.
3   Any salt of a substance specified in paragraph 1 or 2.
4   Any preparation or other product containing a substance specified in any of paragraphs 1 to 3, not being a preparation specified in Schedule 5.

Schedule 4: Part I

Controlled Drugs excepted from the prohibition on importation, exportation and, when in the form of a medicinal product, possession and subject to the requirements of Regulations 22, 23, 25, 26 and 27

1   The following substances and products, namely:

Alprazolam	Ketazolam
Aminorex	Loprazolam
Bromazepam	Lorazepam
Brotizolam	Lormetazepam
Camazepam	Medazepam
Chlordiazepoxide	Mefenorex
Clobazam	Mesabolene (2003)
Clonazepam	Mesocarb
Clorazepic acid	Midazolam
Clotiazepam	Nimetazepam
Cloxazolam	Nitrazepam
Delorazepam	Nordazepam
Diazepam	Oxabolene (2003)
Estazolam	Oxazepam
N-Ethylamfetamine	Oxazolam
Ethyl loflazepate	Pemoline
Fencamfamin	Pinazepam
Fenproporex	Prazepam
Fludiazepam	Pyrovalerone
Flurazepam	Tetrazepam
Halazepam	Triazolam
Haloxazolam	Zolpidem.
4-Hydroxy-*n*-butyric acid	

2   Any stereoisomeric form of a substance specified in paragraph 1.
3   Any salt of a substance specified in paragraph 1 or 2.
4   Any preparation or other product containing a substance or product specified in any of paragraphs 1 to 3, not being a preparation specified in Schedule 5.

Schedule 4: Part II

Controlled Drugs excepted from the prohibition on possession when in the form of a medicinal product; excluded from the application of offences arising from the prohibition on importation and exportation when imported or exported in the form of a medicinal product by any person for administration to himself; and subject to the requirements of Regulations 22, 23, 26 and 27

1   The following substances and products, namely:

4-Androstene-3,17-dione	Bolandiol
5-Androstene-3,17-diol	Bolasterone
Atamestane	Bolazine

Boldenone	Mibolerone
Bolenol	Nandrolone
Bolmantalate	19-Nor-4-androstene-3,17-dione
Calusterone	19-Nor-5-androstene-3,17-diol
4-Choromethandienone	Norboletone
Clostebol	Norclostebol
Drostanolone	Norethandrolone
Enestebol	Ovandrotone
Epitiostanol	Oxandrolone
Ethyloestrenol [ethylestrenol]	Oxymesterone
Fluoxymesterone	Oxymetholone
Formebolone	Prasterone
Furazabol	Propetandrol
Mebolazine	Quinbolone
Mepitiostane	Roxibolone
Mestanolone	Silandrone
Mesterolone	Stanolone
Methandienone	Stanozolol
Methandriol	Stenbolone
Methenolone [metenolone]	Testosterone
Methyltestosterone	Thiomesterone
Metribolone	Trenbolone

2   Any compound (not being trilostane or a compound for the time being specified in paragraph 1 of this part of this Schedule) structurally derived from 17-hydroxyandrostan-3-one or from 17-hydroxyestran-3-one by modification in any of the following ways:

(a)   by further substitution at position 17 by a methyl or ethyl group;

(b)   by substitution to any extent at one or more positions 1, 2, 4, 6, 7,9, 11 or 16, but at no other position;

(c)   by unsaturation in the carbocyclic ring system to any extent, provided that there are no more than two ethylenic bonds in any one carbocyclic ring;

(d)   by fusion of ring A with a heterocyclic system.

3   Any substance which is an ester or ether (or, where more than one hydroxyl function is available, both an ester and an ether) of a substance specified in paragraph 1 or described in paragraph 2 of this Part of the Schedule.

4   The following substances:

Chorionic gonadotrophin (HCG)
Somatotropin
Clenbuterol
Somatrem
Non-human chorionic gonadotrophin (HCG)
Somatropin.

5   Any stereoisomeric form of a substance specified or described in any of paragraphs 1 to 4 of this Part of this Schedule.

6   Any salt of a substance specified or described in any of paragraphs 1 to 5 of this Part of this Schedule.

7   Any preparation of other product containing a substance or product specified or described in any of paragraphs 1 to 6 of this Part of the Schedule, not being a preparation specified in Schedule 5.

Schedule 5

Controlled Drugs excepted from the prohibition on importation, exportation and possession and subject to the requirements of Regulations 24 and 25.

1   (1) Any preparation of one or more of the substances to which this paragraph applies, not being a preparation designed for administration by injection, when compounded with one or more other active or inert ingredients and containing a total of not more than 100 milligrams of the substance or substances (calculated as base) per dosage unit or with a total concentration of not more than 2.5 per cent (calculated as base) in undivided preparations.

   (2) The substances to which this paragraph applies are acetyldihydrocodeine, codeine, dihydrocodeine, ethylmorphine, nicocodine, nicodicodine (6-nicotinoyldihydrocodeine), norcodeine, pholcodine and their respective salts.

2   Any preparation of cocaine containing not more than 0.1 per cent of cocaine calculated as cocaine base, being a preparation compounded with one or more other active or inert ingredients in such a way that the cocaine cannot be recovered by readily applicable means or in a yield which would constitute a risk to health.

3   Any preparation of medicinal opium or of morphine containing (in either case) not more than 0.2 per cent of morphine calculated as anhydrous morphine base, being a preparation compounded with one or more other active or inert ingredients in such a way that the opium or, as the case may be, the morphine, cannot be recovered by readily applicable means or in a yield which would constitute a risk to health.

4   Any preparation of dextropropoxyphene, being a preparation designed for oral administration, containing not more than 135 milligrams of dextropropoxyphene (calculated as base) per dosage unit or with a total concentration of not more than 2.5 per cent (calculated as base) in undivided preparations.

5   Any preparation of difenoxin containing, per dosage unit, not more than 0.5 milligrams of difenoxin and a quantity of atropine sulphate equivalent to at least 5 per cent of the dose of difenoxin.

6   Any preparation of diphenoxylate containing, per dosage unit, not more than 2.5 milligrams of diphenoxylate calculated as base, and a quantity of atropine sulphate equivalent to at least 1 per cent of the dose of diphenoxylate.

7   Any preparation of propiram containing, per dosage unit, not more than 100 milligrams of propiram calculated as base and compounded with at least the same amount (by weight) of methylcellulose.

8   Any powder of ipecacuanha and opium comprising:

   10 per cent opium, in powder

   10 per cent ipecacuanha root, in powder, well mixed with

   80 per cent of any other powdered ingredient containing no Controlled Drug.

9   Any mixture containing one or more of the preparations specified in paragraphs 1 to 8, being a mixture of which none of the other ingredients is a Controlled Drug.

The Poisons List Order 1982

Non-medicinal poisons are listed in the Schedule to this order (SI 1982 No.217, as amended) made under the Poisons Act 1972. Those substances in Part I of the list may not be sold by retail except by a person lawfully conducting a retail pharmacy business. Those in Part II of the list may only be sold by a person lawfully conducting a retail pharmacy business or by a person whose name is entered in a local authority's list.

The Poisons List: Part I

Aluminium phosphide
Arsenic; its compounds, other than those
  specified in Part II of this list
Barium, salts of, other than barium sulphate
  and the salts of barium specified in Part II
  of this list
Bromomethane
Chloropicrin
Fluoroacetic acid; its salts, fluorocetamide
Hydrogen cyanide; metal cyanides, other than
  ferrocyanides and ferricyanides
Lead acetates; compounds of lead with acids
  from fixed oils
Magnesium phosphide
Mercury, compounds of, the following:
  nitrates of mercury; oxides of mercury;
  mercuric cyanide oxides; mercuric
  thiocyanate; ammonium mercuric
  chlorides; potassium mercuric iodides;

organic compounds of mercury
  which contain a methyl group
  directly linked to the mercury atom
Oxalic acid
Phenols
  (phenol; phenolic isomers of the
  following: cresols, xylenols,
  monoethylphenols) except in
  substances containing less than 60
  per cent, weight in weight, of
  phenols; compounds of phenol with
  a metal, except in substances
  containing less than the equivalent
  of 60 per cent, weight in weight, of
  phenols
Phosphorus, yellow
Strychnine; its salts, its quaternary
  compounds
Thallium, salts of.

The Poisons List: Part II

Aldicarb
Alpha-chloralose
Ammonia
Arsenic, compounds, of; the following:
    Calcium arsenites
    Copper acetoarsenite
    Copper arsenates
    Copper arsenites
    Lead arsenates
Barium, salts of; the following:
    Barium carbonate
    Barium silicofluoride
Carbofuran
Cycloheximide
Dinitrocresols (DNOC); their compounds with
    a metal or a base
Dinoseb; its compounds with a metal or a
    base
Dinoterb
Drazoxolon; its salts
Endosulfan
Endothal; its salts
Endrin
Fentin, compounds of
Formaldehyde
Formic acid
Hydrochloric acid
Hydrofluoric acid; alkali metal bifluorides;
    ammonium bifluoride; alkali metal
    fluorides; ammonium fluoride; sodium
    silicofluoride
Mercuric chloride; mercuric iodide; organic
    compounds of mercury except compounds
    of mercury which contain a methyl (CH_3)
    group directly linked to the mercury atom

Metallic oxalates
Methomyl
Nicotine; its salts; its quaternary
    compounds
Nitric acid
Nitrobenzene
Oxamyl
Paraquat, salts of
Phenols (as defined in Part I of this List)
    in substances containing less than 60
    per cent, weight in weight, of
    phenols; compounds of phenols with
    a metal in substances containing less
    than the equivalent of 60 per cent,
    weight in weight, of phenols
Phosphoric acid
Phosphorus compounds, the following:
    Azinphos-methyl, chlorfenvinphos,
    demephion, demeton-S-methyl,
    demeton-S-methyl sulphone, dialifos,
    dichlorvos, dioxathion, disulfoton,
    fonofus, mecarbam, mephosfolan,
    methidathion, mevinphos,
    omethoate, oxydemeton-methyl,
    parathion, phenkapton, phorate,
    phosphamidon, pirimiphos-ethyl,
    quinalphos, schradan, sulfotep,
    thiometon, thionazin, triazophos,
    vamidothion
Potassium hydroxide
Sodium hydroxide
Sodium nitrate
Sulphuric acid
Thiofanox
Zinc phosphide.

The Poisons Rules 1982

The Poison Rules 1982 (SI 1982 No.218, as amended), made under the Poisons Act 1972, are described in Chapter 18. In this appendix are set out eight of the Schedules to the rules. NB Schedules 2, 3, 6 and 7 were deleted by the Poisons Rules (Amendment) Order 1985 (SI 1985 No.1077).

Schedule 1

Rules 5, 6, 7, 9, 10(1), 17(2) and 21(2)

Poisons included in the Poisons List to which special restrictions apply unless exempted by Rule 7 (see pp. 218 and 221–226).

Aldicarb
Alpha-chloralose
Aluminium phosphide
Arsenic; its compounds, except substances containing less than the equivalent of 0.0075 per cent of arsenic (As)
Barium, salts of (other than barium sulphate)
Bromomethane
Carbofuran
Chloropicrin
Cycloheximide
Dinitrocresols (DNOC); their compounds with a metal or a base; except winter washes containing not more than the equivalent of 5 per cent of dinitrocresols
Dinoseb; its compounds with a metal or a base
Dinoterb

Drazoxolon; its salts
Endosulfan
Endothal: its salts
Endrin
Fentin, compounds of
Fluoroacetic acid; its salts, fluoroacetamide
Hydrogen cyanide except substances containing less than 0.15 per cent, weight in weight, of
    hydrogen cyanide (HCN); metal cyanides, other than ferrocyanides and ferricyanides,
    except substances containing less than the equivalent of 0.1 per cent, weight in weight, of
    hydrogen cyanide (HCN)
Lead, compounds of, with acids from fixed oils
Magnesium phosphide
Mercuric chloride; except substances containing less than 1 per cent of mercuric chloride;
    mercuric iodide except substances containing less than 2 per cent of mercuric iodide:
    nitrates of mercury except substances containing less than the equivalent of 3 per cent,
    weight in weight, of mercury (Hg); potassio-mercuric iodides except substances contain-
    ing less than the equivalent of 1 per cent of mercuric iodide; organic compounds of
    mercury except substances, not being aerosols, containing less than the equivalent of 0.2
    per cent, weight in weight, of mercury (Hg)
Methomyl
Nicotine; its salts; its quaternary compounds
Oxamyl
Paraquat, salts of
Phosphorus compounds, the following:
    Azinphos-methyl
    Chlorfenvinphos
    Demephion
    Demeton-S-methyl
    Demeton-S-methyl sulphone
    Dichlorvos
    Dioxathion
    Disulfoton
    Fonofos
    Mecarbam
    Mephosfolan
    Methidathion
    Mevinphos
    Omethoate
    Oxydemeton-methyl
    Parathion
    Phenkapton
    Phorate
    Phosphamidon
    Pirimiphos-ethyl
    Quinalphos
    Thiometon
    Thionazin
    Triazophos
    Vamidothion
Strychnine; its salts; its quaternary compounds; except substances containing less than 0.2
    per cent of strychnine
Thallium, salts of
Thiofanox
Zinc phosphide.

Schedule 4

Rule 8

Articles exempted from the provisions of the Act and Rules (see p.214)

Group I: General Exemptions

Adhesives; anti-fouling compositions; builders' materials; ceramics; cosmetic products; distempers; electrical valves; enamels; explosives; fillers; fireworks; fluorescent lamps; flux in any form for use in soldering; glazes; glue; inks; lacquer solvents; loading materials; matches; medicated animal feeding stuffs; motor fuels and lubricants; paints other than pharmaceutical paints; photographic paper; pigments; plastics; propellants; rubber; varnishes; vascular plants and their seeds.

Group II: Special Exemptions

Poison	Substance or article in which exempted
Ammonia	Substances not being solutions of ammonia or preparations containing solutions of ammonia; substances containing less than 5 per cent, weight in weight, of ammonia (NH_3); refrigerators
Arsenic; its compounds	Pyrites ores or sulphuric acid containing arsenic or compounds of arsenic as natural impurities; in reagent kits or reagent devices supplied for medical or veterinary purposes, substances containing less than 0.1 per cent, weight in weight, of arsanilic acid
Barium, salts of	Witherite other than finely ground witherite; barium carbonate bonded to charcoal for case hardening; fire extinguishers containing barium chloride; sealed smoke generators containing not more than 25 per cent, weight in weight, of barium carbonate
Bromomethane	Fire extinguishers
Carbofuran	Granular preparations
Drazoxolon; its salts	Treatments on seeds
Fenaminosulf	Granular preparations
Formaldehyde	Substances containing less than 5 per cent, weight in weight, of formaldehyde (H.CHO); photographic glazing or hardening solutions
Formic acid	Substances containing less than 25 per cent, weight in weight, of formic acid (H.COOH)
Hydrochloric acid	Substances containing less than 10 per cent, weight in weight, of hydrochloric acid
Hydrogen cyanide	Preparations of wild cherry; in reagent kits supplied for medical or veterinary purposes, substances containing less than the equivalent of 0.1 per cent, weight in weight, of hydrogen cyanide

Poison	*Substance or article in which exempted*
Lead acetate	Substances containing less than the equivalent of 2.5 per cent, weight in weight, of elemental lead
Mercuric chloride	Batteries
Mercuric chloride	Treatments on seeds or bulbs
Mercuric iodide	Treatments on seeds or bulbs
Mercury organic, compounds of	Treatments on seeds or bulbs
Mercury, oxides of	Canker and wound paints (for trees) containing not more than 3 per cent, weight in weight, of yellow mercuric oxide
Methomyl	Solid substances containing not more than 1 per cent, weight in weight, of methomyl
Nicotine; its salts; its quaternary compounds	Tobacco; in cigarettes, the paper of a cigarette (any part of that paper forming part of or surrounding a filter), where that paper in each cigarette does not have more than the equivalent of 10 milligrams of nicotine; preparations in aerosol dispensers containing not more than 0.2 per cent, weight in weight, of nicotine; other liquid preparations, and solid preparations with a soap base containing not more than 7.5 per cent, weight in weight, of nicotine
Nitric acid	Substances containing less than 9 per cent, weight in weight, of nitric acid (HNO_3)
Nitrobenzene	Substances containing less than 0.1 per cent of nitrobenzene
Oxalic acid; metallic	Laundry blue; polishes; cleaning powders or scouring oxalates products containing the equivalent of not more than 10 per cent of oxalic acid dihydrate
Oxamyl	Granular preparations
Paraquat, salts of	Preparations in pellet form containing not more than 5 per cent of salts of paraquat calculated as paraquat ion [see p. 218]
Phenols	Creosote obtained from coal tar; liquid disinfectants or antiseptics containing phenol less than 0.5 per cent phenol and containing less than 5 per cent of other phenols (as defined in the Poisons List); motor fuel treatments not containing phenol and containing less than 2.5 per cent of other phenols; in reagent kits supplied for medical or veterinary purposes; solid substances containing less than 60 per cent of phenols; tar (coal or wood), crude or refined; in tar oil distillation fractions containing not more than 5 per cent of phenols
Phenylmercuric salts	Antiseptic dressings on toothbrushes; in textiles containing not more than 0.01 per cent of phenylmercuric salts as bacteriostat and fungicide

Poison	Substance or article in which exempted
Phosphoric acid	Substances containing phosphoric acid, not being descaling preparations, containing more than 50 per cent, weight in weight, of ortho-phosphoric acid
Phosphorus compounds, the following:	
Chlorfenvinphos	Treatments on seeds; granular preparations
Dichlorvos	Preparations in aerosol dispensers containing not more than 1 per cent, weight in weight, of dichlorvos; materials impregnated with dichlorvos for slow release; granular preparations; ready for use liquid preparations containing not more than 1 per cent, weight in volume, of dichlorvos
Disulfoton	Granular preparations
Fonofos	Granular preparations
Oxydemeton-methyl	Aerosol dispensers containing not more than 0.25 per cent, weight in weight, of oxydemeton-methyl
Parathion	Granular preparations
Phorate	Granular preparations
Pirimiphos-ethyl	Treatments on seeds
Thiazophos	Granular preparations
Thionazin	Granular preparations
Potassium hydroxide	Substances containing the equivalent of less than 17 per cent of total caustic alkalinity expressed as potassium hydroxide; accumulators; batteries
Sodium fluoride	Substances containing less than 3 per cent of sodium fluoride as a preservative
Sodium hydroxide	Substances containing the equivalent of less than 12 per cent of total caustic alkalinity expressed as sodium hydroxide
Sodium nitrite	Substances other than preparations containing more than 0.1 per cent of sodium nitrite for the destruction of rats or mice
Sodium silicofluoride	Substances containing less than 3 per cent of sodium silicofluoride as a preservative
Sulphuric acid	Substances containing less than 15 per cent, weight in weight, of sulphuric acid (H_2SO_4); accumulators; batteries and sealed containers in which sulphuric acid is packed together with car batteries for use in those batteries; fire extinguishers
Thiofanox	Granular preparations

In Group II in this Schedule, the expression *granular preparation* in relation to a poison means a preparation:

(a)   which consists of absorbent mineral or synthetic solid particles impregnated with the poison, the size of the particles being such that not more than 4 per cent, weight in weight, of the preparation is capable of passing a sieve with a mesh of 250 microns, and not more than 1 per cent, weight in weight, a sieve with a mesh of 150 microns;

(b)   which has an apparent density of not less than 0.4 grams per millilitre if compacted without pressure; and

(c)   not more than 12 per cent, weight in weight, consists of one or more poisons in respect of which an exemption is conferred by this Schedule in relation to granular preparations.

Schedule 5

Rule 10(2)

Part A

Form to which the poisons specified are restricted when sold by listed sellers of Part II poisons (see p. 220)

Poison	*Form to which sale is restricted*
Aldicarb	Preparations for use in agriculture, horticulture or forestry
Alpha-chloralose	Preparations intended for indoor use in the destruction of rats or mice and containing not more than 4 per cent, weight in weight, of alpha-chloralose; preparations intended for indoor use in the destruction of rats or mice and containing not more than 8.5 per cent, weight in weight, of alpha-chloralose, where the preparation is contained in a bag or sachet which is itself attached to the inside of a device in which the preparation is intended to be so used and the device contains not more than 3 grams of the preparation
Arsenic, compounds of;	Agricultural, horticultural and forestal insecticides or fungicides
Calcium arsenites	Agricultural, horticultural and forestal insecticides or fungicides
Copper acetoarsenite	Agricultural, horticultural and forestal insecticides or fungicides
Copper arsenates	Agricultural, horticultural and forestal insecticides or fungicides
Copper arsenites	Agricultural, horticultural and forestal insecticides or fungicides
Lead arsenates	Agricultural, horticultural and forestal insecticides or fungicides
Barium carbonate	Preparations for the destruction of rats or mice
Carbofuran	Preparations for use in agriculture, horticulture or forestry
Cycloheximide	Preparations for use in forestry
Dinitrocresols (DNOC); their compounds with a metal or a base	Preparations for use in agriculture, horticulture or forestry
Dinosam; its compounds with a metal or a base	Preparations for use in agriculture, horticulture or forestry

Poison	Form to which sale is restricted
Dinoseb; its compounds with a metal or a base	Preparations for use in agriculture, horticulture or forestry
Drazoxolon; its salts	Preparations for use in agriculture, horticulture or forestry
Endosulfan	Preparations for use in agriculture, horticulture or forestry
Endothal; its salts	Preparations for use in agriculture, horticulture or forestry
Endrin	Preparations for use in agriculture, horticulture or forestry
Fentin, compounds of	Preparations for use in agriculture, horticulture or forestry
Mercuric chloride	Agricultural, horticultural and forestal fungicides, seed and bulb dressings, insecticides
Mercuric iodide	Agricultural, horticultural and forestal fungicides, seed and bulb dressings
Mercury, organic compounds of	Agricultural, horticultural and forestal fungicides, seed and bulb dressings, solutions containing not more than 5 per cent, weight in volume, of phenylmercuric acetate for use in swimming baths
Metallic oxalates other than potassium quadroxalate	Photographic solutions or materials
Methomyl	Preparations for use in agriculture, horticulture or forestry
Nitrobenzene	Agricultural, horticultural and forestal insecticides
Oxamyl	Preparations for use in agriculture, horticulture or forestry
Paraquat, salts of	Preparations for use in agriculture, horticulture or forestry
Phosphorus compounds, the following:	Preparations for use in agriculture, horticulture or forestry

    Azinphos-methyl
    Chlorfenvinphos
    Demephion
    Demeton-S-methyl
    Demeton-S-methyl sulphone
    Dialifos
    Dichlorvos
    Dioxathion
    Disulfoton
    Fonofos
    Mecarbam
    Mephosfolan
    Methidathion
    Mevinphos
    Omethoate
    Oxydemeton-methyl
    Parathion
    Phenkapton
    Phorate

Poison	Form to which sale is restricted
Phosphamidon	
Pirimiphos-ethyl	
Quinalphos	
Thiometon	
Thionazin	
Triazophos	
Vamidothion	
Thiofanox	Preparations for use in agriculture, horticulture or forestry
Zinc phosphide	Preparations for the destruction of rats or mice

Part B

Poisons which may be sold by listed sellers of Part II poisons only to persons engaged in the trade or business of agriculture, horticulture or forestry and for the purpose of that trade or business.

Aldicarb
Arsenic, compounds of
    Calcium arsenites
    Copper acetoarsenite
    Copper arsenates
    Copper arsenites
    Lead arsenates
Carbofuran
Cyclohexamide
Dinitrocresols (DNOC); their compounds with a metal or a base; except winter washes containing not more than the equivalent of 5 per cent of dinitrocresols
Dinosam; its compounds with a metal or a base
Dinoseb; its compounds with a metal or a base
Dinoterb
Drazoxolon; its salts
Endosulfan
Endothal; its salts
Endrin
Fentin; compounds of
Mercuric chloride; mercuric iodide; organic compounds of mercury, except solutions containing not more than 5 per cent, weight in volume, of phenylmercuric acetate for use in swimming baths
Methomyl
Oxamyl
Paraquat, salts of
Phosphorus compounds, the following:
    Azinphos-methyl
    Chlorfenvinphos
    Demephion
    Demeton-S-methyl
    Demeton-S-methyl sulphone
    Dialifos
    Dichlorvos
    Dioxathion

Disulfoton
Fonofos
Mazidox
Mecarbam
Mephosfolan
Methidathion
Mevinphos
Mipafox, except in the form of a cap on a stick or wire
Omethoate
Oxydemeton-methyl
Parathion
Phenkapton
Phorate
Phosphamidon
Pirimiphos-ethyl
Quinalphos
Thiometon
Thionazin
Triazophos
Vamidothion
Thiofanox

Schedule 8

Rule 24(1)

Form of application for entry in the list kept by a local authority under section 5 of the Act
(see p. 219).

POISONS ACT 1972
(1972 c.66)

*Form of application by a person to have his name entered in a local authority's list of persons
entitled to sell non-medicinal poisons included in Part II of the Poisons List.*

To the Chief Executive of ....
  I,...
being engaged in the business of..
hereby apply to have my name entered in the list kept in pursuance of section 5 of the above Act
in respect of the following premises, namely,...
....
....
....
....
as a person entitled to sell from those premises non-medicinal poisons included in Part II of the
Poisons List.
  I hereby nominate ....
....
to act as my deputy (deputies) for the sale of non-medicinal poisons in accordance with Rule
10(1) of the Poisons Rules 1982
Signature of applicant ....
Date...
This space is for the use of the local authority.
....
....
....
....

Schedule 9

Rule 24(2)

Form of the list to be kept by a local authority in pursuance of section 5(1) of the Act (see p. 219).

POISONS ACT 1972
(1972 c. 66)

List of persons entitled to sell non-medicinal poisons in Part II of the Poisons List

Full name	Address of premises	Description of business carried on at the premises	Name of deputy (or deputies) permitted to sell

Schedule 10

Rule 25

Certificate for the purchase of non-medicinal poison (see pp. 219 and 223–226).

For the purposes of section 3(2)(a)(i) of the Poisons Act 1972 I, the undersigned, a householder occupying (a) ....
hereby certify from my knowledge of (b) .... of (a) ....
that he is a person to whom (c) .... may properly be supplied.
   I further certify that (d) .... is the signature of the said
(b) ....

....
Signature of the householder giving
certificate
Date
(a) Insert full postal address.
(b) Insert full name of intending purchaser.
(c) Insert name of poison.
(d) Intending purchaser to sign his name here.

Endorsement required by Rule 25 of the Poisons Rules 1982 to be made by a police officer in charge of a police station when, but only when, the householder giving the certificate is not known to the seller of the poison to be a responsible person of good character.
I hereby certify that in so far as is known to the police of the district in which * resides he is a responsible person of good character.

Signature of Police Officer.................................
Rank..
In charge of Police Station at ....
Date..

Office Stamp of
Police Station.

*Insert full name of householder giving the certificate.

Schedule 11

Rule 26

Form of entry to be made in a book to be kept by sellers of poisons in accordance with section 3(2)(b) of the Act (see p. 219).

Date of Sale	Name and quantity of poisons supplied	Purchaser's			Purpose for which the poison stated to be required	Date of certificate (if any)	Name and address of person giving certificate (if any)	Signature of purchaser or, where a signed order is permitted by the Poisons Rules 1982 the date of the signed order
		Name	Address	Business, trade or occupation				

Schedule 12

Rule 12

Restriction of sale and supply of strychnine and certain other poisons (see pp. 219 and 224–226).

Part I

Cases of sale or supply to which provisions of Rule 12 do not apply.

1   The provisions of Rule 12 shall not apply in the case of the sale of substance to be exported to purchasers outside the United Kingdom.
2   The provisions of Rule 12 shall not apply in the case of the sale of a substance to a person or institution concerned with scientific education or research or chemical analysis, for the purposes of that education or research or analysis.
3   The provisions of Rule 12 shall not apply in the case of the sale of a substance by way of wholesale dealing.
4   The following provision of Rule 12, namely paragraph (1) (strychnine etc.), shall not apply in the case of the sale of a substance to a person producing a written authority in the form set out in Part II of this Schedule issued, in England by a person duly authorised by the Minister of Agriculture, Fisheries and Food, or, in Scotland, or Wales, by a person duly authorised by the Secretary of State, authorising the purchase of the substance for the purpose of killing moles; so, however, that the authority in question has been issued within the preceding three months and the quantity sold does not exceed the quantity, not being more than 100 grams, specified therein.

5   The following provisions of Rule 12, namely, paragraph (1) (strychnine etc.), shall
not apply in the case of the sale of a substance to:

(a)   an officer of the Ministry of Agriculture, Fisheries and Food who produces a
written authority in the form set out in Part III of this Schedule issued by a
person duly authorised by the Minister of Agriculture, Fisheries and Food; or

(b)   an officer of the Department of Agriculture and Fisheries for Scotland or the
Welsh Office who produces a written authority in the form set out in Part III of
this Schedule issued by a person duly authorised by the Secretary of State,
authorising the purchase by that officer of the substance for the purpose of
killing foxes (other than foxes held in captivity) in an infected area within the
meaning of the Rabies (Control) Order 1974 (SI 1974 No.2212); so, however,
that the authority in question has been issued within the preceding four weeks
and the quantity sold does not exceed specified therein.

6   (1)   The following provision of Rule 12, namely, paragraph (2) (fluoroacetic acid
etc.), shall not apply in the case of the sale of a substance:

(a)   to a person producing a certificate in form 'A' of the forms set out in Part IV of
this Schedule issued by the proper officer of a local authority or port health
authority certifying that the substance is required for use as a rodenticide by
employees of that local authority or port health authority being such use:

(i)   in ships or sewers in such places as are identified in the certificate; or
(ii)   in such drains as are identified in the certificate, being drains which are
situated in restricted areas and wholly enclosed and to which all means
of access are, when not in actual use, kept closed; or
(iii) in such warehouses as are identified in the certificate, being warehouses
which are situated in restricted dock areas and to which all means of
access are, when not in actual use, kept securely locked or barred; or

(b)   to a person producing a certificate in form 'B' of the said forms issued by the
proper officer of a local authority or port health authority certifying that the
substance is required for use as a rodenticide by such person or by the
employees of such body of persons, carrying on a business of pest control, as is
named in the certificate, being such use as is mentioned in sub-paragraph
(1)(a)(i) or (ii) of this paragraph; or

(c)   to a person producing a certificate in form 'B' of the said forms issued, in
England by a person duly authorised by the Minister of Agriculture, Fisheries
and Food or, in Scotland or Wales, by a person duly authorised by the
Secretary of State certifying that the substance is required for use as a
rodenticide by officers of the Ministry of Agriculture, Fisheries and Food or of
the Department of Agriculture and Fisheries for Scotland, or the Welsh Office
being such use as is mentioned in sub-paragraph (1)(a)(i) or (ii) of this
paragraph;

so, however, that the certificate in question has been issued within the preceding three
months and the quantity sold does not exceed the quantity specified therein.

(2) In this paragraph the following expressions have the meanings hereby respectively assigned to them, that is to say:

dock area means an area in the vicinity of a dock as defined in section 57(1) of the
Harbours Act 1964;

drain and *sewer* have the meanings respectively assigned to them by section 343(1)
of the Public Health Act 1936;

local authority in Greater London means the Common Council of the City of
London or the council of a London borough, elsewhere in England or Wales means
the council of a county or a district and, in Scotland, means an islands or district
council;

port health authority means, in England or Wales, the port health authority of the Port of London or a port health authority for the purposes of the Public Health Act 1936 and, in Scotland, a port health authority as constituted in terms of section 172 of the Public Health (Scotland) Act 1897;

restricted in relation to any area, means controlled in such manner that access to the area by unauthorised persons is in normal circumstances prevented.

7   (1) The following provisions of Rule 12, namely, paragraph (3) (salts of thallium), shall not apply in the case of the sale of a substance:

(a)   to a local authority or a port health authority for the purpose of the exercise of its statutory powers; or

(b)   to a government department or an officer of the Crown, for the purposes of the public service; or

(c)   other than thallium sulphate, to a person, or body of persons, carrying on a business in the course of which salts of thallium are regularly used in the manufacture of other articles, for the purposes of that business; or

(d)   other than thallium sulphate, as an ingredient in any article, not being an article intended for internal consumption by any person or animal.

(2) The following provision of Rule 12, namely paragraph (3) (salts of thallium) shall not apply as regards thallium sulphate in the case of the sale of a substance to a person producing a written authority in the form set out in Part V of this Schedule issued, in England or Wales, by a person duly authorised by the Minister of Agriculture, Fisheries and Food, or, in Scotland, by a person duly authorised by the Secretary of State, authorising the purchase of salts of thallium for use by him or by the employees of such body of persons as is named in the authority for the purpose of killing rats, mice or moles in the course of a business of pest control; so, however, that the authority in question has been issued within the preceding twelve months.

(3) In this paragraph the expressions *local authority* and *port health authority* have the meanings assigned to them by paragraph 6(2) of this Part of this Schedule.

8   (1) The following provision of Rule 12, namely, paragraph (4) (zinc phosphide) shall not apply in the case of the sale of a substance:

(a)   to a local authority for the purpose of the exercise of its statutory powers; or

(b)   to a government department or an officer of the Crown, for the purposes of the public service; or

(c)   to a person, or body of persons, carrying on a trade or business, for the purposes of that trade or business.

(2) In this paragraph the expression *local authority* has the meaning assigned to it by paragraph 6(2) of this Part of this Schedule.

NB The Ministry of Agriculture, Fisheries and Food has been replaced by DEFRA.

Part II

Form of authority for the purchase of strychnine or a salt or quaternary compound thereof for killing moles.

For the purposes of Rule 12(1) of the Poisons Rules 1982 and of paragraph 4 of Part I of Schedule 12 thereto I hereby authorise ....
to purchase within three months from the date hereof .... of
.... for the purpose of killing moles.

....
A person authorised by [the Minister of
Agriculture Fisheries and Food]
[the Secretary of State for Scotland]
Date..   [the Secretary of State for Wales]

Part III

Form of authority for the purchase of strychnine or a salt or quaternary compound thereof for killing foxes.

For the purposes of Rule 12(1) of the Poisons Rules 1982 and of paragraph 5 of Part I of Schedule 12 thereto I hereby authorise ....
(an officer of [the Ministry of Agriculture, Fisheries and Food] [the Department of Agriculture and Fisheries for Scotland]) [the Welsh Office] to purchase within four weeks of the date hereof .... of .... for the purpose of killing foxes (other than foxes held in captivity) in the following infected area (within the meaning of the Rabies (Control) Order 1974), namely the infected area in .... (locality).

....

A person authorised by [the Minister of
Agriculture, Fisheries and Food]
[the Secretary of State for Scotland]
Date ....   [the Secretary of State for Wales]

Part IV

Forms of certificate authorising the purchase of fluoroacetic acid, a salt thereof or fluoroacetamide as a rodenticide.

FORM A

Certificate authorising the purchase of fluoroacetic acid, a salt thereof or fluoroacetamide as a rodenticide for use by employees of a local authority or a port health authority (in Scotland, a port local authority or joint port authority)

For the purposes of Rule 12(2) of the Poisons Rules 1982 and of paragraph 6 of Part I of Schedule 12 thereto, I hereby certify that ....
of .... is required for use by employees of.................................
as a rodenticide in [ships] [sewers]situated at...
[the following warehouses] viz...
situated in the restricted dock area at...
being warehouses to which all means of access are, when not in actual use, kept securely locked or barred.
[the following drains] viz...
situated in the restricted area at..
being drains which are wholly enclosed and to which all means of access are, when not in actual use, kept closed.

....

The officer appointed for this purpose by
Date ....

FORM B

Certificate authorising the purchase of fluoroacetic acid, a salt thereof or fluoroacetamide as a rodenticide for use by a person, or the employees of a body of persons, carrying on a business of pest control or for use by officers of the Ministry of Agriculture, Fisheries and Food or of the Department of Agriculture and Fisheries for Scotland or of the Welsh Office

For the purposes of Rule 12(2) of the Poisons Rules 1982 and of paragraph 6 of Part I of Schedule 12 thereto, I hereby certify that ....
of .... is required for use by [....
....] [employees of] ....
[officers of the Ministry of Agriculture, Fisheries and Food/Department of Agriculture and Fisheries for Scotland/Welsh Office] as a rodenticide in:
    [ships] [sewers] situated at ....
    [the following drains] viz ....
    situated in the restricted areas at..
    being drains which are wholly enclosed and to which all means of access are, when not in actual, use, kept closed.

                                             ....
                                             [The officer appointed for this purpose by]
                                             ....
                    [A person authorised by the Minister of Agriculture, Fisheries and Food]
                            [A person authorised by the Secretary of State for Scotland]
                                             [A person authorised by the Secretary of
Date ....   State for Wales]

Part V

Form of authority for the purchase of salts of thallium for killing rats, mice or moles.

For the purpose of Rule 12(3) of the Poisons Rules 1982 and of paragraph 7 of Part I of Schedule 12 thereto I hereby authorise...
to purchase salts of thallium within twelve months from the date hereof for the purpose of killing rats, mice or moles.

                                             ....
                    [A person authorised by the Minister of Agriculture, Fisheries and Food]
                            [A person authorised by the Secretary of State for Scotland]
                                             [A person authorised by the Secretary of
Date ....   State for Wales]

Dangerous substances and preparations dangerous to supply

The Chemicals (Hazard Information and Packaging for Supply) Regulations 1994 (SI 1994 No.3247, as amended) made under the Health and Safety at Work etc. Act 1974 are described in Chapter 20. An Authorised and Approved List of Dangerous Substances is set out in *Information Approved for the Classification and Labelling of Substances Dangerous for Supply* (3rd edn, January 1996, HMSO). There are five parts to the list:

Part I: List of Dangerous Substances and Articles
Part II: List of Substances Dangerous for Supply (Solvents)
Part III: List of Substances Dangerous for Supply (paints, varnishes, printing inks, adhesives and similar products)
Part IV: List of Risk Phrases
Part V: List of Safety Phrases

The classification of and symbols for substances dangerous for supply are set out in Schedule 1 to the Regulations.

Part I

	List of 'dangerous substances'		
Name of substance	Indication of general nature of risk (references are to the relevant entry in Schedule 1)	Indication of particular risks (references are to the relevant entry in Part IV)	Indications of precautions required (references are to the relevant entry in Part V)
	1	2	3
Acetic acid more than 90%	Corrosive	10, 35	2, 23, 36
Acetone	Highly Flammable	11	2, 9, 16, 23, 33
Ammonia more than 10%	Corrosive	34, 37	1/2, 7, 26, 45
Ammonia 5–10%	Irritant	36/37/38	1/2, 7, 26, 45
Amyl acetate	Flammable	10	23
Carbon tetrachloride more than 1%	Carcinogenic Toxic, dangerous for the environment	23/24/25, 40, 48/23, 59	1/2, 23, 36/37, 45, 59, 61
Chlorfenvinphos	Toxic	26/27/28	26/27/28
Chloroform	Carcinogenic Harmful	22, 38, 40, 48/20/22	2, 36/37
Copper sulphate	Harmful	22, 36/38	22
Dichlorvos	Toxic	23/24/25	2, 13, 44
Ephedrine, salts of	Harmful	22	22, 25
Ethanol (ethyl alcohol)	Highly flammable	11	7, 16
Ethylene glycol	Harmful	22	2
Fluoroacetates, soluble salts	Toxic	28	1/2, 20, 22, 26, 45
Formaldehyde solution more than 25% 5–25% 1–5%	Carcinogenic Toxic Harmful Harmful	23/24/25, 34, 40, 43 20/21/22, 36/37/38, 40, 43 40, 43	1/2, 26, 36/37, 45 51 (all)
Hydrochloric acid more than 25% 10–25%	Corrosive Irritant	34, 37 36/37/38	1/2, 26, 45 1/2, 26, 45
Hydrogen peroxide more than 60% 20–60% 5–20%	Oxidising Corrosive Irritant	8 34 36/38	1/2, 3, 28, 36/39 45 (all)

Mercurous chloride	Harmful	22	2

Methylated spirits
    more than 20%
    3–20%
	Highly flammable
	Harmful
		11, 23/25
		20/22
			1/2, 7, 16, 24, 45
			1/2, 7, 16, 24, 45

Mevinphos	Toxic	26/27/28	1, 13, 28, 45
Oxalic acid	Harmful	21/22	2, 24/25
Paraquat, and salts of	Toxic	26/27/28	1, 13, 45
Potassium chlorate	Oxidising, harmful	9, 20/22	2, 13, 16, 27
Potassium permanganate	Oxidising, harmful	8, 22	2
Sodium chlorate	Oxidising, harmful	9, 20/22	2, 13, 16, 27

Sodium hydroxide
    more than 5%
    2–5%
    0.5–2%
	Corrosive
	Corrosive
	Irritant
		35
		34
		36/38
			1/2, 26, 37/39, 45
			1/2, 26, 37/39, 45
			1/2, 26, 37/39, 45

Strychnine, salts of	Toxic	26/28	1, 13, 28, 45
Sulphuric acid	Irritant	36/38	2, 26

NB This is a selection only (see above).

Part IV

Indication of particular risks

1:	Explosive when dry
2:	Risk of explosion by shock, friction, fire or other sources of ignition
3:	Extreme risk of explosion by shock, friction, fire or other sources of ignition
4:	Forms very sensitive explosive metallic compounds
5:	Heating may cause an explosion
6:	Explosive with or without contact with air
7:	May cause fire
8:	Contact with combustible material may cause fire
9:	Explosive when mixed with combustible material
10:	Flammable
11:	Highly flammable
12:	Extremely flammable
13:	Extremely flammable liquefied gas
14:	Reacts violently with water
15:	Contact with water liberates highly flammable gases
16:	Explosive when mixed with oxidising substances
17:	Spontaneously flammable in air
18:	In use, may form flammable/explosive vapour–air mixture
19:	May form explosive peroxides
20:	Harmful by inhalation
21:	Harmful in contact with skin
22:	Harmful if swallowed
23:	Toxic by inhalation
24:	Toxic in contact with skin
25:	Toxic if swallowed

26:	Very toxic by inhalation
27:	Very toxic in contact with skin
28:	Very toxic if swallowed
29:	Contact with water liberates toxic gas
30:	Can become highly flammable in use
31:	Contact with acids liberates toxic gas
32:	Contact with acids liberates very toxic gas
33:	Danger of cumulative effects
34:	Causes burns
35:	Causes severe burns
36:	Irritating to eyes
37:	Irritating to respiratory system
38:	Irritating to skin
39:	Danger of very serious irreversible effects
40:	Possible risk of irreversible effects
41:	Risk of serious damage to eyes
42:	May cause sensitisation by inhalation
43:	May cause sensitisation by skin contact
44:	Risk of explosion if heated under confinement
45:	May cause cancer
46:	May cause heritable genetic damage
47:	May cause birth defects
48:	Danger of serious damage to health by prolonged exposure

Combination of particular risks

14/15:	Reacts violently with water, liberating highly flammable gases
15/29:	Contact with water liberates toxic, highly flammable gas
20/21:	Harmful by inhalation and in contact with skin
20/21/22:	Harmful by inhalation, in contact with skin and if swallowed
20/22:	Harmful by inhalation and if swallowed
21/22:	Harmful in contact with skin and if swallowed
23/24:	Toxic by inhalation and in contact with skin
23/24/25:	Toxic by inhalation, in contact with skin and if swallowed
23/25:	Toxic by inhalation and if swallowed
24/25:	Toxic in contact with skin and if swallowed
26/27:	Very toxic by inhalation and in contact with skin
26/27/28:	Very toxic by inhalation, in contact with skin and if swallowed
26/28:	Very toxic by inhalation and if swallowed
27/28:	Very toxic in contact with skin and if swallowed
36/37:	Irritating to eyes and respiratory system
36/37/38:	Irritating to eyes, respiratory system and skin
36/38:	Irritating to eyes and skin
37/38:	Irritating to respiratory system and skin
42/43:	May cause sensitisation by inhalation and skin contact

Part V

Indication of safety precautions required

1:	Keep locked up
2:	Keep out of reach of children
3:	Keep in a cool place
4:	Keep away from living quarters

5:      Keep contents under. . .(appropriate liquid to be specified by the manufacturer)

6:      Keep under. . .(inert gas to be specified by the manufacturer)

7:      Keep container tightly closed

8:      Keep container dry

9:      Keep container in a well ventilated place

12:     Do not keep the container sealed

13:     Keep away from food, drink and animal feeding stuffs

14:     Keep away from. . .(incompatible materials to be indicated by the manufacturer)

15:     Keep away from heat

16:     Keep away from sources of ignition – No Smoking

17:     Keep away from combustible material

18:     Handle and open container with care

20:     When using do not eat or drink

21:     When using do not smoke

22:     Do not breathe dust

23:     Do not breathe gas/fumes/vapour/spray (appropriate wording to be specified by manufacturer)

24:     Avoid contact with skin

25:     Avoid contact with eyes

26:     In case of contact with eyes, rinse immediately with plenty of water and seek medical advice

27:     Take off immediately all contaminated clothing

28:     After contact with skin, wash immediately with plenty of. . .(to be specified by the manufacturer)

29:     Do not empty into drains

30:     Never add water to this product

33:     Take precautionary measures against static discharges

34:     Avoid shock and friction

35:     This material and its container must be disposed of in a safe way

36:     Wear suitable protective clothing

37:     Wear suitable gloves

38:     In case of insufficient ventilation, wear suitable respiratory equipment

39:     Wear eye/face protection

40:     To clean the floor and all objects contaminated by this material use. . .(to be specified by the manufacturer)

41:     In case of fire and/or explosion do not breathe fumes

42:     During fumigation/spraying wear suitable respiratory equipment (appropriate wording to be specified)

43:     In case of fire, use. . .(indicate in the space the precise type of fire-fighting equipment. If water increases the risk, add – Never use water)

44:     If you feel unwell, seek medical advice – show the label where possible

45:     In case of accident or if you feel unwell, seek medical advice immediately – show the label where possible

46:     If swallowed seek medical advice immediately and show this container or label

47:     Keep at temperature not exceeding. . .degrees C (to be specified by the manufacturer)

48:     Keep wetted with. . .(appropriate material to be specified by the manufacturer)

49:     Keep only in the original container

50:     Do not mix with. . .(to be specified by the manufacturer)

51:     Use only in well ventilated areas

52:     Not recommended for interior use on large surface areas

Combination of safety precautions required

1/2:	Keep locked up and out of reach of children
3/7/9:	Keep container tightly closed, in a cool well ventilated place
3/9:	Keep in a cool, well ventilated place
3/19/14:	Keep in a cool, well ventilated place away from. . .(incompatible materials to be indicated by the manufacturer)
3/9/14/49:	Keep only in the original container in a cool, well ventilated place away from. . .(incompatible materials to be indicated by the manufacturer)
3/9/49:	Keep only in the original container in a cool, well ventilated place
3/14:	Keep in a cool place away from. . .(incompatible materials to be indicated by the manufacturer)
7/8:	Keep container tightly closed and dry
7/9:	Keep container tightly closed and in a well ventilated place
20/21:	When using do not eat, drink or smoke
24/25:	Avoid contact with skin and eyes
36/37:	Wear suitable protective clothing and gloves
36/37/39:	Wear suitable protective clothing, gloves and eye/face protection
36/39:	Wear suitable protective clothing and eye/face protection
37/39:	Wear suitable gloves and eye/face protection
47/49:	Keep only in the original container at temperature not exceeding. . . (degrees C (to be specified by the manufacturer)

Schedule 1 to the Regulations

Indication of danger

 Toxic or Very Toxic

 Dangerous for the Environment

 Corrosive

 Explosive

 Oxidising

 Harmful

 Highly or Extremely Flammable

 Irritant

The above symbols shall be in black on an orange–yellow background.

APPENDIX THIRTEEN

Section 60 Order under the Health Act 1999

An outline

Part III of s.60 of the Health Act 1969 sets out the requirement for regulating the professions listed. It states:

(1)   Her Majesty may by Order in Council modify the regulation of the professions mentioned in subsection 2 to improve regulation of that profession or its services

(2)   Profession regulated by the Pharmacy Act 1954 (amongst other health professions)

The Society has had protracted discussions since 1999 with the Department of Health regarding the modernising of the Society by the use of powers under the Health Act 1999, and at the time of going to print consultation on these proposed changes was expected in January 2005. Subsequently, the consultation was further delayed until 30th May 2005 allowing time for details to be given before publication. However the Department of Health has informed the Society that consultation has been put back for the fourth time, and will not take place at least until August 2005 with the Order itself being made in April 2006 (*Pharm J* 21 May 2005 p. 601).

As authors, we regret the position we find ourselves in, but it will be appreciated it is a situation beyond our control. The Society has informed us of the Council's recommendations which it has made to the Department for implementation in the Order and the changes are likely to affect the following major areas (see below). However, no one can be sure what the Department will or will not accept until the consultation document is published and some areas may already have been covered by the 2004 Supplemental Charter. A summary of the Council's decisions on what should be covered in the section 60 Order is available on the RPSGB website (www.rpsgb.org.uk).

Areas likely to be subject to section 60 Order:

*   The Council:

    —Structure
    —Scotland and Wales
    —Committees

- Registration:

  —Powers of the Registrar
  —Format of the Register
  —Removal from the Register
  —Retirement from the Register
  —Provision of certificates

- Education and training:

  —UK and EU degrees
  —Overseas degrees (other than EU degrees)
  —Pre-registration training
  —Use of the English language
  —Character requirements for registration (including information on criminal and health status)

- Fitness to practise:

  —A pharmacist's fitness to practise
  —The fitness of a person to be registered as a pharmacist
  —The fitness of a person applying to be restored to the Register
  —The fitness of a person applying to lawfully conduct a retail pharmacy

- Impairment due to:

  —A conviction or caution in the UK for a criminal offence
  —A conviction elsewhere for an offence which if committed in the UK would be an offence
  —Misconduct
  —Impaired competence
  —Deficient professional performance
  —A physical or mental health condition
  —A determination by a body in the UK with statutory responsibility for health or social care to the fact that a person's fitness to practise is impaired

- Discipline

  —Appointments Committee
  —Investigating Committee [replacing the Infringements Committee]
  —Disciplinary Committee [Replacing Statutory Committee]
  —Health Committee

- Pharmacy technicians

  —Registration
  —Fitness to practise

Byelaws and Regulations of the Royal Pharmaceutical Society of Great Britain

June 2005

Section I: Preliminary

1. All the byelaws heretofore passed are hereby revoked, and these byelaws shall be the byelaws of the Society.

2. In these byelaws, unless the context otherwise requires, the following expressions have the meanings hereby respectively assigned to them, that is to say:

"The Council" means the Council of the Society.
"Member" means a member of the Society other than an honorary member.
"Pharmacist" means a pharmaceutical chemist.
"Preregistration Trainee" means a graduate with a degree granted in respect of pharmacy that has been approved by the Council or a student undertaking a pharmacy degree sandwich course approved by the Council who is engaged in preregistration training approved by the Council.
"Register" means the register of pharmaceutical chemists.
"Registered" means, in relation to a pharmacist, duly registered in the register.
"Registrar" means the Registrar appointed under Section 1 of the Pharmacy Act, 1954.
"Registration examination" means the examination for the purpose of Section 3 of the Pharmacy Act 1954.
"Retention fee" means the retention fee referred to in Section 2(3) of the Pharmacy Act, 1954.
"The Society" means the Royal Pharmaceutical Society of Great Britain and any reference to the Pharmaceutical Society of Great Britain in any Act of Parliament or other legislative instrument shall be so construed.

"Student" means a student of the Society, who is an undergraduate student at a school of pharmacy in Great Britain reading for a degree granted in respect of pharmacy that has been approved by the Council for the purpose of registration as a pharmaceutical chemist in Great Britain, or a graduate who has been awarded such a degree, who is not registered as a pharmaceutical chemist and who is undertaking postgraduate research or studies leading to a higher degree, or who is undertaking a period of preregistration training in Great Britain.

"Supplementary Prescriber" means a pharmacist who holds a Practice Certificate in Supplementary Prescribing approved by the Council and who having paid the required fee and satisfied the Registrar that all conditions have been complied with has the annotation "sp" against his name in the Register signifying that he is qualified to order drugs, medicines and appliances as a Supplementary Prescriber."

In these byelaws, unless the context otherwise requires, words importing the singular number only shall include the plural number and vice versa, words importing the masculine gender only shall include the feminine gender and vice versa.

Section II: Members and fees payable to the Society

1. No person shall be a member of the Society unless he is registered as a pharmacist.

Annual retention fee

2. Subject to paragraph (3), each member wishing to retain his name in the register shall pay an annual retention fee as set out in the fourth Schedule to these Byelaws.

3. A pharmacist who on 30 December 1933, was a life-member in accordance with the Byelaws then in force shall pay no retention fee.

Application fee and procedure for recognition as a Supplementary Prescriber

4. Any pharmacist applying to be recognised as a Supplementary Prescriber shall pay an application fee as set out in the fourth Schedule to these Byelaws.

5. Any pharmacist applying to be recognised as a Supplementary Prescriber shall produce evidence to satisfy the registrar that he holds a practising certificate in Supplementary Prescribing approved by the Council.

6. Upon -

    (a) receipt of the application fee set out in the fourth Schedule to these Byelaws; and

    (b) being satisfied of the matters set out in paragraph (5), the Registrar shall annotate the Register of Pharmaceutical Chemists to signify that the pharmacist is qualified to order drugs, medicines and appliances as Supplementary Prescriber, in accordance with Section XXI (5) of these Byelaws.

Due date for fees

7. Every retention fee shall be due and payable on the first day of January in each year in respect of which such fee is payable.

8. Every application fee shall be due and payable upon the making of the application.

Procedure where fees have not been paid by due date

9. The Registrar may send to any pharmacist who has not paid his retention fee on the date specified in paragraph (7) above, a demand for payment.

10.   The demand for payment shall be:

(a)   sent by registered or recorded delivery to the address of the pharmacist as it appears on the register; and

(b)   deemed to have been served on the pharmacist on the day after it was posted.

11.   Where a pharmacist has failed to pay his retention fee to the Society within two months of the date of service of the demand for payment:

(a)   the Registrar shall bring the matter to the attention of the Council; and

(b)   the Council may direct the Registrar to remove the name of the pharmacist from the register.

12.   The Registrar shall refuse to consider or progress any application until the appropriate application fee has been paid.

Section III: Fellows

1.   All members registered as pharmaceutical chemists on or before the first day of February, 1951, shall be designated fellows of the Society.

2.   The Council may designate as a fellow of the Society any member who before 1st February, 1955, either (a) was registered as a pharmaceutical chemist with the provisions of the Pharmacy Act, 1852, or (b) is registered as a pharmaceutical chemist in accordance with the provisions of the Pharmacy Act, 1954, and who but for the passing of that Act would have been registered as a pharmaceutical chemist in accordance with the provisions of the Pharmacy Act, 1852, provided, in either case, that he was eligible for registration as an apprentice or student before 1st June, 1948, and that he commenced in or before the session 1951-52 a recognised course of study of at least two years for a final examination in pharmacy or being registered as a chemist and druggist commenced in or before that session the last year of such a course.

3.   The Council may designate as fellows of the Society such members of the Society of not less than five years' standing as in the opinion of the Council have made outstanding original contributions to the advancement of pharmaceutical knowledge or have attained exceptional proficiency in a subject embraced by or related to the practice of pharmacy.

A member desiring to be designated a fellow under this byelaw shall apply in writing, enclosing the evidence on which he bases his application. The application shall be considered by assessors appointed for the purpose by the Council. The assessors may at their discretion call the applicant for interview and examine him upon his work either orally or in writing. The assessors shall report to the Education Committee of the Council who shall submit the report to the Council with or without a recommendation.

4.   Notwithstanding the provisions of the last preceding byelaw the Council may appoint a panel of fellows not being members of Council who shall have power to designate as a fellow a member of not less than 12 years' standing who in their opinion has made outstanding original contributions to the advancement of pharmaceutical knowledge or attained distinction in the science, practice, profession or history of pharmacy.

5.   Designation under the two preceding byelaws shall take place only at the June or December meeting of Council in any year.

6.   Members designated as fellows of the Society shall be so designated only so long as they remain members.

Section IV: Honorary fellows and honorary members

1. The Council may at their discretion elect as honorary fellows such scientific workers as have distinguished themselves in any of the branches of knowledge embraced in the educational objects of the Society and persons who are eminent in the national life.

2. The Council may at their discretion elect as honorary members such persons as have rendered distinguished service to the Society or to pharmacy.

3. A person who is nominated by the Privy Council to be a member of Council, under the provisions of the Pharmacy Act, 1954, shall, if not registered as a pharmacist, be an honorary member while so holding office.

4. The Council may from time to time determine the number of persons to be honorary fellows and honorary members, other than members of Council nominated by the Privy Council. A member of the Society may suggest the names of persons for election as honorary fellows or honorary members by writing to the Secretary, providing biographical information on the person nominated. At the meeting of the Council held in April of each year, the Secretary shall report in confidence the names of those so nominated and provide to the Council biographical details of the persons concerned. The Council, at its meeting in June of each year, shall consider the names proposed and may select persons to be elected honorary fellows and honorary members respectively.

Section V: Students

1. There shall be a section of the Society entitled 'The British Pharmaceutical Students' Association', membership of which shall be open to all students. Additionally, the Executive of the Association may include members of the Society who have been registered initially for not more than twelve months.

2. The Association shall be regarded by the Council as the representative body for students. It shall act within the policies of the Council, but may make recommendations to the Council.

3. The Association shall be administered by an elected Executive and in accordance with a constitution to be decided jointly by the Association and the Society.

4. The Association shall be jointly financed by the Society and the membership of the Association. The subscription to be paid by the membership shall be decided by the Council, following consultation with the Executive of the Association.

5. There shall be an annual meeting between representatives of the Council and the Executive, and regular discussions between the Executive and officials of the Society.

6. The Association shall be able to participate in the Branch Representatives' Meeting and shall be permitted to send up to two representatives, to submit up to three motions directly related to students, and, at the President's discretion, to participate in the discussion of other motions directly related to students.

7. Members of the Association shall be eligible to receive The Pharmaceutical Journal and The Journal of Pharmacy and Pharmacology at special subscription rates, to be decided by the Council.

8. Members of the Association shall be permitted to serve as co-opted members on the committees of the Society's Branches and Regions.

9.   All students, whether or not members of the Association, shall:

   (a)   be able to attend meetings of the Society's Branches and Regions;
   (b)   be eligible to receive assistance from the Benevolent Fund.

Section VI: Annual and special general meetings

1.   The annual general meeting of members shall be held in each year in the month of May on such date and at such time and place as the Council may determine.

2.   The Council shall prepare a report of their proceedings in respect of each calendar year, which together with the financial statement prepared by the Council, with the Auditors' report thereon, shall be presented at the annual general meeting held in the next subsequent calendar year and the said report of the Council's proceedings and a summary of the financial statement shall be sent to members to arrive not less than 10 days before the day appointed for the said meeting.

3.   A member may raise any matter or move any motion at any annual general meeting of which he has given the Secretary notice in writing not later than the 20th day of April in the year in which the said meeting is to be held. The Rules of Procedure for debating such motions shall be proposed by the Council and presented for adoption at each annual general meeting at which such a motion is to be moved.

4.   The Council shall meet previous to each annual general meeting and arrange the order of business to be transacted thereat.

5.   Special general meetings of members shall be held on such dates and at such times and places and for such purposes as the Council may determine. Upon the requisition in writing of not less than 30 members requiring the Council to convene a special general meeting for the purpose specified in the requisition, such meeting shall accordingly be convened within such reasonable time as the Council shall think fit.

6.   All general meetings shall be summoned by the Secretary by notice published in The Pharmaceutical Journal not less than 10 clear days before the day thereby appointed for the meeting, or by notice sent by prepaid post not less than 10 clear days before the day thereby appointed for the meeting and addressed to each member at his address in the register. Any such notice shall specify the general nature of the business to be transacted at the meeting.

7.   Notwithstanding the provisions of the last preceding byelaw, any special general meeting to be convened for the purpose of considering whether to confirm any alteration, amendment or addition to the Supplemental Charter granted to the Society on December 31st, 1953 shall be summoned in all respects as though the references in the said byelaw to 10 clear days were each of them to 40 clear days.

8.   At all general meetings the President or in his absence the Vice-President or in the absence of the President and the Vice-President such member of the Council as shall be elected by the members present at the meeting shall preside, or if there be no such member of the Council present then such other member of the Society as shall be elected to preside by the members present.

9.   Every member shall have one vote and no more at a general meeting and such vote shall be given personally and not by proxy.

10.   Any question to be decided by a general meeting, if not resolved on without a division, shall be decided by a simple majority of votes and subject to a demand for a ballot the voting shall be by show of hands.

11.   In any case of an equality of votes the chairman shall have a second or casting vote.

12. The chairman of any general meeting may adjourn such meeting from time to time and from place to place, but no such adjournment shall extend beyond a period of four days. It shall not be necessary to give members notice of such adjourned meeting, but no business shall be transacted thereat other than the business left unfinished at the meeting from which the adjournment took place.

13. The proceedings of any general meeting shall be considered perfect in themselves without the necessity of reading or confirming the minutes of the preceding general meeting.

Section VII: Council and meetings of Council

1. The Council shall consist of the persons nominated by the Privy Council in accordance with the provisions of Section 15 of the Pharmacy Act, 1954, and for the time being holding office as members of the Council, and 21 members of the Society elected by the members of the Society in accordance with the provisions of these byelaws.

2. The Council shall meet not less than four times in each calendar year, at such day and hour as may from time to time be decided by the Council. Such further meetings of the Council shall be held as are notified by the Secretary upon direction of the President or any eight members of Council in writing under his or their hands.

3. Members of Council shall be entitled to receive a fee which shall be determined by the Council from time to time by resolution but not exceeding £200 for each day or part of a day for attending any meeting of the Council or any meeting of a committee of the Council or subcommittee of such a committee or on such other occasions as the Council may from time to time by resolution determine. A member of Council who personally incurs expenditure in employment of a pharmacist to take personal control of registered retail pharmacy premises in order to comply with the requirements of the Medicines Act 1968 whilst the member of Council is engaged on Council business shall be entitled to reimbursement of sums expended not exceeding £200 per day.

4. Members of the Council shall be entitled to be reimbursed for expenditure on travel incurred on business of the Society and for costs for accommodation and subsistence and any other expense outlined in Section VII, paragraph 3 up to limits to be determined by resolution of the Council and reported to the Annual General Meeting each year.

5. Eight members shall constitute a quorum, and without that number being present no business shall be transacted. Before other business is entered on, the minutes of the preceding monthly and of any subsequent meeting shall be confirmed.

6. All meetings of the Council shall be summoned by the Secretary by notice left at the place of business or residence of, or sent by prepaid post addressed to the place of business or residence of, the person summoned not less than four clear days before the day thereby appointed for the meeting. Any such notice shall specify the general nature of the business to be transacted at the meeting.

7. The President shall preside at all meetings of the Council, or in his absence the Vice-President. If the President and Vice-President are both absent, a chairman shall be chosen by the members present. In any case of an equality of votes, the chairman of the meeting shall have a second or casting vote.

8. The Council may, from time to time, frame and adopt standing orders for the regulation of their procedure, but the chairman may, notwithstanding the standing orders, require any ordinary motion or proposition to be in writing and signed by the proposer and seconder. Any member of the Council desirous of bringing any special

motion or proposition before the Council shall give written notice to the Secretary of the terms of the motion at least fourteen clear days before the ordinary meeting of the Council, and in default of such notice the motion may be postponed or adjourned by the chairman until the next ordinary meeting. A ballot may be demanded by any member of the Council on any motion put from the chair.

9.   All council members shall comply with the Code of Conduct for such members, as adopted from time to time by the Council, and with the procedures for its enforcement in the Council governance handbook. Such procedures shall include provision for the sanctions available in respect of breach of the Code including suspension or removal from office as a Council member.

10.   Subject to the provisions of these byelaws, all resolutions carried at the meetings of the Council shall be acted upon without confirmation.

11.   The Council may, from time to time, in their discretion appoint from amongst their members or otherwise such committees as shall appear expedient, and may from time to time modify or dissolve any committee.

12.   Nothing in this section shall apply to the Statutory Committee appointed in accordance with Section 7 of the Pharmacy Act, 1954.

Section VIII: Casual vacancies in the Council

1.   If any elected member of the Council shall cease to be a member of the Society, he shall thereupon cease to be an elected member of the Council. Any elected member of the Council may at any time resign his office by giving notice in writing of his resignation to the Secretary.

2.   In the event of any casual vacancy occurring in the elected members of Council, the Council shall appoint a member of the Society to fill the place of such elected member of Council and the member so appointed shall hold office for such period as the person whom he has replaced would have held office.

3.   The Secretary shall report any casual vacancy in the elected members of Council, and the cause thereof, to the next ensuing meeting of the Council, and shall also report the same if time shall permit in the notice summoning the said meeting.

4.   At the meeting of Council next following that at which the casual vacancy is reported nominations of persons to fill the vacancy shall be made, and at the meeting of the Council held next following the meeting at which nominations are made the Council shall proceed to the election of a member to fill the casual vacancy except that if the meeting of the Council at which the vacancy is reported is the March meeting, the Council may, if they so decide, disregard the May meeting for the purpose of this procedure.

Section IX: Officers of the Society

1.   The Council shall at their first meeting held after each annual general meeting elect from among their number who are pharmacists a President, a Vice-President and a Treasurer and they together with the Immediate Past President shall be designated as the Officers of the Society.

2.   The President, Vice-President and Treasurer shall hold office until the first meeting of the Council held after the next following annual general meeting and they or any one or more of them shall be eligible for re-election.

3.   If any President, Vice-President or Treasurer shall cease to be a member of Council, he shall thereupon cease to be President, Vice-President or Treasurer, as the case may

be. The President, Vice-President or Treasurer may at any time resign his office by giving notice in writing of his resignation to the Secretary. If the Immediate Past President ceases to be a member of the Council, he shall thereupon cease to be designated Officer of the Society within the terms of paragraph 1. Until the next election under the terms of paragraph 1 above, his place as an Officer will be taken by the person who preceded him in the office as President and who continues to serve on the Council.

4. In the event of any vacancy occurring in the office of President, Vice-President or Treasurer, the Secretary shall report the same, and the cause thereof, to the next meeting of the Council, and shall also report the same if time shall permit in the notice summoning the said meeting, and the Council shall at that or the next subsequent meeting proceed to elect one of their number to fill such vacant office. Any person so elected shall hold office for such period as the person whom he has replaced would have held office.

5. It shall be the duty of the Treasurer to take charge of all moneys, to pay such accounts as the Council may order by resolution, and to render his account at each monthly meeting.

Section X: Secretary

1. The Council shall at their first meeting held after each annual general meeting appoint a person to be Secretary of the Society.

2. The Secretary shall hold office until the first meeting of the Council held after the next following annual general meeting, and shall be eligible for reappointment.

3. The Secretary shall have such powers, duties and obligations as, subject to the provisions of these byelaws, may be determined by the Council.

4. The Secretary shall be under a duty to superintend and administer the affairs of the Society under the direction of the Council and committees. He shall conduct the correspondence, and issue all summonses and notices, take the minutes of all meetings for business and read them, and make a report of all matters that come under his cognisance for the information of the Council and committees. He shall consult and act on the instructions of the President or Vice-President on any business requiring attention between the various meetings, and be responsible for the safe custody of all the documents and property belonging to the Society which shall be under his control. He shall receive all subscriptions, fees and donations, and give a printed receipt for the same, and no other, except where payment is received by cheque in which case the issue of a receipt, unless specifically requested by the payer, shall be in his discretion. He shall promptly pay to the Society's bankers on behalf of the Treasurer the amount of moneys so received by him. He shall receive such a sum in advance for current expenses as the Council may order, and account for the same to the Council.

5. If at any time more than one person is appointed to be secretary of the Society, the Council shall assign all the powers, duties and obligations referred to in paragraph 4 hereof to one of such persons.

6. In the event of a casual vacancy occurring in the office of Secretary, the President or Vice-President shall appoint some person, pro tempore, to fulfil the duty of the office, and shall report the same and the cause thereof to the next meeting of the Council, and shall also cause the same, if time shall permit, to be reported in the notice summoning the said meeting. At the said meeting the Council shall take appropriate action with a view to filling the vacancy and at some subsequent meeting shall appoint a person to fill the vacancy. The person so appointed shall hold office for such period as the person whom he has replaced would have held office.

7.   If at any time more than one person is appointed to be Secretary of the Society, the provisions of the last preceding byelaw shall be deemed to refer only to the Secretary to whom all the powers, duties and obligations referred to in paragraph 4 hereof have been assigned.

Section XI: Auditors

1.   The Council shall appoint an auditor or auditors of the accounts of the Society.

2.   No person may be appointed as an auditor unless he is a member of a body of accountants established in the United Kingdom and for the time being recognised for the purposes of Section 25(1) of the Companies Act 1989 or Article 28 of the Companies (Northern Ireland) Order 1990.

3.   The Council shall determine the term for which the auditor or auditors shall hold office, and shall fix his or their remuneration as it sees fit.

4.   The auditors shall audit and prepare a report to the Council on the annual statement of income and expenditure and of liabilities and assets prepared by officials of the Society.

Section XII: Election of Council

Section XII of, and the First Schedule to, the Society's Byelaws were replaced on 22 February 2005 by Regulation 1 of the Society's Regulations (see pp. 507–513).

Section XIII: Common seal

1.   The common seal of the Society shall consist of the armorial bearings, crest, and motto, registered in Her Majesty's College of Arms.

2.   The said seal shall be deposited in the custody of the Secretary.

3.   The common seal may be set or affixed to any deed, instrument, or writing, only in pursuance of an order or minute of the Council, entered in their minute book, which shall be laid on the table at each monthly Council meeting. The affixing of the common seal shall be recorded in a seal register, and be certified by the persons present.

4.   The affixing of the common seal shall be attested by the President, or Vice-President, or two members of Council.

Section XIV: Funds and property

1.   The whole property of or under the control of the Society shall be subject to the management, direction and control of the Council, and may, under the direction of the Council (but subject always to any special trusts upon which any particular fund may be held), be invested:

   (1)   in or upon any investments authorised by Part I or II of the first schedule to the Trustee Investments Act, 1961, as amended from time to time; or

   (2)   in or upon any of the securities of the government of the United Kingdom or of any of the countries mentioned in paragraph 2 of this byelaw or of the government of any province or state within any such country that has a separate legislature; or

   (3)   in or upon any mortgages or other securities of any municipality, county or district council or local or public authority or board in any country mentioned

in the last preceding sub-paragraph or in any province or state within any such country that has a separate legislature; or

(4)   in or upon any mortgages or other securities the capital whereof or a minimum rate of interest or dividend whereon is guaranteed by the government of any country mentioned in sub-paragraph (2) above or of any province or state within any such country that has a separate legislature; or

(5)   in or upon the bonds or mortgages or the fully paid guaranteed or preference or ordinary stock or shares or ordinary preferred or deferred or other stock or shares of any company incorporated either by Royal Charter or under any general or special Act of the United Kingdom Parliament or any general or special enactment of the legislature of any country mentioned in sub-paragraph (2) above having an issued and paid up share capital of at least £1 000 000 or its equivalent at current rates of exchange, being stocks or shares which are quoted upon a recognised stock exchange within any such country, and so that in the case of a company having shares of no par value such paid up capital shall be deemed to include the capital sum (other than capital surplus) appearing in the company's accounts in respect of such shares. Provided always that no investment shall be made in any ordinary stocks or shares unless in each of the four years immediately preceding the calendar year in which the investment is made, the company shall have paid a dividend and that the total amount at any time standing invested in investments authorised by this sub-paragraph as shown by the books of the Society shall not exceed 75 per centum of the total amount at such time standing invested in any of the investments hereby authorised as appearing by such books. For the purpose of this sub-paragraph a company formed to take over the business of another company or other companies, or for either of those purposes, shall be deemed to have paid a dividend in any year in which such a dividend has been paid by the company or all the other companies. For the purpose of valuing the investments authorised by this sub-paragraph and held by the Society the minimum price to be taken for each security shall be the cost price thereof to the Society; or

(6)   in the purchase of freehold ground rents or freehold or leasehold land, messuages, tenements and hereditaments within England and Wales provided that as regards leaseholds, the term thereof shall have at least 60 years to run; or in the purchase of lands or house property, feu duties or ground annuals, in Scotland; or

(7)   upon the security of freehold property, freehold ground rents, land charges or rent charges in England and Wales or upon heritable security in Scotland, by way of first mortgage or bond, up to the limit of two-thirds of the value.

2.   Notwithstanding the provisions of Paragraph 1, the Society may, under the direction of the Council, acquire any property and/or rights for the purpose of furthering the publishing activities of the Society (including the acquisition of such property and/or rights by the purchase of shares in a body corporate or other legal entity), provided that the aggregate purchase price in respect of any acquisition of such property and/or rights does not exceed £2 000 000. In calculating the aggregate purchase price, there shall be taken into account the amount of any liabilities assumed by the Society.

3.   This byelaw shall authorise investment in the securities of countries situated outside the United Kingdom only of the following: Australia, Austria, Belgium, Canada, Denmark, France, Federal Republic of Germany, Italy, Japan, Luxembourg, Netherlands, New Zealand, Norway, Portugal, Republic of South Africa, Spain, Sweden, Switzerland, United States of America.

4. The property and funds of the Society, other than moneys from time to time in the hands of the Secretary, shall not be disposed of, or otherwise dealt with, except in pursuance of an order of the Council.

5. Notwithstanding the provisions of Paragraph 1, the Society may, under the direction of the Council, invest funds in the purchase of stock or shares of a body corporate for the purpose of furthering the activity of testing and analysis of medicinal products or chemical substances and related activity, provided that the funds so invested shall not exceed in aggregate the sum of £2 000 000.

Section XV: Benevolent funds

1. There shall be a fund known as 'the Benevolent Fund' consisting of donations and subscriptions and such grants as may from time to time be made by the Council from the general funds of the Society and the investments for the time being in respect of the said fund.

2. Such subscriptions, donations, grants and interest on investments as are not required for current needs shall be invested.

3. The whole of the Benevolent Fund, both as to capital and interest, shall be applicable, in the discretion of the Council, towards the relief of distressed persons being:

   (1) members;
   (2) persons who at any time have been members or have been registered as pharmaceutical chemists or as chemists and druggists;
   (3) widows, orphans or other dependants of deceased persons who were at any time members or registered as aforesaid; or
   (4) students.

4. There shall be a fund known as 'the Orphan Fund', and the provisions of paragraphs 1, 2 and 3 hereof shall apply to the said fund as though references in the said byelaws to the Benevolent Fund were references to the Orphan Fund, save that the Orphan Fund shall be applicable towards the relief of distressed persons who are the orphan children of deceased persons who were at any time members and not otherwise.

5. There shall be a fund known as 'the Birdsgrove House Fund', and the provisions of paragraph 1, 2 and 3 hereof shall apply to the said fund as though references in the said byelaws to the Benevolent Fund were references to the Birdsgrove House Fund, save that the Birdsgrove House Fund shall be applicable towards the establishment and maintenance of convalescent homes for the relief of distressed persons being:

   (1) members;
   (2) persons who at any time have been members or have been registered as pharmaceutical chemists or as chemists and druggists; or
   (3) widows, orphans or other dependants of deceased persons who were at any time members or registered as aforesaid.

Section XVI: Branches and branch representatives' meetings

1. The Council shall establish and maintain a system of local Branches of the Society.

2. Each local Branch shall be constituted and governed in such manner and have such functions as may be determined by the rules for the time being in force in respect of that Branch. The rules of each Branch shall be based upon the model rules set out in the second schedule to these byelaws with such modifications in respect of any Branch as the Council may from time to time approve.

3. The Council shall arrange the holding from time to time and from place to place of meetings of members representative of the local Branches. The number of Representatives of each local Branch, the mode of their appointment, and the procedure to be adopted at the meetings of Representatives, shall be determined by the Council.

4. The functions of the meetings of Representatives shall be to inform the Council of the views of the Branches on matters of concern to the Society, to inform the Representatives of the Council's activities or proposed activities and the reasons therefore, and to ascertain the views of the Branches upon the said activities or proposed activities.

Section XVII: Membership groups

1. The Council may from time to time establish and determine the constitution of special groups of members based on the nature of their occupations or special interests. The function of any such group shall be the discussion of matters of a professional and technical character of common interest to the members of the group.

Section XVIII: Meetings for the reading of papers

1. Meetings of the Society may be held for the reading of papers and discussion of subjects relating to the objects of the Society.

2. Notice of such meetings shall be given in The Pharmaceutical Journal.

Section XIX: Registration of overseas pharmacists

1. The Council may by resolution enter into a reciprocal agreement with the Pharmaceutical Society of Northern Ireland, for the registration as a pharmaceutical chemist under the Pharmacy Act 1954, of a person registered as a pharmaceutical chemist in Northern Ireland who is able to satisfy the Registrar that he registered in Northern Ireland after qualifying in pharmacy in the United Kingdom or by virtue of holding an appropriate European diploma as specified in Schedule 1A to the Pharmacy Act, 1954.

2. Persons making application for registration pursuant to an agreement entered into in accordance with the provisions of the preceding byelaw shall:

   (a) produce evidence to satisfy the Registrar:

       (i) as to his identity;
       (ii) that he is of good character;
       (iii) that he is in good health, both physically and mentally;
       (iv) that he is registered as a pharmaceutical chemist in Northern Ireland within the terms of such agreement; and

   (b) pay to the Registrar a fee specified in the fourth Schedule to these Byelaws; whereupon, subject to the Registrar being satisfied that all conditions have been complied with, he shall be registered.

3. Any person wishing to apply for registration pursuant to an agreement between the Society, in the exercise of powers conferred on the Council of the Society under any previous byelaws, and the authorities responsible for the registration of pharmacists:

   (a) in South Africa; or
   (b) in Australia; or
   (c) in New Zealand

shall apply to the Registrar no later than noon on Friday 30th June 2006 in accordance with the provisions of paragraph 4.

4.   A person making application referred to in paragraph 3 shall:

(a)   produce evidence to satisfy the Registrar:

  (i)   that he is resident in the United Kingdom;
  (ii)   as to his identity;
  (iii)   that he is of good character;
  (iv)   that he is in good health, both physically and mentally;
  (v)   that he has passed a qualifying examination specified in such agreement;
  (vi)   that he is registered as a pharmacist in the country or state, as the case may be, in which he passed that examination and is in good standing with the pharmacists registration authority of the country or state concerned;

(b)   produce a declaration made in accordance with the Statutory Declarations Act, 1935, that he is the person referred to in the documents produced by him and that they are his property;

(c)   in the case of a person who was granted a certificate of qualification to practise pharmacy in any State of the Commonwealth of Australia or in New Zealand after March 31, 1968:

  (i)   produce a certificate from the Registrar of the pharmacists registration authority concerned that, subsequent to the date of his statutory registration, he completed, normally within the jurisdiction of that authority, a period of one years' employment in pharmacy as a registered pharmacist;
  (ii)   produce evidence satisfactory to the Registrar that he has completed in Great Britain a period of four weeks' experience in the practice of pharmacy in a pharmacy or pharmacy department of a hospital under the direct personal control and supervision of a pharmacist registered in Great Britain; and
  (iii)   produce a declaration made in accordance with the Statutory Declaration Act, 1835, that he has studied the laws affecting the practice of pharmacy and the current Code of Ethics (as amended) and Notes for Guidance; and

(d)   pay to the Registrar a fee specified in the fourth Schedule to these Byelaws; whereupon subject to the Registrar being satisfied that all conditions have been complied with, he shall be registered.

5.   The Council, shall authorise the registration as a pharmaceutical chemist under the Pharmacy Act, 1954, of a national from a Member State of the European Community other than the United Kingdom who:

(a)   produces evidence to satisfy the Registrar:

  (i)   as to his identity;
  (ii)   that he is of good character;
  (iii)   that he is in good health, both physically and mentally; and
  (iv)   that he holds an appropriate European diploma as specified in Schedule 1A to the Pharmacy Act, 1954; and

(b)   pays to the Registrar a fee specified in the fourth Schedule to these Byelaws; whereupon, subject to the Registrar being satisfied that all conditions have been complied with, he shall be registered.

6.   The Council may by resolution authorise the registration as a pharmaceutical chemist under the Pharmacy Act, 1954, of a person who:

(a) produces evidence to satisfy the Registrar:

    (i) as to his identity;

    (ii) that he is of good character;

    (iii) that he is in good health, both physically and mentally;

    (iv) that he holds a pharmaceutical qualification or qualifications comparable with an approved degree in pharmacy awarded in the United Kingdom but granted by a University, or a body of comparable academic status, outside the United Kingdom; and

    (v) that he is registered or is qualified to be registered as a pharmacist in the country, state or province in which the university or body is situated, or is registered as a pharmacist in another country;

(b) satisfies an adjudicating committee appointed by the Council as to the content and standard of the course and examination in pharmacy taken by him, his knowledge of pharmacy in relation to current practice in Great Britain and of the English language if that is not his mother tongue;

(c) subsequently produces evidence to satisfy the adjudicating committee:

    (i) that he has completed a period of employment in Great Britain in the practice of pharmacy under conditions laid down by the adjudicating committee; and

    (ii) that he has satisfied the examiners in such part or parts of an examination or examinations approved by the Council for the purposes of this byelaw as may be required by the adjudicating committee and if the committee requires passing of the registration examination, he will be treated as if he was a preregistration trainee in accordance with paragraphs 27, 28 and 29 of Section XX;

(d) pays the Registrar the fee prescribed in paragraph 26 of Section XX of the Byelaws; and

(e) pays to the Registrar:

    (i) a fee specified in the fourth Schedule to these Byelaws in respect of the examination of the evidence produced under (a); and

    (ii) a fee specified in the fourth Schedule to these Byelaws in respect of the inquiry under (b); and

    (iii) a fee specified in the fourth Schedule to these Byelaws in respect of registration;

whereupon, subject to the Registrar being satisfied that all conditions have been complied with, he shall be registered.

Section XX: Registrar and registrations

1. In the event of a vacancy occurring in the office of Registrar, the President or Vice-President shall appoint some person, pro tempore, to fulfil the duty of the office, and shall report the same, and the cause thereof to the next meeting of the Council, and shall also cause the same if time shall permit to be reported in the notice summoning the said meeting. At the said meeting the Council shall take appropriate action with a view to filling the vacancy and at some subsequent meeting shall appoint a person to fill the vacancy.

1A. The subjects for the registration examination shall include: The Practice of Pharmacy including the implementation in practice of laws governing pharmacy and the application in practice of the Code of Ethics and Standards of Professional Practice of the Royal Pharmaceutical Society of Great Britain.

1B. The Council, under the terms of the Supplemental Charter of 1953, hereby delegates to the Education Committee appointed by the Society's Officers its duties and responsibilities set out in Paragraphs 2, 4, 5, 6, 7, 12, 18, 18A, 19 and 22 of this Section of the Byelaws but reserves to itself the consideration of withdrawal of approval of a pharmacy degree course, previously approved within the terms of Paragraph 2.

2.   A person who holds a degree of a University of the United Kingdom or of the Council for National Academic Awards, granted in respect of pharmacy at the conclusion of a course of study undertaken in the United Kingdom and in accordance with European Community obligations and provisions, and approved by the Council, need not be examined in the latin language, botany, materia medica, pharmaceutical chemistry and general chemistry and need not be granted the certificate mentioned in Section 3(5) of the Pharmacy Act 1954 and shall be eligible to be registered as a pharmaceutical chemist provided he produces evidence to satisfy the Registrar:

    (i)   as to his identity;
    (ii) that he has attained the age of 21 years;
    (iii) that he has obtained the appropriate degree;
    (iv) in the case of a pharmacy trainee who commenced Preregistration training after June 30, 1992, or a pharmacy student in a pharmacy degree sandwich course approved by the Council who commenced his 27th week of preregistration training after that date, that he has passed a registration examination.
    (v)   that he is of good character;
    (vi) that he is in good health, both physically and mentally;
    (vii) by a declaration upon an official form obtainable from the Registrar that he has satisfactorily undergone a period of preregistration training in accordance with this Section;
  (viii) that in the event of his having obtained the degree at a date when the degree was not recognised by the Council, he has complied with such other requirements as may be prescribed by the Council;
    (ix) that he has not failed an examination set by the Pharmaceutical Society of Northern Ireland for registration as a pharmacist in Northern Ireland.

3.   A person making application for registration in accordance with byelaw 2 of this section shall pay to the Registrar a fee specified in the fourth Schedule to these Byelaws, whereupon, subject to the Registrar being satisfied that all conditions have been complied with, he shall be registered.

4.   Preregistration training shall be gained in not more than two of the following pharmaceutical establishments in Great Britain approved by the Council for these purposes, subject to the provisions of byelaws 13 to 20 of this Section:

    (a)   a community pharmacy, or up to three community pharmacies owned by a pharmacist, partnership, or corporate body provided no period of less than 10 consecutive weeks is spent in any one pharmacy;
    (b)   the pharmaceutical department of a hospital or similar institution or more than one pharmaceutical department within a group of hospitals;
    (c)   a pharmaceutical industrial establishment;
    (d)   a school of pharmacy;
    (e)   a registered pharmacy engaged solely in the supply of animal and agricultural products.

Unless the Council otherwise determines in any particular case, establishments referred to in (a) and (e) shall be required to have been a registered pharmacy for at least one year before the commencement of a period of preregistration training.

5.   Except in the case of schools of pharmacy, applications from registered pharmaceutical chemists for the approval of pharmaceutical establishments for the purposes of preregistration training shall be made on forms provided by the Council and shall be considered by the Council, in accordance with aims, objectives and guidance agreed

by resolution of the Council as to the training and the establishment in which it is to be undertaken and if necessary following inspection by a member of the Society appointed by the Council. Approval for these purposes shall normally be given for a period of five years. Approval will be given without further consideration by the Council to any school of pharmacy offering a course leading to a degree in pharmacy approved by the Council for the purposes of registration as a pharmaceutical chemist in Great Britain, and the conditions of preregistration training in a school of pharmacy shall be agreed by resolution of the Council.

6. In an application for the approval of a pharmaceutical establishment a registered pharmacist shall be named as the preregistration tutor who, except in circumstances approved by the Council, shall ensure that during any period of preregistration training, each preregistration trainee is under the supervision of a registered pharmacist. In an approved establishment at any time there must be no more preregistration trainees and pharmacy students working in the premises than pharmacists, except for periods totalling 13 weeks or less in any year corresponding with a trainee's full 52 weeks' preregistration training, or for periods totalling seven weeks or less in any period corresponding with a trainee's engagement in a lesser number of weeks' preregistration training, in partial fulfilment of the total training requirement.

7. The preregistration tutor shall have practised for at least three years as a registered pharmaceutical chemist in the aspect of pharmacy with which the establishment is concerned, shall undertake to provide the training required by the Council, and shall fulfil such other requirements as may be resolved by the Council from time to time.

8. In any period of training in one approved establishment, the preregistration tutor shall be engaged full time in the same premises as the trainee, except in those programmes of training within an approved establishment where preregistration trainees move from one premises to another to undertake the full range of training, in which case the preregistration tutor shall undertake to meet each trainee in the place of employment at least once a month.

9. In a school of pharmacy each preregistration trainee shall have a different preregistration tutor, who shall be a member of staff and a registered pharmacist. The head of the school may be one of the preregistration tutors if he is a registered pharmacist, and will be expected to co-ordinate the arrangements within the school.

10. If for any reason the preregistration tutor ceases to occupy the position mentioned in the pharmaceutical establishment concerned, the preregistration trainee concerned shall be permitted to complete the period of preregistration training under the supervision of the registered pharmacist who succeeds the preregistration tutor, without a further application for approval of the establishment. For the remainder of the five-year approval period, the establishment shall only be acceptable for preregistration training if a pharmacist who fulfils the necessary requirements for preregistration tutors undertakes in writing to the Society to provide the training described in the original application.

11. The Council, at its discretion, may decide that any pharmaceutical establishment is unacceptable for this purpose, either upon application or if, during a period of approval, the training gained therein or the facilities provided are found to be no longer satisfactory.

12. The Council may approve any establishment, other than those mentioned above, if satisfied that it is suitable for this purpose.

13. The total duration of preregistration training shall be full-time employment, for at least 52 weeks, including the normal holiday entitlement for the establishment concerned and public holidays. The Registrar shall be informed of any sick leave exceeding the equivalent of one week's full-time employment and any allowance for sick leave or for other reasons will be at the discretion of the Registrar.

14. It will be acceptable for a 52-week period to be undertaken in either an approved community pharmacy or hospital pharmaceutical department.

15. Experience in two approved establishments shall be acceptable, provided each 52-week programme contains:

(i) at least one period of not less than 26 weeks in a community pharmaceutical department; and

(ii) no more than one period in either an industrial establishment, a school of pharmacy or a registered pharmacy engaged solely in the supply of animal and agricultural pharmaceutical products.

16. The periods of training in two establishments may vary in length, provided at least 26 weeks is undertaken in a community pharmacy or hospital pharmaceutical department.

17. When the two periods are of equal duration and are in community and hospital pharmacy practice, the 52-week programme shall be lodged with the Society in advance.

18. When only one of two periods is in community or hospital pharmacy practice the 52-week programme of training shall be approved by the Council in advance.

18A. With the prior approval of the Council, up to 13 weeks of the total period of preregistration training may be undertaken in a pharmacy establishment in another member state of the European Union, provided the placement overseas is continuous, takes place within or for the duration of the period between the 13th and 26th week of the total period and is an integral part of a complete programme which meets the Council's requirements and includes a single placement of at least six months' duration in a community or hospital pharmacy in Great Britain.

19. When two separate periods of acceptable training are undertaken, the second shall be completed within three years immediately following the end of the first, except in circumstances specifically approved by the Council.

20. Within a 52-week programme undertaken in one establishment it shall be permissible, with the mutual agreement of the preregistration tutor and the preregistration trainee, to include up to four weeks' training in another approved establishment, and up to a total of one weeks' experience, normally in another aspect of practice or for a specific training purpose, in a pharmaceutical establishment or establishments which need not be approved by the Council for this purpose.

21. For the purposes of these byelaws, a person wishing to undertake preregistration training shall, prior to the commencement of each period:

(a) inform the Registrar on the prescribed form of the name and address of the establishment concerned, the name of the preregistration tutor and the date of commencement of the period;

(b) pay a fee specified in the fourth Schedule to these Byelaws to the Society for a 52-week period, or, where applicable, a proportion of that amount for any shorter or additional period.

22. The preregistration tutor and the preregistration trainee concerned shall complete the assessment procedure approved by the Council and the trainee shall attend appropriate study days when necessary to complete the required training.

23. Preregistration training shall not be acceptable in an establishment in which the preregistration trainee has a controlling interest.

24. The Registrar shall have discretion to accept, as an exceptional circumstance, a period of preregistration training which does not comply with the byelaws or with

the guidance approved by the Council, but which fulfils the aims and objectives of the Council to his satisfaction.

25. Periods of preregistration training shall commence normally between July 1st and August 15th. The commencement date of preregistration training may be between the last day of the final term of the pharmacy degree course and the date that the Registrar is informed by the appropriate authority that the graduate has successfully completed the examinations of an approved pharmacy degree. In these circumstances, training will only be acceptable from that date if the Registrar is subsequently informed by the appropriate authority that the applicant has successfully completed the degree examinations held during that term.

26. Subject to a satisfactory appraisal report by the preregistration tutor after at least 39 weeks of preregistration training have been undertaken, and in the case of a pharmacy degree sandwich course student after the final degree examinations have been taken, a preregistration trainee shall be eligible, after payment of an examination fee specified in the fourth Schedule to these Byelaws to the Registrar not later than six weeks before the examination, or after payment of a late-entry fee specified in the fourth Schedule to these Byelaws to the Registrar not later than four weeks before the examination, and after completion of at least 45 weeks of preregistration training, to sit the registration examination within eighteen months of such completion.

27. After payment of a fee specified in the fourth Schedule to these Byelaws to the Registrar not later than six weeks before the examination, or after payment of a late entry fee specified in the fourth Schedule to these Byelaws to the Registrar not later than four weeks before the examination a preregistration trainee who:

    (a) fails to pass the registration examination at the first attempt may take the examination again within the following 18 months;

    (b) fails to pass the examination at the second attempt shall be required to complete a period of six months' employment acceptable to the Registrar in a community or hospital pharmacy notified in advance to the Registrar, and may take the examination for a third time within 12 months of satisfactory completion of such period of employment.

28. A preregistration trainee who:

    (a) does not sit the registration examination within 18 months of satisfactory completion of preregistration training; or

    (b) fails to pass the registration examination at the first attempt and does not resit the examination within 18 months; or

    (c) fails to pass the registration examination at the second attempt and does not resit the examination within 12 months of completing his period of employment as required under paragraph 27(b) shall be required to fulfil such requirements as are specified by the Registrar before being eligible for registration as a pharmaceutical chemist.

29. A person who fails the registration examination at the third attempt will not normally be eligible for registration as a pharmaceutical chemist. In circumstances considered by the Council to be exceptional, the Council may specify conditions under which it is prepared to permit a preregistration trainee to sit the examination on one further occasion.

30. On completion of the period of preregistration training the applicant shall submit to the Registrar:

    (1) a declaration:

        (a) that a period or periods of preregistration training of 52 weeks total duration have been completed at the establishment or establishments named in the declaration, stating the dates of commencement and the completion of each period;

(b)   that in the opinion of the preregistration tutor for the full period or second period as the case may be, the applicant is able to apply in practice the knowledge of the law relating to the practice of pharmacy gained during the degree course and is a fit and proper person to be registered as a pharmaceutical chemist;

(2)   a report, in a prescribed form, on each period of preregistration training. The declaration and the report shall be signed by the preregistration tutor for each approved establishment.

31.   A person who satisfies the Registrar that his original certificate of registration has been lost or destroyed shall be issued with a replacement certificate on payment of a fee to be determined by the Council.

Section XXI: The Register of Pharmaceutical Chemists

1.   Each entry in the Register of Pharmaceutical Chemists shall include the full name of the person concerned, his address, a distinguishing registration number, the date of registration, whether the person is a practising or non-practising pharmacist and particulars of such person's qualification for registration.

2.   The entries in the said register shall be arranged in alphabetical order according to the surnames.

3.   Each annual register of pharmaceutical chemists shall contain the particulars and be in the form set forth in the third schedule to these byelaws.

4.   The entries in each annual Register of Pharmaceutical Chemists shall be arranged in alphabetical order according to the surnames.

5.   The Council may by resolution amend the Third Schedule to the Byelaws to enable the annotation of the annual register to indicate particular qualifications, specialist areas of practice or status as determined by the Council or as prescribed by Regulations.

Section XXII: Certificates of registration

1.   The period referred to in paragraph 9 of the second schedule to the Pharmacy Act, 1954 (being the period during which a certificate of registration as a chemist and druggist is deemed to be a certificate of registration as a pharmaceutical chemist), shall be a period of five years commencing the 1st day of January, 1954.

Section XXIII: Scottish Department

1.   The Scottish Department of the Society shall consist of those members of the Society whose addresses in the Register are in Scotland and shall be governed by a body – to be called "the Executive of the Scottish Department" and hereinafter called "the Executive" – acting under the authority of the Council.

2.   The Executive shall consist of the President, the Vice-President and such other members of Council as may be resident in Scotland, ex officio, and, in addition, 18 members of the Society elected from and by members whose addresses in the Register are in Scotland.

3. Six of the elected members shall go out of office in each year, and the vacancies shall be filled by election, the retiring members being eligible for re-election. The six elected members who go out of office shall be the elected members who have been longest in office without re-election.

4. The elections shall be conducted upon such dates and in such manner as may be determined by the Executive. Casual vacancies occurring in the elected members shall be filled in such manner and subject to such conditions as the Executive may determine.

5. The Executive shall elect from among their number a Chairman and a Vice-Chairman to hold office for such period as may be determined by the Executive.

6. There shall be a Secretary of the Scottish Department of the Society resident in Scotland whose duties shall be determined by the Council and who shall be appointed by the Council after considering any recommendation of the Executive.

7. The functions of the Executive will include the implementation in Scotland of the policies of the Society, the management of the Society's House in Edinburgh, the arrangement of meetings in Scotland for the advancement of the objects of the Society, the organisation and supervision of the local Branches of the Society in Scotland, and the making of recommendations to the Council upon any matters affecting the Society and their members.

8. The Executive may appoint from their members such committees or subcommittees as may be necessary to assist them in carrying out their functions. Persons not being members of the Executive may be co-opted in an advisory capacity to any such committee or subcommittee.

9. The Secretary shall submit to the Secretary of the Society a report of each of the meetings of the Executive and such reports upon the Scottish Department of the Society as he may be requested by the Council to submit.

10. Members of the Executive shall be entitled to receive such fee and reimbursement of expenditure incurred on travel, accommodation and subsistence as they may by resolution from time to time determine, but not exceeding the fee and sums for reimbursement of expenses incurred payable to members of Council, for attendance at meetings of the Scottish Department Executive or any meeting of a committee of the Executive or subcommittees of such a committee.

Section XXIV: Welsh Executive

1. The Welsh Executive, acting under the authority of the Council, shall consist of the President, the Vice-President and such other members of Council as may be resident in Wales, ex officio, and, in addition, 12 members of the Society elected from and by members whose addresses in the Register are in Wales.

2. Four of the elected members shall go out of office in each year, and the vacancies shall be filled by election, the retiring members being eligible for re-election. The four elected members who go out of office shall be the elected members who have been longest in office without re-election.

3. The elections shall be conducted upon such dates and in such manner as may be determined by the Executive. Casual vacancies occurring in the elected members shall be filled in such manner and subject to such conditions as the Executive may determine. The member so appointed shall hold office for such period as the person whom he has replaced would have held office.

4. The Executive shall elect from among their number a Chairman and a Vice-Chairman to hold office for one year and be eligible for re-election.

5.   There shall be a Secretary of the Welsh Executive resident in Wales and based in the Society's headquarters in Cardiff whose duties shall be determined by the Council and who shall be appointed by the Council after considering any recommendation of the Executive.

6.   The full title in English of the Welsh Executive shall be: "Royal Pharmaceutical Society of Great Britain – Welsh Executive" and the full title in Welsh shall be: "Cymdeithas Fferyllol Frenhinol Prydain Fawr – Gweithgor Cymru."

7.   The Executive shall be responsible under the authority of the Council for the implementation in Wales of the policies of the Society, the organisation and super-vision of the local Branches of the Society in Wales, and the making of recommenda-tions to the Council upon matters affecting the Society and its members.

8.   The Executive may appoint from their members such committees or subcommittees as may be necessary to assist them in carrying out their functions. Persons not being members of the Executive may be co-opted in an advisory capacity to any such committees or subcommittees.

9.   The Secretary shall submit to the Secretary of the Society a report of each of the meetings of the Executive and such other reports upon the Welsh Executive as may be requested by the Council.

10.   Members of the Executive shall be entitled to receive such fee and reimbursement of expenditure incurred on travel, accommodation and subsistence as they may by resolution from time to time determine, but not exceeding the fee and sums for reimbursement of expenses incurred payable to members of Council, for attendance at meetings of the Welsh Executive or any meeting of a committee of the Executive or subcommittees of such a committee.

Section XXV: Journal and transactions

1.   The Pharmaceutical Journal shall be edited, printed and published in such manner as the Council shall from time to time direct.

2.   The transactions of the Society required to be published shall be inserted in the said Journal, and all notices shall be considered duly given if inserted therein.

Section XXVI: Museum

1.   The Society shall maintain a museum for the benefit of members and students of the Society, and members of the public interested in the profession of pharmacy.

2.   The museum will reflect the principles and practice of British pharmacy and the history of the Society.

3.   The Council shall establish a constitution for the maintenance and management of the museum collection.

Section XXVII: Regulations

1.   The Council shall have power to make regulations for any of the following purposes:

(1)   For prescribing the qualifications of and fees to be paid by persons seeking to be registered as students.

(2)   For prescribing the times, places, forms, fees and dates of entry for, and methods of conducting, the examinations to be held in accordance with the Pharmacy Acts.

(3) For prescribing the subjects and the standard of knowledge thereof to be required of candidates presenting themselves for examination.

(4) For prescribing the scope and length of training to be undergone by candidates presenting themselves for examination and the evidence thereof to be submitted by the candidate.

(5) For prescribing the character and length of curricula to be taken by candidates, the institutions at which such curricula may be taken, and the evidence thereof to be submitted by the candidate.

2. All such regulations and all altered or new regulations shall, before becoming operative, receive the approval of the Privy Council and copies shall immediately thereafter be obtainable by members and students free of charge upon application to the Registrar. The approval of the Privy Council to regulations shall be notified in The Pharmaceutical Journal immediately after its being received.

Section XXVIII: Byelaws

1. Any proposal to make, alter or revoke a byelaw shall be in writing and, being delivered at a Council meeting by a member of Council to the Chairman, or brought up on the report of a committee, shall thereupon be read, and, if seconded and approved, notice of the approval by the Council of the said proposal and of the intention of the Council to make, alter or revoke the said byelaw, as the case may be, at the expiry of not less than 60 days from the date of the said notice, shall be given to the members in The Pharmaceutical Journal.

2. Any member applying to the Secretary for a copy of any proposal to make, alter or revoke a byelaw shall be entitled to receive a copy free of charge.

3. At the meeting of the Council held next after the expiry of 60 days from the date of The Pharmaceutical Journal in which notice of a proposal to make, alter or revoke a byelaw was given, the Secretary shall report any observations received by him upon the said proposal. If the Council shall thereupon confirm the said proposal and make, alter or revoke the said byelaw, as the case may be, but not otherwise, the Secretary shall forthwith submit the byelaw so made, altered or revoked, as the case may be, to the Privy Council for confirmation and approval.

4. If no observations are received by the Secretary upon the said proposal he shall notify the Council in writing, and shall forthwith submit the byelaw as prepared to the Privy Council for confirmation and approval and report this at the next meeting of the Council.

5. Notice of the confirmation and approval by the Privy Council of the making, alteration or revocation of any byelaw shall be given in The Pharmaceutical Journal.

6. Every person upon becoming a member and every person upon becoming a student shall be entitled to receive a copy of the byelaws free of charge.

First schedule

Form of voting paper

Section XII of, and the First Schedule to, the Society's Byelaws were replaced on 22 February 2005 by Regulation 1 of the Society's Regulations (see p. 512).

Second schedule

Model Rules for Branches

1. The name of the Branch shall be* .... Branch of the Royal Pharmaceutical Society of Great Britain.

2. The objects of the Branch shall be to further the interests of the Society and its members more particularly by:

    (1)   serving as a medium of contact between the Council of the Society and members in the Branch area;

    (2)   co-operating with the Council generally in the work of the Society;

    (3)   promoting a corporate spirit amongst members and securing the observance of such standards of professional conduct as will uphold the dignity of the Society;

    (4)   providing opportunity for members to raise and discuss matters of common interest and to express their collective opinion thereon;

    (5)   arranging lectures and courses of instruction for members and students upon scientific and other subjects appertaining to pharmacy;

    (6)   organising social functions and encouraging social intercourse between members;

    (7)   promoting friendly relations and co-operation between members of the Society and members of the medical and allied professions;

    (8)   urging upon members the claims of the Benevolent Fund to their support.

3. Membership of the Branch shall be limited to members of the Society and, except as hereinafter provided, all such persons residing in the Branch area shall be members of the Branch. A member of the Branch may, subject to the approval of the Council of the Society, transfer his membership to another Branch and a member of another Branch may, subject to the approval of the Council of the Society, transfer his membership to the Branch.

4. The Branch area shall be such as the Council of the Society may from time to time decide after consultation with the Branches concerned.

5. The Officers of the Branch shall be: a Chairman, a Vice-Chairman, a Secretary, a Treasurer and such others as may be decided in general meeting.

6. The affairs of the Branch shall be under the control and management of a Committee consisting of the Chairman, the Vice-Chairman, the Secretary, the Treasurer, and any other officers and not more than† .... other members. The Committee may appoint from their number subcommittees for educational, Benevolent Fund, social and other purposes, and delegate to them the powers of the committee in such respects.

7. General meetings of the Branch shall be held annually in‡ .... at such other times as the committee may think fit, and at any time on the written requisition to the Secretary of not fewer than† .... members.

8. The business of the annual general meeting shall include the presentation by the committee of a report of the work of the Branch, and an audited statement of accounts for the past year, and the election of committee and† .... auditors. The committee shall forward to the Secretary of the Society a copy of the audited statement of accounts as soon as possible after the meeting.

---

* Insert name of the branch
† Insert the desired number
‡ Insert the name of a month not later in the year than May

9.   The officers of the Branch shall be elected§ .... The representatives of the Branch to attend the British Pharmaceutical Conference or any Branch Representatives' Meeting shall be elected at a general meeting of the Branch.

10.   The officers and committee shall retire at the annual general meeting, but shall be eligible for re-election. Any vacancy occurring during the year may be filled by the committee.

11.   The committee shall, on request, furnish the Council of the Society with such information about the activities and finances of the Branch as the Council may require.

Third schedule

The Annual Register of Pharmaceutical Chemists

Date of registration	Number	Name	Postal town	Status

The letters in the last margin to the right indicate the status of the member as follows:

F indicates that the member is a Fellow of the Royal Pharmaceutical Society
P indicates that the member is a practising pharmacist*
NP indicates that the member is a non-practising pharmacist*
sp indicates that the member is qualified to order drugs, medicines and appliances as a Supplementary Prescriber

* a practising pharmacist is a member who undertakes any work in, or gives advice in relation to, the science of medicines or the practice of pharmacy or healthcare.
   * a non-practising pharmacist is a member who does not engage in pharmacy practice, is not involved in patient care and does not work in or give advice in relation to, the science of medicines or the practice of pharmacy or healthcare.

Fourth schedule

Fees payable to the Society

Annual retention fee

1.   The annual retention fee payable by a member in accordance with Section II(2) of these Byelaws shall be as follows:

(a)   non-practising pharmacists shall pay a retention fee of £46; and
(b)   practising pharmacists shall pay a retention fee of £256.

Upgrade fee

2.   The fee payable in respect of any pharmacist who wishes to upgrade his registration status from non-practising to practising, shall be £210.

§ Insert either ".... by the annual general meeting" or "by the Committee at a meeting to be held as soon as convenient after the annual general meeting"

Restoration fee

3.   The fee payable by any person whose name has been erased from the register:

(a)   for non payment of the annual retention fee; or
(b)   following a direction issued by the Society's Statutory Committee,
and who applies to the Society to have his name restored to the register, shall be £494.

4.   A person whose application for the voluntary removal of his name from the register is accepted by the Society, and who then subsequently applies to the Society to have his name restored to the register, shall pay an application fee of £125.

5.   Any person whose name is restored to the register shall pay, in addition to the fee specified in paragraph (3) or (4) above, the annual retention fee specified in paragraph (1)(a) or (1)(b).

Application fee for recognition as a Supplementary Prescriber

6.   Any pharmacist applying to be recognised as a Supplementary Prescriber shall pay an application fee of £35.

Application fee for registration of overseas pharmacists under reciprocal arrangements

7.   The application fee for registration pursuant to an agreement entered into in accordance with the provisions of Section XIX (1) and (3) of these Byelaws shall be £125.

Fees for persons wishing to be registered under the Pharmacy Act 1954

8.   The application fee for registration in accordance with the provisions of Section XIX (5) and XIX (6)(e)(iii) of these Byelaws shall be £125.

9.   The fees payable in respect of Section XIX (6)(e)(i) and (ii) of these Byelaws shall be as follows:

(a)   the fee for examination of evidence shall be £556; and
(b)   the fee for inquiry before, and interview by, the Adjudicating Committee shall be £556.

Application Fee for registration by persons having completed pre-registration training within Great Britain

10.   The fee for applications pursuant to Section XX (3) of these Byelaws shall be £125.

Fees in respect of pre-registration training

11.   The fees payable in respect of Section XX (21)(b) of these Byelaws shall be £140.

12.   The fees payable in respect of Section XX (26) of these Byelaws shall be as follows:

(a)   the examination fee shall be £165;
(b)   the late entry fee shall be £330.

13.   The fees payable in respect of Section XX (27) of these Byelaws shall be as follows:

(a)   the examination resit fee shall be £165;
(b)   the late entry fee shall be £330.

Regulations

Preamble

The Royal Pharmaceutical Society of Great Britain ('the Society'), in exercise of the powers conferred upon it by the Supplemental Charter of 2004, and with the approval of the Privy Council, has made these Regulations.

Index to regulations

1. Election of Council members

*This Regulation is made pursuant to articles 8 and 9(2) of the Supplemental Charter of 2004 and supersedes Section XII of, and the First Schedule to, the Society's byelaws.

2. Appointed Council members[†]

[†] This Regulation is made pursuant to articles 8 and 9(2) of the Supplemental Charter of 2004.

Regulation 1 – Election of Council members

Elections

1.1   Elections to elect pharmacists or pharmacy technicians to membership of the Council shall be held in accordance with this regulation.

Interpretation

1.2   In this regulation:

'the Effective Date' means the day after the day of the Annual General Meeting ('AGM') of the Society in 2005.

'Secretary' means the Secretary (or chief executive officer by whatever title known) of the Society and includes any deputy or acting Secretary or other person fulfilling the office of Secretary and any person (not being a member of the Council) authorised by the Secretary.

'general election' means an election held on the expiry of the terms of office of members of the Council.

'Register of Pharmacists' means the register of pharmaceutical chemists.

'Register of Pharmacy Technicians' means the register of pharmacy technicians maintained by the Society.

'pharmacy technician' means a person registered in the Register of Pharmacy Technicians and not registered in the Register of Pharmacists.

Returning Officer

1.3   (1) The Secretary shall act as Returning Officer for elections under this regulation.

(2) The Returning Officer shall invite each candidate to supply by an appointed date and time and in the form specified:

(a)   particulars of his qualifications;
(b)   information about his professional activities;
(c)   an election statement; and
(d)   a recent photograph of himself.

(3) The Returning Officer shall not be required to publish an election statement, information about professional activities and statement of relevant interests relating to a candidate which together exceed 630 words.

(4) The Returning Officer shall not be required to publish anything which in the Returning Officer's opinion is or may be libellous or untrue on matters of fact.

(5) The Returning Officer may, in consultation with the candidate, issue a statement of clarification if in his opinion any part of an election statement refers to matters outside the current functions, powers and duties of the Society.

(6) The Returning Officer shall inform all candidates of the outcome of an election and shall publish the results of the election.

Reserved places for constituencies

1.4   (1) Three places on the Council shall be reserved for pharmacists who are normally resident in each of three national constituencies.

(2) The three national constituencies shall be:

(a)   England, the Isle of Man and the Channel Islands;
(b)   Scotland; and
(c)   Wales.

Election to reserved places and remaining places

1.5   (1) Pharmacists filling the reserved places referred to in paragraph 1.4(1) shall be elected by ballot of pharmacists whose addresses in the Register are in the relevant national constituency.

(2) Pharmacists shall be elected to the reserved places on the Council on a first past the post basis.

(3) A pharmacist may be nominated as a candidate in a national constituency and as a candidate for election to a place on the Council not reserved to a national constituency in the same election.

(4) In the circumstances referred to in paragraph (3) above, the candidate receiving the highest number of votes in a national constituency shall be deemed to have been elected in that constituency and any votes he has received in respect of a place on the Council not reserved to a national constituency in the same election shall be void.

(5) Pharmacists filling places on the Council other than the reserved places referred to in paragraph 1.4(1) shall be elected by ballot of all pharmacists.

(6) Pharmacists shall be elected to the Council on a first past the post basis.

(7) An election ('the first election') to elect the seventeen pharmacists who shall be elected members of the Council from the Effective Date shall be held before that date.

Period of office

1.6 (1) At the first election, the three pharmacists elected in national constituencies and the three pharmacists elected with the highest numbers of votes to places on the Council not reserved to a national constituency shall be elected for a period of three years.

(2) The six pharmacists elected with the next highest numbers of votes to places on the Council not reserved to a national constituency shall be elected for a period of two years.

(3) The remaining five pharmacists elected to the Council shall be elected for a period of one year.

(4) At subsequent elections (other than a by-election to fill a casual vacancy) elected members of the Council shall be elected for a period of three years.

(5) After the first election, elections to places on the Council for pharmacists shall be held every year.

(6) The members of the Council leaving office shall be reported to the Council by the Returning Officer before the notice of election is issued.

Provisions for pharmacy technicians

1.7 (1) An election shall be held before the Effective Date to elect the two pharmacy technicians who shall be members of the Council from that date (the 'first pharmacy technician members').

(2) Candidates in the election of the first pharmacy technician members shall be self-nominated.

(3) The first pharmacy technician members shall be elected by ballot of all registered pharmacy technicians on a first past the post basis.

(4) Of the first pharmacy technician members, the one elected with the highest numbers of votes shall serve for three years and the other shall serve for two years.

(5) All subsequent pharmacy technician members shall be elected to the Council for a period of three years by ballot of all registered pharmacy technicians on a first past the post basis.

Eligibility for election

1.8 (1) A pharmacist or pharmacy technician shall only be eligible for election to the Council if his name appears within Part 1 (practising) of the Register of Pharmacists or, as the case may be, the Register of Pharmacy Technicians.

(2) A pharmacist or pharmacy technician shall only be eligible for election to the Council if he is normally resident in Great Britain, the Isle of Man or the Channel Islands.

(3) If in the opinion of the Council any elected member of the Council ceases to be normally resident in Great Britain, the Isle of Man or the Channel Islands, he shall cease to be a member of the Council.

(4) A pharmacist shall only be eligible for election in a national constituency if he is normally resident in that constituency.

(5) If in the opinion of the Council any member of the Council elected in a national constituency ceases to be normally resident in that constituency, he shall cease to be a member of the Council.

(6) If a pharmacist or pharmacy technician ceases to be a member of the Council under this regulation the resulting vacancy shall be treated as a casual vacancy.

(7) No pharmacist or pharmacy technician shall be eligible for election if he has failed to pay by the date and time fixed for the return of nomination forms any retention fee or penalty then due and payable by him to the Society.

(8) Subject to paragraphs (9) and (10) below:

(a)   No person may be elected as a member of the Council for more than three consecutive terms of office, each of up to three years; and

(b)   No person who has served as a member of the Council for three consecutive terms of office shall be eligible for re-election until a period of three years after leaving office has expired.

(9) Any member of the Council elected in the first election who has served six or more consecutive years on the Council immediately prior to that election shall be eligible to serve only one consecutive term from the Effective Date.

(10) Any member of the Council elected in the first election who has served less than six consecutive years on the Council immediately prior to that election shall be eligible to serve three consecutive terms from the Effective Date.

Eligibility to vote

1.9   (1) Subject to paragraphs (2) to (4) below:

(a)   all pharmacists registered with the Society shall be entitled to vote in the election of pharmacist members of the Council; and

(b)   all pharmacy technicians registered with the Society shall be entitled to vote in elections to seats on the Council for such technicians.

(2) Only pharmacists whose addresses in the Register are in the relevant constituency on the date when the electoral roll is passed to the election organisers shall be entitled to vote in an election in a national constituency.

(3) A person who becomes registered with the Society after the date on which the electoral roll is passed to the election organisers shall not be entitled to receive a voting paper in that election.

(4) A person whose registration with the Society is suspended on the date when the electoral roll is passed to the election organisers shall not be entitled to vote in an election under this regulation.

Notice of election

1.10   (1) The Returning Officer shall fix the time and date by which nomination forms shall be returned and at least 21 days before that date shall publish a notice of the election.

(2) For the first election, the requirement referred to in paragraph (1) above shall be treated as having been met provided that a notice of the first election has been published at least 21 days before the deadline fixed for the return of nomination forms.

(3) The notice shall specify:

(a)   the number of persons to be elected;
(b)   any national constituency in which a vacancy arises;
(c)   the place to which nomination forms are to be returned; and
(d)   the time and date by which they are to be returned.

Nominations

1.11   (1) Nominations for election shall be made on a nomination form provided by the Returning Officer.

(2) Each prospective candidate for election shall be nominated on a nomination form signed by ten nominators in the case of a pharmacist candidate or by five nominators in the case of a pharmacy technician candidate.

(3) All nominators shall be persons eligible to vote for the candidate in question.

(4) A duly completed nomination form shall include:

(a)   the registered name, registered address, registration number and age of the prospective candidate;
(b)   the registered names and registration numbers of the required nominators and their signatures.

(5) A prospective candidate shall also provide with the nomination form:

(a)   a signed declaration that:

(i) the information provided in the nomination form is correct;
(ii) he consents to be nominated;
(iii) he will accept office if duly elected; and
(iv) he is eligible to serve as the trustee of a charity;

(b)   details of the date and terms of any relevant adverse decision of which he has been the subject, including adverse decisions by the Society or another regulatory body on his fitness to practise, and of any criminal convictions, or a statement that he has not been the subject of any relevant adverse decision; and
(c)   a statement of relevant interests or that he has no relevant interests.

(6) Every nomination form shall, on or before the deadline fixed for the return of nomination forms, be delivered by post, by hand or by fax (or by such other method as may be determined by the Returning Officer) at the place appointed.

(7) A nomination form which has not been properly completed, or is not accompanied by the items mentioned at paragraph (5) (a) to (c) above, or is received after the due deadline, shall be invalid.

(8) A nomination form may be withdrawn by notice in writing signed by the prospective candidate and delivered at the place appointed on or before that deadline.

(9) If a prospective candidate dies or ceases to be eligible for election before the close of the nomination period, the nomination form shall be treated as having been withdrawn.

Holding of election

1.12   (1) If the number of pharmacist or pharmacy technician candidates (for pharmacists, in a national constituency or for election to places on the Council not reserved to a national constituency) is equal to the number of vacancies for such candidates and the period for voting has not commenced, the Returning Officer shall declare the candidates elected.

(2) If the number of candidates is fewer than the number of vacancies, the Returning Officer shall declare the candidates elected and a by-election shall then be held to secure the remaining Council members.

(3) If the number of candidates is greater than the number of vacancies, the Returning Officer shall cause an election to be held.

Voting

1.13 (1) The Returning Officer shall fix the time and date by which voting forms must be returned.

(2) At least 14 days before this deadline, the Returning Officer shall send a voting form to each person entitled to vote in that election at his registered address.

(3) The voting form shall include:

(a) a list of the candidates in alphabetical order giving in respect of each candidate his:

 (i) registered name;
 (ii) age; and
 (iii) registered address;

(b) the national constituency in which each candidate is standing for election (if applicable);
(c) the deadline for return of voting forms; and
(d) instructions on the voting procedure.

(4) The voting forms shall disclose the information provided by candidates under sub-paragraphs 1.11(5)(b) and (c).

(5) The period for voting commences on the date on which the first voting forms in an election are dispatched.

(6) If a serious interruption of postal services occurs after the Returning Officer has fixed the deadline for the return of voting forms, he may fix a new deadline for the return of voting forms.

(7) If after the period for voting commences a candidate dies or withdraws his nomination or is found by the Returning Officer to be ineligible to be elected or becomes ineligible to be elected, the votes cast for that candidate shall be void.

(8) The Returning Officer may replace a voting form on request being made to him in writing stating that the original form has not been received or has been lost, destroyed or spoiled.

(9) Votes shall only be cast on a voting form provided by or on behalf of the Returning Officer.

(10) Only one voting form may be completed and returned by each voter.

(11) The voter shall record his vote or votes on the voting form in accordance with the instructions thereon, placing a mark thus X against the name in the voting form of each candidate for whom he wishes to vote. Each voter shall have as many votes as there are vacancies for which he is eligible to vote.

The Scrutineer and outcome of election

1.14 (1) The completed voting forms shall be sent by post to the body appointed by the Council to examine voting forms, count votes and determine the result of the election ('the Scrutineer').

(2) The Scrutineer shall make a report to the Returning Officer specifying:

(a) the total number of voting forms received;
(b) the number of voting forms rejected as invalid;
(c) the number of votes cast for each candidate;
(d) the names of those elected; and

(e) if an election has been decided under paragraph (3) below, a note to that effect.

(3) In the event of a tie, the election shall be decided between the tied candidates by the drawing of lots conducted by or on behalf of the Scrutineer.

Casual vacancies

1.15 (1) In the event of any casual vacancy occurring in the elected members of Council, a by-election shall be held to fill the vacancy.

(2) The person so elected shall hold office for the remainder of the period of office of the outgoing member.

(3) If the relevant unexpired term is less than a year, the Council may determine that the vacancy need not be filled.

By-election

1.16 A by-election shall be conducted as nearly as possible in accordance with the provisions relating to a general election under this regulation.

Resignation and non-eligibility to remain an elected member of Council

1.17 (1) If any elected member of the Council shall cease to be registered within Part 1 (practising) of the Register of Pharmacists or, as the case may be, the Register of Pharmacy Technicians, or to be eligible to serve as trustee of a charity, he shall thereupon cease to be an elected member of the Council.

(2) Any elected member of the Council may resign his office at any time by giving notice in writing of his resignation to the Secretary except where such resignation would cause there to be less than two trustees of any charity of which the member is a trustee.

Effect of non-compliance with provisions

1.18 No election held under this regulation shall be invalidated by reason of any non-compliance with these provisions, or of the non-delivery, loss or miscarriage of any document required under this regulation, if it appears to the Returning Officer: that the election was conducted substantially in accordance with this regulation, and that the result of such failure, non-compliance, non-delivery, loss or miscarriage did not affect the return of any candidate at the election. On this and any other matter concerning the election the decision of the Returning Officer shall be final.

Regulation 2 – Appointed Council members

Number of appointed Council members

2.1 The Charter provides that there shall be 11 appointed members of the Council:

(a) ten persons appointed by the Privy Council; and
(b) one registered pharmacist appointed by the universities in Great Britain awarding degrees accredited by the Society for the purposes of registration as a pharmacist.

Eligibility for appointment

2.2 (1) The Registrar shall ask the Privy Council to bear in mind the eligibility requirements that apply to candidates for election to the Council concerning residence and capacity to serve as the trustee of a charity.

(2) If any appointed member of the Council ceases to be eligible to serve as trustee of a charity, he shall thereupon cease to be a member of the Council.

(3) The following sub-paragraphs shall apply to the appointments under 2.1(a) above only:

(a)   No person may be appointed as a member of the Council for more than three consecutive terms of office, each of up to three years.

(b)   No person who has served as a member of the Council for three consecutive terms of office shall be eligible for re-appointment until a period of three years after leaving office has expired.

(c)   Any appointed member of the Council who, on the day after the day of the Annual General Meeting of the Society in 2005, has served six or more consecutive years on the Council immediately prior to that date, whether as an appointed or elected member, shall be eligible to serve only one consecutive term of office from that date.

(d)   Any appointed member of the Council who, on the day after the day of the Annual General Meeting of the Society in 2005, has served less than six consecutive years on the Council immediately prior to that date, whether as an appointed or elected member, shall be eligible to serve three consecutive terms of office from that date.

Statutory Committee Regulations

The Regulations – The Pharmaceutical Society (Statutory Committee) Order of Council 1978 (SI 1978 No.20)

The Pharmaceutical Society (Statutory Committee) Order of Council 1978 (SI 1978 No.20) came into effect on 1 February 1978.

Part I: General

1 (a)   In these Regulations:
        the Act of 1954 and *the Act of 1968* mean respectively the Pharmacy Act 1954 and the Medicines Act 1968;
        the Committee, the Chairman and *the Secretary* mean respectively the Statutory Committee appointed under section 7 of the Act of 1954 and the Chairman and the Secretary of that Committee;
        the register unless the context otherwise requires and *the Registrar* have respectively the same meanings as in the Act of 1954;
        registered pharmaceutical chemist has the same meaning as in the Act of 1954;
        representative has the same meaning as in section 72(4) of the Act of 1968;

> *the person affected* means the registered pharmaceutical chemist, body corporate, representative or other person affected by any information received by the Committee;
>> *retail pharmacy business* has the same meaning as in the Act of 1968; and
>> *the relevant Acts* has the same meaning as in section 80 of the Act of 1968.

(b) The Interpretation Act 1889, applies to the interpretation of these Regulations as it applies to the interpretation of an Act of Parliament.

2 These Regulations shall come into operation on the 1st day of February 1978, and the Regulations approved by the Royal Pharmaceutical Society (Statutory Committee) Order of Council 1957 are hereby revoked save in relation to the procedure to be followed by the Statutory Committee in the exercise of the jurisdiction conferred on them by the Pharmacy and Poisons Act 1933:
Provided that:

(a) such revocation shall not affect anything duly done or suffered under those Regulations; and

(b) any notice, direction, inquiry, application, proceeding or thing given, made, instituted or done under the Regulations confirmed on the 4th day of May 1957, shall, if in force immediately before these Regulations come into operation, continue in force and be deemed to be given, made, instituted or done under the corresponding provisions of these Regulations on the actual dates when the same were respectively given, made, instituted or done;

(c) without prejudice to the generality of the foregoing, such revocation shall not affect any inquiry or proceeding which has been stayed, postponed or adjourned or where decision has been postponed and such inquiry and proceeding shall be resumed and the decision therein given under the provisions of these Regulations.

Part II: Cases arising out of convictions or misconduct

3 When the Secretary receives information from which it appears that:

(a) a registered pharmaceutical chemist, or a person employed by him in the carrying on of his business, has been convicted of a criminal offence, or been guilty of misconduct; or

(b) a body corporate carrying on a retail pharmacy business has been convicted of an offence under the relevant Acts; or

(c) a member of the board or any officer of or person employed by a body corporate carrying on a retail pharmacy business has been convicted of an offence, or been guilty of misconduct; or

(d) a representative or person employed by a representative in the retail pharmacy business in respect of which he is the representative has been convicted of a criminal offence, or been guilty of misconduct; or

(e) a person applying to be registered as a pharmaceutical chemist has been convicted of a criminal offence, or been guilty of misconduct; or

(f) a person whose name has been removed from the register under section 12(1) of the Act of 1954 or a person employed by him in the carrying on of his business, has been convicted of a criminal offence, or been guilty of misconduct; the Secretary shall submit the information, or a summary thereof, to the Chairman.

4 Where the information in question is in the nature of a complaint charging misconduct, the Chairman may require that any allegation of fact contained therein shall be substantiated by a written statement signed by a responsible person, or, if he

thinks fit, by a statutory declaration and any such statement or statutory declaration shall specify as respects any fact not within the personal knowledge of the declarant, the source of his information and the grounds for his belief in its truth.

5   The Chairman may in any case direct the Secretary to invite the person affected to submit in writing any answer or explanation which he may wish to offer.

6   When he has considered the information, the evidence available in support thereof and any answer or explanation submitted by the person affected, the Chairman shall deal with the matter as follows:

(i)   if he is of the opinion that:

(a)   the case is not within the jurisdiction of the Committee; or

(b)   the complaint is of a frivolous character; or

(c)   owing to the lapse of time or other circumstances the complaint may properly be disregarded;

he shall decide that the case shall not proceed further;

(ii)   if he is of opinion that the conviction or misconduct alleged is not of a serious nature or is for any other reason of such a character that the matter can be disposed of without an inquiry, he may, after consultation orally or by letter with the other members of the Committee, decide that the case shall not proceed further but may direct the Secretary to send a reprimand to the person affected and caution him as to his future conduct;

(iii)   in any other case he shall direct the Secretary to take the necessary steps for the holding of an inquiry by the Committee:

Provided that, if it appears to the Chairman in a case arising under paragraph (b) or paragraph (c) of Regulation 3 that the person affected has no present intention of continuing or commencing to carry on a retail pharmacy business, or in a case arising under paragraph (f) of that Regulation that the person affected has no present intention of practising pharmacy, or seeking employment in a pharmaceutical capacity, he may postpone dealing with the matter until evidence of such an intention is submitted to him.

7   The Chairman shall report to the Committee any case in which he has not directed an inquiry to be held.

8   Where the Chairman has directed an inquiry to be held, the Secretary shall give such notices and take such other steps as are required by Part III of these Regulations, and shall instruct a solicitor to investigate the facts of the case and to present (or brief counsel) to present the case to the Committee at the inquiry:

Provided that, where a complainant undertakes to present his case to the Committee, it shall not be necessary for the Secretary to instruct a solicitor.

9   If the solicitor instructed as aforesaid reports that, as a result of his investigations, he is of the opinion that the evidence available is insufficient to prove the conviction or misconduct alleged, the Committee shall consider his report and decide whether an inquiry shall be held, and give such directions as they think fit. In the interval all proceedings shall be stayed and the Secretary shall give any necessary notices to persons concerned, including the complainant.

10   If at any time after an inquiry has been directed and before it has been held information is received by the Secretary or by the solicitor instructed as afore-mentioned which might have justified the Chairman in not directing an inquiry in the first instance any such information shall be referred to him and he may direct that the inquiry shall not proceed further, and in that case, shall report such direction to the Committee.

Part III: Inquiries

11   (a)   Where directions have been given for an inquiry to be held, the Secretary shall, not less than twenty-eight days before the day appointed for holding the inquiry, send to the person affected a notice specifying generally the matters into which the inquiry will be held, and stating the day, hour and place appointed for holding the inquiry:

         Provided that where the person affected and the complainant (if any) so agree the period of notice required by this Regulation may be reduced to such period as may be agreed.

   (b)   The notice shall be in the form set out in the Schedule to these Regulations, (not reproduced) with such variations as circumstances may require, or in a form to the like effect, and shall be accompanied by a copy of these Regulations.

Where a complainant has undertaken to present his case to the Committee, the Secretary shall send to him copies of the notice and of these Regulations.

12   A notice required by the last preceding Regulation to be sent to any person shall be sent by registered letter or recorded delivery letter addressed to him, in the case of a registered pharmaceutical chemist at his address in the register, in the case of a body corporate at its registered office, or where the body corporate is a firm or partnership in Scotland, its usual place of business, in the case of a representative at his address last notified to the Registrar and in the case of any other person at his last known place of abode.

13   A notice sent to any person in accordance with Regulations 11 and 12 may be amended with the consent of the Committee or of the Chairman and written notice of the amendment shall be sent to such person in the manner provided by Regulation 12 or otherwise brought to his notice by the Secretary before the inquiry is held or in the course of the inquiry:

      Provided that the person affected shall have the right to demand an adjournment of the inquiry if reasonable notice of any amendment materially affecting the particulars of the misconduct alleged in the notice of inquiry has not been given before the inquiry commenced.

14   The person affected shall, after giving reasonable notice to the Secretary, be entitled free of charge to inspect, and to be supplied with a copy of, any information or summary sent to the Chairman in pursuance of Regulation 3 or any written statement or statutory declaration sent to the Committee in pursuance of Regulation 4 and the notice of inquiry shall direct his attention to this Regulation. A complainant who has undertaken to present his case to the Committee shall, after giving reasonable notice to the Secretary, be entitled free of charge to inspect, and to be supplied with a copy of, any answer or explanation submitted in pursuance of Regulation 5 by the person affected.

15   The Chairman may at any time postpone the opening of the inquiry and direct the Secretary to give any necessary notices to persons concerned, including the complainant.

16   The inquiry shall be held in public except that the Committee may at any time direct that the public shall be excluded from an inquiry or any part thereof if it appears to the Committee that in the interests of justice or for some other compelling reason the public should be so excluded.

17   The person affected and a complainant presenting his case to the Committee may be represented by a solicitor, or counsel; alternatively, a body corporate may be represented by a director or officer thereof.

18   At the opening of the inquiry, the Secretary shall read the notice of inquiry and, if the person affected be not present or represented, satisfy the Committee that the notice was duly sent to him. The person affected or the person representing him in

accordance with Regulation 17 may waive the right for the notice of inquiry to be read.

19   If a complainant who has undertaken to present his case to the Committee does not appear, or fails in the opinion of the Committee to present his case properly, the Committee may nevertheless proceed with the inquiry or may adjourn the inquiry, in which case they may instruct a solicitor in accordance with Regulation 8, and Regulations 9 and 10 shall apply during the adjournment.

If the person affected does not appear and the Committee are satisfied that notice of the inquiry was duly sent to him, they may proceed with the inquiry in his absence, or may adjourn the inquiry.

20   Subject to the foregoing provisions with respect to non-appearance, the order of proceedings shall be as follows:

(a)   statement of the case against the person affected and production of evidence in support of it;

(b)   statement of the case of the person affected and production of evidence in support of it;

(c)   reply to the case of the person affected: provided that, except by leave of the Committee, a reply shall not be allowed where the person affected has produced no evidence other than his own.

21   Evidence may be received by the Committee by oral statement, written and signed statement, or statutory declaration. A witness shall first be examined by the person producing him, then cross-examined and then re-examined. The Committee shall disregard oral evidence given by any person who refuses to submit to cross-examination may, in their discretion, decline to admit the written statement or declaration of a person who is not present, and shall disregard it if, being present, he refuses to submit to cross-examination.

22   Members of the Committee may put through the Chairman, or on his invitation, such questions as they think desirable.

23   The Committee may at any stage of the proceedings adjourn the inquiry to a subsequent meeting of the Committee and, where the day, hour and place for such meetings are not appointed at the time of the adjournment, the Secretary shall, not less than twenty-one days before the day appointed, and in the manner specified in Regulation 12 give notice to the person affected and to the complainant, if any, of the day, hour and place appointed:

Provided that, where the person affected and the complainant (if any) so agree the notice may be waived or modified.

24   When the inquiry is resumed, no fresh evidence shall, except by leave of the Committee, be produced unless either:

(a)   the substance thereof has, not less than ten days before the resumed hearing, been communicated to the Secretary and to the person against whom it is to be produced; or

(b)   it is in the nature of a reply to any such evidence.

25   On the conclusion of the hearing the Committee shall deliberate in private and shall decide:

(a)   whether the conviction or misconduct alleged is proved;

(b)   if so, except in a case falling only under paragraph (b) of Regulation 3, whether such conviction or misconduct is such as to render the person with regard to whom it is proved, or is such as would if he were a registered pharmaceutical chemist render him, unfit to be on the register;

(c)   if so, whether one of the directions specified in section 8(1) of the Act of 1954, section 80(1) of the Act of 1968 or section 80(2) of the Act of 1968 or section 80(4) of the Act of 1968 should be made; and

(d)   whether any reprimand or admonition should be addressed to the person affected:

Provided that the Committee may postpone their decision or any part of it, either generally or on such terms as they may approve.

26   The Chairman shall announce in public the decision of the Committee and if the decision or any part of it is postponed the Chairman shall announce such postponement and shall state the terms, if any, on which it is made.

27   If the Committee postpone their decision under paragraph (c) or (d) of Regulation 25, they may when the case is resumed take into account before reaching a decision thereon any information then or previously given to them concerning the conduct of the person affected since the original hearing, provided that they shall not take into account any adverse report without giving the person affected a reasonable opportunity of answering it.

28   The Secretary shall communicate to the person affected and to the complainant, if any, the decision of the Committee and to the Registrar any direction to be acted upon by him.

29   Where under any of the foregoing provisions of these Regulations an inquiry is adjourned from one meeting to another, or a decision or any part of it is postponed to a future meeting, the validity of the proceedings at the later meeting shall not be called into question by reason only that members of the Committee who were present at the earlier meeting were not present at a later meeting, or that members of the Committee who were present at the later meeting were not present at the earlier meeting.

Part IV: Applications for relief from consequences of previous decisions

30   An application to the Committee:

(a)   under section 8(2) of the Act of 1954 for the restoration of the name of the applicant to the register; or

(b)   under section 8(1) of the Act of 1954 for variation of a direction given by the Committee under that subsection; or

(c)   under section 83(1) of the Act of 1968 for the revocation of a direction given by the Committee under section 80 of the Act of 1968, shall be made in writing to the Secretary stating the grounds on which it is made and must be signed by the applicant, or, in the case of a body corporate, by a member of the board thereof.

31   No application for restoration of a name to the register shall be entertained by the Committee unless supported by a statutory declaration made by the applicant and accompanied by at least two certificates of the applicant's identity and good character. One of such certificates must be given by a registered pharmaceutical chemist and another must be given by a registered pharmaceutical chemist, a fully registered medical practitioner for the purpose of the Medical Acts 1956 to 1969, a justice of the peace or a legally qualified holder of a judicial office. The statutory declaration must identify the applicant with his application, the statements made therein and with the required certificates.

32   In a case where the name of an applicant for restoration was removed from the register under section 8(1) of the Act of 1954 on a complaint made by a person who himself appeared to present the facts of his complaint to the Committee, the Secretary shall, if he knows that person's address, give notice of the application to him and inform him that he may submit in writing to the Committee any objection to restoration. The Secretary shall communicate the substance of any such objection to the applicant and the applicant may reply thereto in writing.

33   In considering an application under this part of these Regulations, the Committee may take into account any information in their possession concerning the conduct of the applicant during the period which has elapsed since the original direction was given. The Chairman may direct that the substance of any adverse report be sent to the applicant who shall be given an opportunity of submitting a reply thereto in writing. In these circumstances consideration of the application shall not take place until after such reply is received or a reasonable time for submitting a reply has, in the opinion of the Committee, elapsed. No adverse report shall be taken into account unless these steps have been taken.

34   Unless the Chairman directs that the application shall be considered in public, the Committee shall consider the application in private.

35   (a)   Unless the Committee decide to grant the application without a hearing, the Committee shall afford to the applicant if he wishes an opportunity of appearing before them in person or by a solicitor or counsel and of adducing evidence.

      (b)   The Committee shall inform the applicant of his rights under the preceding paragraph of this Regulation but shall be entitled to proceed with the application if the applicant declines to appear or to adduce evidence before them or if the applicant fails to appear or adduce evidence on an occasion fixed for such purpose of which notice in writing shall have been sent by post to the applicant at the address to which a notice under Regulation 12 would have been sent to him.

      (c)   If the original direction was given following a complaint, the Committee may afford the complainant an opportunity of being heard or of submitting evidence as to any matter which appears to the Committee to be material.

36   Subject to the provisions of Regulation 35, the procedure of the Committee in connection with the application shall be such as they may determine.

37   The Committee may if they think fit adjourn consideration of the application from one meeting to another, and the provisions of Regulation 29 shall apply with the necessary modifications to the later meeting.

38   The Secretary shall communicate to the applicant and to the objector, if any, the decision of the Committee and to the Registrar any direction to be acted upon by him. Any such communication to the Registrar shall, in an appropriate case, direct his attention to section 11(2) of the Act of 1954.

Code of Ethics and Standards

May 2005

Part 1: Pharmacists' ethics

The public places great trust in the knowledge, skills and professional judgement of pharmacists. This trust requires pharmacists to ensure and maintain, throughout their career, high standards of personal and professional conduct and performance, up-to-date knowledge and continuing competence relevant to their sphere of practice whether or not they work in direct contact with the public.

The Royal Pharmaceutical Society of Great Britain seeks to safeguard and promote the interests of the public and the profession by identifying the key responsibilities of a pharmacist.

Ethics has been described as the systematic study of moral choices; it concerns the values that lie behind them, the reasons people give for them and the language used to describe them. Ethical decision making is the process whereby one recognises that a problem needs to be overcome or a difficult choice made, identifies the possible courses of actions, chooses one, takes it and then accepts responsibility.

The exercise of professional judgement requires identification and evaluation of the risks and benefits associated with possible courses of action. On occasions there may not be a right or wrong answer. Different people may reach different decisions on a single set of circumstances and each may be justifiable.

Many of the issues pharmacists are called upon to resolve are unambiguous and the decision will be obvious. However, when faced with ethical dilemmas pharmacists are expected to use their professional judgement in deciding on the most appropriate course of action. They must be able to justify their decisions to their peers, and to any person or organisation which may be affected by their actions, including individual patients, the public, the National Health Service, their employers, and other health care professionals. Pharmacists may be accountable to any of these.

Disreputable behaviour or breach of a professional responsibility or requirement identified in the Code could form the basis of a complaint of professional misconduct. The Society's disciplinary committees, in considering whether or not action should follow, take into consideration the circumstances of an individual case and do not regard themselves as being limited to those matters which are mentioned in this document.

Key responsibilities of a pharmacist

Pharmacists understand the nature and effect of medicines and medicinal ingredients, and how they may be used to prevent and treat illness, relieve symptoms or assist in the diagnosis of disease. Pharmacists in professional practice use their knowledge for the wellbeing and safety of patients and the public.

- At all times pharmacists must act in the interests of patients and other members of the public, and seek to provide the best possible health care for the community in partnership with other health professions. Pharmacists must treat all those who seek their professional services with courtesy, respect and confidentiality. Pharmacists must respect patients' rights to participate in decisions about their care and must provide information in a way in which it can be understood.
- Pharmacists must ensure that their knowledge, skills and performance are of a high quality, up to date, evidence based and relevant to their field of practice.
- Pharmacists must ensure that they behave with integrity and probity, adhere to accepted standards of personal and professional conduct and do not engage in any behaviour or activity likely to bring the profession into disrepute or undermine public confidence in the profession.

Part 2: Standards of professional performance

A. Personal responsibilities

Pharmacists' prime concern, irrespective of their sphere of work, must be for the wellbeing and safety of patients and the public. Some roles pharmacists undertake attract specific professional responsibilities. For example, pharmacists who own a pharmacy, superintendent pharmacists, or pharmacist managers in hospitals and trusts must ensure that procedures designed to minimise risks are formulated and applied. Pharmacists providing professional services in any sphere of practice must ensure that their own work procedures are safe and effective.

The public and the profession are entitled to expect that pharmacists providing services will comply with the specific professional responsibilities associated with them and comply with any other accepted codes of practice and statutory requirements applicable to their sphere of practice.

A.1 Pharmacists providing professional services

Pharmacists assuming responsibility for any pharmacy function whether as an employee, locum, adviser or otherwise are professionally accountable for all decisions to supply a medicine or offer advice, and must ensure that:

(a) they only accept work where they have the requisite skills and fitness for the tasks to be performed. All pharmacists must establish sufficient information about the work to enable an assessment to be made;

(b) they undertake continuing professional development relevant to their professional duties;

(c) all activities they undertake are covered by professional indemnity arrangements;

(d)   they do not work in conditions that do not enable them to comply with the key responsibilities of a pharmacist;

(e)   the requisite facilities, equipment and materials are accessible to enable the provision of the service to professionally accepted standards;

(f)   if any tasks are to be delegated they are delegated to persons competent to perform them, for example, any assistant who is given delegated authority to sell medicines under a protocol should have undertaken, or be undertaking, an accredited course relevant to their duties;

(g)   they and other staff work within standard operating procedures where these exist;

(h)   they agree terms and conditions and abide by them;

(i)   they honour commitments to provide professional services unless this is impossible. If they are not able to honour a commitment the pharmacy owner or other responsible person must be informed at the earliest opportunity in order that alternative arrangements may be made;

(j)   they take action to report to the prescriber and relevant authorities, suspected adverse drug reactions where this is likely to assist in the future treatment of the patient, or the future use of the medicine;

(k)   before accepting employment pharmacists must disclose any factors which may affect their ability to provide services. Where pharmacists' religious beliefs or personal convictions prevent them from providing a service they must not condemn or criticise the patient and they or a member of staff must advise the patient of alternative sources for the service requested;

(l)   if they become aware that a person has received pharmaceutical care of a standard less than the person had a right to expect they provide, if possible, an explanation of what happened, whether or not they are the person responsible;

(m)   they act quickly to protect patients and the public from risk by reporting the matter to an appropriate person, authority or regulatory body if they have good reason to believe that they or a colleague from their own or another profession may not be fit to practise for reasons of health, conduct or competence. The safety of patients and the public must be the prime consideration, over-riding any personal, professional or commercial loyalties.

A.2 Pharmacists who own a pharmacy, superintendent pharmacists and pharmacist managers in hospitals and trusts or other fields of practice

Before assuming the role of pharmacist owner, superintendent pharmacist or pharmacist manager in a hospital or trust pharmacists must be satisfied that they are able to comply with the responsibilities set out below. Pharmacist owners, superintendent pharmacists and pharmacist managers in hospitals and trusts or other fields of practice have a personal professional responsibility:

(a)   to ensure the observance of all legal and professional requirements in relation to pharmaceutical aspects of the business. They are responsible for ensuring that a retrievable record of the pharmacist taking responsibility for the provision of each pharmacy service is maintained and that an identifiable pharmacist is accountable for all activities of non-pharmacists involved in the provision of pharmacy services;

(b)   to ensure that all professional activities undertaken by them or under their control are covered by adequate professional indemnity arrangements;

(c)   to satisfy themselves that the supplier, the source and the quality of any medicines or pharmaceutical ingredients are reputable. Medicines must normally be obtained from licensed wholesalers, the manufacturer or via a central purchasing or inter-branch transfer system. Records must be kept of the source of all medicines obtained by any other means and of measures taken to ensure the safety and efficacy of them. This standard is not intended to cover loans from professional colleagues;

(d)   to ensure that all staff are informed of the professional activities they are expected to undertake. Clear instructions should be provided, designed to identify and minimise risks and reviewed regularly. Where possible standard operating procedures should be drafted;

(e)   not to seek to impose conditions on pharmacists which may adversely affect their ability to comply with their professional and legal duties;

(f)   to ensure that adequate support staff and information about the pharmacy are provided to enable all pharmacists, including temporary staff and locums, to perform their duties effectively;

(g)   to satisfy themselves that pharmacists employed or engaged by them are aware of the need to undertake continuing professional development relevant to their professional duties;

(h)   to ensure that pharmacists and other staff employed by them or under their management have the requisite knowledge, skills and fitness to perform work delegated to them and comply with work instructions;

(i)   to ensure that pharmacists and other staff employed by them are sufficiently competent in English. Competency in other languages common to the area is desirable;

(j)   to ensure that working conditions, facilities, equipment and materials enable the provision of services to professionally accepted standards;

(k)   to have procedures to deal with incidents where there is a threat to the health of a patient or the public and review practices in the light of incidents;

(l)   to ensure that effective measures are in place for protecting the confidentiality of person identifiable data;

(m)   to ensure that an effective complaint handling procedure exists, whereby all complaints are dealt with promptly, constructively and honestly;

(n)   to report to the Society concerns that a pharmacist's professional competence or ability to practise may be impaired and put the public at risk;

(o)   to notify the Society in writing of any changes in the ownership of registered pharmacy premises, or superintendent pharmacist of a body corporate.

A.3 Preregistration tutors and pharmacists supervising preregistration trainees

Preregistration tutors and preregistration managers must ensure that Section XX of the Society's Byelaws, relating to preregistration training, is complied with.

Tutors and preregistration managers must ensure that:

(a)   preregistration trainees they assess understand and comply with the key responsibilities of a pharmacist and are competent. The public may be put at risk if a tutor or manager confirms the competence of a trainee who has not attained the required standard;

(b)   preregistration trainees receive wide-ranging experience of professional practice;

(c)   preregistration training meets the needs of the trainee;

(d)   preregistration trainees are properly supervised, in particular in relation to their responsibilities for services to the public;

(e)   the progress of preregistration trainees is reviewed regularly, with honest and constructive feedback;

(f)   preregistration trainees are encouraged to self-appraise their performance;

(g)   reports of trainees' performance provided to the Society are honest and objective;

(h)   they reflect on work processes and outcomes, evaluate their own performance and take action to develop their expertise and knowledge.

A.4 Co-operation with Inquiries into Fitness to Practise

(a)   Pharmacists must co-operate fully with any investigation or formal inquiry by a committee into their or another pharmacist's, pharmacy technician's or other health care professional's fitness to practise.

(b)   Where pharmacists have given a signed undertaking to the Statutory Committee they must abide fully with the terms and spirit of that undertaking.

(c)   A breach of any signed undertaking given by a pharmacist to the Statutory Committee could form the basis of a complaint of professional misconduct.

B. Professional competence

The public, the profession and the NHS expect pharmacists to develop their professional performance to provide a high level of care to patients. Practising pharmacists are expected to maintain records of their continuing professional development (CPD) and make the records available for review by the Society on request. CPD records should contain evidence that a practising pharmacist:

(a)   continually reviews the skills and knowledge required for their field(s) of practice, identifies those skills or knowledge in need of development or improvement and audits their performance as part of the review;

(b)   plans appropriate learning activities to address identified learning needs and implements their plans;

(c)   evaluates what they have learned and effectively translates their learning into improved professional practice.

C. Confidentiality

The public expects pharmacists and their staff to respect and protect confidentiality. This duty extends to any information relating to an individual which pharmacists or their staff acquire in the course of their professional activities. Confidential information includes personal details and medication, both prescribed and non-prescribed.
   Pharmacists must ensure that:

(a)   the confidentiality of information acquired in the course of their professional activities is respected and protected, and is disclosed only with the consent of the individual other than in the circumstances defined below in (b).

(b)   information is disclosed without the patient's consent only in the following circumstances:

    (i) where the patient's parent, guardian or carer has consented to the disclosure and the patient's apparent age or health makes them incapable of consent. Pharmacists should be aware that information about services provided to adolescents should not normally be disclosed to their parents.

    (ii) where disclosure of the information is to a person or body empowered by statute to require such a disclosure;

   (iii) where disclosure is directed by a coroner, judge or other presiding officer of a court, Crown Prosecution Office in England and Wales and Procurator Fiscal in Scotland;

   (iv) to a police officer or NHS Fraud Investigation Officer who provides in writing confirmation that disclosure is necessary to assist in the prevention, detection or prosecution of serious crime;

   (v) where necessary to prevent serious injury or damage to the health of the patient, a third party or to public health;

(c)   they do not disclose information relating to the prescribing practices of identifiable prescribers or their practices, other than for the necessary purposes of the NHS or other health care provider, unless the prescriber has given his written informed consent to the disclosure;

(d)   access to confidential information within the pharmacy is restricted to those who require that information and who are themselves subject to an obligation of confidentiality;

(e)   the requirements of data protection legislation for data collection and use are complied with;

(f)   confidential information is effectively protected against improper disclosure when it is disposed of, stored, transmitted or received;

(g)   pharmacy computer and manual systems which include patient specific information incorporate access control systems to minimise the risk of unauthorised or unnecessary access to the data. Pharmacy computer systems which include patient specific information and which are linked to the internet or other networks must incorporate measures such as data encryption to eliminate the risk of unauthorised access to confidential data.

Part 3: Service specifications

The application of the key professional responsibilities described in Part 1 to the following activities indicates that the provision of these services should incorporate the following professional requirements. Pharmacists should build upon these requirements when developing professional services to enable the public to receive services that reflect the best possible pharmaceutical practice. These service specifications must be read in conjunction with each other to ensure that in providing a service account is taken of all relevant professional requirements.

    When providing any professional service pharmacists should ensure that the tenets of clinical governance are followed:

- that an identifiable pharmacist is accountable for all activities undertaken;
- that they and staff providing services are suitably trained and competent to perform the tasks required;
- that any necessary equipment and suitable facilities are available for the provision of the service and that these are maintained in good order;
- that risk assessment and management procedures have been identified and are followed;
- that adequate records are maintained to enable the service to be monitored.

The following service specifications cover a range of services; some are core services which will be provided by the majority of pharmacies, others are additional professional services which pharmacists may wish to be involved in.

1. Publicity, promotion and information

It is in the public interest for pharmacies to provide information about their opening hours and services available. Any information or publicity material regarding pharmacy services must be accurate and honest. The public and the profession would not expect any products or services advertised or otherwise promoted, to be injurious to health when properly and responsibly used.

(a)   All information and publicity for goods and services must be legal, decent and truthful; be presented and distributed in a manner so as not to bring the profession into disrepute; and not abuse the trust or exploit the lack of knowledge of the public.

(b)   Information and promotional material relating to professional services must be compatible with the role of pharmacists as skilled and informed advisers about medicines, common ailments, general health care and well being. It should be presented so as to allow the recipient to decide independently whether or not to use a service and should not disparage the professional services of other pharmacies or pharmacists.

(c)   Pharmacists must not make any unsolicited approach, for promotional purposes, directly to a member of the public by way of a telephone call, e-mail, or visit made without prior appointment.

(d)   Pharmacists must ensure that promotions (materials and campaigns) for medicines aimed at the public:

　　(i) emphasise the special nature of medicines;
　　(ii) do not make any medicinal claim not capable of substantiation;
　　(iii) are consistent with the summary of product characteristics approved by the Medicines and Healthcare products Regulatory Agency as part of the licensing procedures;
　　(iv) do not promote a medicine by way of endorsement by a pharmacist, or comparison with other products. A pharmacist may recommend a product in response to a request for advice from an individual patient;
　　(v) do not promote inappropriate or excessive consumption or use of medicines or their misuse, injudicious or unsafe use which may be injurious to health.

(e)   Pharmacists may advertise the prices at which they sell medicines and price discounts. Promotions for pharmacy medicines which seek to persuade consumers to obtain medicines that are not wanted or quantities substantially in excess of those wanted are considered to be professionally unacceptable.

2. Stock

The public and the profession are entitled to expect all stock to be obtained from a reputable source and be of high quality and fit for the intended purpose.

(a)   Pharmacists must not purchase or supply any medicines, food supplement or health care related product where they have reason to doubt its quality or safety.

(b)   Pharmacists must report to the Royal Pharmaceutical Society, the Medicines and Healthcare products Regulatory Agency, Veterinary Medicines Directorate or the marketing authorisation holder any instance where they suspect that they have been offered or have been supplied with counterfeit or defective medicines. Such medicines must be isolated from other pharmacy stock and withheld from sale or supply.

(c)   Pharmacy stock must be stored under suitable conditions appropriate to the nature and stability of the product concerned. Particular attention must be paid to protection from contamination, sunlight, atmospheric moisture and adverse temperatures.

During storage medicines must be retained in the manufacturer's original packaging. Pharmacists must exercise their knowledge of stability of materials to segregate for disposal any substances that are likely to have deteriorated, or have been in stock for unduly long periods or have reached their expiry dates.

(d)   All stocks of medicines in the pharmacy must have batch and expiry details. Medicines may only be removed from blister or foil packs at the time of dispensing to assist an individual patient.

(e)   Medicines returned to a pharmacy from a patient's home, a nursing or residential home must not be supplied to any other patient.

(f)   Pharmacists must not purchase for sale on registered pharmacy premises, any product which may be injurious to public health or bring the profession into disrepute. This includes tobacco products other than nicotine replacement therapies, alcohol and products intended to mask signs of alcohol or drug consumption.

3. Pharmacy premises and facilities

The profession expects all parts of pharmacy premises to be kept clean and orderly to reflect the professional health care image of pharmacy, and to facilitate a safe system of work. The public is entitled to expect that any part of premises from which professional services are provided is readily identifiable and well maintained. The public and the profession expect a pharmacy offering professional services to have the resources to ensure competent provision of the service. These requirements apply to both registered retail pharmacy premises and hospital pharmacies.

(a)   Premises must be safe for the public and people working there. All statutory requirements must be complied with, eg, health and safety, occupier's liability, disability discrimination legislation, etc, and high standards of hygiene must be ensured.

(b)   A designated area reserved for pharmacy services should be easily identifiable and arranged to enable services to be provided efficiently. Arrangements for the sale of pharmacy medicines must ensure that the sale is made by a pharmacist or a person acting under the supervision of a pharmacist. Pharmacy medicines must not be accessible to the public by self-selection.

(c)   The size and organisation of the dispensary must reflect the volume and work flow, and facilitate effective communication and supervision.

(d)   Refrigerators used for pharmaceutical stock must be capable of storing products between 2°C and 8°C. They must be equipped with a maximum/minimum thermometer which is checked on each day the pharmacy is open and the maximum and minimum temperatures recorded. Appropriate action must be taken to rectify any identified deficiency.

(e)   Arrangements must be made for the regular collection and safe disposal of pharmaceutical waste and other refuse.

4. Supply of prescribed medicines

4.1 Dispensing procedures in community pharmacies and for hospital outpatients

The public is entitled to expect the service to be accurate, accessible and reasonably prompt, and the medicines to be of appropriate quality, with a sufficiently long expiry date to cover the course of treatment, and to be suitably packaged and labelled for the intended recipient. The profession expects pharmacists to seek to maintain adequate stock holdings.

(a)   Dispensing must be under the supervision of a pharmacist, who must be available to intervene and advise.

(b)   Every prescription must be professionally assessed by a pharmacist to determine its suitability for the patient. Pharmacists must ensure that the patient receives sufficient information and advice to enable the safe and effective use of the medicine.

(c)   Pharmacists must implement procedures to minimise the risks of dispensing errors or contamination of medicines, incorporating checks to reduce special risks associated with particular products.

(d)   Where a product is ordered on a prescription a pharmacist must supply a product with a marketing authorisation, where such a product exists and is available, in preference to an unlicensed medicine or food supplement.

(e)   Except in an emergency, pharmacists must not substitute any other product for a specifically named product without the approval of the patient or carer and the prescriber, or a hospital drug and therapeutics committee.

(f)   All solid dose and all oral and external liquid preparations must be dispensed in reclosable child resistant containers unless:

   (i) the medicine is in an original pack or patient pack such as to make this inadvisable;
   (ii) the patient has difficulty in opening a child resistant container;
   (iii) a specific request is made that the product shall not be dispensed in a child resistant container; or
   (iv) no suitable child resistant container exists for a particular liquid preparation;
   (v) the patient has been assessed as requiring a compliance aid.

(g)   Labelling of dispensed products must be clear and legible and include the details required by the labelling regulations under the Medicines Act and where appropriate any cautionary and advisory labelling recommended by the current British National Formulary.

(h)   Where it is not possible to dispense a prescription in its entirety, the patient, their carer or representative, should be informed at the outset and be given the opportunity to take the prescription to another pharmacy. A legible note detailing the name and quantity of the medication outstanding must be provided and a record kept in the pharmacy. Wherever possible the patient, their carer or representative, must be informed when the balance will be available for collection.

(i)   Dispensed medicines should normally be supplied directly to the patient or their carer in the pharmacy, where there is an opportunity for face-to-face contact, and the pharmacist has access to records and references which enable him to provide the best pharmaceutical service. Service Specification 8 must be complied with whenever dispensed medicines are not to be handed over in the pharmacy direct to the patient, their carer or representative.

4.2 Medicines for hospital inpatients

Patients, hospital staff and management teams are entitled to expect pharmacists involved in the supply of medicines to ensure that the systems in place are adequate to assure the safe and accurate supply and usage of medicines.

This service specification applies to all supplies of medicines for hospital in-patients whether supplied as ward stocks or on an individual named patient basis.

(a)   Pharmacists must adopt procedures to support appropriate use of medicines and minimise the risks of dispensing errors or contamination of medicines, incorporating checks to reduce special risks associated with particular products.

(b)   Medication must be clearly and legibly labelled.

(c)   Sufficient information must be provided to ensure that all medicines supplied to in-patients are likely to be used safely, effectively and appropriately. Patient information leaflets must be available to the ward.

(d)   Medicines brought in to hospital by patients remain the property of the patient; they must not be supplied to anyone else.

(e)   All medicines returned from a ward or hospital department must be examined under the direction of a pharmacist, to assess their suitability for being returned into stock. Date expired medicines must be destroyed.

5. Patient medication records

The public is entitled to expect the best available pharmaceutical care from pharmacies. In order to provide that care, pharmacists and their staff need timely and accurate information to be held on pharmacy computer systems or in manual records.

Patients are entitled to expect that any information stored about them will be pertinent, accurate and up to date, stored securely and treated as confidential and used only for the purpose for which it is was obtained.

Pharmacists must be aware that individual patients have a right, under data protection legislation, to inspect records held about them provided that suitable notice is given.

The pharmacy patient medication record system must:

(a)   be notified to the Information Commissioner;

(b)   incorporate access control mechanisms to minimise the risk of unauthorised or unnecessary access to patient specific data;

(c)   have the facility to identify drug interactions and be able to highlight those which are potentially hazardous;

(d)   provide for the collection, storage and display of patient medication records containing the following as a minimum:

    (i) sufficient information about the patient to allow accurate identification;
    (ii) the identity of the patient's GP;
    (iii) prescription details (quantity supplied, directions, date of dispensing, any balance owed).

6. Repeat medication services

A repeat medication service is a service operated in co-operation with local prescribers, in which pharmacists will provide professional support to assist in the rational, safe, effective and economic use of medicines.

(a)   The pharmacy must operate a patient medication record (PMR) system, notified to the Information Commissioner, and ensure that an audit trail exists to identify each request and supply so as to enable the service to be monitored.

(b)   The request for the service must come from the patient or their carer and be recorded in writing. Pharmacists may not act as the carer for this purpose.

(c)   Unless this information is already available from the prescription form, pharmacists must establish with the prescriber the period for which repeat prescriptions will be issued. Pharmacists must be alert to the possibility of the patient needing earlier review. On dispensing the final repeat the pharmacist must remind the patient or their carer, preferably in writing, of the need to visit the prescriber.

(d)   Pharmacists may institute a patient reminder system but may not request a repeat prescription from a surgery before obtaining the patient or carer's consent.

(e)   At the time of each request the pharmacist must establish which items the patient or their carer considers are required and ensure that unnecessary supplies are not made. At this stage pharmacists must also use their professional judgment to decide whether concordance or other problems encountered by the patient may require early reference to the prescriber.

(f)   Records of all interventions should be kept in order to be able to deal with any queries that may arise and to advise the prescriber.

7. Prescription collection services

Prescription collection services encompass any scheme whereby a pharmacy receives prescriptions other than directly from the patient, their carer or representative.

(a)   Prescriptions must be collected by individuals acting in accordance with directions given by the pharmacist.

(b)   Pharmacists must ensure that the procedures for the collection of prescriptions safeguard patient confidentiality and the security of prescriptions.

(c)   The request for the ongoing service must come from the patient or carer and the pharmacy must ensure that a procedure for recording the initial request, preferably consisting of written authorisation, exists.

(d)   All requests to the doctor for repeat prescriptions must be initiated by the patient or carer and be made directly to the surgery unless the pharmacy is offering a repeat medication service in compliance with Service Specification 6.

(e)   On receipt of prescriptions pharmacists must ensure that the pharmacy is authorised to receive and dispense them. Any prescriptions received for which the pharmacy does not have the patient's or their carer's consent must be returned to the surgery for collection by the patient or carer or be directed to the pharmacy authorised to receive the prescription.

8. Delivery services

A delivery service is one where medicines are handed over to a patient or their carer other than on the registered pharmacy premises. The provisions detailed in this service specification also apply to rural collection points. On each occasion a service is requested pharmacists must use their professional judgment to assess whether direct face-to-face contact with the patient or their carer is necessary.

In addition to complying with all other professional requirements relating to the sale or supply of medicines pharmacists are responsible for ensuring that the delivery mechanisms used:

(a)   are safe and that the medicines will be delivered promptly to the intended recipient with instructions for use. Unless alternative delivery arrangements have been made, medicines must only be handed over to the patient or their carer and before doing so the delivery person must confirm with the patient or their carer that the name and address of the patient is correct;

(b)   cater for any special storage requirements of the product;

(c)   enable a verifiable audit trail to be kept identifying the initial request for the service and each delivery and attempted delivery so that the service can be monitored. Wherever possible a signature should be obtained indicating safe delivery of the medicines.

9. On-line pharmacy services

The public is entitled to expect the same high quality pharmaceutical care irrespective of whether the service is provided on-line or face-to-face on pharmacy premises. At all times pharmacists must act in the best interests of the patient and seek to provide the best possible health care.

Pharmacy websites must clearly display the name of the owner of the business, the address of the pharmacy at which the business is conducted and where applicable the name of the superintendent pharmacist. Details of how to confirm the registration status of the pharmacy and pharmacists must be provided.

In addition to complying with all other professional requirements relating to the sale or supply of medicines pharmacists must ensure compliance with the following:

(a)   Security and confidentiality

    (i) Pharmacists must ensure that the confidentiality and integrity of all patient information is protected. All patient data transmissions must be encrypted to prevent the possibility of access by the internet service provider or any other unauthorised party;

    (ii) National Health Service patient data must comply with security standards and other requirements determined by the NHS Executive;

(b)   Request for supply of medicines

    (i) In all cases where a Pharmacy Medicine is requested or recommended, pharmacists must ensure that sufficient information is available to enable a professional assessment of the request and that they have an opportunity to provide appropriate counselling or advice. Advice must be available to all prospective purchasers of General Sale List Medicines and vitamin and mineral supplements;

    (ii) The patient must be able to identify the pharmacist assuming professional responsibility for the supply of medicines to them;

    (iii) Pharmacists providing on-line pharmacy services must advise patients to consult a convenient pharmacy whenever a request for a medicine or the symptoms described indicate that the patient's interests would be better served by a face-to-face consultation;

(c)   Information and advice

    (i) All information related to specific products must comply with the marketing authorisation, the patient information leaflet and the Medicines (Advertising) Regulations;

    (ii) Information relating to medicines must include all relevant details of contra-indications and side-effects;

    (iii) Non-patient specific health care advice, such as that relating to the treatment of symptoms or specific conditions, first aid, travel precautions, etc, provided on pharmacy web sites must be of a high professional standard and the pharmacist assuming professional responsibility for the provision of that advice must be identified;

    (iv) Product recommendations may only be given in respect of individual patients. A record must be kept of the pharmacist assuming professional responsibility for the recommendation and this pharmacist must be identified to the patient;

    (v) Before a patient receives a Pharmacy or Prescription Only Medicine pharmacists must ensure that the patient receives sufficient information to enable the safe and effective use of the medicine. Procedures for dealing with requests for supplies of medicines and/or delivery arrangements must ensure that this occurs;

(d)   Record keeping

(i) The pharmacy must maintain information about supplies of medicines sufficient to guard against risks of abuse or misuse;

(ii) Records must be kept to identify the pharmacist authorising every supply of a P or POM medicine following an e-mail request to purchase.

(e)   Complaints procedures – the website must contain details of how to make a complaint about the on-line pharmacy services provided.

10. Sales of Pharmacy Medicines

The public is entitled to expect that medicines purchased over the counter will be safe, effective and appropriate for the condition to be treated and the intended recipient. The following requirements apply to Pharmacy Medicines intended for human use and pharmacy only veterinary medicines.

All staff whose work regularly includes the sale of Pharmacy Medicines must be competent and instructed to refer customers to the pharmacist where appropriate. Pharmacists responsible for the provision of professional services in a pharmacy must ensure that the following standards are observed in the sale of Pharmacy Medicines.

(a)   Pharmacists or assistants asked for advice on treatment must obtain sufficient information to allow an assessment to be made that self-medication is appropriate, and to enable a suitable product or products to be recommended. Advice on the use of products must be provided.

(b)   Pharmacists must ensure that when a product is requested by name the procedures for sales of medicines provide for professional advice and intervention whenever this can assist in the safe and effective use of pharmacy medicines. Pharmacists or assistants must provide any advice relevant to the product and the intended consumer.

(c)   Pharmacists must be personally involved whenever this is necessary to provide an acceptable standard of pharmaceutical care. Assistants must be trained to know when the pharmacist should be consulted.

(d)   Procedures must ensure that the particular care needed is provided when supplying products for children, the elderly and other special groups or individuals or where the product is for animal use.

(e)   Pharmacists must ensure that they are involved in the decision to supply any medicine, which requires their intervention. Such medicines may include those that have recently become available without prescription, that may be subject to abuse or misuse, or where the marketing authorisation for non-prescription use is restricted to only selected conditions. Pharmacists and their staff must be aware of the abuse potential of certain OTC products and should not supply where there are reasonable grounds for suspecting misuse.

11. The supply of emergency hormonal contraception as a Pharmacy Medicine

Pharmacists in personal control of a pharmacy must ensure that the following standards are observed in the supply of emergency hormonal contraception as a Pharmacy Medicine. As with all medicines pharmacists must have sufficient knowledge of the product to enable them to make an informed decision when requests are made.

(a)   Pharmacists must deal with the request personally and decide whether to supply the product or make a referral to an appropriate health care professional.

(b)   Pharmacists must ensure that all necessary advice and information is provided to enable the patient to assess whether to use the product.

(c)   Requests for emergency hormonal contraception must be handled sensitively with due regard being given to the patient's right to privacy.

(d)   Only in exceptional circumstances should pharmacists supply the product to a person other than the patient.

(e)   Pharmacists should whenever possible take reasonable measures to inform patients of regular methods of contraception, disease prevention and sources of help.

12. Complementary therapies and medicines

The public trusts pharmacists to offer informed advice on treatments and medicines, and the profession expects pharmacists to ensure that they are competent in any area in which such advice is given.

Pharmacists providing homoeopathic or herbal medicines or other complementary therapies have a professional responsibility:

(a)   to ensure that stocks of homoeopathic or herbal medicines or other complementary therapies are obtained from a reputable source of supply;

(b)   not to recommend any remedy where they have any reason to doubt its safety or quality;

(c)   only to offer advice on homocopathic or herbal medicines or other complementary therapies or medicines if they have undertaken suitable training or have specialised knowledge.

13. Health care information and advice

Pharmacists are encouraged to contribute to the promotion of healthy lifestyles. By increasing public awareness of health promotion issues and participating in disease prevention strategies pharmacists can work actively towards improving the nation's health.

The public and other health care professions are entitled to expect pharmacists and their staff to be able to provide up to date, accurate and reliable advice and information on a wide range of health care issues.

Pharmacists and staff providing information and advice on health related issues must:

(a)   have an adequate level of current knowledge and information about relevant subjects;

(b)   ensure that all advice is independent and not compromised by commercial considerations;

(c)   seek appropriate and sufficient information from the enquirer to enable them to provide informed advice;

(d)   continually review their knowledge and keep up to date regarding new products and new policies for health promotion;

(e)   be aware of local and major national and topical health promotion initiatives;

(f)   work in partnership with patients and other health care professionals in seeking to promote healthy lifestyles and respect patients' rights to be involved in decisions about their health.

14. Diagnostic testing and health screening

Pharmacists working in primary care are well placed to provide diagnostic testing and health screening services to the public, who would expect any such service to be safe and accurate.

Pharmacists providing diagnostic testing or health screening services must:

(a)   ensure that before providing a service all staff have completed any training required to ensure competency with the equipment and procedures to be used and in the interpretation of results. They must be aware of the limits of the tests provided. The pharmacy must have a designated area, not in the dispensary, with suitable facilities to perform the tests and provide counselling;

(b)   institute and operate an appropriate quality assurance programme in order to ensure the reliability of the results produced;

(c)   ensure that equipment is maintained in good order to ensure that performance is unimpaired;

(d)   keep up to date with developments in the field and ensure that they are aware of current advice or local guidance on when to refer patients to their general medical practitioner;

(e)   before undertaking a test provide an explanation to the patient of the procedure to be adopted and obtain the patient's consent;

(f)   communicate test results to the patient in a manner in which they can be understood. Patients should be fully informed about the significance of the results and must be provided with any necessary counselling and available information;

(g)   ensure that adequate documentation is maintained to enable the service to be audited.

15. Emergencies

Increasingly the public looks to pharmacists in community practice for help and assistance, sometimes in emergencies.

(a)   Pharmacists must consider using their rights to make emergency supplies of medicines whenever a patient has an urgent need for a medicine. They must consider the medical consequences, if any, of not supplying.

(b)   Where pharmacists are not able to make an emergency supply of a medicine they should do everything possible to advise the patient how to obtain essential medical care.

(c)   Pharmacists must assist persons in need of emergency first aid or medical treatment whether by administering first aid within their competence or by summoning assistance and/or the emergency services. The Society's booklet, 'Emergency first aid: guidance for pharmacists', provides guidance on action in life-threatening situations.

16. Collection and disposal of pharmaceutical waste

These services include the collection and disposal of unwanted medicines returned to the pharmacy by patients and other members of the public, or from wards, clinics or other departments in a hospital, and the disposal of obsolete pharmacy stock.

(a)   Within the hospital sector pharmacists must ensure that a standard operating procedure dealing with waste management, including pharmaceutical waste, is in place.

(b)   Pharmacists must ensure that a contract has been made with an authorised carrier for the collection and disposal of pharmaceutical waste at regular intervals or on demand.

(c)   All pharmaceutical waste must be segregated from pharmacy stock and promptly transferred to disposal containers.

(d)   Pharmacists must ensure that consignment notes and any other requisite documentation are completed and copies kept to comply with legal requirements.

17. Advisory services to nursing and residential homes

This service specification applies to any service intended to facilitate the safe, effective, and appropriate usage of medicines, dressings and appliances, their storage, stock control or disposal, and the associated record keeping in nursing and residential homes and hospices.

Pharmacists providing advisory services must ensure that:

(a)   they have undertaken adequate training relevant to the services being provided;

(b)   they visit the home regularly by appointment. All staff visiting the home should carry identification;

(c)   they have contact, regularly and as frequently as needed, with medical and nursing personnel responsible for the care and medical treatment of residents;

(d)   they undertake professional assessments to ensure appropriate usage of medicines in the home;

(e)   they assess and advise on procedures to ensure safe and accurate administration of medicines;

(f)   all necessary supplementary information, eg, patient information leaflets, is available at the home;

(g)   they advise on the safe disposal of unwanted medicines supplied by the pharmacy and of other pharmaceutical and clinical waste, in compliance with legal requirements;

(h)   adequate records are maintained to enable them to deal with any queries that may arise and to enable audit of the service;

(i)   where they do not supply the medicines to the home they liaise with the pharmacy that does.

18. Domiciliary oxygen services

Domiciliary oxygen services comprise the supply of oxygen and associated equipment to a patient's home and the provision of advice on the use of oxygen in the home.

(a)   The pharmacy must operate a patient medication record system, notified to the Information Commissioner.

(b)   The pharmacy must have the facilities, as laid down in statute, for the safe storage of oxygen cylinders and oxygen concentrators and display the required statutory warning signs.

(c)   Personnel involved in the provision of domiciliary oxygen services must be suitably trained to undertake the tasks required of them and should carry identification.

(d)   All patients receiving domiciliary oxygen for the first time must be visited by the pharmacist or a suitably trained and competent member of staff to instruct the patient or their carer on the use of oxygen in the home.

(e)   Pharmacists must ensure that all necessary safety information is provided to the patient or their carer.

(f)   Sets must be serviced regularly in accordance with the manufacturer's recommendations.

(g)   Pharmacists must maintain adequate records of supplies and advice given to enable the regular audit of the service.

19. Services to drug misusers

Services to drug misusers include the dispensing and/or supervision of patient self-administration of methadone and other products dispensed on instalment prescriptions.

(a)   The pharmacy must operate a patient medication record system, notified to the Information Commissioner.

(b)   Pharmacists must liaise with health care professionals and others involved in the care of the patient having due regard for the patient's confidentiality.

(c)   If pharmacists anticipate or experience problems of unacceptable behaviour by a patient they should enter into an agreement with the patient for the future provision of the service. This should detail the services that the pharmacist will provide and also outline the pharmacist's expectations of the patient, the reasons why and any action to be taken if the patient's conduct becomes unacceptable. Pharmacists may decline to provide a service to a patient whose conduct is unacceptable.

(d)   The pharmacy must not deviate from the instructions given on the prescription. Sugar-and/or colour-free products have a greater potential for abuse than syrup based and coloured products and must not be dispensed unless specifically prescribed.

(e)   Patients must be treated with respect and courtesy and where self-administration occurs due regard must be given to the provision of a quiet area in order to provide some privacy for both the patient and other members of the public.

(f)   Only in exceptional circumstances should pharmacists supply clean injecting equipment for drug misusers if the pharmacy has no arrangements for taking back contaminated equipment. Purchasers of injecting equipment should be advised of the availability of disposal facilities at the pharmacy and should always be encouraged to dispose of used syringes and needles safely.

20. Needle and syringe exchange schemes

Needle and syringe exchange schemes involve the provision of clean syringes and needles and the collection of contaminated equipment used by substance and drug misusers.

(a)   Pharmacists must be aware of local facilities for drug misusers and have established contacts with other health care professionals involved in the care of drug misusers.

(b)   All staff who may be involved in the service must be instructed on procedures to be followed to minimise risks.

(c)   Supplies of syringes and needles must be made by pharmacists or trained staff.

(d)   Individuals must be encouraged to return used contaminated equipment in approved disposal containers, but a supply of clean equipment must not be refused if they omit to do so.

(e)   Used equipment must be disposed of, preferably by the individual, into a properly designed sharps container available in the pharmacy.

(f)   Suitable arrangements must be made for the disposal of full sharps containers.

21. Extemporaneous preparation/compounding

This service specification is not intended to cover the reconstitution of dry powders with water or other diluents.

The public is entitled to expect that products extemporaneously prepared in a pharmacy will be prepared accurately, suitable for use and meet the accepted standards for quality assurance.

Pharmacists wishing to be involved in extemporaneous preparation must ensure that they, and any other staff involved, are competent to undertake the tasks to be performed and that the requisite facilities and equipment are available.

(a)   A product should only be extemporaneously prepared when there is no product with a marketing authorisation available and where the pharmacist is able to prepare the product in compliance with accepted standards.

(b)   Equipment must be maintained in good order to ensure that performance is unimpaired.

(c)   Pharmacists must be satisfied as to the safety and appropriateness of the formula for the product.

(d)   Ingredients must be sourced from recognised pharmaceutical manufacturers and be of a quality accepted for use in the preparation and manufacture of pharmaceutical products. All calculations and, where possible, measurements should be checked. Pharmacists must pay particular attention to substances which may be hazardous and require special handling techniques.

(e)   The product must be labelled with the necessary particulars, including any special requirements for the safe handling or storage of the product, and an expiry date.

(f)   Records must be kept for a minimum of two years but if possible for five years. The records must include the formula, the ingredients and the quantities used, their source, batch number and expiry date. Where the preparation is dispensed in response to a prescription the records must also include the patient's and prescription details and the date of dispensing. A record must be kept of personnel involved including the identity of the pharmacist taking overall responsibility.

22. Aseptic dispensing services from non-licensed units

Aseptic dispensing includes manipulations such as reconstitution, dilution and transfer of a sterile preparation avoiding microbiological contamination and maintaining a physicochemical stability, under the supervision of a pharmacist.

(a)   The preparation of products intended for administration to humans must be in accordance with the principles of Good Manufacturing Practice throughout the process. This is encompassed in the documents 'Quality assurance of aseptic preparation services' and 'Aseptic dispensing for NHS patients' and any subsequent revisions.

(b)   The decision to prepare a product aseptically should be made in the context of the clinical needs of the patient. The pharmacist must ensure that the product complies with the standards to be expected for that product.

(c)   Personnel involved in aseptic dispensing must be suitably trained to enable them to work safely and competently.

(d)   The facilities and the service as a whole must be regularly audited and faults and deficiencies once identified must be promptly rectified.

23. Patient group directions

Pharmacists involved in writing and/or approving patient group directions are accountable for their content and must therefore ensure that:

(a)   they only approve directions which comply with legal requirements;

(b)   the staff training specified will enable safe operation of the patient group direction;

(c)   the appropriate people have been involved in the drafting and approval of the patient group direction;

(d)   they have up-to-date knowledge relating to the clinical situation covered by the patient group direction, the medicine and its use for the indications specified in the patient group direction;

(e)   they are familiar with their role and responsibilities and the government advice set out in relevant guidance.*

Pharmacists involved in the supply and/or administration of a Prescription Only Medicine under a patient group direction must:

(f)   ensure that they have up-to-date knowledge relating to the clinical situation covered by the patient group direction, the medicine and its use for the indications specified;

(g)   ensure that they have undertaken any training required for operation of the patient group direction;

(h)   be satisfied that the patient group direction is legally valid and that it has been approved by the relevant health authority or other NHS body;

(i)   ensure that when supplies are made the agreed protocol is followed and that the information specified in the patient group direction is recorded. These records must include the identity of the pharmacist assuming responsibility for each supply.

---

* HSC 2000/026 (England only), WHC: (2000) 116 (Wales only) or HDL (2001) 7 (Scotland only).

17

Proposals for new National Health Service contract

England

The proposals for England fall into three areas:

- new rules on 'control of entry': the conditions which must be met before a Primary Care Trust (PCT) may approve an application for inclusion in a pharmaceutical list of NHS community pharmacies (note: this process is often described in terms of the pharmacy 'obtaining an NHS contract');
- reform of the financial mechanisms for supply and reimbursement of generic medicines supplied against NHS prescriptions in the community; and
- A new contract for NHS community services.

Control of entry

Pharmacies may obtain an NHS contract without fulfilling the 'necessary or desirable' tests in the regulations if they fall into one of the following categories:

- open for the provision of NHS pharmaceutical services for at least 100 hours per week;
- located in a one-stop primary care centre, developed in accordance with the PCT's Strategic Services Development Plan (SSDP);
- located in a 15 000 m² retail development; or
- wholly Internet or mail order based.

Certain conditions must then be met to qualify for the above exemptions.

Reimbursement of generics

A consultation document published in September 2003 invited comments from interested parties in the pharmaceutical industry, the NHS and others on the Government's proposed arrangements for the long-term supply and reimbursement of generic medicines to the NHS in primary care in England. The proposal when implemented would also replace the current Maximum Price Scheme for generic medicines. The scheme will be based on a voluntary agreement under section 33 of the Health Act 1999 and those that opt out of such a scheme would be subject to a statutory scheme under sections 34 to 38 of that Act. Under the scheme, issues which are not resolved amicably between the Department of Health and industry, are referred to an arbitration body. The Department of Health intends to report to Parliament annually on the scheme. Publication of consultation responses in mid-2004 suggest changes to the system for calculating the Drug Tariff and a system for monitoring the generics market, while ensuring that all parts of the supply chain obtain a fair return for their businesses. The financial arrangements for reimbursement of generics will almost certainly be linked to the financial arrangements for the new contract (see below).

New community pharmacy contract

The details below are taken from www.psnc.org.uk/contract (November 2004).

The proposed structure consists of three different levels of service: essential services, advanced services and enhanced services. The suggested services are divided into essential, advanced and enhanced services.

Essential services

Essential services would be offered by all contractors and include:

> *dispensing*: supply of medicine or appliance, advice to patient about the medicines being dispensed, advice about 'significant' interactions with other medicines, recording medicines dispensed and possibly advice provided, providing Compliance Aids needed by disabled patients (in line with the Disability Discrimination Act 1995)
> *repeat dispensing*: in partnership with the patient and prescriber, ascertaining the patient need for a repeat supply of a particular medicine, communicating all significant issues to the prescriber and dispensing medicines for a period of up to one year, without the need for patients to return monthly to the prescriber for further prescriptions
> *signposting patients to other healthcare providers*: pharmacist and staff referring patients to other health professionals or providers where appropriate
> *clinical governance*: requirements include use of standard operating procedures, adverse incident reporting to the National Patient Safety Agency, evidence of pharmacist continual professional development, service audits and patient questionnaires, intervention monitoring
> *public health*: healthy lifestyle promotion; opportunistic one-to-one counselling on smoking cessation and risk factors for coronary heart disease, promotion of influenza vaccination uptake, educating the public about the appropriate use of antibiotics
> *medication waste disposal*: disposal of unwanted medicines via pharmacies; service standards would apply to disposal companies; special arrangements may apply to Controlled Drugs (post Shipman Inquiry).

Advanced services

Advanced services would require accreditation, for example that training had been completed and that facilities were available. These would include:

> *medicines use review*: pharmacist would undertake medicines use review, face-to-face with patient using a concordance-centred review, which assesses patient's problems with current medication and its administration; patient's knowledge of the medication regimen is assessed and developed and a report is fed back to the patient's GP;

the patient's knowledge of their medication and why they are taking it is increased and problems with their medication are identified and addressed

prescription intervention service: similar to the medicines use review service but initiated by a significant issue with a patient's prescription; interventions may include prescription synchronisation, dose optimisation, suggestions for therapeutic substitutions based on local protocols, recommendations of changes to help with patient concordance; the pharmacist would feedback suggestions and comments to the prescriber using standardised paperwork or electronically and the scheme is intended to improve the quality of prescribing and hence patient care.

Enhanced services

Enhanced services would have a specification and value agreed nationally but be commissioned locally by PCTs. Services *may* include:

- minor ailments management
- diabetes screening
- substance misuse services
- coronary heart disease screening/healthy living service
- disease-specific medicines management services
- palliative care services
- emergency hormonal contraception service
- full clinical medication review
- concordance services
- out of hours service
- care home and intermediate care services
- prescriber support services (medical practice based)
- home care services – domiciliary assessments
- head lice management service
- smoking cessation service
- gluten-free food supply service
- needle exchange scheme
- services to schools.

It is envisaged that the contract framework will develop over time to keep pace with the changing needs of patients and the NHS. This gradual contract development may, for example, see advanced services becoming part of the essential category and enhanced services become part of the advanced or even essential services.

Information on the new contract arrangements in England and Wales is also available from the National Primary and Care Trust Development Programme (http://www.natpact. nhs.uk).

Scotland

The Community Pharmacy Contract in Scotland is likely to comprise four core services: a minor ailment service, a chronic medication service, an acute medication service and a public health service (*Pharm. J* 14 August 2004 p. 211).

The chronic medication service and minor ailment service will be based on capitation payments, possibly on top of a basic allowance; the public health service will be based on a basic allowance weighted to reflect the pharmacy population's 'health profile'; the acute medication service will be paid with a flat 'per item' dispensing fee. There will also be set allowances for maintaining IM & T and premises, and a fund to facilitate system developments and improvements (*Chemist and Druggist* 14 August 2004 p. 4).

Information is available on www.show.scot.nhs.uk/publicationsindex.htm and at Scottish Pharmaceutical General Council: www.spgc.org.uk.

Wales

The NHS Community Pharmacy Contract in Wales is likely to follow broadly similar lines to that in England. However, Wales has rejected changes to the control of entry arrangements and has not adopted provisions for local pharmaceutical services. Wales also intends to remove prescription charges in the future.

Details will be on the Community Pharmacy Wales website: http://www.cpwales.org.uk.

National Health Service: England and Wales terms of service for chemists

The following terms of service are as set out in Schedule 2 to the National Health Service (Pharmaceutical Services) Regulations 1992 (SI 1992 No.662, as amended). In the following, HA stands for health authority.

General

Interpretation (reg.1)

1   In this Schedule, unless the context otherwise requires, any reference in a paragraph to a numbered sub-paragraph is a reference to the sub-paragraph bearing that number in that paragraph.

Incorporation of provisions (reg.2)

2   Any provisions of the following affecting the rights and obligations of chemists and doctors who provide pharmaceutical services shall be deemed to form part of the terms of service for chemists or, as the case may be, of the terms of service of doctors who provide pharmaceutical services:

(a)   these regulations;

(b)   the *Drug Tariff* in so far as it lists drugs and appliances for the purpose of section 41 of the Act;

(c)   so much of Part II of the National Health Service (Service Committees and Tribunal) Regulations 1992 (SI 1992 No.664) as relates to:

      (i) the investigation of questions arising between chemists and persons receiving pharmaceutical services and other investigations to be made by the pharmaceutical discipline committee and the joint discipline committee and the action which may be taken by the HA as a result of such investigations; and

(ii) appeals to the Secretary of State from decisions of the HA.

Part II: Terms of Service

Directed services (reg.2A)

A chemist with whom an HA makes an arrangement for the provision of any directed service shall comply with the terms and conditions of the arrangement.

Directed services means *additional pharmaceutical services* (s.41A of the 1977 Act).

Provision of pharmaceutical services (reg.3)

3   (1) Where any person presents on a prescription form:

(a)   an order for drugs, not being scheduled drugs, or appliances, signed by a doctor; or

(b)   an order for drugs specified in Schedule 11 to the medical regulations, signed by, and endorsed on its face with the reference 'SLS' by a doctor; or

(c)   an order for listed drugs or medicines, signed by a dentist or his deputy or assistant; or

(d)   an order for listed drugs or medicines, or listed appliances, signed by a nurse prescriber,

a chemist shall, with reasonable promptness, provide the drugs or medicines so ordered, and such of the appliances so ordered as he supplies in the normal course of his business.

(1A) If the person presenting the prescription form asks the chemist to do so;

(a)   he shall give an estimate of the time when the drugs, medicines or appliances will be ready;

(b)   and if they are not ready by then, he shall give a revised estimate of time when they will be ready (and so on).

(1B) Where a chemist reasonably believes that a form presented to him as a prescription form in accordance with paragraph 3(1) is not a genuine order for the person named on the form (for example because he reasonably believes the form has been stolen or forged), he may refuse to provide the drugs or medicines or listed appliances specified on the form.

(1C) Before providing the drugs or medicines or listed appliances ordered on a prescription form as specified in paragraph 3(1):

(a)   the chemist shall ask any person who makes a declaration on the prescription form, that the person named on the prescription form does not have to pay charges by virtue of either:

(i) entitlement to exemption to charges under the Charges Regulations (SI 1989 No. 419, as amended); or

(ii) entitlement to remission of charges, under the Remission of Charges Regulations (SI 1988 No. 551, as amended)

to produce satisfactory evidence of such entitlement unless the declaration is in respect of entitlement to exemption and at the time of the declaration the chemist already has such evidence available to him; and,

(b)   if no satisfactory evidence is produced to the chemists the chemists shall endorse the prescription form to that effect.

(2) Any drug which is provided as part of pharmaceutical services and included in the *Drug Tariff,* the *British National Formulary* including any Appendix published as part of that Formulary, the *Dental Practitioners' Formulary,* the *European Pharmacopoeia,* or the *British Pharmaceutical Codex,* shall comply with the standard or formula specified therein.

(3) Subject to any regulations in force under the Weights and Measures Act 1985 and subject to sub-paragraphs (4) to (12) a chemist shall provide pharmaceutical services only in response to and in accordance with an order on a prescription form, signed as specified in sub-paragraph (1)

(4) Where an order, not being an order to which the Poisons Rules 1982 or the Misuse of Drugs Regulations 1985 apply, which is issued by a doctor, a dentist or a nurse prescriber on a prescription form for drugs does not prescribe their quantity, strength or dosage, a chemist may provide the drugs in such strength and dosage as in the exercise of his professional skill, knowledge and care he shall consider to be appropriate, and, subject to sub-paragraph (5), in such quantity as he so considers to be appropriate for a course of treatment, for the patient to whom the order relates, for a period not exceeding five days.

(5) Where an order to which sub-paragraph (4) applies is for:

(a) an oral contraceptive substance; or
(b) a drug which is available for supply as part of pharmaceutical services only together with one or more drugs; or
(c) an antibiotic in a liquid form for oral administration in respect of which pharmaceutical considerations require its provision in an unopened package;

which is not available for provision as part of pharmaceutical services except in such packages that the minimum available package contains a quantity appropriate to a course of treatment for a patient for a period of more than five days, the chemist may provide that minimum available package.

(6) Where any drug, not being one to which the Misuse of Drugs Regulations 1985 apply, ordered by a doctor, dentist or nurse prescriber on a prescription form, is available for provision by a chemist in a pack in a quantity which is different to the quantity which has been so ordered, and that drug is:

(a) sterile;
(b) effervescent or hygroscopic;
(c) a liquid preparation for addition to bath water;
(d) a coal tar preparation;
(e) a viscous preparation; or
(f) packed at the time of its manufacture in a calendar pack or special container;

the chemist shall, subject to sub-paragraph (7), provide the drug in the pack whose quantity is nearest to the quantity which has been so ordered.

(7) A chemist shall not provide, pursuant to sub-paragraph (6), a drug in a calendar pack where, in his opinion, it was the intention of the doctor, dentist or nurse prescriber who ordered that drug that it should be provided only in the exact quantity ordered.

(8) In this paragraph:

(a) *calendar pack* means a blister or strip pack showing the days of the week or month against each of the several units in the pack;
(b) *special container(s)* means any container with an integral means of application or from which it is not practicable to dispense an exact quantity.

(9) Where, in the case of emergency, a doctor or nurse prescriber personally known to the chemist requests him to provide a drug, the chemist may provide that drug before receiving a prescription form, provided that:

(a)   that drug is not a scheduled drug;

(b)   that drug is not a Controlled Drug within the meaning of the Misuse of Drugs Act 1971 other than a drug which is for the time being specified in Schedule 4 or 5 to the Misuse of Drugs Regulations 1985; and

(c)   the doctor or nurse prescriber undertakes to give the chemist such a prescription form within 72 hours.

(10) Except as provided in sub-paragraph (11), a chemist shall not provide a scheduled drug, by way of pharmaceutical services or otherwise, in response to an order by name, formula or other description on a prescription form.

(11) Where a drug has an appropriate non-proprietary name and it is ordered on a prescription form either by that name or by its formula, a chemist may provide a drug which has the same specification notwithstanding that it is a scheduled drug, provided that where a scheduled drug is a pack which consists of a drug in more than one strength, such provision does not involve the supply of part only of the pack.

(12) Where a drug which is ordered as specified in sub-paragraph (11) combines more than one drug, that sub-paragraph shall apply only if the combination has an appropriate non-proprietary name, whether the individual drugs which it combines do so or not.

(13) A chemist shall provide any drug which he is required to supply under this paragraph in a suitable container.

(14) A chemist shall not give, promise or offer to any person any gift or reward (whether by way of a share of or dividend on the profits of the business or by way of discount or rebate or otherwise) as an inducement to or in consideration of his presenting an order for drugs or appliances on a prescription form.

Premises and hours (reg.4)

4   (1) Pharmaceutical services shall be provided at each of the premises from which the chemist has undertaken to provide pharmaceutical services at such times as, following an application in writing by the chemist, shall have been approved in his case by an HA or, on appeal, the Secretary of State, in accordance with the following provisions of this paragraph.

(2) An HA shall not approve any application submitted by a chemist in relation to the times at which he is to provide pharmaceutical services unless it is satisfied that:

(a)   the times proposed are such that a pharmacist will normally be available:

(i) subject to sub-paragraph (4) for no less than 30 hours in any week; and

(ii) on five days in any such week; and

(b)   the hours when a pharmacist will normally be available in any week are to be allocated between the days on which he will normally be available in that week in such a manner as is likely to meet the needs of persons in the neighbourhood for pharmaceutical services on working days between the hours of 09.00 and 17.30 (or 13.00 on an early closing day).

(3) In this paragraph *available* means, in relation to a pharmacist, available to provide pharmaceutical services of the kind he has undertaken to provide and *availability* shall be construed accordingly. *Working day* means Monday to Saturday excluding a Good Friday, Christmas Day, 28th December if 26th December is a Saturday or a bank holiday which falls on any such day; and *an early closing day* means any working day when most shops in the neighbourhood are habitually closed after the hour of 13.00.

(4) The HA may approve an application to provide pharmaceutical services for less than 30 hours in any week provided that it is satisfied that the provision of pharmaceutical services in the neighbourhood is likely to be adequate to meet the need for such services on working days between the hours of 09.00 and 17.30 (or 13.00 on an early closing day) at times when the pharmacist is not available.

(5) An application for approval pursuant to sub-paragraph (2) shall be made in writing to an HA.

(6) The HA shall determine an application within 30 days of receiving it.

(7) Subject to sub-paragraph (8), in determining any application, the HA shall either:

(a)   grant approval;
(b)   grant approval subject to any requirement that it considers appropriate for the purpose of ensuring that a pharmacist is available for the provision of pharmaceutical services at such times as are necessary to meet the need for such services on working days between the hours of 09.00 and 17.30 (or 13.00 on an early closing day); or
(c)   refuse approval.

(8) Where the HA is considering whether to grant approval subject to any requirements, as mentioned in sub-paragraph (7)(b), it shall consult the Local Pharmaceutical Committee before determining the application.

(9) An HA shall notify the chemist in writing of its determination, and, where it refuses an application or grants an application subject to any requirements under sub-paragraph (7)(b), it shall send the chemist a statement in writing of the reasons for its determination or, as the case may be, for the imposition of the requirements and of the chemist's right of appeal under sub-paragraph (10).

(10) A chemist may, within 30 days of receiving a notification pursuant to sub-paragraph (9), appeal in writing to the Secretary of State against any refusal of approval or against any condition imposed pursuant to sub-paragraph (7)(b).

(11) The Secretary of State may, when determining an appeal, either confirm the determination of the HA or substitute his own determination for that of the HA.

(12) The Secretary of State shall notify the chemist in writing of his determination and shall in every case include with the notification a written statement of the reasons for the determination.

(13) At each of the premises at which a chemist provides pharmaceutical services he shall exhibit:

(a)   a notice provided by the HA specifying the times at which the premises are open for the provision of drugs and appliances; and
(b)   at times when the premises are not open, a notice, where practicable legible from outside the premises, specifying the addresses of other chemists in the pharmaceutical list and the times at which drugs and appliances may be obtained from those addresses.

(14) An HA shall notify the chemist in writing of the names and addresses of other chemists included in the pharmaceutical list whose premises are in the neighbourhood and of the times at which they are required to provide pharmaceutical services.

(15) Where a chemist is prevented by illness or other reasonable cause from complying with his obligations under this paragraph he shall, where practicable, make arrangements with one or more chemists whose premises are situated in the neighbourhood for the provision of pharmaceutical services during that time.

(16) A chemist may apply to an HA for a variation of the times at which, in accordance with a determination under this paragraph (*the earlier determination*), a pharmacist is required to be normally available, and sub-paragraphs (3) to (13) shall apply to the making and determination (*the subsequent determination*) of an

application under this sub-paragraph as if it were the first application by that chemist for the purpose of this paragraph.

(17) Where an application made under sub-paragraph (16) is approved, the earlier determination mentioned in sub-paragraph (16) shall cease to have effect and the subsequent determination mentioned in that sub-paragraph shall have effect instead:

(a)   where the subsequent determination is made by an HA and no appeal is made, from the day falling eight weeks after the date on which the chemist receives notification of that HA's determination; or

(b)   where the subsequent determination is made on appeal, from the day falling eight weeks after the date on which the chemist receives notification of the Secretary of State's determination.

(18) Where it appears to the HA, after consultation with or at the request of the Local Pharmaceutical Committee, that the times at which a pharmacist is available no longer meet the needs of persons in the neighbourhood for pharmaceutical services on working days between the hours of 09.00 and 17.00 (or 13.00 on an early closing day) it may review the terms of:

(a)   any approval granted by the HA under sub-paragraph (7)(a) or (b) or by the Secretary of State under sub-paragraph (12); or

(b)   any direction given under sub-paragraph (20)(a) by the HA or, on appeal, by the Secretary of State.

(19) On any review under sub-paragraph (18), the HA shall:

(a)   give notice to the chemist of its proposed changes in the times at which the pharmacist is to be available; and

(b)   allow him 30 days within which to make representations to the HA about its proposals.

(20) After considering any representations made in accordance with sub-paragraph (19)(b), the HA shall either:

(a)   direct the chemist to revise the times at which the pharmacist is to be available in the manner specified in the direction; or

(b)   confirm that the existing times of availability continue to meet the need for pharmaceutical services on working days between the hours of 09.00 and 17.00 (or 13.00 on an early closing day).

(21) The HA shall notify the chemist in writing of its determination under sub-paragraph (20), and where it gives a direction under head (a) of that sub-paragraph it shall include with the notification a statement in writing of the reasons for its determination and of the chemist's right of appeal under sub-paragraph (22).

(22) A chemist may, within 30 days of receiving a notification under sub-paragraph (21), appeal in writing to the Secretary of State against a direction under sub-paragraph (20)(a).

(23) Sub-paragraphs (11) and (12) shall apply to any appeal made under sub-paragraph (22) but as though in sub-paragraph (12) any reference to a determination were a reference to a direction.

(24) A chemist in respect of whom a direction is given under sub-paragraph (20) shall revise the times of availability of the pharmacist so as to give effect to the direction:

(a)   where the direction is given by the HA and no appeal is made, not later than eight weeks after the date on which he receives notification under sub-paragraph (21); or

(b)   where the direction is given or confirmed on appeal, not later than eight weeks after the date on which he receives notification of the Secretary of State's decision.

(25) Where it appears to the HA, after consultation with the Local Pharmaceutical Committee, that the times at which a pharmacist is available:

(a)   on working days before the hour of 09.00 or after the hour of 17.30 (13.00 on an early closing day); or

(b)   on any Sunday, Good Friday, Christmas Day or bank holiday;

are not adequate to meet the needs of persons in the neighbourhood for pharmaceutical services at those times or on those days, the HA may, subject to sub-paragraphs (26) to (28), direct the chemist to revise the times at which the pharmacist is to be available in the manner specified in the direction.

(26) If the HA has been directed under section 41A(1)(a) or (b) of the Act that it must or may make arrangements for a pharmacist to be available to any person in the HA's area for consultation outside the hours referred to in sub-paragraph (25), no direction shall be given unless sub-paragraph (26A) have been complied with.

    (26A) The requirements referred to in sub-paragraph (26) are that:

(a)   the HA must have offered to make such arrangements with the chemist; and

(b)   the arrangements offered must have been such that under them a pharmacist would have been available at the revised times which the HA proposes to require in its direction under sub-paragraph (25)

but it is immaterial whether or not the chemist accepted the offer of such arrangements.

    (26B) If the HA has not been directed in the manner referred to in sub-paragraph (26) no direction shall be given under sub-paragraph (25) unless a fee, allowance, or other remuneration to be paid to any chemist so directed is included in the *Drug Tariff* or has been determined by the HA by virtue of regulation 18(1A) (as the case may be).

    (27) Before giving any direction under sub-paragraph (25) the HA shall:

(a)   give notice to the chemist of the revised times at which it proposes the pharmacist is to be available; and

(b)   allow the chemist 30 days within which to make representations to the HA about its proposals and shall take any such representations into account.

    (28) The HA shall notify the chemist in writing of a direction under sub-paragraph (25), and shall include with the notification a statement in writing of the reason for its direction and of the chemist's right of appeal under sub-paragraph (29).

    (29) A chemist may within 30 days of receiving notification under sub-paragraph (28), appeal in writing to the Secretary of State against a direction under sub-paragraph (25).

    (30) Sub-paragraphs (11) and (12) shall apply to any appeal made under sub-paragraph (29) but as though any reference to a determination:

(a)   in sub-paragraph (11) were to a direction; and

(b)   in sub-paragraph (12) were to a decision.

    (31) A chemist in respect of whom a direction is given under sub-paragraph (25) shall revise the times of availability of the pharmacist so as to give effect to the direction:

(a)   where the direction is given by the HA and no appeal is made, not later than eight weeks after the date on which he receives notification under sub-paragraph (28); or

(b)   where the direction is given or confirmed on appeal, not later than eight weeks after the date on which he receives notification of the Secretary of State's decision.

Provision of drugs and fitting of appliances (reg.5)

5   (1) Drugs shall be provided either by or under the direct supervision of a pharmacist.

(1A) Where the pharmacist referred to in sub-paragraph (1) is employed by a chemist, the pharmacist must not be one:

(a)   who having been disqualified under section 46(2)(b) of the Act (or under any corresponding provision in force in Scotland or Northern Ireland) from inclusion in the pharmaceutical list of a HA (or in Scotland of a Health Board, or in Northern Ireland of a Health and Social Services Board), is also the subject of a declaration under section 46(2)(c) of the Act (or any corresponding provision in force in Scotland or Northern Ireland) that he is not fit to be engaged in any capacity in the provision of pharmaceutical services; or

(b)   who is suspended by direction of the Tribunal, other than in a case falling within section 49B(3) of the Act.

(2) Subject to paragraph 3(1) a chemist shall make all necessary arrangements:

(a)   for measuring a person who presents a prescription for a truss or other appliance of a type requiring measurement and fitting by the chemist; and

(b)   for fitting the appliance.

Particulars of chemists (reg.6)

6   A chemist shall give the HA, if it so required, the name of any pharmacist employed by him for the provision of drugs for persons from whom he has accepted an order for the provision of pharmaceutical services under paragraph 3.

Charges for drugs (reg.7)

7   (1) Subject to regulations made under section 77 of the Act, all drugs, containers and appliances supplied under these terms of service shall be supplied free of charge.

(2) Where a chemist supplies a container in response to an order for drugs signed by a doctor under paragraph 43 of Schedule 2 to the medical regulations or by a nurse prescriber or supplies an oxygen container or oxygen equipment, other than equipment specified in the *Drug Tariff* as not returnable to the chemist, the container and equipment shall remain the property of the chemist.

Remuneration of chemists (reg.8)

8   (1) A chemist who has undertaken to provide supplemental services within the meaning of regulation 16 shall, on request, make available to the HA all records made in accordance with regulation 16(2)(b).

(1A) A chemist who has undertaken to provide additional professional services within the meaning of regulation 16A shall, on request, permit the HA or another person on its behalf at any reasonable time to inspect the premises from which those services are provided for the purpose of satisfying itself that those services are being provided in accordance with the undertaking.

(2) The HA shall make payments, calculated in the manner provided by the *Drug Tariff* or in accordance with any determination made by virtue of regulation 18(1A) subject to any deduction required to be made by regulations made under section 77 of the Act) to chemists in respect of drugs and appliances, containers, medicine measures and dispensing fees.

(2A) The HA shall make such payments, if any, as are provided for by the *Drug Tariff* or in accordance with any determination made by virtue of regulation 18(1A) to chemists who provide additional professional services within the meaning of regulation 16A.

(3) Where a chemist so requires, the HA shall afford him reasonable facilities for examining all or any of the forms on which the drugs or appliances provided by him were ordered, together with particulars of the amounts calculated to be payable in respect of such drugs and appliances and the HA shall take into consideration any objections made by the chemist in relation to those amounts.

(4) Where so required by the Local Pharmaceutical Committee or any organisation which is, in the opinion of the Secretary of State, representative of the general body of chemists, the HA shall give the Local Pharmaceutical Committee or the organisation in question similar facilities for examining such forms and particulars relating to all or any of the chemists which it represents.

Professional standards (reg.8A)

8A (1) A pharmacist whose name is on the pharmaceutical list shall provide pharmaceutical services and exercise any professional judgment in connection with the provision of such services in conformity with the standards accepted in the pharmaceutical profession.

(2) A chemist who employs a pharmacist in connection with the provision of such services shall secure that the pharmacist complies with the requirements set out in sub-paragraph (1).

Incorporation of provisions (reg.9)

Deleted by SI 1995 No.644.

Withdrawal from pharmaceutical list (reg.10)

10 (1) Subject to sub-paragraph (2), a chemist may at any time give notice in writing to the HA that he wishes to withdraw his name from the pharmaceutical list and his name shall be removed accordingly at the expiry of three months from the date of such notice or of such shorter period as the HA may agree.

(2) Where representations are made to the Tribunal under the provisions of section 46 of the Act (disqualification of a practitioner) that the continued inclusion of a chemist in the pharmaceutical list would be prejudicial to the efficiency of pharmaceutical services, he shall not, except with the consent of the Secretary of State, be entitled to have his name removed from such list pending the determination of the proceedings on those representations.

Complaints (regs.10A and 10B)

10A (1) Subject to sub-paragraph (2), a chemist shall establish, and operate in accordance with this paragraph, a procedure (in this paragraph and in paragraph 10B referred to as a *complaints procedure*) to deal with any complaints made by or on behalf of any person to whom he has provided pharmaceutical services.

Rider A

10   (2) The complaints procedure to be established by a chemist may be such that it also deals with complaints made in relation to one or more other chemists.

    (3) The complaints procedure to be established by a chemist who provides pharmaceutical services from more than one set of premises may be such that it relates to all those premises together.

    (4) A complaints procedure shall apply to complaints made in relation to any matter reasonable connected with the chemist's provision of pharmaceutical services and within the reasonable control of:

(a)   the chemist;

(b)   where the chemist is a body corporate, any of its directors or former directors;

(c)   a former partner of a chemist;

(d)   any pharmacist employed by the chemist;

(e)   any employee of the chemist other than one falling within sub-paragraph (d);

and in this paragraph and paragraph 10B references to complaints falling within this sub-paragraph.

    (5) A complaint may be made on behalf of any person with his consent, or:

(a)   where he is under 16 years of age:

        (i) by either parent, or in the absence of both parents, the guardian or other adult person who has care of the child; or

        (ii) where he is in the care of an authority to whose care he has been committed under the provisions of the Children's Act 1989 or in the care of a voluntary organisation, by that authority or voluntary organisation; or

(b)   where he is incapable of making a complaint, by a relative or other adult person who has an interest in his welfare.

    (6) A complaint may be made as respects a person who has died by a relative or other adult person who has an interest in his welfare, or where he was as described in paragraph (a)(ii) of sub-paragraph (5), by the authority or voluntary organisation.

    (7) A complaints procedure shall comply with the following requirements:

(a)   the chemist must specify a person (who need not be connected with the chemist and who, in the case of an individual, may be specified by his job title) to be responsible for receiving and investigating all complaints;

(b)   all complaints must be:

        (i) recorded in writing;

        (ii) acknowledged, either orally or in writing, within the period of three days (excluding Saturdays, Sundays, Christmas Day, Good Friday and bank holidays) beginning with the day on which the complaint was received by the person specified under paragraph (a) or where that is not possible as soon as is reasonably practicable;

        (iii) properly investigated;

(c)   within the period of 10 days (excluding Saturdays, Sundays, Christmas Day, Good Friday and bank holidays) beginning with the day on which the complaint was received by the person specified under paragraph (a) or where that is not possible as soon as is reasonably practicable, the complainant must be given a written summary of the investigations and its conclusions;

(d)   where the investigation of the complaint requires consideration of any records relating to the person as respects whom the complaint is made, the person specified under paragraph (a) must inform him or the person acting on his behalf, if the investigation will involve disclosure of information contained in those records to a person other than the chemist, or a director, partner, or employee of the chemist; and

(e)   the chemist must keep a record of all complaints and copies of all correspondence relating to complaints, but such records must be kept separate from any records relating to the person by whom the complaint is made.

(8) At each of the premises at which the chemist provides pharmaceutical services, he must provide information about the complaints procedure and give the name (or title) and address of the person specified under sub-paragraph (7)(a).

10B   (1) A chemist must co-operate with any investigation of a complaint by the HA in accordance with the procedures which it operates in accordance with directions given under section 17 of the 1995 Act, whether the investigation follows one under the chemist's complaints procedure or not.

(2) The co-operation required by sub-paragraph (1) includes:

(a)   answering questions reasonably put to the chemist by the HA;

(b)   providing information relating to the complaint reasonably required by the HA;

(c)   attending any meeting to consider the complaint (if held at a reasonably accessible place and at a reasonable hour and due notice has been given), if the chemist's presence at the meeting is reasonably required by the HA.

NB The various forms for application to the pharmaceutical list are listed in the schedules but are not included in this appendix.

National Health Service: Scotland terms of service for chemists

The following terms of service are as set out in Schedule 1 to the National Health Service (Pharmaceutical Services) (Scotland) Regulations 1995 (SI 1995 No.414 (S.28), as amended). HB stands for Health Board in the following text.

Schedule I: Terms of Service for Pharmacists

Interpretation (reg.1)

1   In these terms of service unless the context otherwise requires:

    (a)   *prescription form* means a form provided by the Agency for issue by a doctor or dentist or nurse prescriber to enable a person to obtain pharmaceutical services;

    (b)   except in relation to a pharmacist who has notified the Board or Primary Care NHS Trust under regulation 3(7) that he wishes to be excluded from the arrangements for the supply of contraceptive substances and appliances referred to in regulation 3, *drugs* includes contraceptive substances and *appliances* includes contraceptive appliances;

    (c)   any reference to a numbered paragraph is a reference to the paragraph bearing that number in these terms of service and any reference to a numbered sub-paragraph is a reference to the sub-paragraph bearing that number in that paragraph.

Incorporation of provisions (reg.2)

2   Any provisions of the following affecting the rights and obligations of pharmacists shall be deemed to form part of the terms of service:

(a)   these regulations;

(b)   the *Drug Tariff*;

(c)   any scheme made under Regulation 8;

(d)   so much of Part II of the National Health Service (Service Committees and Tribunals) (Scotland) Regulations 1992 as relates to:

> (i) the investigation of complaints made by or on behalf of persons against pharmacists and other investigations to be made by the pharmaceutical service committee and the joint services committee and the action which may be taken by the Board or Primary Care NHS Trust as a result of such investigations, including the withholding of remuneration from pharmacists where there has been a breach of the terms of service;
>
> (ii) appeals to the Secretary of State from decisions of the Board.

Provisions of pharmaceutical services (reg.3)

3   (1) Subject to sub-paragraphs (2) and (3) a pharmacist shall supply, with reasonable promptness, to any person who presents on a prescription form:

(a)   an order for drugs, not being scheduled drugs, or for appliances signed by a doctor;

(b)   an order for a drug specified in Schedule 11 to the National Health Service (General Medical Services) (Scotland) Regulations 1995, signed by, and endorsed on the face with the reference 'SLS' by a doctor;

(c)   an order for listed drugs, or for drugs, not being scheduled drugs signed by a dentist or nurse prescriber;

(d)   an order for listed drugs or listed appliances signed by a nurse prescriber;

such drugs and appliances as may be so ordered, and any drugs so supplied shall be in a suitable container.

(2) A pharmacist shall not accept for dispensing any prescription form transmitted from or received at a registered pharmacy which is not included in the pharmaceutical list.

(3) A pharmacist shall not supply any drugs or listed appliances ordered on a prescription form other than at a registered pharmacy which is included in the pharmaceutical list.

(3A) (a) Subject to sub-paragraph (b), a pharmacist shall, before supplying a prescribed item to any person presenting a prescription form with a declaration claiming either charge exemption under regulation 7 of the National Health Service (Charges for Drugs and Appliances) (Scotland) Regulations 1989 or charge remission under the National Health Service (Travelling Expenses or Remission Charges) (Scotland) Regulations 1988, request the evidence of the patient's entitlement to such exemption or remission;

(b)   sub-paragraph (a) shall not apply in respect of claims for exemption under regulation 7(1)(a) to (f) of the 1989 regulations where the pharmacists has information in his possession at the time of supplying the item which confirms that the patient is entitled to the exemption claimed;

(c)   where the person presenting the prescription form does not show valid evidence of entitlement and the pharmacist, in respect of a claim for exemption does not have evidence in his possession to confirm that the patient is entitled to make that claim, the pharmacist shall mark that patient's prescription form accordingly before supplying the prescribed item.

(4) Where an order, not being an order to which the Poisons Rules 1982 or the Misuse of Drugs Regulations 1985 apply, issued by a doctor or a dentist or a nurse prescriber on a prescription form for drugs or listed drugs does not prescribe the quantity, strength or dosage thereof, a pharmacist may supply such strength and

dosage of drugs or listed drugs so ordered as he shall consider to be appropriate, and, subject to the provisions of sub-paragraph (5), in such quantity as he considers to be appropriate for a course of treatment of the patient to whom the order relates, for a period not exceeding five days.

(5) Where an order to which sub-paragraph (4) applies is for:

(a)   an oral contraceptive; or

(b)   a drug or listed drug which is available for supply as part of pharmaceutical services only together with one or more drugs or listed drugs; or

(c)   an antibiotic in a liquid form for oral administration in respect of which pharmaceutical considerations require supply in an unopened package;

which is not available for supply as part of pharmaceutical services except in such packages that the minimum available package contains a quantity appropriate to a course of treatment for a patient for a period of more than five days, the pharmacist may supply for the patient to whom the order relates, such minimum available package.

(6) Where any drug, not being one to which the Misuse of Drugs Regulations 1985 apply, ordered by a doctor or dentist or nurse prescriber on a prescription form, is available for provision by a pharmacist in a pack in a quantity which is different to the quantity which has been so ordered, and that drug is:

(a)   sterile;

(b)   effervescent or hygroscopic;

(c)   a liquid preparation for addition to bath water;

(d)   a coal tar preparation;

(e)   a viscous preparation;

(f)   packed at the time of its manufacture in a calendar pack or special container;

the pharmacist shall subject to sub-paragraph (7) provide the drug in the pack whose quantity is nearest to the quantity which has been so ordered.

(7) A pharmacist shall not provide, pursuant to sub-paragraph (6), a drug in a calendar pack where, in his opinion, it was the intention of the doctor or dentist or nurse prescriber who ordered the drug that it should be provided only in the exact quantity ordered.

(8) In this paragraph:

(a)   *calendar pack* means a blister or strip pack showing the days of the week or month against each of the several units in the pack;

(b)   *special container* means any container with an integral means of application or from which it is not practicable to dispense an exact quantity.

(9) All drugs and preparations supplied by pharmacists shall, where a standard or formula is specified in the *British Pharmacopoeia,* the *British Pharmaceutical Codex,* the *British National Formulary* (including any appendix published as part of that formulary) or the *Drug Tariff,* conform to the standard or formula so specified, and in any other cases shall be of a grade or quality not lower than the grade ordinarily used for medicinal purposes.

(10) All appliances supplied by pharmacists shall conform to the specifications included in the *Drug Tariff.*

(11) Subject to any regulations in force under the Weights and Measures Act 1985, a pharmacist shall provide pharmaceutical services only in response to and, subject to sub-paragraphs (4), (5) and (6) in accordance with an order on a prescription form, signed as specified in sub-paragraph (1), except that in a case of urgency where a doctor or nurse prescriber personally known to a pharmacist requests him to dispense a drug or appliance the pharmacist may supply that drug or appliance before receiving such a prescription form, only if:

(a)   that drug is not a scheduled drug;

(b)   that drug is not a Controlled Drug within the meaning of the Misuse of Drugs Act 1971 other than a drug which is for the time being specified in Schedule 5 to the Misuse of Drugs Regulations 1985; and

(c)   in any case, the doctor or nurse prescriber undertakes to furnish the pharmacist, within 72 hours, with such a prescription form.

(12) Except as provided in sub-paragraph (13) a pharmacist shall not supply by way of pharmaceutical services under the Act or otherwise, any scheduled drug which is ordered by name, formula, or other description on a prescription form.

(13) Where a drug has an appropriate non-proprietary name and it is ordered on a prescription form either by that name or by its formula, a pharmacist may supply a drug which has the same specification notwithstanding that it is a scheduled drug.

(14) Where a drug which is ordered as specified in sub-paragraph (12) combines more than one drug, that sub-paragraph shall apply only if the combination has an appropriate non-proprietary name, whether the individual drugs which it combines do so or not.

(15) A pharmacist shall not give, promise or offer to any person any gift or reward (whether by way of a share of or dividend on the profits of the business or by way of discount or rebate or otherwise) as an inducement to or in consideration of his presenting an order for drugs or appliances on a prescription form.

(16) A pharmacist shall not, except with the consent of the Secretary of State, provide at a health centre services other than pharmaceutical services in accordance with section 27 of the Act.

Premises and hours of business (reg.4)

4   (1) Pharmaceutical services shall be provided at the premises specified in the application made by the pharmacist for inclusion in the Board's or Primary Care NHS Trust's list, and the premises shall be open for the supply of pharmaceutical services during the hours specified in the scheme to be made by the Board or Primary Care NHS Trust for that purpose under the regulations.

(2) At every premises from which pharmaceutical services are provided there shall be exhibited a notice to be provided by the Board or Primary Care NHS Trust in the form prescribed in Schedule 2. There shall also be exhibited at such premises, at times when those premises are not open, and in such a manner as to be visible at all times, a notice in a form approved by the Board or Primary Care NHS Trust indicating the facilities available for securing the dispensing of medicines urgently required.

(3) Pharmaceutical services shall not, except with the consent of the Board or Primary Care NHS Trust or, on appeal, of the Secretary of State, be provided by a pharmacist in premises occupied by a doctor other than at a health centre.

(4) No pharmacist shall provide pharmaceutical services from any pharmacy or other premises which are not included in the pharmaceutical list in respect of that pharmacist.

Dispensing of medicines (reg.5)

5   (1) The dispensing of medicines shall be performed either by or under the direct supervision of a pharmacist.

(2) Where the pharmacist referred to in sub-paragraph (1) is employed by a chemist, the pharmacist must not be one:

(a)   who having been disqualified under section 29(3)(b) of the Act (or under any corresponding provision in force in England or Wales or Northern Ireland) from inclusion in the pharmaceutical list of any Board or Primary Care NHS Trust (or in England and Wales of a Health Authority, or in Northern Ireland of a Health and Social Services Board), is also the subject of a declaration under section 29(3)(c) of the Act (or any corresponding provision in force in England and Wales or Northern Ireland) that he is not fit to be engaged in any capacity in the provision of pharmaceutical services; or

(b)   who is suspended by direction of the Tribunal, other than in a case falling within section 32B(3) of the Act.

Names of registered pharmacists (reg.6)

6   A pharmacist contractor shall, if so required by the Board or Primary Care NHS Trust, furnish to the Board or Primary Care NHS Trust the name or names of pharmacists employed by him in dispensing medicines.

Drugs etc. to be supplied without charge (reg.7)

7   (1) Subject to the provisions of any regulations made under section 69 of the Act, all drugs, containers and appliances supplied under these terms of service shall be supplied free of charge.

(2) Where a pharmacist supplies an oxygen container or oxygen equipment, other than equipment specified in the *Drug Tariff* as not returnable to the pharmacist, the container and equipment shall remain the property of the pharmacist, who shall have no claim against the Board or Primary Care NHS Trust in the event of the loss of, or damage to, such container or equipment except as may be provided in the *Drug Tariff*.

Method of payment (reg.8)

8   (1) A pharmacist is required to furnish to the Board or Primary Care NHS Trust or to such other person or body as they may direct, on dates to be appointed by the Secretary of State after consultation with an organisation which is in his opinion representative of the general body of pharmacists, the prescription forms and other forms upon which the orders for drugs and appliances supplied by him were given, arranged in such manner as the Board or Primary Care NHS Trust may direct, together with a statement of accounts containing such particulars relating to the provision by him of pharmaceutical services as the Board or Primary Care NHS Trust, with the approval of the Secretary of State, may from time to time require.

(2) A pharmacist whose name is included in the pharmaceutical list shall supply, in response to a request from the Secretary of State and within one month of the notification of the request, any information which the Secretary of State may require for the purpose of conducting any inquiry into the prices, payments, fees, allowances and remuneration specified in these regulations.

(3) The Board or Primary Care NHS Trust shall, if any pharmacist so requires, afford him reasonable facilities for examining all or any of the forms on which the drugs or appliances supplied by him were ordered, together with particulars of the amounts calculated to be payable in respect of such drugs and appliances and if he takes objection thereto, the Board or Primary Care NHS Trust shall take such objection into consideration.

(4) The Board or Primary Care NHS Trust shall, if so required by any organisation which is, in the opinion of the Secretary of State, representative of the general body of chemists, afford the said organisation similar facilities for examining such forms and particulars relating to all or any of the pharmacists and shall take into consideration any objection made thereto by the said organisation.

(5) Payment will be made for drugs and appliances in the *Drug Tariff* at the prices specified therein and for drugs or appliances not in the tariff in the manner set forth therein. The payment to be made for containers and in respect of dispensing fees shall be calculated in the manner set forth in the tariff: provided however in either case

that the amount payable shall be reduced by an amount equal to any charge made or recoverable under regulations made under section 69 of the Act.

(6) If the Secretary of State, after consultation with such organisation as is mentioned in sub-paragraph (1) of this paragraph, is satisfied at any time that the method of payment herein before provided for in this paragraph is such that undue delay in payment may be caused thereby, he may direct that the amounts to be payable to a chemist shall be calculated by such other method, whether by averaging the amounts payable to a pharmacist or otherwise, as appears to him designed to secure that:

(a)   payment may be made within a reasonable time; and
(b)   payments to a pharmacist shall, as nearly as may be, remain the same as if the payments had been calculated in accordance with the first mentioned method of payment;

and payments calculated by any such other method shall be deemed for all purposes to be payments made in accordance with these regulations.

(7) No pharmacist shall be paid in respect of the supply of drugs or listed appliances indicated on a prescription form unless that supply takes place at a registered pharmacy included in the pharmaceutical list in respect of that pharmacist.

Professional standards (reg.8A)

8A   Without prejudice to any rule or implication of law to that effect, a pharmacist who provides pharmaceutical services in accordance with arrangements made in the regulations shall do so in conformity to standards generally accepted in the pharmaceutical profession.

Complaints (reg.9A and 9B)

9A   (1) Subject to sub-paragraph (2), a pharmacist or pharmacist contractor shall establish, and operate in accordance with this paragraph, a procedure (in this paragraph and in paragraph 9B) referred to as a *complaints procedure* to deal with any complaints made by or on behalf of any person to whom he has provided pharmaceutical services.

(2) The complaints procedure to be established by a pharmacist may be such that it also deals with complaints made in relation to one or more other pharmacists.

(3) The complaints procedure to be established by a pharmacist or a pharmacist contractor who provides pharmaceutical services from more than one set of premises may be such that it relates to all those premises together.

(4) A complaints procedure shall apply to complaints made in relation to any matter reasonable connected with the pharmacist's or pharmacist contractor's provision of pharmaceutical services and within the reasonable control of:

(a)   the pharmacist;
(b)   where the pharmacist is a body corporate, any of its directors or former directors;
(c)   a former partner of a pharmacist;
(d)   any pharmacist employed by the pharmacist contractor;
(e)   any employee of the pharmacist or pharmacist contractor other that one falling within sub-paragraph (d);

and in this paragraph and paragraph 9B references to complaints falling within this sub-paragraph.

(5) A complaint may be made on behalf of any person with his consent, or:

(a)   where he is under 16 years of age:

    (i) by either parent, or in the absence of both parents, the guardian or other adult person who has care of the child; or

    (ii) in the care of an authority under Part II of the Social Work (Scotland) Act or in the care of a voluntary organisation, by that authority or voluntary organisation; or

(b)   where he is incapable of making a complaint, by a relative or other adult person who has an interest in his welfare.

(6) A complaint may be made as respects a person who has died by a relative or other adult person who has an interest in his welfare or, where he was as described in (a)(ii) of sub-paragraph (5), by the authority or voluntary organisation.

(7) A complaints procedure shall comply with the following requirements:

(a)   the pharmacist or pharmacist contractor must specify a person (who need not be connected with the pharmacist or the pharmacist contractor and who, in the case of an individual, may be specified by his job title) to be responsible for receiving and investigating all complaints;

(b)   all complaints must be:

    (i) recorded in writing;

    (ii) acknowledged, either orally or in writing, within the period of three days (excluding Saturdays, Sundays, Christmas Day, Good Friday and bank holidays) beginning with the day on which the complaint was received by the person specified in (a) of this sub-paragraph or where that is not possible as soon as is reasonably practicable; and

    (iii) properly investigated;

(c)   within the period of 10 days (excluding Saturdays, Sundays, Christmas Day, Good Friday and bank holidays) beginning with the day on which the complaint was received by the person specified under paragraph (a) or where that is not possible as soon as is reasonably practicable, the complainant must be given a written summary of the investigations and its conclusions;

(d)   where the investigation of the complaint requires consideration of any records relating to the person as respects whom the complaint is made, the person specified in paragraph (a) must inform him or the person acting on his behalf, if the investigation will involve disclosure of information contained in those records to a person other than the chemist, or a director, partner, or employee of the pharmacist; and

(e)   the pharmacist or pharmacist contractor shall keep a record of all complaints and copies of all correspondence relating to complaints, but such records must be kept separate from any records relating to the person by whom the complaint is made.

(8) At each of the premises at which the pharmacist provides pharmaceutical services, he must provide information about the complaints procedure and give the name (or title) and address of the person specified under paragraph (7)(a); and where he supplied supplemental services he must provide the same information to the person referred to in regulation 3(3)(a).

9B   (1) A pharmacist must co-operate with any investigation of a complaint by the Board or Primary Care NHS Trust in accordance with the procedures which it operates in accordance with directions given under section 17 of the 1995 Act, whether the investigation follows one under the chemist's complaints procedure or not.

(2) The co-operation required by sub-paragraph (1) includes:

(a)   answering questions reasonably put to the pharmacist by the Board or Primary Care NHS Trust;

(b)   providing information relating to the complaint reasonably required by the Board or Primary Care NHS Trust;

(c)   attending any meeting to consider the complaint (if held at a reasonably accessible place and at a reasonable hour and due notice has been given), if the pharmacist's presence at the meeting is reasonably required by the Board or Primary Care NHS Trust.

Withdrawal from pharmaceutical list (reg.10)

10   (1) Subject to sub-paragraph (2), a pharmacist may at any time give notice in writing to the Board or Primary Care NHS Trust that he desires to withdraw his name from the pharmaceutical list and his name shall be removed therefrom at the expiration of three months from the date of such notice or of such shorter period as the Board may agree.

(2) Where representations are made to the Tribunal under the provisions of section 29 of the Act that the continued inclusion of a pharmacist in the pharmaceutical list would be prejudicial to the efficiency of the service, he shall not, except with the consent of the Secretary of State and subject to such conditions as the Secretary of State may impose, be entitled to withdraw his name from the list pending the termination of the proceedings on such representations.

(3) The name of any pharmacist whose business is carried on by representatives in accordance with the provisions of the Medicines Act 1968, shall not be removed from the list so long as the business is carried on by them in accordance with the provisions of that Act, and the representatives agree to be bound by the terms of service of the pharmacist.

Records to be made available (reg.11)

11   A pharmacist who has undertaken to provide supplemental services within the meaning of paragraph (3) of regulation 3 shall on request make available to the Board or Primary Care NHS Trust all records kept in accordance with sub-paragraphs (b) and (c) of that paragraph.

Index